Child, Parent, and State

LAW AND POLICY
READER

Child, Parent, and State

■ LAW AND POLICY READER

Under the sponsorship of the
University of Pennsylvania Law Review

Edited by

S. Randall Humm
Beate Anna Ort
Martin Mazen Anbari
Wendy S. Lader
William Scott Biel

TEMPLE UNIVERSITY PRESS

Philadelphia

Temple University Press, Philadelphia 19122
Copyright © 1994 by Temple University, except Chapter 5 copyright
© 1994 by Elizabeth Bartholet. All rights reserved
Published 1994
Printed in the United States of America

The paper used in this publication meets the minimum requirements of
American National Standard for Information Sciences—Permanence of
Paper for Printed Library Materials, ANSI Z39.48-1984   ⊗

Library of Congress Cataloging-in-Publication Data
Child, parent, and state : law and policy reader / under the
    sponsorship of the University of Pennsylvania law review, edited by
    S. Randall Humm . . . [et al.].
        p.   cm.
    Includes bibliographical references and index.
    ISBN 1-56639-133-4 (acid-free paper). — ISBN 1-56639-134-2 (pbk.:
acid-free paper)
    1. Children—Legal status, laws, etc.—United States.   2. Parent
and child (law)—United States.   3. Child welfare—United States.
4. Children—Government policy—United States.   I. Humm, S.
Randall.   II. University of Pennsylvania law review.
KF479.A75C475   1994
346.7301'7—dc20
[347.30617]   93-8223

To the children of America

CONTENTS

PART II: CHILDREN AND THE SOCIAL SERVICE SYSTEM

Section 3: Child Abuse

Section 4: Foster Care

Section 5: Homelessness

PART III: Children and School

PART IV: Children and Health Policy

ACKNOWLEDGMENTS

LAW REVIEWS are unique in American academia since they are run by students. This book is an extension of that tradition, conceived and edited by members of the *University of Pennsylvania Law Review*. We would like to thank the following for their editorial contributions: Andrew Africk, Raquel Alvarez, Martin Arias, Kathy Bakst, Naomi Biswas, Claudia Brett, Rachel Ekery, Teri Firmiss, Tamara Gelboin, Olga Gomez, Brian Graff, Mark Greene, Douglas Halijan, Brent Hooker, John Hovendon, José Ibietatorremendía, Gary Ignatin, Jason Isralowitz, Megan Jacobson, Amy Kim, Joel Mick, Eniko Miksche, Derek Pew, Beth Rushing, John Schloerb, Adam Silverstein, Cynthia Soohoo, David Wachen, and Jeffrey Wallack. The assistance of Professor Barbara Bennett Woodhouse and of Ellen Chung was invaluable.

We express our appreciation to Doris Braendel, senior acquisitions editor at Temple University Press, who supported this project from beginning to end. We also thank Jennifer French and Jane Barry as well as two anonymous readers for their excellent work in helping shape the final product.

The Editors

Introduction

The Editors

PERSONS UNDER THE age of eighteen make up just over a quarter of the United States population.[1] "America's future is forecast in the lives of its children and the ability of their families to raise them."[2] Children become the parents, workers, and leaders upon whom the progress of the nation depends. We continue to hold a special regard for children, and their welfare and well-being remain a primary focus of law and public policy.

The well-being of children depends to a large extent on their rights under the law. Children may be said to have a variety of important rights. These include the right to physical safety, adequate parental supervision and rearing, adequate education, adequate standard of living, adequate health care, freedom from exploitation, freedom of speech and religion, equal treatment, and adequate representation in their own right in legal proceedings.[3] American law guarantees these rights to varying degrees, but never completely.[4]

The law permeates the lives of all children at every turn, but is particularly relevant for the child "at risk." This child comes in many types. A child may be the subject of a custody battle, or be in foster care, or be up for adoption. She may be abused or homeless or ill. She may be a five-year-old living in poverty and dependent on Medicaid, a middle-class teenager, or a public school student. Some children are criminals and delinquents. Many are several of the above.

"Although many children grow up healthy and happy in strong, stable families, far too many do not."[5] As the bipartisan National Commission on Children[6] observed, many children grow up in families whose lives are in turmoil. Their parents are too stressed and too drained to provide the nurturing, structure, and security that protect children and prepare them for adulthood. Some of these children are unloved and ill tended. Others are unsafe at home and in their neighborhoods. Many are poor, and some are homeless and hungry. Often, they lack the rudiments of basic health care and a quality education. Almost always, they lack hopes and dreams. . . . America's future depends on these children too.[7]

Perhaps the key theme in the law of children is that children do not act in the legal world in isolation; rather, they are one part of a triangle that also includes the parents and the state. Historically, parental control over children until they reach the age of majority has been very strong. In general, this society has had great respect for the child–parent relationship and for the values of family privacy and freedom from governmental intrusion; accordingly, we are reluctant to intervene in that relationship. Even the U.S. Supreme Court has stated that "[t]he history and culture of Western civilization reflect a strong tradition of parental concern for the nurture and upbringing of their children. This primary role of the parents in the upbringing of their children is now established beyond debate as an enduring American tradition."[8]

On the other hand, we have become aware that the family environment and the way a child is treated and reared, especially in her younger years, have a tremendous impact on the child's emotional and physical well-being and her role as a useful member of society. For that reason, the state may sometimes find it appropriate to limit parental discretion in the interest of the child's welfare. In other words, while parental rights are fundamental, they are not absolute.

As a result, laws regulating the child–parent relationship often strike a balance between these two competing interests. State education laws provide a good illustration. Compulsory education laws are more than a century old, and now every state has statutes requiring that children attend school between the ages of six and sixteen, unless the child completes high school earlier.[9] The state's interest here is in a productive and informed citizenry. The state also acts in the best interests of the child against her parents' neglect and apathy. These interests, however, are pitted against societal assumptions about the centrality of the family to the transmission of social values from generation to generation and the paramount interest of parents in making decisions about the education of their children.

Court decisions reflect this balance. While the state may require school attendance, the school need not be a public school.[10] States' control of what is taught in private schools is limited.[11] Parents whose religious beliefs conflict with the concept of compulsory education—the Amish, for example—retain the constitutional right to avoid those laws.[12] Even in public schools, parents retain some control over curriculum and library books, and the attendance of their children in sex education classes. At the same time, parental control is not permitted to interfere with very important state goals such as school desegregation.[13]

Another example of state intervention in the child–parent relationship is in the area of child custody. The courts must intervene on behalf of children when the family unit has to dissolve. "Each year, more than a million American children are affected by their parents' decision to separate or end their marriages."[14] Since about half of all divorces involve children, and since a substantial number of divorced parents bring more than one custody action, the volume of custody litigation is massive.[15]

Early English law had a simple rule that, absent unusual circumstances, the child's father was entitled to custody. This rule did not have a strong hold on American courts. Indeed, until recently, under the so-called tender years doctrine, there was a rebuttable presumption that custody of young children should normally go to the mother.[16] The constitutional mandate for gender equality as well as modification of state laws changed all that. "Nearly all judicial discussion of custody cases begins with the statement that custody must be so awarded as to promote the child's best interests."[17]

The Uniform Marriage and Divorce Act defines the child's best interests as follows:

> (1) the wishes of the child's parent or parents as to his custody; (2) the wishes of the child as to his custodian; (3) the interaction and interrelationship of the child with his parent or parents, his siblings and any other person who may significantly affect the child's best interest; (4) the child's adjustment to his home, school and community; (5) the mental and physical health of all individuals involved. The court shall not consider conduct of a present or proposed custodian that does not affect his relationship to the child.[18]

In addition to custody cases, courts apply this standard in cases of adoption, cases in which neither natural parent is available or fit to have custody, and cases in which a natural parent is engaged in a custody dispute with a foster parent, a grandparent, or other nonparent.

A new breed of cases may soon become common: cases where children sue on their own behalf to determine who will have custody of them. Two recent celebrated examples are the case of "Gregory K.," a twelve-year-old boy who wished to "divorce" his natural mother in order to remain permanently with his foster family, and the case of Kimberly Mays, the fourteen-year-old who wished to remain with the man who raised her, after an inadvertent switch at birth in a hospital, rather than live with, or spend any time with, her biological parents. While the courts in both cases did the children's bidding, the concept of a child suing on his own behalf in a custody battle met considerable resistance.[19]

The best interests standard is decidedly vague. Custody litigation therefore has a certain ad hoc quality and is very fact-intensive. Factors considered in the best interests calculus include continuity, stability, and permanence. If the child is mature enough, courts take her preferences into account. But in any event the meaning of the standard remains a major question in the law of children.

Along with custody decisions, courts must issue property distribution, alimony, and child support decisions. These decisions, again, are multifactorial and made on a case by case basis. It is widely known that divorce frequently results in a precipitous decline in the former wife's standard of living. Since custody is usually given to the mother, the children suffer equally. Child support awards are usually adequate on paper, but the enforcement of these awards is frequently difficult and thorny. A network of state and federal laws exist to maximize enforcement. The federal government has an interest in proper child support enforcement to decrease the burdens on federal welfare programs. Thus, the federal government assists the individual states in locating the defaulting parents.

The child–parent relationship breaks down in other ways that bring the child into the hands of the state and its social service system. One unfortunate but particularly common form of breakdown is child abuse and neglect. Reports of child maltreatment have been increasing in recent years. "In 1974, there were about 60,000 cases reported, a number that rose to 1.1 million in 1980 and more than doubled during the 1980s to 2.4 million."[20] This increase reflects to some extent an increase in public awareness, but there is still much reason to believe that the reported cases constitute just a fraction of the actual incidence of abuse and neglect.[21]

Every state has in place a number of mechanisms to deal with the problem. Child protection systems investigate allegations of abuse and neglect and intervene if needed. Because of respect for the integrity of the family and the child–parent relationship, these systems' first preference is to address the abusive situation while keeping the child with her parents. Indeed, the law requires child protection workers to make reasonable efforts to keep families together. Thus, child protection systems may provide home-based services to troubled families, day care and homemaker services, counseling and other therapeutic services, parent education, and other forms of support.

Child protection agencies resort to criminal sanctions only in extreme situations of abuse and neglect, and even within the repertoire of civil remedies, child protection workers proceed with caution. They do not resort lightly to such drastic remedies as depriving the parent of her parental rights and assuming full control of the abused or neglected child. Even when they do so, federal and state laws have a presumption in favor of reuniting the child with the abusive parent whenever possible. In accord with this presumption, the U.S. Supreme Court decided in 1982 that the state must meet a high standard of proof before terminating parental rights.[22]

When it becomes impossible for the abused or neglected child to stay in the parental home, the child is placed elsewhere. Foster care is a common form of out-of-home placement, since it assumes the possibility of future reunification of parent and child should circumstances permit. Child protection agencies expend much time and energy recruiting and training foster parents. If abusive parents relinquish their parental rights or if these rights are terminated, adoption becomes possible. Again, much effort is spent to find suitable adoptive homes. Finding such homes for minority children is difficult; it is particularly challenging for special needs children whose handicap or ill health requires committed and well-trained adoptive parents.

Most legal issues surrounding these procedures are straightforward and largely settled. The chronic problems associated with child protection services are usually ones of adequate funding and staffing, especially in the face of one of the most daunting social problems of our time. The funding crisis has spawned in recent years a special type of litigation in which children, through a guardian or advocate, sue the state. In these suits the children allege that the state has been negligent in not intervening quickly enough to stop their abuse at the hands of a parent or foster parent. The more elaborate of these suits try to prove a pattern of inadequacy and ask for court orders obligating the child protection systems to accomplish a number of specified changes and improvements.

In a landmark 1989 case,[23] by a vote of 5 to 4, the U.S. Supreme Court closed the door to suits filed on behalf of abused children against child protection agencies alleging that these agencies negligently failed to stop the abuse and demanding damages for these children. Suits against the state on behalf of children are permitted to some extent in the case of foster children. Very delicate issues come to the fore in this context: Financially strapped child welfare systems have now to deal with court orders specifying areas of needed change, poorly compensated social workers become the target of child advocates, and courts start dabbling with the business of running complex bureaucracies.

The law and policy behind these suits raise timely questions of extreme importance. For example, the federal courts are split on whether child victims of sexual abuse may sue the state when the abuse was committed in a public school.[24] The U.S. Supreme Court may have to take up the question in the near future.

For those children not faced with threats to their very safety, education is a paramount issue. As the National Commission on Children recently noted, "American students continue to lag behind their counterparts in many developed and developing nations. . . . Far too many of the nation's youth drop out of school, and even among those who complete high school, a substantial number lack the basic skills and knowledge needed to get a job."[25] Their parents' poverty or lack of education, or other problems in the home, cause many children to be ill prepared for school. In other cases, the commission points the finger of blame at the schools:

> Many schools across the country lack the basic ingredients and flexibility to be lively, innovative learning centers. They often lack a common educational vision and strong leadership. They fail to set rigorous academic standards and do little to foster initiative, innovation, and creativity among teachers and staff. Many do not encourage parents to be active partners in their children's education, and some are unable to maintain order and discipline.[26]

Often this state of affairs reflects inadequate funding.

In the constitutional lexicon, education is not a "fundamental right" in the way speech, privacy, and freedom of religion are. For example, disparities in the quality of education across school districts do not raise federal constitutional concerns. The most interesting education-related litigation, therefore, is occurring in state courts. In these cases, students and their advocates sue the state based on state constitutions and state statutes. The most celebrated cases are those in which courts interpret the state constitutional guarantee of equal treatment under the law to compel the state to eliminate financial disparities between school districts. In Texas, for example, public education is financed with taxes on property. Consequently, poorer parts of the state necessarily operate with smaller budgets. The Texas Supreme Court held that this situation was inconsistent with the state constitution's guarantee of equality under the law.[27]

Another paramount issue for children is health care. Health care is one of the most complex policy issues of our time. The health status of children is a key indicator of how well we as a society and polity are treating them, and the current picture is not encouraging. Between 8 and 10 million children have no form of health insurance.[28] The infant mortality rate in this country remains higher than that in twenty-one other industrialized nations, and more than forty thousand babies a year die before their first birthday.[29] Low birth weight is associated with poor health and reduced chances of survival among infants. The rate of low birth weight is high, and "[n]o progress has been made since 1980 in reducing the rate of babies born with low weights; for black babies, the rate has risen."[30] The National Commission on Children has attributed these figures to the relative unavailability of early prenatal care for women without health insurance and to the "growing epidemic of alcohol and illegal drug use, especially use of crack cocaine, by pregnant women [which] severely threatens the health and development of as many as 375,000 babies each year."[31]

Children currently have health insurance either under Medicaid or under private insurance policies held by their parents, usually in an employment context. Many children, as we saw above, are uninsured. But even for those insured under Medicaid, access remains problematic. This is so because, in contrast to Medicare (the federal insurance program that serves the elderly), Medicaid is poorly funded, and low reimbursement rates make many health care providers unwilling to treat large numbers of Medicaid patients.

Health care for children raises the same issues as our health care system as a whole. It is widely held that the system has twin problems: inadequate access, in that some people have no insurance, and high cost, in that individuals have difficulty affording health insurance and government spending on health care is increasing more rapidly than other areas of the budget. Solving one problem, however, exacerbates the other. If we are to insure everyone fully, the government will spend more. If we are to contain costs, we will have to provide fewer services for the poor or provide services to fewer of them.

In the past few years, the federal government has put in place some cost-containment measures. In the mid-1980s, the government introduced the Diagnosis Related Group (DRG) method of payment into the Medicare program. Under the DRG system, government regulators could now decide how much the typical case of every illness should cost, and reimburse hospitals for no more than that amount. Ostensibly, this fosters efficiency and cost consciousness. A few years later, the government turned its attention to physician fees. Empowered by Congress to address, in a budget-neutral fashion, the income disparities between generalists and specialists, government regulators went further. Rules issued in 1991 cut physician income under Medicare across the board, including the incomes of general internists.

The individual states have also sought ways to save money. In a particularly controversial proposal, Oregon set out to cover more people under its Medicaid program by providing fewer services to each of them. It has engaged in a complicated ranking of medical interventions so that only the more "useful" and "cost-effective" ones are covered. The Oregon plan received the blessing of the Clinton administration,[32] preventing a full Congressional debate on the issues involved.[33] Implementation of the plan will be closely watched, since it will inform the ongoing intense debate[34] over the general concept of rationing health care. A variety of options for improving the health status of children continue to be discussed as society and government tackle the complex task of designing an optimal health care system.

Beyond what we do and do not do for and to young people, many legal issues arise out of what they do to others. Too many juveniles are finding themselves on the wrong side of the law. "Today, younger and younger children are committing more serious and violent crimes than in years past. Assaults, robberies, and murders have become commonplace on many city streets and even in schools. Today, more teenage boys in the United States die of gunshot wounds than of all natural causes combined."[35]

In most cases, juveniles accused of crime are processed in the juvenile court. This court's raison d'être is to handle a variety of issues related to the young, including abuse and neglect, foster care, truancy, and running away from home. In dealing with juvenile crime, the juvenile court's watchword is rehabilitation. "Since 1899 when the first juvenile court was founded, society's commitment to young people charged with the commission of a crime has been to rehabilitate rather than to punish them."[36] Indeed, one key assumption underlies the treatment of juvenile delinquents and criminals in this country: We assume that minors are immature and impressionable and thus should not be held to the same standards of culpability and responsibility as adults. Accordingly, we punish juvenile crime less severely, and, indeed, often opt for rehabilitation as the only means of dealing with juvenile crime.

Originally, it was believed that the court's emphasis on the best interests of the child and on a decided preference for rehabilitation over punishment made elaborate procedural safeguards unnecessary. In 1967, however, the U.S. Supreme Court heard the appeal of Gerald Gault, a fifteen-year-old who, after making a number of obscene phone calls to a neighbor, was adjudged a delinquent and committed to a state rehabilitation institution for six years, the remainder of his minority. An adult committing the same offense would have been fined up to fifty dollars and imprisoned a maximum of two months.[37] The Supreme Court found that "[d]epartures from established principles of due process have frequently resulted not in enlightened procedure, but in arbitrariness."[38]

The Court has since extended to juveniles such rights as representation by counsel and conviction beyond a reasonable doubt. It has, however, balked at extending other rights, such as trial by jury[39] and the use of strict standards before the accused is confined pending trial.[40] There is still a tradeoff between benevolent treatment and procedural rights.

For very serious crimes, the state is permitted to "waive" the accused juvenile into criminal court, after sufficient hearings, so that the juvenile may be tried as an adult. In that situation, the juvenile enjoys all the procedural protections, constitutional and otherwise, afforded criminal defendants. In return, the juvenile is subject to severe punishment, including, in rare cases, the death penalty.

Drawing on many of the points just discussed, this book addresses some of the most important and timely issues related to law and policy affecting children. The book is intended to be as comprehensive as possible, and to represent a variety of viewpoints and perspectives. Three questions resonate throughout and arise, in some form or another, in most of the contexts we address. What rights do children have? How similarly to adults should they be treated? How subject to the will of adults should they be?

This book has five parts. Part I is concerned with the regulation of the child–parent relationship, especially when there is a need to decide anew who should perform parenting functions for a child. As we noted earlier, in making custody decisions after divorce, courts have as their guidepost the best interests of the child. Similar concerns govern decisions about adoption and deprivation of parental rights. Part I discusses the many meanings of this standard both in theory and in reality, and such special problems as the use of religion as a factor in custody decisions, the impact of a parent's homosexuality on custody decisions, the role of race and race matching in adoption, and the particularly vexing issue of drug-addicted pregnant women.

Part II looks at children's interactions with the social service system. Child abuse is prominent here. These chapters consider the legal and, perhaps more importantly, the policy issues that child advocates have to contend with in their efforts to negotiate this problem. We concentrate on suits filed on behalf of children alleging a pattern of defective governmental response to child abuse and demanding significant restructuring of the system. Two perspectives are presented: that of concerned advocates and that of welfare system workers doing the best they can with the resources they have. In addition, contributors to Part II address the particular difficulties homeless families face and the legal and policy issues affecting them.

Part III discusses children and schools. The state of our public school system is the main issue here, but the role of state and federal policies in improving the system and recent controversies about inequities in the financing of public schools are addressed as well.

Part III also addresses, briefly, the issue of students' free speech rights. A series of Supreme Court decisions give school authorities significant leeway in controlling what students can write about for the consumption of other students.

This matter is not only important in itself, but also represents one side of a coin, the other side of which is the exclusion of library and curriculum books by school authorities. The recent controversy about whether, in requiring first graders to learn about homosexuality and AIDS, the New York school system is making students know *too much* incorporates values and conflicts integral to the debate about student speech rights.

Part IV tackles the interaction of children with the health care system. The section entitled "Paying for Children's Health Care" focuses on the availability of health insurance to children and provides the legal background against which current policy options should be considered. This extremely complex area is covered as thoroughly as possible.

Another important health-related issue is the allocation of the power to make decisions about medical care among children, parents, and third parties, including the state. Part IV specifically addresses seriously ill newborns and the right of adolescents to consent to or decline care. Three chapters concern children with AIDS, with emphasis on schoolchildren who have the disease.

The last part discusses children and the criminal justice system. Part V starts with a debate about the assumptions and workings of the juvenile court. One contributor argues that the juvenile court has outlived its usefulness, while others argue that juveniles are indeed different from adults and that as a society we recognize that difference in many ways.

The chapters then briefly consider two situations in which our basic assumptions about juveniles and the tradeoff between punishment and procedure are played out. The first is pretrial detention, which affects many thousands of juveniles and is permitted by the Supreme Court under much looser standards than would apply to adults.[41] The debate about pretrial detention mirrors and illustrates in concrete terms the conflict about how we treat our juvenile delinquents. In the chapters on the death penalty, we deal with the most serious crimes that juveniles commit and ask what is literally a life or death question: How much responsibility are we entitled to expect of this society's youth? And does it make much sense to speak of impressionable, misunderstood youngsters when they commit the most horrendous crimes?

Issues related to the place of children in society have implications for both law and policy. The editors have, therefore, designed the book to appeal to readers from a variety of backgrounds: law, medicine, education, social work, sociology, psychology, public health, and other social sciences. We hope that the book will fulfill our intentions.

NOTES

1. *See* Center for the Study of Social Policy, Kids Count Databook: State Profiles of Child Wellbeing 9 (1991).
2. National Commission on Children, Beyond Rhetoric: A New American Agenda for Children and Families 2 (1991) [hereinafter Beyond Rhetoric].

3. This list parallels the list of rights outlined by the United Nations Convention on the Rights of the Child. *See* Children's Rights in America: U.N. Convention on the Rights of the Child Compared with United States Law (C. Cohen & H. Davidson eds., 1990). This convention is the "gold standard" that might be used to evaluate any society's performance in guaranteeing children's legal rights.

4. *Id.*

5. Beyond Rhetoric, *supra* note 2, at vii.

6. The commission was set up in 1989 to serve as a forum on behalf of the children of the nation. Its thirty-four members were appointed by the President, the President *pro tempore* of the Senate, and the Speaker of the House of Representatives. The commission was chaired by Senator Jay Rockefeller of West Virginia. Then-Governor Bill Clinton was a member.

7. Beyond Rhetoric, *supra* note 2, at 2.

8. Wisconsin v. Yoder, 406 U.S. 205, 232 (1972).

9. *See* 2 H. Clark, The Law of Domestic Relations in the United States § 20.4 (2d ed. 1988).

10. *See* Pierce v. Society of Sisters, 268 U.S. 510 (1925).

11. *See* Meyer v. Nebraska, 262 U.S. 390 (1923).

12. *See Yoder.*

13. *See* H. Krause, Family Law in a Nutshell 200–201 (1986).

14. Beyond Rhetoric, *supra* note 2, at 6.

15. *See* Clark, Law of Domestic Relations, *supra* note 9, at 476–77.

16. *See id.* at 477.

17. *Id.* at 479 (footnote omitted).

18. § 402, Uniform Marriage and Divorce Act.

19. The trial court in the Gregory K. case gave him the right to sue on his own behalf to determine his own custody status. On appeal, a Florida appellate court held that Gregory had no such right, and that children may not sue to deprive their parents of their parental rights. The court left Gregory with his foster family on other grounds. *See* Kingsley v. Kingsley, 1993 Fla. App. LEXIS 8645 (Fla. Ct. App. Aug. 18, 1993). Likewise, the court in the Mays case acceded to Kimberly's wishes, but sidestepped the issue of whether she could sue on her own behalf to determine her custody status.

20. U.S. Advisory Board on Child Abuse and Neglect, Child Abuse and Neglect: Critical First Steps in Response to a National Emergency, at x (1990).

21. *See id.*

22. *See* Santosky v. Kramer, 455 U.S. 745 (1982) (holding that the state must prove by "clear and convincing evidence" that a child was abused or neglected before parental rights are terminated).

23. *See* DeShaney v. Winnebago County Dep't of Soc. Servs., 489 U.S. 189 (1989).

24. *See* Doe v. Taylor Indep. Sch. Dist., 975 F.2d 137 (5th Cir. 1992) (holding that public school student's constitutional rights were violated when she was sexually molested by a teacher); D.R. v. Middle Bucks Area Vocational Technical Sch., 972 F.2d 1364 (3d Cir. 1992) (reaching the opposite conclusion).

25. Beyond Rhetoric, *supra* note 2, at 48.

26. *Id.* at 49–50.

27. *See* Edgewood Indep. Sch. Dist. v. Kirby, 804 S.W.2d 491 (Tex. 1991).

28. *See* Children's Defense Fund, The State of America's Children 1991, at 56 (1991); Beyond Rhetoric, *supra* note 2, at 12.

29. *See* Beyond Rhetoric, *supra* note 2, at 12.

30. *Id*. (endnote omitted).

31. *Id*. (endnote omitted).

32. The Bush administration had denied Oregon an administrative waiver on the ground that the rationing plan would violate the Americans with Disabilities Act.

33. Since the Oregon plan affects beneficiaries of Medicaid, a joint federal–state program, Oregon could not act alone. The federal government—either the administration or Congress—had to approve the plan before it could go forward.

The place of health rationing in any reform scheme Congress will adopt remains unclear.

34. *See* Symposium, The Law and Policy of Health Care Rationing: Models and Accountability, 140 U. Pa. L. Rev. 1505 (1992).

35. *Id*. at 13 (endnote omitted).

36. T. Stein, Child Welfare and the Law 28 (1991).

37. *See id*.

38. *In re* Gault, 387 U.S. 1, 19 (1967).

39. McKeiver v. Pennsylvania, 403 U.S. 528 (1971).

40. *See* Schall v. Martin, 467 U.S. 253 (1984).

41. *See id*.

■ PART I

Regulating the Child–Parent Relationship

■ CHAPTER ONE

Awarding Custody: The Best Interests of the Child and Other Fictions

Andrea Charlow

THE "BEST INTERESTS of the child" is the standard for awarding child custody in the United States, a standard that presumably places paramount importance on the child's physical and psychological well-being. While in theory this standard appears enlightened, in practice custody decisions focus on parents rather than children and are marred by personal and cultural bias. Predictions are made without a scientific foundation and, frequently, in contravention of research findings and constitutional equal protection requirements. Because the "best interests of the child" standard is more a vague platitude than a legal or scientific standard, it is subject to abuse both by judges who administer it and parents who use it to further their own interests.

This chapter begins with an explanation of the best interests standard and the problems caused by the vagueness of the standard. The second section critiques attempts to simplify the decision-making process through presumptions in favor of the mother, the primary caretaker, the psychological parent, and joint custody. The third section discusses research findings, which suggest that minimized familial conflict and continued contact with both parents should be the most important goals in custody awards. The final section of the chapter proposes a new method for achieving these goals, by awarding custody to the party most willing and able to minimize conflict for the benefit of the child.

Published originally in 5 Yale L. and Pol'y Rev. 267 (1987). Copyright 1987 Yale Law and Policy Review. Reprinted by permission.

The Current Standard

Child custody law in the United States has evolved from the early European concept of absolute paternal power,[1] to a presumption that the mother should be granted custody of young children,[2] to the current standard, which dictates that the custody award be made in the best interests of the child.

The Best Interests of the Child

Some states provide a list of factors to be considered in determining the best interests of the child,[3] while others leave the determination of which facts are material to the discretion of the court.[4] In either case, courts make custody decisions on an individual basis. Statutes do not establish the weight to be accorded to any particular factor. Furthermore, it is not clear whether the "best interests of the child" means a "happy" childhood or a childhood that leads to a well-adjusted adult regardless of the happiness experienced during minority. The answer to that question, like the weight to be given to each factor, depends on judicial discretion.

Despite its shortcomings, the current best interests standard provides a welcome departure from the rigidity of previous rules. Rules that automatically prefer one parent on the basis of sex are not sensitive to the unique characteristics of each family or to the needs of individual children. Furthermore, the best interests standard ostensibly focuses the inquiry on the child's needs rather than the parents' rights. Given the relative fragility of the child and the fact that the child did not participate in decisions concerning its conception or the divorce, this focus on the child is admirable.

Theory and practice in custody decisions, however, do not coincide. Frequently, the hearing and the law attend more to the competing claims of the parents than to any consideration of the child's interests. Proceedings revolve around the fitness of the respective parents; courts frequently do not request children's opinions; and children routinely do not receive legal representation. The deference paid to the parents is so obvious that one author has suggested that the courts abandon the best interests charade and openly consider the parents' interests along with the child's.[5]

The Problem

The landmark case of *Painter v. Bannister*[6] demonstrates the problems inherent in the current application of the best interests of the child standard. That case involved a custody contest between the father and the maternal grandparents (after the mother's death). The trial judge awarded custody to the father; the Iowa Supreme Court reversed and awarded custody to the grandparents. In its decision, the court conceded that both parties were fit parents. However, the court characterized the father's lifestyle as "unstable, unconventional, arty, Bohemian, and probably intellectually stimulating,"[7] while that of the grandparents was characterized as "stable, dependable, conventional, middleclass, middlewest."[8]

The *Painter* decision offered trial judges little instruction for deciding future custody cases. The court did not identify factors that determine what best serves the interests of the child, making the decision appear arbitrary, based on the justices' personal preference for one lifestyle over that chosen by the lower court judge. Perhaps the decision indicated that stability constitutes the single most important factor in determining the best interests of the child. But because the decision did not explicitly rely on stability or any other factor, it sets no useful precedent. The decision is imprecise because the standard is vague. The *Painter* case illustrates that "the best interests of the child" is not a standard, but a euphemism for unbridled judicial discretion.

The vagueness of the best interests of the child standard does not represent its only shortcoming: Judges also express discomfort with the decisions they have made utilizing the standard. One study, conducted to determine whether judges could identify the "psychological parent" as ably as mental health professionals, found no significant difference in their ability to do so but found that the judiciary was less comfortable with its determinations.[9] Unlike mental health professionals, however, judges grant custody on the basis of their assessments. Judges cannot be certain that their decisions are best for the children involved; science has not yet provided a sound basis for such decisions. Nor can judges be certain that their decisions are legally correct, because the law remains undefined. Judicial action lacks a scientific or legal foundation and must be based on guesswork.

The high level of discretion not only increases the possibility of error but also may encourage litigation. The outcome is hard to predict in a child custody case because the court applies a vague standard to a unique fact pattern. When the outcome is uncertain, each party is more likely to litigate, believing that he or she will prevail. In fact, the relitigation rate in divorces that include children is ten times greater than in those without children.[10]

Recent studies have attempted to determine if there is any pattern in the application of the best interests standard by judges. In one study, Kentucky circuit court judges and commissioners reported on their weighting of twenty factors in child custody decisions.[11] The study indicated that the most important factors were the judge's assessment of each parent's (1) maturity and judgment, (2) mental stability, (3) ability to provide access to schools, (4) moral character, (5) ability to provide continuing involvement in the community, (6) financial sufficiency, and (7) sense of responsibility for the child. Only the last of these factors involves the parent's relationship with the child, as opposed to characteristics of the parent as an individual. The study also revealed a limited emphasis on factors related to the continuity and diversity of social relationships within the custodial home.

The evidence from the Kentucky study supports the argument that judicial inquiry generally focuses on the parents' rather than the child's best interests. The focus on the parents is justified by the need to assess parental character in making judicial predictions of the child's future welfare. However, the advisability of such speculation is questionable. In the absence of scientific indication that particular characteristics will translate into successful custody arrangements, the decision must be based on the judge's personal values and bias. Many of the Kentucky judges readily admitted that their decisions were based on "gut" reactions.[12]

The authors of the Kentucky study also pointed out that some of the criteria utilized by the judges demonstrated a failure to comply with legislation and to accept the results of current psychological research. Specifically, one-fourth of the judges gave priority to the mother over the father when the parents were in conflict.[13] The father was never given preference over the mother solely on the basis of his sex.[14] Scientific research, however, has disproved the sex-based "tender years" doctrine—the proposition that young children are best placed with their mothers.[15]

A more recent study of judicial decision making, in contested custody cases in Colorado,[16] concluded that older judges (averaging 63.7 years of age, with an average of 19.1 years on the bench) were more likely to award custody to mothers than fathers in contested cases and that the burden in those cases was on the fathers to prove that the mothers were unfit. Younger judges (averaging 38.2 years of age, with an average of 3.2 years on the bench) also granted custody to mothers more often than to fathers but rejected the tender years doctrine or a general maternal preference.[17] Younger judges reported greater reliance on interim custody arrangements than older judges.[18] Most of the judges in both groups, however, stressed the need for discretion and individual analysis in child custody disputes.[19]

The Colorado judges, like those in Kentucky, reported that they were not fond of domestic relations cases. In the words of one, "I am playing God. . . . You can do extreme damage. Usually before a decision I do not sleep. My stomach hurts. I would rather send someone to life in the penitentiary."[20]

These studies lead to several conclusions. First, the results of this research must be interpreted with caution. Self-reporting is a highly suspect research method because of inaccuracies and biases that occur absent an objective control methodology. At the same time, it is hard to believe that a judge who admits noncompliance with a statute or higher court ruling is not being candid. One judge admitted that he concealed his reliance on temporary custody awards, an action prohibited by the state supreme court, by couching his decision in terms of psychological parenting.[21]

Second, judges' backgrounds and values strongly influence custody decisions. The gut feeling admission cited above and the protestations of the authors of the *Painter* decision indicate that subconscious values affect the process judges use to decide contested custody cases even if it is impossible to measure this influence precisely.

In addition, the studies demonstrate that the current decision-making process allows too much judicial discretion. Use of the indeterminate best interests standard permits individual judges to ignore the results of scientific research and to substitute their prejudices and values for those of legislatures—specifically, to substitute sex-biased custody decisions for sex-neutral statutory standards. Although limited judicial discretion is necessary to ensure that case-specific issues are addressed, the current best interests standard provides too much latitude in which judges can obscure the rationales for their decisions and allows them to base custody awards on their personal values.

Finally, broad judicial discretion may exacerbate the conflict between parents. With outcomes uncertain, some parents may be encouraged to litigate. Others may enter "bad" settlements because they perceive sex bias on the part of the court that might lead a judge to deprive them of custody altogether. For example, fathers may be discouraged from seeking custody because they believe that mothers always win, or mothers may be discouraged from seeking custody when fathers contest because statistics show that fathers now win contested cases more often than mothers.

Failed Solutions

Courts have attempted to confront the dilemma caused by the current approach to the best interests standard through establishment of a rebuttable presumption in favor of one parent. The presumption simplifies the task of the adjudicator by narrowing the scope of inquiry, and by providing for mechanical application of a simple legal rule. When the presumption is rebuttable, the judge may engage in a more detailed inquiry, but the likelihood of such an inquiry is decreased. A presumption may settle the disquiet felt by many judges by allowing them to abdicate responsibility for the custody decision to a legal norm. The tender years doctrine and the psychological parent theory epitomize efforts to establish these presumptions, attempts that ultimately fail because they ignore research concerning the best interests of children from divorced families.

The Tender Years Doctrine

The tender years doctrine, which has now been formally abolished in most states, creates a rebuttable presumption in favor of granting custody to the mothers of young children. The doctrine reflects the societal stereotype that healthy development occurs most readily if young children are raised by their mothers. Unless a mother is proven unfit, courts following the tender years doctrine routinely award her custody.

Although the tender years doctrine may still claim widespread cultural support, recent psychological and sociological research challenges the notion that the mother is the best parent for a young child.[22] While mothers may be the primary caretakers of children in most American families today, some fathers fulfill that role. The rationale for the presumption is not sufficiently compelling in light of the current emphasis on the importance of fatherhood, the prevalence of two-career families, and the evidentiary burden the presumption places on fathers. As a result, most states now prohibit a presumption in favor of awarding custody to the mother.[23]

Despite legislative and appellate court action eliminating express reliance on the tender years doctrine, studies of custody decisions indicate that some judges continue to grant the mother a preference.[24] The broad discretion and lack of guidelines inherent in the best interests of the child standard allow the tender years doctrine to survive. As a result, some fathers do not request custody because they believe that they would not obtain custody in a contested case.

The Primary Caretaker and Psychological Parent Theory

The presumption that the primary caretaker should be granted custody is a gender-neutral version of the tender years doctrine. Instead of presuming that the mother is the primary caretaker, the court inquires into the child-rearing practices of the family in question. In most cases the primary caretaker will be the mother. The new standard provides flexibility, however, for the more recent phenomenon of homemaker fathers and two-career homes.

A more sophisticated variation on the primary caretaker presumption is the psychological parent doctrine, originally espoused by Goldstein, Freud, and Solnit.[25] Goldstein and colleagues define the psychological parent as the person who maintains the strongest bond with the child as a result of daily attention to the child's physical and psychological needs.[26] Although the psychological parent is not necessarily synonymous with the primary caretaker, the psychological parent concept is essentially an extension of the primary caretaker concept. The primary caretaker is generally the psychological parent because continuity of care is the primary basis for the psychological bonding between parent and child.

Goldstein identifies four principles upon which custody decisions should be based: (1) the importance of continuity of relationships and physical environment; (2) the child's sense of time with regard to continuity and separation (since young children experience a greater sense of urgency than most adults); (3) the law's inability to supervise interpersonal relationships; and (4) the limitations of human knowledge in making long-range predictions.[27] Based on these guidelines, Goldstein concludes that the psychological parent should be granted custody, except where it is destructive to the child;[28] children should not be shifted around pending a final custody decision;[29] and all custody decisions should be final.[30] In addition, according to Goldstein, the custodial parent should determine all matters regarding visitation.[31]

Goldstein's theories follow logically if one accepts the proposition that continuity is the most important factor in child placement. Psychological studies demonstrate, however, that parental reaction to divorce may alter parenting abilities and change existing parent–child relationships.[32] As a result, placement with the psychological parent may not provide the desired continuity. In addition, studies show that continuity is *not* the determinative factor in healthy adjustment to divorce;[33] decreased parental conflict more directly influences child development following divorce.[34] The Goldstein proposal, unfortunately, does little to minimize such conflict.

The Goldstein proposition that the custodial parent have complete control over visitation is an invitation to cut off all contact between the noncustodial parent and the child. In those few custody cases that are contested, both parties are generally seeking sole custody. Often these parties are motivated more by anger against the other party than by feelings of love and concern for the child. As a result, custody and visitation rights may repeatedly be litigated after the court enters its original order. The Goldstein proposal would allow the prevailing parent to limit or prevent visitation with the noncustodial parent. According to research, however, children develop better when they continue their relationships with both parents.[35] Thus, granting the custodial parent complete control over visitation is not in the best interests of the child.

Goldstein apparently dismisses the possibility of more than one psychological parent. If there is more than one psychological parent, the logical conclusion from Goldstein's theory would be that the child requires a continuous relationship with both parents. But by granting absolute control to one parent, the other is likely to be cut off from the child, and the child is likely to experience a strong sense of loss.

Paradoxically, Goldstein recommends finality while emphasizing the inability of the court to predict future events. This view is merely a corollary of the principle of primacy of continuity: No change of circumstances assumes more importance than the continuity of custody. Despite the need for finality in custody decisions, however, the inability of the court accurately to predict the future requires that the courts not terminate access to the legal system. Although Goldstein correctly argues that recourse to the courts should be limited after the initial custody award, total preclusion would be dangerous. The importance of continuity in parent–child relationships, and the danger of frivolous custody relitigation, does not justify prohibition of all modification actions.

Joint Custody

Joint custody appears to provide a simple and egalitarian solution to the contested custody dilemma. By awarding joint custody, the judge need not decide who is the better parent or speculate about the child's future. As research concerning divorced families recommends, children would have the benefit of contact with both parents. Neither parent would face the stigma of losing a custody dispute, and extensive inquiries into the backgrounds and habits of the parents would not be necessary. In fact, contested cases might cease if the parties were certain that they would be ordered to share custody.

Unfortunately, joint custody is not a panacea. Perhaps even more unfortunately, legislatures already have passed statutes creating joint custody presumptions, without fully considering the consequences of their actions.[36] The reality of joint custody differs markedly from its conceptual ideal.

Joint legal and joint physical custody have been artificially separated in the law and have very different meanings. Legal custody relates to the legal rights of a guardian to make major decisions concerning the child and to obtain information about the child that ordinarily would be available only to a parent or guardian.[37] Physical custody refers to the actual daily care, control, and responsibility for the child.[38]

Joint legal custody may be granted to both parents, even though the court grants sole physical custody to one parent. Joint physical custody does not require that half of the child's time be spent living with each parent. Custody may alternate daily, weekly, monthly, or yearly; the types of arrangements are as varied as the number of families who adopt them.[39] In an uncontested case, where the parties are amicable or the noncustodial parent is not particularly interested in daily care of the children, joint legal custody without joint physical custody does not present much of a problem. In a contested case, however, splitting legal and physical custody may increase confusion and hostility without providing any benefit to the child.[40]

Preliminary results of one joint custody study[41] indicate that parents relitigate joint custody decisions less frequently than sole custody decisions. This study suggests that either the joint custody experience is more satisfactory to the parents or that they do not feel compelled or able to relitigate the issue. However, the study cannot be considered conclusive regarding court-ordered joint custody, since only 18 of the 138 joint custody families sampled had joint custody pursuant to court order. Thirty-three percent of those 18 families relitigated their custody arrangement, as compared with a 32 percent relitigation rate for sole custody arrangements.

A number of other studies illustrate the difficulty of assuming that joint custody is as appropriate in contested cases as in voluntary agreements.[42] Although most researchers surveyed relatively small groups of highly motivated families,[43] children frequently reported problems with divided loyalties and movement between households.[44] One researcher found that within one year of her initial interviews, one-third of the research sample had abandoned joint physical custody.[45] An earlier study indicated that voluntary joint custody arrangements benefited all parties, but that the few families with involuntary joint custody experienced substantial conflict and instability.[46]

Research indicates that children develop better when conflict levels decrease after divorce. The studies of joint custody demonstrate that voluntary joint custody provides continued contact with both parents, to a child's benefit. Involuntary joint custody, however, can maintain or increase conflict between warring parents, thus impairing the child's development. As a result, most proponents of joint custody do not recommend court-ordered joint custody in contested cases.

The Role of Research

Legal presumptions are useful shortcuts, but they must be based on reality. Research provides clues about the reality of child development following divorce, research that judges do not apply to their decisions. Admittedly, the social and psychological sciences have not provided definitive models for parenting or for identifying and predicting the most beneficial environment for child development. Nevertheless, conclusions from available research can provide useful guides for judges and legislators.

Wallerstein and Kelly found that the psychological adjustment of children of divorce depends more on the development and characteristics of children at the time of divorce than on those of their parents.[47] The psychological stability of the parents affected adjustment after divorce, but did not always result in better parenting.[48] Despite these findings, the factors considered by judges when deciding custody cases usually focus on the parents.[49]

In Wallerstein and Kelly's research sample, children whose parents adjusted poorly to divorce, children of "stressed custodial parents," experienced more developmental or psychological problems than children whose parents did not have serious adjustment problems.[50] At first glance, this finding would seem to indicate the appropriateness of focusing on the parents; however, the study also revealed that parental care before and after the divorce was not the same. Most children experienced a decreased level of care in the year immediately following the divorce.[51] Some parents who neglected their children prior to divorce improved with the alleviation of the problems of the marriage, while some who were good parents prior to divorce did not adjust well, exhibiting poor parenting skills long after the initial one-year adjustment period. Still others were consistent in their parenting patterns before and after divorce. Thus, parenting at the time of divorce may not be a dependable indicator of parenting following the divorce.[52]

Isolation of the factors that most significantly affect postdivorce child development is the most important contribution of the Wallerstein and Kelly research. The one consistent finding of Wallerstein and Kelly and subsequent studies is that the level of parental conflict is the most important factor in child development after divorce. Children in families with decreased conflict levels fare better than their counterparts who experience continued or increased family hostilities.[53]

In a review of child development research, Emery argues that interparental conflict is the principal cause of children's problems, rather than separation from one parent.[54] Emery's theory draws support from research findings that: (1) there are more behavioral problems in families with only one parent because of divorce than in families with only one parent because of death; (2) children of divorced parents from homes without conflict fare better than children from intact homes with conflict; (3) children's responses to divorce and discord are similar; (4) children of divorce who no longer live with conflict do better than children of divorce with conflict present after the divorce; and (5) the problems of children of divorce are frequently present before the divorce. In addition, studies show that the negative effects of separation from a parent are only present for a limited time.[55]

Although not as critical as decreased conflict, close contact with both parents has been identified as a positive factor in several studies.[56] Research also shows that without frequent contact, fathers eventually tend to lose all connection with their children.[57] These findings underscore the need for adequate visitation with the noncustodial parent.

A Proposal

The legal system cannot eliminate all of the problems caused by antagonistic parents, but it can minimize the damage that conflict inflicts on the child. The research discussed above suggests the need to decrease parental conflict yet maintain contact between the child and both parents. It follows logically that the parent who is best able to separate parental discord from his or her relations with the child should have custody. This parent should be able to place the child's interests above his or her own in order to avoid conflict, and to allow the other parent access to the child.[58]

Improving the Odds

A custody battle is not in a child's best interests unless one of the parents clearly is unfit.[59] In the majority of cases when parents fight about custody and neither is clearly unfit, at least one of them is not putting the interests of the child above his or her own. Research confirms this hypothesis. As Scott and Derdeyn state:

> Some parents may seek custody to better maintain a sense of purpose and of continuity in the parental identity. . . . Maneuvers to punish the offending spouse are particularly prominent. By sustaining the anger, the rejected spouse may avoid the sadness that would accompany acceptance of the extent and the finality of loss. . . . [T]hese issues also provide the major route by which the couple can continue to attempt to control and frustrate each other.[60]

Wallerstein and Kelly's research also suggests that interest in the child's welfare may be only one factor motivating a parent seeking custody:

> Fighting between parents for the child's loyalty and affection at the time of divorce is often related to each parent's need for that child's presence to maintain self-esteem and to ward off self-criticism and depression. Litigation over custody thus may reflect the dependence of the adult on the child, and the adult's need to hold on to the child to maintain his or her psychic balance.[61]

Although the research addresses reduced conflict levels in general, a judge cannot review all pretrial conflict to determine which parent is more contentious.

Such an investigation would consume an inordinate amount of time, involve innumerable factual questions concerning reported statements by the parties, and allow judges once more to make subjective decisions in determining which parent was contentious and which was "justified" in any particular dispute.

Instead, inquiry at the custody hearing should be limited to a determination of the reasons that the custody dispute has not been resolved through negotiation. The judge should ask what has been offered and why each party has refused to agree to the other's offer. If the parents know that decreased conflict is best for the child and if neither parent is clearly unfit, they should be required to justify the court battle in terms of the child's best interests. Of course, if one parent is clearly unfit, the judge would be free to award custody to the fit parent. If both parents are unfit, the court could remove the child from both of them and place it in foster care, or terminate parental rights and place the child up for adoption.[62]

By forcing the parents to justify their failure to settle out of court on the basis of the best interests of their children, the judge may discover the ability and willingness of a parent to decrease conflict and to allow access by the noncustodial parent. If the reason the parents cannot agree is that they are incapable of speaking civilly to each other, then the court could offer mediation services. If the parents cannot agree through the intervention of a neutral third party, then the parent who is blocking agreement should justify his or her refusal to agree in terms of the needs of the child. If he or she cannot, then that parent has demonstrated his or her inability to place the child's best interests over personal needs. Custody should then be granted to the other parent.

As noted above, this approach is not appropriate in cases where one or both parents are unfit. An abusive parent clearly does not avoid conflict and, therefore, would not be granted custody under the above criteria. The neglectful parent may want to do what is right to help the child, but may not have the ability or training to do so. As a result, the hearing might cover all areas of inquiry presently explored and result in the same problems as the present system. Allegations of unfitness would be specified in the initial petition. In the proposed system an unfit parent is not a less effective one, but an ineffective one. If a parent is petty or spiteful in his or her allegations of unfitness, he or she is not placing the child's interests above his or her own to avoid conflict. The accusing parent, therefore, would be denied custody. The knowledge that frivolous allegations of unfitness may lead to loss of custody should discourage such allegations.[63]

One parent might insist on custody because of a belief that he or she is the better parent or that the other parent, although not legally unfit, is not a "good" parent. Many gradations of parenting skills fall short of the legal definition of unfitness. Arguably, a parent should not be granted custody over one much more able to care for the child. If one parent is truly better, however, he or she is likely to understand the need to reduce conflict for the sake of the children and less likely to raise as an issue the inadequacies of the legally fit but less capable parent.

Even if the parents lack such foresight, the proposed system should cause few problems. The parent charged with insufficient parenting skills presumably helped to raise the child prior to the divorce. The presence of both parents might have mitigated the effects of bad parenting by one, and the same might result if the parents worked out a joint custody arrangement. If the judge were allowed to decide which parent is "more fit," the system would be no different than the present one, with the same problems of broad discretion and decisions based on personal rather than scientific or legal standards. In addition, research demonstrates that decreased conflict levels correlate with healthy child development following divorce; similar findings do not exist regarding any particular style of parenting. Thus, the court should not attempt to choose between two competent parents on the basis of parenting techniques or personalities, but rather on the basis of willingness and ability to decrease conflict levels.

Benefits of the System

The possible benefits of the proposed approach are numerous. Hearings would be brief and to the point. The court would escape the protracted testimony concerning personalities and parenting techniques that is necessary under the current system.[64] By decreasing the period of parental conflict caused by the custody hearing, both children and the courts would benefit. In addition, although the task of predicting which parent will provide a better home for the child would remain, the criteria for that prediction generally would be more reliable. Judges would be constrained in their use of subjective factors, and the operative criteria—ability and willingness to place the child's best interests over the parent's to minimize conflict and allow contact with the noncustodial parent—would correlate with scientific findings.

Subsequent hearings to alter custody would be discouraged because the petitioning parent would have to justify the renewed conflict in terms of the child's best interests. The petitioning parent would have to show why the conflict created by repeated recourse to the courts was beneficial for the child. If the petition claimed anything short of the other's unfitness or a substantial increase in detrimental conflict, the petition would be dismissed. Relitigation for harassment purposes would be less likely because of the certainty of dismissal.

The proposed system would limit the amount of conflict in the family by shortening the custody hearing and reducing the likelihood of future legal disputes. Although parents may continue to fight after divorce, the legal system would not prolong or encourage conflict. Speedy hearings and reduced relitigation also would meet Goldstein's concern about the child's sense of urgency and need for continuity, without sacrificing recourse to the courts in the event of a substantial change in circumstances.

Potential Problems

Although the above proposal may provide benefits over current procedures, it creates some problems as well. The proposed system fails to eliminate all judicial discretion, since the judge still must determine whether a parent has been unreasonable in blocking agreement on custody issues. No decision-making process can eliminate all judicial discretion, however, while protecting the best interests of the child. Discretion under the proposed system would be limited to a determination of whether refusal to accept a custody settlement offer is reasonable. Although judges' opinions will differ, the "reasonable persons" standard and determinations of "good faith" are common in our legal system. Judges are trained to determine issues of reasonableness, but they are not trained to predict accurately the effects of parenting situations on healthy child development.

Another possible objection to the proposed system is that pretrial negotiations would be divulged to the court. Our legal system generally discourages such disclosure to facilitate and encourage private settlement of disputes.[65] Presumably, parties are more likely to reach agreement if they can speak freely, confident that statements and offers will not be repeated in court if they fail to settle. Without confidentiality, the parties might fear that settlement offers would imply admission of liability or would affect the amount of a possible court judgment.

Child custody negotiations, however, involve issues different than most settlement negotiations. There is no question of liability, and there is no monetary award that could be affected by prior offers. Suggestions for custody or visitation arrangements might be made during custody negotiations, but if the child is of ultimate importance to the parties and the proposed arrangements are reasonable, disclosure of such suggestions would not be unfair. Presumably, the parent would only make offers during negotiations that he or she felt were acceptable. Knowing that the judge might be influenced by statements made during negotiation, a parent might only offer the arrangement that he or she deems ideal and refuse to make concessions, rendering settlement more difficult. Under the proposed system, however, parents would be required to show that they were reasonable during negotiations and that they failed to agree because although one was trying to protect his or her children, the other was not.

Obstinate refusal to make concessions also could be interpreted by the judge as an inability or unwillingness to decrease conflict, especially when such concessions would be beneficial to the children. Refusal to make a concession would have to be supported by a reasonable argument that the concession would not be in the child's best interests. Likewise, unreasonable demands would indicate an inability or unwillingness to decrease conflict in the child's best interests and could result in loss of custody. Thus, the proposed system would facilitate settlement by encouraging the parties to make reasonable offers and demands and to be flexible during negotiations.

To the extent that this proposal inhibits negotiation for child custody based on divorce issues unrelated to the child's welfare, it would improve the present system. Our legal system should not encourage the use of children as bargaining chips to obtain monetary benefits. Under the current system, parents can threaten to contest custody or visitation to obtain a beneficial property settlement or decreased child or spousal support. The case may be settled out of court, but not until one parent has forfeited valuable rights in order to avoid a custody battle.[66]

The proposed system would eliminate the possibility of such unfair bargaining producing "unfair" settlements.

Modification of the rules of evidence in child custody cases is not without precedent. General rules of evidence have been altered for other legal issues involving children. For example, hearsay may be admissible in child neglect and abuse hearings.[67] The importance of protecting children from child abuse and the difficulty of proof in abuse and neglect cases justifies admission of hearsay evidence. Similarly, the importance of protecting children from marital discord justifies admission of settlement negotiations. Because of other incentives in the proposed system, disclosure would not tend to discourage negotiation. Relaxation of the general rule to admit statements made during negotiations, therefore, should cause less of a legal dilemma than the admission of hearsay evidence in abuse and neglect hearings.

Encouraging Settlement

The proposed system could be characterized as an attempt to compel parties to settle custody disputes by themselves, through their attorneys, or by mediation through third parties or the court. That is exactly what should happen, if the resulting agreements further the best interests of the child. Under the current system, approximately 90 percent of all custody matters are settled by private agreement without court intervention.[68] Presumably this is because the parents know more about themselves and their children than a court can learn during a hearing. Parents also may settle because they prefer their agreements to the ones that might be produced by court orders.[69] No research is available to prove whether parents who settle are better at determining what is best for their children than judges. Given the large number of cases settled privately at present, however, the proposed system would not create problems if it produced an increase in the number of families who use these agreements rather than deferring to the court.

In addition to an increase in negotiated agreements, the proposed system might encourage an increase in mediated agreements. Results of the Denver Custody Mediation Project show that couples who reach agreement through mediation relitigate at less than half the rate of their adversarial counterparts.[70] Parents who utilized mediation expressed greater satisfaction with the process and final settlements than parents who used the adversarial process without mediation.[71] Project results also showed that parents who mediated agreed to more frequent visitation for the noncustodial parent than parents who did not.[72] Perhaps the most important and unexpected result of this research was that parents who failed to reach agreement through mediation nevertheless reported that the process helped them "to understand and communicate" with their ex-spouses.[73]

Although the Denver research did not test for long-term gains[74] or for the effects of mediation on the adjustment and mental health of the children involved, the study provides some early indication of the possible advantages of mediation over the adversarial system. Since litigation increases parental conflict, reduced relitigation benefits the children of divorce and frees up the court's docket in the process. In addition, the increased understanding and communication between divorced parents that results from the mediation process is likely to decrease conflict after the divorce, even when the parents do not mediate an agreement. Finally, the increased visitation of noncustodial parents as a result of mediation contributes to healthy child development following divorce.

Mediation does not provide an answer for the problems of all divorcing parents. As with joint custody, some states have legislated compulsory mediation in custody disputes without recognizing that not all couples can mediate successfully.[75] In addition, because mediation of custody disputes is relatively new in the United States, a number of other problems, including the practice of law without a license by nonattorney mediators, informed consent, attorney-mediators who represent neither party, attorney–client privilege in the mediation session, fee sharing, the role of independent counsel, and other issues must be resolved.[76] Despite the problems with mediation, however, increased mediation under the proposed system would represent an improvement over the current system.

Summary

In summary, legislation should be enacted to clarify the best interests of the child standard in custody proceedings as follows:

1. After initial finding that neither parent is clearly unfit, the determinative factor for granting custody in the best interests of the child is the ability of a parent to place the child's interests above his or her own in order to decrease parental conflict and allow access to the child by the noncustodial parent.
2. A parent who claims that the other parent is unfit must allege in the petition for custody the specific actions or omissions of the allegedly unfit parent that make him or her unfit. Frivolous allegations of unfitness will be held against the claimant, and claims of relative fitness will not be considered.
3. Parents should be informed that research indicates that reduced conflict and access to both parents have been found to be in the best interests of the child. They also should be informed that if the court finds that they are contesting custody for reasons other than the child's best interests, they will not be granted custody.
4. Custody hearings where neither parent is clearly unfit should focus on the reasons that the parents cannot agree. The purpose of this inquiry is to determine whether one or both parents are putting their own interests above the child's to instigate or prolong a conflict. The parent who cannot justify his or her refusal of a proposal on the basis of the child's best interests should not be granted custody.
5. Mediation services should be provided to parents who appear to be concerned primarily with their children's welfare but lack the ability to

agree. If the judge feels that he or she can solve the impasse quickly
during the hearing, he or she may do so without engaging formal mediation services for the parties.

6. Child custody hearings should be expedited and held before any other
   contested issues of divorce are considered. Custody awards should be
   appealable prior to final decisions of divorce and should be given calen-
   dar preference.

7. The only grounds for modification of final custody orders should be that
   the custodial parent is unfit, or that the custodial parent has consistently
   failed to comply with the terms of the custody portion of the divorce
   decree in a manner that increases parental conflict and/or unduly interferes with the noncustodial parent's visitation rights. Visitation rights
   also may be modified if there is a substantial change in circumstances,
   such as a change of residence by one parent that makes the prior visitation schedule impractical.

Conclusion

Nearly one in every two marriages in the United States ends in divorce; 60 percent of the divorces involve couples with minor children.[77] Between 8 and 17
percent of those families will be involved in custody disputes,[78] and those who do
not go to court to resolve custody conflicts nonetheless will be heavily influenced
in their negotiations by the legal standard. The lack of definition of the best interests of the child standard and the broad discretion it allows produce uneven results for the children whose lives are directed by this system, increase the likelihood and frequency of litigation, and leave judges uneasy about the wisdom of
their decisions.

The index to the Krause casebook on family law includes a cryptic reference to
"vultures" under the child custody section.[79] The associated text contains an article from the *New York Times* regarding the behavior of a pair of California condors
who were fighting over which one of them would take care of their egg. They
fought for hours until their struggle resulted in the accidental destruction of the
egg.[80]

The implication is clear. The egg was destroyed because, in their enmity, the
vultures were more interested in themselves than in the egg. They lost sight of
the object of their fight. As the battle intensified, their attention became so focused on each other that they destroyed the egg.

Parents who fight over custody of their children often wage war with little
regard for their offspring. Although the children, unlike the egg, may not be
totally destroyed, damage is almost certain to follow. If the inquiry in contested
child custody cases is confined to determination of which parent is best able to
place the child's interests above his or her own in order to reduce conflict, then all
of the parties involved—the court, the parents, and the attorneys—will focus on
the reason for their deliberations: the protection and nurturance of the child.

AWARDING CUSTODY: UPDATE

In my original article, I argued that the standard for determining child custody increases the likelihood of protracted litigation and is not related to the best interests of the child. I suggested that custody be granted to the parent who is better able to reduce conflict, and that actions for modification be severely limited. In the five years since that article was published, research into the factors affecting postdivorce child development has continued. Although the law has not changed significantly, research has refined the theories that formed the basis for the original article.

In the article, I concluded that although joint custody is a viable alternative to sole custody, it should not be ordered in contested cases. Research remains equivocal on the benefits of joint custody for child development.[81] One recent study found no correlation between custody arrangements and child development; that is, children living in joint custody arrangements fared no better than those in sole custody homes.[82] Another researcher, working with families who were compelled to adopt joint custody, recommends that joint custody, not be ordered against parents' wishes.[83] Thus, although joint custody is promising in theory, it is not the answer to a contested case.

Psychological and sociological studies available when the original article was written stressed the negative impact of interparental conflict on child development. Research continues to support that conclusion. In attempting to identify the process by which interparental hostility affects children, researchers have theorized that styles of conflict resolution and healthy parent–child relationships may buffer the adverse effects of parental conflict. One study indicates that when parents attempt to resolve their disagreements through compromise, their children tend to cope better with the divorce. Conversely, when parental hostility manifests itself in avoidance, or physical or verbal attack, children are more likely to experience emotional problems.[84] In another study, researchers theorize that interparental conflict indirectly affects child adjustment by impairing the parent–child relationship.[85] These researchers conclude that the deleterious effects of divorce can be mediated if one or both parents remain empathic, communicate expectations for age-appropriate behavior, and avoid involving the child in parental conflicts or using the child for emotional support.[86] Their conclusion suggests that if either parent can maintain a healthy relationship with the child, the level of conflict is not determinative of the child's adjustment. However, the authors state that parenting during the divorce is affected by preseparation conflict,[87] and previous studies show that parenting before the divorce is not necessarily consistent with parenting after divorce.[88] Although research has not yet identified why interparental conflict harms children, the fact that it does so is not disputed. Until new studies further define causation and provide factors enabling us to predict healthy child development following divorce, custody determinations should be based on a parent's ability to avoid conflict over the child.

Martin Guggenheim suggests in Chapter 2 that the proposed system may encourage a parent to agree to an unreasonable demand in order to appear more compromising. By conceding to all demands, reasonable or otherwise, the parent assures himself or herself custody. The opposite should be true. If the demand is unreasonable, it is not unreasonable to refuse to comply, and the parent who *makes* the unreasonable demand is less likely to obtain custody than the parent who refuses to comply with it. Thus, the proposed system should protect a parent from unreasonable demands. One might argue, moreover, that a parent must second-guess what a judge believes to be reasonable before deciding to accept or reject an offer. However, if a judge determines that a proposal was reasonable but that the rejection was based on a parent's bona fide belief that the compromise was not in the child's best interests, the judge may still grant custody to the rejecting parent. The final decision is based on the conflict resolution behavior of each party, not on the judge's agreement with a particular plan. For example, the parents may disagree because of fundamental religious beliefs. The fact that the judge finds one's parent's ideas more compatible with his or her own should not determine the final outcome of the case.

In addition, Guggenheim suggests that if one parent is risk-averse, the other parent may exact a better settlement. In other words, one parent may agree to almost anything to avoid the appearance of being unreasonable. This suggestion implies a misconception of the proposed system and the theory on which it is based. Research suggests that the degree of conflict in parents' interaction as spouses or ex-spouses is not the sole indicator of harm. Rather, it is conflict in their parental roles that damages the child.[89] Under the proposed system, conflict over all issues in the divorce except child custody is irrelevant. Inquiry at the custody hearing would focus solely on the conflict related to custody and visitation. Hopefully, then, parents will not be able to use custody to obtain favorable monetary settlements, as they do today. In addition, they should be encouraged to be more reasonable in their negotiations concerning custody, and conflict both in and out of the courtroom should be reduced.

If decreasing conflict should be the sole goal of child custody law, then it may be better to adopt a simpler resolution mechanism than that proposed, such as a rule that custody goes to the primary caretaker. Although determination of the primary caretaker appears simpler than determination of the more reasonable parent, it is not. In families where both parents work, the situation in most American homes today, it may be unclear who is the primary caretaker. This is especially a problem when the inquiry affects school-age children who do not require much direct parental care. For example, if the father takes the children to play while the mother cleans the house and prepares the meals, who is the primary caretaker? In addition, the astute parent who knows that she or he will file for divorce may take a more active role in parenting prior to divorce to create a primary caretaker issue. The other parent is then less certain about the outcome of the custody dispute. The "conniving" parent has improved his or her bargaining position and can exact a better monetary settlement.

It has been suggested that the proposed system also fails to decrease conflict. Although the primary caretaker presumption may lead to decreased custody litigation, it does not decrease out-of-court conflict. If one parent is contentious, he or she may continue to instigate fights after the divorce. Granting custody to the less contentious parent, the argument goes, will not alter the level of out-of-court conflict. Clearly nothing can stop someone from being contentious, but the custodial parent may apply to the court to limit visitation if the noncustodial parent repeatedly employs confrontation in child custody matters. It is easier to persuade a judge to limit visitation than to persuade one to transfer custody because the custodial parent is excessively hostile. Thus, the noncustodial parent should be discouraged from employing such tactics. In addition, if custody is granted to the more contentious parent, he or she might be encouraged to limit access to the child by the noncustodial parent and to instigate conflict. Anyone who has dealt with divorce knows that a determined custodial parent can frustrate the noncustodial parent with little chance of effective intervention by the courts. The proposed system discourages postdivorce conflict by either parent because the parent who engages in such conduct or brings litigation solely to harass the other parent will not only lose, but may find his or her custody or visitation rights limited because of his or her insistence on prolonging the conflict.

If, as recent studies hypothesize, children experience postdivorce adjustment problems in part because they learn negative conflict resolution styles from their parents,[90] then children should be placed with parents who resolve disputes in a positive manner. Thus, placement on the basis of conflict resolution style is more likely to result in healthy child development than placement based on primary caretaker status alone.

As long as the legal system purports to premise custody decisions on the best interests of the child, an attempt should be made to draft laws on the basis of scientific evidence regarding those interests. Current scientific methods are inexact, and perhaps no scheme can truly forward the child's interests, but surely a system based on the realities of divorce has a better chance to succeed than one based on mere conjecture. Although the proposed system is far from perfect, it should address many of the problems now faced by the courts while focusing more accurately on the child's best interests.

NOTES

Acknowledgments: I gratefully acknowledge the invaluable assistance of Joseph Lenz and Robin Charlow for their review of earlier drafts of this chapter. I would also like to thank Robin Anthony Sears and Steven Mauer for their research assistance.
1. Under this concept of paternal power, the child was treated as a chattel and the father was granted complete rights, including the power to terminate the child's life. *See, e.g.,* Rex v. Greenhill, 11 Eng. Rep. 922 (1836).

2. *See, e.g.,* Boone v. Boone, 150 F.2d 153 (D.C. Cir. 1945).

3. *See, e.g.,* Ky. Rev. Stat. Ann. § 403.270 (Bobbs-Merrill 1984); Wis. Stat. Ann. § 767.24 (West 1981).

4. *See, e.g.,* N.J. Stat. Ann. § 9:2–4 (West 1976); Tenn. Code Ann. §36-6-101 (1986).

5. Chambers, Rethinking the Substantive Rules for Custody Disputes in Divorce, 83 Mich. L. Rev. 477, 499–503 (1984).

6. 140 N.W.2d 152 (Iowa 1966).

7. 140 N.W.2d at 156.

8. 140 N.W.2d at 154. Two years later, the child decided to live with his father, and the grandparents acquiesced. W. Wadlington & M. Paulsen, Cases and Other Materials on Domestic Relations 663 n.1 (successor ed. 1984).

9. Charnas, Practice Trends in Divorce Related Child Custody, 4 J. Divorce 57 (1981).

10. Scott & Derdeyn, Rethinking Joint Custody, 45 Ohio St. L.J. 455, 493 (1984). Unfortunately, the available data do not make clear whether custody issues alone are being disputed. Similarly, the data do not disclose whether noncustodial parents relitigate because they believe they can regain lost custody rights or whether they relitigate because they simply cannot accept the loss of their child.

11. Lowery, Child Custody Decisions in Divorce Proceedings: A Survey of Judges, 12 Prof. Psychology 492 (1981).

12. S. Settle & C. Lowery, Child Custody Decisions: Content Analysis of a Judicial Survey, Therapists, Lawyers & Divorcing Spouses 125, 136 (1982).

13. *Id.* at 127.

14. *Id.* at 134. This phenomenon occurred despite the fact that Kentucky had passed legislation four years earlier requiring equal consideration for both parents regardless of the age of the child. *See* Ky. Rev. Stat. Ann. § 403.270 (Bobbs-Merrill 1984).

15. Settle & Lowery, Child Custody Decisions, *supra* note 12, at 134.

16. Pearson & Ring, Judicial Decision-Making in Contested Custody Cases, 21 J. Fam. L. 703 (1982–83).

17. *Id.* at 719. Despite the apparent sex bias found in these two studies, other research shows that men are more likely to obtain custody than women in contested cases. Sheppard, Unspoken Premises in Custody Litigation, 7 Women's Rts. L. Rep. 229 (1982). Contested custody case estimates range from 8 to 13 percent of all divorces involving children. In the remaining 87 to 92 percent of the cases, the mother is overwhelmingly agreed between the parties to be the parent with physical custody. Weitzman & Dixon, Child Custody Awards: Legal Standards and Empirical Patterns for Child Custody, Support and Visitation After Divorce, 12 U.C. Davis L. Rev. 473, 517–19 (1979). Perhaps these data indicate a reverse sex bias in contested cases, although since these studies are based on statistics rather than interviews with judges, it is difficult to interpret their findings.

18. Pearson & Ring, Judicial Decision-Making, *supra* note 16, at 720.

19. *Id.* at 723.

20. *Id.* at 722.

21. *Id.* at 720.

22. *See* Santrock & Warshak, Father Custody and Social Development in Boys and Girls, 35 J. Soc. Issues 112 (1979); Settle & Lowery, Child Custody Decisions, *supra* note 12, at 134. *See also* Watts v. Watts, 77 Misc. 2d 178, 181–82, 350 N.Y.S.2d 285, 289–90 (Fam. Ct. 1973).

23. *See, e.g.,* Or. Rev. Stat. § 107.137(3) (1983); Md. Fam. Law Code Ann. § 5-203(c)(2) (1986); Watts v. Watts, 77 Misc. 2d. 178, 350 N.Y.S.2d 285 (1973).

24. Lowery, Decisions in Divorce Proceedings, *supra* note 11, at 495; Pearson & Ring, Judicial Decision-Making, *supra* note 16, at 715; Settle & Lowery, Child Custody Decisions, *supra* note 12, at 134.

25. J. Goldstein et al., Beyond the Best Interests of the Child (1979).

26. *Id.* at 19.

27. *Id.* at 31–52.

28. *Id.* at 19–20, 53.

29. *Id.* at 38–39.

30. *Id.* at 35.

31. *Id.* at 38.

32. J. Wallerstein & J. Kelly, Surviving the Breakup 108–20, 158–60, 224–25 (1980).

33. Emery, Interparental Conflict and the Children of Discord and Divorce, 92 Psychological Bull. 310, 313 (1982). One group of authors suggests that it is beneficial to move male children to new communities after divorce because behavior problems in boys following divorce are not forgotten by adults long after the boys have readjusted and discontinued their antisocial behavior. Hetherington et al., Play and Social Interaction in Children Following Divorce, 35 J. Soc. Issues 26, 44 (1979).

34. Ellison, Issues Concerning Parental Harmony and Children's Psychosocial Adjustment, 53 Am. J. Orthopsychiatry 73 (1983); Emery, Interparental Conflict, *supra* note 33, at 313; Wallerstein & Kelly, Surviving the Breakup, *supra* note 32, at 215, 223.

35. *See* Hess & Camara, Post-Divorce Family Relationships as Mediating Factors in the Consequences of Divorce for Children, 35 J. Soc. Issues 79 (1979); Wallerstein & Kelly, Surviving the Breakup, *supra* note 32, at 215.

36. *See, e.g.,* Cal. Civ. Code § 4600.5 (West 1983 & Supp. 1987); Iowa Code Ann. § 598.21 (West 1981 & Supp. 1987).

37. *See* Dodd v. Dodd, 93 Misc. 2d 641, 644–45, 403 N.Y.S.2d 401, 403 (Sup. Ct. 1978); Iowa Code Ann. § 598.41 (West Supp. 1987).

38. *See, e.g.,* Iowa Code Ann. § 598.41 (West Supp. 1987).

39. *See, e.g.,* Dodd v. Dodd, 93 Misc. 2d 641, 645, 403 N.Y.S.2d 401, 404 (Sup. Ct. 1978).

40. Many states specifically provide for or allow joint legal custody without joint physical custody. *See, e.g.,* Frey v. Wagner, 433 So. 2d 60 (Fla. Dist. Ct. App. 1985); Del. Code Ann. tit. 13, § 728 (1981); Iowa Code Ann. § 598.41 (West Supp. 1987).

41. F. Ilfield et al., Joint Custody and Shared Parenting 136 (1984).

42. *See* Scott & Derdeyn, Rethinking Joint Custody, *supra* note 10, at 484–88.

43. The Ilfield and Luepnitz studies included a few cases of court-ordered joint custody, and Luepnitz included several "reluctant" joint custody agreements. Il-

field et al., Custody and Parenting, *supra* note 41, at 137; D. Luepnitz, Child Custody 38 (1982).

44. Steinman, The Experience of Children in a Joint-Custody Arrangement: A Report of a Study, 51 Am. J. Orthopsychiatry 403, 410 (1981). The Luepnitz study also reported problems, but only two children (8 percent) complained. Luepnitz, Child Custody, *supra* note 43, at 46.

45. Steinman, Joint Custody: What We Know, What We Have Yet to Learn, and the Judicial and Legislative Implications, 16 U.C. Davis L. Rev. 739, 748 (1983).

46. Luepnitz, Child Custody, *supra* note 43, at 149.

47. Wallerstein & Kelly, Surviving the Breakup, *supra* note 32, at 213.

48. *Id*. at 215.

49. *See* Fla. Stat. Ann. § 61.13 (West 1984); Mich. Stat. Ann. § 25.312(3) (Callaghan 1984). *See generally* Lowery, Decisions in Divorce Proceedings, *supra* note 11, at 496; Pearson & Ring, Judicial Decision-Making, *supra* note 16.

50. Wallerstein & Kelly, Surviving the Breakup, *supra* note 32, at 224.

51. *Id*. at 99–102.

52. One group of authors suggests that parents alter their behavior temporarily at the time of divorce to obtain a favorable review for custody. Scott & Derdeyn, Rethinking Joint Custody, *supra* note 10, at 496.

53. One might argue that problems with research methodology in this area weaken conclusions based on these studies. However, as Emery notes, because independent studies each with a different methodology problem have reached the same conclusions, one may place great weight on their findings. Emery, Interparental Conflict, *supra* note 33, at 311–12.

54. Emery, Interparental Conflict, *supra* note 33, at 313.

55. *Id*. at 314.

56. In the case of an abusive parent, however, children fare better when they are separated from that parent. Wallerstein & Kelly, Surviving the Breakup, *supra* note 32, at 215.

57. Scott & Derdeyn, Rethinking Joint Custody, *supra* note 10, at 488–90 nn.162–77.

58. It could be argued that custody should be granted to the more contentious party in the hope that he or she would then stop fighting. This would encourage prehearing conflict, however, which would be detrimental to the child. In addition, there may be a greater likelihood that a contentious parent who is granted custody will interfere with visitation.

59. The term "unfit" as used in this article is distinguished from the use of the term in a situation where one parent is not as effective as the other, but he or she remains an adequate parent.

60. Scott & Derdeyn, Rethinking Joint Custody, *supra* note 10, at 493.

61. Wallerstein & Kelly, Surviving the Breakup, *supra* note 32, at 103.

62. *See, e.g.*, Conn. Gen. Stat. § 46b-129 (1986); Minn. Stat. § 260.191, § 260.221 (1986).

63. Unfortunately, at times serious allegations might appear frivolous because the complaining parent has failed to gather sufficient proof. Although the proposed system cannot alleviate this problem, the present system presents this issue as well. It is unlikely that the proposed system would exacerbate the problem.

64. This testimony still may be necessary in the case of allegations that a parent is unfit. Unfounded allegations of unfitness should be discouraged, however, because they almost certainly would lead to loss of custody by the parent who made them.

65. *See, e.g.,* Fed. R. Evid. 408; N.Y. Civ. Prac. L. & R. 3221 (McKinney 1983).

66. It should be noted that the parent who loses in this case is the parent who most likely would win a custody battle under the proposed system—that is, the parent who is more concerned about the child and about avoiding continued conflict.

67. *See, e.g.,* N.Y. Fam. Ct. Act § 1046 (McKinney 1983).

68. Weitzman & Dixon, Child Custody Awards, *supra* note 17, at 504.

69. This hypothesis is supported by the finding that parents who litigated felt that the process and final orders in their cases were unfair more often than parents who negotiated or mediated a custody agreement. Pearson et al., Mediation of Contested Custody Disputes, Colo. Law., Feb. 1982, at 337, 342.

70. *Id.* at 354.

71. *See id.* at 342.

72. *Id.* It should be noted, however, that the differences were not great in terms of overall visitation time. Noncustodial parents with successful mediation set visitation at 7.7 days per month, unsuccessful mediation clients had 5.5 days per month, and parents who did not mediate were granted 4.9 days of visitation per month. *Id.*

73. *Id.*

74. The last set of results was obtained six to twelve months after final court orders were issued. *Id.* at 338. It should be noted that even in this short period, some dissipation of the beneficial effects of mediation was found. *Id.* at 354.

75. *See, e.g.,* Cal. Civ. Code § 4607 (West 1983 & Supp. 1987); Iowa Code Ann. § 598.41(2) (West Supp. 1987).

76. Discussion of such problems is beyond the scope of this chapter. For a detailed analysis of the issues, see Mediation Debated, Explored at ABA Section Meeting, 8 Fam. L. Rep. 2641 (1982).

77. Glick, Children of Divorced Parents in Demographic Perspective, 35 J. of Soc. Issues 170, 174–75 (1975). Glick estimates that this number represented 28 percent of all children under the age of eighteen in 1976, and that by 1990 the figure will be approximately 33 percent. *Id.*

78. Weitzman & Dixon, Child Custody Awards, *supra* note 17, at 518; Lowery, Decisions in Divorce Proceedings, *supra* note 11, at 497.

79. H. Krause, Family Law Cases, Comments, & Questions xlvii (2d ed. 1983).

80. N.Y. Times, Mar. 6, 1982, § 1, at 6, *reprinted in* Krause, Family Law Cases, *supra* note 79, at 711.

81. Kline et al., Children's Adjustment in Joint and Sole Physical Custody Families, 25 Developmental Psychol. 430 (1989).

82. *Id.*

83. Johnston et al., Ongoing Postdivorce Conflict: Effects on Children of Joint Custody and Frequent Access, 59 Am. J. Orthopsychiatry 576, 590 (1989). Unlike most studies of joint custody, this research involved families who were undertaking joint custody arrangements on recommendation of a court official or by order of a judge.

84. Camara & Resnick, Styles of Conflict Resolution and Cooperation Between Divorced Parents: Effects on Child Behavior and Adjustment, 59 Am. J. Orthopsychiatry 560 (1989). *See also* Johnston et al., Ongoing Postdivorce Conflict and Child Disturbance, 15 J. Abnormal Child Psychol. 493 (1987).

85. Tschann et al., Family Process and Children's Functioning During Divorce, 51 J. Marriage and the Family 431 (1989). *See also* Johnston et al., Ongoing Postdivorce Conflict, *supra* note 84.

86. Tschann et al., *supra* note 85, at 443.

87. *Id.* at 440.

88. Wallerstein & Kelly, Surviving the Breakup, *supra* note 32, at 99–102.

89. Camara & Resnick, Styles of Conflict Resolution, *supra* note 84, at 572.

90. Both the Tschann study and the Camara and Resnick study theorize that parental aggression may serve as a model of aggressive behavior as a means of settling disputes, resulting in unhealthy behavior on the part of the child. Tschann et al., Family Process, *supra* note 85, at 442; Camara & Resnick, Styles of Conflict Resolution, *supra* note 84, at 560. If this is true, it provides further support for the proposition that the child should be placed in the home of the parent who is willing to compromise to resolve conflict.

■ CHAPTER TWO

The Best Interests of the Child: Much Ado about Nothing?

Martin Guggenheim

THERE IS A fundamental paradox in the way child custody disputes are resolved. Under the traditional standard for resolving such disputes, the court must decide the case on the basis of the "best interests" of the child. Yet the very use of this standard often produces results that are inconsistent with the "best interests" of the particular child or children.

The Dilemma of the Best Interests Standard

The best interests standard has many defects. It gives judges unbounded discretion, yet provides them with no guidance on matters such as burden of proof and presumptions. It encourages costly litigation that often is detrimental to children and their parents. Finally, because the "best interests" concept is so elusive, it invites judges to engage in open-ended inquiry and to rely on their own value-laden preferences. As a result, one simply cannot be confident that a court's final conclusion about a child's best interests is anything other than a reflection of the judge's personal values.[1]

Scholars have struggled to formulate standards of judicial inquiry that would better serve children and that would ensure that children's needs were taken into acount when child custody disputes are adjudicated. Andrea Charlow writes in this tradition. In the second half of this chapter I will return to a discussion of her specific proposals and why I think they will not have the impact on the system that she expects. First, however, I want to take a broader look at the landscape of parent–child interaction as it touches the law.

Depending on how one views the law relating to child rearing, one might say either that children's interests are a central part of the law or that they have virtually nothing to do with it. In summary terms, parents are free to raise their children as they see fit, subject only to limitations on the most extreme forms of child abuse or neglect. These limitations compel parents to feed, clothe, shelter, educate, and provide health care for their children. But beyond these minima, parents are free to decide how to raise their children, even though the children feel—and even if most other adults would feel—that the parents' choices are misguided or contrary to the children's best interests.

Why do parents have this virtually unbridled power? The child-focused answer would be that our society has made a judgment that these noninterventionist rules are best for children. It is not possible for society to oversee the rearing of all children, and young children especially must have others make decisions for them. Empowering parents, therefore, represents a means of ensuring that such decisions will be made by someone who presumably will act in the children's best interests. On careful review, however, this child-focused answer does not quite work. Even when it can be demonstrated that a parent's decision is not in a child's best interests, that decision is immune to attack or even to review, at least so long as the parent has not breached the minimum level of care society demands of all parents.

In short, it is misleading to explain broad-based parental authority in terms of children's best interests. This becomes particularly apparent when one restates the legal rule on child rearing from the child's perspective. The corollary of nearly absolute parental authority would be that children have a right to be raised by minimally fit people. But children's legally enforceable rights are violated only when their caretakers neglect or abuse them. Children do not have any positive rights when it comes to child custody. At best, they have negative rights. Children have a right not to be harmed by their caretaker, but this right can be exercised only when the harm results from their caretaker's failure to meet the minimum standard of acceptable parenting established by law. This is such a limited right that it makes speaking in terms of rights almost meaningless.

I prefer to think about parental authority to rear children from the parent's perspective. As David Richards has eloquently written: "Child-rearing is one of the ways in which many people fulfill and express their deepest values about how life is to be lived."[2] Parents are free to send their children to whatever school the parents choose; parents are free to live where they wish; and parents select the values of importance in the family, including religion, morality, and eating habits. The specific decisions parents make when raising their children are beyond the state's area of concern.[3]

There is still a third possible explanation for the principle that the family is off-limits to state intervention or review except when children are palpably suffering harm. Unless the charge against a parent rises to the level of unfitness (meaning a serious danger to a child's life or health), families are not at any risk of being forced into court to explain their intimate lives. This principle drastically reduces the number of cases that ever get to court. That is a major benefit. Although this rule means that some children are forced to live with parents when they would be better off elsewhere, the majority of children and parents are saved the awful costs that arise when parents are forced into court to defend themselves. Judging parents when they have not fallen below minimal standards of parenting is just not worth the time, effort, and uncertainty. Following such an inquiry, we cannot even be confident that the review means very much or that a negative judgment of particular parents is not the product of prejudice, discrimination, or the judge's application of his or her highly individualized set of values.

This background must be kept in mind when discussing child custody disputes upon the breakup of a family. Parental disagreements about who should raise the children or how they should be raised are disagreements in which the state has virtually no interest. When parents in an intact family agree on how to raise their children, the state may not intervene. Even upon a breakup of the family unit, parents are entitled to decide between themselves who the primary caretaker will be. When parents disagree, they are free to choose the mechanism by which their disagreement will be resolved; either parent is free not to agree and to use the state court system. However, once that system is invoked, parents are bound by its rules, including the substantive standard used by the court to resolve the matter. This is the circuitous route by which a child's best interests suddenly become a matter of state concern. And even here, the state serves only as an arbiter of a purely private dispute.

Perhaps the clearest way to recognize how limited the state's interest actually is—and how non-child-focused the rules on child rearing really are—is to consider a typical case of divorcing parents embroiled in a custody dispute. In a standard case of this sort, each parent has accused the other of being a poor parent. Each is represented by a lawyer, who has employed a set of experts. Each parent has been before the court for scores of hours giving testimony. All of this has been done in the name of achieving the child's best interests. But if the parents suddenly settle the matter, or if one of the parents dies or becomes physically unable to take the child, the other parent will get custody without so much as a whimper from the state.

This typical case suggests that child custody cases are not really about children at all. They are about adults. These disputes are over which parent shall be given legal entitlement to raise a child. They are not, as some would have it, child-centered inquiries determining the best environment for the child. They are far more restricted than that; the deciding court is limited to choosing between the two competing adults. Moreover, the court is involved only because of a decision by one or both of the parents; the child was neither consulted nor considered.

Still further evidence that custody disputes are really about parental rights is obtained by looking at how judges view these proceedings. It is a commonplace that judges agonize over child custody cases and consider them to be among the most difficult cases on their docket. This is extraordinary when one thinks for a moment what it means to judge a difficult child custody case. By definition, a difficult child custody case is one in which the judge cannot easily choose between the competing parties. In other words, it is unclear to the judge whether one parent or the other would be a better custodian and caretaker. Thus, in a significant percentage of all child custody cases, the judge is unable to figure out how best to serve the child's best interests.

If these cases were really about children's interests, wouldn't judges see them as exceedingly easy? Even if a judge cannot determine which outcome is ideal, it is readily apparent that—*from the child's point of view*—either outcome will do. Both parents are quite capable of serving the child's needs, or else the case would not be agonizing to the judge in the first place. Why then are these cases so difficult for judges? Because—from the court's perspective and from the perspective of the adult litigants—they really are about parents and their rights to be with their children. As Jon Elster explains, "[T]he knowledge that the decision will have momentous importance for the parties directly involved and the recognition that it may not be possible to have a rational preference for one parent over the other[] conspire to create a psychological tension in decision makers that many will be unable to tolerate."[4]

This lengthy backdrop to a discussion of child custody disputes is necessary because the focus in this area of the law is commonly so misleading. Typically, a discussion of child custody disputes quickly turns into a discussion of the best interests of children. This is understandable: The best interests standard for resolving such disputes has become ingrained.

In Search of a More Realistic Standard

In the early 1970s, Joseph Goldstein, Anna Freud, and Albert Solnit advanced our conception of child custody disputes by trying to shift the focus from adults to children and from an unrealistic standard to a more realistic one.[5] They proposed that courts stop talking about the best interests of children and reconceive the judicial function as trying to find the least detrimental alternative. This shift in language was meant to remind judges and scholars that once parents divorce and are unable to settle the question of custody amicably and outside the formal judicial process, it is hopeless to speak in terms of children's best interests. Rather, the most courts can hope for is to minimize damage.

But the influence of Goldstein and colleagues has been broader than that; his proposal has also continued to encourage scholars to focus attention on the harm litigation imposes on children. In her very thoughtful chapter in this volume, Andrea Charlow takes this notion seriously and suggests that if courts really care about children, they will begin to find ways to minimize the damage done to children by contested custody cases. The best way to minimize damage, she suggests, is to minimize litigation. She attempts to develop rules that will encourage settlements and discourage trials. There is nothing wrong with this goal. She observes correctly that although the best interests standard may appear "enlightened, in practice custody decisions focus on parents rather than children and are marred by personal and cultural bias."[6]

It seems, however, to me that she takes too seriously the need to decide cases in accordance with children's best interests. She wants to be certain we focus on the child, "[g]iven the relative fragility of the child and the fact that the child did not participate in decisions concerning its conception or the divorce."[7] Of course, it is true that children did not pick their parents, but that does not mean we ought to give children the right to be liberated from their parents and to live with the best adults they can find.

After all, why make such a fuss to ensure that children's best interests are being served after a divorce, especially if (as we have seen) there is no requirement to ensure that children's best interests are being served *before* divorce? Children are forced to live with adults whose parenting skills are limited or even inadequate so long as the parenting does not fall below a minimum standard of fitness. "Forcing" children to live with one of two fit parents without determining which parent is more "fit" or "better" (assuming for these purposes that it is even possible to do so) is not significantly different from "forcing" children to live with parents without making a preliminary determination of their fitness as parents. Why is it that we are so comfortable eschewing this inquiry before divorce, and yet so manifestly uncomfortable with the prospect of a court saying to divorcing parents that it is neither capable of, nor interested in, determining which parent is better for the child?

As I have already suggested, this discomfort does not stem from our concern for the children; it actually has to do with parental concerns. Parents want the opportunity to prove that they have the right to be with their child, not that their child has the right to be with them. The best interests standard blinds us to this central truth. As David Chambers says, "[A]ll states expect courts to make the children's interests the sole focus of their attention. The parents' interests are to be ignored."[8] The best interests standard also distorts our thinking and causes scholars like Charlow to try to do even more to find true best interests. But this search is in vain.

Problems with Alternative Best Interests Standards

Charlow is certainly right to be concerned that substantive rules may lead to unnecessary, harmful litigation. She is also correct to expose the connection between the indeterminacy of the best interests standard and the parental incentive to litigate custody disputes. Indeterminacy does indeed encourage litigation.

One of the more intriguing—and welcome—suggestions in Charlow's article is to make the negotiation process visible to the court and thereby force parties to say publicly what our current settlement process allows them to say privately. There have been few attempts to study the bargaining process in custody cases. Robert Mnookin and Lewis Kornhauser suggest, however, that it may not be possible to realize Charlow's goal of ensuring more settlements by allowing courts to punish the parent who does not place the child's interests above all else when negotiating a custody resolution.[9] They observe that the parameters of the bargaining process are quite complicated, and, wholly apart from the legal rules that loom in the background, the characteristics of the individual parties—including their willingness to take risks—unavoidably affect outcomes in settlements.[10]

Charlow proposes that rules be created that will make parents more likely to work out a satisfactory custody arrangement between themselves. She proposes to punish the parent who unreasonably refuses to settle when the case gets to court. Her proposal is reminiscent of King Solomon's celebrated judgment, which depended on his use of data obtained during the custody litigation itself. As in Solomon's decision, a modern party who fails to place the child's interests above all else loses under Charlow's proposed rule. However, when one takes into account the reality of bargaining, it is unlikely that Charlow's proposed change in the substantive standard for deciding custody cases will have the effect she envisions. Consider, for example, what would have happened had both litigants before Solomon known on what basis the king was going to decide the case. Perhaps Solomon was "outguessed by the woman who declared she would rather give up the child."[11]

Charlow fails to look carefully enough at the realities of bargaining. Placing so much emphasis on blaming the parent who unreasonably refuses to settle is likely to *increase* the stress responsible parents will feel during the settlement process. A quick look at a hypothetical case may help to illustrate this point. In our hypothetical, the mother is a reasonable, caring, loving caretaker of her daughter. But she is also highly risk-averse and takes very seriously the normative rules that are explained to her by her attorney. Her attorney tells her that the court expects the parties to settle the case and will insist that both parties make the child's interests the paramount consideration. Moreover, her lawyer tells her, the court places such emphasis on avoiding trial that it will punish the parent who unreasonably fails to settle the case.

The father, on the other hand, is a gambler who is quite comfortable taking risks. His lawyer gives him the same description of the legal rules and the shadow they cast over the bargaining process. The father quickly realizes the leverage he has over his wife. He knows that he can live with the uncertainty of a fully litigated contest, but she cannot. The father may assess his chances of getting custody through a contested trial process to be poor. In that case, this shrewd assessor of risks understands, his leverage is increased by not settling. The father's advantage in the bargaining process is that he knows his wife cannot bear the least prospect that she might be judged unreasonable by the court. Because he can play the game better than his wife, the father has a better chance of forcing her to capitulate in the bargaining process.

Wholly apart from the impact Charlow's proposal would have, in what sense can we say that settlement furthers the child's best interests? The answer is simply that the case was not litigated; the conflict was reduced quickly. But if that is the goal, there are other ways to make litigation unlikely or even impermissible.

Charlow, of course, knows there are other ways to avoid litigation, but she disapproves of them.

The Promise of Alternative Litigation Avoidance Standards

If child custody disputes were really about what is best for children, society would do whatever it could to keep cases out of court; even flipping coins to settle cases would seem to do just fine. Indeed, flipping coins has been seriously advanced as a means to resolve these disputes,[12] most recently by Elster in a thoughtful proposition.[13] Proponents of the coin flip solution, however, fail to consider its impact on bargaining. Most child custody disputes are resolved without trial. This is undoubtedly because in many cases it is obvious to the parents which parent should have primary custody after divorce. It is not just a matter of both parents agreeing upon what makes the most sense for their children; there is also a shared understanding of what a neutral fact-finder would say after hearing the full story. Knowing that the court will decide the dispute if they are unable to do so, many parents choose to do the right thing in order to avoid litigation expenses. But if the ultimate decision-maker were a coin, many "less worthy" parents would see their leverage greatly increased. They could threaten the "more worthy" parent with utilizing the coin flip in order to extract concessions in the bargaining process. Adding arbitrariness to the process will almost certainly disadvantage the parent who all knowledgeable parties would agree should obtain child custody.

Still, there are other ways to avoid trials. For example, substantive rules that favor one parent, such as the tender years presumption or the gender-neutral primary caretaker presumption, serve the same purpose. I personally prefer a return to the tender years presumption that gives custody of young children to mothers,[14] but I recognize that this would be inconsistent with modern efforts to fashion gender-neutral rules of decision making. The primary caretaker presumption is also preferable to current law. Under it, there is little incentive for the nonprimary caretaker to litigate because the rules are stacked against him or her. Unless the nonprimary caretaker can show that the primary caretaker is unfit, there is nothing to litigate. Charlow never quite tells us what is wrong with this alternative standard. She says that the primary caretaker preference places too much emphasis on continuity of care when that is not the only criterion by which to determine a child's best interests, but that objection is misplaced. It is insufficient to complain that the primary caretaker rule does not guarantee serving a child's best interests, for policy-makers cannot try to do the best thing for everyone. Instead, policy-makers must be more modest and try to do the least harm to the fewest, and on this standard the primary caretaker rule is quite powerful. Certainly the rule is not irrational.

Chambers has endorsed the primary caretaker presumption for yet another reason. Chambers wants parental interests to be formally counted when making custody decisions.[15] As a result, he prefers the primary caretaker because he or she is likely to be more anguished by the loss of custody.[16] Even if it fails to state perfectly a rule for serving a child's best interests, the primary caretaker presumption would avoid contested custody cases. Since Charlow highly values litigation avoidance, she should embrace a child-centered rule, such as the primary caretaker rule, that discourages litigation.[17] On the other hand, the primary caretaker rule does not tell us what the result should be when both parents work or are away from the home an equal amount of time. It also does not avoid litigation when the substantive meaning of "primary" is enhanced by subjective factors, as occurs in at least some jurisdictions.[18]

It may well be that the primary caretaker standard makes improper assumptions about children's best interests. Children may, for example, do better in cases where they are sent to live with the nonprimary caretaker; but for every child who would be better off if shifted from the primary to the nonprimary caretaker, there may be another four or five children who will suffer needless harm by being subjected to a contested custody battle. The transactional costs of litigating the best interests of the child simply are not worth the gains. Even if we knew that some children would be better off with the nonprimary caretaker, it is important to consider that even those children will be saved by the primary caretaker rule from the trauma of litigation and uncertainty. In addition, best interests litigation does not guarantee that courts will correctly identify those children who would be better off if moved. How many children who would be better off with their primary caretakers will an erroneous judicial decision place with the other parent? And how many children who would be better off with the other parent will wrongfully be determined to be better off with the primary caretaker?[19]

Conclusion

In the final analysis, the more clearly defined rule is vastly superior to an open-ended standard such as a child's best interests or even Charlow's most reasonable parent rule. Adults, not children, will lose under fixed rules. It is adults—whether they be legislators, law professors, or judges who see themselves as potential disputants in a postdivorce custody case—who are unwilling to be cut off from the possibility of trying to obtain custody of their children. Children are simply not empowered by child custody cases, and we would be far better off if we stopped deluding ourselves into thinking otherwise.

In the modern era, as in the past, the family courts of this country operate on the unwarranted premise that judges are capable of making fine-tuned judgments about a child's best interests. While the underlying ideal and rhetoric are laudable, the unfortunate reality is that enormous amounts of time, money, and emotional energy are being expended in contested custody proceedings, often solely to the benefit of the divorce lawyers. For every case in which the outcome can truly be said to benefit a child, a far larger number of cases are litigated for no good purpose. Preserving a system that produces protracted and costly custody litigation whenever parents are unwilling to resolve their custody disputes is in the best interests of only a very small number of people.

NOTES

1. *See* Mnookin, Child-Custody Adjudication: Judicial Functions in the Face of Indeterminacy, 39 Law & Contemp. Probs., Summer 1975, at 226, 255–62.

2. Richards, The Individual, the Family, and the Constitution: A Jurisprudential Perspective, 55 N.Y.U. L. Rev. 1, 28 (1980).

3. The Supreme Court has characterized the state's interest in these circumstances as "de minimus." Stanley v. Illinois, 405 U.S. 645, 657 (1972). In addition, the Court has recognized the rights of parents and families to be free from unnecessary state interference under various theories: privacy, *see, e.g.*, Roe v. Wade, 410 U.S. 113, 152–53 (1973); Griswold v. Connecticut, 381 U.S. 479, 485–86 (1965); liberty, *see, e.g.*, Cleveland Bd. of Educ. v. LaFleur, 414 U.S. 632, 639–40 (1974); Wisconsin v. Yoder, 406 U.S. 205, 230–34 (1972); Stanley v. Illinois, 405 U.S. 645, 651 (1972); Pierce v. Society of Sisters, 268 U.S. 510, 534–35 (1925); and integrity, *see, e.g.*, Stanley v. Illinois, 405 U.S. 645, 651 (1972); Griswold v. Connecticut, 381 U.S. 479, 500 (1965) (Harlan, J., concurring); Poe v. Ullman, 367 U.S. 497, 551–52 (1961) (Harlan, J., dissenting).

4. J. Elster, Solomonic Judgements: Studies in the Limitations of Rationality 124 (1989).

5. J. Goldstein et al., Beyond the Best Interests of the Child (1973).

6. See Chapter 1 in this volume.

7. *Id.*

8. Chambers, Rethinking the Substantive Rules for Custody Disputes in Divorce, 83 Mich. L. Rev. 477, 499 (1984).

9. Mnookin & Kornhauser, Bargaining in the Shadow of the Law: The Case of Divorce, 88 Yale L.J. 950 (1979).

10. *Id.* at 973–77.

11. Elster, Solomonic Judgements, *supra* note 4, at 128.

12. Chambers, Rethinking the Substantive Rules, *supra* note 8, at 485; Mnookin, Child-Custody Adjudication, *supra* note 1, at 226, 289–92; Mnookin & Kornhauser, Bargaining in the Shadow, *supra* note 9, at 970–71.

13. Elster, Solomonic Judgements, *supra* note 4, at 123–74.

14. *See* Uviller, Fathers' Rights and Feminism: The Maternal Presumption Revisited, 1 Harv. Women's L. J. 107 (1978).

15. Chambers, Rethinking the Substantive Rules, *supra* note 8, at 478–79.

16. *Id.* at 502.

17. The rule may have an adverse political impact. In order to fulfill traditional expectations of the primary caretaker role, and thereby avoid the danger of losing custody in the event of a divorce, mothers may decide not to work full-time.

18. *See* Chambers, Rethinking the Substantive Rules, *supra* note 8, at 538 n.230.

19. Elster, Solomonic Judgements, *supra* note 4, at 147–48.

■ CHAPTER THREE

The Use of Religion as Part of the "Best Interests" Test in Child Custody Decisions

Donald L. Beschle

PROFESSOR CHARLOW'S desire to reduce both the incidence of conflict and the indeterminacy of judicial discretion in child custody decisions through the promotion of voluntary agreement is entirely understandable. Her position that the willingness to place a child's interests over one's own is the strongest factor supporting a parent's claim to custody can, as Professor Guggenheim notes in Chapter 2, trace its lineage at least as far back as the days of King Solomon. Still, it is highly unlikely that courts will be relieved of the responsibility of determining the best interests of children on a case by case basis within the foreseeable future.[1] One specific issue in judicial determination of best interests has been especially problematic for the courts: the legitimacy of the use of religion as a factor. This chapter will address whether courts may consider the presence of a religious environment in the home of a parent to be a positive factor without violating the First Amendment prohibition of government establishment of religion.

Uncertainty as to when or whether a traditional religious upbringing is in the best interests of the child may make courts reluctant to assert that state promotion of traditional religion serves a legitimate secular purpose. Furthermore, favoring traditional religion places the courts in the untenable position of favoring particular types of religion. However, the First Amendment should not be seen as preventing all inquiry into the effect of parental values—be they called moral or religious—on the home environment. Social scientists and other observers have noted that despite surface perceptions that our society is thoroughly secular, religion remains quite important to a large number of Americans.[2] Meanwhile, the increasing religious diversity of the United States and the simultaneous increase in religiously mixed marriages make it more likely that parents will have different religious views.[3] This in turn indicates an increase in the likelihood that courts will be asked to choose between those religious views in the context of child custody disputes. At the same time, however, the constitutional commitment to religious neutrality contained in the First Amendment raises serious questions about the legitimacy of judicial consideration of religion as a factor in custody decisions. In addressing the constitutionality of such decisions, we must first address the related question of whether religion may, in fact, be seen as a factor promoting the best interests of the child.

The Religion Clauses of the First Amendment: Standards

The First Amendment provides that "Congress shall make no law respecting an establishment of religion" and that "Congress shall make no law . . . prohibiting the free exercise [of religion]."[4] However, neither the establishment clause nor the free exercise clause is an absolute bar to government activity that has some impact on religious belief. Rather, the Supreme Court has attempted to develop standards that will preserve the core values which led to the erection of a "wall of separation between church and state,"[5] but that will also take into account the frequent and inevitable intersection of the concerns of religion with the concerns of government.

Since 1971, the prevailing test for weighing government action challenged under the establishment clause has been the three-part test set forth in *Lemon v. Kurtzman*.[6] Under *Lemon*, to avoid invalidation a government act must: (1) "have a secular legislative purpose"; (2) have a "principal or primary effect . . . that neither advances nor inhibits religion"; and (3) avoid "an excessive . . . entanglement with religion."[7] The *Lemon* test may, however, be applied with varying degrees of rigor, and influential voices have recently called for its refinement or abandonment.

Justice O'Connor has maintained that *Lemon* should be applied in a way that primarily focuses on whether the challenged government action can reasonably be seen as "government endorsement or disapproval of religion. Endorsement sends a message to nonadherents that they are outsiders, not full members of the political community, and an accompanying message to adherents that they are insiders, favored members of the political community."[8] Incidental benefits to religion will not invalidate a government action that is not intended or reasonably perceived to convey such a message. This approach has received much favorable commentary,[9] and may soon emerge as the primary tool of establishment clause analysis.

Justice Kennedy, however, has put forward a different standard, which also has its adherents. This approach would largely replace the *Lemon* test with the question of whether the challenged government action constitutes "coercion" or "proselytization."[10] The most lenient of the three tests, Justice Kennedy's approach would permit government action short of that intended or likely to bring about religious conformity through the use of government's coercive power. Still, regardless of whether this test or Justice O'Connor's nonendorsement test ultimately prevails, the same core questions set forth by *Lemon* must be examined. Is government acting with the purpose of furthering religious belief, or for a secular reason? What effect is the government action likely to have on secular concerns? And is the secular effect of the action sufficient to outweigh whatever aid it may give or be perceived to give to a particular faith?

The free exercise clause may also be relevant to child custody cases. During the 1960s and early 1970s, the Supreme Court adopted an approach which required that any government act placing a significant burden on the practice of religion must be justified by showing that the restriction was narrowly tailored to protect a "compelling state interest."[11] In 1990, the Court significantly narrowed the scope of the free exercise clause in the controversial case *Employment Division v. Smith*.[12] A narrow majority of the Court held that the clause would be applied strictly only against government attempts actually to change beliefs or prevent communication of religious doctrine, or where a state prohibited action only because of state hostility to a particular religious message or belief.[13] Thus, if the government acts for a legitimate secular reason and regulates action rather than belief or speech, an individual may not claim exemption from the law based on its impact on his or her religion. At the core of both establishment and free exercise analyses, then, is a necessary determination of the existence and strength of the secular reasons underlying government acts that favor or disfavor religion.

Religion as a Factor in Child Custody: What Have Courts Done?

Religion has been used as a factor in child custody cases for as long as courts have attempted to assess a child's best interests.[14] Courts have diverged in their views of what weight can or should legitimately be given to religious factors. Most states give courts great leeway in determining what factors contribute to a child's best interests. While the term "religion" is rarely used, most courts hold that "moral" concerns are relevant;[15] some courts have made reference to the child's "spiritual" welfare.[16]

Some states, sensitive to First Amendment concerns, have limited the role of religion. Some have held that religion may be neither the sole nor the dominant factor in custody decisions.[17] Others have held that religion may be considered only upon a showing that it will have a clear effect on the secular well-being of the child.[18] In these states, the argument for child custody may be based on evidence that the presence or absence of religion will cause physical, emotional, or social benefits or harm to a child,[19] but an argument based on spiritual welfare or the assumption that religion is per se beneficial would be improper.[20]

Some courts have held that religion is relevant where a child has "actual religious needs."[21] Thus, if a child has acquired a religious preference or feels religion to be part of his or her identity, the relative ability of parents to provide for religious needs is a proper consideration. This position presents some practical difficulties, not the least of which is the problem of determining when a child acquires actual religious needs. Do they exist from the earliest stages of religious training, or, at the other extreme, do only mature minors have such needs?[22] Despite these difficulties, this distinction does seem attractive in its insistence that the focus remain squarely on the child, rather than on the feelings of the parents.

In addition to questions concerning the presence or absence of religion, courts may also be called upon to weigh situations where both parents intend to provide religious training, but each adheres to a different faith. If there is an undisputed core to the jurisprudence of the religion clauses, it is that government may not prefer one religion to another.[23] Most courts consistently refuse to weigh the relative value of religions, even highly unconventional sects. Thus, a California court refused to find necessarily contrary to a child's best interests the fact that a mother was a member of a religious sect that prohibited social contact with non-members, participation in civic or political activity, ownership of radios or televisions, or giving toys to children.[24] There are occasional exceptions to the general rule against judicial evaluation of religious beliefs. The Nebraska Supreme Court upheld a finding that a mother's adherence to the beliefs of an ultraconservative sect, which required the mother to shun her daughter if she disobeyed church rules and taught that "a master plot on the part of Jews and Communists [threatened] to gain control of the world,"[25] weighed against her claims to custody.

Quite the opposite situation presents itself when there is no denominational split between parents. When both parents express allegiance to the same set of religious values, yet one parent claims to be in a better position than the other parent to communicate those values to the child, courts can consider easily ascertainable factors, and no choice need be made between religions or between religion—however defined—and irreligion. The court merely accepts the parents' agreed choice of religious values and seeks to determine how they may best be conveyed. Thus relieved of the burden of seeming to declare one religion better than another, courts often attempt to determine which parent will provide the better religious environment for the child. Courts have considered factors ranging from relatively objective matters, such as the fact that only one parent lives in a community that has religious facilities for the child to attend,[26] to more subjective matters, such as whether a parent's moral conduct is consistent with his or her professed beliefs.[27] Regular church attendance,[28] a parent's participation in church-related activities,[29] or insistence that the child attend church services or parochial school[30] have all been favorably noted by various courts. Once in a while, a court has even found that too much religious activity on the part of a parent is bad for the child. The Alabama Supreme Court held that a trial judge might properly consider evidence that an evangelist's intense religious involvement was adversely affecting her children.[31]

Thus, where parents profess the same denominational beliefs, a number of courts have been willing to weigh the presence of a religious environment as a factor—almost always positive—in the overall determination of best interests. Even here, however, care must be taken to ensure that the court is not actually being asked to choose between competing religious philosophies. Parents may belong to the same denomination but differ sharply on value questions. This may be reflected in such things as frequency of church attendance or the rigor with which official church teaching is followed at home. Unlike cases involving the availability of religious facilities in two different communities, here the court may actually be faced with a choice between different religious conceptions, even though they share a common denominational label. Courts should certainly attempt to avoid making decisions regarding who is the "better" member of a certain religion.[32]

Only in extreme cases will courts choose one of two competing denominations as better for the child. However, courts are less reluctant to endorse one parent's greater commitment to providing the child with an upbringing in the faith shared by both parents, or to favor the presence of some religion in the home over its complete absence. These latter bases for custody decisions raise serious constitutional concerns. May courts make such decisions and remain faithful not only to the best interests of the child, but also to the demands of the First Amendment?

Can the Use of Religion Be Justified?

Government may not promote religion for its own sake, but must put forward some plausible secular reason for an action that touches on, and perhaps has the effect of benefiting, religion.[33] Thus, the use of religion as a factor in child custody disputes, if it is to be constitutionally justified, must promote legitimate, secular ends.

However skeptical one may be of the value of the best interests test, it would seem clear that the promotion of the best interests of the child qualifies as secular. It has been noted that best interests can be thought of in two ways.[34] Best interests may be seen as related to the happiness or welfare of the individual, as defined by that individual, or measured against a set of socially approved standards: Is the child likely to become a well-educated, law-abiding, productive member of society?[35] It may be somewhat artificial to separate these two approaches to a best interests analysis. Individual happiness surely has some relationship to the rewards society bestows on those who exhibit approved behavior. Still, it will be helpful for purposes of analysis to look separately at the individual's subjective view of a good life and the community's view of the same thing.

A significant amount of research has examined the relationship between religion and emotional well-being. Reviewing studies conducted from 1951 through 1979 that correlated religiousness with indices of emotional health (such as self-esteem, ego strength, or adjustment) or pathology (such as hostility, anxiety, or neuroticism), Allen Bergin found mixed results, but on the whole the studies provided "marginal support for a positive effect of religion."[36]

More recent studies have attempted to be more precise in their measurement of religion and have produced interesting results. Rather than using traditional, and perhaps not very reliable, indicators of the presence of religion such as church attendance, formal church membership, or agreement with statements of orthodox belief,[37] Raymond Paloutzian and Craig Ellison have attempted to measure an individual's orientation to what Ellison calls "transcendence, or the capacity to find purpose and meaning beyond one's self and the immediate and to relate positively to God, parenting and life experiences which promote trust and fundamental optimism."[38] They have attempted to measure this orientation through the use of a twenty-item questionnaire called the Spiritual Well-Being Scale (SWB).[39] In several studies, high SWB scores have been found to correlate positively with a sense of hope,[40] purpose in life,[41] self-esteem,[42] and social skills,[43] and to correlate negatively with loneliness.[44]

Perhaps most interesting, however, is the division of the SWB into two distinct submeasures. Ten of the twenty items, referred to as the Religious Well-Being (RWB) subscale, specifically refer to God and the extent to which the respondent feels a sense of transcendence in traditional theistic terms.[45] The other ten items, referred to as the Existential Well-Being (EWB) subscale, measure a sense of transcending self, but without overt traditional theistic overtones.[46] While the SWB, RWB, and EWB scales all consistently correlate positively with measures of emotional health and well-being, the EWB subscale provides much stronger support for this correlation than does the RWB subscale.[47]

Thus, empirical studies have shown that well-being is furthered by a sense of "transcendence, or the capacity to find purpose and meaning beyond one's self and the immediate," but that traditional theism is not the sole, or perhaps even the most effective, path to achieving that end.[48] These findings suggest that the inconsistency of earlier studies may arise less from any lack of correlation between religion and well-being than from disagreement over the meaning of the term "religion." To successfully analyze the role of religion in child custody, or in any other context, requires an initial attempt to define the term.

At the end of the nineteenth century, the Supreme Court drew its definition of religion around conventional Western notions of theism, prayer, and worship. The court stated: "The term 'religion' has reference to one's views of his relations to his Creator, and to the obligations they impose of reverence for his being and character, and of obedience to his will."[49] Religion was explicitly theistic, primarily oriented toward otherworldly concerns, and usually practiced as a member of a recognized church. Assuming that this was an accurate definition at the time of the framers, is such a definition still valid?

In tracing the history of religion, Robert Bellah has noted a shift in the degree to which it has focused on transcendent, otherworldly concerns as opposed to social questions.[50] Bellah has observed that primitive religion was nearly indistinguishable from other aspects of community life. But religion evolved into what

Bellah calls "historic religion": religion that is separate from worldly concerns and that exalts "another realm of reality" as alone true and infinitely valuable.[51] Over the past century, "historic religion" has evolved into "modern religion," which attempts to reunite transcendental and social concerns.[52] The law has not failed to notice this change.

In 1961 the Supreme Court noted that there could be religions "which do not teach what would generally be considered a belief in the existence of God."[53] Later, in addressing the eligibility of draft-age men for conscientious objector status based on "religious training and belief," the Court held that "religion" could include any comprehensive system of ultimate concerns that creates "duties superior to those arising from any human relation."[54] This system of beliefs did not have to be articulated in traditional theistic terms or practiced within a traditional church or sect.[55] Such a broad definition, the Court held, would permit the law to grant an exemption based upon "religious" concerns without violating the establishment clause.[56]

The significance of the definition of religion should be apparent. To single out for special treatment traditional theism or "historic religion," which comprise the types of religions most familiar to the framers of the First Amendment, raises serious constitutional problems. To define the term more broadly, however, may mitigate such concerns. This fits quite nicely with the findings of modern studies discussed above.[57] Social science gives us little reason to believe that, if religion is narrowly and traditionally defined, it will promote the best interests of the child. But religion broadly defined as a commitment to an "ultimate concern," a coherent set of beliefs that transcend and give meaning to everyday existence, does seem to be a source of mental and emotional well-being. Thus, we may not easily dismiss the proposition that religion may be used in custody decisions for the legitimate secular purpose and effect of promoting the welfare of the child.

The best interests test may also be seen from society's point of view as a means of promoting the shaping of "good" children, as well as merely happy children. As long as the definition of a "good" person does not include religion for its own sake, this social goal would clearly seem to qualify as secular. It has been argued that community values will inevitably affect custody decisions, and that open acknowledgment of this is entirely proper. One commentator states that "a court would be justified in *candidly* . . . preferring the parent whose values more closely reflect such qualities as tolerance, charity, compassion, a sense of social duty, respect for independence of mind . . . whether the cultural values in conflict have a secular or religious origin."[58] Is there evidence that religion promotes these ends, and is such a secular use of religion appropriate?

Social science has explored the connection between religious belief and social attitudes. Early research failed to establish a clear link between religion and prosocial values. Studies disagree on whether religion has any correlation with juvenile delinquency or other antisocial behavior.[59] Some early studies even indicated that racial prejudice and intolerance are positively linked to religiousness.[60] However, later research, giving more precise consideration to the evidence, presents a somewhat different picture. Evidence exists that certain types of religion—distinguished from religion per se—are linked to positive social values and behavior. The crucial distinction among religions is not between denominations, but rather between two types of religiousness, labeled by the sociologist Gordon Allport "intrinsic" and "extrinsic."[61]

Intrinsic religious believers treat their beliefs as ends, valuable by virtue of their very existence.[62] Extrinsic believers, on the other hand, conform their beliefs and actions to religious norms in order to achieve other ends, such as social acceptance.[63] Allport's early research indicated a positive correlation between religion and racial prejudice,[64] but he modified his position on the basis of the intrinsic–extrinsic distinction. Intrinsic religious belief was found to indicate low levels of prejudice; extrinsic religiosity, however, was "entirely compatible with prejudice."[65] Further research has demonstrated links between intrinsic religiosity and traits such as friendliness and helpfulness.[66]

Others have challenged the value of the intrinsic–extrinsic distinction and suggested alternative ways to categorize religion that will correlate with positive social attitudes even more reliably.[67] Perhaps the most interesting approach is that of Daniel Batson and his colleagues. Their research indicates that the best religious indicator of low prejudice is a religion that is regarded as "an open-ended process of pursuing ultimate questions more than ultimate answers," one in which religion is a "quest."[68] On the other hand, where religion represents a commitment to a closed set of norms, it does not lead to low levels of prejudice.[69] Thus, despite continuing skepticism on the part of some observers,[70] there is substantial evidence that some forms of religious belief—types that cut across denominational lines—can promote socially desirable attitudes and behavior. While this alone may not be determinative, it provides further support for the proposition that secular purposes and effects may legitimate some consideration of religion in applying the best interests test.

The furtherance of best interests, of course, is not the only possible legitimate secular reason for taking account of religion. Courts have held that the protection of the right of free exercise of religion is a legitimate secular goal and may justify actions otherwise seen as aid to religion and threats to establishment clause values.[71] To insist that a parent violate religious precepts or curtail religious practices in order to gain or retain custody or visitation rights raises parental free exercise concerns, even after the narrowing of the scope of the free exercise clause by the Supreme Court in *Smith*.[72] At the very least, rules pursuing the best interests of the child should attempt to achieve that goal with minimal interference with parents' free exercise of religion.

Similarly, the free exercise rights of the child should be respected. These independent, potentially competing rights are often difficult to weigh. Although the notion of a child, especially a younger child, having a religion independent of that of the parents can be troublesome,[73] a child who is old enough to articulate particular religious beliefs and feel a sense of membership in some religious group should be properly regarded as having independent free exercise rights.

Respect for these rights may serve as a legitimate purpose for consideration of religious factors in custody disputes.

Using Religion as a Factor in
Child Custody Decisions

What does all of this tell us about the legitimacy of the use of religious factors as part of the determination of the best interests of the child? In short, consideration of religion is by no means always unconstitutional, but the scope of this consideration must be carefully limited. Presumptions that traditional religion is always a positive factor may, in many instances, be not only unwise, but also unconstitutional.

It seems clear, and relatively uncontroversial, that where there are clear, individualized showings of physical or emotional consequences to a child, positive or negative, from the presence of religion in the home environment, religion may be considered in the determination of best interests.[74] Similarly, where a mature child has "actual" religious needs, taking them into account will both help fulfill the child's need for stability and further the child's emerging free exercise rights. When courts go further, to regard the presence of religion as a positive factor across the board, critics are right to feel uneasy. Social science indicates that a commitment to values beyond self promotes a happier, better-adjusted life, but this commitment need not be framed in traditional theistic terms. The proper response, therefore, is not to exclude consideration of religion from the best interests test, but to pay close attention to the definition of religion.

There is insufficient evidence that religion defined as traditional theism or church affiliation will produce happier children or children who will mature into "better" citizens. Therefore, to consider traditional religiosity as better than its absence clearly runs afoul of Justice O'Connor's test by endorsing traditional religion for its own sake. It may even violate the noncoercion test by influencing parents to profess beliefs that they do not genuinely hold in order to qualify for custody.

If, however, the expansive definition of religion as "ultimate concern" is used, far different conclusions are warranted. The evidence that people whose values transcend self-interest report higher levels of emotional well-being provides a legitimate secular purpose for considering the values espoused by contending parents. Evidence that a parent believes, acts pursuant to, and will convey the message that life is meaningful, and that transcendent values demand commitment beyond self-interest, need not be excluded from the best interests calculus.

One might legitimately argue that if the parent whose values are rooted in secular philosophies must be treated the same as parents with theistic value systems, all references to religion in custody disputes might be replaced with references to morals or ethics. While a case might be made for a conclusion that all references to these issues should be made in nontheistic terms, doing so might unfairly disadvantage those whose approach to providing values to their children is closely linked to traditional religion. A large part of the American public enunciates its transcendent commitments in traditional religious terms.[75] To privilege those who do not would be just as improper as favoring those who do. Thus, religious values may be considered in determining the overall home environment, but traditional religiosity cannot hold a privileged place compared with other coherent systems of value not rooted in traditional religion.

Of course, coherent value systems may not always promote beliefs regarded as socially desirable. This leads to the much more delicate question of whether, in the presence of two coherent value systems, courts may prefer one to the other. Certain types of religiosity, which cut across denominational lines, correlate better than others with valued social attitudes such as tolerance, charity, and social duty.[76] Promotion of these values by placing children in religious environments more likely to promote them might be seen as having a secular purpose and effect. Still, to permit such choices conflicts with what is generally regarded as the minimal core of the establishment clause. Even those who contend that government may favor religion over irreligion concede that government may not prefer one religion over another.[77] And even if this is expressed not as a choice of denominations, but rather as a preference for "inner-directed," "quest-oriented," or "liberal" religion, it is extremely troubling and almost surely improper under current First Amendment standards.

An occasional voice has challenged the conventional wisdom here. In a recent article, Daniel Conkle suggests that the true concern of the establishment clause was the effect of "inerrant" religion, one in which beliefs are not subject to rational dialogue.[78] He suggests, at least tentatively, that in some contexts government may give more respect to the beliefs of "dialogic" religions whose members are open to rational persuasion, at least on issues of worldly concern.[79] Joseph Mucci argues that decision-makers cannot avoid taking social values into account, and therefore explicit approval of religions that teach tolerance and other liberal values is preferable to approval that is disguised in court decisions.[80] These critics may have a point, but explicit judicial approval of some religious values as preferable to others is so inconsistent with historic First Amendment doctrine that the likelihood that such rulings will be found permissible in the foreseeable future seems exceptionally slim. While there will, no doubt, be occasional exceptions in extreme cases of concrete, demonstrable harm to particular children,[81] the establishment clause will not allow courts in general to label some systems of religious belief as preferable to others.

Conclusion

The connection between traditional religion and a secularly defensible contribution to the best interests of the child is tenuous at best. This does not mean that the establishment clause precludes any use of religion in child custody determinations. The use of a traditional, narrow definition of religion causes constitutional problems. If, however, the definition of religion is not limited to traditional theism practiced in familiar denominations, but includes a much broader range of expression and commitment to value systems transcending self-interest, consideration of religion as a factor in determining a child's best interests is not only supported by social science, but also, when carried out with sensitivity to the limits discussed above, consistent with the demands of the First Amendment.

NOTES

Acknowledgment: An expanded treatment of the subject of this essay can be found in Donald L. Beschle, *God Bless the Child? The Use of Religion as a Factor in Child Custody and Adoption Proceedings*, 58 Fordham L. Rev. 383 (1989).

1. Even under rules granting strong presumptions to one or another parent, some considerations of the child's welfare inevitably appear, even if considered only to be exceptions. *See generally* Einhorn, Child Custody in Historical Perspective: A Study of Changing Social Perceptions of Divorce and Child Custody in Anglo-American Law, 4 Behav. Sci. & L. 119 (1986) (reviewing the historical biases of Anglo-American courts in making decisions based on sexual stereotypes, rather than individual competence).

2. Survey data from the 1980s indicate that 90 percent or more of Americans pray at least occasionally, about one-half say that religion is very important to them, and about 40 percent attend church in a typical week. *See* R. Wuthnow, The Restructuring of American Religion: Society and Faith Since World War II, at 164–65 (1988).

3. Most American marriages are religiously homogeneous, but the incidence of interfaith marriage appears to be increasing. The percentage of religiously heterogeneous marriage is substantially higher among younger couples. *See* Alston et al., Extent of Interfaith Marriages Among White Americans, 37 Soc. Analysis 261, 262–63 (1976). This is mitigated by the fact that over time, most couples from different religions eventually achieve religious unity through conversion of one or both spouses. *See* Wuthnow, The Restructuring of American Religion, *supra* note 2, at 90. Still, "[f]or every major denomination, a smaller proportion of married people are currently wedded to a spouse who has the same religion as theirs than was the case a few decades ago." *Id.*

4. U.S. Const. amend. I.

5. The phrase comes from Thomas Jefferson. *See* A Reply to a Committee of the Danbury Baptist Association, in 8 The Writings of Thomas Jefferson 113 (H. A. Washington ed., 1854).

6. 403 U.S. 602 (1971).

7. *Id.* at 612–13.

8. Lynch v. Donnelly, 465 U.S. 668, 688 (1984) (O'Connor, J., concurring).

9. *See* Dellinger, The Sounds of Silence: An Epistle on Prayer and the Constitution, 95 Yale L.J. 1631 (1986); Loewy, Rethinking Government Neutrality Towards Religion Under the Establishment Clause: The Untapped Potential of Justice

O'Connor's Insight 64 N.C. L. Rev. 1049 (1986); Rostain, Note, Permissible Accommodations of Religion: Reconsidering the New York *Get* Statute, 96 Yale L.J. 1147, 1159–64 (1987).

10. County of Allegheny v. ACLU, 492 U.S. 573, 664 (1989) (Kennedy, J., concurring in part and dissenting in part).

11. *See* Wisconsin v. Yoder, 406 U.S. 205 (1972); Sherbert v. Verner, 374 U.S. 398 (1963).

12. 110 S. Ct. 1595 (1990).

13. *Id.* at 1599.

14. One of the earliest reported cases in which a court determined custody by examining the likely effects of the decision on the child, rather than simply applying the then prevalent rule that the father had the right to determine a child's upbringing, turned largely on the atheistic beliefs of the father, the poet Percy Bysshe Shelley. *See* Shelley v. Westbrooke, 37 Eng. Rep. 850 (Ch. 1817).

15. *See, e.g.,* Hild v. Hild, 157 A.2d 442, 446 (Md. 1960); *In re* Adoption of "E," 279 A.2d 785, 792 (N.J. 1971). For statutes with the same approach, see Ohio Rev. Code Ann. § 3109.04(B)(1)(c) (Anderson 1989); Utah Code Ann. § 30-3-10(1)(1989).

16. *See, e.g.,* Burnham v. Burnham, 304 N.W.2d 58, 61 (Neb. 1981); Dean v. Dean, 232 S.E.2d 470, 471–72 (N.C. Ct. App. 1977); Pruss v. Pruss, 344 A.2d 509, 510 (Pa. Super. Ct. 1975). For statutes with similar references, see Haw. Rev. Stat. § 571-46(5) (1985); S.C. Code Ann. § 20-3-160 (1976).

17. *See, e.g.,* Frank v. Frank, 167 N.E.2d 577, 580 (Ill. App. Ct. 1960).

18. *See, e.g., In re* Marriage of Short, 698 P.2d 1310, 1311–12 (Colo. 1985); Osier v. Osier, 410 A.2d 1027, 1030 (Me. 1980); *In re* Marriage of Hadeen, 619 P.2d 374, 382 (Wash. Ct. App. 1980).

19. *See, e.g., Burnham,* 304 N.W.2d at 61.

20. *See, e.g.,* Gould v. Gould, 342 N.W.2d 426, 432 (Wis. 1984).

21. *See* Bonjour v. Bonjour, 592 P.2d 1233, 1239–40 (Alaska 1979); *In re* Vardinakis, 160 Misc. 13, 17–18, 289 N.Y.S. 355, 361 (N.Y. Dom. Rel. Ct. 1936); *see also* Note, The Establishment Clause and Religion in Child Custody Disputes: Factoring Religion Into the Best Interests Equation, 82 Mich. L. Rev. 1702, 1727–32 (1984) (discussing a number of factors limiting the use of a child's religion-based preference).

22. *See* Ramsey, The Legal Imputation of Religion to an Infant in Adoption Proceedings, 34 N.Y.U. L. Rev. 649 (1959). Some courts have held that younger children are too immature to meaningfully choose their religion. *See, e.g.,* Wojnarowicz v. Wojnarowicz, 137 A.2d 618, 621 (N.J. Super. Ct. 1958); Schwarzman v. Schwarzman, 88 Misc. 2d 866, 874, 388 N.Y.S.2d 993, 999 (N.Y. Sup. Ct. 1976).

23. This principle is affirmed even by justices generally seen as accommodationists. *See* Wallace v. Jaffree, 472 U.S. 38, 113 (1985) (Rehnquist, J., dissenting).

24. Quiner v. Quiner, 59 Cal. Reptr. 503 (Cal. Ct. App. 1967).

25. Burnham v. Burnham, 304 N.W.2d 58, 60 (Neb. 1981).

26. T. v. H., 245 A.2d 221, 221 (N.J. Super. Ct. 1968), *aff'd* 264 A.2d 244 (N.J. Super. Ct. App. Div. 1970).

27. *See, e.g.,* McNamara v. McNamara, 181 N.W.2d 206 (Iowa 1970).

28. *See, e.g.,* Strickland v. Strickland, 235 So. 2d 833, 835 (Ala. 1970); Lewis v. Lewis, 537 P.2d 204, 208 (Kan. 1975); Welch v. Welch, 307 So. 2d 737, 739 (La. Ct. App. 1975).

29. *See, e.g.,* Meyer v. Hackler, 54 So. 2d 7, 10 (La. 1951); *In re* Custody of King, 181 S.E.2d 221, 222 (N.C. Ct. App. 1971).

30. *See, e.g.,* Woodard v. Woodard, 244 So. 2d 595, 597 (Ala. Civ. App. 1971); Johnson v. Johnson, 536 S.W.2d 620, 621 (Tex. Civ. App. 1976).

31. Hilley v. Hilley, 405 So. 2d 708, 711 (Ala. 1981).

32. Recent research indicates that the most significant religious differences among Americans are no longer denominational. Robert Wuthnow's major premise in his recent book is that most denominations are informally dividing into liberal and conservative groups who may have less in common with those having an opposite approach to their own denomination than with those having a similar approach to other denominations. R. Wuthnow, Introduction, in The Religious Dimension: New Directions in Quantitative Research 1, 5–6 (R. Wuthnow ed., 1979) [hereinafter The Religious Dimension].

33. *See supra* notes 4–10 and accompanying text.

34. *See* Chambers, Rethinking the Substantive Rules for Custody Disputes in Divorce, 83 Mich. L. Rev. 477, 488–94 (1984).

35. *Id.*

36. Bergin, Religiosity and Mental Health: A Critical Revaluation and Meta-Analysis, 14 Prof. Psychology Res. & Prac. 170 (1983). Bergin found religion positively linked to mental health in 47 percent of reported effects, negatively linked in 23 percent, with 30 percent showing no relationship. *Id.* at 176. Most of the positive and negative results were quite weak; only seven of thirty outcomes produced statistically significant relationships between religion and mental health (five of these were positive relationships, two negative). *Id.*

37. For an extensive survey of approaches to measuring religiosity, see W. Roof, Concepts and Indicators of Religious Commitment: A Critical Review, in The Religious Dimension, *supra* note 32, at 17–41. The use of any single, static measure of religiosity, especially self-identification with a denomination, is criticized in Larson et al., Systematic Analysis of Research on Religious Variables in Four Major Psychiatric Journals, 1978–1982, 143 Am. J. Psychiatry 329 (1986). That study concludes that psychiatric research in this area has been less sophisticated than the work of psychologists or sociologists. *Id.* at 333.

38. Ellison, Spiritual Well-Being: Conceptualization and Measurement, 11 J. Psychology & Theology 330, 338 (1983). The classic work in this area is R. Paloutzian & C. Ellison, Loneliness, Spiritual Well-Being, and the Quality of Life, in Loneliness: A Sourcebook of Current Theory, Research and Therapy 224 (L. Peplau & D. Perlman, eds., 1982).

39. *See* Ellison, Spiritual Well-Being, *supra* note 38, at 332–33.

40. *See* Carson et al., Hope and Its Relationship to Spiritual Well-Being, 16 J. Psychology & Theology 159, 163 (1988).

41. *See* Dufton & Perlman, The Association Between Religiosity and the Purpose-in-Life Test: Does It Reflect Purpose or Satisfaction?, 14 J. Psychology and Theology 42, 47 (1986).

42. *See* Ellison, Spiritual Well-Being, *supra* note 38, at 336.

43. *See id.* at 335.

44. *See* Paloutzian & Ellison, Loneliness, *supra* note 38, at 234.

45. *See* Ellison, Spiritual Well-Being, *supra* note 38, at 332–33.

46. *Id.*

47. *See id.* at 333–35 (data summarized in tables 1–3); *see also* Carson et al., Hope and Spiritual Well-Being, *supra* note 40, at 165–66.

48. *See* Ellison, Spiritual Well-Being, *supra* note 38, at 338.

49. Davis v. Beason, 133 U.S. 333, 342 (1890).

50. Bellah, Religious Evolution, 29 Am. Soc. Rev. 358, 374 (1964).

51. *Id.* at 359–60. Historic religions, then, are transcendental, stressing the separateness of religious and political structures and seeking to set the believer apart from ordinary worldly concerns.

52. *Id.*

53. Torcaso v. Watkins, 367 U.S. 488, 495 n.11 (1961).

54. United States v. Seeger, 380 U.S. 163, 173–85 (1965). *See also* Welsh v. United States, 398 U.S. 333 (1970). The Court drew heavily on liberal Protestant thought, citing the work of Paul Tillich and John Robinson. *See Seeger*, 380 U.S. at 180–81.

55. *See Seeger*, 380 U.S. at 177–78.

56. The Court cautioned that it was adopting this definition only for the purpose of interpreting § 6(j) of the Military Selective Service Act of 1948, Pub. L. 80–759, 62 Stat. 604, 613 (codified as amended at 50 U.S.C. § 456(j) (1988)). Without such a broad definition, the § 6(j) provision of eligibility for conscientious objector status based on "religious training and belief" might have been unconstitutional. *See Welsh*, 398 U.S. at 344–67 (Harlan, J., concurring). Nevertheless, the definition of religion has been widely cited in other contexts. *See generally* L. Tribe, American Constitutional Law 1179–88 (2d ed. 1988).

57. *See supra* notes 36–46 and accompanying text.

58. Mucci, The Effect of Religious Beliefs in Child Custody Disputes, 5 Can. J. Fam. Law 353, 360–61 (1986).

59. *See* G. Jensen & M. Erickson, The Religious Factor and Delinquency: Another Look at the Hellfire Hypotheses, in The Religious Dimension, *supra* note 32, at 157–77. Jensen and Erickson summarize the conflicting findings of earlier research, and conclude on the basis of their own research that "the view that organized religion is ineffective or irrelevant [in controlling delinquency]" is both supported and refuted "depending on the particular findings one chooses to highlight." *Id.* at 174–75.

60. *See* T. W. Adorno et al., The Authoritarian Personality 212 (1950); Allport & Kramer, Some Roots of Prejudice, 22 J. Psychology 25–26 (1946).

61. Allport, The Religious Context of Prejudice, 5 J. Sci. Study of Religion 447, 454–56 (1966).

62. *Id.* at 455.

63. *Id.*

64. *See* Allport & Kramer, Some Roots of Prejudice, *supra* note 60, at 378.

65. Allport, Religious Context, *supra* note 61, at 456. *See also* Allport & Ross, Personal Religious Orientation and Prejudice, 5 J. Personality & Soc. Psychology 432, 434–35 (1967).

66. *See* Donahue, Intrinsic and Extrinsic Religiousness: Review and Meta-Analysis, 48 J. Personality & Soc. Psychology 400, 415–16 (1985); Morgan, A Research Note on Religion and Morality: Are Religious People Nice People?, 61 Soc. Forces 683, 691 (1983).

67. *See, e.g.,* Griffin et al., A Cross-Cultural Investigation of Religious Orientation, Social Norms, and Prejudice, 26 J. Sci. Study of Religion 358, 364–65 (1987) (suggesting that intrinsic religiosity correlates negatively with prejudice only where the overall culture sends the message that prejudice is socially undesirable); Roof, Religious Orthodoxy and Minority Prejudice: Causal Relationship or Reflection of Localistic World View?, 80 Am. J. Soc. 643, 660–61 (1979) (arguing that racial prejudice and certain religious beliefs do not stand in a cause–effect relationship with each other, but are rather both consequences of narrow world views and limited social perspectives).

68. Batson et al., Social Desirability, Religious Orientation and Racial Prejudice, 17 J. Sci. Study of Religion 31, 40 (1978).

69. *Id.* Batson and his colleagues agree with Griffin and his colleagues, *supra* note 67, that intrinsic religiousness is a reliable indicator of the absence of prejudice only when tolerance is supported by social norms. They find, however, that "quest" religious orientation correlates with low prejudice regardless of the social desirability of prejudice. *See* Batson et al., Social Desirability, *supra* note 68, at 36–40.

70. *See, e.g.,* Griffin et al., A Cross-Cultural Investigation, *supra* note 67, at 363–65.

71. *See, e.g.,* Widmar v. Vincent, 454 U.S. 263 (1981).

72. For a discussion of how courts have approached and should approach problems involving religious practices by the noncustodial parent during visitation periods, see Beschle, God Bless the Child? The Use of Religion as a Factor in Child Custody and Adoption Proceedings, 58 Fordham L. Rev. 383, 403–404, 421–23 (1989).

73. *See generally* Ramsey, Legal Imputation of Religion, *supra* note 22.

74. *See supra* note 21.

75. *See supra* note 2.

76. *See supra* notes 59–69.

77. *See supra* note 23.

78. Conkle, Religious Purpose, Inerrancy, and the Establishment Clause, 67 Ind. L.J. 1, 10–11 (1991).

79. *Id.* at 23–24.

80. *See* Mucci, Religious Beliefs, *supra* note 58, at 360–61 (writing on the freedom of religion clause of the Canadian Charter of Rights and Freedoms).

81. *See, e.g.,* Burnham v. Burnham, 304 N.W.2d 58, 61 (Neb. 1981).

■ CHAPTER FOUR

Custody Denials to Parents in Same-Sex Relationships: An Equal Protection Analysis

Anne I. Seidel

THE PARAMOUNT consideration in child custody disputes is the best interests of the child.[1] Applying this standard, some state courts deny custody to parents who are labeled, by themselves or by their ex-spouses, "homosexual." These courts reason that custody with such parents might result in stigmatization or harassment, harm the children's moral well-being, or adversely affect their sexual orientation.

This chapter argues that the equal protection clause of the Fourteenth Amendment[2] limits the states' ability to deny custody based on homosexuality. The first part examines cases predicating custody determinations on the parents' sexual orientation. The second part argues that, although such custody denials are commonly viewed as classifying parents based on sexual orientation, they are better understood as based on same-sex relationships and gender classifications. The second part also argues that these decisions should be subject to strict or intermediate scrutiny[3] under two theories: that same-sex relationship classifications require heightened scrutiny and that custody decisions turning on same- sex relationships employ gender classifications. The third part examines the justifications courts give in denying child custody to parents in such relationships and concludes that these purported state interests are inadequate to withstand any level of equal protection scrutiny.

Originally printed in 102 Harv. L. Rev. 617 (1989). Reprinted by permission. Copyright © 1989 by the Harvard Law Review Association.

Child Custody Cases Involving a Parent's Sexual Orientation

Child custody decisions determine with whom the child will reside, who will have primary responsibility for the child's welfare, and the extent of the noncustodial parent's visitation rights.[4] Case law and statutes typically require courts to resolve custody disputes based on the best interests of the child.[5] If the dispute is between a parent and a nonparent, a presumption is usually made in favor of the parent.[6]

A parent's homosexuality generally becomes an issue in a child custody case only if the parent is in a serious intimate relationship with a person of the same gender. Although both courts and litigants tend to couch the issue in terms of the parent's sexual orientation, custody denials or restrictions almost always turn on the existence of a same-sex relationship, rather than on the parent's sexual orientation in the abstract.[7] In fact, courts often grant custody or visitation on the condition that the child not be exposed to the relationship.[8] Therefore courts would probably not deny custody based solely on a stipulation that the parent is a celibate homosexual.[9]

State courts give different weights to a parent's same-sex relationship when applying the best interests standard. In some jurisdictions, a parent's relationship with a companion of the same gender gives rise to an apparently irrebuttable presumption that a grant of custody to that parent is not in the child's best interests.[10] Although a second set of jurisdictions claims to reject such a per se rule of unfitness,[11] many of these courts require a parent to prove that his or her same-sex relationship will not harm the child, effectively creating a rebuttable presumption against that parent.[12] In a third set of jurisdictions, courts cannot deny or restrict custody based solely on a parent's sexual orientation.[13]

Courts use four rationales to support their findings that custody by a parent in a same-sex relationship will adversely affect the child.[14] First, courts fear that children raised by such parents will be stigmatized or harassed because of their parents' sexual orientation.[15] Second, courts worry that exposure to the relationship might affect the child's own sexual orientation.[16] Third, courts believe that a custody award to a homosexual parent will affect the child's moral well-being.[17] Finally, some courts justify their decisions either by asserting that state "sodomy statutes," which typically forbid consensual sexual acts involving contact between the genitals of one person and the mouth or anus of another, embody a state interest against homosexuality, or by assuming that a homosexual parent is a criminal and therefore not a fit parent.[18]

Heightened Equal Protection Scrutiny for Custody Denials Based on Same-Sex Relationships

This section argues that the equal protection clause demands that courts apply heightened scrutiny to presumptions that custody by or visitation with a parent in a same-sex relationship is not in the child's best interests. In focusing on same-sex relationships, this chapter departs from the approach advocated by those judges and commentators who have argued for heightened scrutiny based on sexual orientation status. Such arguments presuppose that an individual's sexual orientation either is something over which an individual has no control or is fundamental to an individual's identity.

Neither of these assumptions, however, is necessarily true for any individual, and both have potentially harmful consequences for eliminating bias against gay people. First, because there are people who are not exclusively homosexual by orientation but choose to have only same-sex partners, the assumption that homosexuality is not freely chosen is not uniformly true.[19] Furthermore, heightened scrutiny arguments premised on the involuntary nature of homosexuality denigrate gay people by implying that they are helpless in the face of their same-sex attractions.[20] A person who feels only same-sex attractions, however, can choose not to act upon those attractions and can therefore effectively remove himself or herself from the group. Homosexuality thus differs from race and sex characteristics. Rather than predicating heightened scrutiny on assertions that gay people cannot change, a more positive approach would be to apply heightened scrutiny because gay people should not be required to change. Within the confines of the sexual orientation status approach, however, this requires viewing sexual orientation as a critical component of self-definition. Yet this assumption that homosexuality is a "defining characteristic . . . essential to personhood"[21] depends on and emphasizes rigid sexual orientation categories that are "central to the oppression" of those whom they define as different.[22] If society did not have the concept of sexual orientation or did not view it as important to individuals' identities, society would be less likely to deem those with minority orientations as aberrant, and government actors would therefore be less likely to classify on such a basis. Furthermore, bisexuals, as well as others, may not view their current partner's gender as fundamental to their own identity or even as relevant.

In contrast, arguments premised on committed same-sex relationships avoid these pitfalls. The existence of a loving and intimate relationship with a companion is certainly important to an individual, even if the gender of that companion is not. Similarly, applying heightened scrutiny on the ground that treating individuals in same- and opposite-sex relationships differently constitutes gender discrimination does not treat the companion's gender as a part of the individual's identity. Conceptualizing these child custody decisions in terms of their impact on same-sex relationships, moreover, sharpens their equal protection defect.

Heightened Scrutiny of Classifications Burdening Same-Sex Relationships

Presumptions against awarding custody to parents in same-sex relationships demand rigorous judicial scrutiny because of the combined effect of their burden on intimate relationships and their regulation of a group that displays features warranting suspect classification.[23] *Plyler v. Doe* best exemplifies that such a combination can trigger heightened scrutiny.[24] In *Plyler*, the Supreme Court struck down a state statute denying public education to children of illegal aliens. Although holding that illegal aliens are not a suspect class and that education is not a fundamental right,[25] the Court nevertheless found that the unique vulnerability of these children combined with the importance of education warranted more rigorous scrutiny than the deferential rational basis review usually employed.[26]

Because custody denials premised solely on a parent's same-sex relationship involve a similar combination of circumstances, they also warrant heightened scrutiny. First, individuals in same-sex relationships exhibit many of the indicia of a suspect class. As some commentators have noted, such individuals have a history of discrimination,[27] are singled out for reasons that "bear[] no relation at all to [their] ability to contribute fully to society,"[28] and are politically powerless partly because of the "serious social costs" associated with openly participating in the political process as a homosexual.[29]

Second, presumptions against awarding custody to parents in same-sex relationships impinge on the right to intimate association. Although the Supreme Court has never clearly delineated the scope of this right, it has held that implicit in the due process clause is a fundamental right that "afford[s] the formation and preservation of certain kinds of highly personal relationships a substantial measure of sanctuary from unjustified interference by the State."[30] The Court has discerned the restriction of this right primarily in regulations burdening marriage and family relationships;[31] however, the Court has "not held that constitutional protection is restricted to relationships among family members."[32] Rather, these relationships merit protection because they "cultivat[e] and transmit[] shared ideals and beliefs . . . thereby foster[ing] diversity and act[ing] as critical buffers between the individual and the power of the State."[33] "Moreover, the constitutional shelter afforded such relationships reflects the realization that individuals draw much of their emotional enrichment from close ties with others."[34]

Relationships between parents and their same-sex companions also deserve this increased protection.[35] These loving and committed relationships—sometimes formalized by a ceremony of union[36]—serve the same functions and have the same characteristics as protected relationships.[37] In fact, the parent, the companion, and the child typically view themselves as a family.

Bowers v. Hardwick,[38] which held that the substantive due process right to privacy does not extend to same-sex sodomy, does not foreclose heightened scrutiny for same-sex relationships. A same-sex relationship is in no way defined by, nor dependent upon, sodomy. The sexual aspects of same-sex relationships do not necessarily involve sodomy, and same-sex sodomy does not depend on an intimate relationship. Rather, sodomy and the relationship are two separate phenomena that sometimes happen to coexist. Just as it does not follow that Mormons enjoy no right to worship freely because a state can outlaw polygamy—a practice in which many Mormons at one time engaged—without violating the free exercise of religion clause of the First Amendment,[39] so too it does not follow that those in same-sex relationships enjoy no right to intimate association solely because some same-sex couples engage in behavior that can be outlawed without violating the right to privacy.[40]

Gender Discrimination

In most states that deny custody based on same-sex relationships, opposite-sex relationships outside marriage are less of a bar to custody or visitation than are same-sex relationships.[41] Based on the gender of their companions, parents with same-sex cohabitants are treated differently from parents with opposite-sex companions.[42] Presumptions against custody awards to parents in same-sex relationships thus employ a gender classification. The fact that these presumptions equally affect men and women does not negate the gender-based nature of the classification because a disproportionate effect on a protected group is not necessary to trigger heightened scrutiny when state action employs a suspect or quasi-suspect classification.[43] In the race context, the Court has held that race-based classifications that equally affect blacks and whites nonetheless merit strict scrutiny. In *McLaughlin v. Florida*,[44] for example, the Court invalidated a statute prohibiting interracial cohabitation. In a case analogous to custody decisions premised on same-sex relationships, the Court held in *Palmore v. Sidoti*[45] that custody awards based on the race of a remarried parent's spouse violated equal protection. These cases can be read as holding that any explicit use of a suspect or quasi-suspect classification triggers heightened scrutiny[46] because the very use of such a classification is presumed to reflect an illicit purpose.[47]

Indeed, the *McLaughlin* line of cases is pertinent even if read to require a showing of animus toward the protected group, because discrimination against those in same-sex relationships embodies animus toward women.[48] Traditional gender roles, and classifications that perpetuate them, subordinate women. Such traditional conceptions constrain the scope of women's choices, locking them into a cultural model that assumes that "the female [is] destined solely for the home and the rearing of the family, and [that] only the male [is qualified] for the marketplace and the world of ideas."[49] Equal protection doctrine "aims to break down [such] legally created or legally reenforced systems of subordination."[50] Classifications predicated on traditional conceptions of gender roles also merit heightened scrutiny because they are more likely to reflect "outmoded notions of the relative capabilities of men and women" rather than "meaningful considerations."[51]

Because bias and discrimination against those in same-sex relationships derive from and reinforce these traditional, constraining conceptions of gender roles, such classifications require heightened scrutiny.[52] The censure attached to being labeled a "homosexual," a stigma that partially derives from and is reinforced by legal disabilities, pressures men and women to stay within the boundaries of their roles. Thus, for example, to avoid having their heterosexuality questioned, women are less likely than they would be otherwise to enter traditionally male occupations or to fail to conform to socially acceptable forms of dress and behavior.[53]

In addition, because same-sex relationships do not fit the dominant-male/submissive-female mold, they show that traditional sex roles are not necessary for intimate relationships, thereby providing a different, and threatening, alternative.[54] The link that antigay writers frequently make between homosexuality and the demise of traditional male/female roles shows that antigay bias to some extent reflects hostility to this threat to traditional roles.[55] Likewise, language in some custody decisions supports the view that the desire to maintain gender roles underlies courts' hostility toward same-sex relationships.[56]

Indeed, the very existence of the concept of sexual orientation derives from and perpetuates biased conceptions of gender roles.[57] The labeling of people as homosexual or heterosexual dates only from the mid-nineteenth century.[58] In the nineteenth century, homosexuality was seen as "'sexual inversion,' a complete exchange of gender identity."[59] Seeing "homosexual" men as women and vice versa allowed society to reconcile the existence of same-sex attractions and relationships with the belief in the inevitability of rigid gender roles.[60] In a similar but less severe fashion, the attachment of a sexual orientation to a person allows society to smooth over the challenge same-sex relationships pose to assumptions about gender differences. By labeling those who do not conform to gender-related expectations as homosexual and deviant, those who do conform can continue to believe that heterosexuality and gender differences are natural, innate, and unchanging for everyone except homosexuals.

As society's views of an individual's capabilities become less dependent upon the individual's gender, the importance placed on the gender of an individual's companion will decrease. The gender of a person's companion could become as relevant to that individual's identity as is the companion's race, which is not thought to be part of who a person is. Thus, just as interracial couples stand out less in societies with more racial equality and integration, it would appear less peculiar to have two men or two women in an intimate relationship if society did not expect men and women to act in very different ways. Eliminating gender-based classifications that exhibit antigay bias moves society in this direction.

Sufficiency of State Interests

This section applies equal protection analysis to custody denials or restrictions premised on a parent's same-sex relationship. As discussed above, courts justify these decisions under four rationales: that the child might be harassed or stigmatized, that the child's sexual orientation might be affected, that the child's moral development might be harmed, and that the state sodomy statute mandates the custody denial or restriction.[61]

Legitimacy of Justifications

Recognizing a classification as suspect or quasi-suspect entails treating as illegitimate any state interest in harming the group protected by such a classification.[62] Because they cannot be defined independently of animus toward women or persons in same-sex relationships, all four rationales fail.[63] Insofar as the sodomy statute rationale embodies a state interest against homosexuality, it too explicitly rests on animus toward gay people. Similarly, concerns about the child's moral development make sense only on the assumption that the state has an interest in promoting the belief that same-sex relationships are immoral. The fear that the child might "become" homosexual if raised by a gay parent may also result from animus toward homosexuals.

Other rationales, although not directly based on animus toward those in same-sex relationships, attempt to shield the child from the consequences of others' prejudices and thus depend indirectly on bias. The justification that a child in a gay parent's custody will be harassed, for example, reflects a state interest in protecting the child from unpleasant experiences. Similarly, the state may want to diminish the likelihood that the child will be nonheterosexual because it believes that prejudice causes nonheterosexuals unhappiness.

Under *Palmore v. Sidoti*,[64] these justifications are illegitimate. In *Palmore*, the Supreme Court held that a custody denial based on the potential stigmatization of the child because of the mother's subsequent interracial remarriage violated equal protection. The Court recognized that "[t]here is a risk that a child living with a stepparent of a different race may be subject to a variety of pressures and stresses not [otherwise] present,"[65] but nevertheless held that a court could not predicate denial of custody on "private biases and the possible injury they might inflict."[66] "The Constitution cannot control such prejudices but neither can it tolerate them."[67]

Indeed, stigma is an illegitimate justification even under rational basis review. In *City of Cleburne v. Cleburne Living Center, Inc.*,[68] the Court quoted *Palmore* for the proposition that "'[p]rivate biases may be outside the reach of the law, but the law cannot, directly or indirectly, give them effect.'"[69] The *Cleburne* Court held that the government's fears that students of a nearby junior high school might harass residents of a home for the mentally retarded was not a constitutionally sufficient reason to justify denying a zoning permit for the home.[70] "[D]enying a permit based on such vague, undifferentiated fears," the Court reasoned, "permit[s] some portion of the community to validate what would otherwise be an equal protection violation."[71] Although *Cleburne* was perhaps decided on a standard stricter than the rational basis test that the Court claimed to apply,[72] the Court's holding that government action predicated on others' biases violated equal protection does not appear to rest on heightened scrutiny.

Justifications that violate other constitutional requirements are also illegitimate. Thus, a court cannot justify a custody denial based on the child's moral well-being because it believes that the child's best interests require him or her to be inculcated in society's antipathy toward gay people[73] or to learn "society's mores."[74] This attempt to control beliefs violates the First Amendment. As the Court has noted, "at the heart of the First Amendment is the notion that an individual should be free to believe as he will, and that in a free society one's beliefs should be shaped by his mind and his conscience rather than coerced by the State."[75] The goal of promoting morals is sometimes sufficient to justify state action that regulates conduct.[76] There is a critical difference, however, between prohibiting conduct deemed immoral and attempting to control supposedly immoral beliefs.[77] Thus, although the state can outlaw homosexual sodomy without violating the First Amendment, it cannot require parents to teach their children that such conduct is immoral. Because the justification of controlling the child's moral beliefs is impermissible under the First Amendment, it fails even the weakest level of scrutiny.

Correlations Between Justifications and State Interests

As argued above,[78] heightened scrutiny should be applied to presumptions against custody awards to parents in same-sex relationships. Under heightened scrutiny, the state must prove that a classification is substantially related to achievement of the state interest.[79] Even under the rational relationship test, a classification cannot be completely arbitrary; there must be some connection between the classification and the state interest. Under the rational relationship test's weakest formulation, state action is constitutional as long as a conceivable justification exists, even if the justification is not supported by evidence.[80] Under less toothless formulations, however, the Court examines the justifications to ascertain whether they actually serve the asserted state interest.[81]

Because the presumption against awarding custody to a parent in a same-sex relationship is judge-made rather than legislative in origin, the rationales for the most deferential test are weak. Courts, unlike legislatures, hear and weigh evidence, record their reasoning, and are composed of fewer individual decision-makers. Thus, it is easier for a reviewing court to know whether a decision-maker actually used a conceivable justification.[82]

The rationales that children raised by gay parents might "become" homosexual or might be stigmatized are factually unsupportable. The concern that being raised by a gay parent will affect a child's sexual orientation is unsupported by studies, which find no correlation between the parent's and the child's sexual orientations.[83] Likewise, the fear that the child will be stigmatized, although not subject to as much empirical examination, finds little support in reported studies.[84] Perhaps more importantly, only one reported case contains any evidence of harassment,[85] implying that specific evidence of harassment is rarely available.

Similarly, justifications invoking the sodomy statute, on the assumption that the statute reflects a state interest against homosexuality or that the parent is a criminal and therefore unfit to raise a child, lack factual support. First, because the vast majority of these statutes do not specify the gender of the participants, and thus apply equally on their face to heterosexual and homosexual acts,[86] the statutes cannot be read as reflecting a state interest against homosexuality.

The assumption that the gay parent has engaged in criminal conduct is likewise unsupportable. In many of the child custody cases relying on sodomy statutes, no evidence exists that the parent in question actually participated in any statutorily prohibited conduct or that the other parent did not.[87] Nor can courts assume that all persons defining themselves as gay or homosexual engage in proscribed conduct. According to studies, a significant minority of lesbians rarely or never engage in activities covered by sodomy statutes;[88] moreover, the most common lesbian sexual practice does not violate the statutes.[89] Likewise, in an effort to reduce their potential exposure to the HIV virus, many gay men also refrain from such activities.[90]

Finally, the argument that the parent is engaging in criminal activities and therefore subject to arrest[91] is also unsupportable.[92] Even assuming that the gay parent engages in proscribed activities and the heterosexual parent does not, arrests for private consensual sexual activities are virtually nonexistent.[93] Furthermore, a decision premised solely on the specific sexual acts engaged in by the parent has no connection to the child's best interests and therefore fails rational basis review. Surely, assuming that the child is not present during the sexual activity, the difference between the parent receiving sexual gratification through oral or manual stimulation will not affect the child's well-being.[94]

Conclusion

Although custody denials based on a parent's homosexuality are generally viewed as sexual orientation discrimination, they are better understood as dependent upon same-sex relationships. In fact, the fears behind the four rationales for denying gay parents' custody of their children are much more likely to be realized when the parent openly engages in a same-sex relationship. Because such custody decisions employ same-sex relationship and gender classifications, they merit heightened scrutiny. The four justifications for denying custody to parents in same-sex relationships all fail both heightened scrutiny and rational relationship review. If courts refused to take into account the gender of a parent's companion, they would help both to deemphasize the categories of sexual orientation that lead to antigay prejudice and to reduce the subordination of women that such prejudice derives from and engenders.

NOTES

Acknowledgments: The author would like to thank Dan M. Kahan, Karen M. McGaffey, and Francesca Ortiz for their assistance.
1. *See, e.g.*, A. Haralambie, Handling Child Custody Cases § 3.06, at 24, § 7.07, at 82–83 (1983).
2. U.S. Const. amend. XIV, § 1.
3. This chapter uses the term "heightened" to refer to either strict or intermediate scrutiny. When a law makes a classification (that is, distinguishes between two groups of people), it may be subject to different levels of scrutiny by the federal courts. Some classifications, such as those based on race or ethnic origin, are

subjected to strict scrutiny. This means that, to be constitutional, the classification has to be "necessary" to accomplish a "compelling state interest." Palmore v. Sidoti, 466 U.S. 429, 432 (1984). Other classifications, such as those based on gender, are subject to intermediate scrutiny. This means that the classification has to be "substantially related" to an "important state interest." Craig v. Boren, 429 U.S. 190, 197 (1976). If a classification is not subject to strict or intermediate scrutiny, the equal protection clause requires only that it be "rationally related to a legitimate government purpose." Kadrmas v. Dickinson Pub. Schools, 487 U.S. 450, 458 (1988).

4. This chapter uses the term "custody" to refer to both visitation and custody decisions.

5. *See, e.g.,* Pikula v. Pikula, 374 N.W.2d 705, 711 (Minn. 1985); Alaska Stat. § 25.20.060 (1983); Ga. Code Ann. § 19-9-3 (1982); Ky. Rev. Stat. Ann. § 403.270 (Baldwin 1983); Va. Code Ann. § 20-107.2 (1983).

6. *See* H. Clark, The Law of Domestic Relations in the United States § 19.6 (2d ed. 1988).

7. *See, e.g.,* Jacobson v. Jacobson, 314 N.W.2d 78, 81 (N.D. 1981) ("Sandra's homosexuality may, indeed, be something which is beyond her control. However, living with another person of the same sex in a sexual relationship is not"); M.J.P. v. J.G.P., 640 P.2d 966, 967 (Okla. 1982) (holding that an "acknowledged, open homosexual relationship" sufficiently justified a change of custody). Moreover, references in the cases to the parent's choice to remain in a same-sex relationship imply that it is the relationship, and not the parent's sexual orientation, that primarily disturbs the courts. *See, e.g.,* Roe v. Roe, 324 S.E.2d 691, 694 (Va. 1985). This emphasis on the relationship rather than on the parent's perceived sexual orientation is also evident in cases granting custody to parents when there is evidence of only past homosexual conduct. *See* Buck v. Buck, 233 S.E.2d 792 (Ga. 1977); Gay v. Gay, 253 S.E.2d 846 (Ga. Ct. App. 1979).

8. *See, e.g.,* N.K.M. v. L.E.M., 606 S.W.2d 179, 183 (Mo. Ct. App. 1980) (changing custody to the father based on the mother's violation of a condition in the original custody decree requiring her to "discontinu[e] any relationship whatsoever with . . . and not be in [the] presence or company" of "Betty"); M.P. v. S.P., 404 A.2d 1256, 1261 (N.J. Super. 1979) (noting that the trial court had ordered the lesbian friend "banish[ed] . . . from the presence of the children"); Conkel v. Conkel, 509 N.E.2d 983, 984 (Ohio Ct. App. 1987) (allowing the father visitation on the condition that it not be exercised in the presence of unrelated male persons); A. v. A., 514 P.2d 358, 359 (Or. Ct. App. 1973) (prohibiting the custodial father, who denied any homosexual activity but admitted the possibility of homosexual "tendencies," from allowing males to reside with him and the children); Dailey v. Dailey, 635 S.W.2d 391, 395–96 (Tenn. Ct. App. 1982) (modifying, sua sponte, the trial court's order to prevent visitation in the home the mother shared with her same-sex cohabitant or "from having the child in the presence of [the cohabitant] or any other homosexual with whom the [mother] might have a lesbian relationship").

9. A custody denial based solely on a stated but unactualized same-sex attraction would raise additional constitutional concerns because it would be based on a status, *cf.* Robinson v. California, 370 U.S. 660 (1962) (invalidating a statute criminalizing the status of narcotic addiction), and would be even more difficult to reconcile with the best interests standard than custody denials premised on a same-sex relationship.

10. Judicially created irrebuttable presumptions currently appear to exist in Missouri and Virginia. *See* G.A. v. D.A., 745 S.W.2d 726, 728 (Mo. Ct. App. 1987); *id.* at 728 (Lowenstein, J., dissenting) (arguing that current Missouri law creates an irrebuttable presumption that should be rebuttable); N.K.M. v. L.E.M., 606 S.W.2d 179, 186 (Mo. Ct. App. 1980) (stating that the "court does not need to wait . . . till the damage is done"); Roe v. Roe, 324 S.E.2d 691, 691 (Va. 1985).

11. *See, e.g.,* Nadler v. Superior Court, 255 Cal. App. 2d 523, 525, 63 Cal. Rptr. 352, 354 (1967); D.H. v. J.H., 418 N.E.2d 286, 292 (Ind. Ct. App. 1981); Hall v. Hall, 291 N.W.2d 143 (Mich. Ct. App. 1980); *In re* J.S. & C., 324 A.2d 90, 92 (N.J. Super. Ct. 1974).

12. A few courts have placed the burden of disproving harm explicitly on the gay parent, *see, e.g.,* Constant A. v. Paul C.A., 496 A.2d 1, 5 (Pa. Super. Ct. 1985), or have stated that there is a presumption of harm, *see, e.g.,* Thigpen v. Carpenter, 730 S.W.2d 510, 513 (Ark. Ct. App. 1987). Many courts effectively create a rebuttable presumption of harm even though their holdings are not in terms of presumptions or burdens of proof. Despite the lack of evidence of any actual or potential harm to the child from the parent's same-sex relationship, these courts award custody to the avowedly heterosexual parent presumably because the other parent failed to prove the lack of harm. *See, e.g.,* Jacobson v. Jacobson, 314 N.W.2d 78, 80 (N.D. 1981) (viewing mother's lesbianism as the "overriding factor"); M.J.P. v. J.G.P., 640 P.2d 966 (Okla. 1982).

13. *See* S.N.E. v. R.L.B., 699 P.2d 875, 879 (Alaska 1985); D.H. v. J.H., 418 N.E.2d at 291 (dictum); Doe v. Doe, 452 N.E.2d 293 (Mass. App. Ct. 1983); Stroman v. Williams, 353 S.E.2d 704 (S.C. Ct. App. 1987). Courts sometimes also phrase this rule as requiring an adverse effect on the child. *See, e.g.,* D.H., 418 N.E.2d at 293 ("[H]omosexuality standing alone without evidence of any adverse effect upon the welfare of the child does not render the homosexual parent unfit as a matter of law to have custody of the child"). This approach is sometimes referred to as a "nexus" requirement. *See, e.g.,* S.N.E., 699 P.2d at 878; Rivera, Queer Law: Sexual Orientation Law in the Mid-Eighties (pt. 2), 11 U. Dayton L. Rev. 275, 330 (1986).

14. *See generally* Clark, Law Of Domestic Relations, *supra* note 6, § 19.4, at 805; Rivera, Queer Law, *supra* note 13, at 329; Comment, Burdens on Gay Litigants and Bias in the Court System: Homosexual Panic, Child Custody and Anonymous Parties, 19 Harv. C.R.–C.L. L. Rev. 497, 526–37 (1984); Comment, Assessing Children's Best Interests When a Parent Is Gay or Lesbian: Toward a Rational Custody Standard, 32 UCLA L. Rev. 852, 869–84 (1985).

15. *See, e.g., Thigpen,* 730 S.W.2d at 514; *Jacobson,* 314 N.W.2d at 81; Roe v. Roe, 324 S.E.2d 691, 694 (Va. 1985). *But see S.N.E.,* 699 P.2d at 879 (holding that "it is impermissible to rely on any real or imagined social stigma attaching to Mother's status as a lesbian"); M.P. v. S.P., 404 A.2d 1256, 1263 (N.J. Super. Ct. 1979) (noting that the community's intolerance may cause the children to "emerge better equipped to search out their own standards of right and wrong").

16. *See, e.g.,* S. v. S., 608 S.W.2d 64, 66 (Ky. Ct. App. 1980) (citing expert's admittedly speculative testimony), *cert. denied,* 451 U.S. 911 (1981); N.K.M. v.

L.E.M., 606 S.W.2d 179, 186 (Mo. Ct. App. 1980) (fearing that the child might "be condemned . . . to sexual disorientation").

17. *See, e.g., Thigpen*, 730 S.W.2d at 514 (approving the lower court's finding that "it was contrary to the court's sense of morality to expose the children to a homosexual lifestyle"); S.E.G. v. R.A.G., 735 S.W.2d 164, 166 (Mo. Ct. App. 1987).

18. *See, e.g.*, Chaffin v. Frye, 45 Cal. App. 3d 39, 47, 119 Cal. Rptr. 22, 26 (Ct. App. 1975); L. v. D., 630 S.W.2d 240, 243 (Mo. Ct. App. 1982); *Roe*, 324 S.E.2d at 694. Even courts in states without sodomy statutes occasionally use other states' statutes to support custody decisions. *See, e.g.*, Constant A. v. Paul C.A., 496 A.2d 1, 5 (Pa. Super. Ct. 1985) (claiming that the lesbian mother might be subject to arrest if she traveled with her children to states with sodomy statutes).

19. Sexual orientation exists on a continuum between exclusively heterosexual and exclusively homosexual orientations. *See, e.g.*, A. Kinsey et al., Sexual Behavior in the Human Male 636–55 (1948). Thus, although a bisexual individual's place on the sexual orientation continuum may be immutable, she can still choose to act in a completely heterosexual or homosexual way even though she cannot choose not to be attracted to both men and women.

A significant proportion of adults have had sexual contact with persons of both genders. *See id.* at 650; A. Kinsey et al., Sexual Behavior in the Human Female 453 (1953).

20. *See* D'Emilio, Making and Unmaking of Sexual Minorities: The Tensions Between Gay Politics and History, 14 N.Y.U. Rev. L. & Soc. Change 915, 921 (1986).

21. Note, The Constitutional Status of Sexual Orientation: Homosexuality as a Suspect Classification, 98 Harv. L. Rev. 1285, 1300 (1985).

22. *See* D'Emilio, Sexual Minorities, *supra* note 20, at 920.

23. A "suspect" classification is a classification subject to heightened scrutiny. *See supra* note 3.

24. 457 U.S. 202, 221–23 (1982) (justifying heightened scrutiny).

25. *See id.* at 223.

26. *See id.* at 223–24. For an explanation of the three standards of equal protection, see *supra* note 3.

27. *See* Law, Homosexuality and the Social Meaning of Gender, 1988 Wis. L. Rev. 187, 192–96; Note, An Argument for the Application of Equal Protection Heightened Scrutiny to Classifications Based on Homosexuality, 57 S. Cal. L. Rev. 797, 799–807, 824–25 (1984).

28. L. Tribe, American Constitutional Law § 16-33, at 1616 (2d ed. 1988).

29. *See* J. Ely, Democracy and Distrust 163 (1980). This political powerlessness is underscored by the presence of official government discrimination. *See* Note, Homosexuality, *supra* note 27, at 799–807, 825–27.

30. Roberts v. United States Jaycees, 468 U.S. 609, 618 (1984).

31. *See, e.g.*, Zablocki v. Redhail, 434 U.S. 374, 383–86 (1978) (marriage); Moore v. City of East Cleveland, 431 U.S. 494, 498–99 (1977) (plurality opinion) (cohabitation with extended family); Stanley v. Illinois, 405 U.S. 645, 651 (1972) (parent–child relationship).

32. Board of Directors of Rotary, Int'l v. Rotary Club, 481 U.S. 537, 545 (1987) (dictum).

33. *Roberts*, 468 U.S. at 619.

34. *Id*. The Court in *Roberts* saw these relationships as characterized by "relative smallness, a high degree of selectivity in decisions to begin and maintain the affiliation, and seclusion from others in critical aspects of the relationship." *Id*. at 620.

35. *See* Karst, The Freedom of Intimate Associations, 89 Yale L.J. 624, 682–86 (1980) (arguing that the freedom of intimate association applies to homosexual relationships); Richards, Constitutional Legitimacy and Constitutional Privacy, 61 N.Y.U. L. Rev. 800, 853 (1986) (same).

36. *See, e.g.*, S. v. S., 608 S.W.2d 64, 65 (Ky. Ct. App. 1980), *cert. denied*, 451 U.S. 911 (1981); M.J.P. v. J.G.P., 640 P.2d 966, 967 (Okla. 1982).

37. *See* Karst, Intimate Associations, *supra* note 35, at 682.

38. 478 U.S. 186 (1986).

39. *See* Reynolds v. United States, 98 U.S. 145 (1879).

40. The dicta in Bowers v. Hardwick, 478 U.S. 186 (1986), implying that recognition of a privacy right requires a connection between the would-be protected activity and "family, marriage, or procreation," 478 U.S. at 191, also do not destroy the viability of the right-to-association argument. *Id*. The right to live in an alternative to heterosexual marriage is at least as connected to marriage as the right to choose an abortion is connected to procreation.

41. *Compare* S.E.G. v. R.A.G., 735 S.W.2d 164 (Mo. Ct. App. 1987) (holding that custody with mother in same-sex relationship is "an unhealthy environment") *and* G.A. v. D.A., 745 S.W.2d 726, 728 (Mo. Ct. App. 1987) (Lowenstein, J., dissenting) (stating that Missouri has an irrebuttable presumption that custody with a homosexual parent is detrimental to the child) *with* Wilhelmsen v. Peck, 743 S.W.2d 88 (Mo. Ct. App. 1987) (holding that a mother's extramarital heterosexual cohabitation was insufficient to warrant a change of custody); Jacobson v. Jacobson, 314 N.W.2d 78 (N.D. 1981) (reversing a custody award because of the mother's same-sex relationship) *with* Lapp v. Lapp, 336 N.W.2d 350 (N.D. 1983) (affirming a denial to change custody because of unmarried cohabitation and expressly distinguishing Jacobson on the ground that it involved "a homosexual relationship"); Constant A. v. Paul C.A., 496 A.2d 1 (Pa. Super. Ct. 1985) (holding that a lesbian relationship raises a presumption of detrimental effect on the child) *with* Michael T.L. v. Marilyn J.L., 525 A.2d 414, 416 (Pa. Super. Ct. 1987) (stating that nonmarital opposite-sex relationships are "relevant only if they could be shown to have an adverse effect on the child").

42. Certain other states, although claiming to apply the same standard to those involved in same-sex and opposite-sex cohabitation, tend to deny custody more readily to those in same-sex relationships. *Compare, e.g.*, Thigpen v. Carpenter, 730 S.W.2d 510 (Ark. Ct. App. 1987) (denying custody to a mother in a lesbian relationship) *with* Ketron v. Aguirre, 692 S.W.2d 261 (Ark. Ct. App. 1985) (granting custody to a mother living with a married man).

43. *See* Baehr v. Lewin, 852 P.2d 44 (Haw. 1993) (holding that statute barring same-sex marriages implicates state constitution's equal protection clause despite equal burden on both genders). Courts, however, have rejected similar gender discrimination arguments in two other contexts because the state action equally affected men and women. *See* DeSantis v. Pacific Tel. & Tel. Co., Inc., 608 F.2d 327, 330–31 (9th Cir. 1975) (rejecting an argument that discrimination against ho-

mosexuals is sex discrimination under Title VII); State v. Walsh, 713 S.W.2d 508, 510–11 (Mo. 1986) (en banc) (rejecting a gender discrimination challenge to a statute criminalizing only same-sex sexual activity). Neither of these cases, however, confronted the analogy to race discrimination cases discussed below.

44. 379 U.S. 184 (1964); *see also* Loving v. Virginia, 388 U.S. 1 (1967) (holding a ban on interracial marriages unconstitutional).

45. 466 U.S. 429 (1984).

46. *See, e.g.,* McLaughlin, 379 U.S. at 191; *see also* Personnel Adm'r v. Feeney, 442 U.S. 256, 274 (1979) (implying that an examination into whether a law is invidious proceeds only if the classification is not explicitly gender-based).

47. Similarly, the Court has struck down legislation disadvantaging men in part because the use of the classification was presumed to perpetuate *women's* subjugation. *See* Mississippi Univ. for Women v. Hogan, 458 U.S. 718, 729–30 & n.15 (1982).

48. This animus does not have to be recognized as such by the responsible state actors. For example, in Loving v. Virginia, 388 U.S. 1 (1967), both the state trial and appeals courts found that the miscegenation statute's purpose was to promote racial purity. *See id.* at 3, 7. The Supreme Court read this as evidencing "an endorsement of . . . White Supremacy," *id.* at 7; however, it is possible that legislatures could believe in racial purity without purposely desiring to harm nonwhites. Similarly, state actors disadvantaging same-sex relationships may not intend to harm women but instead intend to promote heterosexuality.

49. Stanton v. Stanton, 421 U.S. 7, 14–15 (1975).

50. *See* Tribe, American Constitutional Law, *supra* note 28, § 16-21, at 15.

51. City of Cleburne v. Cleburne Living Center, Inc., 473 U.S. 432, 441 (1985).

52. Professor Law has noted:

> Homosexual relationships challenge dichotomous concepts of gender [and] the notion that social traits, such as dominance and nurturance, are naturally linked to one sex or the other. Moreover, those involved in homosexual relations implicitly reject the social institutions of family, economic and political life that are premised on gender inequality and differentiation.

Law, Homosexuality and Gender, *supra* note 27, at 196.

53. *See, e.g.,* Radicalesbians, The Woman-Identified Woman, in Out of the Closets 173 (K. Jay & A. Young eds., 1972) ("Lesbian is the word, the label, the condition that holds women in line. When a woman hears this word tossed her way, she knows . . . she has crossed the terrible boundary of her sex role. She recoils, she protests, she reshapes her actions to gain approval"). Feminists are frequently called "lesbian," *see, e.g.,* R. Morgan, Going Too Far 7 (1978); G. Steinem, Outrageous Acts and Everyday Rebellions 9, 22 (1983); because this is seen as a terrible stigma, it serves to discourage women from being "too" feminist.

54. *See* Law, Homosexuality and Gender, *supra* note 27, at 210.

55. *See, e.g.,* A. Bryant, The Anita Bryant Story 53–55 (1977) (linking the women's movement, "family breakdown," and homosexuality); F. Dumas, Gay Is Not Good 141 (1979); J. Falwell, Listen America! 183 (1980) ("We would not be having the present moral crisis regarding the homosexual movement if men and women accepted their proper roles as designated by God").

56. For example, some cases find disturbing the mother's submissive role vis-à-vis her companion, although they would approve of such behavior if her companion were male. Thus, what disturbs these courts is the companion's donning of a male role. *See, e.g.*, N.K.M. v. L.E.M., 606 S.W.2d 179, 184 (Mo. Ct. App. 1980) (describing as "most telling" a conversation that shows the mother "to be quite passive and servient in her relation to Betty, while Betty occupies a dominant role"); Dailey v. Dailey, 635 S.W.2d 391, 394 (Tenn. Ct. App. 1981) ("Given the choice of whether a homosexual relationship involving a mother in the submissive role or a normal relationship wherein males and females adhere to their roles, [the father's expert] voiced his opinion that the situation involving the natural father would be preferable for [the child]"); *see also* Newsome v. Newsome, 256 S.E.2d 849, 851 (N.C. Ct. App. 1979) (quoting a witness' testimony that "'[t]here were a lot of magazines, M.S. [sic] magazines'" in the alleged lesbian mother's home).

57. *See* Arriola, Sexual Identity and the Constitution: Homosexual Persons as a Discrete and Insular Minority, 10 Women's Rts. L. Rep. 143, 166 (1988) ("In the 20th century, that a man or a woman might be marked as 'gay,' lesbian or homosexual, we owe to the dominance of rigid sexual roles and the notions of patriarchy that fostered them"); Law, Homosexuality and Gender, *supra* note 27, at 197–206, 230 ("History suggests that a primary purpose and effect of state enforcement of heterosexuality is to preserve gender differentiation and the relationships premised upon it"); Note, The Miscegenation Analogy: Sodomy Law as Sex Discrimination, 98 Yale L.J. 145, 158–60 (1988).

58. *See* M. Foucault, 1 History Of Sexuality 43 (R. Hurley trans., 1978); D'Emilio, Sexual Minorities, *supra* note 20, at 917 (1986).

59. J. D'Emilio & E. Freedman, Intimate Matters: A History of Sexuality in America 226 (1988).

60. In fact, medical literature at this time considered "normal" the "feminine' member of a female couple," J. Katz, Gay/Lesbian Almanac 144 (1983), thus demonstrating that normality was determined more by sex-role conformity than by sexual orientation.

61. *See supra* notes 15–18 and accompanying text.

62. *See, e.g.*, Loving v. Virginia, 388 U.S. 1, 11 (1967) (stating that racial classifications must be "necessary to the accomplishment of some permissible state objective, independent of . . . racial discrimination").

63. Under the gender discrimination argument, the state is foreclosed from pursuing state interests dependent upon antigay prejudice because animus against homosexuals derives from and reinforces gender bias. *See supra* notes 45–60 and accompanying text.

64. 466 U.S. 429 (1984).

65. *Id.* at 433.

66. *Id.*

67. *Id.*

68. 473 U.S. 432 (1985).

69. *Id.* at 448 (quoting *Palmore*, 466 U.S. at 433).

70. *See id.* at 449.

71. *Id.*

72. *See, e.g., id.* at 456 (Marshall, J., concurring in part and dissenting in part); Tribe, American Constitutional Law, *supra* note 28, § 16-3, at 1444.

73. *See* S.E.G. v. R.A.G., 735 S.W.2d 164, 166 (Mo. Ct. App. 1987) (fearing that custody would adversely affect the "development of a child's values and character").

74. *See, e.g.,* Roe v. Roe, 324 S.E.2d 691, 693 (Va. 1985). In addition, some courts fear a potentially harmful conflict between the parent's and society's morals. *See* M.J.P. v. J.G.P., 640 P.2d at 969; Kallas v. Kallas, 614 P.2d 641, 643 (Utah 1980) (finding that a lesbian mother "may, as a role model, at least to some extent cause serious conflict in the minds of the children concerning certain basic life-styles"). The assumption that it is better for the child to grow up prejudiced than to experience any "conflict" contradicts basic notions of tolerance critical to our pluralistic society. In fact, some courts cite the potential for children raised by gay parents to be more tolerant as a reason to *award* custody to the gay parent. *See, e.g.,* M.P. v. S.P., 404 A.2d 1256, 1263 (N.J. Super. Ct. 1979).

75. Abood v. Detroit Bd. of Educ., 431 U.S. 209, 234–35 (1977); *see also* West Virginia Bd. of Educ. v. Barnette, 319 U.S. 624, 642 (1943) ("If there is any fixed star in our constitutional constellation, it is that no official, high or petty, can prescribe what shall be orthodox in politics, nationalism, religion, or other matters of opinion").

76. *See, e.g.,* Bowers v. Hardwick, 478 U.S. 186, 196 (1986).

77. *See, e.g.,* United States v. O'Brien, 391 U.S. 367 (1968) (distinguishing between government control of conduct and regulation of speech).

78. *See supra* notes 19–60 and accompanying text.

79. *See* Craig v. Boren, 429 U.S. 190, 197 (1976). Under strict scrutiny, classifications must be necessary to accomplish a compelling government interest. *See* Palmore v. Sidoti, 466 U.S. 429, 432 (1984).

80. *See* Vance v. Bradley, 440 U.S. 93, 111 (1979). However, even if a justification survives this weak formulation of the rational relationship test, if the correlation between the justification and the child's best interests is insufficient, the custody decision will be statutorily impermissible.

81. *See, e.g.,* Hooper v. Bernalillo County Assessor, 472 U.S. 612 (1985); Lindsey v. Normet, 405 U.S. 56, 76–79 (1971).

82. *Cf.* Tribe, American Constitutional Law, *supra* note 28, § 16-2, at 1440 (attributing judicial deference toward what constitutes a public purpose partly to "sympathy for the difficulties of the legislative process").

83. *See, e.g.,* Golombok et al., Children in Lesbian and Single-Parent Households: Psychosexual and Psychiatric Appraisal, 24 J. Child Psychology & Psychiatry 551, 564 (1983); Green, The Best Interests of the Child with a Lesbian Mother, 10 Bull. Am. Acad. Psychiatry & L. 7, 13 (1982); Green et al., Lesbian Mothers and Their Children: A Comparison with Solo Parent Heterosexual Mothers and Their Children, 15 Archives Sexual Behav. 167, 181 (1986).

84. *See, e.g.,* Hotvedt & Mandel, Children of Lesbian Mothers, in Homosexuality 282 (W. Paul et al., eds., 1982) (finding that no difference existed between sons of heterosexual and lesbian mothers in terms of peer relations and that daughters of lesbians rated their own popularity higher).

85. In the only reported case that mentioned evidence of teasing, the teasing had occurred while the child was in the custody of the nongay parent and was used to deny a change of custody from the avowedly heterosexual father to the lesbian mother. *See* L. v. D., 630 S.W.2d 240, 244 (Mo. Ct. App. 1982).

86. *See* Note, Miscegenation Analogy, *supra* note 57, at 151 (noting that statutes in only seven states apply solely to same-sex sodomy).

87. *See, e.g.,* Constant A. v. Paul C.A., 496 A.2d 1 (Pa. Super. Ct. 1985); Roe v. Roe, 324 S.E.2d 691 (Va. 1985); *see also* P. Blumstein & P. Schwartz, American Couples 236 (1983) (finding that same-sex couples engaged in oral sex only slightly more frequently than opposite-sex couples).

88. *See, e.g.,* Blumstein & Schwartz, American Couples, *supra* note 87, at 236 (finding that 23 percent of lesbians rarely or never engage in oral sex). Oral sex is the only prohibited activity in which two women can engage.

89. *See* A. Bell & M. Weinberg, Homosexualities 109 (1978) (finding that manual stimulation of or by a partner is the technique most commonly employed by lesbians).

90. *See, e.g.,* Martin, The Impact of AIDS on Gay Male Sexual Behavior Patterns in New York City, 77 Am. J. Pub. Health 578, 580 (1987); *see also* Blumstein & Schwartz, American Couples, *supra* note 87, at 549 n.12, 578 n.45 (finding that before the AIDS crisis, mutual masturbation, a practice not covered by sodomy statutes, was the sexual practice in which male couples most frequently engaged).

91. *See Constant A.,* 496 A.2d at 5 (maintaining that, despite Pennsylvania's lack of a sodomy statute, the mother could be subject to arrest if she traveled to other states).

92. *See* Comment, Gay Litigants, *supra* note 14, at 529 (arguing that denying custody because of sodomy statute violations would require similar denials based on any crime).

93. *See, e.g.,* Bowers v. Hardwick, 478 U.S. 186, 198 n.2 (1986) (Powell, J., concurring) (noting the lack of any "reported decision involving prosecution for private homosexual sodomy under [Georgia's sodomy] statute for several decades").

94. There is no evidence in any reported case that the child at issue witnessed the parent engaging in sexual conduct. In any case, the important distinction in terms of the child's welfare is the child's awareness of the sexual activity, not the specific sexual activity in which the parent engaged.

CHAPTER FIVE

Where Do Black Children Belong? The Politics of Race Matching in Adoption

Elizabeth Bartholet

THIS CHAPTER explores the meaning and the wisdom of racial matching policies in adoption—the policies in effect throughout the nation requiring that children available for adoption be placed with same-race parents. I question why it is that these policies seem to have made so much sense to so many people over the years—why it is that blacks and whites, conservatives and liberals and radicals, judges and legislators and social workers, have found common cause in preventing the mixing of the races in this adoption context. I argue that these policies should not be seen as any form of legitimate "affirmative action."

My thesis is that current racial matching policies represent a coming together of powerful and related ideologies—old-fashioned white racism, modern-day black nationalism, and what I will call "biologism," the idea that what is "natural" in the context of the biological family is what is normal and desirable in the context of adoption. Biological families have same-race parents and children. The laws and policies surrounding adoption in this country have generally structured adoption in imitation of biology, giving the adopted child a new birth certificate as if the child had been born to the adoptive parents, sealing off the birth parents as if they had never existed, and attempting to match adoptive parents and children with respect to looks, intellect, and religion. The implicit goal has been to create an adoptive family that will resemble as much as possible "the real thing"—

Adapted from a much longer article originally published in 139 U. Pa. L. Rev. 1163 (1991). Copyright 1991 The University of Pennsylvania Law Review. *See also* E. Bartholet, Family Bonds: Adoption and the Politics of Parenting (1993).

the "natural" or biological family that it is not. These laws and policies reflect, I believe, widespread and powerful feelings that parent–child relationships can only work, or at least will work best, between biologic likes. They also reflect widespread and powerful fears that parents will not be able to truly love and nurture biologic unlikes. These feelings and fears have much in common with the feelings and fears among both blacks and whites in our society about the dangers of crossing racial boundaries. It is thus understandable that there would be sympathy for racial matching in the adoption context.

But the question is whether we *should* be so reluctant to cross boundaries of racial "otherness" in the context of adoption—whether today's powerful racial matching policies make sense from the viewpoint of either the minority children involved or the larger society. It is a question of growing practical importance today. Minority children are pouring, in increasing numbers, into the already overburdened foster care system,[1] and current policies stand in the way of placing these children with available adoptive families. In addition, how we deal with the race matching issue will affect how we deal with the related issues involved in the adoptive placement of children from a variety of different ethnic and national backgrounds. It will therefore affect our thinking about the growing phenomenon of international adoption, which involves the adoption by whites in this country of many dark-skinned children from foreign countries and cultures. Racial matching policies also pose a question of powerful symbolic importance. How we deal with race in the intimate context of the family says a lot about how we think about and deal with race in every other context of our social lives.

Current Racial Matching Policies

The available evidence indicates that today most public and private adoption agencies are governed by powerful race matching policies in making placement decisions for the children who come under their jurisdiction. My own investigation has included interviews with a wide array of leaders in the adoption world and experts on racial matching policies, together with a review of the relevant literature.[2] This investigation has made clear to me that race is used as the basis for official decision making in adoption in a way that is unparalleled in a society that has generally endorsed an antidiscrimination and prointegration ideology. This investigation has also made clear that current policies have a severe impact on minority children, often causing serious delays in or permanent denial of adoptive placement.

An initial order of business for most adoption agencies is the separation of children and prospective parents into racial classifications and subclassifications. Children in need of homes are typically separated into black and white pools. The children in the black pool are then classified by skin tone—light, medium, dark— and sometimes by nationality, ethnicity, or other cultural characteristics. The prospective parent pool is similarly divided and classified. An attempt is then made to match children in the various "black" categories with their parent counterparts. The goal is to assign the light-skinned black child to light-skinned parents, the Haitian child to Haitian parents, and so on. The white children are matched with white prospective parents.

This matching scheme confronts a major problem in the fact that the numbers of children falling into the black and the white pools do not "fit," proportionally, with the number of prospective parents falling into their own black and white pools. In 1987, 37.1 percent of the children in "out-of-home placement" were black as compared with 46.1 percent white.[3] Although no good statistics are available, the general understanding is that a very high percentage of the waiting adoptive parents are white. In addition, many whites interested in adopting do not bother to put themselves on the waiting lists because of their understanding that the number of children available to them is so limited.[4]

The matching policies of today place a high priority on expanding the pool of prospective black adoptive parents so that placements can be made without utilizing the waiting white pool. As discussed below, programs have been created to recruit black parents, subsidies have been provided to encourage them to adopt, and traditional parental screening criteria have been revised.

Nonetheless, the numbers mismatch continues. There are many more black children than there are waiting black families. There is a large pool of waiting white families.

Today's matching policies generally forbid the immediate placement of black children available for adoption with waiting white families. These policies tend to preclude such placements, either implicitly or explicitly, for periods ranging from six to eighteen months to several years or longer. In many instances the policies preclude transracial placement altogether.

The matching process surfaces, to a degree, in written rules and documented cases. But it is the unwritten and generally invisible rules that are central to understanding the nature of current policies. Virtually everyone in the system agrees that, all things being equal, the minority child should go to minority parents. Thus by the universal rules of the official game, race matching *must* be taken into account in the placement process. But this vastly understates the power of racial matching policies in the official adoption world. The fact is that the entire system has been designed and redesigned with a view toward promoting inracial placements and avoiding transracial placements. The rules generally make race not simply *a* factor, but an overwhelmingly important factor in the placement process.

The Impact of Current Policies

A major issue is the degree to which racial matching policies result in delaying or denying permanent placement for minority children. What we know is that minority children are disproportionately represented in the population of children waiting for adoptive homes, they spend longer waiting than white children, and they are less likely to be eventually placed. Estimates indicate that of the population of children waiting for homes, black children make up over one-third and children of color make up roughly one-half.[5] A recent study found that minority children waited an average of two years, compared with an average one-year wait for nonminorities.[6] Minority placement rates were 20 percent lower than nonminority placement rates. The minority children were comparable in age with the nonminorities and had other characteristics that, had race not been an issue, should have made it easier to find adoptive placements—they had fewer disabilities and fewer previous placements in foster care. The study concluded that racial status was a more powerful determinant of placement rate than any other factor examined.[7] These findings are consistent with the general understanding.[8] Informed observers of the adoption scene—people who know the policies and see them in operation—believe there is a strong causal connection between the policies and the delays and denial of placement that minority children face.

We know that many minority children never receive adoptive homes, and many others spend years waiting in foster care or institutions. We know that while most prospective white adopters prefer to adopt healthy white infants, many are interested in adopting black children and many are interested in adopting older children with serious disabilities. There can be no doubt that the current racial matching regime, by barring and discouraging white parents from transracial adoptions, rather than welcoming them in the agency doors, denies adoptive homes to minority children.

The Law

Current racial matching policies are in conflict with the basic law of the land on race discrimination. And they are anomalous. In no other area do state and state-licensed decision-makers use race so systematically as the basis for action. In no other area do they promote the use of race so openly. Indeed, in most areas of our community life, race is an absolutely impermissible basis for classification.

The Federal Constitution, state constitutions, and a mass of federal, state, and local laws prohibit discrimination on the basis of race by public entities. Private entities with significant power over our lives are also generally bound by laws prohibiting discrimination on the basis of race. In the past twenty-five years, this body of law has grown so that today there are guarantees against race discrimination not only in housing, employment, and public accommodations, but in virtually every area of our community life.

It is true that the antidiscrimination norm has been limited by the principles of respect for privacy and freedom of association. People are permitted to act on the basis of racial preference in choosing their friends and companions, and in forming truly private social clubs. Small employers and rooming houses were exempted from the employment and the housing provisions of the 1964 Civil Rights

Act partly on the basis of these principles.[9] But the state is not permitted to *insist* that race count as a factor in the ordering of people's most private lives. And so in *Loving v. Virginia*[10] the Supreme Court held it unconstitutional for the state to prohibit interracial marriage, and in *Palmore v. Sidoti*[11] the Court held it unconstitutional for the state to use race as the basis for deciding which of two biological parents should have custody of a child. *Palmore* involved the issue of whether a white child could be removed from the custody of its biological mother on the basis of the mother's relationship with a black man. The Court unanimously held that in this context reliance on race as a decision-making factor violated the equal protection clause of the Fourteenth Amendment.[12] The Court rejected arguments that removal of the child from a racially mixed household was justified by the state's goal of making custody decisions on the basis of the best interests of the child. Conceding that there was a "risk that a child living with a stepparent of a different race may be subject to a variety of pressures and stresses not present if the child were living with parents of the same racial or ethnic origin," the Court nonetheless had no problem concluding that these were constitutionally impermissible considerations.[13]

The antidiscrimination principle has been interpreted to outlaw almost all race-conscious action by the state and by the various agencies that control our community lives. There need be no showing that the action is designed to harm or that it results in harm. Race-conscious action has generally been allowed only where it can be justified on the grounds of compelling necessity, or where it is designed to benefit racial minority groups either by avoiding or preventing discrimination[14] or by remedying its effects, as in the case of affirmative action. But these exceptions have been narrowly defined.[15]

The necessity doctrine was used to justify the exclusion for national security reasons of Japanese-Americans from military areas in this country during World War II. But it is a sign of how limited this doctrine is that the Supreme Court decision upholding this exclusion as constitutional[16] stands essentially alone in our constitutional jurisprudence and has been significantly discredited.[17]

Affirmative action has always been controversial in this country.[18] The antidiscrimination norm has generally been expressed in individualistic and race-neutral terms—forbidding discrimination "on the basis of race" or mandating "the equal protection of the laws"—and has accordingly been interpreted to protect whites as well as blacks. Action designed to promote black group interests has often been challenged as discriminatory against whites. The courts have generally insisted that for affirmative action programs to be upheld as legitimate they must be justified on the basis of a remedial rationale.[19]

In recent years the Supreme Court has held that for federal law purposes, even "benign" racial classifications are highly suspect and must be limited to narrowly defined situations.[20] In *City of Richmond v. J.A. Croson Company*,[21] the Court held that state and local programs designed to benefit minority groups are subject to the same kind of strict constitutional scrutiny as programs designed to burden such groups. It held further that affirmative action can be justified as constitutional only if shown to be absolutely essential to remedying prior discrimination.[22]

The adoption world is an anomaly in this legal universe in which race-conscious action is deemed highly suspect and generally illegal. In agency adoptions, as we have seen, race-conscious action is one of the major rules of the child allocation game. The fact that race is a recognizable factor in decision-making is enough under our general antidiscrimination norm to make out a case of intentional discrimination.[23]

The racial matching policies fit none of the recognized exceptions to the antidiscrimination norm. There is no compelling necessity for racial matching, on a level comparable to a national emergency threatening the survival of the nation. Nor can racial matching policies be rationalized as programs designed to eliminate or to remedy the effects of prior discrimination, or otherwise to benefit blacks as a group. It is easy to argue that there has been such discrimination. The problem is that racial matching policies do not look like the kinds of remedial affirmative action programs that the courts have accepted as legitimate. The policies are blatantly inconsistent with the Supreme Court's recent *Croson* decision, which places severe limits on legitimate affirmative action, requiring a near-exact fit between a given affirmative action program and the discriminatory actions it is designed to remedy. *Croson* prohibits the use of affirmative action that is designed more broadly to counter the effects of historical or societal discrimination.[24] But even apart from *Croson*, the courts have generally insisted that affirmative action programs look backward more than they look forward, be limited in duration, and be designed to help move society to a point where race can be eliminated as a decision-making factor.[25] By contrast, racial matching policies seem to look forward at least as much as they look backward. They require race matching on an ongoing basis, without apparent limit in time. They are not designed to eliminate the role of race in agency decision making in the future, but to perpetuate its importance.

Racial matching policies are in addition fundamentally inconsistent with traditional affirmative action rationales because racial matching promotes racial separatism rather than racial integration. By contrast, affirmative action programs that have had any general level of acceptance have been consistent with the orthodox view in this country on the nature of the racial problem and of appropriate solutions to that problem. That orthodox view holds that the problem lies in the segregation of an oppressed class, and the solution can be found in the integration of that class with those who have enjoyed the privileges of life in this society. Both antidiscrimination law and affirmative action programs have been designed to break down segregatory barriers and to promote integration.

In addition, and even more significantly, race-conscious action that has any level of principled support in today's world relies on arguments that it *benefits* racial minorities. Even those courts and Supreme Court Justices most sympathetic to affirmative action have argued that allegedly benign racial classifications should be scrutinized carefully to ensure that they are truly benign in impact and do not serve to disadvantage their supposed beneficiaries.[26] Racial matching policies are not clearly beneficial in any short-term or long-term sense to blacks as a group, and in fact they seem quite harmful to a significant part of that group—the children in need of adoptive homes.

There is no particular reason to believe that blacks as a group would support these policies. They are policies developed and promoted by the leaders of one black social workers organization in the absence of any evidence of general support in the black community and with limited vocal support from any other organization.[27] Reported surveys of black community attitudes indicate substantial support for transracial adoption and very limited support for the kinds of powerful matching principles embodied in today's adoption policies.[28] The underlying motivations for these policies seem quite clearly to include a complex mix, with white opposition to race mixing in the context of the family playing a part. There is no obvious answer to the question whether racial matching policies are likely to benefit or burden the black community, advance or impede black group interests. It is certainly questionable whether imposing on the black community an obligation to take care of "its own," while providing limited resources for the job, does much to help that community.

What *does* seem clear is that current policies are harmful to the group of black children in need of homes. Affirmative action is not supposed to do concrete harm to one group of blacks in the interest of promoting what are at best hypothetical benefits to another.[29]

And adoption is not supposed to be about parent or community rights and interests, but rather about serving the best interests of children. Adoption laws throughout this country provide that agencies are to make children's interests paramount in placement decisions. Arguments can be made that black children in general will benefit from efforts to strengthen the black community, and that racial matching policies represent one such effort. The problem is that, as indicated above, racial matching policies seem contrary to the immediate and long-term interests of the specific black children waiting for homes.

Advocates for racial matching of course argue that growing up with same-race parents is a benefit of overriding importance to black children. But the claim that a black person, by virtue of his or her race, will necessarily be more capable than a white of parenting a black child is the kind of claim that courts have generally refused to allow as justification for race-conscious action.[30] The near-absolute presumption under our antidiscrimination laws is that race is irrelevant to qualifications. Moreover, the available evidence does not support the claim that same-race placement is beneficial to black children, much less that it outweighs the harm of delayed placement.[31] Ultimately, the argument that racial matching policies are beneficial rather than harmful to the children immediately affected rests on the unsupported assumption that black children will be significantly better off with "their own kind." This may or may not be true; empirical studies involving human beings and the attempt to measure human well-being may not be capable of proving the proposition one way or another. But it is not the kind of assumption that has been permitted under our nation's antidiscrimination laws. More importantly, it is not an assumption that should be permitted in a situation where there is evidence that by insisting on a racial match we are doing serious injury to black children.

Directions for the Future

Adoption agencies should be prohibited from exercising *any significant preference* for same-race families. *No delays* in placement—whether for six months or one month—should be tolerated in the interest of ensuring a racial match. Delay harms children because it causes discontinuity and disruption and because any delay creates a risk of further delay.

Accordingly, any preference for same-race placement that involves delay or that otherwise threatens the interest of the children involved in receiving good homes should be viewed as unlawful racial discrimination, inconsistent not simply with traditional limits on affirmative action,[32] but with *any* legitimate concept of affirmative action. The courts and administrators responsible for interpreting and enforcing the law should apply established legal principles to find any such preference in violation of the equal protection clause of the Constitution, Title VI of the 1964 Civil Rights Act,[33] and other applicable antidiscrimination mandates.

The only real question, then, is whether agencies should be allowed to exercise a genuinely mild preference. A mild preference would mean that if an agency had qualified black and white families waiting to adopt, it could take race into account in deciding how to allocate the children waiting for homes. But there would be real dangers in a rule involving even a mild preference. On a symbolic level, it is problematic for the state to mandate or even tolerate a regime in which social agencies, rather than private individuals, decide what shall be the appropriate racial composition of families. It is similarly problematic for the state to decide what the "appropriate" racial identity for a child is and how it is best nurtured. The Supreme Court decided some time ago that the state should not be in the business of deciding whether interracial marriages are wise. Indeed, we would not want to live in a regime in which social agencies prevented such marriages, or prevented interracial couples from producing children. Transracial adoption is, of course, different from interracial marriage in that it involves minor children, many of whom are unable to express their own desires with respect to the kind of family they would like. But it seems dangerous for the state or its agencies to assert that children should not or would not choose to ignore race if they could exercise choice in the formation of their families, and to conclude that it is presumptively in the child's best interests to have a same-race upbringing.

Moreover, the existence of transracial adoptive families in which blacks and whites live in a state of mutual love and commitment, and struggle in this context to understand issues of racial and cultural difference, seems a positive good to be celebrated. The state should not be in the position of discouraging the creation of such families.

On a pragmatic level, there is a real question as to whether it is *possible* to create a genuinely mild preference for same-race placement—a real danger that if *any* racial preference is allowed, enormous weight will in fact be given to race no matter what the formal rule of law. After all, agencies and courts commonly describe today's matching policies as if race functioned simply as one of many factors in decision making, with nothing more than a mild preference for same-race placement at work. Current adoption law is that race should *not* be used in the absolute and determinative way in which we know it systematically *is* used. Given the extraordinary level of commitment by adoption professionals to same-race placement and the amount of discretion they have traditionally enjoyed to make placement decisions, it may well be that the only practicable way to prevent race from playing the kind of determinative role that it plays today is to prohibit its use as a factor altogether.

On balance then, it seems that even a mild preference is unwise as a matter of social policy. The generally applicable legal rule that race should not be allowed to play *any* role in social decision making should be held to apply in the adoption area as well. Policy-makers should not treat such a preference as an appropriate form of affirmative action.

A no-preference regime would remove adoption agencies from the business of promoting same-race placement. It would not mean that racial considerations must be ignored altogether in the agency process. Agencies could act in their educational and counseling capacity to advise prospective parents with respect to racial matters. They could encourage parents to explore their feelings with respect to race, and they could try to educate parents as to issues involved in raising a child of a different race. They could try to guide prospective parents in the direction of the children they seem most fit to raise. But neither agencies nor courts should use their decision-making powers to approve prospective parents as parentally fit, in order to match parents with a same-race child, or to prescribe and enforce rules as to appropriate attitudes regarding a child's racial identity. It is important for agencies to try to help parents think through what they should do to affirm their child's racial identity. But it is dangerous for the state to be in the business of mandating how people should think about their child's racial heritage, and for the state to establish requirements regarding who they should have as friends, where they should go to church, and where they should live.

Conclusion

Both common sense and the available evidence from empirical studies indicate that racial matching policies are doing serious harm to black children. Accordingly, these policies violate the principle at the core of our nation's adoption laws, namely that the best interests of the child should govern the placement process.

They also violate the antidiscrimination norm contained in the nation's various civil rights laws and in the equal protection clause of the Constitution.

The evidence from the empirical studies indicates uniformly that transracial adoptees do as well on measures of psychological and social adjustment as black children raised inracially in relatively similar socioeconomic circumstances. The evidence also indicates that transracial adoptees develop comparably strong senses of black identity. They see themselves as black, and they think well of blackness. The difference is that they feel more comfortable with the white community than blacks raised inracially. This evidence provides no basis for concluding that there are inherent costs in transracial placement from the children's viewpoint.

By contrast, the evidence from the empirical studies, together with professional opinion over the decades and our common sense, indicates that the placement delays of months and years that result from our current policies impose very serious costs on children. Children need permanency in their primary parenting relationships. They may be destroyed by delays when those delays involve, as they so often do, abuse or neglect in inadequate foster care or institutional situations. They will likely be hurt by delays in even the best of foster care situations, whether they develop powerful bonds with parents they must then lose, or live their early years without experiencing the kind of bonding that is generally thought crucial to healthy development.

Current policies also significantly increase the risk that minority children who are older and who suffer serious disabilities will never become part of a permanent family. Advocates of these policies claim that prospective white parents do not want these children anyway. But the last two decades have demonstrated that efforts to educate and recruit adults of all races are successful in changing attitudes and making people aware of the satisfactions involved in parenting children with special needs. Current policies mean that virtually no such education and recruitment is going on in the white community with respect to the waiting minority children. These are the children who wait and wait. They represent a significant piece of the foster care problem. It defies reason to claim that we would not open up many homes to these children if agencies were willing to look for such homes in the white community.

It is true, as advocates of current policies often say, that more could be done to find black families. More substantial subsidies could be provided, and more resources could be devoted to recruitment. But it is extremely unlikely that our society will anytime soon devote more than lip service and limited resources to putting blacks in a social and economic position where they are capable of providing good homes for all the waiting black children. It will always be far easier to get white society to agree on the goal of placing black children in black homes than to get an allocation of financial resources that will make that goal workable. The danger in using black children as hostages to pry the money loose is that white society will not see these lives as warranting much in the way of ransom. Moreover, in a desperately overburdened and underfinanced welfare system, those who care about children should take children's many needs into account as they make decisions about allocating any new funds that might be available. Money is desperately needed to provide services that will enable biological families to function so that children are not unnecessarily removed from parents who could provide them with good parenting were it not for adverse circumstances. It is desperately needed to protect children from abuse and neglect. It is desperately needed to improve the adoption process so that children who should be permanently removed from their families are freed up for adoption and placed as promptly as possible with permanent adoptive families. Money is needed in these and other areas to help ensure some very basic protections for children that should take priority over the essentially adult agenda of promoting racial separation.

NOTES

1. Unfortunately, no really accurate figures are available. The federal government stopped gathering statistics on a uniform, national basis in the mid-1970s. The United States National Center for Social Statistics issued its last report on adoption in 1975. *See* Hollinger, Introduction to Adoption Law and Practice, in Adoption Law and Practice 1-52 (J. Hollinger ed., 1988). However, in recent years the federal government has begun to maintain national statistics on adoption, based on information collected on a voluntary basis from state substitute care systems. Dr. Toshio Tatara, director of the Research and Demonstration Department of the American Public Welfare Association (APWA), heads this Voluntary Cooperative Information Systems (VCIS) effort. His statistics indicate that the number of children in "out-of-home placement" increased from a total of 262,000 in 1982 to 280,000 in 1986 to 360,000 in 1989, with the percentage of black children in such placement rising from 34.2 percent in 1982 to 34.9 percent in 1986 to 37.1 percent in 1987. Telephone interview with Dr. Toshio Tatara, director of Research and Demonstration Department, American Public Welfare Association (Jan. 29, 1991) [hereinafter Tatara Interview].

Other estimates generally show that roughly half of the children in out-of-home placement are children of color, with a somewhat smaller percentage being children characterized as black. *See* House Select Committee on Children, Youth, and Families, No Place to Call Home: Discarded Children in America, H.R. Rep. No. 395, 101st Cong., 2d Sess. 5, 38 (1990) [hereinafter No Place to Call Home] (noting that "[i]n 1985, minority children comprised 41% of the children in foster care," more than twice the proportion of minority children in the nation's total child population); J. Munns & J. Copenhaver, The State of Adoption in America 3–4 (1989).

Most adoption professionals believe there has been an enormous increase in children coming into foster care in the last few years, with young minority children representing a large part of the increase. In No Place to Call Home, *supra,* the Select Committee on Children, Youth, and Families of the United States

House of Representatives estimates that if current trends continue, the out-of-home placement population will increase 68 percent by 1995, rising from a figure of 500,000 to 840,000. *See id.* at 5. These figures include children under the jurisdiction of juvenile correctional and mental health authorities, who are not included in the APWA statistics. Among the reasons named for this rise are increases in drug and alcohol abuse, other deteriorating social conditions, and inadequacies in social services provided. Telephone interview with Eileen Pastorz, director of the Adoption Subcommittee of the Child Welfare League (Jan. 28, 1991); *see also* Waiting for a Home, Boston Globe, Nov. 30, 1989, at 1 (discussing policies opposing transracial adoption in the context of escalating numbers of black children in foster care); New York Sees Rise in Babies Hurt by Drugs, N.Y. Times, Oct. 18, 1989, at B1, B2 (discussing the reasons for the increase in the number of infants in need of special services).

2. I conducted a series of interviews, some by telephone and some in person, with dozens of adoption world professionals, students of the adoption system, and related experts, including both critics and supporters of current racial matching policies. Those interviewed include the following: Richard Barth, professor, School of Social Welfare, University of California, Berkeley; Betsy Burch, director, Single Parents for the Adoption of Children Everywhere (SPACE); Alice Bussiere, National Center for Youth Law; Carol Coccia, president, National Coalition to End Racism in America's Child Care System; Sydney Duncan, director, Homes for Black Children; Jane Edwards, former director, Spence Chapin Adoption Service; Susan Freivalds, Adoptive Families of America; Carolyn Johnson, executive director, National Adoption Center; Joe Kroll, executive director, North American Council on Adoptable Children; Betty Laning, Open Door Society; Ernesto Loperena, New York Council on Adoptable Children; Phyllis Lowenstein, former director, International Adoptions Inc.; Leora Neal, executive director, New York Chapter of Association of Black Social Workers Child Adoption Counselling and Referral Service; William Pierce, president, National Committee for Adoption; Dr. Alvin Poussaint, Department of Psychiatry, Harvard Medical School; Nancy Rodriguez, supervisor, Adoption Subsidy Program, Massachusetts Department of Social Services; Mary Beth Seader, National Committee for Adoption; Rita Simon, co-author of one of the leading empirical studies of transracial adoption; Carolyn Smith, Massachusetts Adoption Resource Exchange; Peggy Soule, director, the CAP Exchange; Linda Spears, director, Office of Special Projects, Massachusetts Department of Social Services; Toshio Tatara, director, Research and Demonstration Department, American Public Welfare Association; Ken Watson, Child Welfare League of America Adoption Task Force and Chicago Child Care Society; Mary Wood, Native American Adoption Resource Exchange.

3. These are APWA statistics obtained during my interview with Dr. Toshio Tatara. Tatara Interview, *supra* note 1. Of the children legally free for adoption, 34.1 percent were black and 52.5 percent were white in 1987. *Id.*

By contrast to their numbers in the foster care population, blacks represent only 12.3 percent of the general population. *See* U.S. Department of Commerce, Bureau of the Census, Statistical Abstract of the United States 1990, at 12 (1990).

4. The APWA statistics do not include information on waiting families. However, a study done for the Child Welfare League provides some documentation of the

numbers mismatch. *See* Munns & Copenhaver, State of Adoption, *supra* note 1, at 8. The 1991 figures for the National Adoption Center exchange, which lists hard-to-place children waiting for homes as well as waiting families, provide further documentation. They show that 67 percent of the listed children are black, and 26 percent are white. *See* Memorandum from Director Carolyn Johnson to Staff 1–2 (Mar. 28, 1991) (on file with author). Of the waiting families, 31 percent are black and 67 percent are white. *See* Fax Transmittal Memorandum from Director Carolyn Johnson to Elizabeth Bartholet (Apr. 16, 1991) (on file with author). The Massachusetts Adoption Resource Exchange figures for December 1990 show that, of the children registered with the exchange, 121 were of color and 198 were white. Of the families registered, 41 were of color and 281 were white. Of the 281 white families, 161 were listed as being interested in children over the age of six and 120 were listed as being interested in children under six. Telephone interview with Carolyn Smith, Massachusetts Adoption Resource Exchange (Jan. 24, 1991).

5. *See supra* note 1. By contrast, blacks make up 12.3 percent of the total population, and people of color make up approximately 17 percent. *See* U.S. Department of Commerce, Statistical Abstract 1990, *supra* note 3, at 12.

6. *See* 1 WESTAT, Inc., Adoptive Services for Waiting Minority and Nonminority Children (Apr. 15, 1986).

7. *See id.*, at x–xi, 3-7 to 3-8, 3-17 to 3-44, 6-1.

8. *See* Mason & Williams, The Adoption of Minority Children, in Adoption of Children with Special Needs 83–84 (1985) (noting that minority children are disproportionately represented and spend longer in foster care than white children); No Place to Call Home, *supra* note 1, at 38–39. There is, however, some conflict in the findings regarding the connection between race and delay in placement. *See* Benedict & White, Factors Associated with Foster Care Length of Stay, 70 Child Welfare League J. Pol'y, Prac. & Program, Jan.–Feb. 1991, at 45, 48, 50.

9. *See* 42 U.S.C. § 2000e (b) (1988); *id.* § 2000a (b)(1).

10. 388 U.S. 1 (1967). The Court held that Virginia's ban on interracial marriage constituted a racial classification in violation of the equal protection clause as well as a denial of liberty without due process of law under the Fourteenth Amendment.

11. 466 U.S. 429 (1984).

12. *See id.* at 434. The Court noted that a core purpose of the Fourteenth Amendment was "to do away with all governmentally imposed discrimination based on race" and that "classifying persons by race is more likely to reflect racial prejudice than legitimate public concerns." *Id.*

13. *Id.* at 433.

14. *See, e.g.,* United Jewish Orgs. v. Carey, 430 U.S. 144 (1979) (upholding consideration of race in legislative reapportionment on grounds that it was designed to avoid abridging the right to vote on the basis of race).

15. *See* L. Tribe, American Constitutional Law 1466 & n.4 (2d ed. 1988).

16. *See* Korematsu v. United States, 323 U.S. 214 (1944).

17. *See* Tribe, American Constitutional Law, *supra* note 15, at 1466.

18. *See id.* at 1523.

19. *See id.* at 1537–44.

20. *See* City of Richmond v. J.A. Croson Co., 488 U.S. 469 (1989); Johnson v.

Transportation Agency, 480 U.S. 616 (1987); United States v. Paradise, 480 U.S. 149 (1987); Local 28, Sheet Metal Workers Int'l Ass'n v. Equal Employment Opportunity Comm'n, 478 U.S. 421 (1986); Wygant v. Jackson Bd. of Educ., 476 U.S. 267 (1986).

21. 488 U.S. 469 (1989).

22. The Supreme Court held in 1990 that the United States Congress had greater leeway than the states to mandate affirmative action, in the only case in which the Court has specifically endorsed a nonremedial form of affirmative action. *See* Metro Broadcasting v. F.C.C., 110 S. Ct. 2997, 3009 (1990) (holding that congressionally mandated affirmative action measures are not subject to "strict scrutiny" review, but will be upheld if "they serve important governmental objectives within the power of Congress and are substantially related to achievement of those objectives").

23. The standard is "but for" causation. In cases where race is one of a number of factors contributing to a decision, the Supreme Court has placed the burden on the decision-makers to demonstrate that they would have come to the same result on the basis of nonracial factors. *See* Price Waterhouse v. Hopkins, 490 U.S. 228 (1989); Mt. Healthy City Bd. of Educ. v. Doyle, 429 U.S. 274 (1977).

24. I find the *Croson* holding enormously problematic and inconsistent with the purpose of the Fourteenth Amendment and with much of the development of the meaning of the amendment over the years. *Croson*, however, is quite clearly binding on the public adoption agencies and other public entities, subjecting their racial matching policies to strict scrutiny review.

25. *See supra* notes 17–21 and accompanying text. The Supreme Court's recent decision in Metro Broadcasting v. F.C.C., 110 S. Ct. 2997 (1990), stands as an important but nonetheless very limited exception to these general principles. It held that Congress can legitimately mandate race-conscious measures designed to benefit minority-owned businesses in the broadcast industry, where the purpose was to enhance programming diversity in the future, not simply to remedy discrimination against minority broadcasters in the past. *See id.* at 3009–10.

26. *See, e.g.,* Regents of the Univ. of California v. Bakke, 438 U.S. 265, 324, 361 (Brennan, J., concurring and dissenting) (arguing for "strict and searching review" of affirmative action because of the "significant risk that racial classifications established for ostensibly benign purposes can be misused, causing effects not unlike those created by invidious classifications"); United Jewish Orgs. v. Carey, 430 U.S. 144, 172–74 (1977) (Brennan, J., concurring in part) ("[A] purportedly preferential race assignment may in fact disguise a policy that perpetuates disadvantageous treatment of the plan's supposed beneficiaries. . . . [Therefore, the Court must give] careful consideration [to] the operation of any racial device, even one cloaked in preferential garb").

27. *See* Bartholet, Where Do Black Children Belong? The Politics of Race Matching in Adoption, 139 U. Pa. L. Rev. 1163, 1174–82 (1991).

28. For example, a study designed to assess the black community's attitudes regarding the transracial adoption debate found significant support for transracial adoption and very limited support for the National Association of Black Social Workers' [NABSW] position among a sample black population. *See* Howard et al., Transracial Adoption: The Black Community Perspective, 22 Soc. Work 184 (1977).

A majority (56.7 percent) had an "open" attitude toward transracial adoptions, while 6.7 percent were "most unfavorable" and 19.3 percent "somewhat unfavorable." *See id.* at 185–86. Three-fourths of all respondents felt that transracial adoption might be beneficial if no black home was available, while only 16 percent disagreed. Eighty-one percent preferred transracial adoption over keeping a child in a foster home or institution, while 14 percent did not. *See id.* In looking at rationales, the study concluded: "While the respondents were concerned about the child's possible loss of identification with the black community, the needs of the individual child were seen to be of prime importance." *Id.* at 188.

An earlier study involved interviews with blacks and whites with some awareness of issues related to the placement of black children. The group included adoptive parents, adoption professionals, and representatives of the black community. The black respondents divided evenly for and against transracial placements. In general, persons with direct experience with transracial adoption came out two to one in favor of it. *See* Herzog et al., Some Opinions on Finding Families for Black Children, 18 Children 143, 146 (1971).

A third study asked a sample of "educated middle-class blacks" the general question of whether they approved of the practice of whites adopting black children and found opinion divided, with slightly under half (45 percent) approving of the practice. *See* Simon, Black Attitudes Toward Transracial Adoption, 39 Phylon 135, 140 (1978).

29. *See* United States v. Starrett City Assocs., 840 F.2d 1096 (2d Cir. 1988). At issue was the use of racial quotas that limited black access to a housing complex in the interest of maintaining racial integration. The case thus involved a conflict between blacks interested in living in adequate and integrated housing and blacks interested in gaining access to that housing. The court struck down the access-limiting quotas as inconsistent with the Fair Housing Act's antidiscrimination mandate, relying on the Supreme Court's affirmative action cases discussed *supra* note 26.

30. Again, the Supreme Court's decision in Metro Broadcasting v. FCC, 110 S. Ct. 2997 (1990), stands as an important but limited exception to this principle. In upholding a preference for minority-owned businesses in the broadcast industry, a 5–4 majority of the Court indicated some acceptance, for the first time, of the idea that race might be intrinsically related to qualifications—here the ability to promote diversity in programing. *See id.* at 3011. But, as noted previously, the significance of this case is limited by the fact that since Congressional action was involved, the Court applied a uniquely lenient standard of constitutional review. In previous cases dealing with action by state entities, the Supreme Court has never been willing to endorse "role model" or other nonremedial rationales for affirmative action. For example, in Wygant v. Jackson Bd. of Educ., 476 U.S. 267 (1986), the Court was presented with an affirmative action program involving the hiring of schoolteachers, where the goal for minority hiring had been set with a view toward providing minority children in the school system with a roughly proportionate number of same-race teachers. *See Wygant*, 476 U.S. at 270. The Court struck down the plan for a variety of reasons, with four Justices indicating they felt that the goal of providing students with same-race teachers was not a constitutionally appropriate one. *See id.* at 275–76.

31. *See* Bartholet, Where Do Black Children Belong?, *supra* note 27, at 1207–26.
32. *See supra* text accompanying notes 18–26, 29–30.
33. Pub. L. No. 88-352, 78 Stat. 252 (codified as amended at 42 U.S.C. § 2000d (1988)) ("No person in the United States shall, on the ground of race, color, or national origin, be excluded from participation in, be denied the benefits of, or be subjected to discrimination under any program or activity receiving Federal financial assistance").

■ CHAPTER SIX

Prosecution of Mothers of Drug-Exposed Babies: Constitutional and Criminal Theory

Doretta Massardo McGinnis

DURING THE LATE 1980s, a new prosecutorial trend developed: Women who had used drugs during pregnancy and subsequently delivered drug-exposed babies were charged with a variety of crimes, including criminal neglect, delivery of drugs to a minor, and involuntary manslaughter. It was estimated that eighteen such cases were pending nationwide as of October 1989, representing an abrupt increase in the wake of the Supreme Court's July 1989 decision in *Webster v. Reproductive Health Services*.[1] Early in 1990 the American Civil Liberties Union counted at least thirty-five cases across the country as this prosecutorial trend continued into the new decade. By October 1992, at least 160 women in twenty-four states and the District of Columbia had been charged with crimes related to their delivery of drug-exposed babies.

These prosecutions uniformly involve the application of laws previously applied to redress offenses committed against children after birth. Arguably, prosecutors have misconstrued existing statutes to create new offenses in contravention of legislative intent, while denying defendants the due process requirements of notice and fair warning. Several state legislatures have passed or are considering legislation specifically aimed at prohibiting and punishing the use of illicit drugs by pregnant women. Passage of such legislation will likely be accompanied by clear expressions of legislative intent, and potential defendants will likely be

---

Reprinted in redacted form with permission of the University of Pennsylvania Law Review. Originally appeared in 139 U. Pa. L. Rev. 505 (1990). Copyright 1990 The University of Pennsylvania Law Review.

granted notice and fair warning. Other potential constitutional problems, however, will remain. The fundamental right to bear a child will be denied to a class of women—drug addicts—based on their status as addicts and the effects that their addictive behaviors are likely to have on their children. The rights of privacy and reproductive freedom currently accorded all women may be further eroded. Such restrictions may, however, be found constitutional if courts accept the view that fetal rights outweigh women's rights in the context of a pregnant woman's behavior likely to cause fetal harm.

Even if the current constitutional defects are remedied through the passage of narrowly tailored statutes and increased recognition of fetal rights, prosecutions of pregnant drug users still cannot be justified under prevailing theories of criminal law. These prosecutions may involve punishing women on two inappropriate grounds: their involuntary, addictive behavior and their status as pregnant addicts. Involuntary behavior typically does not justify punishment, and status crimes are categorically prohibited. The involuntary nature of addiction makes it unlikely that these prosecutions will have any significant deterrent effect. In the absence of general deterrence, these prosecutions will fail to benefit potential defendants, their children, or society as a whole. In fact, it is likely that criminogenic effects[2] will ensue: Crimes associated with the evasion of these prosecutions may increase; respect for the legal system may be diminished as the public observes the spectacle of the state prosecuting poor, disenfranchised drug users while the wealthy avoid prosecution and enjoy the benefits of discriminatory law enforcement; prosecutorial resources may be diverted from more effective uses (such as the prosecution of drug suppliers and dealers) to the prosecution of women whose children are already permanently drug-affected and who require medical, not penal, attention. Drug-addicted women and their actual and potential children need medical help, which the criminal justice system is neither designed nor equipped to provide.

In May 1989, Melanie Green of Rockford, Illinois, became the first woman in the United States to be charged with manslaughter for the death of a baby who died (after being born alive) of complications resulting from prenatal maternal cocaine use.[3] Green was also charged with delivering drugs to a minor.[4] A Winnebago County grand jury refused to indict Green, and all charges were dropped.

In July 1989, the Seminole County Court in Sanford, Florida, convicted Jennifer Johnson of delivering drugs to a minor. Johnson had used cocaine during her pregnancy, and her child was born with traces of the drug in his system. An attempt to convict Johnson of child abuse was unsuccessful. The prosecutor ultimately applied a statute typically used against drug traffickers. Johnson was sentenced to fifteen years of probation, attendance at a drug rehabilitation program, and mandatory prenatal supervision should she become pregnant again. Ultimately, however, the Florida Supreme Court reversed Johnson's conviction.

This chapter will first discuss the constitutional ramifications of these prosecutions. It will then analyze the prosecutions in the context of criminal legal theory. Finally, the prosecutions will be discussed in the context of the national debates on abortion and drug abuse. This chapter concludes that the criminal justice system is ill-suited to intervene in the complex medical and sociological problems associated with drug use and pregnancy, which may be more effectively and humanely addressed by drug treatment programs for pregnant addicts.

Constitutional Issues

The constitutional concerns raised by the prosecution of mothers who have delivered drug-exposed babies are twofold. First, the unforeseeable application against pregnant drug abusers who harm their fetuses of statutes usually construed to protect live-born children does not satisfy the requirements of due process. Prosecutors have crafted new offenses that are not sanctioned by state legislatures, and potential defendants are subjected to criminal liability without notice or fair warning. Second, such prosecutions further expand fetal rights at an impermissible cost to women's rights. This section evaluates these two aspects of the dubious constitutionality of the recent prosecutions.

Due Process Violations

Prior to the spate of prosecutions at issue here, statutes criminalizing child abuse, manslaughter, or the delivery of drugs to a minor had been used against adults who abused, killed, or sold drugs to children, not against mothers whose prenatal drug use caused fetal harm.[5] The statutes typically use such terms as "child" or "person";[6] their application in cases involving live-born children harmed after birth fell within the bounds of legislative intent[7] and avoided delicate determinations concerning the beginnings of "personhood." Endorsement by the courts of prosecutors' applications of such statutes to mothers who have harmed their fetuses by using drugs during pregnancy may, however, constitute the impermissible judicial creation of new offenses. The legislature, not the courts, should create new offenses. In addition, the prosecuted mothers were not on notice that their activity was a crime vis-à-vis their fetuses. This unforeseeable classification of certain acts as offenses is a violation of the constitutional requirements of notice and fair warning. The requirements of due process that (1) the legislature, not the courts, define crimes and (2) potential defendants be granted notice or fair warning that their conduct is criminal are considered below.

Legislative Definitions of Crimes

The Supreme Court of California provided an instructive discussion of the role of the legislature in defining crimes in the landmark case of *Keeler v. Superior Court*.[8] The defendant, charged with murder in connection with the stillbirth of a baby that had suffered a fractured skull in utero, had beaten the child's mother during the eighth month of pregnancy with the intent to kill the fetus.

The California court began by noting the language of the state's murder statute, which proscribed the "unlawful and malicious killing of a *human being*."[9] Examining legislative intent, the court concluded that a fetus was not a human being within the meaning of the statute; the defendant, therefore, was not guilty of murder.[10] The *Keeler* court stated that "the power to define crimes and fix penalties is vested exclusively in the legislative branch. . . . [T]he courts cannot go so far as to create an offense by enlarging a statute . . . or by giving the terms used false or unusual meanings."[11] Given the codification of criminal law in the United States and the attendant demise of common law crimes, these statements describe the general American rule, not simply the law of California.[12] The California state legislature responded to the *Keeler* decision by revising the state's murder statute to encompass feticide.[13]

Fair application of a statute in a manner consistent with legislative intent requires an inquiry into the meaning of the statutory terms. In *Keeler*, for example, the court had to determine whether a fetus came within the statutory term "human being." One issue raised by the current prosecutions of mothers who bear drug-exposed babies is whether the fetuses are "children" or "persons" within the meaning of the applied statutes. For example, the drug delivery complaint against Melanie Green characterized her fetus as a person under eighteen years of age.[14] Several prosecutors have evaded considerations of legislative intent by arguing that drugs were delivered to a child born alive via the umbilical cord in the moments before the cord was clamped.[15] If a fetus was not intended by the legislature to come within the ambit of a statutory term such as "person," this application of the statute to cases of fetal harm may constitute the creation of a new offense by enlarging the statute to encompass harm to fetuses as well as to persons, or by according an unusual or unintended meaning to the term "person." Either of these consequences would constitute prosecutorial usurpation of the legislature's power to define crimes.

While an analysis of the legislative history of the relevant statutes in each state where prosecutions have occurred is beyond the scope of this chapter, it is apparent that prosecutors have applied laws in novel ways. In the *Green* case, prosecutor Paul Logli "sought to apply the involuntary manslaughter statute because there [were] no laws in Illinois directly applicable to the case."[16] Logli himself has speculated that the grand jury failed to indict Green because "the jurors were uncomfortable with the use of statutes that were not intended to be used in these circumstances."[17] Such prosecutorial initiatives may contravene legislative intent and ostensibly create new offenses of fetal harm. Creation of offenses is a role that is properly assumed by the legislature, not prosecutors.[18]

It is possible that state legislatures will respond to the courts' failure to convict pregnant drug users under existing statutes by passing laws that are more narrowly tailored to prosecutorial goals. The statutory definition of a child or person may be expanded to include fetuses,[19] or the definition of abuse or neglect may be amended to mention explicitly maternal drug use during pregnancy. It has been suggested that "states could promote the unborn's potentiality for life by outlawing fetus endangerment, abandonment, neglect and nonsupport."[20] Such legislation would parallel the protections commonly in place for live-born children. To date, most legislative responses have been in the area of civil, rather than criminal, law. After the Illinois grand jury refused to indict Melanie Green for manslaughter, the state legislature expanded the statutory definition of a neglected or abused minor to include "any newborn infant whose blood or urine contains any amount of a controlled substance . . . or a metabolite of a controlled substance."[21] The amended statute facilitates judicial jurisdiction over drug-exposed newborns and their removal from their mothers.[22] Several other states have amended or enacted laws under which a child who is born drug-dependent or drug-exposed is considered to be abused or neglected.[23] The Pennsylvania legislature considered similar legislation,[24] but did not pass it.

The Illinois legislature failed to pass a new criminal statute prohibiting "conduct injurious to a newborn."[25] The bill stated in part:

> Any woman who is pregnant and without a prescription knowingly or intentionally uses a dangerous drug or a narcotic drug and at the conclusion of her pregnancy delivers a newborn child, and such child shows signs of narcotic or dangerous drug exposure or addiction, or the presence of a narcotic or dangerous drug in the child's blood or urine, commits the offense of conduct injurious to a newborn.[26]

The proposed crime would have been a felony punishable by probation or a prison term of one to three years. Instead, the legislature passed a bill creating a pilot drug treatment program for pregnant women, who would lose custody of their children if they refused treatment.

The passage of legislation criminalizing certain maternal behavior during pregnancy and imposing liability for the harmful effects of such behavior on children would satisfy the due process requirement that the legislature, rather than the courts, define criminal offenses. Substantively, it appears that such legislation would be constitutional. While the Supreme Court in *Roe v. Wade*[27] held that a fetus is not a person within the meaning of the Fourteenth Amendment, it "did not prohibit lawmakers from extending to the unborn the benefits of personhood in other cases."[28] This part of the *Roe* holding has been strengthened by the Court's opinion in *Webster*: Legislators may now attribute the qualities of legal personhood even to previable fetuses.[29] States arguably have a compelling interest in promoting the welfare of fetuses from the moment of conception, and this interest may support legislation such as that contemplated here. The state's interest, however, must be balanced against women's constitutional right to privacy.[30]

The correction of constitutional defects through legislative responses to the prosecution of pregnant drug users has not been uniform across the nation. Prosecutors continue to employ existing statutes that facially protect children only after their birth.[31] It is unlikely that there will be much incentive for more specific legislation in states where prosecutors have obtained convictions. Successful prosecutors may find it unnecessary to support new legislation.[32] As long as prosecutors continue to apply existing statutes in derogation of the basic principle of statutory construction that requires reliance on legislative intent, the due process requirements of notice and fair warning will be violated.

Requirements of Notice and Fair Warning

The *Keeler* court provided a useful discussion of the notice and fair warning concerns that are currently raised by prosecutors' implicit inclusion of fetuses (or babies who suffered lasting injury as fetuses) within the ambit of child abuse or drug trafficking statutes. The court stated that "[t]he first essential of due process is fair warning of the act which is made punishable as a crime."[33] This requirement of fair warning is rooted in the Constitution's prohibition against legislative enactment of ex post facto laws.[34] Relying on the Supreme Court's decision in *Bouie v. City of Columbia*,[35] the *Keeler* court noted that "unforeseeable judicial enlargement" of existing statutes—a situation analogous to enactment of ex post facto laws[36]—violates the due process requirement of fair warning, and concluded that the inclusion of fetuses within the state murder statute constituted such an unforeseeable enlargement.[37]

A comparable unforeseeable judicial enlargement of existing laws is the use of drug delivery statutes in the current prosecutions of addicted mothers. These statutes had typically been used against drug dealers; their application to pregnant addicts was novel and unanticipated. Recognizing the connection between novelty and unforeseeability, the *Keeler* court rejected the prosecutor's interpretation of the murder statute in part because of its novelty.[38] While innovative approaches to the drug problem were arguably forthcoming in light of the much-discussed national "war on drugs," foreseeable actions included the stricter but uncreative enforcement of laws prohibiting drug delivery, possession, and sale, rather than the novel applications of such laws. With regard to the current prosecutions, it has been noted that "[t]hese drug [delivery] statutes were not intended to apply to fetuses and prenatal behavior and it was not considered a crime to take drugs during pregnancy when these woman did that. They could not have known they were committing a crime."[39]

The unforeseeability of a statute's application must be analyzed from the defendant's perspective if the due process requirements of "notice" and "fair warning" are to have any content.[40] Potential defendants must be warned or put on notice that their behavior may subject them to criminal liability. A critical method of notice is the reporting of other cases within the jurisdiction. The *Keeler* court based its decision in part on its finding "no reported decision of the California courts which should have given petitioner notice that the killing of an unborn but viable fetus was prohibited by [the state murder statute]."[41] Certainly people do not consult local case reporters before engaging in criminally questionable conduct; groundbreaking cases, however, do generate a great deal of publicity in the popular media. Arguably, Jennifer Johnson's conviction put pregnant Floridians who use drugs on notice that they may be prosecuted.

At least one defendant, charged with gestational child abuse after giving birth to two premature, cocaine-exposed babies, has questioned the foreseeability of including a fetus within Florida's child abuse statute. She stated: "I don't feel I'm a child abuser. . . . Being in my shoes, you wouldn't look at it like child abuse. I was abusing myself, and something grew inside me."[42] This argument has been echoed by lawyers who decry the consequences of according women and their fetuses separate, conflicting interests.[43]

Fetal Rights Versus Women's Rights

Since the Supreme Court's 1973 decision in *Roe v. Wade,* fetal rights have been continuously expanded. This trend is likely to continue in the wake of *Webster v. Reproductive Health Services,* which expanded the states' right to limit abortions based on an asserted state interest in potential life that may be found compelling throughout pregnancy without regard for fetal viability. Continued expansion of fetal rights engenders concern that women's rights to privacy and self-determination may be compromised. The prosecution of drug-addicted pregnant women raises the additional problem of essentially punishing for "status."

Privacy Interests

The fundamental right to bear a child[44] is virtually unregulated by state law.[45] A pregnant woman certainly may choose to carry her baby to term regardless of fetal defects or ill effects on her own health. It has been argued that states permissibly could impose more regulations on birth in order to promote the interests of the unborn. States may be unwilling to do so because of constitutional precedent concerning the privacy of personal decisions regarding procreation, marriage, and contraception. *Webster,* with its recognition of the state's interest in fetal welfare from the moment of conception,[46] and its widening of the state's opportunity to prohibit abortions, may represent a move toward promoting birth.[47]

To what extent does a woman's decision to carry a baby to term affect her exercise of other fundamental rights, such as the right to privacy? It has been argued that "[o]nce she decides to forgo abortion and the state chooses to protect the fetus, the woman loses the liberty to act in ways that would adversely affect the fetus."[48] Endorsement of this position could open the floodgates to prosecutions of pregnant women for any activity that might conceivably harm their fetuses, *even* if such activity could *benefit* the mothers.[49] The state would effectively create an adversarial relationship between mother and fetus that might threaten a woman's fundamental rights by controlling her behavior during pregnancy.[50]

Maternal behaviors that may cause fetal harm can be distinguished on a number of bases, such as the magnitude of the risk of harm, the likely severity of the harm, the potential benefits to the mother, and the likelihood that these benefits will be achieved. The distinction most frequently noted, however—that between legal and illegal maternal activity—bears no relation to fetal harm, the danger ostensibly sought to be avoided by prosecuting pregnant drug users. Further, it is axiomatic that illegal acts are illegal regardless of the actor's reproductive status, so that pregnant women who commit drug-related crimes are already subject to prosecution regardless of their pregnancies. The legal–illegal distinction is particularly problematic in the context of prosecuting addicts.

A New Status Crime?

Drug addiction has been judicially designated a status, which cannot be penalized as such. The Supreme Court in *Robinson v. California*[51] held unconstitutional a state law that criminalized the condition of being a drug addict and accepted the validity of a disease model of drug addiction.[52] At least a portion of the medical community currently regards substance abuse as a disorder warranting medical intervention and treatment. Recent prosecutions of women who were pregnant drug addicts have been criticized for essentially punishing a status, or the coexistence of two statuses that alone would be unpunishable and undeserving of punishment. As determined by *Robinson,* the status of being a drug addict cannot constitute a crime. Even drug use, a symptom of addiction, is not ordinarily a crime. If drug addiction or drug use is not a crime, "then what is being punished [by these prosecutions] is the status of being pregnant"[53] when it coexists with the status of drug addiction or with drug use. The result of criminalizing the coexistence of two unpunishable statuses—drug addiction and pregnancy—is the creation of a new status crime.[54] The harm to others, such as the babies of drug addicts, which may result from the convergence of addiction and pregnancy may be addressed by independent statutes that focus on harm, not status.[55] Indeed, it is typically the case that when drug or alcohol use results in harm to another person, the harmful "undesirable behavior is ordinarily proscribed by another criminal statute [and] the prosecution is limited to the crime . . . independent of drug use."[56] If drug use alone is not a crime, but drug use by pregnant women is, then pregnancy constitutes "a necessary element of a remarkable new status-based criminal offense: [p]regnancy by a drug-dependent person, or drug use by a pregnant woman."[57]

The recent expansion of fetal rights, as demonstrated by prosecutions of pregnant drug addicts, may effectively deny the fundamental right of reproduction to a particular class of sick women (drug addicts) whose symptoms (compulsive drug use) may injure their fetuses. This emphasis on fetal rights may lead to further incursions on the rights of ill women to bear children. There can be no justification for imposing criminal sanctions on diseased persons simply because they are sick. The question becomes whether the fact that a person is ill may be used as the basis for regulating that person's behavior to the point of circumscribing rights that she would be accorded if she were healthy. From the perspective of furthering fetal and childhood well-being, it is clearly not in the best interests of children to be born of women who are HIV-positive, cancer patients, or alcoholics. Alcoholic women, women who are infected with HIV, and women who refuse medical treatment for pregnancy-related ailments place their fetuses at an increased risk of illness and physical and developmental abnormalities.[58] Pregnant women who have cancer or epilepsy often require drugs that may harm their fetuses.[59] The constitutional protections that preserve such persons' right to procreate should extend to substance abusers as well. Adults have a right to procreate, while children have no corollary right to be born healthy, financially secure, or into a two-parent family. In each of these cases the potential parent's right to reproduce predominates over any imagined right of the fetus to be born to a healthy mother. The prosecutions of drug-addicted mothers could foreseeably lead to procreation being considered a privilege to be granted by the state rather than a right rooted in the Constitution.

Criminal Theory

The current prosecutions of pregnant drug users demonstrate a disregard for commonly accepted theories and objectives of the criminal law. We now turn to two aspects of this problem. First, the general prohibition against punishing persons for their involuntary behavior will be considered in light of the nature of drug addiction and the attendant potential for deterrence. Second, Sanford Kadish's criminogenesis analysis will be applied to the current prosecutions, which arguably create more harm than good.

Punishing Involuntary Behavior

The Anglo-American criminal law tradition has consistently recognized the immorality and futility of punishing individuals for involuntary behavior. Culpability generally requires a voluntary act; people do not deserve punishment for acts they neither intended nor controlled. The Model Penal Code (MPC), for example, imposes no criminal liability in the absence of a voluntary act or omission.[60] The voluntary act requirement exists, among other reasons, to foster deterrence, a primary goal of the criminal law.[61] Distinguishing between voluntary and involuntary acts has proved difficult, and behavior associated with drug addiction presents unique problems of classification. This section will describe involuntary aspects of drug addiction and analyze the problems associated with punishing addicts for the consequences of their involuntary acts.

The Supreme Court has long recognized that drug addiction is an illness, stating that addicts "are diseased and proper subjects for [medical] treatment."[62] The disease model of addiction is widely accepted by the medical community,[63] and the American Psychiatric Association categorizes substance-use disorders as mental disorders.[64] These disorders, including the cocaine dependence plaguing many mother-defendants, are addictions, identified in part by the diagnostic criterion of "continued use despite knowledge of having a persistent or recurrent . . . problem that is caused or exacerbated by the use of the . . . substance."[65] This loss of control over drug intake may be particularly pronounced in crack users. "The drug's hold is so vicious, so absolute, that it overrides even the most basic of human drives. . . . [This] is why a woman can keep getting high while she's pregnant, or interrupt the delivery of twins to call her dealer, or forget that she delivered a baby altogether."[66] Such addictive behavior may be considered compulsive or irresistible. Women who want to take proper care of their children, during pregnancy and after, find themselves unable to do so because of the overpowering effect of drugs.

Punishing involuntary, addictive behavior is unlikely to deter that behavior, because the actor is unable to control her behavior. Nonetheless, courts have been unwilling to excuse liability for acts resulting from irresistible impulses.[67] Punishment is often justified on the basis of protecting third parties from harm caused by substance abusers' uncontrollable acts.[68]

The risk-to-others analysis is unsatisfactory in the pregnancy context because it is unlikely that pregnant addicts are culpable within the accepted terms of criminal law.[69] A woman who does not know that she is pregnant clearly must be unaware that her drug use is injuring anyone but herself. This case is clearly distinguishable from that of the drunk driver who knows or should know that other cars have access to the road, or the crack addict who forms and carries out the intent to rob while under the influence of drugs. Moreover, an addict who knows she is pregnant may be unaware of the drug's effects on her fetus. When a pregnant addict takes drugs, she often will not view the fetus as a victim, and she probably intends no harm to the baby at all.[70] It may be difficult even to prove that taking drugs during pregnancy is reckless. To convict Melanie Green of involuntary manslaughter, prosecutor Logli would have had to prove that she acted recklessly in taking drugs when pregnant—that she took a risk that a reasonable person would not have taken. The grand jury determined that Logli had not proved this mens rea requirement of the offense.

Conceptually, pregnant addicts may be likened to the "temporarily insane" who successfully defend against criminal charges on the grounds of lack of culpability. It must be noted, however, that defendants who have committed criminal acts under the influence of drugs have been unsuccessful in arguing that drugs produced temporary insanity that should excuse their behavior.[71] This defense is typically rejected on the ground that the drugs were taken voluntarily with knowledge of the likely effects on behavior.[72] It is, however, possible that this argument may be applied with greater success in the context of the prosecutions at issue here, because of the involuntary nature of drug taking by addicts.

Although the pathogenesis of crack addiction may consist of initial voluntary drug use, falling within the MPC's definition of self-induced intoxication, this stage is often followed by involuntary drug use. Once a person is addicted, she may be considered to have a "mental disease" within the terms of the MPC.[73] If a woman becomes pregnant after she is addicted and when her drug use has become involuntary, it can be argued that drug-induced temporary insanity prevented her from recognizing or considering the likely ill effects of the drug on her fetus. Indeed, addicts' descriptions of the effects of crack can be deemed consistent with temporary insanity. Even when a pregnant addict knows that crack is injurious to her fetus, the insanity-like effects of the drug may render her unable to act in accordance with this knowledge.

Criminogenesis

In the late 1960s, some lawyers attempted to limit the scope of the criminal law by analyzing the effects of laws on the overall functioning of the criminal justice system.[74] According to Sanford Kadish, the enforcement of certain laws has a criminogenic effect: Enforcement breeds more harm than ignoring the offenses. Kadish concluded that three classes of offenses should be abolished because of their criminogenic effects. These categories are morals offenses, offenses that serve to permit police or prosecutorial intervention into what is more properly the realm of social service agencies, and offenses that manufacture police authority to apprehend suspected criminals with slight cause.[75] Although these offenses have been characterized as "private" or "victimless" crimes,[76] terms inapplicable to drug abuse by pregnant women whose babies are considered victims, the prosecution of these women may be viewed as an attempt by the criminal justice system to provide services such as drug counseling or medical care in the face of default by social service agencies.[77]

Kadish's analytical framework is well suited to these prosecutions. He considers "how the inevitable process of actual enforcement of . . . laws (a) so poorly serves the objectives [of enforcement], and (b) in any event produces a variety of substantial costs, including adverse consequences for the effective enforcement of the criminal law generally."[78] This two-step analysis requires a determination of the legal objectives in question and a weighing of the costs and benefits of enforcement. The objectives of prosecuting women who deliver drug-exposed babies have been identified as deterring prosecuted women from having more drug-exposed children, and providing drug counseling or other care. Kadish identifies four types of enforcement costs that may outweigh the benefits of enforcing laws that poorly serve their asserted objectives: (1) diminished respect for law; (2) unenforceability, corruption, and discrimination; (3) the crime tariff; and (4) misallocation of enforcement resources.[79]

This section will argue that these prosecutions do not fulfill their objectives, and that the costs of enforcing sanctions against drug-using mothers outweigh the benefits. Costs incurred in Kadish's categories (1), (2), and (4) will be discussed. Category (3) is inapplicable because it is identified as a special cost of using the criminal law "to prohibit commercial transactions in goods and services."[80]

Objectives of the Prosecutions

The asserted and implicit objectives of the prosecutions have been discussed above. Briefly, prosecutors hope to deter pregnant women from taking drugs and drug addicts from having children. While general deterrence may be unachievable because of the involuntary nature of drug use by addicts, incapacitation and specific deterrence are hailed as viable goals to be attained by the incarceration or monitoring of pregnant addicts. For example, prosecuted addicts may be sentenced to attend rehabilitation programs to which they were previously denied admission.

It is too early to tell what the long-term effects of these prosecutions will be on the mothers and children involved. For children born of drug addicts, the intervention wrought by prosecuting their mothers may prove futile. The children may suffer the long-term effects of their mothers' drug use regardless of medical, legal, or social intervention. If the mothers prove unable to care for their children adequately, the legal system may resort to proceedings to determine maternal fitness regardless of drug-addiction status. The alleged benefits of the prosecutions discussed in this chapter may accrue to the as-yet-unconceived babies of addicts and former addicts.

Florida prosecutor Jeff Deen asserted that the goal of prosecuting women who deliver drug-exposed babies is to deter them from having more afflicted children. The attainment of this goal, however, turns on the deterrent function of these prosecutions. The nature of addiction makes it unlikely that these prosecutions will have much deterrent value. In addition, the goal of insuring fetal health may be better served by providing pregnant addicts with drug treatment and prenatal care. It may be that the only goal served by these prosecutions is punishment, an objective denied by prosecutors. Thus, under the first prong of Kadish's analysis, the enforcement of sanctions against women who deliver drug-exposed babies poorly serves the objectives of enforcement.

Loss of Respect

Whether these prosecutions engender a loss or gain of respect for the criminal justice system depends upon the sociopolitical views of the speaker. Some see the prosecutions as creative approaches to a seemingly insoluble problem.[81] Prosecutors may be viewed as "making a difference," reducing the drug problem to individual terms, and vindicating the rights of innocent child-victims. Others, however, feel that prosecutors have misused their power and authority, terrorizing poor women who lead desperate lives rather than prosecuting those who make drugs available in the first place.[82] It may be increasingly difficult to maintain respect for a system that prosecutes drug-addicted mothers, arguably the victims of profit-seeking drug dealers, while the dealers are perceived as going free. The failure of the Winnebago County grand jury to indict Melanie Green has been construed as a victory of compassion and common sense over prosecutorial gamesmanship.[83] At the very least, these prosecutions send a message about the new willingness of government to interfere in the most intimate aspects of women's lives.

Unenforceability

The enforcement of criminal sanctions against women who deliver drug-exposed babies raises serious concerns about the proper role of the medical profession in identifying defendants. Currently, some states require medical professionals to report the drug-dependence of newborns or the presence of drugs in their systems.[84]

Many medical professionals are uncomfortable about being forced to set these

prosecutions in motion.[85] Some health care providers believe that potential liability will discourage pregnant drug addicts from seeking prenatal care. "Health
care providers fear that they will lose the struggle to bring pregnant women into
prenatal care and that mothers will not deliver their babies in hospitals. They
foresee more abandoned babies, more seriously disabled babies, more infant
deaths."[86] Some women whose babies test positive for drugs may be enrolled in
substance abuse programs or may voluntarily seek treatment with the help of
supportive families; medical professionals may deem criminal intervention in
such cases to be inappropriate. Prenatal drug treatment is difficult to obtain,[87] and
many medical professionals believe that rather than being penalized, women who
are successful in locating such programs should be rewarded and encouraged to
take care of themselves and their babies. These considerations may make health
care providers resist compliance with reporting requirements, and such resistance
could render criminal sanctions unenforceable.

Attempts to evade reporting requirements may also have criminogenic effects.
As Kadish states, the creation of a new category of crime is likely to breed an
increase in other related crimes.[88] For example, medical personnel may refuse to
reveal their drug findings in an effort not to lose their patients, or potential defendants may attempt to bribe hospital staff to suppress their reports. Furthermore,
demand for abortions may also increase, and if states continue to limit the legal
availability of abortions, this increased demand will be for illegal procedures.

Corruption and Discrimination

Corrupt or discriminatory enforcement of sanctions lessens respect for the law
and may generate more crime. For example, women who are likely to be prosecuted may bribe officials, while those unlikely to face charges engage in criminal
behavior undeterred. Discriminatory enforcement of the reporting requirement—
the preliminary stage in the prosecution of pregnant drug users—has already
been reported in Pinellas County, Florida. A study found that black mothers were
9.58 times more likely to be reported for their substance abuse even though white
women were 1.09 times more likely to have abused a substance just prior to their
first visit for prenatal care.[89] This pattern is consistent with the notion that the real
motivating factor behind these prosecutions is drug hysteria, aimed specifically at
poor, minority addicts who are often viewed as causes of the drug problem rather
than its victims. More than half of the women who have been prosecuted thus far
are women of color. As crack spreads beyond the inner city and gains a hold in
suburbia, there will be more middle- and upper-class white addicts. It remains to
be seen whether they will face prosecution as frequently as their poorer black and
white counterparts.

The prosecutions at issue poorly serve the goals asserted by prosecutors. In
addition, substantial harms to the criminal justice system are introduced: People
may lose respect for the system, lack of compliance by medical personnel may
render the underlying reporting statutes unenforceable, and corruption and discrimination may ensue as women and their health care providers seek to avoid

criminal intervention and as the judicial system disproportionately sanctions poor, minority women. Thus, under Kadish's analysis, this prosecutorial approach should be abandoned in favor of intervention by medical and social service agencies.

Protecting Life Or Combating Drug Abuse?

Prosecutions of women who deliver drug-exposed babies may also be seen as an expression of national concern about two major social issues: abortion and drug abuse. It appears to be more than coincidence that the rash of these prosecutions during the summer of 1989 followed the *Webster* decision and accompanied a heightened public focus on abortion and the "war on drugs." At first glance, these prosecutions appear perfectly consistent with "right to life" policies and objectives, such as the promotion of birth and the acknowledgment of fetal rights. Further analysis, however, reveals that such prosecutions actually may lead to consequences that ardent supporters of fetal rights would not condone. Pregnant drug addicts may be less likely to seek medical care that could benefit their unborn children and themselves, or they may seek abortions.

Many health care providers have expressed concern about the chilling effect these prosecutions are likely to have on pregnant drug addicts' seeking medical attention.[90] They believe that incentives should be structured to encourage these women to seek prenatal care, which may include drug counseling, rather than avoid it because of fear of prosecution. Supporters of fetal rights, who envision a fetal right to a drug-free, healthy gestation,[91] must recognize that this goal can be accomplished more fully by encouraging drug addicts to seek medical care than by threatening them with criminal sanctions.[92] The women who have been prosecuted to date had already delivered drug-exposed babies when they were charged with criminal offenses. It is obvious that both these women and their babies would have enjoyed a healthier pregnancy had their drug abuse been detected and treated as early as possible. Their prosecutions send a message to others in their position that an attempt to find proper medical care during pregnancy will lead to criminal court.

It also is likely that some pregnant addicts will choose to abort rather than run the risk of delivering a baby whose birth will be the subject of criminal investigation and sanctions. Surely this is not the outcome sought by right-to-life supporters of such prosecutions. If abortion restrictions are enacted and enforced as states respond to *Webster*, the pregnant addict may find herself choosing between an illegal abortion and an "illegal" delivery. Both mother and child are likely to suffer either way, as the mother faces prosecution and the child loses any chance for a healthy life.

It is no exaggeration to state that the nation is deeply concerned about drug abuse. News reports and incidents of daily urban life barrage us with the horrors of addiction. Drug-addicted babies are the youngest victims in a social system characterized by violence and desperation. The babies of drug addicts are not, however, the only ones who may suffer the ill consequences of maternal behavior during pregnancy: the deleterious effects of alcohol[93] and tobacco[94] on fetuses also have been well documented. Widespread and insidious as illegal drug use is, liquor and cigarettes are even more accessible and widely used. If the primary objective of prosecuting women who deliver drug-exposed babies is to foster fetal well-being, prosecution of women who smoke cigarettes or drink while pregnant is a logical extension.

Why have women who smoke and drink while pregnant largely avoided the prosecutions leveled at their drug-addicted counterparts? The answer may be found in society's unwillingness to tolerate drugs and drug users, in contrast with its general acceptance of alcohol and tobacco. Drugs are illegal while liquor and cigarettes are not.[95] The legality distinction fails in the context of maternal prosecutions, however, because most successful prosecutions of drug-addicted mothers have been based on laws prohibiting the delivery of drugs to a minor; similar statutes regulate the sale of alcoholic beverages and cigarettes to minors. If the schoolyard crack dealer and the pregnant crack addict may be prosecuted under the same statute, there is no reason why the liquor store clerk who sells to an underage customer and the pregnant alcoholic should not face the same liability under an analogous statute. Perhaps such prosecutions will follow as the logical extension of the current prosecutorial trend. That this has not yet occurred may be symptomatic of the nation's rage and desperation in the face of a seemingly intractable drug epidemic—such strong emotions are not engendered by the health epidemics of smoking and drinking. In addition, addiction to drugs, especially crack, is perceived as a plague of the urban poor, whereas "everyone" smokes and drinks. If prosecutions for the fetal effects of drugs are aimed at the middle class, society's attitude toward these prosecutions may change.

Drug Treatment: An Alternative to Criminal Prosecution

Increasing the availability of drug treatment programs tailored to the needs of women would more humanely and effectively address the problem of drug-exposed babies. Prosecutors have asserted that their goals are to get mothers into drug rehabilitation programs and to foster the birth of healthy babies. Indeed, women convicted of delivering drugs to their babies prenatally may be sentenced to attend drug treatment programs. Ironically, a criminal conviction may be required to help these women obtain the social services that they are unable to avail themselves of by choice.

Pregnant addicts who seek drug treatment face frustration when they confront an overburdened social welfare system that is largely unresponsive to their needs. Women are routinely turned away from programs that exclude pregnant women, pregnant women on Medicaid, or pregnant crack abusers on Medicaid.[96]

Many residential treatment programs will not permit mothers to keep their children with them,[97] thereby forcing a woman to forgo either treatment or her children. Many women choose to delay treatment because they fear the consequences of relinquishing their children to the welfare system.[98] The failure of many programs to accommodate children is one facet of the male orientation of most programs,[99] which were designed to serve male convicts and which have not adjusted their emphasis in response to the increasing number of female drug addicts.[100] Drug treatment is often punitive and confrontational, and this style may be particularly ineffective for women: "It's not necessary to humiliate a substance-abusing woman; she already has lost her self-esteem."[101]

The lack of treatment programs for women may lead them to criminal prosecution despite their best intentions and efforts. One pregnant heroin addict in Butte County, California, was motivated by fear of fetal harm to seek drug treatment[102] and, through persistence and determination, gained admittance to an outpatient methadone maintenance clinic in Sacramento. After months of attending the program, which required her to travel 140 miles round trip each day, she fell behind in her payments and lost her only available means of transportation. Following sound medical advice, she went back to using heroin because a sudden withdrawal from drugs might have been fatal to her fetus. Soon after she gave birth and discussed her drug problem with hospital personnel, her baby was taken away from her by Child Protective Services and the district attorney announced plans to prosecute her. If this woman had been able to attend an affordable treatment program close to her home, she might have overcome her drug problem, kept her baby, and avoided prosecution.

Successful treatment programs for women must provide residential care for mothers and children. One such program is New Image, "a therapeutic community for homeless, addicted women and their children"[103] in Philadelphia. This program reported a dropout rate of 50 percent in its first year of operation, which is lower than expected.[104] Parenting training, psychological assessments, and a series of workshops on development of life skills and job-readiness complement drug therapy in this program.[105] Other innovative community programs have been developed in Miami, Los Angeles, and Chicago.[106] Federal legislation may increase funding for drug treatment programs designed to serve women addicts, especially during pregnancy.

Conclusion

The recent wave of prosecutions of women who deliver drug-exposed babies represents a flawed approach to a critical social problem. These prosecutions flagrantly violate the Constitution by denying defendants their due process rights of notice and fair warning. Moreover, the prosecutions represent judicial enlargement of existing statutes without regard for legislative intent or for the legislature's role in defining crimes. In addition, women's rights have been further eroded by these prosecutions as courts follow *Webster*'s lead in asserting a compelling interest in fetal well-being that may come at the expense of women's health and welfare. Criminal theory also is flouted by the current prosecutions: Involuntary behavior is punished, the major goal of deterrence is not promoted, and criminogenesis results as the criminal justice system intrudes into the realm of medical and social services.

The moral outrage and prosecutorial resources aimed at women whose children are drug-exposed might be more effective if directed against the conditions that breed drug abuse and against the suppliers of drugs, who essentially prey on the insatiable needs of addicts. A reduction in the available supply of drugs, coupled with education about their harmfulness, would be a more humane and potentially successful approach to this intractable problem. There is a dearth of drug treatment facilities for the poor, especially for pregnant crack addicts. If such services were provided without resort to criminalization and prosecution, more women might overcome their drug habits while suffering no infringement of their constitutional rights. The solution to the social tragedy of drug use by pregnant women does not lie in strained interpretations of the law that create more harm than good.

NOTES

1. 109 S. Ct. 3040 (1989).
2. *See infra* text following note 74.
3. The complaint read in part: "Melanie Green committed the offense of involuntary manslaughter in that she . . . killed her child . . . by recklessly performing the act of ingesting a controlled substance containing cocaine while pregnant with [the child]." *See* Logli, Drugs in the Womb: The Newest Battlefield in the War on Drugs, 9 Crim. Just. Ethics 23, 29 n.9 (1990).
4. The complaint read in part: "Melanie Green committed the offense of violation of the controlled substances act in that she, a person over eighteen years of age, delivered to a person under eighteen years of age a controlled substance containing cocaine, to wit: while pregnant . . . she knowingly ingested a controlled substance containing cocaine which was thereby delivered to the bloodstream and body of her fetus." *Id.* at 29 n.10.
5. For example, the drug delivery statute used against Jennifer Johnson had previously been used against drug dealers. *See* Chavkin, Help, Don't Jail, Addicted Mothers, N.Y. Times, July 18, 1989, at A21.
6. *See, e.g.*, Fla. Stat. Ann. § 893.13(1)(a)(3)(c) (West 1976) (criminalizing delivery of drugs to "a person under the age of 18 years"); Ill. Ann. Stat. ch. 56 1/2, para. 1407 (Smith-Hurd 1985 & Supp. 1990) (same).
7. A child born alive is indisputably a person under eighteen years of age, regardless of whether a child conceived but not yet born is such a person.
8. 470 P.2d 617 (Cal. 1970).
9. *Id.* at 619 (quoting Cal. Penal Code § 187 (1872) (amended 1970) (emphasis added)).

10. *See id.* at 618.

11. *Id.* at 624–25 (citations omitted).

12. *See* S. Kadish et al., Criminal Law and Its Processes 354 (4th ed. 1983).

13. *See* Cal. Penal Code § 187 (West 1988).

14. *See supra* note 4.

15. *See, e.g.,* Paltrow, When Becoming Pregnant Is a Crime, 9 Crim. Just. Ethics 42 (1990)(describing the prosecutor's argument in the *Johnson* case); Hoffman, Pregnant, Addicted—And Guilty?, N.Y. Times, Aug. 19, 1990, § 6 (Magazine), at 34 (describing the prosecutor's contention in the case of a Michigan woman charged with delivering crack to her son through the umbilical cord and noting that such arguments "avoid . . . debates over when the fetus becomes a person"). The personhood debate, however, is unavoidable when drug exposure occurred well before birth, so that drug metabolites could not be passed through the umbilical cord after birth.

Dr. Ira J. Chasnoff, founder and president of the National Association of Perinatal Addiction Research and Education, questions the medical validity of the theory that cocaine can be passed through the umbilical cord immediately before it is clamped. He has said, "Good ethics and good law have to be based on good science . . . and we just don't have that kind of data." *Id.* at 35.

It should be noted that finding that a fetus is a person within the meaning of a state statute could be constitutional, and would contravene neither *Roe v. Wade,* 410 U.S. 113 (1973) (which held that a fetus is not a person under the Fourteenth Amendment), nor *Webster v. Reproductive Health Services,* 109 S. Ct. 3040 (1989) (which left *Roe's* Fourteenth Amendment holding intact). *See infra* text accompanying notes 27–30. Such a finding, though constitutional, may still be violative of legislative intent.

This chapter will presume that the state legislatures in question did not intend to include fetuses within the ambits of the statutes currently being used to prosecute pregnant drug users.

16. Wilkerson, Jury in Illinois Refuses to Charge Mother in Drug Death of Newborn, N.Y. Times, May 27, 1989, at A10.

17. Logli, Drugs in the Womb, *supra* note 3, at 24; and see Chapter 8 in this volume.

18. *See supra* notes 11–12 and accompanying text.

19. In order for a statute to be used with a sound legal basis against a woman whose prenatal behavior harms her fetus, the statute should include language or legislative history that supports such application; merely stating that the law encompasses fetal harm is insufficient, as is shown by the case of *People v. Stewart.* Stewart was charged with criminal neglect under a statute that makes it a misdemeanor for a parent to "willfully omit[] without lawful excuse, to furnish necessary clothing, food, shelter or medical attendance, or other remedial care for his or her child" and states that a "child conceived but not yet born is an existing person insofar as this section is concerned." Cal. Penal Code § 270 (West 1988). Although Stewart had allegedly injured a "child conceived but not yet born," charges were dismissed for failure to state a charge: The judge ruled that the state legislature intended the law to be used only to require child support. *See* A Judge Dismissed Thursday the Criminal Prosecution of a Mother Accused of Contributing to Her

Baby's Death, UPI, Feb. 26, 1987, AM cycle, Domestic News (LEXIS, Nexis library, UPI file). Stewart's attorney, Lynn Paltrow of the American Civil Liberties Union (ACLU), argued that the statute was intended to require fathers to pay for pregnancy care. *See id.* The statute had been amended in 1925 to include fathers within its ambit. *See id.*

20. Parness & Pritchard, To Be or Not to Be: Protecting the Unborn's Potentiality of Life, 51 U. Cin. L. Rev. 257, 270 (1982) (footnotes omitted); *see also* Cal. Penal Code § 270 (West 1988) (making it a misdemeanor for a parent to fail to provide necessities for a minor child, including "a child conceived but not yet born").

21. Ill. Rev. Stat. ch. 37, para. 802-3(c) (1989); *see also* Logli, Drugs in the Womb, *supra* note 3, at 27 (supporting the proposition that the statute was responsively amended).

22. *See id.*

23. *See, e.g.,* Fla. Stat. Ann. § 415.503(9)(a)(2) (West Supp. 1990); Haw. Rev. Stat. § 587-2 (1985); Ind. Code Ann. § 31-6-4-3.1 (West Supp. 1990); Okla. Stat. Ann. tit. 10, § 1101(4) (West 1987). *See generally* Development in the Law, Fetal Drug or Alcohol Addiction Syndrome: A Case of Prenatal Child Abuse?, 25 Willamette L. Rev. 223, 224 & n.7 (1989) (listing amendments to Oklahoma and Florida child abuse and neglect statutes). For a discussion of state court action in the absence of explicit statutory directives, see *id.* at 224–29.

24. *See* Gen. Assembly Of Pa., Senate Bill No. 575, § 3 (1989) (proposing an expansion of Pennsylvania's definition of child abuse to include a "substance-abused child," defined as "a child who is born with fetal alcohol syndrome, neonatal abstinence syndrome or the systemic presence of a substance listed in . . . 'The Controlled Substance, Drug, Device and Cosmetic Act'").

25. *See* Logli, Drugs in the Womb, *supra* note 3, at 27.

26. *Id.*

27. 410 U.S. 113 (1973).

28. Parness & Pritchard, To Be or Not to Be, *supra* note 20, at 258.

29. *See* Webster v. Reproductive Health Servs., 109 S. Ct. 3040, 3057 (1989) (noting that there was no reason "why the State's interest in protecting potential human life should come into existence only at the point of viability, and that there should therefore be a rigid line allowing state regulation after viability but prohibiting it before viability").

30. *See infra* notes 44–50 and accompanying text.

31. *See, e.g.,* Hoffman, Pregnant and Guilty, *supra* note 15, at 34 (noting that prosecutor Tony Tague "ordered Kimberly Hardy arrested on the same charge prosecutors routinely use against drug dealers: delivering drugs in the amount of less than 50 grams, a felony in Michigan"); *id.* at 35 (noting that a prosecutor in North Carolina "charged an addicted mother whose newborn had a positive toxicology test with . . . assault with a deadly weapon").

32. Conversely, prosecutors who have failed to convict women who used drugs during pregnancy may successfully urge state legislatures to pass "corrective" legislation. *See* Logli, Drugs in the Womb, *supra* note 3, at 27.

33. Keeler v. Superior Court, 470 P.2d 617, 626 (Cal. 1970). The court further explained:

> That the terms of a penal statute creating a new offense must be sufficiently explicit to inform those who are subject to it what conduct on their part will render them liable to its penalties, is a well-recognized requirement, consonant alike with ordinary notions of fair play and the settled rules of law.

Id. (quoting Connally v. General Constr. Co., 269 U.S. 385, 391 (1926)).

34. *See id.* at 626 (citing U.S. Const. art. I, §§ 9, 10).

35. 378 U.S. 347 (1964).

36. The court explained that

> when an "unforeseeable state-court construction of a criminal statute is applied retroactively to subject a person to criminal liability for past conduct, the effect is to deprive him of due process of law in the sense of fair warning that his contemplated conduct constitutes a crime." . . . "Indeed, an unforeseeable judicial enlargement of a criminal statute, applied retroactively, operates precisely like an *ex post facto* law [which] . . . the Constitution forbids."

Keeler, 470 P.2d at 626 (quoting *Bouie*, 378 U.S. at 354–55).

37. *See id.* at 630.

38. *See supra* notes 10–11 and accompanying text.

39. Punishing Pregnant Addicts: Debate, Dismay, No Solution, N.Y. Times, Sept. 10, 1989, at E5 [hereinafter Punishing Pregnant Addicts] (quoting Kary L. Moss, an attorney with the ACLU Women's Rights Project, New York); *see also* Logli, Drugs in the Womb, *supra* note 3, at 24 (acknowledging that manslaughter and drug delivery statutes were not intended to be used in prenatal injury cases). Because of the courts' duty to enforce laws in consonance with legislative intent, it may be argued that an appliction of a law in derogation of legislative intent is unforeseeable.

40. *See, e.g., Keeler*, 470 P.2d at 627 (accentuating the importance of evaluating due process rights from the defendant's point of view by asking, "[W]ould the judicial enlargement of section 187 now proposed have been foreseeable to this petitioner?").

41. *Id.* at 628.

42. Linn, The Corruption of Motherhood, Phila. Inquirer, Sept. 17, 1989, Magazine, at 14, 34.

43. One Boston lawyer has described the prosecution of women for conduct during pregnancy as "preposterous. . . . It is conceptually splitting a woman in half by saying that she is not only doing [something harmful] against herself but that she's also [willfully] doing it against another." Sherman, Keeping Babies Free of Drugs, Nat'l L.J., Oct. 16, 1989, at 1, 28 (quoting Nancy Gertner of the law firm of Silvergate, Gertner, Fine & Good); *see also infra* notes 44–50 and accompanying text.

44. The fundamental right of all persons, married or single, to choose freely whether or not to conceive or bear children was recognized by the Supreme Court in *Eisenstadt v. Baird*, 405 U.S. 438, 453–54 (1972).

45. For a discussion of states' general refusal to regulate births, see Parness & Pritchard, To Be or Not to Be, *supra* note 20, at 286–93. Parness and Pritchard found that "[s]tate laws compelling birth . . . are rather scarce" despite the states' constitutional power to "promote the interest of the unborn in attaining the full potential of life." *Id.* at 287. Similarly, "while state laws prohibiting the birth of one already conceived might be imaginable [and not necessarily unconstitutional] there seem to be no such laws." *Id.* at 288–89. In sum, "most state laws affecting the birth of the unborn regulate only the circumstances of birth and leave the ultimate decision regarding birth to the prospective parents." *Id.* at 292.

46. *See* Webster v. Reproductive Health Servs., 109 S. Ct. 3040, 3057 (1989)(noting that the "[s]tate has compelling interests in ensuring maternal health and in protecting potential human life, and these interests exist 'throughout pregnancy'" (quoting Thornburgh v. American College of Obstetricians & Gynecologists, 476 U.S. 747, 828 (1986) (O'Connor, J., dissenting))).

47. Arguably, however, the interests of the state and the unborn would be better served by encouraging the abortion of certain fetuses, such as those affected by maternal drug use. *See* Parness & Pritchard, To Be or Not to Be, *supra* note 20, at 298 (suggesting that, in some cases, "[l]egal protection of the unborn can be achieved by . . . promoting the unborn's interest in not being born").

48. Robertson, Procreative Liberty and the Control of Conception, Pregnancy, and Childbirth, 69 Va. L. Rev. 405, 437 (1983).

49. Behaviors that pose potential risks to fetuses, regardless of maternal benefit, and that could result in a mother's liability include failing to eat nutritious foods, using drugs (prescription, nonprescription, or illegal), smoking, drinking alcoholic beverages, permitting exposure to infectious disease or to workplace hazards, engaging in immoderate exercise or sexual activity, residing at high altitudes for prolonged periods, and using a general anesthetic or labor-inducing drugs. *See* Note, The Creation of Fetal Rights: Conflicts with Women's Constitutional Rights to Liberty, Privacy, and Equal Protection, 95 Yale L.J. 599, 606–607 (1986); *see also* Paltrow, Becoming Pregnant, *supra* note 15, at 42 (noting the fetal hazards posed by radiation exposure during airplane flights and the risk of toxoplasmosis, a disease contracted through contact with cat feces).

50. *See* Note, Creation of Fetal Rights, *supra* note 49, at 600. It has been further argued that "[b]y substituting its judgment for that of the woman, the state deprives women of their right to control their lives during pregnancy—a right to liberty and privacy protected by the Constitution. Furthermore, by regulating women as if their lives were defined solely by their reproductive capacity, the state perpetuates a system of sex discrimination that is based on the biological difference between the sexes, thus depriving women of their constitutional right to the equal protection of the laws." *Id.* at 613; *see also* Note, Rethinking [M]otherhood: Feminist Theory and State Regulation of Pregnancy, 103 Harv. L. Rev. 1325, 1333–42 (1990) (criticizing the rights-based construction of mother and fetus as adversaries, particularly in the context of maternal substance abuse, and emphasizing instead the intimate connection between mothers and their fetuses).

51. 370 U.S. 660, 667 (1962).

52. The Court explained that narcotic addiction "is apparently an illness which may be contracted innocently or involuntarily . . . [and] that persons addicted to narcotics 'are diseased and proper subjects of [medical] treatment.'" *Id.* at 667 & n.8 (quoting Linder v. United States, 268 U.S. 5, 18 (1925)).

53. Mariner et al., Pregnancy, Drugs and the Perils of Prosecution, 9 Crim. Just. Ethics 30, 31 (1990).

54. *See id.*; Paltrow, Becoming Pregnant, *supra* note 15, at 41–42.

55. *See* Mariner et al., Perils of Prosecution, *supra* note 53, at 31; *see also infra* notes 67–70 and accompanying text (discussing the legal infirmities of prosecuting pregnant addicts in light of the need to show intent).

56. Mariner et al., Perils of Prosecution, *supra* note 53, at 31.

57. *Id.*; *see also* Paltrow, Becoming Pregnant, *supra* note 15, at 41–42 (stating that "none of the women have been arrested for the crime of illegal drug use or possession. Instead, they are being arrested for a new and independent crime: becoming pregnant while addicted to drugs").

58. *See* Nolan, Protecting Fetuses from Prenatal Hazards: Whose Crimes? What Punishment?, 9 Crim. Just. Ethics 13, 15 (1990).

59. *See* Paltrow, Becoming Pregnant, *supra* note 15, at 42.

60. *See* Model Penal Code § 2.01(1) (1962) ("A person is not guilty of an offense unless his liability is based on conduct that includes a voluntary act or the omission to perform an act of which he is physically capable"). Drug taking is an act, not an omission; the discussion in this chapter will be restricted, therefore, to voluntary and involuntary acts, rather than to omissions.

61. *See id.* § 2.01 comment 1 ("[T]he law cannot hope to deter involuntary movement or to stimulate action that cannot physically be performed").

62. Linder v. United States, 268 U.S. 5, 18 (1925).

63. *See, e.g.,* Smith, Substance Use Disorders: Drugs & Alcohol, in Review Of General Psychiatry 278, 279 (H. Goldman ed., 1984) (describing the World Health Organization's definition of addiction).

64. *See* Diagnostic and Statistical Manual of Mental Disorders 165–85 (rev. 3d ed. 1987).

65. *Id.* at 169.

66. Linn, The Corruption of Motherhood, *supra* note 42, at 26.

67. The definition of an involuntary act has been explained as follows:

> [I]n the criminal law an act is not to be regarded as an involuntary act simply because the doer does not remember it. . . . Nor is an act to be regarded as an involuntary act simply because the doer could not control his impulse to do it. . . . Nor is an act to be regarded as an involuntary act simply because it is unintentional or its consequences are unforeseen.

Kadish et al., Criminal Law, *supra* note 12, at 253; *see also* Powell v. Texas, 392 U.S. 514, 521 (1968) (refusing to recognize chronic alcoholism as a defense to a charge of appearing drunk in public despite the prevailing medical view that "a chronic alcoholic does not appear in public by his own volition but under a compulsion symptomatic of the disease of chronic alcoholism").

68. *See supra* notes 55–56 and accompanying text. Jeff Deen, the Florida prosecutor who initiated proceedings against Jennifer Johnson, stated that one policy goal of such prosecutions is "to interrupt the cycle, so we don't end up with another cocaine baby." Linn, The Corruption of Motherhood, *supra* note 42, at 25. In addition, it is hoped that punishment may prevent convicted addicts from repeating injurious behavior by incapacitating them through imprisonment. It is important to note, however, that even the incarceration of pregnant drug users cannot guarantee that they do not use drugs, as noted by Dr. Brian Udell of Broward General Medical Center, who "had two patients who were smoking coke in jail on the day of their delivery." *Id.* at 26; *see also* Nolan, Protecting Fetuses, *supra* note 58, at 19 (stating that "[d]rug use can continue despite imprisonment, and medical attention for pregnant women in prisons may be sorely inadequate").

69. *See* Model Penal Code § 2.02(1) (1962) (describing the culpability requirement that the defendant must have acted purposely, knowingly, recklessly, or negligently).

70. James Bopp, general counsel to the National Right to Life Committee, believes that prosecutions of pregnant drug users are flawed because it is nearly impossible to prove that the women intended to injure their babies. He stated that such prosecutions "are rarely justified because it must be proven that a woman knowingly intended to pose substantial risk of harm to the unborn child. It's unlikely a woman takes drugs to harm her child. Cocaine addiction is compulsive behavior." Punishing Pregnant Addicts, *supra* note 39, at E5.

71. *See, e.g.,* State v. Hall, 214 N.W.2d 205 (Iowa 1974) (rejecting defense of temporary drug-induced insanity by defendant who committed murder under the influence of LSD).

72. *See id.* at 208; *see also* Model Penal Code § 2.08(5) (1962) (defining self-induced intoxication, which is not a defense).

73. Under the Model Penal Code, intoxication alone is not evidence of a mental disease. *See* Model Penal Code § 2.08(3) (1962). A bona fide mental disease, however, may constitute a defense to criminal charges. *See id.* § 4.01(1) ("A person is not responsible for criminal conduct if at the time of such conduct as a result of mental disease or defect he lacks substantial capacity either to appreciate the criminality [wrongfulness] of his conduct or to conform his conduct to the requirements of the law").

74. *See* Kadish, The Crisis of Overcriminalization, 374 Annals 157 (1967); Kadish, More on Overcriminalization: A Reply to Professor Junker, 19 UCLA L. Rev. 719, 719–20 (1972).

75. *See* Kadish, The Crisis of Overcriminalization, *supra* note 74, at 157, 159.

76. Junker, Criminalization and Criminogenesis, 19 UCLA L. Rev. 697, 698 (1972).

77. Prosecutor Jeff Deen argues that the purpose of these prosecutions is to get drug-addicted mothers into treatment programs, not to punish them. *See* Linn, The Corruption of Motherhood, *supra* note 42, at 25, 34. Jennifer Johnson, who was prosecuted by Deen, was sentenced to mandatory drug treatment. *See id.* at 34. Unfortunately, pregnant drug addicts may find that conviction is their only certain path to drug treatment. Many poor, pregnant women are unable to get drug treatment without judicial intervention because they are routinely excluded from treatment programs. For example, a survey of seventy-eight drug treatment programs in New York City found that 54 percent excluded pregnant women, 67 percent excluded pregnant Medicaid recipients, and 87 percent excluded pregnant crack addicts on Medicaid. *See* Sherman, Keeping Babies, *supra* note 43, at 29. Melanie Green sought drug treatment but was confronted by six-month waiting lists. *See* McNamara, Fetal Endangerment Cases on the Rise, Boston Globe, Oct. 3, 1989, at 1, 11. Such waiting periods are particularly problematic for pregnant women, who may be unable to enter treatment until after considerable harm has been done to their fetuses. *See also* One Drug-Using Mother's Story, 11 Youth L. News 19 (1990) (describing a pregnant heroin addict's attempts to obtain treatment, her loss of child custody, and her possible prosecution).

78. Kadish, More on Overcriminalization, *supra* note 74, at 720.

79. *See* Junker, Criminalization and Criminogenesis, *supra* note 76, at 700; Kadish, The Crisis of Overcriminalization, *supra* note 74, at 160, 163–64.

80. Junker, Criminalization and Criminogenesis, *supra* note 76, at 707. Crime tariff costs may militate in favor of decriminalizing narcotics. *See* Kadish, The Crisis of Overcriminalization, *supra* note 74, at 163–65. The illegality of substances used by pregnant women is not at issue here, however. *See infra* text accompanying note 95. The other elements of the cost–benefit analysis (1, 2, 4) apply to the prosecutions in question here as well as to the potential extension of prosecutions to pregnant users of alcohol and tobacco.

81. For example, Dr. Jan Bays, director of child abuse programs at Emanuel Hospital in Portland, Oregon, has stated:

> We must up the ante to criminalize or impose reproductive controls on people who are out of control. . . . I'm fed up with seeing damaged babies born who have lost the right to make what they can out of life. . . . I don't see that the courts have had any impact.
>
> We thought we were getting tough when we tried voluntary contracts that required the parents to go into drug treatment, gave the state legal custody or allowed it to monitor the child. But it doesn't work. . . . We can't say forever that people have unlimited rights to have a child.

Punishing Pregnant Addicts, *supra* note 39, at E5.

Plymouth County, Massachusetts, Prosecutor William C. O'Malley has said, "I'd much rather see this problem dealt with by the more subtle systems of public health, social services and education. But, damn it, we've had nothing but failures. . . . It's time to invoke the mechanism of last resort." *Id.* at E5.

82. Neonatologist Dr. Loretta Finnegan, founder of a program for pregnant addicts in Philadelphia, notes that most of the women she treats have been the victims of childhood sexual or physical abuse, rape as adolescents, and domestic violence at the hands of husbands or boyfriends as adults. *See* Linn, The Corruption of Motherhood, *supra* note 42, at 25; *see also* Paltrow, Becoming Pregnant, *supra* note 15, at 42 (noting that several recently prosecuted women have been battered); *id.* at 45 (noting that many drug-addicted women were victims of rape or incest).

George J. Annas argues that "[t]o prosecute people who make money off drugs can be useful. But to drag in pregnant women is not, because they have real problems [in addition to] drugs. Usually it's poverty, discrimination, living where services aren't available." Punishing Pregnant Addicts, *supra* note 39, at E5.

83. *See* Colen, Reining in Runaway Prosecutors, Newsday, June 6, 1989, at 13 (Nassau & Suffolk ed.).

84. *See, e.g.,* D.C. Code Ann. § 2-1352 (Supp. 1990); Fla. Stat. Ann. §§ 415.503 (9)(a)(2), 415.504 (West 1986 & Supp. 1990); Haw. Rev. Stat. §§ 350-1.1(a), 587-2(1985 & Supp. 1989); Ill. Ann. Stat. ch. 23, para. 2053, 2054 (Smith-Hurd 1988 & Supp. 1990); Mass. Ann. Laws ch. 119 § 51A (Law. Co-op. 1990); N.Y. Soc. Serv. Law § 412(9) (McKinney Supp. 1990); Okla. Stat. Ann. tit. 21, § 846A (West Supp. 1989).

85. *See* Pinkney, Drugs in Pregnancy: A Growing Crisis with No Easy Solution, Am. Med. News, Oct. 6, 1989, at 30 (discussing pressures on the medical community to identify women who use drugs during their pregnancies).

86. Larsen, Creating Common Goals for Medical, Legal and Child Protection Communities, in A.B.A. Center on Children and the Law, Drug Exposed Infants and Their Families: Coordinating Responses of the Legal, Medical and Child Protection System 3, 6 (1990).

87. *See* Chavkin, Help, Don't Jail, Addicted Mothers, *supra* note 5, at A21 (discussing surveys of the availability of prenatal programs for pregnant addicts); *see also* Sherman, Keeping Babies, *supra* note 43, at 29; *supra* note 77 and accompanying text.

88. *See* Kadish, The Crisis of Overcriminalization, *supra* note 74, at 164 (finding that the criminalization of gambling and selling narcotics has spawned organizations that engage in "satellite forms of crime" such as bribery, loan-sharking, and labor racketeering).

89. *See* Sherman, Keeping Babies, *supra* note 43, at 28–29.

90. Attorneys and defendants have also expressed concern about the consequences of candid discussion with health care professionals—consequences that, if foreseen by other pregnant addicts, may deter them from seeking prenatal care.

Jennifer Johnson's attorney has noted the legal significance of his client's discussion of her addiction with medical personnel:

> The interview [with the hospital's social worker] became the backbone of the prosecution's case. . . . [A]fter a while, she was also interviewed by a police investigator . . . and she talked with him and he discussed if she used cocaine while she was pregnant. She said yes. She didn't anticipate that this was going to lead to an arrest. She thought this is what she had to do to get the child back.

Linn, The Corruption of Motherhood, *supra* note 42, at 25.

Lynn Bremer, who discussed her cocaine addiction with her obstetrician during prenatal office visits, describes herself as "a perfect example of someone who tried to reach out, and it's all coming back in my face. . . . I feel betrayed. . . . Everyone I talked to about my drug problem has been subpoenaed." Hoffman, Pregnant and Guilty, *supra* note 15, at 55.

91. Such a right has been found by at least one state court. *See In re* Baby X, 293 N.W.2d 736, 739 (Mich. Ct. App. 1980) (stating that "a child has a legal right to begin life with a sound mind and body" (citing Womack v. Buchhorn, 187 N.W.2d 218, 222 (Mich. 1971))).

92. Criminal sanctions are not likely to deter involuntary addictive behavior, but they may deter the voluntary behavior of seeking medical care. Not all behavior is involuntary in the addict; rather, it is the ingestion of the drug that is involuntary. On the deterrent effect of threatened criminal sanctions on women seeking prenatal care, see Mariner et al., Perils of Prosecution, *supra* note 53, at 37 (stating that "[t]here is reason to believe that women will avoid prenatal delivery care if detection of their drug use could lead to their arrest or loss of child custody"); Paltrow, Becoming Pregnant, *supra* note 15, at 44–45 (noting that "prosecutions and convictions deter pregnant women from getting what little health care is available . . . [and further that] women who do seek care are often too frightened to speak openly to their doctors about their problems"). *But see* Hoffman, Pregnant and Guilty, *supra* note 15, at 57 (noting comments of Muskegon General Hospital staff psychologist Cheryl Gawkowski that some pregnant addicts have sought drug treatment because of their fear of incarceration, while others have avoided prenatal care because of this same fear).

93. Fetal alcohol syndrome (FAS) is the name given to the set of abnormalities resulting from maternal alcohol use during pregnancy. The syndrome is characterized by the presence of one or more of the following developmental defects:

> (1) low birth weight and small size with failure to catch up in size or weight;
> (2) mental retardation, with an average IQ in the 60s; and (3) a variety of
> birth defects, with a large percentage of cardiac abnormalities. The fetuses
> are very quiet in utero, and there is an increased frequency of breech presentations [which may lead to delivery complications]. There is a higher incidence of delayed postnatal growth and behavior development. The risk
> factors are appreciably higher when more than 6 drinks are ingested each
> day.

Current Medical Diagnosis & Treatment 662 (M. Krupp et al. eds., 1987). Infants who exhibit FAS suffer from irreversible, long-term sequelae such as growth deficiencies and are likely to have difficulty in school. *See, e.g.,* Current Pediatric Diagnosis & Treatment 92 (C. Kempe et al., 9th ed. 1987) (noting that the severity of outcome is not influenced by socioeconomic or educational factors). For a description of a family's attempts to deal with an adopted son's FAS complications, see M. Dorris, The Broken Cord (1989).

94. The fetal effects of maternal cigarette smoking can be similar to the effects of maternal drinking. *See* Current Medical Diagnosis & Treatment, *supra* note 93, at 662.

> Maternal smoking has been conclusively associated with decreased birth
> weight at every gestational age after 30 weeks. . . . [I]nvestigators have
> found that light smoking as well as heavy smoking . . . is associated with increased perinatal death. . . . Preliminary results of follow-up for 5 years have
> shown an increase in postneonatal deaths, hospital admissions, physical and
> mental impairments, and respiratory and skin diseases in children of smoking compared to nonsmoking mothers.

Current Pediatric Diagnosis & Treatment, *supra* note 93, at 92–93.

95. Plymouth County Prosecutor William C. O'Malley relies on the illegality of drugs to distinguish the current wave of prosecutions from any possible extension into prosecutions of women who use legal substances. *See* Punishing Pregnant Addicts, *supra,* note 39, at E5 "I can't foresee the prosecution of a case where the underlying facts are not illegal. I don't see myself as a pregnancy cop. I don't think that's the role of the DA." Wong, DA Calls for Guidelines in Fetal Injury Cases, Boston Globe, Nov. 4, 1989, at 25.

96. *See* Diesenhouse, Drug Treatment Is Scarcer Than Ever for Women, N.Y. Times, Jan. 7, 1990, at E26. In November 1989, the ACLU Women's Rights Project filed a lawsuit on behalf of women who had been refused admission to drug treatment programs in New York. *See* Paltrow, Becoming Pregnant, *supra* note 15, at 47 n.45. The state's highest court recently ruled that a drug treatment program's blanket exclusion of all pregnant women constitutes facial sexual discrimination. *See* Elaine W. v. Joint Diseases North General Hospital, Inc., 81 N.Y.2d 211, 216 (1993). Such a policy may be justified, however, if "it is medically unsafe to treat pregnant women at [a] facility, either because all pregnant addicts require immediate on-site obstetrical services [which the facility lacks] or because it cannot be predicted with reasonable medical certainty which ones might require such services." Id. at 218.

97. Only 50 of about 7,000 programs nationwide provide child and obstetric care to female patients. *See* Paltrow, Becoming Pregnant, *supra* note 15, at 47 n.45.

98. *See* Tracy, Women Suffer Most from Drugs, Phila. Inquirer, Nov. 27, 1988, at E7.

99. *See id.*

100. *See* Diesenhouse, Drug Treatment, *supra* note 96, at E20.

101. Tracy, Women Suffer Most from Drugs, *supra* note 98, at E7.

102. *See* One Drug-Using Mother's Story, 11 Youth L. News 19 (1990).

103. New Image Newsletter, Spring 1990, at 1 (on file with the author).

104. *See id.* at 6.

105. *See id.*

106. *See* Larsen, Creating Common Goals, *supra* note 86, at 53.

CHAPTER SEVEN

Poor Mothers, Poor Babies: Law, Medicine, and Crack

Barbara Bennett Woodhouse

MY CONTRIBUTION to this reader is light on law and heavy on policy. I am a law professor, specializing in children's law. I freely admit that my bias, in situations that truly pit the child's welfare against the parent's autonomy, is toward protecting the child. In this chapter, however, I will step outside my area of competence and talk very little about law and primarily about medicine. I believe the journey to skepticism I traveled as the crack epidemic unfolded may set a cautionary example for all those committed to better lives for children and their families. I learned, along the way, not to trust too quickly in the science of scientific studies, especially when the answers they give take the familiar form of assigning blame for poor children's health problems to the immorality and criminality of their mothers.[1]

Criminal law's beauty, of course, is its power to reduce a complex story to the individualist essentials of personal responsibility and retribution, of a Defendant brought to justice by the People, for bad acts perpetrated against a Victim. In response to the rise in crack use among pregnant women, many prosecutors sought indictments of pregnant crack users for delivering drugs to their infants, and legislatures drafted laws criminalizing crack use by pregnant women. The power of this story of victim and victimizer was seductive. It failed, however, to capture the complex relationships of interdependency and shared need that characterize pregnancy. It relied on a simplistic story about bad mothers victimizing their babies in place of a rigorous review of medical research on crack and a realistic evaluation of the role it plays in the broader picture of maternal and child health.

While lawmakers wrangle over the moral, legal, and pragmatic dilemmas presented by issues of criminal intent, deterrence, and retribution, medicine is still trying to understand the actual effects of crack on the fetus. We know that too many babies are born prematurely, sick, and at dangerously low birth weights, and that too many infants fail to develop normally into school-ready children.[2] Is crack cocaine use by pregnant women the public enemy behind these statistics? Or is crack cocaine, as recent studies suggest, only one part of a massive public health failure, linked to low socioeconomic status and affecting poor mothers and poor babies generally?

To place these questions in perspective, let me trace the cocaine epidemic as it has played out nationally and in my community, the City of Philadelphia. Crack first appeared in America in the early 1980s. In striking contrast to earlier drug epidemics, crack seemed to hit hardest among women of childbearing age. By 1988, studies were reporting from 11 percent to a high in some urban hospitals of 25 percent of newborns testing positive for cocaine.[3] The legal system began to address the problem of drug-using mothers in a series of highly publicized criminal cases in the late 1980s.[4] Supporters of criminal sanctions pointed to rising numbers of mothers testing positive for cocaine at delivery, arguing that these mothers must be deterred from inflicting irreparable harm on their fetuses.[5] Early studies suggested a connection between cocaine use and low birth weight (LBW), placental abruption (separation of the placenta prior to delivery of the infant), premature onset of labor, and congenital malformations.[6] The most alarming note was sounded in studies detecting evidence of injury to the fetal central nervous system, raising the specter of children with long-term developmental handicaps.[7] The *New York Times* spoke of damaged children incapable of love, and reported that crack interfered with "the central core of what it is to be human."[8] These so-called Crack Kids rapidly captured public attention, making the cover of *Time* Magazine on May 13, 1991, with the caption, "Their mothers used drugs, and now it's the children who suffer."[9] The article reported that in some major cities "the percentage of newborns showing the effects of drugs is 20 percent or even higher" and warned of a "lost generation" suffering from "behavioral aberrations" and likely to become an "unmanageable multitude of disturbed and disruptive youth."[10]

Not only the media and prosecutors but legislatures and judges treated medical studies, understood within the medical community to be in their tentative first stages, as if they had produced conclusive findings.[11] Social service and health departments followed suit. Some child protective services departments adopted policies treating a positive drug screen as prima facie abuse or even proof of "nonaccidental serious physical injury" to the child.[12] In New York City, babies' birth certificates began to include notations identifying them as cocaine-exposed.[13] Around the country, hospitals responding to the agencies' demand for information developed drug testing protocols that, in retrospect, seem structurally biased to pass over the affluent cocaine user and select the young, indigent, minority mother and her infant for screening.

Substance abuse, it must be remembered, takes different forms in different families and neighborhoods, different ethnic, racial, and geographic communities, and different economic strata. Philadelphia's experience with crack mirrored that of many other urban centers with heavy concentrations of poor, unemployed, and largely minority populations. Crack was a relatively new form of cocaine, reaching epidemic levels in a new population of users—pregnant women. As a legal academic involved in local child advocacy circles, I shared my community's learning curve on the drug and its in utero effects. In 1989, estimates of the percentage of inner city mothers delivering with crack in their systems in Philadelphia hospitals were running as high as 16 percent.[14] The City of Philadelphia has a high concentration not only of poor families but also of medical schools, law schools, and children's advocates. As in other urban centers, individuals from the Philadelphia community concerned about children and families began to gather in panels and symposia to debate not only sanctions aimed at deterrence but also strategies for drug abuse treatment and prevention.[15] At these conferences, doctors, lawyers, and social service professionals shared both information and perspectives on medical and legal issues ranging from protocols for drug testing to chances for rehabilitation. We heard stories about mothers who had abandoned their babies in crack dens without a backward glance and stories from mothers who, for the sake of their babies, challenged enormous odds to break their cocaine habits.[16] Not all of the anecdotal news was bad. Residential treatment centers like Gaudenzia New Image reported with amazement that they had seen crack-addicted mothers who entered the program as late as their third trimester of pregnancy deliver normal-weight, full-term babies.[17]

The "crack baby" studies that had created the greatest alarm, those early reports of neurological damage affecting child development, had been based primarily on statistics about and direct observation of babies that had been identified to the investigators as "drug-exposed." Conclusions drawn from studies that are not blind, longitudinal, or controlled are particularly problematic. It is unclear why these early studies on cocaine received such wide, relatively uncritical acceptance and exposure. Racism and class bias surely played a part.[18] And, of course, we tend to prefer a new crisis and an identifiable culprit to an old and chronic woe.[19]

As the first studies linking cocaine with neurological effects were being published, neonatologists and specialists in early neurological development embarked on the painstaking process of constructing prospective longitudinal studies that would follow drug-exposed babies over months and years and compare them, in careful, blind studies, with matched control groups. I first heard early results from one such study at a conference in December 1990, in a presentation by Dr. Hallam Hurt, director of neonatology at Albert Einstein Medical Center in Philadelphia.[20] Cautioning us that her results were, as yet, extremely tentative, she told us that they cast doubt on earlier drastic reports of neurological damage. I, like many other lawyers at the conference, felt the ground shift under me, as I had naively believed doctors "knew" crack was the pathogen and that we were gathered primarily to debate whether various alternative legal interventions presented a viable and constitutional cure. Ironically, it became clear that the medical people at the conference also suffered from their own myopia. They understood that the data on crack's medical effects were inconclusive, but seemed to accept, as a matter of arcane lawyers' logic, that a sufficient legal basis existed for ordering and reporting test data, detention of infants, or other state interventions.[21]

Legal issues aside, many doctors shared the American Academy of Pediatrics' concern about the public health and policy ramifications of the public's reaction to the incomplete data on cocaine's effects.[22] In January 1992 a group of doctors from the Yale Study Center, the National Institute of Child Health and Human Development, and the Boston University School of Medicine published an article in the *Journal of the American Medical Association*,[23] challenging the factual basis for labeling cocaine-exposed infants as damaged. The authors expressed deep concern that a rush to judgment about the effects of cocaine on the fetus had resulted in stigmatizing crack-exposed babies and had "exempted society from having to face other possible explanations of the children's plight—explanations such as poverty, community violence, inadequate education, and diminishing employment opportunities that require deeper understanding of wider social values."[24] The authors focused on a number of critical methodological issues: poorly defined study populations, flaws in identifying levels and patterns of cocaine use, difficulty isolating effects of cocaine from those of other drugs, including alcohol and cigarettes, difficulty disentangling the intrauterine from the pre- and postnatal sociological impact of cocaine. Disentangling such factors is especially difficult in populations and communities already at risk for poor medical care, environmental toxins, and "poverty, violence, abandonment, hopelessness, multiple short-term foster placements, and inadequate or abusive parenting."[25]

Early studies had suggested an association between cocaine use and maternal complications such as placental abruption, premature rupture of membranes, premature labor, and spontaneous abortion.[26] Many of these maternal complications had yet to be consistently substantiated in methodologically rigorous studies. Reviewing the data as of May 1992, Dr. Laurence Slutsker of the Centers for Disease Control noted that the data on maternal complications, with the exception of placental abruption, appeared inconsistent.[27] Repeated findings, he noted, indicate a link between cocaine use and placental abruption.[28] In one controlled study, however, such risks became statistically insignificant with adequate prenatal care.[29]

Among the adverse neonatal outcomes that early studies had identified were LBW, prematurity, fetal growth retardation, sudden infant death syndrome (SIDS), congenital abnormalities, and neurobehavioral abnormalities. The association with SIDS, still unproven, appears to have been substantially overestimated.[30] Evaluations of the findings on LBW, prematurity, and fetal growth retardation, while certainly not exonerating crack, have stressed that data must be treated cautiously, as all three conditions are closely related and all three are sensitive to factors such as smoking,[31] race,[32] alcohol consumption,[33] maternal age,[34] and prenatal care.[35] While it is clear that pregnant women should abstain from using cocaine to avoid risks to themselves and their fetuses, medical science has not yet determined cocaine's precise effects or how they compare with, interact with, and are affected by myriad other socioeconomic, environmental, chemical, and genetic factors influencing maternal and fetal health.[36] It seems the jury is still out on the basic factual predicate that supposedly justified harsh sanctions:[37] the association between crack use by pregnant women and a high risk of serious physical harm to the fetus.

As this chapter goes to press, Dr. Hurt's Philadelphia study[38] numbers over one hundred cocaine-exposed babies and a similar number of control group non-exposed babies of comparable birth weight, gestational age, and natal condition and, most significantly, matched for low socioeconomic status (SES). These babies, all born at or near term and nonasphyxiated,[39] are evaluated at birth, and every six months thereafter,[40] by examiners blind to their group assignment. Videotapes of the children at play, at eighteen and twenty-four months, are submitted, in a double-blind research design, for evaluation of complexity of play.[41]

It is still too early to draw any clear conclusions. But results from this study continue to challenge the alarming earlier reports of cocaine babies' neurological deficits. At birth, there is no difference between the neurologic status of the cocaine-exposed group and that of the control group. In addition, the study, thus far, has found no statistically significant differences in the early language development or videotaped play behavior of the two groups.[42] Sadly, the Bayley Mental Development Index scores of both have *decreased* significantly over time, most likely reflecting the cumulative effects of indigence, poor parenting skills, and other environmental deficits. While there is no guarantee that specific learning disorders will not emerge later, overall these blind studies fail to detect the frightening evidence of neurological damage that seemed so pronounced to early researchers, who were aware that the babies under observation were drug-exposed. Dr. Hurt and her colleagues have begun to suspect that the single most significant statistical correlation with poor development, across both groups, may be indigence.

The leading role played by poverty should surprise no one. Recent data collected by the bipartisan National Commission on Children document yet again the overlapping and mutually reinforcing nature of family risk factors such as low income, minority race, and divorce or single parenthood.[43] These risks are compounded and magnified for families in dense urban environments where community resources are lacking and where one's neighbors are likely to suffer from many of the same deficits of human and social capital.[44] Urban poverty, especially, is associated with a host of environmental and social ills, including poor nutrition, poor or no health care, epidemic diseases like measles and tuberculosis, infections like syphilis and hepatitis, lack of social and family support structures, substandard or nonexistent housing, violence, lack of community services, and increased exposure to toxic substances and illegal and legal street drugs like tobacco and alcohol. Many of these factors begin to affect babies' opportunities and futures before conception and continue long after they leave the uterus.

It is important not to fall into the very trap criticized by this essay: the trap of treating early reports as definitive findings. Nevertheless, the reports from Dr. Hurt's study and others like it ought to give us pause. While it seems likely that *some* children are affected in utero,[45] it is becoming increasingly apparent that *most*, at least as measured by current tools, are not. There is reason to question whether we ought to approach prenatal cocaine exposure as a qualitatively different intrauterine harm to the fetus or as just another variable in the ecology of poor health and material deprivation that the indigent fetus shares with its mother.

If the latter, then the focus on criminal sanctions and coercive state intervention, in some jurisdictions triggered by no more than a positive drug test, will have served only to distract us from the real battle facing infants born in poverty. By treating maternal cocaine use as a crime or as child abuse, rather than as a public health problem, we may have driven mothers away from essential prenatal care.[46] We will have drained scarce dollars from education, nutrition, and health programs needed not only by crack-involved mothers and their babies but by so many poor mothers and their at-risk babies. Worst of all, we will have stigmatized the children. Deemed defective, they may become victims of a self-fulfilling prophecy, facing greater risks of being aborted or abused, or becoming "boarder babies" unable to find adoptive or foster homes.[47] They will be weighted down by their teachers' and caregivers' lowered expectations, because we have planted the suggestion that the "classic symptoms of prenatal exposure to crack" lurk in every inner-city child who has difficulty sitting still.[48]

The evolution I have traced in our understanding of crack's effects does not eliminate crack as an issue on legal dockets. Much of the legal discussion to date has focused on constitutional infirmities of criminalization of maternal substance use. However, if we were to do away with criminal sanctions today, drug use during pregnancy would remain a pressing issue. Legislatures and judges have clear legal authority in their role as protectors of children to pass and enforce laws that, *in effect*, if not by stated purpose, punish women for conduct during pregnancy. Heavy drug use during pregnancy continues to bear on children's well-being after delivery quite aside from its effects on the fetus. Substance abuse by caregivers (of which a drug screen at delivery is evidence) is a prime marker for environmental risks to infants, including risks of poverty and malnutrition, violence, and abusive or neglectful parenting.[49] Across the country, states, counties and municipal agencies process tens of thousands of civil cases of abuse or neglect involving drug-exposed babies or drug-involved families for every crack baby case that reaches a criminal docket.[50] Many of the claimed constitutional infirmities of the criminal arena are attenuated or absent in the child protective services (CPS) context. In CPS, where the issue is not guilt but protecting the child, the state need not show intent to harm in order to remove a child from her parent or to terminate parental rights.[51] In CPS, the analysis turns not on mens rea but on functional unfitness, a "status" that may be found to warrant removal and termination of rights even when the addicted, mentally ill, or retarded parent acts "involuntarily" or lacks the capacity to change.[52] Fifth and Sixth Amendment protections against self-incrimination and hearsay are attenuated in CPS proceedings.[53] Standards of proof may be relaxed. Due process and equal protection are narrowly construed.[54] Unlike criminal law, CPS is explicitly in the business of extrapolating present and future misconduct from prior bad acts and intervening not to punish but to prevent harm. In the predictive world of CPS, the admissibility of a positive drug or alcohol screen at delivery does not turn on whether a fetus is a person. It turns on whether the past drug abuse is indicative of future risks.[55] The reasons for these differences are apparent—the sanctions imposed by CPS are collateral effects of protecting children and, unlike incarceration, can work to protect and reunite children and families as well as separate them.[56] My point is simply that opponents of criminal sanctions could prevail in their legal arguments, or even succeed in decriminalizing street drugs generally, and they still would not banish the issue of drug use by pregnant women from the legal arena.

If the crack saga has taught one lesson, however, it must be that it is dangerous to waste time in doctrinal skirmishing while the real battle for maternal and child health is being waged on other fronts. Although knotty legal issues remain, these legal questions are dwarfed by the stark public policy choices that confront us. The fundamental policy choice is this: How shall we respond to the devastation we are witnessing in the lives of so many children and their families? Does coercive intervention hold the answers, or do the answers lie elsewhere?[57] The shortfall in prenatal care and access to substance abuse programs for pregnant drug users remains acute or has worsened.[58] Child protective systems are virtually collapsing under the onslaught of new cases. Our ability to detect drug use and write laws penalizing it far outpaces our wisdom or fiscal capacity to deal effectively with the needs of children and families who are drawn into the CPS systems of foster care and state supervision in the wake of such tests and proceedings.[59] In growing recognition of our inability to replicate or replace children's families, there is a new emphasis on prevention and "family preservation" in CPS. Newer initiatives rely heavily on interdisciplinary cooperation between health care, social work, and legal systems to minimize family disruption and prevent or treat the risks of drug abuse without removing children from their homes.[60]

The most basic challenge for law, medicine, and policy is to learn from past mistakes and avoid a rush to judgment, whether in the criminal or the civil context. The easy answer that makes outlaws of so many mothers—almost one in five in my community!—as victimizers of their children is an illusion. The costs of nursing our illusions are enormous, not only to individuals but to society, as we squander our resources on the not-so-cheap thrills of punishment rather than long-term economies of prevention.[61] Perhaps lawyers and politicians can move beyond the deadlock over individual versus public blame,[62] maternal versus fetal rights, to develop a family policy that recognizes the essential unity and interdependence of mothers and children and, ultimately, communities and nations, by promoting our shared interests in a healthy start. We must avoid pitting mother and child against each other in a zero sum game for which all of us will bear the costs.[63]

Legal recognition of the shared interests of mother, child, and community in strengthening families would be a fitting partner to a public policy that cared for children by caring for their mothers and families. Such a partnership would focus less on intervention and more on prevention, investing in health care and services for pregnant women, including but not limited to drug and alcohol treatment, and in community and material resources for parents, infants, and children. While not minimizing the risks of drugs, it would focus less on whether mothers and babies are drug-involved and more on the health and educational needs that drug-exposed babies (and drug-involved families) share with many of their drug-free peers. In the absence of such a community of support, penalties against pregnant women remain a sideshow, distracting policy-makers, legal theorists, and the public from attending to the real mothers and real children all around us.

NOTES

Acknowledgments: Special thanks to Dr. Hallam Hurt, director of neonatology at Albert Einstein Medical Center in Philadelphia, for her inspiration and explanations, to Joanne Fischer of the Maternity Care Coalition of Greater Philadelphia for advice, to Cathryn Miller and Cheryl Hardy for their excellent research, and to Debbie Nearey Walsh for her secretarial assistance. Thanks also to Seth Kreimer and Stephen Morse for their comments. Any errors are my own.

1. *See* Austin, Sapphire Bound!, 1989 Wis. L. Rev. 539, 554–55 (noting the "exaggerated hostility" generated by the pregnancies of the poor and the tendency to blame black mothers for their daughters' failings).

2. *See* National Commission on Children, Beyond Rhetoric: A New American Agenda for Children and Families 119–121 (1991) (noting long-term consequences of neonatal complications, and observing that progress in preventing prematurity and low birth weight slowed in the 1980s and that low birth weight is actually increasing among blacks) [hereinafter Beyond Rhetoric].

3. *See* Roberts, Punishing Drug Addicts Who Have Babies: Women of Color, Equality, and the Right to Privacy, 104 Harv. L. Rev. 1419, 1428–29 (1991); Committee on Substance Abuse of the American Academy of Pediatrics, Drug-Exposed Infants, 86 Pediatrics 639 (1990) [hereinafter Committee on Substance Abuse].

4. For a profile of the legal developments through the late 1980s, see McGinnis, Prosecution of Drug-Exposed Babies: Constitutional and Criminal Theory, 139 U. Pa. L. Rev. 505–508 (1990), reprinted as Chapter 6 in this book. Initiatives to prosecute drug-using mothers for exposing their fetuses to controlled substances have met with little success on appeal. For example, Jennifer Johnson's conviction, discussed in Chapter 6, was unanimously overturned by the Florida Supreme Court. Johnson v. State, 602 So. 2d 1288 (Fla. 1992). *See* Lewin, Mother

Cleared of Passing Drug to Babies, N.Y. Times, July 24, 1992, at B7. This was the first such case to reach a state's highest court. *Id.* The fact that appellate courts have almost universally struck down these convictions does not, however, mean that criminalization has had no substantive impact, since many women charged under criminal statutes have pled guilty. *Id.*

5. The theories of these cases ranged from criminal child abuse, to delivery of drugs to a minor, to involuntary manslaughter, but all were predicated on the belief that cocaine causes irreparable damage to the fetus in utero. *See* Chapter 6. The proposed Illinois law cited by McGinnis, for example, bases a crime of "conduct injurious to a newborn" on the presence of cocaine in the child's blood or urine. *Id. See also id.* at n.31 (noting that one prosecutor charged the mother with "assault with a deadly weapon" based on a positive toxicology test); and McGinnis' original law review article, *supra* note 4, at 527–28 (prosecutor describes purpose as deterring mothers from having "afflicted children").

6. For a paper gathering research, current as of 1989, see Bandstra, Medical Issues for Mothers and Infants Arising from Perinatal Use of Cocaine, in Drug Exposed Infants and Their Families: Coordinating Responses of the Legal, Medical, and Child Protection System 19, 21–26 (ABA Center on Children and the Law ed., 1990) [hereinafter Drug Exposed Infants].

7. *See id.* at 22–23. Perhaps most prominent among researchers asserting evidence of neurological impairment was Dr. Ira J. Chasnoff of the National Association for Perinatal Addiction Research and Education (NAPARE) in Chicago.

8. Blakeslee, Crack's Toll on Infants Found to Be Emotional Devastation, N.Y. Times, Sept. 17, 1989, at 1.

9. Time, May 13, 1991, cover.

10. Toufexis, Innocent Victims, Time, May 13, 1991, at 56, 57. Among the inaccuracies in *Time's* reporting was the 20 percent figure, which reflected percentages of newborns testing positive for drug exposure, not documented evidence of effects. In fact, even studies linking intrauterine cocaine exposure with neonatal sequelae find less than half of the drug-exposed neonates demonstrating any observable effects. Chasnoff et al., Drugs, Alcohol, Pregnancy, and the Neonate, 266 JAMA 1567, 1568 (1991). Although cautioning that the studies were under debate, *Time* went on to report drastic neurological complications as if relating conclusive findings. *See* Toufexis, *supra*, at 58–60.

11. The medical community itself was not immune to seduction. *See* Mayes et al., The Problem of Prenatal Cocaine Exposure: A Rush to Judgment, 267 JAMA 406 (1992). Nevertheless, the medical community early on took a nonpunitive stance. *See, e.g.,* Committee on Substance Abuse, Drug-Exposed Infants, *supra* note 3, at 641 (opposing criminalization, advocating nonpunitive access to prenatal care and services, and urging prevention and treatment); Chavkin & Kandall, Between a Rock and a Hard Place: Perinatal Drug Abuse, 85 Pediatrics 223, 224 (1990) (advocating services for pregnant addicts).

12. *See In re* Smith, 496 N.Y.S.2d 331 (N.Y. Fam. Ct. 1985) (basing neglect petition on mother's prenatal conduct); *In re* Ruiz, 500 N.E.2d 935 (Ohio Com. Pl. 1986) (same). *See also* Scheffey, Trailing 66 Amici, Valerie D. Case Heads for High Court, Conn. L. Trib., May 4, 1992, at 2 (noting that the Connecticut Appellate Court allowed a termination of parental rights to be "based solely on a mother's prenatal conduct"). *In re Valerie D.* was reversed on appeal, with the Supreme Court of Connecticut finding that the state's parental termination statute applies only to "postnatal parental conduct." *In re* Valerie D., 1992 Conn. LEXIS 274, at *28 (Conn. August 18, 1992).

13. Lewin, Page Two on Birth Certificates: The Confidential Portion, N.Y. Times, July 28, 1991, § 4, at 16. New York officials defended the collection of this information and insisted that it would be used only for research, but civil libertarians questioned why in that case the records should not carry identifying numbers rather than names, to preserve confidentiality. *Id.*

14. Goldman and Woodall, Children with No Place to Go, Phila. Inquirer, Dec. 27, 1989, at A1 (reporting on an April 1989 Philadelphia Perinatal Society study, which found that 16 percent of women delivering at eight city hospitals either "admitted using cocaine during their pregnancies or tested positive for the drug").

15. My first interdisciplinary exposure to the issues was a May 1989 community-based conference on "Support for Families of Cocaine Addicted Mothers" sponsored by Philadelphia's Maternity Care Coalition. Whatever perspective I now claim I owe to the many presenters and participants who gathered in Philadelphia in 1990 and 1991 to explore the issue of maternal drug use. These meetings ranged from large public conferences to small professional exchanges and included "From the Streets to Recovery," a symposium on drug use among homeless mothers, convened by the Philadelphia and U.S. Departments of Health in June 1990; "Cocaine, The Youngest Victims," a multidisciplinary conference sponsored by the Children's Rights Committee of the Philadelphia Bar Association, Philadelphia's Support Center for Child Advocates, the Juvenile Law Center, and the Education Law Center; "A Fair Chance for Every Newborn," the annual conference of the Philadelphia Perinatal Society held in April 1991; and the Albert Einstein Hospital Division of Neonatology's Pediatric Mortality-Morbidity Conference of June 4, 1991.

16. Speaking at "From the Streets to Recovery," *supra* note 15, a crack-involved mother and her daughters told of loading the children and grandchildren too young to walk into a shopping cart and trudging many miles across Philadelphia to Mayor Wilson Goode's office to beg for admission to a drug treatment center.

17. Presentation by Christine Blakely, program supervisor, Philadelphia Gaudenzia New Image, June 19, 1990.

18. *See* Roberts, Punishing Drug Addicts, *supra* note 3, at 1432–36. Claire Coles of Emory University, whose research indicates that neglect and not brain damage may explain behaviors observed by teachers and caregivers, suggests that the "crack baby" label attracted media attention because "crack is exotic and happening mostly in 'marginal' populations among 'bad people' who are not like 'us.'" *See* Goodman, The Myth of the "Crack Babies," Boston Globe, Jan. 12, 1992, at 69 (quoting Coles). *See also* Chasnoff et al., The Prevalence of Illicit Drug or Alcohol Use During Pregnancy and Discrepancies in Mandatory Reporting in Pinellas County, Florida, 322 New Eng. J. Med. 1202, 1204 (1990) (although the rate of illicit drug use was similar across race and economic lines, black women were ten times more likely to be reported to authorities); Sege, Role of Crack Babies' Environment Studied, Boston Globe, May 14, 1992, at 1 (reporting that Dan R. Griffith of the NAPARE believes that cocaine's frequent association with other factors is more dangerous for children than cocaine's impact on the fetus).

19. One factor may have been a built-in bias against the null hypothesis—most people (even scientific investigators) prefer news to no news. As early as 1989, a paper published in *The Lancet* looked at fifty-eight abstracts on cocaine's effects on the fetus submitted for presentation at the annual meeting of the Society for Pediatric Research between 1980 and 1989; it noted that 57 percent of the studies showing adverse effects were accepted, while only 11 percent of those showing *no* effects were accepted, although the studies showing no effects were methodologically more rigorous. *See* Koren et al., Bias Against the Null Hypothesis: The Reproductive Hazards of Cocaine, The Lancet, Dec. 16, 1989, at 1440.

20. *See* "Cocaine, The Youngest Victims," *supra* note 15.

21. I recall one telling interchange in a panel discussion of legal and medical professionals. A perinatologist complained of potential misuse of test results by prosecutors and social service agencies. Seeking a clearer understanding of why testing was medically necessary, I asked how a positive test would affect the medication or indicated treatments for mother and child. He startled the lawyers by remarking that it had little or no effect. "Why do you test?" "We test because you say we have to." This dialogue, we all realized, was incomplete—an epigrammatic rendering of a complex problem. But it illustrated how lawyer and doctor each had assumed that the drug screening was justified under the arcane principles of the other's art. In fact, the key to the crucial legal issues lay in medical research and practice. Panel Discussion, "A Fair Chance for Every Newborn," Annual Meeting of Philadelphia Perinatal Society, Apr. 9, 1991.

22. *See supra* note 11.

23. *See* Mayes, Rush to Judgment, *supra* note 11, at 406–408.

24. *Id*. at 406.

25. *Id*. at 406–408. Probably the best known of the environmental toxins referred to by the Mayes article is lead paint poisoning. *See* Rosen, The Killing Walls, N.Y. Times, April 11, 1992, at 25 (reporting as chair of a Center for Disease Control (CDC) advisory panel that lead poisoning is the most common preventable pediatric illness in the United States). Poor and minority communities also bear a disproportionate share of toxic chemical risks from landfills, smelters, factories, incinerators, and hazardous waste sites. *See* Austin & Schill, Black, Brown, Poor and Poisoned: Minority Grassroots Environmentalism and the Quest for Eco-Justice, 1 Kansas J. L. & Pub. Pol. 69 (1991) (minority and poor populations bear a disproportionate share of toxic chemical risks); Kennedy & Rivera, Pollution's Chief Victims: The Poor, N.Y. Times, Aug. 15, 1992, at 19.

26. *See* Bandstra, Medical Issues, *supra* note 6, at 21–23. Placental abruption increases risks of both infant and maternal mortality. *See* Slutsker, Risks Associated with Cocaine Use During Pregnancy, 79 Obstetrics & Gynecology 778, 780 (1992). Not surprisingly, frequent cocaine use was also associated with increased risk of a mother's becoming a victim of violence. *See* Amaro et al., Violence During Pregnancy and Substance Use, 80 Am. J. Pub. Health 575 (1990).

27. *See* Slutsker, Cocaine Use During Pregnancy, *supra* note 26, at 780.

28. *Id*.

29. *Id*. (citing MacGregor et al., Cocaine Abuse During Pregnancy: Correlation

Between Prenatal Care and Perinatal Outcome, 73 Obstetrics & Gynecology 715, 715–20 (1989)).

30. *See* Slutsker, Cocaine Use During Pregnancy, *supra* note 26, at 787. The SIDS scare is an example of the instability of early findings. A 1987 retrospective chart review by Dr. Ira Chasnoff found that 10 of 66 cocaine-exposed infants had died of SIDS. In a controlled prospective study at Boston City Hospital, 1 of 175 cocaine-exposed infants died of SIDS, compared with 4 of 821 unexposed infants. *Id.* (comparing Chasnoff et al., Cocaine Use in Pregnancy: Perinatal Morbidity and Mortality, 9 Neurotoxicology Teratology 291 (1987) with Bauchner et al., Risk of Sudden Infant Death Syndrome Among Infants with In Utero Exposure to Cocaine, 113 J. Pediatrics 831 (1988)).

31. One study indicated that smoking accounted for 18 percent of singleton low birth weights in whites and 35 percent of singleton low birth weights in blacks. *See* Petitti & Coleman, Cigarette Smoking and the Risk of Low Birth Weight: A Comparison in Black and White Women, 1 Epidemiology 201 (1990). Estimates of increased risks of LBW from smoking ranged from 3.6 to 5.1, *see id.*; risks from cocaine ranged from 3.0 to 6.6, *see* Slutsker, Cocaine Use During Pregnancy, *supra* note 26, at 783.

32. Black babies' mortality rate in the United States is twice as high as white babies'. *See* Schoendorf et al., Mortality Among Infants of Black as Compared with White College-Educated Parents, 326 New Eng. J. Med. 1522 (1992). This reflects both a higher mortality rate among normal weight black infants and a higher incidence of LBW. *Id.* at 1525. Although socioeconomic factors play a role, the reasons for this discrepancy are still unclear. A recent CDC study found that black infants born to college-educated parents were more than twice as likely to be low birth weight as the infants of white college-educated parents. *Id.* at 1524.

33. *See* McLaughlin et al., Randomized Trial of Comprehensive Prenatal Care for Low-Income Women: Effect on Infant Birth Weight, 89 Pediatrics 128 (1992).

34. Infants born to very young mothers face higher risks of prematurity and LBW. *Id.* at 130.

35. One study, for example, showed that 25 percent of a 407-gram weight decrement in infants was attributable to cocaine use while the remainder was attributable to cigarettes, marijuana, other drugs, and poor nutrition. *See* Zuckerman et al., Effects of Maternal Marijuana and Cocaine Use on Fetal Growth, 320 New Eng. J. Med. 762, 762–68 (1989).

36. Indeed, there is considerable evidence that *preconception* drug and alcohol use by *male* parents may adversely affect fetal development. *See* Yazigi et al., Demonstration of Specific Binding of Cocaine to Human Spermatozoa, 266 JAMA 1956, 1956–59 (1991) (finding that human spermatozoa exposed to cocaine may act as vectors to transport cocaine into an ovum, but noting that the findings have not been replicated in studies on human users outside the laboratory).

37. *See, e.g.,* Logli, Drugs in the Womb: The Newest Battlefield in the War on Drugs, 9 Crim. Just. Ethics 23, 24 (1990) (describing the factual assumptions behind such prosecutions).

38. *See supra* note 20 and accompanying text.

39. Dr. Hurt observes that the sample does not attempt to evaluate problems stemming from prematurity or placental abruption but is designed to examine cocaine exposure itself. The infants were all born at or beyond 34 weeks gestational age and were not asphyxiated (their Apgar scores were at or above 5 at five minutes of age), a complication associated with placental abruption. *But see* Singer et al., Neurobehavioral Sequelae of Fetal Cocaine Exposure, 117 J. Pediatrics 667, 671 (1991) (noting that studies restricted to full-term infants may underestimate morbidity). However, even high-end estimates of prematurity range from 12 percent to 15 percent of cocaine-exposed infants, and thus the study's population is typical of the large majority of such infants. For accounts of others reporting similar early findings, *see* Goodman, Myth of the "Crack Babies," *supra* note 18; Sege, Environment Studied, *supra* note 18.

40. Bayley Scales of Infant Development (BSID) are administered at 6, 12, 18, and 24 months.

41. The videotaped children are scored for cognitively complex play behavior (unfocused, nonpretense, total pretend) by off-site trained scorers, blind to group assignment and test purpose.

42. *See also* Chasnoff et al., Cocaine/Polydrug Use in Pregnancy: Two-Year Follow Up, 89 J. Pediatrics 284 (1992) (also finding no developmental differences between drug-exposed and control groups as measured by the Bayley Scales, but finding smaller head circumference in the exposed children).

43. Beyond Rhetoric, *supra* note 2, at 24–25.

44. *Id.* at 29.

45. *See e.g.*, Slutsker, Cocaine Use During Pregnancy, *supra* note 26.

46. The American Academy of Pediatrics Committee on Substance Abuse noted the absence of evidence that criminal sanctions prevented in utero drug exposure. *See* Committee on Substance Abuse, *supra* note 3, at 641. While some evidence exists that civil court intervention may improve outcomes, coercive interventions raise substantial concerns about driving women away from care. *Id.*; Johnson v. State, 602 So. 2d 1288 (Fla. 1992) (criminal sanctions deter prenatal care). William Gibbons, Esq., of Philadelphia's Community Legal Services, told discussants at "A Fair Chance for Every Newborn," *supra* note 15, of a client in labor who left Philadelphia by train to give birth in another city because she had heard she would be tested. Her escape failed, since that city also screened mothers suspected of drug use, but, as Gibbons remarked, "There is something wrong when mothers in labor are running away from our help." *See also* Chavkin & Kandall, A Rock and a Hard Place, *supra* note 11, at 224 ("A mother's love cannot be coerced by jailing pregnant women and errant mothers").

47. *See, e.g.*, Barden, Hospitals Housing Healthy Infants, N.Y. Times, July 26, 1992, at 20 (reporting on the difficulty of finding foster and adoptive homes); Koren, Null Hypothesis, *supra* note 19, at 1441; Mayes, Rush to Judgment, *supra* note 11, at 407 (noting the danger that alarm will lead to unnecessary abortions). To note yet another unforeseen consequence, breast feeding programs, particularly important to low income infants, have been decimated in inner city hospitals because hospital personnel cannot be sure whether a mother is drug-involved and fear that crack in the mother's milk will irreparably damage the infants. Interview with Mary Beth Haas of NORTH, Inc., a Philadelphia-area Women Infants and Children Program (WIC) provider, in Philadelphia (Oct. 20, 1992).

48. *See* Van Tassel, Schools Trying to Cope with "Crack Babies," N.Y. Times, Jan.

5, 1992, §12, at 1. The author relates teachers' estimates that 15 percent of children now entering school exhibit "classic symptoms" of crack abuse such as inability to concentrate, "itchiness," and being "up the wall." *Id.* She also notes teachers' disbelief at parents' denial of drug involvement. *Id.*

An ugly rumor, once started, is difficult to kill. Even as New York Judge Francis Murphy chastised the press for its "near hysterical" stories and urged bench and bar to educate themselves, a Justice of the Ohio Supreme Court wrote that *"any* person of ordinary intelligence has to know that *in utero* exposure to cocaine poses an unacceptable risk to the unborn child." *Compare* Murphy, Prejudice Attacks Victims of Prenatal Drug Abuse, N.Y.L.J., Jan. 29, 1992, at 37, *with* State v. Gray, 584 N.E.2d 710, 714 (Ohio 1992) (Wright, J., dissenting) (emphasis in the original). Moreover, classifying as unlawfully "high risk" any behavior that is as prevalent as maternal substance abuse raises definitional issues. *See infra* note 61 and accompanying text.

49. *See* Mayes, Rush to Judgment, *supra* note 11, at 407–408. Elevated risks, it must be noted, are present in affluent as well as indigent families, and among drug-involved parents of both sexes and all races.

50. Currently, some 430,000 children are in foster care in the United States, many of them because of drug exposure or parents' drug involvement. *See* Barden, Housing Healthy Infants, *supra* note 47. One study of hospitals in twelve cities identified 7,000 boarder babies either abandoned or detained in one year, 85 percent of whom had been exposed to alcohol or drugs before birth. *Id.; see also* Beyond Rhetoric, *supra* note 2, at 284 (projecting 550,000 children in foster care by 1995). Each of these half-million children has a CPS docket number, although overburdened judges can spend only an average of ten minutes on each case. *Id.* at 283. In addition to CPS intervention, it appears many states may be pursuing civil commitment as a means of controlling pregnant drug users. *See* Popovits, Criminalization of Pregnant Substance Abusers: A Health Care Perspective, 24 J. Health & Hosp. L. 169, 182 (1991).

51. *See, e.g.,* State v. Demarest, 599 A.2d 937, 941 (N.J. Super. Ct. App. Div. 1991) (comparing civil scheme's purpose of protecting child with criminal law purpose of determining culpability).

52. *See, e.g.,* Minn. Stat. §260.015(2a)(8) (1982 & 1991 Supp.) (defining a child in need of protection or services as, inter alia, a child who lacks proper parental care because of the "emotional, mental, or physical disability, or state of immaturity" of her parent); *Id.* §260.221(b)(5) (parent's rights may be terminated on showing that, after reasonable efforts by state agency, condition leading to placement has not been corrected). *See also In re* Joyce T., 489 N.Y.S.2d 705, 712 (N.Y. 1985) (termination of mentally retarded parent's rights survives due process challenges); *In re* Christina A., 262 Cal. Rptr. 903, 905 (Cal. Ct. App. 1989) (rejecting a due process challenge to termination of parental rights based on "mental disability").

53. *See* Baltimore v. Bouknight, 110 S. Ct. 900, 908–909 (1990) (holding that a mother could not invoke the Fifth Amendment as a defense to noncompliance with an order to produce her child or disclose the child's whereabouts). Sixth Amendment confrontation rights are attenuated in civil proceedings, affecting hearsay and other evidentiary rules. *Compare* Idaho v. Wright, 110 S. Ct. 3139,

3145–52 (1990) (construing hearsay rules strictly) *with* 42 Pa. Cons. Stat. § 5986 (relaxing hearsay rules in civil cases); 23 Pa. Cons. Stat. § 6381 (same).

54. *See, e.g., In re* T.D. & S.D., 536 N.E.2d 211 (Ill. App. 1989) (applying preponderance of the evidence standard in civil child sexual abuse case); *In re* S.K. and V.L., 564 A.2d 1382 (D.C. 1989) (preponderance of the evidence); *In re* Katherine C., 471 N.Y.S.2d 216 (N.Y. Fam. Ct. 1984) (fair preponderance of evidence).

55. The status of the fetus may be relevant to whether prenatal conduct constitutes a direct violation of child abuse and neglect laws. *See* Chapter 6; *In re* Ruiz, 500 N.E.2d 935, 939 (Ohio Com. Pl. 1986) (holding that a viable fetus is a "child" under the child abuse statute). Even a finding that the statute does not reach abuse in utero, however, does not render the conduct irrelevant. Sound policy counsels against regulations that deem a positive drug test to be a prima facie case of past neglect. *See* Robin-Vergeer, The Problem of the Drug-Exposed Newborn: A Return to Principled Intervention, 42 Stan. L. Rev. 745, 749 (1990) (opposing *automatic* removal of any "prenatally drug-abused newborns from their mothers"). Nevertheless, most CPS courts do consider prenatal drug use, along with other data, as evidence of future risk. *See id.* at 761–62; *see also* Brown v. Dept. of Health, 582 So. 2d 113, 115 (Fla. Ct. App. 1991) (finding evidence of drug abuse to be a sufficient basis to support a finding of "prospective neglect"); *In re* Troy D., 215 Cal. App. 3d 889 (1989) (juvenile court's jurisdiction established by positive toxicology); *In re* Stepfanel Tyesha C., 556 N.Y.S.2d 280 (1st Dept. 1990) (positive toxicology sufficient to allege cause of action for neglect). It is commonplace in CPS for evidence of past conduct that would be inadmissible in a criminal trial to be admitted as relevant. For example, neglect or abuse of one sibling is relevant to a finding of risk to another sibling. *In re* Henry, 530 N.E.2d 571, 580–81 (Ill. App. Ct. 1988); *In re* Katherine C., 471 N.Y.S.2d at 220 (N.Y. Fam. Ct. 1984) (finding siblings to be neglected children based on sexual abuse of their sister and without evidence of harm to them).

56. *See* A.J. Solnit et al., When Home Is No Haven: Child Placement Issues (1992) (illustrating how nonvoluntary interventions have potential to restore dysfunctional families).

57. The debate over policies to address poor maternal and child health is starkly posed in the contrasting positions of the majority of the commissioners in Beyond Rhetoric and the Minority Report on Health, subscribed to by nine commissioners. The majority report advocated public health initiatives such as drug treatment, education and immunization, as well as expanding prenatal and pediatric care and providing adequate nutrition to the poorest Americans. *Id.* at 118. The Minority Report contended that the root cause of high infant mortality rates and poor maternal outcomes was lack of personal responsibility and high-risk health and sexual behavior, problems that could not be rectified by increased public spending. *See id.* at 159–75.

58. Although the crack crisis brought pressure for residential and outpatient treatment for addicted women, drug treatment programs for pregnant women remain scarce. *See* Krauss, Pregnant Cocaine Addicts Facing Harsher Sentences in the Courts, N.Y.L.J., May 1, 1992, at S-10; Toufexis, Innocent Victims, *supra* note 10 (only 11 percent of pregnant addicts obtain treatment). One in four infants in this country is born to a mother who did not receive early prenatal care, and the

proportion remained stagnant or increased as public health funding decreased in the eighties. *See* Beyond Rhetoric, *supra* note 2, at 123. Nine percent of pregnant mothers (433,000 women at any given time) are without any health coverage, public or private. *Id.* at 137. Although food supplements as provided under the WIC program can reduce incidents of prematurity and LBW by 15 percent to 25 percent, WIC receives funding for only half of the poor mothers who are eligible. *Id.* at 151.

59. A study by the Child Welfare League of America and the National Association of Public Hospitals states: "The child welfare system is virtually collapsing under burgeoning caseloads as the number of children reported abused and neglected, drug exposed, homeless and severely troubled has skyrocketed." Barden, Housing Healthy Infants, *supra* note 47, at 20. The number of children in foster care has risen from 273,000 in 1986 to 429,000 as of 1991, an increase in substantial part attributable to drug-related cases. *Id.*

60. *See* Beyond Rhetoric, *supra* note 2, at 306–308 (urging preventive services as more cost-effective and humane).

61. Ironically, even the data in the debate about costs may be compromised by uncertainties about the effects of cocaine and about our response to maternal drug use. Drs. Niel Miele and David Benson, responding to Phibbs et al., The Neonatal Costs of Maternal Drug Use, 266 JAMA 1521 (1991), point out that statistics on the high cost of maternal cocaine use may be influenced by doctors' and social service agencies' decisions to place neonates in intensive care or to keep them in protective custody—decisions that were, in turn, influenced by misinformation about the effects of cocaine. *See* Miele and Benson, Controversial Costs of Cocaine, 267 JAMA 507 (1992) (letter to the editor).

62. *See* Minority Report on Health, in Beyond Rhetoric, *supra* note 2, at 162–63 (attributing LBW and infant mortality to parents' lifestyles and opposing "simply increasing funding for [WIC]").

63. The federally funded "Healthy Start" infant–maternal pilot program, coordinating outreach, education, and a broad spectrum of preventive services in community-based settings, is a beginning. *See* Beyond Rhetoric, *supra* note 2, at 172.

CHAPTER EIGHT

Prosecution of Mothers of Drug-Exposed Babies: A Response to McGinnis

Paul A. Logli

THE VICTIMIZATION of children by means of maternal substance abuse during pregnancy has generated a continuing debate not only in the courtrooms of our nation but also in the writings of its legal scholars. Doretta Massardo McGinnis in Chapter 6 summarizes some of the more compelling issues at stake in the controversy.[1] Her chapter is written largely in reaction to the actions of this prosecutor and others like me in addressing the problems of children damaged at birth by their mothers' continuing use of illegal drugs during pregnancy.

It is a well-settled rule in criminal cases that prosecutors, having the burden of proving the charge, have the right to open and close the evidence and the arguments.[2] Having opened the controversy by virtue of our decisions to prosecute,[3] it is now our task to respond to the arguments advanced by McGinnis and similar critics.

The May 1989 prosecution of Melanie Green within my own jurisdiction of Winnebago County, Illinois, served as a starting point in much of the ensuing debate regarding maternal substance abuse and the protection of newborn children. While the summary of the incident in Chapter 6 is accurate, it fails to convey the real-life factors that compelled our response.

The death of Melanie Green's two-day-old infant on February 4, 1989, was reported by local hospital authorities to the Rockford Police Department and the Illinois Department of Children and Family Services as the drug-related death of a child. The report was clearly mandated by the Abused and Neglected Child Reporting Act of the State of Illinois.[4] As medical reports and other evidence were gathered, it became clear that the death of the baby was indeed due to the maternal use of cocaine immediately prior to the delivery of the child.[5] The subsequent filing of criminal charges was motivated by the prosecutors' desire to react vigorously to the tragic and unnecessary death of a full-term and otherwise healthy infant. Although the prosecution was unsuccessful, the intent of the action was to hold the mother responsible under the law for the death of her child, to deter her from continuing to engage in behavior that could place future children at risk, and, last, to serve as a general deterrent to others who might also harm their children through illegal and dangerous activity. In the absence of either precedent or custom, prosecutors attempted to work with existing law and at the same time fulfill community expectations that they should do all in their power to protect life and deter future criminal conduct.

Prosecutors do not argue that drug use by a pregnant woman is always harmful to the fetus, or that prosecution is always appropriate for maternal substance abuse during pregnancy. However, harm to the newborn as a result of maternal drug use during pregnancy does frequently occur, and the death of Melanie Green's baby is a stark example of that harm. What we argue is that these prosecutions have a role in society's efforts to stem the tide of drug abuse and child abuse. These prosecutions and similar juvenile court proceedings often have the result of returning the drug-abusing mother to the social welfare system. This is crucial in the prevention of further child abuse, given the high correlation between drug abuse and continuing child abuse and neglect.[6]

McGinnis raises questions regarding the constitutionality of the prosecutions as well as their suitability under various criminal legal theories. This chapter will deal with each of the areas in the order in which they are raised, and then discuss the important role that prosecutors can play in society's efforts to deal with the difficult problem of substance-abused children.

Constitutional Issues

Chapter 6 properly raises constitutional concerns regarding the prosecution of mothers who have delivered drug-exposed infants.[7] The issues that are most compelling and more readily addressed are those involving due process and fair notice and relate to the use of statutes by prosecutors in situations not originally intended by the enacting legislature. Courts in at least two states have now addressed these issues and have disallowed prosecutions that have used existing statutes dealing with the delivery of controlled substances to persons as the basis of charges against women who delivered drug-exposed children.[8]

It appears to be almost a settled proposition that the prosecution of mothers who deliver drugs to fetuses while in the womb will have to rest on statutes specifically passed to address the issue. McGinnis points out one such legislative enactment: the Illinois legislature's expansion of the definition of a neglected or abused minor to include "any newborn infant whose blood or urine contains any amount of a controlled substance."[9] The amendment affects the jurisdiction of Illinois juvenile courts by declaring such a child to be a ward of the court for purposes of protective orders.[10] It does not constitute the basis for an adult criminal prosecution.

A bill intended to establish a new category of offense entitled "Conduct Injurious to a Newborn" was introduced in 1990. The nature of the proposed statute is set out in Chapter 6.[11] The bill was introduced in the legislature at my request following the unsuccessful prosecution of Melanie Green. Although the bill was not passed, it clearly constitutes an attempt to address the due process issues raised by McGinnis. Other legislative schemes have been proposed by other authors, but they have not yet met legislative approval.[12] It appears that a narrowly structured statute that specifically addresses the issues involved in substance abuse of newborns may very well satisfy the constitutional requirements of notice and fair warning.[13]

The other issues raised involve the balance between fetal rights and a woman's rights, especially as they pertain to the perceived privacy interest of an expectant mother.[14] Compelling discussions on both sides of the issue have appeared in legal publications,[15] and a detailed restatement of the arguments that frame the issue is not necessary here. McGinnis herself acknowledges the persuasiveness of arguments on both sides.[16] However, she argues that increased protection of fetal rights would "effectively create an adversarial relationship between mother and fetus."[17] Such a conclusion is logically suspect and difficult to justify. If the state were to proscribe certain actions by the mother, such as the use of illegal drugs during pregnancy, then the interest of the mother in maintaining good health and remaining in conformity with prevailing law would be entirely consistent with the best interests of the fetus and the good health of a newborn.

A more rational and legally justifiable approach is used by E. B. Myers in his discussion of the constitutional law implications of fetal protection versus maternal privacy rights. Although he personally disagrees with punitive state action in this regard, and instead encourages a juvenile court response to the problem, his ideology is consistent with solid legal analysis.[18]

> In sum, I am not persuaded by the argument that prosecution places an unconstitutional burden on procreative privacy. As the Supreme Court pointed out in *Wisconsin v. Yoder*, the State has considerable authority to restrict parental decision making that "will jeopardize the health or safety of the child."
>
> Turning to another important constitutional right, individuals enjoy a right to physical liberty and freedom from restraint. This right may well be implicated by State action *during* pregnancy to coerce women to refrain from activity that harms the fetus. When it comes to prosecution *following* the birth of a damaged child, however, the right to freedom from restraint is not implicated.[19]

McGinnis further argues that a new status crime is created by criminalizing coexistent conditions that are otherwise unpunishable by themselves, namely, drug addiction and pregnancy.[20] This argument is simply extremist ideology carried to an absurd conclusion. In both criminal and civil contexts, persons have been found to be in possession of drugs on the basis of blood or urine tests.[21] The Supreme Court case of *Robinson v. California*[22] does not prohibit the prosecution of an individual for actual use of drugs. When blood test results at the time of birth clearly indicate the use of drugs by a woman during pregnancy, then certainly the *Robinson* test is met insofar as actual possession of narcotics within the body is at issue and not mere status as an addict.[23]

The possession of illegal drugs is a crime, and there is no fundamental right to use psychoactive drugs.[24] Any legislation that would allow state criminal action in the event of a drug-affected birth would presumably be based on blood or urine tests showing the possession or use of drugs by the mother. Adding pregnancy to the equation is not constitutionally suspect. "Consequently, different treatment may be justified on the basis of pregnancy where the treatment bears a rational relationship to the governmental objective or interest."[25] The governmental objective or interest in the case of substance-abused infants is the avoidance of harm to a child and the resulting financial consequences to society. Surely these legitimate state interests far outweigh the perceived privacy rights of a woman to possess or use illegal drugs during pregnancy.

McGinnis has advanced legitimate criticism of early prosecution efforts in cases involving substance-abused infants. As indicated earlier, some state courts have agreed that due process and fair notice rights were violated by the use of statutes in a manner not originally intended. Other constitutional issues raised dealing with privacy rights and maternal autonomy, however, must be evaluated in light of the goals of society to protect the health of newborns and provide protection to otherwise helpless victims of another person's drug abuse.[26] Even in denying a civil cause of action by a fetus against the mother for the unintentional affliction of prenatal injuries, the Illinois Supreme Court left open the door for future legislative action by holding "that if a legally cognizable duty on the part of pregnant women to their developing fetuses is to be recognized, the decision must come from the legislature only after thorough investigation, study and debate."[27]

Criminal Law Theory

McGinnis goes to great lengths to attack the idea of holding pregnant drug users criminally responsible for their actions, arguing that the prosecutions are intended to punish persons for involuntary behavior. She cites Anglo-American legal tradition: the Model Penal Code and the general proposition that drug addiction is an illness or disease.[28] Surprisingly, McGinnis dismisses too readily a body of case law wherein courts have refused to insulate individuals from criminal responsibility for their acts on the basis of a temporary mental state that is voluntarily self-induced.[29]

The Illinois Supreme Court reduced the consideration of such a defense to rather basic elements.

> The essential consideration is not whether the medical profession characterizes the defendant's use of intoxicants resulting in a psychosis as a mental disease or defect, but rather whether society should relieve from criminal responsibility a defendant who voluntary ingests such intoxicants and then commits criminal acts. It is obvious to us that an actor should not be insulated from criminal responsibility for acts which result from a temporary mental state that is voluntarily self-induced.[30]

The court goes on to note that a majority of jurisdictions agree with its holding.[31]

McGinnis attempts to argue the issue both ways. The behavior of the addict, according to McGinnis, is involuntary, and the addict has no control over her actions.[32] Yet she also argues that the addict, out of fear of apprehension, will avoid prenatal care and the possibility of being reported to authorities.[33] Apparently McGinnis believes that the addict has enough mental ability to avoid apprehension but not enough to seek to conform her actions to the requirements of law and behave in the best interests of the baby. McGinnis' conjecture as to a pregnant addict's reaction to the possibility of criminal liability dispels the notion that the same addict is not able to act knowingly in ingesting drugs and causing harm to her baby.

Other courts have agreed with the Illinois court in finding that even if a defendant was psychotic at the time surrounding the criminal acts and was not capable of understanding that the act committed was wrong, this type of temporary insanity is no defense because it was not of a settled and permanent nature and was clearly the product of the voluntary ingestion of drugs.[34] In the absence of specific intent requirements, a general prohibition regarding the use of illegal drugs during pregnancy by a woman would not be subject to the defense of voluntary intoxication or even a resulting temporary insanity. A person who could otherwise control her actions and seek to avoid apprehension and prosecution should be legally responsible for not conforming her actions to law. To remove McGinnis' argument from the context of this issue and apply it to other criminal acts would seriously impair the prosecution of anyone for a criminal act while in a drugged or drunken condition.

McGinnis goes on to cite the work of Sanford Kadish, who advances the theory that the enforcement of certain laws has a criminogenic effect: Enforcement breeds more harm than ignoring the offense.[35] McGinnis postulates that this description would apply to laws against mothers' harming their newborns through drug use during pregnancy.[36] The fact is that such laws are outside the realm of Kadish's original work.[37]

In his work, Kadish discusses laws used for the enforcement of morals.[38] Laws against maternal drug use during pregnancy do not fall into this category, since the proscribed behavior is distinguishable from actions among consenting adults, such as sex offenses, abortion, gambling, and narcotics.[39] While the proposed laws do involve narcotics use, they differ from the narcotics laws that Kadish discusses because the proposed statutes involve a nonconsenting victim who has been directly harmed by the conduct of another.

Kadish also discusses laws that are used not to protect against serious misbehavior, "but to provide social services to needy segments of the community," such as nonsupport laws and laws against public drunkenness.[40] While laws against drug-abusing mothers should be designed to get them into treatment programs, they are not solely for that purpose. The conduct that these laws are intended to prevent creates victims other than the drug user and inflicts harm on parties who are unable to protect themselves.

Even if these laws were the kind that Kadish refers to, arguments regarding loss of respect for law and unenforceability can be countered. The argument is made that enforcing laws against drug-using mothers could create a diminished respect for law and for prosecutors.[41] It is said that "it may be increasingly difficult to maintain respect for a system that prosecutes drug-addicted mothers . . . while the dealers are perceived as going free."[42] Such a statement misleadingly implies that these women would be prosecuted instead of drug suppliers when, in reality, their cases would be conducted in addition to those cases involving dealers that are currently prosecuted in every jurisdiction in the country.

The failure of the Winnebago County grand jury to indict Melanie Green has been attributed to loss of respect for the law.[43] This failure "has been construed as a victory of compassion and common sense over prosecutorial gamesmanship."[44] It is more likely that the jurors were uncomfortable with the use of statutes that were not intended to be used in this circumstance.[45] With legislation directed specifically to the issue, the grand jury would not have to face this problem, and it would be more willing to indict. Conversely, a loss of respect for prosecutors may occur if they do not respond to the needs of the child at risk. By prosecuting violations vigorously, the prosecutors protect victims who, as children, are unable to protect themselves. Additionally, it is hardly justifiable that the possible loss of respect for prosecutors should dictate the rights of the victims.

McGinnis further argues that such laws would be unenforceable because health care providers would resist compliance with reporting requirements.[46] However, harm to a newborn through drug use is no less child abuse than the infliction of other injuries, such as a contusion or broken bone, that the Abused and Neglected Child Reporting Act requires health care providers to report. Viewed in this light, the argument of unenforceability is weakened.[47]

McGinnis also argues that laws against these mothers would only discourage pregnant drug addicts from seeking prenatal care. Health professionals fear that mothers will not deliver their babies in hospitals, and they foresee more abandoned babies, more seriously disabled babies, and more infant deaths.[48] There is more than one response to this. First, there are no studies or objective measures to show this; it is merely speculative. In addition, medical literature states that even without the possibility of prosecution, most women using illicit drugs receive little or no prenatal care.[49] Thus, the deterrent effect of prosecution on women seeking prenatal care would be minimal. A woman cannot be driven from a system in which she is not participating in the first place.

McGinnis also argues that discriminatory enforcement of sanctions will create problems. She cites a study in Pinellas County, Florida, which found that black mothers were 9.58 times more likely to be reported for their substance abuse than white mothers.[50] More than half of the women who have been prosecuted thus far are women of color.[51] However, McGinnis misses the point in placing the blame on the prosecutors. The implication that prosecutors go out of their way to prosecute only black women overlooks the fact that prosecutors can only deal with those cases that are reported to them. Ira Chasnoff and colleagues give several possible reasons for the reporting of black women in a higher proportion than white women.[52] Among them were the fact that the white women in Pinellas County were more likely to have private obstetricians, who may be less aware of current techniques to identify drug-exposed children and more reluctant to refer infants with drug exposure, since reporting would be disruptive to a private practice.[53] Universal testing for newborns would help ensure that fewer newborns would slip through the cracks of the health care and legal systems.

The Issue in Broader Context

The remainder of McGinnis' arguments prompts a largely personal response. McGinnis postulates that prosecutions such as the case against Melanie Green are motivated by a prosecutorial prolife conspiracy hatched in the wake of *Webster v. Reproductive Health Services*.[54] This is an especially dubious assertion in regard to the *Green* case, since the charge was brought several months before the *Webster* decision was announced. The insertion of the highly politicized question of abortion rights into the discussion of how society can best respond to the problem of substance-abusing pregnant women is disturbing. Once a mother, either intentionally or by default, has decided to carry a baby to term, the issues of procreative liberty and abortion rights should be left at the doorway of the courthouse or legislative chamber. Unfortunately, it appears that the abortion rights lobby views attempts by a state to protect fetal health as the start of a large-scale intrusion into the ability of a woman to control her own body.[55] It is not too simplistic to suggest that while a woman has a right either to have a baby or to not have a baby, there can be no right under the law to have a drug-damaged baby.

It is truly unfortunate that what began in the minds of prosecutors as a child protection issue has become entangled in the volatile and distracting issue of abortion rights. The best argument for removing this discussion from the issue of abortion is evidenced by McGinnis' own comment that prosecution of substance-abusing pregnant women is subject to attack by both sides of the abortion issue.[56] This is clearly a no-win situation for a prosecutor. It is even more disturbing to consider that the insertion of abortion rights into this discussion may effectively paralyze the effort of state governments to address constructively and rationally the issue of fetal health and a pregnant woman's obligation to avoid obviously illegal behavior that can produce extensive and permanent damage to a helpless child.

McGinnis will find little disagreement from most prosecutors with her stated concerns regarding the availability and suitability of drug treatment programs for women and especially pregnant women. Clearly state action taken in either adult court or juvenile court to coerce or motivate a woman to seek treatment will not succeed if no appropriate drug treatment program is available. By raising the profile of the problem of substance-exposed infants, prosecutors have motivated communities to adopt programs to respond to the problem. Since the prosecution of Melanie Green in 1989, the City of Rockford has seen the beginning of both inpatient and outpatient programs for substance-abusing women, including pregnant women. "Drug Free Families with a Future" is an aggressive local outreach program intended to identify women at risk and bring them into the drug treatment and prenatal health care systems. The program is coordinated by a committee with representatives from several local and state agencies, including public health, public aid, the Department of Children and Family Services, the Department of Alcohol and Substance Abuse, local medical providers, *and* the office of the local prosecutor. The program was initially one of a few pilot programs that received state funding. Unfortunately, a fiscal crisis not unlike that facing other states has substantially reduced the funding for these pilot programs. Nationally, as many as four hundred private-sector treatment programs have closed their doors in the last three years.[57]

Nor would most prosecutors disagree with McGinnis' assessment of the long-term solution to the problem. In fact, many of us have long insisted that the long-term solution does not rest with local prosecutors. "Society, including the medical and social welfare establishment, must be more responsive in providing readily accessible prenatal care and treatment alternatives for pregnant addicts."[58]

The difference between McGinnis and many prosecutors lies in how best to motivate the woman to seek care. Both sides can probably cite numerous anecdotes indicating that the fear of prosecution may motivate a woman to seek treatment or produce the opposite result. It is my belief that the chances of a woman's entering and successfully completing a drug-treatment program are certainly not hindered and are probably enhanced when that person is under the pressure of a court order or threat of legal action.

As a local prosecutor I have adopted a policy of using the juvenile court as a primary response to reports of drug-affected births. In many of our cases, drug-exposed children will remain with their mothers as they enter the child care and drug treatment network. In still other cases, we have agreed that another responsible family member may assume the care of the newborn, and thus preserve the important contact between mother and child. In cases in which a mother is unwilling or unable to come into the drug treatment program, we have moved under Illinois law to have the child declared abused and neglected so as to activate the protective orders of the juvenile court.[59] The results of such juvenile court involvement are clearly mixed, and although we have never formally compiled statistics, we are motivated by the knowledge that saving one child from an abusive environment is an achievement worthy of note. Our experience confirms the results of at least one study that showed a correlation as high as 83 percent between drug and alcohol misuse and continuing child abuse or neglect by the substance abusers.[60] It is very important to note that if the problem of the substance-abused infant is not dealt with at the time of birth, the chances of that child coming back into the court system even further abused or neglected are quite high.

Again, while using the juvenile court to respond to the problem of substance-abused infants, my office continues to believe that a criminal statute similar to the one proposed previously[61] is necessary in those cases in which no child survives or where the mother has proven to be especially difficult to bring into the prenatal or drug treatment systems. An alternative or even an addition to the criminal response would be a civil commitment statute similar to that adopted by the State of Minnesota.[62] Such a plan allows for the involuntary civil commitment into a drug treatment program of a pregnant woman who is found to be abusing drugs, a move that would avoid the infliction of harm on a newborn in the first place. Legislators have to establish clear public policy regarding fetal health and deal with the problem in a comprehensive and humane manner.

Conclusion

In the final analysis, I believe that people on both sides of this issue share the goal of guaranteeing fetal health and producing healthy newborns. Much has been made of a relatively small number of actions by the prosecutors of this country. Most prosecutors, like me, do not believe that they are a major player in this issue. Nevertheless, we have unfairly become easy targets for some law review authors and abortion rights advocates.[63] Given the proper legislative tools, it is clear that prosecutors can at least make some inroads into the problem of substance-abused infants, at least until the medical, social welfare, and child-care segments of our society can bring enough political pressure to bear on various federal and state legislative bodies to provide adequate programs to address women's unique prenatal and drug treatment needs.

NOTES

Acknowledgment: The author gratefully acknowledges the assistance of Erika Kruse, a graduate of the University of Illinois Law School, in preparation of this chapter.
1. *See* McGinnis, Prosecution of Mothers of Drug-Exposed Babies: Constitutional and Criminal Theory, 139 U. Pa. L. Rev. 505 (1990), reprinted as Chapter 6 in this book.

2. *See* 75A Am. Jur. 2d *Trial* § 539 (1991).

3. *See* Chapter 6.

4. Ill. Rev. Stat. ch. 23, para. 2051–2061.7 (1989), recodified as 325 Ill. Comp. Stat. 5/1 to 5/11.7 (1992).

5. Enid F. Gilbert-Barness, M.D., professor of pathology and pediatrics and director of surgical pathology at the University of Wisconsin Hospital and Clinics, reviewed the case and concurred in the opinion of Gary L. Anderson, M.D., a pathologist from Rockford, Illinois, that the death of the infant "related to the effects of cocaine and the sequence of events that followed were related to severe fetal hypoxia." Letter from Enid F. Gilbert-Barness, M.D., to Gary L. Anderson, M.D., Mar. 3, 1989 (on file with author).

6. *See* ten Bensel, Assessing the Dynamics of Child Neglect and Abuse, Juv. & Fam. Ct. J., Winter 1984, at 33, 37.

7. *See* Chapter 6.

8. *See* People v. Hardy, 469 N.W.2d 50 (Mich. Ct. App. 1991) (holding that the use of cocaine by a pregnant woman, which may result in the postpartum transfer of cocaine through the umbilical cord to her infant, is not the type of conduct that the legislature intended to be prosecuted). *See also* Johnson v. State, 602 So. 2d 1288 (1992) (reversing the decision of a lower court, 578 So. 2d 419 (Fla. Dist. Ct. App. 1991) and disallowing the prosecution of a mother for delivering cocaine to her child via the umbilical cord under a statute making illegal the delivery of controlled substances to a minor).

9. Ill. Rev. Stat. ch. 37, para. 802–3(c) (1991), recodified as 705 Ill. Comp. Stat. 405/2-3 (1992).

10. *See id.* para. 802–23 (1991), recodified as 705 Ill. Comp. Stat. 405/2-23 (1992).

11. *See* Chapter 6.

12. *See* Schierl, A Proposal to Illinois Legislators: Revise the Illinois Criminal Code to Include Criminal Sanctions Against Prenatal Substance Abuse, 23 J. Marshall L. Rev. 393, 423–24 (1990).

13. *See* Chapter 6. *See also* Myers, A Limited Role for the Legal System in Responding to Maternal Substance Abuse During Pregnancy, 5 Notre Dame J.L. Ethics & Pub. Pol'y 747, 765 (1991).

14. *See* Chapter 6.

15. *See, e.g.,* Balisy, Maternal Substance Abuse: The Need to Provide Legal Protection for the Fetus, 60 S. Cal. L. Rev. 1209 (1987); Barrett, Prosecuting Pregnant Addicts for Dealing to the Unborn, 33 Ariz. L. Rev. 221 (1991); Drendel, When Self Abuse Becomes Child Abuse: The Need for Coercive Prenatal Government Action in Response to the Cocaine Baby Problem, 11 N. Ill. U. L. Rev. 73 (1990); Holland, Criminal Sanctions for Drug Abuse During Pregnancy, The Antithesis of Fetal Health, 8 J. Hum. Rts. 915 (1991); Logli, Drugs in the Womb: The Newest Battlefield in the War on Drugs, 9 Crim. Just. Ethics 23 (1990); Logli, The Prosecutor Steps Into the Fray: Substance-Abused Infants, 90 The Prac. Prosecutor 15 (1990); Mariner et al., Pregnancy, Drugs and the Perils of Prosecution, 9 Crim. Just. Ethics 30 (1990); McNulty, Pregnancy Police: The Health Policy and Legal Implications of Punishing Pregnant Women for Harm to Their Fetuses, 16 N.Y.U. Rev. L. & Soc. Change 277 (1987).

16. *See* Chapter 6.

17. *Id.*

18. *See* Myers, A Limited Role, *supra* note 13, at 760.

19. *Id.* at 761 (citing Wisconsin v. Yoder, 406 U.S. 205, 234 (1972)) (footnotes omitted).

20. *See* Chapter 6.

21. *See* Yanez v. Romero, 619 F.2d 851 (10th Cir. 1980); Schlobohm v. Rice, 510 N.E.2d 43 (Ill. App. Ct. 1987); *see also* Colo. Rev. Stat. Ann. § 18-18-104 (West 1988) (prohibiting use of drugs specifically).

22. 370 U.S. 660 (1962).

23. *Id.* at 666.

24. *See* City of Newport v. Iacobucei, 479 U.S. 92 (1986) (regarding local regulation of alcohol); California v. LaRue, 409 U.S. 109 (1972) (same); Whalen v. Roe, 429 U.S. 589 (1977) (regarding state regulation of the dispensing of drugs).

25. *See* Drendel, When Self Abuse Becomes Child Abuse, *supra* note 15, at 113–14.

26. See discussion of Deborah Mathieu's five factors relevant in evaluating whether state intervention can be limited to ensure minimal intrusion on maternal autonomy, in Balisy, Maternal Substance Abuse, *supra* note 15, at 1233, 1234. The factors are: (1) magnitude of harm to the future child compared with the intrusive harm to the pregnant woman; (2) comparative value of preventing child's suffering as opposed to the value of the woman's ability to use drugs freely; (3) the probability of harm to the child if action is not taken; (4) the probability that harm to the child can be prevented if the mother stopped using the injuring substance; and (5) whether the state intervention will create more harm than it will prevent.

27. Stallman v. Youngquist, 531 N.E.2d 355 (Ill. 1988).

28. *See* Chapter 6.

29. See discussion of case law in People v. Free, 447 N.E.2d 218, 232 (Ill. 1983).

30. *Id.* at 231.

31. *See id.* at 232.

32. *See* Chapter 6.

33. *See id.*

34. *See* People v. Kelly, 516 P.2d 875 (Cal. 1973).

35. *See* Chapter 6.

36. *See id.*

37. *See* Kadish, The Crisis of Overcriminalization, 374 Annals 157 (1967).

38. *See id.*

39. Kadish's article was written before Roe v. Wade, 410 U.S. 113 (1973).

40. Kadish, Overcriminalization, *supra* note 37, at 159.

41. *See* Chapter 6.

42. *Id.*

43. *See id.*

44. *Id.*

45. *See* Logli, Drugs in the Womb, *supra* note 15, at 24.

46. *See* Chapter 6.

47. *See* Abused and Neglected Child Reporting Act, Ill. Rev. Stat. ch. 23, para. 2051, 2054 (1991), recodified as 325 Ill. Comp. Stat. 5/11, 5/14 (1992).

48. *See* Chapter 6.

49. *See* Myers, A Limited Role, *supra* note 13, at 757.

50. *See* Chapter 6.

51. *Id.*

52. *See* Chasnoff et al., The Prevalence of Illicit Drug or Alcohol Use During Pregnancy and Discrepancies in Mandatory Reporting in Pinellas County, Florida, 322 New Eng. J. Med. 1202, 1205 (1990).

53. *Id.*

54. 492 U.S. 490 (1989).

55. *See* McNulty, Pregnancy Police, *supra* note 15, at 288–90; *see also* Roberts, Punishing Drug Addicts Who Have Babies: Women of Color, Equality, and the Right to Privacy, 104 Harv. L. Rev. 1419, 1463 (1991); Romney, Prosecuting Mothers of Drug-Exposed Babies: The State's Interest in Protecting the Rights of a Fetus Versus the Mother's Constitutional Rights to Due Process, Privacy and Equal Protection, 17 J. of Contemp. L. 325, 343 (1991).

56. *See* Chapter 6.

57. *See* Ford, The Incredible Shrinking Utilization, National Ass'n of Addiction Treatment Providers Rev., Fall 1992, at 2.

58. Logli, Drugs in the Womb, *supra* note 15, at 28; *see also* Logli, The Prosecutor's Role in Solving the Problems of Prenatal Drug Use and Substance-Abused Children, 43 Hastings L.J. 559, 565–67 (1992). The report of the meeting of prosecutors and others in July 1990 in Chicago, sponsored in part by the American Prosecutors Research Institute, states clearly that prosecutors must work with all groups to increase treatment resources and encourage a multidisciplinary effort of medical, treatment, social services, and other groups to form an effective approach to substance abuse during and after pregnancy. *See* Substance-Abused Infants: A Prosecutorial Dilemma, NCPCA Update (National Center for Prosecution of Child Abuse), Sept./Oct. 1990.

59. *See* Ill. Rev. Stat. ch. 37, para. 802-3(c) (1991), recodified as 705 Ill. Comp. Stat. 405/2-3(c) (1992).

60. *See* ten Bensel, Assessing the Dynamics, *supra* note 6, at 32.

61. *See* Chapter 6.

62. *See* Minn. Stat. Ann. § 626.556 (West 1983).

63. *See generally* Symposium, Substance Use During Pregnancy: Legal and Social Responses, 43 Hastings L.J. 505 (1992) (containing an article by Dawn Johnsen, legal director, National Abortion Rights Action League, *id.* at 569).

■ PART II

Children and the
Social Service System

■ CHAPTER NINE

In Search of Affirmative Duties toward Children under a Post-*DeShaney* Constitution

Amy Sinden

As PUBLIC AWARENESS and concern about child abuse have increased in recent decades,[1] more and more resources have been directed toward efforts to protect children from dangerous home situations.[2] In the past thirty years, laws have been passed in all fifty states requiring certain professionals to report suspected child abuse and creating state and county agencies to receive and investigate such reports.[3] Since 1960, the number of children reported to child welfare agencies as suspected victims of abuse or neglect has increased dramatically,[4] as has the number of children in foster care.[5] Although most professionals now agree that child abuse and neglect occur in all socioeconomic classes,[6] the vast majority of families reported to and investigated by child welfare agencies are poor.[7]

Thus, the child welfare agency has become a major presence in poor communities. Given the resources and legal authority they possess, such agencies have the power to be both a source of great help and a source of great harm to these communities. While their laudable mission is to save children, child protective social workers also have the capacity to cause serious harm. They must strike a delicate balance between the risk of injury to the child in the home and the risk of destroying desperately needed family bonds through overly intrusive intervention. An error in either direction can have catastrophic consequences for the child. Failure to remove, in the most extreme situations, can lead to serious injury

---

Reprinted in redacted form with permission of the University of Pennsylvania Law Review. Originally in 139 U. Pa. L. Rev. 227 (1990). Copyright 1990 The University of Pennsylvania Law Review.

or even death,[8] but removing a child from her home will inevitably result in emotional injury that may be worse than that which the child might have suffered there.[9] Moreover, foster care itself does not always offer children the safe haven from physical and emotional abuse that it is supposed to provide.[10] Yet despite the importance of the judgments that we trust them to make, and the devastating consequences of error, child protective social workers are generally poorly paid, inadequately trained, and overworked.[11] As a result, the judgments they make may too often be wrong.[12]

Attempts have been made to hold child welfare agencies accountable for the tragic effects of their most egregious mistakes through federal court actions under section 1983 of the Civil Rights Act of 1871 alleging violations of the child-victim's constitutional rights. Yet, while wrongful removal of a child by an agency clearly involves state action in violation of the child's and the parents' rights under the Fourteenth Amendment, many of the other mistakes committed by child welfare agencies and their social workers result not in a clearly definable *action* on the part of the agency, but rather in the agency's *failure to act*. Thus, a child who is seriously injured at the hands of her parents or foster parents may seek to hold the agency liable for its *failure* to take action to protect her. Similarly, a child in foster care who could return home safely if certain protective services were provided to her or her family may seek to hold the agency liable for its *failure* to provide those services.

Imposing liability for a state's failure to act under the Constitution, however, poses very serious difficulties. Judge Richard Posner observed that "the Constitution is a charter of negative rather than positive liberties. The men who wrote the Bill of Rights were not concerned that government might do too little for the people but that it might do too much to them." This view from the Seventh Circuit is gaining wider acceptance among members of the federal bench. In *DeShaney v. Winnebago County Department of Social Services*, the U.S. Supreme Court adopted this Posnerian stance in response to an attempt to hold a child welfare agency liable under the due process clause of the Fourteenth Amendment for its failure to protect four-year-old Joshua DeShaney from near-fatal abuse by his father. Despite the fact that the agency had been supervising the family for over a year and was aware of the serious risk of abuse faced by the child, the Court held that the agency "had no constitutional duty to protect Joshua against his father's violence."

This chapter examines the possibilities that remain after the *DeShaney* decision for imposing affirmative constitutional duties on child welfare agencies. The first part examines the *DeShaney* opinion itself and argues that most courts are reading the decision too broadly. A careful reading of the text indicates that the decision actually forecloses affirmative governmental duties in a smaller range of cases than most courts seem to have assumed. Turning then to the implications of *DeShaney* regarding the liability of child welfare agencies for abuse and neglect of children in foster care, I argue for an interpretation of the opinion that will foreclose such liability in fewer instances. The next section discusses a number of possible factual situations, other than abuse and neglect in foster care, that might escape the *DeShaney* bar and support a finding of an affirmative duty to protect on the part of child welfare agencies. I then consider the potential scope of affirmative constitutional duties beyond a duty of protection that may be imposed on agencies, such as a duty to provide the substantive services necessary to reunite foster children with their natural parents. The final section briefly discusses other constitutional arguments left untouched by *DeShaney* that may also be used to advocate the imposition of affirmative duties on child welfare agencies.

The *DeShaney* Case

The Facts

On March 8, 1984, four-year-old Joshua DeShaney was beaten so severely by his father that half of his brain was destroyed.[13] As a result, Joshua is now permanently brain-damaged and profoundly retarded and is expected to remain institutionalized for the rest of his life. A medical examination indicated that this was not the first time that Joshua was seriously injured by his father's blows. Scars of varying ages were found all over his body, and a neurosurgeon's examination revealed evidence of previous traumatic head injury.

The preceding year Joshua had been taken to the emergency room with suspicious injuries, and the Winnebago County Department of Social Services (DSS) had arranged for the hospital to hold him for several days while it investigated his case. The result of that investigation was to release Joshua back to his father because of insufficient evidence, despite the fact that abuse was strongly suspected. The DSS's petition against the father was subsequently dismissed from court without a hearing, but during the following year DSS continued to monitor the family. Although there were repeated signs of abuse, including several more visits to the emergency room with suspicious injuries, the DSS social worker assigned to the case took no action except to visit the family sporadically—no more than once a month—and during two of these visits she did not actually see the child. It was clear, however, that she believed Joshua to be at serious risk, since afterward she said to his mother, "I just knew the phone would ring someday and Joshua would be dead."

Joshua, through his guardian ad litem and his mother, brought suit under 42 U.S.C. § 1983 against the Winnebago County Department of Social Services, the caseworker assigned to the case, and her supervisor, alleging that their failure to take action to protect Joshua constituted a deprivation of his liberty without due process of law in violation of the Fourteenth Amendment. The district court granted summary judgment in favor of the defendants, and that ruling was affirmed by the Seventh Circuit and then by the Supreme Court. The Supreme Court, in an opinion by Chief Justice Rehnquist, focused on the issue of duty, holding that the due process clause did not impose an affirmative duty on the state to protect Joshua from his father's violence. "The Clause is phrased as a limitation on the State's power to act, not as a guarantee of certain minimal levels of safety and security."[14]

Arguing for a Constitutional Duty: The Special Relationship Theory

It is well established that the Constitution generally does not impose duties on the state to provide care or protection to its citizens.[15] The *DeShaney* plaintiffs, however, argued that this case involved a special circumstance in which the state did have a constitutional duty to act by virtue of the "special relationship" that existed between the state and Joshua. The defendants were specifically aware of the particular danger faced by Joshua: They "proclaimed, by word and by deed, [their] intention to protect him against that danger"[16] and actually undertook to so protect him. Moreover, the defendants were specifically charged under Wisconsin law with the responsibility of protecting children from abuse. For these reasons, the plaintiffs claimed, the defendants had a special relationship with Joshua, which imposed on them a special constitutional duty to protect him that they did not owe to the public at large.[17]

At the time the case was argued, this special relationship theory had been endorsed by the Third and Fourth Circuits in cases similar to *DeShaney*. *Estate of Bailey v. County of York*[18] involved a five-year-old girl who was beaten to death by her mother or her mother's paramour while the family was under the supervision of the county child welfare agency. The Third Circuit held that the facts alleged—that the agency was specifically aware of the child's plight and had in the past temporarily removed her from her mother's custody because of suspected abuse—were sufficient to establish a special relationship between the agency and the child, such that the agency could be found constitutionally liable for its failure to protect her. The Third Circuit relied heavily on a recent Fourth Circuit case, *Jensen v. Conrad*,[19] which had dismissed a similar claim on immunity grounds but suggested in dicta that a special relationship could exist under such facts.

This concept of a special relationship triggering an affirmative duty to act has been borrowed directly from common law tort doctrine, which shares with constitutional law a sharp distinction between action and inaction. Tort law imposes liability on parties for their "misfeasance" or affirmative acts that cause injury to others, but not for their "nonfeasance" or failure to protect or help another person.[20] When, however, a "special relationship" between the parties exists, there is an exception to this rule, and the defendant may be held liable for failing to act in aid of another.[21]

The Relevance of Common Law Tort Doctrine

Although Joshua DeShaney's claim could be described as a "constitutional tort," it is clear that common law tort doctrine is not controlling in such a case.[22] Just as negligently inflicted injury does not rise to the level of a constitutional deprivation under the Supreme Court's holding in *Daniels v. Williams*,[23] there is no reason to assume that all of the duties imposed by common law under the special relationship doctrine are also imposed on government officials by the Constitution. Because constitutional torts impose liability on government rather than private persons, the policy considerations involved are clearly different. Additionally, constitutional torts must be anchored in the Constitution, which generally is read to impose limits on government action rather than inaction.[24] In fact, the federal courts generally have been unwilling to expand constitutional liability for government officials' failure to act as far as the common law has expanded liability for nonfeasance under the "special relationship" doctrine.[25]

Still, with an understanding that the common law is not controlling, it is helpful to look to the original common law definition of "special relationship" in analyzing the attempts that have been made to import this theory into constitutional law. Tort law enumerates four basic types of special relationships: (1) that which arises when the defendant acts affirmatively to cause the peril faced by the plaintiff; (2) that which arises when the defendant undertakes to rescue the plaintiff; (3) that dependent upon the status of the parties (e.g., parent and child, landlord and tenant); and (4) that which arises when there is a contract between the parties.[26]

The plaintiffs in *DeShaney* argued that a special relationship of the second and/or third types made the defendants liable for their inaction.[27] Thus, the DSS had a special relationship with Joshua both because it had already undertaken to rescue him through its prior involvement with his family and because of its status as the child protective agency that was monitoring his situation. While the Supreme Court clearly rejected these proffered definitions of a special relationship, it did not reject altogether a special relationship doctrine for constitutional torts. Indeed, the Court could not have done so without breaking with a well-established line of precedent imposing a constitutional duty on government officials to protect prisoners and the institutionalized mentally disabled. I argue that the Supreme Court's analysis in *DeShaney* essentially limited the special relationship theory as applied to constitutional torts to situations in which the peril is caused by the defendant (type 1 above). Thus the Court's holding that the state was under no constitutional duty to protect Joshua was based on its finding that the state had not created the danger that he faced.

Precedent for a Special Relationship in Constitutional Torts

The Duty to Those in State Custody

Prior to *DeShaney*, the Supreme Court had already found government officials constitutionally liable for their failure to act in certain circumstances. In *Estelle v. Gamble*,[28] the Court held that prison officials' failure to provide medical treatment to prisoners could be a constitutional violation actionable under section 1983. Although this decision rested on the cruel and unusual punishment clause of the

Eighth Amendment, the principle was later extended to institutional settings outside the prison context under the due process clause of the Fourteenth Amendment. *Youngberg v. Romeo*[29] established an affirmative duty on the part of state officials to provide mentally retarded persons who are involuntarily committed to state institutions with reasonable safety, freedom from unnecessary restraint, and the training necessary to ensure such safety and freedom.

In the language of tort doctrine, these cases stand for the proposition that in certain circumstances a "special relationship" exists between the state and the individual such that the Constitution imposes on the state an affirmative duty to act to provide care and/or protection to the individual.[30] The plaintiffs in *DeShaney* relied heavily on *Estelle* and *Youngberg* in their argument, and the Court in ruling against them was forced to distinguish these cases. Most of the *DeShaney* opinion, in fact, is devoted to defining the boundaries of *Youngberg* and *Estelle* so as to place *DeShaney* clearly outside those boundaries. It is important to look closely at how the Court made this distinction in order to understand exactly where the contours of the special relationship theory now lie.

While the Court in *DeShaney* clearly rejected the plaintiffs' argument that a special relationship was established by the state's undertaking to rescue Joshua (type 2) or by the defendant's status as a child protection agency (type 3), a superficial reading of *DeShaney* suggests that the Court has set up another status-based test for special relationship, asking whether or not the plaintiff is in the custody of the state. Under this reading, the Court simply found that the special relationship established in *Youngberg* and *Estelle* need not apply to *DeShaney*, since the plaintiffs in those cases were in state custody and Joshua DeShaney was not. This is in fact how most lower courts have been reading the decision.[31] I argue, however, that the opinion can be more accurately and usefully read as defining a special relationship of type 1. Where the state has played some role in creating the peril faced by the plaintiff, then a special relationship exists such that the state has a duty to act. Situations where the state has taken an individual into custody fit within this definition but constitute only a subset of all possible special relationships.

The Special Relationship Duty
Outside the Custody Context

A state-created danger theory of special relationship in constitutional torts is not new. An earlier line of lower federal court decisions, originating in the Seventh Circuit, has found a constitutional state duty to act in situations where the state created the danger:

> If the state puts a man in a position of danger from private persons and then fails to protect him, it will not be heard to say that its role was merely passive; it is as much an active tortfeasor as if it had thrown him into a snake pit.[32]

In *Byrd v. Brishke*,[33] the Seventh Circuit held that police officers could be liable under section 1983 for their failure to protect a person beaten by other police officers in their presence. In *White v. Rochford*,[34] the court held that police officers who arrested the guardian of three children for drag racing, and then left the children alone in an abandoned automobile along the side of a highway on a cold evening, could be found liable under section 1983 for their failure to protect the children. These decisions have been widely followed in other circuits.[35] They were not mentioned by the Court in *DeShaney*[36] and apparently survive that decision, even though these cases effectively create a constitutional special relationship duty in situations that do not involve state custody.[37]

The Text of the Opinion

A textual examination of the *DeShaney* opinion demonstrates that the Court's analysis actually rested on the state-created danger definition of special relationship, rather than a status-based custody test, even though certain language in the opinion, taken alone, seems to point in the direction of a simple custody test. Thus, after discussing *Estelle* and *Youngberg*, the Court stated that "[these cases] stand only for the proposition that when the State takes a person into its custody and holds him there against his will, the Constitution imposes upon it a corresponding duty to assume some responsibility for his safety and general well-being."[38] However, in the following sentence the Court further refined its characterization of *Estelle* and *Youngberg*, emphasizing not the custodial status of the state's relationship with the individual, but the action taken by the state that placed the individual in a dangerous situation.[39]

> The rationale for this principle is simple enough: when the State by the *affirmative exercise of its power* so restrains an individual's liberty that it renders him unable to care for himself, and at the same time fails to provide for his basic human needs . . . it transgresses the substantive limits on state action set by the Eighth Amendment and the Due Process Clause.[40]

Chief Justice Rehnquist continued by stating, "[I]t is the state's *affirmative act* of restraining the individual's freedom to act on his own behalf . . . which is the 'deprivation of liberty' triggering the protections of the Due Process Clause."[41] Thus, according to Chief Justice Rehnquist, in *Youngberg* and *Estelle* it was the state's act of taking the plaintiff into state custody that set the stage for the ensuing injury. The special relationship analysis in these cases turns not simply on whether the plaintiffs were in state custody, but also on whether the state's act in taking them into custody created the danger. In *DeShaney*, on the other hand, at least in Chief Justice Rehnquist's eyes, the state "played no part in [the] creation [of the dangers that Joshua faced],"[42] and thus there was no special relationship.

The state-created danger test seems to turn, at least partly, on a causal analysis. In order to find an affirmative duty arising from a special relationship, we must be able to point to some affirmative action by the state that is a but-for cause of the injury.[43] Thus, Nicholas Romeo would not have been injured but for the fact that the state committed him to Pennhurst,[44] and a prisoner who was denied medical treatment would presumably have had that treatment but for the fact that she was incarcerated by the state.[45] The "snake pit" line of cases also follow this analysis. Thus, in *White v. Rochford*,[46] the children would not have been left alone on the side of the highway but for the action of the police in arresting their custodian.[47]

Moreover, it is clear that the state's danger-creating act must involve some element of involuntary submission by the individual to the state's power or authority.[48] The *DeShaney* opinion repeatedly emphasized the involuntary nature of the plaintiff's confinement in both *Estelle* and *Youngberg* and the fact that the state had acted coercively in those cases, "restrain[ing] an individual's liberty,"[49] imposing "limitation . . . on his freedom to act on his own behalf,"[50] and "hold[ing] him [in custody] against his will."[51]

Thus, the special relationship test that emerges from *DeShaney* is not simply whether the plaintiff is in state custody. The test asks whether some affirmative state action, taken without the plaintiff's consent, has sufficiently altered the plaintiff's situation such that the action can be said to be a but-for cause of her injury.[52] Certainly, whenever the plaintiff is involuntarily in state custody, it is easy to show that a special relationship exists, but involuntary custody is not the litmus test. Such cases are only a subset of the special relationship cases that survive the *DeShaney* opinion, and there can also be noncustodial situations that fit within the special relationship doctrine.[53]

Majority Versus Dissent: What Constitutes a "State-Created Danger"?

Under this view of the special relationship standard, the dispute between the majority and the dissenters in *DeShaney* appears to be less over which test to apply than over how to apply it. In his dissent, Justice Brennan also articulated a state-created danger standard for special relationships. While Chief Justice Rehnquist, however, characterized the affirmative state action necessary to trigger a special relationship as "restraining the individual's freedom to act on his own behalf," Justice Brennan recognized that such a standard is meaningless in this situation, in which Joshua, a four-year-old child, never had the ability to act on his own behalf at all. This standard is equally inadequate to explain *Youngberg*:

> [T]he Court's exclusive attention to State-imposed restraints of "the individual's freedom to act on his own behalf" . . . suggests that it was the State that rendered Romeo unable to care for himself, whereas in fact—with an I.Q. of between 8 and 10, and the mental capacity of an 18-month-old child . . . [—] he had been quite incapable of taking care of himself long before the State stepped into his life. Thus, the fact of hospitalization was critical in *Youngberg* not because it rendered Romeo helpless to help himself, but because it separated him from other sources of aid that, we held, the State was obligated to replace.[54]

The dissent agreed with the majority that a special relationship exists when the state affirmatively acts without the individual's consent, thereby rendering her more vulnerable and creating the danger she faces. In *Youngberg* and *De-Shaney*, however, cases in which the individual was never capable of acting on his own behalf, the question whether the state had restrained the individual's freedom to act on his own behalf should have been translated into the question whether the state had cut off other private sources of aid to the individual. The dissent further argued that, on the facts of this case, the defendants' actions did actively cut off other sources of aid to Joshua. By establishing the DSS as the sole agency to which all reports of child abuse are made (by private and public persons), and by according the agency the responsibility to investigate reports and take action to protect children, the state "relieved ordinary citizens and government bodies other than the Department of any sense of obligation to do anything more than report their suspicions of child abuse to DSS. If DSS ignores or dismisses these suspicions, no one will step in to fill the gap."[55]

While the majority clearly held that the state did not create the dangers faced by Joshua, such a holding may have been based on a specific factual conclusion that the state did not, in this instance, cut off other sources of aid to Joshua, or it may have been based on a broader legal holding that cutting off other sources of aid does not, in any instance, constitute an act sufficiently harmful to meet the state-created danger standard. Chief Justice Rehnquist's repeated insistence that the state did not "do *anything* to render [Joshua] *any* more vulnerable to [the danger],"[56] and that "it placed him in *no worse position* than that in which he would have been had it not acted at all,"[57] points toward a factual holding that, in this particular situation, the state did not cut off other sources of aid. Such an interpretation leaves open the possibility that the dissent's argument could be adopted in a later case.[58]

It is apparent that the special relationship theory endorsed by the Supreme Court in *DeShaney* does not turn on whether the plaintiff is in state custody at the time of her injury. Instead, after *DeShaney*, a special relationship exists whenever the state acts to create the danger faced by the plaintiff, and the plaintiff is involuntarily subjected to such danger. While the Court in *DeShaney* rejected the argument that the state's action in cutting off other sources of aid to Joshua established a special relationship with him, that holding may be read as limited to the specific facts of the case. Thus, the opinion does not foreclose the possibility that "cutting off other sources of aid" might establish a special relationship under a different set of facts.

The Implications of *DeShaney* for Children Abused in Foster Care

How would the special relationship analysis have differed if Joshua had been beaten while in foster care rather than in the custody of his natural father? The Supreme Court left this question open in the *DeShaney* opinion.[59] Eleven days after *DeShaney* was decided, the Court again declined to consider this question by denying certiorari in *Taylor ex rel. Walker v. Ledbetter*.[60] The Eleventh Circuit in *Taylor* held that the state did owe a special relationship duty, under the due process clause, to a child abused in foster care.

At the time *DeShaney* and *Taylor* reached the Supreme Court, only a handful of courts had considered whether a special relationship exists between the state and foster children. In 1976, two decisions of the Southern District of New York[61] rejected the analogy of foster care to incarceration and found no special relationship duty to exist. "[T]he state's action in taking the child plaintiffs into foster care, whether with an institution or foster parent, is not a deprivation of liberty. The state has merely provided a home for them in substitution for the one the parents failed to provide."[62] Subsequent cases, however, have found a substantive due process duty to protect children in foster care. In 1979, the Southern District of New York held that "[a] child who is in the custody of the state and placed in foster care has a constitutional right to at least humane custodial care."[63] In 1981, the Second Circuit held that the foster care situation was controlled by *Estelle*, and that the child welfare agency therefore had an affirmative duty to protect the plaintiff from sexual abuse in foster care.[64] Finally, in 1985, the Northern District of Illinois held that under *Youngberg*, the state had a duty to protect a foster child from attacks by other foster children.[65]

The *DeShaney* opinion leaves the foster child–plaintiff with two major problems. First, courts are interpreting *DeShaney* to create a simple custody test for special relationship.[66] This test not only derives from an imprecise reading of the *DeShaney* opinion but is unworkable in practice, since it leaves unresolved the ambiguity inherent in the term "custody." Such a test allows the state to argue in virtually all cases that the child is not in its actual custody because the foster parent is a private party over whom the state has limited control.[67] Second, *DeShaney* appears to require the plaintiff to be involuntarily subjected to state action in order for a special relationship to be established. The lower courts have interpreted this requirement to mean that when a child's foster care placement is initially authorized by a "voluntary placement agreement" signed by the parent (as is most often the case),[68] this involuntariness requirement is not met, and there is no special relationship.

Problems Presented by the Custody Test

The meaning of the word "custody" varies significantly depending upon the context in which it is used. Asking whether someone is in "custody" in a *Miranda* case is entirely different from asking whether a child is in "custody" in the context of a domestic relations dispute. "Custody" does not in and of itself clearly designate a specific set of parameters for purposes of a special relationship test.

The word's meaning is especially ambiguous in the foster care context, in which the rights and responsibilities attendant to custody may be shared among a number of entities and individuals.[69] State child welfare agencies retain "legal custody" of foster children in that the court order permitting the placement of the child in foster care normally designates the agency as the custodian. The state agency makes the initial decision to petition the court for placement of the child, along with the subsequent decision as to where to place her.[70] The agency also retains control over decisions pertaining to moving the child from one foster home to another, visiting arrangements with the natural parents, and returning the child to them.[71]

In many instances the state agency contracts with a private foster care agency, which in turn contracts with the foster parents. The private agency decides which foster family will receive the child. The private agency usually employs a social worker who has regular contact with the foster family and exercises some supervisory authority over day-to-day decisions. Her role may overlap substantially with that of the state agency social worker, and the manner in which responsibility is divided between the two agencies may vary significantly from case to case. One or both social workers might be involved in dealing with the child's school, arranging psychological testing and/or treatment, and organizing visits with the natural parents, in addition to a range of other issues relating to the child's care. Although private agencies are not formally parties to dependency proceedings, their social workers are frequently included in case plan meetings and pretrial negotiations and may exert substantial influence over decisions made by the state agency and the court as to parental visitation and the ultimate return of the child.

The foster parent, of course, has physical custody and exercises authority over most of the day-to-day details of the child's life. The natural parents, however, retain substantial rights over a child placed in foster care, including at a minimum the right to make major medical decisions, the right to be consulted before the child is moved, and the right to regular visitation.[72]

Thus, responsibility and decision-making authority with regard to a foster child may frequently be shared among three or four parties. The word "custody" or "custodian," without a more specific definition, is of little value in determining the rights and duties of these various parties.

Two recent Third Circuit opinions, interpreting *DeShaney*'s "custody" test, demonstrate how malleable the term really is. In *Stoneking v. Bradford Area School District*,[73] the court noted that students required by state law to attend public school could be viewed as being in the "functional custody" of the state while at school, such that a special relationship could be held to exist consistent with *DeShaney*.[74] In *Horton v. Flenory*,[75] the plaintiff was beaten to death by a private club owner who was purportedly questioning the plaintiff about a crime. Since the beating occurred with the knowledge and acquiescence of the police, the court held that the plaintiff was in constructive state custody.[76]

While in these cases the meaning of the word "custody" was broadly interpreted to the benefit of the plaintiffs, the term may just as easily be narrowly construed to the detriment of plaintiffs seeking the protection of the state. In *Milburn v. Anne Arundel County Department of Social Services*,[77] the Fourth Circuit dismissed a claim by a child abused in foster care on the grounds that the foster parent was not a state actor.[78] This line of reasoning assumes that "custody," for purposes of special relationship analysis, refers only to the type of physical custody exercised by the foster parent. Assuming that only the foster parents could be said to have "custody" of the child, the court went on to require that the foster parents be state actors in order to be subject to the Fourteenth Amendment.

Milburn involved a child who allegedly suffered repeated serious physical abuse by his foster parents over a period of two years. During that time, the Department of Social Services, which had placed the child in the foster home, took no action to remove him despite reports of suspected abuse from the hospitals where the boy was treated. The child sued the foster parents, the two hospitals, the county, the Department of Social Services, and employees thereof under section 1983, alleging deprivation of his rights under the First, Fourth, Fifth, Ninth, and Fourteenth Amendments.

In upholding the dismissal of the complaint, the Fourth Circuit said that the Supreme Court's decision in *DeShaney* was dispositive and that the facts of *DeShaney* were virtually "indistinguishable" from this case. In the court's view, the child was not in the custody of the state when the injuries occurred, but in the custody of the foster parents, who were private parties in the same sense that Joshua DeShaney's father was a private party. Therefore, just as the state had no obligation to protect Joshua when he was in the custody of his father, it had no duty to protect a child in the custody of private citizens who happened to be foster parents.

Rather than looking to *Youngberg* and *Estelle* to determine what constitutes state custody for purposes of a special relationship (or to determine what constitutes a state-created danger), the court erroneously equated the question whether the plaintiff was in state custody for purposes of special relationship analysis with the question whether the custodian (foster parent) was a state actor and thus subject to the Fourteenth Amendment under *Burton v. Wilmington Parking Authority*[79] and *Jackson v. Metropolitan Edison Co.*[80]

These state action cases, discussed at length by the *Milburn* court, address an issue that is clearly distinct from the issue of a special relationship duty with which *DeShaney* deals. The state action cases ask whether the actions of the defendant can be fairly attributed to the state such that the defendant can be held to have violated the Fourteenth Amendment, which binds only the conduct of states, not private parties. *DeShaney*, on the other hand, asked whether the defendant child welfare agency, which was clearly an arm of the state, could be held to have deprived someone of life, liberty, or property by its failure to protect that person from the acts of a private party. The two inquiries are similar in that they both ask when the state should be held responsible for the actions of a private party, but they are doctrinally distinct. In the language of the due process clause, the special relationship inquiry asks: Has the state *deprived* a person of life, liberty, or property? The state action inquiry asks: Was it the *state* that deprived a person of life, liberty, or property?[81]

The Fourth Circuit's discussion of whether the foster parents were state actors was relevant to the plaintiff's claims against the foster parents themselves.[82] Such a state action inquiry could also be relevant to claims against a county and its department of social services, but only insofar as such claims were made under *Monell v. Department of Social Services*,[83] alleging that a policy or custom of the county caused the foster parents to violate the child's rights.[84] To the extent, however, that the plaintiff was proceeding under a *DeShaney*-type special relationship theory, the question whether the foster parents were state actors was irrelevant to the question of the liability of the DSS and its social workers for failing to protect the child from abuse by his foster parents.[85] Just as the other patients who attacked plaintiff Nicholas Romeo were clearly not state actors in *Youngberg*, those who inflicted injury on Charles Milburn need not have been state actors in order for the state to be held liable for his injury under a special relationship theory.[86]

Thus, the ambiguity inherent in the term "custody" raises significant problems when one is attempting to apply such a test to a specific fact situation. Analyzing the state's duty toward foster children through a state-created danger test for special relationship raises less ambiguity as to meaning and would result in more consistent treatment of foster care cases. Under a state-created danger test, the analogy to *Youngberg* and *Estelle* is fairly straightforward. Just as inmate Gamble would not have been unable to obtain medical care but for the state having incarcerated him, and patient Romeo would not have been injured by other patients at Pennhurst but for the state having committed him, a foster child who suffers abuse by her foster parents clearly would not have suffered such abuse but for the state's affirmative act of placing her in the foster home. The second prong of the *DeShaney* special relationship test, however—the requirement that the plaintiff have been involuntarily subjected to state action—raises an additional set of problems for the foster child–plaintiff, to which we now turn.

The Involuntariness Requirement as Applied to Children

Whether we read *DeShaney* as establishing a custody test or a state-created danger test, the case appears to require some element of involuntary submission by the individual to state power or authority in order to establish a special relationship. *Youngberg* also included this notion. Justice Powell repeatedly noted throughout that opinion that Romeo had been "involuntarily" committed to the institution,[87] although there was no discussion as to what the concept of "involuntary" might mean in reference to someone who is severely mentally retarded. Similarly, the "snake pit" line of cases, establishing a special relationship based on state-created danger, all involve coercive action by the state.

Determining whether a young child or an infant has consented to some action by the state is clearly problematic. Children who are preverbal cannot express their consent or nonconsent. Even decisions to place older children are not usually based on the child's opinion.[88] Most courts construing the special relationship theory in the context of foster care translate this question into whether or not the child was "voluntarily placed" in foster care, meaning whether or not the parents signed an agreement consenting to the placement.[89] Parents do act as proxy for their children in making most decisions about their welfare. Arguably, we should therefore view the parent's signing of a voluntary placement agreement as consent by both parent *and* child to the state's action. For several reasons, however, this is a flawed analysis.

First, the *Youngberg* case itself, which serves as our central model of a special relationship created by involuntary institutionalization, involved a mother who essentially "voluntarily placed" her child in state care. Romeo's mother petitioned the court asking that he be admitted to a state institution for the mentally retarded because she was unable to care for or control him. Romeo, at age thirty-three, had the mental capacity of an eighteen-month-old child and was incapable of consenting on his own behalf. Therefore, pursuant to state law, a commitment hearing was held, and he was "involuntarily committed" to Pennhurst State Hospital. Thus, *Youngberg*, on its facts, supports the idea that a placement consented to by a parent can establish a special relationship.

Second, parents cannot generally act as a proxy for their children in making decisions that affect the children's constitutional rights, such as the fundamental right to an abortion,[90] the right to procedural due process,[91] or, in certain circumstances, the right to counsel.[92] It would be inconsistent with this principle to hold that in this instance a parent's consent on behalf of a child causes the child to lose constitutional rights she would otherwise possess.

Finally, even if consent to placement by the parent were sufficient to vitiate a special relationship, it is not at all clear that a parent's signature on a voluntary placement agreement reliably indicates that the placement was in fact voluntary. Because middle- and upper-class parents have the resources to arrange other alternatives for the care of their children in the face of crisis, those who place their children in state-run foster care are usually poor, uneducated, and without the benefit of legal counsel when they sign such agreements.[93] The extent to which such a parent at a time of crisis may be subtly coerced or intimidated by a social worker, backed by the authority of the state, who confidently pronounces placement to be "in the best interests of the child" is impossible to measure.

Coercion may even take more overt forms. The social worker may threaten the parent with a longer placement or even permanent removal of the child through court intervention if she does not "cooperate" by signing the agreement.[94] Even if the social worker is more honest and explains to the parent that she will be given a chance to convince a judge that she should be able to keep her child, many parents may consider their chances of winning a court case against a government agency to be slim at best and will adopt a conciliatory stance.[95] Thus, even putting aside the question of the child's consent, "voluntary" foster care placement may in fact constitute coercive state action against the parent.

Moreover, voluntary placement agreements are typically valid for only thirty days.[96] In order to keep a child in foster care beyond this initial period, the agency must obtain judicial approval of the agreement.[97] At this point the placement is clearly authorized by the coercive power of the state. Once such an order is entered, the parent may no longer regain custody of her child merely by revoking her consent to placement. Further, while the court orders are frequently entered with the "agreement" of the parents, such an agreement is often the result of a Hobson's choice. It is analogous to a criminal defendant's voluntary plea of guilty. The plea is "a bargain with the [state] for what is seen as the 'least bad' option."[98] Certainly, a prisoner who enters state custody by such a plea is not considered to be voluntarily incarcerated and therefore entitled to fewer constitutional protections.

While most of the courts that have considered the issue so far have found a special relationship to exist between the state and foster children,[99] those holdings are on shaky ground. First, given the dominant reading of *DeShaney* as creating a custody test for a special relationship, many courts will be particularly prone to use an erroneous analysis, similar to that of the Fourth Circuit in *Milburn*. Second, given the significance accorded to voluntary placement agreements by the courts, relief under this theory is, in practical terms, unavailable to most foster children. A careful analysis of the *DeShaney* holding, as well as informed consideration of the special situation of children and how voluntary placements work in practice, however, should lead courts to expand the special relationship doctrine to all children in foster care.

Regarding the first prong of the special relationship test, courts should recognize that simply asking whether or not the plaintiff is in state custody will not yield any clear answers in the foster care context, and additionally that such is not the appropriate test under *DeShaney* anyway. Asking instead whether the state created the danger faced by the foster child by its affirmative act of placing her in foster care, in the same sense that the state created the danger faced by the plaintiffs in *Estelle* and *Youngberg* by placing them in institutions, leads to a clearer analysis and follows more accurately the Supreme Court's analysis in *DeShaney*.

Regarding the second prong of the special relationship test—whether the state acted without the plaintiff's consent—courts should consider that the signing of a voluntary placement agreement may not in practice signify the consent of the child or the parent. Moreover, even if a placement is in fact voluntary on the part of the parent, *Youngberg* teaches us that such action by the parent is not enough to vitiate the state's special relationship with the child.

Thus, children abused in foster care should in virtually all cases meet the requirements for a special relationship with the state. They have been placed in foster care by the state, almost always without their consent, and but for this placement, injury at the hands of their foster parents would not have occurred.

Extending the Right to Safety Beyond Foster Care

After *DeShaney*, it appears that agency supervision in the form of monthly visits by a social worker to the parents' home is not sufficient to create an affirmative duty of protection toward a child, while placing and maintaining a child in foster care may create such a duty. This simple formula does not, however, address the many other child welfare situations that fall somewhere in between these two extremes. Agency intervention takes many forms, some of which are more intensive than monthly home visits but not as extreme as removal. Simply because the minimal intervention in *DeShaney* was held not to create a special relationship, it does not necessarily follow that other forms of agency intervention, short of placement in foster care, will not rise to the level necessary to create a special relationship.

The following are all fact patterns that may arise in this gray area between supervision and foster care, and thus present potential due process claims that are not necessarily foreclosed by *DeShaney*:

- The agency allows a parent to visit her child at the foster home. During one of these visits, the parent severely abuses the child.
- A child in foster care is sent home for an overnight visit with her parents, during which they severely abuse her.
- After a child has been in foster care for two years, the agency decides it is safe to send her home to her parents. Shortly after being returned home, she is severely abused.[100]
- After a child has been in foster care for two years, the agency sends her home but retains legal custody. After being returned home, she is severely abused.
- The agency removes a child from her home and places her temporarily with relatives, during which time the agency retains court-authorized supervision (or legal custody) over the child. The child is subsequently severely abused in the relatives' home.[101]
- As an alternative to placing the children of a mother and father who are mentally retarded in foster care, the agency engages in a program of intensive supervision. Social workers are at the home forty hours a week helping the parents with parenting and homemaking skills. After a year of such supervision, the children are found to have been severely abused.[102]

Applying the state-created danger test to these fact patterns means asking whether the injury would have occurred but for the state's intervention. In the first example, one might be tempted to conclude that if the parent beat the child during the visit, she probably would have done the same had the child been left at home. But what if the parent had never beaten the child before? What if the child was taken away not because of parental abuse but because the parent was homeless and unable to care for the child? What if the parent beat the child because the stress and frustration of not being able to find a home, and being told by judges and social workers that she could not care for her own child, had pushed her to the breaking point? What if she beat the child out of fear and frustration at seeing her own child not respond to or obey her and hearing her call a stranger "Mommy"?[103] If these are the causes of the parent's dysfunction, it becomes much more difficult to view the state's intrusion into the family as completely unrelated to the injury. At some point along this continuum, the state's intervention becomes so substantial that it is no longer possible simply to subtract the state from the equation and honestly say what would have happened without it.

By bringing these "gray area" right-to-protection lawsuits in situations where the effect of the agency's intervention is more pronounced than it was in *DeShaney*, advocates may encourage the courts to consider the continuum that exists between supervision and foster care, and thus prevent the doctrine in this area from evolving into a simplistic bright-line rule that foster care creates a special relationship and supervision does not.

Affirmative Duties Beyond Ensuring Physical Safety

When there is a special relationship, do child welfare agencies have any affirmative duties beyond ensuring physical safety? A number of courts have found that the substantive due process cause of action for failure to protect against physical injury extends to emotional injury as well.[104] Perhaps more significantly, however, two courts have recently been willing to extend the special relationship duty of the state beyond protection to an affirmative duty to assist children in foster care in exercising fundamental constitutional rights such as their right to family integrity and association.

The Duty to Assist in the Exercise of Constitutional Rights

In *Lipscomb v. Simmons*, three foster children challenged Oregon's foster care funding scheme, under which financial assistance was provided only to children who were placed with foster parents who were not related to them. Under this scheme, two of the plaintiffs lived with strangers because their relatives, though willing to care for them, were financially unable to meet the children's needs. The third was in danger of having to leave her aunt and uncle's home because they could not receive foster care payments. The Ninth Circuit held that the state had a special relationship duty toward children in foster care and that this duty encompassed an obligation not only to ensure their safety but also to "assist the children to exercise their constitutional rights."[105] In this instance, therefore, the state was required to fund foster care placements with relatives so as to enable the children to exercise their "constitutionally protected liberty interest in choosing to live with family members."[106]

The court relied primarily on prison cases that held that prison officials have an affirmative duty to assist prisoners in the exercise of their right to abortion,[107] the observance of religious dietary laws,[108] and access to the courts.[109] It concluded that "[t]he State's obligation to ensure that children in its custody are able to exercise their constitutional rights is even greater than its responsibility toward prisoners," since foster children are in the state's custody not because of their own misdeeds but "solely because they were the victims of abuse by others."[110]

In *Aristotle P. v. Johnson*,[111] Judge Williams of the Northern District of Illinois reached a similar conclusion, holding that under the due process clause the state has an affirmative duty to assist foster children in exercising their right to family association by providing visits with siblings who are separately placed.

While these two cases effected fairly narrow and specific changes in the respective state child welfare systems, the principle articulated, if followed, could lead to much broader claims for services on behalf of foster children and their families. If the state must fund placements with relatives and provide visitation with siblings, it logically follows that its duty to assist foster children in exercising this constitutional right to family association also embraces an obligation to ensure the provision of substantive services (such as housing, day care, or drug treatment) that are necessary to reunite foster children with their parents.

Three months prior to *Lipscomb* and *Aristotle P.*, such a claim brought by foster children seeking reunification services was rejected by the Northern District of Illinois in *B.H. v. Johnson*.[112] Several months after *Lipscomb* and *Aristotle P.*, however, another Northern District of Illinois court held that the state's special relationship duty toward foster children *does* require the state to do more than ensure their physical safety. In this case, *Artist M. v. Johnson*,[113] the court found a due process obligation on the part of the state to ensure that caseworkers were promptly assigned to children in foster care.

Until very recently, the Adoption Assistance and Child Welfare Act of 1980[114] appeared to provide an alternative statutory cause of action for such suits seeking reunification services. It requires states receiving federal money under the act to make "reasonable efforts" to reunite foster children with their parents by providing appropriate services.[115] Ironically, it was in the *Artist M.* case itself that the Supreme Court recently held that no private cause of action is available to enforce the "reasonable efforts" provision of the act.[116] While it may still be possible to bring private enforcement actions under other sections of the act, which impose procedural requirements regarding, for example, the development and periodic review of case plans for each child,[117] the possibility of using the act to force agencies to provide substantive services to foster children and their families has now clearly been foreclosed. Perhaps in some cases the substantive due process theory endorsed in *Lipscomb*, *Aristotle P.*, and the district court's opinion in *Artist M.* can provide a viable alternative method to force child welfare agencies to provide reunification services.

Distinguishing the Duty to Provide from the Duty to Protect

A state's duty to protect individuals from private violence can be distinguished from its duty to provide care and services. *DeShaney* clearly involved the former, as do the foster care abuse cases. *Estelle*, however, which established a duty to provide medical care, falls into the latter category, as do *Lipscomb* and *Aristotle P. Youngberg* involved both protection (from the violence of other inmates) and care (adequate food, clothing, and training). Should these two duties be treated the same for purposes of special relationship analysis?

When an individual requests state protection, the harm from which she seeks protection comes from a clearly identifiable source other than the state. The source of Joshua's injuries, for example, was his father. When an individual requests care or services from the state, however, the source of the harm those services will alleviate is more abstract; it may be disease or poverty. To protect the first individual from actions of a third party, the state must inevitably restrain the liberty of the third party in some way. Protecting Joshua DeShaney, for instance, would have required interfering with his father's liberty interest in raising his child. Since such direct and active governmental interference with liberty is exactly what the due process clause most clearly proscribes, courts have reason to be particularly hesitant in imposing such a duty to protect.

Chief Justice Rehnquist expressed this hesitation in *DeShaney*:

> [I]t must also be said that had [the state] moved too soon to take custody of the son away from the father, [it] would likely have been met with charges of improperly intruding into the parent-child relationship, charges based on the same Due Process Clause that forms the basis for the present charge of failure to provide adequate protection.[118]

Thus, the duty of protection potentially sets two constitutional imperatives against each other: the liberty interest of the child to be free from harm and the liberty interest of the third party to be free from governmental interference.

A duty to provide care or services does not present this problem of conflicting constitutional mandates, since there is no identifiable source of harm. Provision of medical care to a prisoner or reunification services to a foster child does not require the state to impose restraints on a third party's liberty. This observation suggests that we should be more willing to impose a duty of care on the state than a duty of protection, and that perhaps the special relationship test should be different in the two instances. Under this analysis, *DeShaney* is binding precedent only with regard to the duty of protection, and advocates asserting a duty to provide care or services are free to argue for a broader definition of a special relationship.[119]

Other Constitutional Arguments
Left Open by *DeShaney*

Other than the alternative of suing under state tort law,[120] which Chief Justice Rehnquist suggested would have been the most appropriate recourse for the plaintiffs in *DeShaney*, the opinion leaves open several other constitutional claims for plaintiffs seeking to impose affirmative duties on child welfare agencies. Depending on the facts involved, children injured as a result of agency inaction may be able to allege violations of their equal protection or procedural due process rights.

First, as the Court pointed out, a plaintiff who is a member of a disfavored minority may be able to make a claim under the equal protection clause that she was selectively denied protective services because of her disfavored status.[121] Additionally, even plaintiffs who are not members of a suspect class may in some instances be able to argue that they have been subject to arbitrary and capricious governmental action in violation of the equal protection clause. It is well established that governmental action that arbitrarily singles out individuals and treats them less favorably than others similarly situated violates the equal protection clause under the minimum scrutiny of the rational basis standard.[122]

It is possible that this kind of equal protection argument could be made in a *DeShaney*-type situation. Admittedly, in most child protection cases such minimum scrutiny would be easy for the state to overcome; if the agency could make any reasonable assertion that the decision to ignore or give less attention to a case was based on a social worker's judgment, the claim would fail. The best factual situation for the assertion of such a claim, therefore, would be one in which the plaintiff's case "fell through the cracks" and was ignored purely because of administrative error, rather than one that received consideration by a social worker. Where it is possible to demonstrate that other, similarly situated children have received greater protection and that the source of the disparate treatment is entirely arbitrary, this type of equal protection claim may lie even in the absence of invidious discrimination.

In *Logan v. Zimmerman Brush Co.*,[123] the Supreme Court indicated that this kind of arbitrary administrative action taken pursuant to a facially neutral law could constitute an equal protection violation. That case involved a plaintiff who filed a complaint before the Illinois Fair Employment Practices Commission. Under the state statute, the commission had 120 days after the filing of the complaint to convene a fact-finding conference. Because the commission, through inadvertence, failed to schedule the conference within the specified time limit, the plaintiff's claim was dropped. The Supreme Court ruled in favor of the plaintiff on procedural due process grounds, but a majority of the Court also indicated in dicta that the state's action violated the equal protection clause. Although the statute on its face did not make explicit classifications,[124] in effect it operated to divide claimants into two categories: those whose claims were processed within 120 days and those whose claims were not. The Court majority found that this distinction did not bear a rational relationship to any legitimate governmental objective. Although there was no creation of a suspect class that would have triggered strict scrutiny, this arbitrary division of claimants violated equal protection even under the less stringent rational basis standard.

Another argument made by the *DeShaney* plaintiffs but not considered by the Court[125] was that the Wisconsin child protection statutes gave Joshua an entitlement to child protective services subject to procedural due process protections.

Under *Board of Regents v. Roth*,[126] benefits conferred by state statute may, depending on the statutory language, constitute an individual entitlement, which is considered to be a property interest and thus not subject to restriction by the state without due process of law.[127] In order for a statutorily conferred benefit to be treated as a property interest, the statute must condition receipt of the benefit on the existence of certain facts that are ascertainable at a due process hearing. Where a statute leaves the issuance of benefits to the discretion of state officials, however, no property interest is created.

In *Taylor ex rel. Walker v. Ledbetter*,[128] the plaintiffs successfully brought such a claim, arguing that state statutes and regulations governing foster care in Georgia required child welfare officials to follow specific guidelines to ensure the well-being and safety of children in foster care. The Eleventh Circuit held that the statutory scheme in Georgia created an entitlement to the state's protection from harm. Thus, the state's withholding of such protection without procedural due process violated the Fourteenth Amendment. Similar procedural due process claims have been rejected, however, in two recent suits brought by foster children in the Northern District of Illinois,[129] and in a recent Seventh Circuit decision in a case with facts similar to those in *DeShaney*.[130] Since these holdings are rooted in the state law of Illinois, however, these cases do not preclude procedural due process claims in other jurisdictions.[131]

Conclusion

Lawsuits seeking to hold child protective agencies liable for their most egregious mistakes are an important tool for ensuring a minimally adequate level of competence among those whom we charge with the immeasurably important task of protecting our children. The *DeShaney* case has significantly reduced the possibility of bringing many such actions in federal court. If advocates and judges pay close attention to what was actually stated by the Supreme Court in *DeShaney*, however, that opinion need not foreclose relief under the due process clause in as many instances as some have assumed.

A number of decisions since *DeShaney* have already found a special relationship duty under the due process clause to protect foster children in some circumstances. Under a careful reading of *DeShaney*, with sensitivity to the special considerations surrounding children and the practical realities of foster care placement, the principle of these cases can be construed to cover all children in foster care. *DeShaney* may also leave room for this duty to be applied in other situations in which an agency's intrusion into a family is substantial. Furthermore, there may still be an opportunity to construe this duty as one to provide care and services to children and their families in addition to physical protection. Finally, there are other claims under the due process and equal protection clauses of the Fourteenth Amendment that were left untouched by *DeShaney* and that remain available to plaintiffs seeking to impose liability on child welfare agencies for their failure to act.

NOTES

1. Social concern about child abuse in the United States has waxed and waned over the past 300 years. For a summary of the history of child protection since the seventeenth century, including the recent resurgence of interest, *see* Oren, The State's Failure to Protect Children and Substantive Due Process: DeShaney in Context, 68 N.C. L. Rev. 659, 665–69 (1990).

2. Whereas the federal government spent only a few million dollars on child protective services in 1963, by 1980 that expenditure had risen to over $325 million. *See* Besharov, Right Versus Rights: The Dilemma of Child Protection, 43 Pub. Welfare 19, 20 (1985).

3. *See* Oren, DeShaney in Context, *supra* note 1, at 668, 702.

4. The number of children reported has increased at least tenfold during this period. *See* Besharov, The Misuse of Foster Care: When the Desire to Help Children Outruns the Ability to Improve Parental Functioning, 20 Fam. L.Q. 213 (1986) (noting approximately 150,000 children reported in 1963 and 1,500,000 reported in 1984); *see also* U.S. Bureau of the Census, Statistical Abstract of the United States: 1989, at 172 (1989) (table 291) (counting over 1,900,000 children reported in 1985).

This dramatic statistical increase may actually reflect the effects of mandatory reporting laws, increased awareness among the public, and a broadening of the definition of child abuse over the past thirty years, rather than an actual increase in the incidence of child abuse. *See* Johnson, Symbolic Salvation: The Changing Meanings of the Child Maltreatment Movement, 6 Stud. Symbolic Interaction 289 (1985).

5. The number of children placed in foster care because of allegations of abuse or neglect rose from approximately 75,000 in 1963 to over 300,000 in 1980. *See* Besharov, The Misuse of Foster Care, *supra* note 4, at 218.

6. *See* Stewart et al., Family Violence in Stable Middle-Class Homes, 32 Soc. Work 529 (1987).

7. A national study conducted in 1986 found that children from families with incomes of less than $15,000 were reported to child protective services and other agencies as maltreated at five times the rate of other children. *See* National Center on Child Abuse and Neglect, Study Findings: Study of National Incidence of Child Abuse and Neglect: 1988, at 5–41 (1988). Another study showed that in 1984 approximately 48 percent of all children reported to child protective services were from families receiving public assistance. *See* U.S. Bureau of the Census, Statistical Abstract, *supra* note 4, at 172 (table 291). Some studies suggest that children from poor and minority families are more likely to be labeled "abused" than middle- and upper-class children, who are more likely to be assumed to be victims of accidents. *See* Hampton, Race, Class and Child Maltreatment, 18 J. Comp. Fam. Stud. 113, 114 (1987).

While middle- and upper-income families can afford to buy the social services they need during crises, indigent families are dependent on public agencies. Many of the cases that come to an agency's attention as neglect cases stem directly from poverty. Thus, a mother may have difficulty caring for her children because of homelessness or inadequate living quarters, lack of day care, or the stresses caused by these conditions. *See* Lowry, Derring-Do in the 1980s: Child Welfare Impact Litigation After the Warren Years, 20 Fam. L.Q. 255, 257–58 (1986). It has also been suggested that since the poor, by virtue of their participation in welfare programs, are more likely to have their private lives scrutinized by state-employed social workers, they are more likely to be reported to child welfare agencies. *See* Wald, State Intervention on Behalf of Neglected Children: Standards for Removal of Children from Their Homes, Monitoring the Status of Children in Foster Care, and Termination of Parental Rights, 28 Stan. L. Rev. 623, 629 n.21 (1976).

8. In 1987, over 1,100 children died from abuse nationwide. *See* Shapiro & Shapiro, Tomorrow: The Epidemic of Child Abuse Turns Deadly, U.S. News & World Rep., Apr. 11, 1988, at 35.

9. *See* J. Goldstein et al., Beyond the Best Interests of the Child 9–25 (1979); Fein & Maluccio, Children Leaving Foster Care: Outcomes of Permanency Planning, 8 Child Abuse & Neglect 425 (1984); Lowry, Impact Litigation, *supra* note 7, at 257; Wald, State Intervention on Behalf of Neglected Children, *supra* note 7, at 644–46. Foster children are often traumatized by being shuffled from home to home without an opportunity to develop bonds with any one set of foster parents. This only compounds the feelings of loss and abandonment that children inevitably feel upon being removed from their natural family. *See* Chapter 11 in this volume.

10. Some studies show the rates of abuse and neglect in foster homes to be substantially higher than those in the general population. *See* Department of Health & Human Services, National Analysis of Official Child Neglect and Abuse Reporting, at 10–11 (1978) (table 2) (showing that rates of substantiated abuse in foster care ranged as high as ten times greater than rates in the general population). Mushlin, nn. 29–30 to Chapter 11, observes that the rate of substantiated abuse and neglect in foster family homes in New York City is one-and-a-half times that in the general population (citing Vera Institute of Justice, Foster Home Child Protection 63–64 (1981)). *See also* Nunno & Motz, The Development of an Effective Response to the Abuse of Children in Out-of-Home Care, 12 Child Abuse & Neglect 521–22 (1988) (discussing a study indicating that fatalities from abuse and neglect in foster homes may be two or three times that of the general population). *But see* M. Wald et al., Protecting Abused and Neglected Children 183–87 (1988) (reporting a multiyear study showing that children may be better off in foster care than with their natural parents in some circumstances).

11. *See* Levine, Caveat Parens: A Demystification of the Child Protection System, 35 U. Pitt. L. Rev. 1, 13–15 (1973); Musewicz, The Failure of Foster Care: Federal Statutory Reform and the Child's Right to Permanence, 54 S. Cal. L. Rev. 633, 649 (1981).

12. Studies in some states have indicated that 25 percent of all child fatalities attributed to abuse or neglect involved children who were previously reported to a child welfare agency. *See* Nunno & Motz, The Development of an Effective Response, *supra* note 10, at 522.

13. *See* Brief for Petitioners at 8, DeShaney v. Winnebago County Dep't of Social Servs., 109 S. Ct. 988 (1989).

14. *DeShaney*, 109 S. Ct. at 1003. Since the Court found no duty to act, it did not reach a number of other issues implicated by this case, including causation, *see* Martinez v. California, 444 U.S. 277 (1980); the "state of mind" on the part of the defendant that is necessary to trigger the protections of the due process clause— i.e., negligence, gross negligence, recklessness, or deliberate indifference, *see* Daniels v. Williams, 474 U.S. 327 (1986); whether the injuries alleged were a result of a policy or custom of the department, as required by Monell v. New York City Dep't of Social Servs., 436 U.S. 658 (1978) and its progeny; or whether the defendants were entitled to qualified immunity, *see* Anderson v. Creighton, 483 U.S. 635 (1987). Clearly, any section 1983 action against a child welfare agency for failure to act that escapes the limitations set by *DeShaney* and establishes a duty to act will still have to face these hurdles, as well as possible Eleventh Amendment immunity problems when the agency is state-run. These additional issues, however, are beyond the scope of this chapter.

15. *See* Youngberg v. Romeo, 457 U.S. 307, 317 (1982) ("As a general matter, a state is under no obligation to provide substantive services for those within its border" (citing Harris v. McRae, 448 U.S. 297, 317–18 (1980) (no duty to provide abortions); Maher v. Roe, 432 U.S. 464, 469 (1977) (no duty to provide medical services)).

16. *DeShaney*, 109 S. Ct. at 1004.

17. *See* Brief for Petitioners, *supra* note 13, at 18–20.

18. 768 F.2d 503 (3d Cir. 1985).

19. 747 F.2d 185 (4th Cir. 1984), *cert. denied*, 470 U.S. 1052 (1985).

20. Prosser & Keeton on the Law of Torts § 56 (W. Keeton et al. eds., 5th ed. 1984) [hereinafter Prosser & Keeton, Torts].

21. *Id.* § 56.

22. *See, e.g.*, Daniels v. Williams, 474 U.S. 327, 335–36 (1986) (stating that the Fourteenth Amendment does not constitutionalize every common law duty owed by government officials).

It is important to note that a section 1983 case like *DeShaney* involves two intellectually distinct levels at which a tort-like analysis might be employed. Thus the question whether an official has subjected the plaintiff to a deprivation of rights secured by the Constitution *under section 1983* is distinct from the question whether the official has deprived the plaintiff of life, liberty, or property *under the due process clause*. Tort law concepts may be imported into either one of these analyses. The *DeShaney* case and this chapter deal only with the due process clause inquiry. Thus the Supreme Court's statement in Monroe v. Pape, 365 U.S. 167, 187 (1961), *overruled on other grounds*, Monell v. New York City Dep't of Soc. Servs., 436 U.S. 658 (1978), that "section [1983] should be read against the background of tort liability" is irrelevant for our purposes here.

23. 474 U.S. 327, 330–31 (1986).

24. *See* Currie, Positive and Negative Constitutional Rights, 53 U. Chi. L. Rev. 864 (1986).

25. *See, e.g.*, Archie v. City of Racine, 847 F.2d 1211, 1223–24 (7th Cir. 1988) (en banc) (holding no constitutional liability for fire dispatcher's refusal to provide rescue services requested by plaintiff), *cert. denied*, 109 S. Ct. 1338 (1989).

26. *See* Prosser & Keeton, Torts, *supra* note 20, § 56.

27. *See* Brief for Petitioners, *supra* note 13, at 18–20.

28. 429 U.S. 97 (1976).

29. 457 U.S. 307 (1982).

30. In the constitutional context the term "special relationship" has generally been used only in cases that extend an affirmative duty of protection beyond situations where the individual is in state custody. *See, e.g.,* Estate of Bailey v. County of York, 768 F.2d 503, 510–11 (3d Cir. 1985) (finding a special relationship between a child welfare agency and a child living at home under agency supervision). The term was not actually used by the Court in *Estelle* or *Youngberg.* In the interests of clarity and consistency, however, I use the term in this chapter to refer to any instance in which the due process clause imposes a duty to act on the state, including *Youngberg*-type cases in which the individual is in state custody.

31. *See, e.g.,* D.R. v. Middle Bucks Area Vocational Technical Sch., 972 F.2d 1364, 1370 (3d Cir. 1992) ("Our court has read *DeShaney* as primarily setting out a test of physical custody"), *cert. denied,* 113 S. Ct. 1045 (1993); Piechowicz v. United States, 885 F.2d 1207, 1215 (4th Cir. 1989) ("The implications of DeShaney . . . are clear, and devastating. The United States did not trigger the due process clause because it never took [the plaintiffs] into its custody"); Griffin v. Carlisle, 1989 WL 107126,* 2 (E.D. Pa. Sept. 15, 1989) (finding food service worker at juvenile detention facility not constitutionally entitled to state protection against inmates because "the relationship between [the] plaintiff and the state [was] not one of custody, but merely one of employment"); *see also* Oren, DeShaney in Context, *supra* note 1, at 683.

32. Bowers v. DeVito, 686 F.2d 616, 618 (7th Cir. 1982).

33. 466 F.2d 6 (7th Cir. 1972).

34. 592 F.2d 381 (7th Cir. 1979).

35. *See* First, "Poor Joshua!": The State's Responsibility to Protect Children from Abuse, 23 Clearinghouse Rev. 525, 532 (1989).

36. This is a conspicuous omission, since the decisions were discussed in the Brief for Petitioners, *supra* note 13, at 12, 17, and in the Seventh Circuit *DeShaney* opinion, 812 F.2d at 303, as well as in virtually every other case involving the special relationship theory. *See, e.g.,* Archie v. City of Racine, 847 F.2d 1211, 1222–23 (7th Cir. 1988) (failure to provide requested rescue squad), *cert. denied,* 109 S. Ct. 1338 (1989); Estate of Bailey v. County of York, 768 F.2d 503, 510 (3d Cir. 1985) (failure to protect abused child); Jensen v. Conrad, 747 F.2d 185, 191–94 (4th Cir. 1984) (same), *cert. denied,* 470 U.S. 1052 (1985).

37. Citing *DeShaney* in support of its holding, a recent Ninth Circuit decision clearly follows this line of cases in finding a special relationship in a noncustodial situation in which the state created the danger. *See* Wood v. Ostrander, 879 F.2d 583, 589–90 (9th Cir. 1989) (holding that a police officer who arrested driver of car for drunk driving, impounded vehicle, and left female passenger stranded at night in high-crime area, where she was raped by a stranger from whom she accepted a ride, had an affirmative duty to protect the passenger because he created the danger she faced), *cert. denied,* 498 U.S. 938 (1990); *see also* cases cited *infra* note 52.

38. *DeShaney,* 109 S. Ct. at 1005.

39. It is possible to read *Youngberg* as defining a status-based special relationship. In finding a special relationship duty to exist, Justice Powell seemed to emphasize Romeo's status in relation to the state, more than the state's affirmative action in institutionalizing him. *See Youngberg*, 457 U.S. at 317 ("When a person is institutionalized—and wholly dependent on the State [—] . . . a duty to provide certain services and care does exist"). Chief Justice Rehnquist, however, as discussed above, cast the decision in a different light.

40. *DeShaney*, 109 S. Ct. at 1005–1006 (emphasis added). Similarly, while the Court observed that "the harms Joshua suffered did not occur while he was in the State's custody," the next sentence indicated that the Court's real concern was whether the state created the danger: "While the State may have been aware of the dangers that Joshua faced in the free world, it played no part in their creation, nor did it do anything to render him any more vulnerable to them." *Id.* at 1006.

41. *Id.*

42. *Id.*

43. It is important to note that this causation inquiry occurs within the duty analysis and is distinct from the standard causation inquiry that ultimately determines tort liability (i.e., the causation element of the duty–breach–causation–damages analysis). The latter inquiry asks whether the defendant's breach (here the failure to act) was a necessary antecedent condition to a reasonably foreseeable injury. In contrast, the duty–causation inquiry asks whether some previous, nonbreaching act (e.g., imprisoning or institutionalizing the plaintiff) was a necessary antecedent condition to the plaintiff's injury. Here the causal chain may be fairly attenuated, the foreseeability requirement is lessened, and intervening causes do not break the causal chain.

44. *See Youngberg*, 457 U.S. at 307.

45. *See Estelle*, 429 U.S. at 97.

46. 592 F.2d 381 (7th Cir. 1979).

47. In *DeShaney*, the majority found no state action that had even incrementally contributed to the cause of Joshua's injuries. Instead, the state "placed him in no worse position than that in which he would have been had it not acted at all." *DeShaney*, 109 S. Ct. at 1006.

48. Without this additional criterion, the but-for causation test alone would produce absurd results. For example, it seems unlikely that Chief Justice Rehnquist meant to argue that since a state's act in issuing an adoption decree is a but-for cause of an adopted child's injuries at the hands of her adoptive parents, the state should owe a special relationship duty of protection to every adopted child. This involuntariness requirement is not the only way the but-for test could have been effectively limited. Notions of proximate cause might have served the same purpose.

49. *DeShaney*, 109 S. Ct. at 1005.

50. *Id.* at 1006.

51. *Id.* at 1005.

52. A few courts have interpreted *DeShaney* in this way to find a special relationship in noncustodial situations in which the state created the danger. In Cornelius v. Town of Highland Lake, 880 F.2d 348 (11th Cir. 1989), *cert. denied*, 494 U.S. 1066 (1990), a town clerk, who was abducted from the town hall, held hostage, and terrorized for three days by prison inmates assigned to a community work squad, sought to hold the town and its officials liable under section 1983 for violation of her due process rights. The Court found that these allegations could support the existence of a special relationship under the standard set forth in *DeShaney*, because "the defendants did indeed create the dangerous situation of the inmates' presence in the community by establishing the work squad and assigning the inmates to work around the town hall." *Id.* at 356.

In a similar case, Swader v. Virginia, 743 F. Supp. 434 (E.D. Va. 1990), the daughter of a prison employee, who was required as a condition of employment to live on the prison grounds, was brutally raped and murdered by an inmate who was negligently permitted outside the fenced-in area of the prison without the accompaniment of a guard. The court observed that "a central part to the [Supreme] Court's analysis [in *DeShaney* was] the fact that the State played no part in the creation of the dangers that harmed Joshua, nor did the state do anything to render him more vulnerable to those dangers." *Id.* at 441. Because in this case "not only did the State play a part in making [the girl] more vulnerable to the dangers which led to her death, but . . . the State actually played a part in the creation of those dangers," the court found a special relationship duty of protection to exist. *Id.; see also* Freeman v. Ferguson, 911 F.2d 52, 55 (8th Cir. 1990) (police officials and department may be held constitutionally liable for their failure to protect plaintiff from a fatal beating by her estranged husband where one official acted affirmatively to prevent other officials from taking steps to protect her); Gibson v. City of Chicago, 910 F.2d 1510, 1521 n.19 (7th Cir. 1990) (city and officials had affirmative constitutional duty to protect victim of shooting by former police officer, who had been removed from duty because of mental health problems, because they had created the danger by training and arming the officer in the first place and failing to disarm him when they removed him from duty); Ward v. City of San Jose, 737 F. Supp. 1502, 1507 (N.D. Cal. 1990) (concluding that, under *DeShaney*, police officers can be held liable pursuant to the Fourteenth Amendment for their failure to protect plaintiff against a danger they created), *aff'd in part, rev'd in part*, 967 F.2d 280 (9th Cir. 1991).

53. *See* White v. Rochford, 592 F.2d 381 (7th Cir. 1979); Byrd v. Brishke, 466 F.2d 6 (7th Cir. 1972); cases cited *supra* note 52.

54. *DeShaney*, 109 S. Ct. at 1006.

55. *Id.* at 1011 (Brennan, J., dissenting). While the petitioners did make the argument adopted by the dissent—that the state cut off private sources of aid—they made this argument in the context of a procedural due process claim that the Court explicitly declined to consider. *See* Brief for Petitioners, *supra* note 13, at 27; *see also DeShaney*, 109 S. Ct. at 1003 n.2. They did not explicitly argue that the defendant's act in cutting off other sources of aid constituted a state-created danger triggering a special relationship duty. This argument, however, was extensively made in the ACLU Amicus Brief. *See* Brief Amicus Curiae of the American Civil Liberties Union Children's Rights Project in support of Petitioners at 28–34.

56. *DeShaney*, 109 S. Ct. at 1006 (emphasis added).

57. *Id.* (emphasis added).

58. A subsequent Seventh Circuit opinion supports this view of the majority opinion in *DeShaney*. In Ross v. United States, 910 F.2d 1422, 1431 (7th Cir. 1990),

the court held that government officials could be constitutionally liable for their failure to rescue a drowning person where they had cut off other sources of aid by actively preventing private persons who were at the scene from attempting a rescue.

59. It explained:

> Had the State by the affirmative exercise of its power removed Joshua from free society and placed him in a foster home operated by its agents, we might have a situation sufficiently analogous to incarceration or institutionalization to give rise to an affirmative duty to protect. . . . We express no view on the validity of this analogy, however, as it is not before us in the present case.

DeShaney, 109 S. Ct. at 1006 n.9.

60. 791 F.2d 881 (11th Cir. 1986), *aff'd in part, rev'd in part on reh'g*, 818 F.2d 791 (11th Cir. 1987) (en banc), *cert. denied*, 109 S. Ct. 1337 (1989).

61. *See* Black v. Beame, 419 F. Supp. 599 (S.D.N.Y. 1976), *aff'd*, 550 F.2d 815 (2d Cir. 1977); Child v. Beame, 412 F. Supp. 593 (S.D.N.Y. 1976).

62. *Child*, 412 F. Supp. at 608. *Child* challenged the failure to provide adoptive homes to foster children, and *Black* challenged the failure to provide housing and welfare benefits necessary to reunite foster children with their family. These cases therefore are arguably distinguishable from cases alleging a right to physical safety in foster care.

63. Brooks v. Richardson, 478 F. Supp. 793, 795 (S.D.N.Y. 1979).

64. *See* Doe v. New York City Dep't of Social Servs., 649 F.2d 134, 141 (2d Cir. 1981), *cert. denied*, 464 U.S. 864 (1983).

65. *See* Rubacha v. Coler, 607 F. Supp. 477, 479 (N.D. Ill. 1985).

66. *See supra* note 31. In most foster care protection cases decided since *DeShaney*, the courts have found that a special relationship duty toward foster children *does* exist under the custody test. *See, e.g.,* Winston v. Children and Youth Servs. of Delaware County, 948 F.2d 1380 (3d Cir. 1991), *cert. denied*, 112 S. Ct. 2303 (1992); Meador v. Cabinet for Human Resources, 902 F.2d 474, 476 (6th Cir. 1990), *cert. denied*, 498 U.S. 867 (1990); Lipscomb v. Simmons, 884 F.2d 1242, 1247 (9th Cir. 1989), *reh'g granted*, 907 F.2d 114 (9th Cir. 1990), *aff'd*, 962 F.2d 1374 (9th Cir. 1992); LaShawn A. v. Dixon, 762 F. Supp. 959, 992 (D.D.C. 1991), *aff'd*, 990 F.2d 1319 (D.C. Cir. 1993); Campbell v. City of Philadelphia, 1990 WL 102945 (E.D. Pa. July 18, 1990); B.H. v. Johnson, 715 F. Supp. 1387 (N.D. Ill. 1989). *But see* Milburn v. Anne Arundel County Dep't of Social Servs., 871 F.2d 474, 476 (4th Cir. 1989), *cert. denied*, 110 S. Ct. 148 (1989) (finding no special relationship because foster child was found not to be in state custody); Pfoltzer v. County of Fairfax, 775 F. Supp. 874, 884 (E.D. Va. 1991) (same), *aff'd*, 966 F.2d 1443 (4th Cir. 1992). A recent Seventh Circuit opinion by Judge Posner, however, applied a state-created danger test for special relationship to conclude that the state owes a duty to children involuntarily placed in foster care. *See* K.H. v. Morgan, 914 F.2d 846 (7th Cir. 1990).

67. This argument may gain additional force when (as is often the case) the state contracts out the provision of foster care to private agencies, which in turn contract with individual foster parents.

68. Estimates of the proportion of all placements that are "voluntary" vary from 50 to 90 percent. *See* note 120 to Chapter 11 in this volume.

69. The Supreme Court has held that foster children are *not* in state "custody" for purposes of habeas corpus relief. *See* Lehman v. Lycoming County Children's Servs. Agency, 458 U.S. 502 (1982). For a discussion of why the concept of custody creates an artificial line with little or no relation to the question of who bears actual responsibility for the child, see Oren, DeShaney in Context, *supra* note 1, at 704.

70. *See* Wald, State Intervention on Behalf of Neglected Children, *supra* note 7, at 631.

71. While these decisions are subject to court approval, many courts with overcrowded dockets frequently rubber-stamp the agency's recommendation.

72. *See* Santosky v. Kramer, 455 U.S. 745, 753 (1982) ("The fundamental liberty interest of natural parents in the care, custody, and management of their child does not evaporate simply because . . . they have lost temporary custody of their child to the State"); *see also* 55 Pa. Code § 3130.68 (1990) (regarding rights of parents to visitation and to be informed before the child is moved); *id.* § 3130.91 (requiring parent's authorization for nonroutine medical treatment).

73. 882 F.2d 720, 723–24 (3d Cir. 1989), *on remand from* 109 S. Ct. 1333 (1989) (remanding in light of *DeShaney*), *aff'g on other grounds* 856 F.2d 594 (3d Cir. 1988), *cert. granted and judgment vacated*, 489 U.S. 1062 (1989).

74. The *Stoneking* court, perhaps anticipating that this finding of functional custody might be regarded by the Supreme Court as too strained a reading of *DeShaney*, ultimately based its finding of liability on alternative grounds. *See* 882 F.2d at 724 (holding the school district liable for the child-plaintiff's injuries from sexual abuse at the hands of a school-employed band director on the basis of the school district's maintenance of "a practice, custom, or policy of reckless indifference to instances of known or suspected sexual abuse of students by teachers" (relying on Monell v. New York City Dep't of Social Servs., 436 U.S. 658 (1978)). *Stoneking's* suggestion that compulsory attendance laws might be viewed as creating a special custodial relationship between schools and students has since been rejected by the Third Circuit, however. *See* D.R. v. Middle Bucks Area Vocational Technical Sch., 972 F.2d 1364, 1370–71 (3d Cir. 1992).

75. 889 F.2d 454 (3d Cir. 1989), *on remand from* City of New Kensington v. Horton, 109 S. Ct. 1334 (1989) (remanding in light of *DeShaney*), *aff'g In re* City of New Kensington, 857 F.2d 1463 (3d Cir. 1988).

76. *See* 889 F.2d at 458.

77. 871 F.2d 474 (4th Cir. 1989).

78. *See id.* at 476–79. The court also based its holding that there was no special relationship on the fact that the child was voluntarily placed in foster care. The court summarily resolved the involuntariness issue by observing that the child "was voluntarily placed in the foster home by his natural parents," without any discussion of whether such consent on the part of the parents could fairly be attributed to the child. *Id.* at 476. This same approach has been taken by every court considering a right to protection claim by a foster child since *DeShaney*; it is discussed above under "The Involuntariness Requirement as Applied to Children."

79. 365 U.S. 715 (1961).

80. 419 U.S. 345 (1974).

81. The Fourth Circuit launched into its state action analysis from a vague reference in the *DeShaney* opinion to the fact that Joshua was "in the custody of his natural father, who was in no sense a state actor." *Milburn*, 871 F.2d at 476 (quoting *DeShaney*, 109 S. Ct. at 1006). Yet this sentence in and of itself hardly indicates that the Court's opinion turns on whether Joshua's father was a state actor in the sense of *Burton* and *Jackson*. It is hard to imagine that the *DeShaney* Court would, in such a cursory manner, import into the special relationship theory all of the complexity and uncertainty of the state action requirement.

82. A claim against the foster parents does not involve a *DeShaney*-type special relationship inquiry, because the foster parents are not being sued for their failure to act but for their acts of abuse. Such a claim does, however, involve a state action inquiry, since it can be argued that the foster parents are private actors. This issue did not come up in *DeShaney*, because the defendants, the Winnebago County Department of Social Services and employees thereof, were all clearly state actors. Joshua's father could not be named as a defendant under section 1983 precisely because he was so clearly not a state actor.

83. 436 U.S. 658, 690 (1978).

84. No such claim was made in *Milburn*.

85. Thus, it is important to note that there are two possible theories under which a child abused in foster care could attempt to hold a municipality or county liable for her injuries. The first alleges that the county had a duty to act to protect the child from her foster parents by virtue of the special relationship that was formed when the county placed the child in foster care. This theory relies on *Youngberg*, *Estelle*, and footnote 9 in *DeShaney*. The second theory alleges that the foster parents are state actors and that because their actions in abusing the child resulted from some county policy or custom, the county is liable for the child's injuries under *Monell*.

86. One district court in the Fourth Circuit has already followed *Milburn*, holding that *DeShaney* forecloses a substantive due process claim by a child abused in foster care where the foster parents are not state actors. *See* Pfoltzer v. County of Fairfax, 775 F. Supp. 874, 884 (E.D. Va. 1991), *aff'd*, 966 F.2d 1443 (4th Cir. 1992).

87. *See Youngberg v. Romeo*, 457 U.S. at 310, 313, 315, 316, 318, 321–22.

88. One study found that 27 percent of children voluntarily placed in foster care were opposed to the decision and that nearly half of all foster children were too young to understand the reasons why they had been placed in foster care. *See* A. Gruber, Children in Foster Care: Destitute, Neglected, Betrayed 141 (1978).

89. *See, e.g.*, *Milburn*, 871 F.2d at 476 (holding of no special relationship between state and foster child based in part on fact that child was voluntarilly placed in foster care by his parents); Black v. Beame, 419 F. Supp. 599, 602 (S.D.N.Y. 1976) (also focusing on voluntary placement of child by parents), *aff'd*, 550 F.2d 815 (2d Cir. 1977); *see also* Aristotle P. v. Johnson, 721 F. Supp. 1002, 1009 (N.D. Ill. 1989) (distinguishing factual circumstances of the case because children involved were not voluntarily placed in foster care as in *Black*). A district court opinion following *Milburn* took this reasoning a step further, holding that the "voluntary" nature of the children's placement precluded a special relationship where, in order to get their children back after an emergency placement, the parents had agreed to a consent order according to which physical custody of the children was returned to the parents but "temporary legal custody" remained with the child welfare agency. Six months later the agency unilaterally removed the children from their parents' home without a court hearing on the basis of that order. Thus, even though the parents had never consented to the actual physical removal of their children, the court found the placement in foster care to be "voluntary." *See* Pfoltzer v. County of Fairfax, 775 F. Supp. 874 (E.D. Va. 1991), *aff'd*, 966 F.2d 1443 (4th Cir. 1992). *But see* LaShawn A. v. Dixon, 762 F. Supp. 959, 993 (D.D.C. 1991), *aff'd*, 990 F.2d 1319 (D.C. Cir. 1993) (in class action suit on behalf of all children in foster care—some of whom were presumably placed there through voluntary placement agreements—the court found a special relationship duty toward all of them and noted "plaintiffs did not come into the District's care by choice").

90. *See* Planned Parenthood v. Danforth, 428 U.S. 52, 74–75 (1976) (holding unconstitutional statute requiring parental consent for minor's abortion where mother's life not threatened).

91. *See* Parham v. J.R., 442 U.S. 584, 604 (1979) (holding that a child's right to procedural due process before being committed to a mental hospital is not waived simply because parent consents to commitment).

92. A number of state courts have held that a minor's right to counsel in delinquency and dependency hearings cannot be waived by the parent where the interests of parent and child are found to be adverse. *See In re* Manuel R., 543 A.2d 719, 726 (Conn. 1988); McBurrough v. Dep't of Human Resources, 257 S.E.2d 35, 36 (Ga. Ct. App. 1979); Stapleton v. Dauphin County Child Care Serv., 324 A.2d 562, 573 (Pa. Super. 1974); *see also* Model Juvenile Court Act § 26(a) (1968) ("If the interests of 2 or more parties conflict separate counsel shall be provided").

93. *See* Smith v. Organization of Foster Families for Equality & Reform, 431 U.S. 816, 833–34 (1977); Musewicz, The Failure of Foster Care, *supra* note 11, at 639; *see also In re* David R., 420 N.Y.S.2d 675, 677 (N.Y. Fam. Ct. 1979) (regarding woman, fluent only in Spanish, who, without the aid of an interpreter, signed a voluntary placement agreement in English relinquishing custody of her grandchild).

94. *See* Chapter 11 in this volume; *see also In re* Burns, 519 A.2d 638, 640–41 (Del. 1986) (finding that seventeen-year-old mother signed voluntary placement agreement on the understanding that if she did sign, her child would stay with her, and that if she did not sign, the court would take him away).

95. *See* Mnookin, Foster Care—In Whose Best Interest?, 43 Harv. Educ. Rev. 599, 601 (1973).

96. *See* Chapter 11 in this volume.

97. *See id.*

98. *Id.*

99. The only post-*DeShaney* decisions so far to find no special relationship have been Milburn v. Anne Arundel County Dep't of Social Servs., 871 F.2d 474 (4th Cir. 1989), and a district court case following *Milburn*, Pfoltzer v. County of Fairfax, 775 F. Supp. 874 (E.D. Va. 1991), *aff'd*, 966 F.2d 1443 (4th Cir. 1992).

100. *See* Lord v. Murphy, 561 A.2d 1013, 1018 (Me. 1989) (Clifford, J., concurring)

(suggesting that the state's special relationship duty under due process extends to a child who, after one-and-a-half years in foster care placement, was returned to his mother, who then abused him). *But see* McComb v. Wambough, 934 F.2d 474, 483 (3d Cir. 1991) (rejecting a state-created danger argument in a *DeShaney*-type case in which a child was severely neglected by natural parent after a two-year stay in foster care).

101. *See* Hampton v. Motley, 911 F.2d 722 (4th Cir. 1990) (holding that children who were removed from their mother's custody and placed with their paternal grandparents, and who then suffered abuse at the hands of their grandparents and their father, had a substantive due process claim against the state based on a special relationship). *But see* Weller v. Dep't of Social Servs., 901 F.2d 387, 392 (4th Cir. 1990) (finding no special relationship that would render the state liable for injuries sustained by a child while in the custody of his grandmother or mother, with whom the child was placed after being removed from the custody of his father).

These first five hypothetical cases could present the plaintiff with the possibility of avoiding the special relationship issue altogether by arguing that the agency's action (in arranging the visit, returning the child, or placing the child with the relative) directly caused the child's injury. The existence of an intervening cause, in the form of the private party who actually delivered the blows, clearly poses a serious problem to this argument, but the Supreme Court's opinion in Martinez v. California, 444 U.S. 277, 285 (1980), suggests that it might not be insurmountable, given the right facts. The plaintiff would also have to be able to assert that the action itself constituted a breach of duty, probably at the level of deliberate indifference, which would require at a minimum that the agency had substantial reason to suspect the danger of abuse before returning the child or arranging the visit.

Even if this direct causation argument is not available, the fact that the chain of causation from agency action to child's injury is shorter in these cases than in *DeShaney* makes more convincing the plaintiff's argument that the state, by its action, created the danger that the plaintiff faced and thus established a special relationship duty. (Under this line of reasoning, the subsequent inquiries under standard tort analysis then become: first, whether the agency's failure to act was a breach of duty, and, second, whether that breach caused the child's injury. *See supra* note 43.)

102. Clearly, in addition to establishing a duty in each of these hypothetical cases, a plaintiff would also have to show a breach of that duty, presumably by showing at a minimum that the agency had reason to suspect that abuse would occur. *See supra* note 43. Here the focus is only on duty, as it is throughout this chapter.

103. For discussions of the emotional reactions of parents whose children are placed in foster care, see Carbino, Group Work with Natural Parents in Permanency Planning, Soc. Work with Groups, Winter 1982, at 7, 12; McAdams, The Parent in the Shadows, 51 Child Welfare 51 (1972).

104. *See, e.g.,* White v. Rochford, 592 F.2d 381, 385 (7th Cir. 1979) (holding that aspects of emotional well-being are protected by the due process clause of the Fourteenth Amendment); B.H. v. Johnson, 715 F. Supp. 1387, 1395 (N.D. Ill. 1989) ("[A] child who is in the state's custody has a substantive due process right to be free from unreasonable and unnecessary intrusions on both its physical and emotional well-being"); Doe v. New York City Dep't of Social Servs., 670 F. Supp. 1145, 1184 (S.D.N.Y. 1987) (holding unconstitutional inadequate shelter and treatment of foster children).

105. 884 F.2d 1242, 1246 (9th Cir. 1989), *aff'd*, 962 F.2d 1374 (9th Cir. 1992).

106. *Id.* at 1244.

107. *Id.* at 1246 (citing Monmouth County Correctional Institutional Inmates v. Lanzaro, 834 F.2d 326 (3d Cir. 1987), *cert. denied*, 486 U.S. 1006 (1988)).

108. *See id.* at 1246–47 (citing McElyea v. Babbitt, 833 F.2d 196 (9th Cir. 1987); Schlesinger v. Carlson, 489 F. Supp. 612 (M.D. Pa. 1980)).

109. *See id.* at 1248 (citing Bounds v. Smith, 430 U.S. 817 (1977)).

110. *Id.* at 1247.

111. 721 F. Supp. 1002 (N.D. Ill. 1989).

112. 715 F. Supp. 1387 (N.D. Ill. 1989). In this case, a class of foster children challenged virtually all aspects of the child welfare system: from abuse and neglect in foster care and the failure to provide services to reunite families, to high caseloads and the agency's failure to react quickly to reports of abuse and neglect. In addition to the substantive due process claim, plaintiffs also made procedural due process claims and federal statutory claims under the Adoption Assistance and Child Welfare Act of 1980, 42 U.S.C. §§ 620–29, 670–79 (1982 & Supp. V 1987). Judge Grady did find a special relationship to exist, such that foster children have a substantive due process right to be "free from unreasonable and unnecessary intrusions upon their physical and emotional well-being . . . and to be provided by the state with adequate food, shelter, clothing and medical care and minimally adequate training to secure these basic constitutional rights," 715 F. Supp. at 1396, but was unwilling to extend this right to parental and sibling visitation and reunification services, *see id.* at 1396–97.

113. 726 F. Supp. 690 (N.D. Ill. 1989). While holding that a special relationship duty did exist, the court nonetheless dismissed the plaintiffs' substantive due process claim, holding that the state's conduct did not rise to the level of "complete indifference to a known significant risk" necessary to trigger the protection of the due process clause. *See id.* at 700. The court did, however, uphold the plaintiffs' claim under the Adoption Assistance and Child Welfare Act of 1980. *See id.* at 697.

114. 42 U.S.C. §§ 620–29, 670–79 (1982 & Supp. V 1987).

115. The act provides, in relevant part:

> In order for a State to be eligible for payments under this part, it shall have a plan approved by the Secretary which . . . (15) . . . provides that, in each case, reasonable efforts will be made (A) prior to the placement of a child in foster care, to prevent or eliminate the need for removal of the child from his home, and (B) to make it possible for the child to return to his home.

42 U.S.C. § 671(a)(15) (1982).

116. *See* Suter v. Artist M., 112 S. Ct. 1360 (1992). Both the district court and the Seventh Circuit had reached the opposite holding, *see Artist M.*, 726 F. Supp. 690, 696–97, *aff'd*, 917 F.2d 980, 990 (7th Cir. 1990), as had other courts. *See, e.g.*, Norman v. Johnson, 739 F. Supp. 1182 (N.D. Ill. 1990).

117. *See, e.g.*, B.H. v. Johnson, 715 F. Supp. 1387, 1401 (N.D. Ill. 1989).

118. *DeShaney*, 109 S. Ct. at 1007. The social worker's dilemma is perhaps exaggerated here by Chief Justice Rehnquist. The standard of care creates a sizable zone of safety, in that an error in either direction that does not rise at least to the level of gross negligence, or perhaps deliberate indifference, will not result in liability. *See* Daniels v. Williams, 474 U.S. 327, 333 (1986).

119. Lower courts so far have not made this distinction but instead have applied *DeShaney* with full force to substantive due process claims asserting a duty to provide services. *See, e.g.,* Alessi v. Commonwealth of Pennsylvania, 893 F.2d 1444, 1448 (3d Cir. 1990) (finding no duty to provide residential treatment services to mentally retarded individuals); Edwards v. Johnston County Health Dep't, 885 F.2d 1215, 1219 (4th Cir. 1989) (finding no duty to ensure safe and sanitary housing); Philadelphia Police & Fire Ass'n for Handicapped Children, Inc. v. City of Philadelphia, 874 F.2d 156, 166–68 (3d Cir. 1989) (finding no duty to continue providing services to mentally retarded individuals who live at home).

120. Depending on state law, such suits may be barred by sovereign immunity, or the amount of damages may be limited. In Wisconsin, for example, where the *DeShaney* case arose, damages in state tort suits are limited to $50,000. *See* Wis. Stat. § 893.80(3) (1983).

121. *See DeShaney*, 109 S. Ct. at 1004 n.3. This type of claim has been brought against police departments by adult women who have been victims of domestic violence and allege that the police department's failure to respond to domestic violence calls as quickly as it responds to reports of other types of assaults violates equal protection. *See, e.g.,* Thurman v. City of Torrington, 595 F. Supp. 1521 (D. Conn. 1984). *But see* McKee v. City of Rockwell, 877 F.2d 409, 413 (5th Cir. 1989) (rejecting plaintiff's claim that the police department's failure to respond to domestic violence calls violated equal protection on the grounds that plaintiffs cannot circumvent *DeShaney* by converting a due process claim into an equal protection claim), *cert. denied*, 110 S. Ct. 727 (1990).

122. *See, e.g.,* Lindsey v. Normet, 405 U.S. 56, 74–79 (1972) (holding that the double bond prerequisite for appealing an action under the Oregon Forcible Entry and Detainer Statute violated the equal protection clause under the minimum rationality standard because it granted appeals to some litigants while "arbitrarily" and "capriciously" denying them to others).

123. 455 U.S. 422 (1982).

124. While Justice Blackmun noted that this made the equal protection claim "an unconventional one," *id.* at 438, the idea that a facially neutral law may violate equal protection because of unequal administration of that law is not new. *See* Yick Wo v. Hopkins, 118 U.S. 356 (1886).

125. *See DeShaney*, 109 S. Ct. at 1003 n.2.

126. 408 U.S. 564 (1972).

127. A plaintiff claiming entitlement to protection (like Joshua DeShaney) might also claim a liberty interest subject to due process protection. *See id.* at 572 (discussing broad due process protection afforded liberty interests); *see also* Vitek v. Jones, 445 U.S. 480, 481 (1980) ("[T]he involuntary transfer of [a prisoner] to a mental hospital implicates a liberty interest that is protected by the Due Process Clause of the Fourteenth Amendment").

128. 818 F.2d 791 (11th Cir. 1987) (en banc), *cert. denied*, 109 S. Ct. 1337 (1989) (certiorari was denied only eleven days after the Court decided *DeShaney*).

129. *See* B.H. v. Johnson, 715 F. Supp. 1387 (N.D. Ill. 1989); K.H. v. Morgan, 1989 WL 105279 (N.D. Ill. Sept. 8, 1989) (dismissing a procedural due process claim because plaintiff did not have a "legitimate claim of entitlement" to the requested benefits), *aff'd in part, remanded in part*, 914 F.2d 848 (1990).

130. *See* Doe v. Milwaukee County, 903 F.2d 499, 502–503 (7th Cir. 1990) (holding that Wisconsin law did not create a property interest in having the child welfare agency conduct an investigation of a report of suspected child abuse because the statute only specified a set of procedures that the agency had to follow, and procedures in and of themselves are not benefits subject to due process protection). *See also* Chrissy F. v. Mississippi Dep't of Pub. Welfare, 925 F.2d 844, 852 (5th Cir. 1991) (court noted but declined to decide state law entitlement procedural due process claim against child welfare agency); LaShawn A. v. Dixon, 762 F. Supp. 959, 994 (D.D.C. 1991) (in class action, following *Taylor* with respect to procedural due process claim of class members in foster care, but declining to decide the issue as to children at home under supervision of child welfare agency), *aff'd* 990 F.2d 1319 (D.C. Cir. 1993).

131. Also of potential interest to the child welfare plaintiff is a recent decision in a wife abuse case from the Eastern District of Pennsylvania. In Coffman v. Wilson Police Dep't, 739 F. Supp. 257, 264 (E.D. Pa. 1990), the court held that though the Pennsylvania Protection from Abuse Act itself did not create a property interest in police protection for battered women, a protective order issued by a court pursuant to the act did create such a property interest. A parallel argument might be made by a child abused while in the custody of her parents but subject to a court order directing the child welfare agency to supervise the child.

CHAPTER TEN

DeShaney and Child Welfare Reform

Cathleen Tucker
Paul Blatt

A GROWING NUMBER of children and families in America are suffering. As reported by Amy Sinden in Chapter 9 in this volume, since 1960 the number of children reported to child welfare agencies as suspected victims of abuse or neglect has increased dramatically, as has the number of children in foster care. A review of some leading indicators of family well-being reveals a disturbing long-term trend:

> Children are now the poorest age group in America. In 1990 one in five, or 12.7 million children, was poor, an increase of 2.7 million from 1979.[1]
> Nationwide in 1980, 271,801 babies, or 7.5 percent of all babies born, were born to single teens. By 1989 the number had climbed to 347,880 babies, or 8.6 percent of all births—a 14 percent increase in the percentage of all births to teens over the decade.[2]
> In 1990 almost 13 million children, 2 million more than in 1980, lived in single-parent families.[3]

The child protective services system, the system with direct responsibility for addressing the most severe problems of family dysfunction, is itself in crisis today. Overwhelmed by a flood of new reports of abused and neglected children, the system increasingly expends its limited staff time and energy on investigation, and its scarce service dollars on out-of-home placement of children. The statistics are shocking:

> In 1991 there were 2.6 million reports of child abuse, an increase of more than 6 percent since 1990 and 40 percent since 1985. Nearly 1,400 children died of maltreatment, almost an 11 percent increase in child abuse

fatalities since 1990. Almost 80 percent of the children who died as a result of abuse or neglect were under the age of five; 56 percent were infants of one year or younger.[4]

From the start of 1986 to the end of 1991, there was a 49 percent increase in out-of-home placements made by public child welfare agencies, from 273,000 to 470,000.[5]

Federal funding for child welfare placements increased almost 600 percent between 1981 and 1991, while funds for prevention rose only 78 percent. When federal and state funds are added together, more than $9 billion was spent on out-of-home placement in 1991.[6]

The strategy that has evolved in this nation to prevent the maltreatment of children is to allocate staff and dollar resources for crisis intervention. Within the context of this strategy, the U.S. Supreme Court held in *DeShaney v. Winnebago County Department of Social Services* that states do not have an affirmative duty under the Federal Constitution to protect children from abuse.[7] Joshua De-Shaney's clearly mishandled case was not an aberration. Through its decision in *DeShaney*, the Supreme Court expressed its displeasure with the current means taken to protect children from harm and presented the nation with a rare glimpse of its child welfare system and the opportunity to examine the systemic problems within it. We contend that in addition to the overarching legal question presented in *DeShaney*, the case also posed a social and public policy question: Why is our current strategy failing?

DeShaney opened a door for advocates and policy-makers seeking an effective and fundamental reform of the child welfare system based on *prevention and early intervention*. It did so by examining the current strategy for preventing and treating child abuse and neglect in this country—a strategy indirectly to blame for the harm inflicted upon Joshua DeShaney—and identifying some of its deficiencies. In this chapter we review the current strategy and advocate the implementation of a new one based on three separate but integral components: supporting families for healthy child development, assisting families and children in need, and protecting abused and neglected children through direct intervention.

The Current Strategy

In 1988 Congress established the U.S. Advisory Board on Child Abuse and Neglect and charged it with the mission of evaluating the nation's efforts to prevent and treat child abuse. The board ominously found that

> 1) each year *hundreds of thousands* of children are being starved and abandoned, burned and severely beaten, raped and sodomized, berated and belittled; 2) the *system* the nation has devised to respond to child abuse and neglect *is failing*; and 3) the United States spends *billions* of dollars on programs that deal with the *results* of the nation's failure to prevent and treat child abuse and neglect.[8]

The board concluded that "[c]hild maltreatment represents the complex interaction of numerous factors." Although all are important, "several are especially significant: poverty, ethnicity, neighborhood dysfunction, mental health problems, substance abuse, and the presence of children with special needs."[9] Thus, while maltreatment occurs at all socioeconomic levels and in all cultural groups, it is disproportionately high in areas with the highest poverty rates and the stressors that accompany poverty. Dysfunctional neighborhoods, lacking support for families under severe stress, tend to have a higher frequency of child maltreatment. Parents suffering from a multitude of mental health problems are also more likely to abuse or neglect their children, as are those addicted to drugs and alcohol. In addition, maltreatment of children with disabilities is disproportionately high.[10]

In 1988 the American Public Welfare Association (APWA) formed the National Commission on Child Welfare and Family Preservation. The twenty-five-member commission consisted of cabinet-level state human service commissioners, local administrators, welfare directors, and representatives of other human service fields such as mental health. The commission conducted a national survey of the human service agencies that provide child welfare services in the fifty states and the District of Columbia. The survey results—two aspects of which are highlighted below—provide insight into why the current child welfare system is failing.

Service and Program Availability

The most commonly used programs in this country generally come into play only after abuse and neglect have already begun and sometimes after they have become entrenched. Prevention and early intervention have been largely excluded as strategies to respond to child maltreatment.

Of forty existing programs to serve children and families, only three are provided by all fifty-one public human service agencies.[11] The first category comprises intra-familial and quasi-familial child protective services, provided in response to an allegation of abuse or neglect. These services include intake, screening, investigation, disposition determination, crisis intervention, and discharge. The second category, foster family care services, place children with licensed or approved family units that provide substitute care on a twenty-four-hour basis. Third are adoptive services for special needs children, whose work includes the entire legal process of adoption.

These services "can generally be accessed only through allegations of abuse/ neglect and agency custody/wardship. In other words, services are only available in the event of a crisis and/or a legal mandate," the commission observed.[12] "Services that address anything beyond the most basic human needs are sadly underrepresented in the standard service offerings of public child welfare agencies."[13]

Staffing

The child protection system today remains primarily a system of investigation and placement. Direct line service workers, the people responsible for service delivery and program implementation, receive too little training and have too few service options to offer families.

Fully 90 percent of the agencies surveyed by the commission reported diffi-culties in recruiting staff for child welfare positions, with the most acute shortages among the direct service workers.[14] More than half expressed dissatisfaction with the administrative structure for screening and hiring child welfare staff.[15] The most commonly cited problems were inadequate or inefficient personnel systems, minimal or no recruiting efforts, few objective measures on which to base hiring decisions, and minimal or ineffective screening procedures.[16]

Of forty-three states reporting on educational requirements for direct service workers, eleven indicated one or more positions that required less than a college degree. Fewer than half of the states provide preservice training to child welfare staff, and only sixteen assess the competence of the trainees.[17] Inservice training is universally available but is mandatory in only 70 percent of the states, and trainee competence is assessed in only 40 percent.[18]

In the *DeShaney* case, the consequences of the inadequacies just cited were readily apparent. Authorities in the Winnebago County Department of Social Ser-vices Child Protection Unit had substantial evidence that Joshua was at great risk. The DSS caseworker assigned to handle Joshua's case repeatedly documented her continued suspicions that someone in the DeShaney home was physically abus-ing him.[19] Neither she nor any member of the multidisciplinary team involved in the case—consisting of doctors, a child psychiatrist, nurses, police, and the county civil attorney and her own supervisor—used the information aggressively to push the team and the court system to respond.[20] Yet the social worker, gener-ally lower-paid and with less education than others on such teams,[21] is the one held accountable when errors are made and children are abused again.

Child welfare positions remain unfilled because of lack of qualified candidates, hiring freezes and other budgetary constraints, staff turnover, unappropriated funds, and recruitment and retention difficulties due to low salaries and high caseloads.[22] Caseload standards for direct service workers do not exist in some states. Where they do exist, the actual average caseload exceeds the state's own standard in the majority of states.[23]

Lack of qualified staff added to a dearth of available services to offer families exposes a system in need of fundamental reform; the current one responds far too late, often after abuse and neglect have already become an established pattern of behavior. This country's current strategy may actually be defined as a *nonstrategy* based on investigation and placement. As a means to prevent and deal with child maltreatment, this response is hopelessly inadequate.

A New Strategy to Prevent and Remedy Child Maltreatment

The U.S. Advisory Board's findings, reported in 1990, were followed in January 1991 by the release of the recommendations of the National Commission on Child

Welfare and Family Preservation. After conducting public hearings across the country, extensive research, and public discussions, the commission issued *A Commitment to Change*, calling for the creation of a new framework for family services.[24]

This new framework is composed of three complementary approaches or components. The first one broadly supports all families, the second assists families in need, and the third protects abused and neglected children. Each component is important individually, but all three must work in concert to support and improve the quality of life for children and families. From a policy and practice perspective, the three components are equal yet distinct, each with its own goals and locus of control. Families receiving help under any one of the components will have access to a "seamless" and unbroken chain of services linked by common goals and a common philosophy. The key to this new system is its ability to respond in a culturally sensitive manner to any and all family needs where and when they arise.

Component I: Supporting Families for Healthy Child Development

Under Component I, community service networks will be responsible for pioneering new ways to organize and offer services and provide or arrange for access to a range of family services currently unavailable in much of the country. The plan relies on establishing community service networks that are able to address a range of family development needs. The emphasis is on helping families use local community and neighborhood resources (both formal and informal) and on forging strong links between traditional health, nutrition, mental health, education, juvenile justice, drug and alcohol, law enforcement, and social service programs.

Component I has four goals: to ensure healthy child development, to preserve families, to strengthen parents' capacity to raise children, and to build community capacity to help families fulfill their responsibilities.[25] Services are to be voluntarily selected by families and build on the family's strengths; they are to be family-focused and readily accessible to all families who need them. The community service network should represent a mix of prevention activities and provide comprehensive developmental assistance aimed at strengthening healthy family functioning and child development.[26]

Local networks under Component I are likely to differ widely, but all should: (1) identify families that may need services, (2) assess the developmental needs of families and children, (3) provide information on available services, (4) help families enroll or register in the services they have selected, and (5) provide access to needed services in local neighborhoods.[27] Finally, to be effective, program directors and staff must coordinate their efforts with private agencies, the corporate sector, and the local departments of state human service agencies.

Component I envisions that the services available in a community should reflect the community's unique needs.[28] In recognition of limitations on funding, states and local communities may give priority to neighborhoods with large numbers of children in poverty. But, in any case, programs and services should be viewed and managed as services needed by and appropriate for *all* families.

Component I comprises a variety of services.[29] For example, prenatal care ensures healthy newborns and prevents low birth weights; it includes regular prenatal examinations, nutrition education, and education on the effects of drugs, alcohol, and tobacco. Parenting education aims to support parents in the everyday tasks of raising children by furnishing information on appropriate discipline, child development, and play activities. Child care services help parents find child care providers and educate them on factors to consider in choosing a provider. Home visitors are paraprofessionals or professionals who visit new parents to provide assistance and education and to identify families at risk for abuse and neglect. Finally, every community should have a strong family planning program and should fully utilize the government-funded Early Periodic Screening, Diagnosis and Treatment (EPSDT) program for children's health.

Component II: Assisting Families and Children in Need

Families served under Component II face problems that are too severe to be resolved solely by services offered in Component I but do not involve child maltreatment, which is the basis for Component III services. Component II services are transitional in the sense that families seek them when their current needs and resources require it; their involvement ends when the problem has been resolved.

Component II has two fundamental goals: to strengthen and preserve families that are experiencing problems before they become too severe, and to improve the capacity of service agencies to deliver coordinated and collaborative family-focused community services. To achieve these goals, human service programs delivered through health, mental health, juvenile justice, substance abuse, education, and social service agencies must invest in and commit themselves to focused interagency collaboration, coordination, and case management.[30]

As in Component I, family service programs under Component II will offer preventive and early intervention services, delivered through a community-based network. At this level, the network must be capable of providing intake and family assessment, referral to service providers, advocacy for service development and interagency coordination, and case management to link clients to the full range of services offered across multiple service systems and to ensure that these services are received completely but without duplication.[31]

Component II establishes outcome indicators to measure child and family well-being in terms of family stability, child safety, the physical and mental health of the child and family, and the educational attainment of the child. The following measures illustrate the kinds of goals this new service network is intended to achieve:

> Improved parental capacity to support the social and educational needs of their children, as measured by improved school performance and reduced incidence of teen pregnancy

Prevention of child abuse and neglect, as measured by fewer referrals to child protection services

Prevention of out-of-home placement, as measured by fewer children placed outside their homes because of education, mental health, delinquency-related, or other problems.[32]

Component II includes intensive, inhome family preservation services provided by specially trained workers and designed to help parents become self-sufficient and avoid behavior that may become abusive or neglectful.[33] Other services are respite care, which is designed to provide temporary relief to a parent or caretaker of a child with a defined need, day treatment, mental health services, substance abuse treatment for children and adults, and services for pregnant adolescents.

Component II focuses on early intervention, targeted to families in which identifiable problems have already emerged but have not yet precipitated a crisis. As in Component I, individual communities should be able to target certain populations to receive priority in service.

Component III: Protecting Abused and Neglected Children

The third and final component has three goals: to protect children and youths who have suffered serious harm or are at risk of suffering serious harm, to ensure that reasonable efforts are made to maintain children in their own homes once abuse or neglect has been substantiated, and to provide permanency as quickly as possible for children who are removed from their family.[34] Component III targets families in which child maltreatment has occurred, defined as "a recent act or failure to act on the part of a parent that results in death or serious physical, sexual, emotional, or imminent risk of serious harm to a child under age 18."[35]

Services in Component III are designed to eliminate abusive or neglectful behavior toward children. Network activities and interaction are directed toward enhancing the child's and family's ability to function. To prevent out-of-home placements, and to support families, communities must have access to intensive inhome services. Court intervention should occur only when necessary to protect the child. When a child cannot be reunited with his or her family, services should focus on providing the child with a stable living arrangement that may include preparation for and support in adoption, long-term foster family or relative care, or independent living.

Building on Components I and II, programs under Component III should be delivered by specially trained workers. Outcome measures might include the following:

The family's ability to minimize or eliminate problems that place the child in jeopardy and to care for its child in a developmentally appropriate fashion

The appropriateness of the child's physical, mental, emotional, social, and
educational development for his or her age and life experience
The child's achievement of a stable living situation and maintainenance of
stable relationships.[36]

The services constituting Component III are, generally, the familiar steps
taken to protect a child after abuse or neglect has started: report taking, report
screening, investigation, risk assessment, determination of disposition, and case
plan development and implementation. Out-of-home placement would be
avoided but, if resorted to, would take such forms as kinship care, foster care,
group home care, and adoption.[37]

Conclusion

The lack of a comprehensive strategy for combatting child maltreatment has resulted in a system that allocates resources disproportionately to out-of-home
placements following substantiated abuse and neglect while failing to support
preventive programs. If we are to prevent tragedies like Joshua DeShaney's, we
must understand the systemic problems that produce them and seek solutions
through systemic reform.

We must first agree on a common definition of child maltreatment. Each state
must examine its child abuse and neglect statutes, policies, and regulations to
ensure that child protective services promote a family-focused approach. States
must develop a range of services from many disciplines to assure that reasonable
efforts are made to keep children in their own homes. The array of services available to children in need of protection must be expanded and adequately staffed
and funded. Preventing out-of-home placements requires the development of a
core group of services to respond to the special needs of children and families at
risk. When children must be removed from their families, services and programs
should be used either to reunify the family or to arrange prompt, permanent
alternative placements and long-term care.

The majority decision in *DeShaney v. Winnebago County Department of Social Services* can be viewed as an opportunity to examine serious shortcomings in the
current child welfare system and create a more prevention-oriented strategy. If
we as a country fail to do so, we can expect the crisis in child abuse and neglect
and its long list of victims to grow. Affirmative duties toward children after *De-
Shaney* stand at a crossroads. Which path will we take?

NOTES

Note: Points of view or opinions expressed in this chapter are those of the authors
and should not be construed as representing the official position of the American
Public Welfare Association.

1. *See* Center for the Study of Social Policy, Kids Count Databook: State Profiles of Child Wellbeing 3 (1991).
2. *See id.*
3. *See id.*
4. *See* U.S. Advisory Board on Child Abuse and Neglect, Creating Caring Communities: Blueprint for an Effective Federal Policy on Child Abuse and Neglect, at vii (1991) (the board's second report).
5. Tatara, Some Additional Explanations for the Recent Rise in the U.S. Child Substitute Care Population, VCIS Research Notes (Voluntary Cooperative Information Systems, American Public Welfare Association) (Nov. 1991) at 1.
6. Select Committee on Children, Youth, and Families, No Place to Call Home: Discarded Children in America, H.R. Rep. No. 395, 101st Cong., 2d sess. 65–74 (1990).
7. *See* DeShaney v. Winnebago County Dep't. of Social Servs., 489 U.S. 189 (1989).
8. U.S. Advisory Board on Child Abuse and Neglect, Child Abuse and Neglect: Critical First Steps in Response to a National Emergency, at vii (1990) [hereinafter Board, Critical First Steps].
9. *Id.*
10. *See id.* at x–xi.
11. *See* National Commission on Child Welfare and Family Preservation, Factbook on Public Child Welfare Services and Staff 3 (1990) [hereinafter Commission, Factbook].
12. *Id.* at 43. "In either case, dire necessity is, in essence, the key criterion for service provision." *Id.*
13. *Id.* Indeed, in a time of increasing interest in comprehensive, "holistic," and preventive services, "intensive home-based services and respite services are among the least available of the 40 services that were examined." *Id.*
14. *See id.* at 50, 71. The salary range for entry-level direct service worker positions was $17,344 to $24,882. *See id.* at 55.
15. *See id.* at 47.
16. *See id.* at 48.
17. *See id.* at 55–61.
18. *See id.* at 56–57.
19. Deshaney v. Winnebago County Dep't. of Social Servs., 489 U.S. 189, 192–93 (1989).
20. *See id.* at 192.
21. *See supra* notes 14, 17–19 and accompanying text.
22. *See* Commission, Factbook, *supra* note 11, at 72.
23. *See id.* at 62.
24. *See* The National Commission on Child Welfare and Family Preservation, A Commitment to Change (1990) [hereinafter Commission, Commitment to Change].
25. *See id.* at 11.
26. The importance of prevention has also been emphasized by the U.S. Advisory Board on Child Abuse and Neglect. Its recommendation 25 states:

> The Secretary of Health and Human Services, in conjunction with his counterparts in the Federal Government . . . , and the Governors of the several

states should ensure that efforts to prevent the maltreatment of children are substantially increased. Such efforts, at a minimum, should involve a significant expansion in the availability of home visitation and follow-up services for all families of newborns.

Board, Critical First Steps, *supra* note 8, at 82. The board noted further that, in the face of budgetary constraints, advocates of prevention and advocates of treatment have "battled to expand the approach they favor," *id.*, hampering the system's ability to respond to child abuse and neglect. Accordingly, recommendation 26 states: "The U.S. Congress and State and local legislative bodies should ensure that, in any expansion of programs concerned with child abuse and neglect, resources devoted to prevention and resources devoted to treatment do not come at the expense of each other." *Id.* at 83.

27. *See* Commission, Commitment to Change, *supra* note 24, at 11.

28. *See id.* at 13.

29. *See id.* at vi.

30. *See id.* at 17.

31. *See id.* at 18–19.

32. *See id.* at 19.

33. *See id.*

34. *See id.* at 23.

35. *Id.* This definition was developed by the National Association of Public Child Welfare Administrators, an affiliate of the APWA.

36. *See id.* at 25.

37. *See id.* at 26–27.

■ CHAPTER ELEVEN

Unsafe Havens: The Case for Constitutional Protection of Foster Children from Abuse and Neglect

Michael B. Mushlin

IN A MIDWESTERN community not long ago, a one-year-old girl who required constant medical attention for epileptic seizures was sent by a state child welfare department to a foster home known by the state to be inadequate.[1] In fact, the caseworker assigned by the state to supervise the home had recommended that the department not use this "marginal" setting except on a temporary, short-term basis. Children sent to this home in the past had been "ill clothed" and had not received attention for medical problems. The warning was ignored. When the child's caseworker reported that the foster parents were not bringing the child to her scheduled medical appointments, again the child welfare department did not respond. Finally, after two-and-one-half years and pressure from the child's physician, the child was removed from the foster home. By this time the child, now three-and-one-half, had not received treatment for her epilepsy and was also experiencing other medical problems.[2] Even after the state registered an official finding of abuse against the home for its failure to care for this child, the state continued without interruption to place abused and neglected children there.

In the same state another foster child was assaulted while in foster care. The state knew of the attack but did nothing. Within four months the child was sexually abused by the foster father in the same home.[3] In a third foster home, a four-

---

year-old girl was whipped by her foster mother and made to stand with her hands extended over her head for thirty minutes. The child was being punished for being dirty. Although the caseworker determined that the child had been beaten, and reported this to her superiors, no action was taken and the child was returned to the home.[4]

In another part of the county, a troubled young boy who wet his bed was placed in a foster home. The foster mother, frustrated at her inability to control his behavior, sought help from the state's child welfare agency. Her pleas were ignored. The situation deteriorated until one night the foster mother forced the child to "drink his urine."[5]

None of these cases received public attention, nor were any the subject of reported court decisions or large damage awards. Each, however, is an example of the stark reality of life in foster homes[6] for too many of the nation's half-million[7] foster children. This chapter assesses the constitutional rights of foster children to protection. Since the early 1960s, the number of children in foster care has increased fivefold.[8] The foster care program now ranks with prisons, mental institutions, and juvenile detention and treatment centers as a major state-operated custodial program.[9]

The chapter argues that foster children have a claim to federal judicial protection from harm while in state care equal to, if not greater than, that of institutionalized persons, who are already accorded significant protections.[10] Yet, in stark contrast to scores of decrees entered to protect institutionalized persons from physical harm, very few federal cases[11] have enforced by injunctive decree a constitutional right of foster children to protection from harm while in foster care.

The six sections of this chapter present the case for direct federal court involvement in aiding children who are at risk of abuse and neglect while in foster care. The first section discusses the extent of abuse and neglect in foster care as well as the structural causes of this maltreatment. It also explains the inevitable failure of the political branches of government to confront the problem. The next section describes the constitutional right to safety and surveys the judicial treatment of that right, including the lack of development of the right for children in foster care. I then examine differences between children in foster family care and institutionalized persons, and argue that none of the differences can account for the failure to accord foster children the benefits of the right to safety. The following section explores remedies and demonstrates that damage remedies are inadequate because their availability is severely circumscribed by a variety of immunity doctrines, and because, even if they were available, monetary awards would deflect attention from the root causes of abuse and neglect of foster children. This section presents the case for structural injunctions as the most practical remedy.

I then consider whether federal courts are the appropriate forum to address the right to safety for foster children. Until the 1960s, federal courts declined to become involved in cases involving custodial conditions because of a self-imposed abstention policy called the "hands-off" doctrine.[12] Under that doctrine, courts deferred entirely to the judgments of administrators.[13] The awakening of interest in the rights of the confined led to the erosion of that doctrine.[14] In 1974 the Supreme Court announced definitively that the hands-off doctrine was inconsistent with constitutional principles.[15] Since then, lower federal courts have intervened on behalf of the institutionalized, at least when necessary to protect against the most severe conditions of confinement.[16] This section concludes that federal courts are also the appropriate forum for foster care right-to-safety cases, and argues that none of the judicially created abstention doctrines bar them.

In the final section I propose four guidelines that, if followed, would maximize the effectiveness of district courts in making foster care safe. The chapter concludes that federal judicial involvement offers the promise of benefiting children in foster care by materially improving a system that thus far has resisted reform. Without judicial scrutiny, the abuse and neglect that many children suffered in their original homes will continue after the state places them in foster care. For these children, the temporary, substitute family system imposed on them by the state will not be a haven, but a hell.

Abuse and Neglect in Foster Care

Foster care is intended to provide a temporary, safe haven for children whose parents are unable to care for them.[17] Too often, however, this purpose is not realized, and children are exposed to abuse and neglect by foster parents, and to serious injury due to the system's failure to provide for stable care or to attend to the children's medical problems. The failure of foster care programs to follow appropriate minimum standards that would ensure the care and protection of children has led to increased rates of foster care abuse and neglect. Despite the considerable costs, to both the children affected and to society generally, the political process has been unresponsive to calls for reform of foster care systems.

Types of Abuse and Neglect

Whatever the reason for placement, foster children have not had a normal upbringing. The bonds to a foster child's permanent family have been disrupted. Foster children suffer disproportionately from serious emotional, medical, and psychological disabilities.[18] To compound matters, it is well established that they are at high risk of further maltreatment while in foster care.[19] Foster children, therefore, are especially vulnerable individuals, prone to become victims unless special care is taken to protect them. Two broad categories of mistreatment have been identified.

Foster Family Abuse and Neglect

No one knows how many children are abused or neglected while in foster care,[20] but the problem is more widespread than is currently acknowledged. Children in foster family care have been reported severely beaten,[21] killed,[22] and subjected to bizarre punishments[23] or parental neglect.[24]

Foster children seem peculiarly vulnerable to sexual abuse. By definition, there is no permanent kinship bond in foster care, so that the traditional incest taboo does not operate.[25] The lack of permanent ties,[26] combined with the cultural and class gaps that often exist between foster families and foster children, can also create an environment in which expressions of verbal hostility may erupt.[27]

While foster care has been frequently criticized for other reasons, some observers claim that, at the very least, children in foster care are protected from a high risk of abuse and neglect.[28] The evidence, however, does not bear out these hopes. One study reported that the rate of substantiated abuse and neglect in New York City foster family care was more than one-and-one-half times that of children in the general population.[29] A national survey of foster family abuse and neglect, completed in 1986 by the National Foster Care Education Project, revealed rates of abuse that, at their highest, were over ten times greater for foster children than for children in the general population.[30]

Program Abuse

An equally dangerous form of mistreatment results when the foster care system itself fails to provide children with a stable and secure home setting, or when it does not provide for the child's medical, psychological, and emotional needs. This type of mistreatment has been termed "program abuse."[31]

Stability of Care. Children entering foster care placement inevitably experience the pain of separation from their family setting, no matter how inadequate that setting has been.[32] The substitute experience compounds that trauma if it does not provide a stable home environment.[33] Unfortunately, foster home placements are frequently extremely unstable. Often foster children are shuffled from home to home without any opportunity to form an attachment to an adult caretaker. Stays in four or more foster homes are common.[34] Aside from the trauma entailed by this movement, the likelihood that the child will be abused at some time during his stay increases with each move.[35]

Medical Care. As the substitute parent, the child welfare program assumes responsibility for the child's medical and psychological care.[36] All children need medical care, but the need is acute for foster children, who are less healthy than any other identifiable group of youngsters in the United States.[37] The provision of treatment cannot await the end of a foster care placement.

Nevertheless, medical care systems for foster children are inadequate "to manage effectively even simple and common child health problems."[38] For example, a comprehensive study of the medical status of foster children found that many of the pre-school-age foster children studied had not received vaccinations for the prevention of childhood diseases.[39] Fourteen percent had received no medical examination upon admission to foster care, and the average physical exam was incomplete.[40] Forty-seven percent of the children had visual problems that had not been evaluated by an optometrist.[41] Over 40 percent needed dental care but had not been to a dentist.[42] Only one-fourth of the children who had identifiable emotional or developmental problems had received treatment.[43]

The Causes and Costs of Maltreatment

Although not all of the facets of abuse and neglect of foster children have been examined, enough is known to dispel notions that maltreatment is inevitable or that responsibility for maltreatment rests entirely with foster parents. Instead, a growing body of evidence links foster family abuse and neglect to the state child welfare agencies that fail to meet minimum professional standards.[44] Such standards require the careful screening and licensing of potential foster care applicants,[45] training of those who are chosen for the job,[46] careful matching of foster children with foster parents,[47] and regular, continual supervision by competent caseworkers[48] of the foster care placement.[49] Training, casework support, and consultation with social workers are often essential for foster parents to understand and guide foster children. Absent these forms of state backup, foster parents can find the behavior of foster children "baffling or inexplicable," or may feel that they are in an endless "struggle for control."[50] Professional standards also provide for the elimination of foster home overcrowding,[51] strict bans on improper punishment,[52] and prompt referrals for outside investigation of suspected maltreatment by foster parents.[53] Failure to follow professional standards results in increased abuse and neglect, with a serious detrimental effect on society. Nevertheless, the legislative and executive branches of government have not responded to calls for foster care reform.

The Failure of Reform: Legislative and Executive Default

Although its deficiencies have been spotlighted almost from its start,[54] the American foster care system has developed a remarkable immunity to reform. It has been the subject of studies at the state and national levels,[55] yet little appreciable improvement has resulted. In 1979 the president of the Children's Defense Fund, Marian Wright Edelman, concluded that conditions in the system remained a "national disgrace."[56] In the same year, the National Commission on Children in Need of Parents[57] issued its unanimous verdict that "[w]ith some admirable exceptions, the foster care system in America is an unconscionable failure, harming large numbers of the children it purports to serve."[58]

It is not difficult to understand the reasons for this failure. Foster care systems are administered by staffs that are "overburdened, poorly paid and often unprepared professionally"[59] for the difficult work they are called upon to perform. Lack of financial support has led to a system that is poorly organized and usually lacks even the most basic information about its own operation.[60] Foster parents as well receive inadequate financial and professional support. Payments offered to foster parents are often less than the cost of caring for the child's basic needs, adding financial stress to the burdens of being a foster parent.[61] Funding is especially important if foster care placements are to be made safe.

Why foster care is "least favored by the legislature"[62] also is not difficult to discern. A service almost always reserved for the children of the poor,[63] in most states foster care is disproportionately used by minority children,[64] who, not unexpectedly, have encountered discrimination in the foster care system.[65] The disparate treatment of minorities also appears to mean that they run an even greater risk of abuse and neglect in foster care than other foster children.[66] While other parents experiencing difficulties with child rearing can rely on private school and paid professional support, the poor and the underclass must resort to their local child welfare agency.

Supporters of foster care reform have concentrated on the states' overreliance on foster care rather than on the issue of safety within the system. Yet even if these reforms are successful, "there will always be some children—the orphans, the abandoned, and the severely abused—for whom substitute care outside of their homes will be necessary."[67]

The Call for Judicial Involvement

Courts would provide a great benefit to society were they to become involved in foster care reform, both by preventing the indignity of abuse and by protecting foster children's futures. Federal courts are understandably reluctant to become involved in the protracted endeavors required by large-scale institutional reform of this kind, yet the case for the exercise of judicial discretion to ensure protection of foster children clearly is compelling.

As discussed below, the right to protection occupies a critical niche in our system of government; it has historical roots in our philosophical conception of the fundamental role of government and the justification for its existence.[68] If a group in society is denied the right to protection, it is difficult to imagine how it can enjoy any other right. Yet foster children are powerless to obtain this right for themselves.[69] Involvement by the federal courts in advancing the right to protection is thus consistent with the notion of the limited intervention of the federal judiciary. An additional justification for judicial involvement in foster care reform is the long history of solicitude for the needs of children, who, because of their obvious dependency, need special protection.[70] As long ago as 1944,[71] the Supreme Court recognized the state's strong interest in safeguarding children from abuse.[72] This interest is reflected in a virtually unbroken line of Supreme Court opinions upholding state actions that might otherwise have been unconstitutional but that were saved by the need to protect children.[73]

Having examined the nature and scope of the problem, the foster care system's resistance to change through the legislature or the executive, and the consistency of judicial involvement in foster care reform with principles of judicial intervention, we now examine which substantive rights justify judicial involvement.

The Constitutional Right to Safety

In 1982, a unanimous court in *Youngberg v. Romeo* held that the state owes an "unquestioned duty" to provide reasonable safety for all residents of a state institution for the mentally retarded.[74] Unquestioned though the right may be, recognition of its existence developed slowly, and it continues to lack clear standards defining its scope. Nevertheless, the right to safety has deep roots in American legal and philosophical thought. This section briefly traces the origin of the right and its development in lower federal courts and in the Supreme Court, and provides a brief comment on the standards that courts have used to determine whether or not the right has been violated. It concludes with a discussion of the application of the right to foster children.

The Development of the Right to Safety

The right to safety for the institutionalized invoked by Justice Powell in *Youngberg* can be traced as far back as Blackstone, Cooke, and Hobbes—progenitors of modern American law—all of whom recognized that the first function of government is protection of the governed.[75] Despite its deep jurisprudential underpinnings, the right to safety has been recognized only recently as an enforceable constitutional right of the institutionalized.

By the late 1960s and early 1970s, federal courts, responding to the Supreme Court's receptive approach to civil rights cases, slowly began to lower the barrier to judicial review of institutional conditions. In 1974 Justice White sounded the Supreme Court's death knell for the "hands-off" doctrine in a single line: "There is no iron curtain between the Constitution and the prisons of this country."[76] With the demise of the "hands-off" doctrine, lower courts were free to consider right-to-safety cases without jurisdictional hindrance.

While the right to safety was first articulated in the context of prisons, and has been most fully developed there, it has been implemented in other institutional settings as well. In 1973 a federal district court held that a class of residents of the Willowbrook State School for the Mentally Retarded had the right "to reasonable protection from harm."[77] The court distinguished this right to safety from a right to treatment, which it declined to recognize. Courts since have followed the Willowbrook decision, applying it in other institutionalized settings as well. It is now firmly established that the mentally ill and retarded,[78] residents of state juvenile training schools,[79] suspects in police custody,[80] and pretrial detainees[81] have a constitutional right to protection.

As in prison cases, the right is most frequently implemented by courts in class action suits seeking injunctive relief, rather than in individual suits for damages, where the plaintiff's claim often founders on one or more of the various immunity doctrines.[82] Injunctive relief has provided significant reforms in several institutional contexts. Courts have ordered institutions for the mentally retarded or ill to make structural improvements,[83] decrease their population,[84] hire more staff,[85] institute staff training programs,[86] and provide training of residents.[87] In pretrial detention decisions, courts have been willing to close jails where deemed necessary to ensure safety.[88]

Since the Eighth Amendment does not apply outside the context of prison,[89] courts have relied on different theories to support the right to safety for those in nonpenal institutions. The due process clause of the Fourteenth Amendment is most frequently invoked. For confinement to meet constitutional standards, the conditions of confinement must bear some relationship to its purpose.[90] If, as in the case of the mentally ill, confinement is supposed to permit them to be treated and protected, the deprivation of liberty lacks constitutional support when it fails to advance those purposes.[91]

In 1982 the Supreme Court explicitly recognized the right to safety in the context of institutionalized mentally retarded persons. *Youngberg v. Romeo*[92] was a damage action brought on behalf of a thirty-three-year-old retarded man with the mental capacity of an eighteen-month-old child. Romeo, confined involuntarily to the Pennhurst State Hospital, was "injured on numerous occasions, both by his own violence and by the reactions of other [inmates] to him."[93] Romeo's mother brought suit on his behalf against Pennhurst's director and two supervisors, alleging at least sixty-three incidents of violence against him. In an amended complaint, Romeo sought compensation for the failure to be protected and provided with "treatment or programs for his mental retardation."[94]

The Supreme Court held that the right to safety for the institutionalized was an "unquestioned duty" of the state and was one of the "essentials of care that the state must provide."[95] The majority included the right to safety within the "historic liberty interests" essential to ensure a person's bodily integrity from unnecessary invasion by the state, thus qualifying the right to safety for substantive protection under the due process clause.[96] The right survives involuntary commitment, and since the mentally retarded, unlike convicts, have not been guilty of any wrongdoing, the Court intimated that their rights may be even greater than those of prisoners.[97]

While the Court had little difficulty identifying the right to safety as a substantive due process entitlement of the involuntarily confined, it struggled to articulate a clear standard for determining when the right had been violated. The Court rejected the "deliberate indifference" standard used in prison right-to-safety cases and by the district court in *Youngberg*.[98] On the other hand, the Court rejected the less demanding "substantial necessity" test as well.[99] It is not entirely clear what test the Court adopted in its place. Justice Powell stated that courts should balance "the liberty [interest] of the individual" in safety against "the demands of an organized society."[100] Restrictions on liberty that are "reasonably related to legitimate government objectives" are not unconstitutional even if they result in a "lack of absolute safety."[101] Just what "relevant state interests" Justice Powell had in mind for this balance are not readily apparent from his opinion. Despite the uncertainty about the appropriate standard, the Court's opinion leaves little doubt that a constitutional right to safety is included in the notion of substantive due process.

The Development of the Right to Safety in Foster Care Case Law

The limited case law suggests a judicial reluctance to accept the notion that foster children should be beneficiaries of the right to safety. *Taylor ex rel. Walker v. Ledbetter*[102] illustrates this trend. On behalf of a two-year-old girl, plaintiff sued the Gwinnett County, Georgia, Department of Family and Children's Services for severe injuries that occurred while the child was in foster care. The original panel in *Taylor* affirmed the district court's dismissal of the complaint for failure to state a claim upon which relief could be granted. The Eleventh Circuit panel declared that "[f]ederal courts should exercise great caution in becoming involved in the decisions of state and local officials charged with the custody and welfare of children."[103] Thus, the court articulated what amounted to another federal abstention doctrine. Although the Eleventh Circuit, sitting en banc, reversed the panel's decision and held that the complaint should not have been dismissed, it left for further proceedings whether or not the child's claim "constitutes a liberty interest protected by the due process clause."[104]

Only in the Second Circuit has the right to safety been squarely recognized and enforced in the foster care context. In *Brooks v. Richardson*, the first reported case to discuss this issue, a district judge in the Southern District of New York refused to dismiss the pro se complaint of a mother who maintained that her child had been abused and neglected for over five years while in foster care.[105] It was not until the Second Circuit's decisions in *Doe v. New York City Department of Social Services*,[106] however, that a court actually awarded damages in a disputed case involving the right to safety. A child who had been beaten and sexually abused by her foster father sued, claiming that her plight had been or should have been known to the agency responsible for her foster care.[107]

Although it found for the plaintiff, the *Doe* court did not identify the source of the constitutional right it invoked or discuss the rationale for finding that the right applied in a foster care setting. The Court of Appeals intimated that attributes of foster care might render the application of right-to-protection concepts developed in the prison field unduly burdensome to foster care administrators. Thus, a constitutional near-vacuum seems to exist with respect to foster children. Several factors may account for this curious state of affairs.

First, foster care is seen as a particularly benevolent service run by the state with the best of intentions.[108] Prisons, jails, mental institutions, and homes for the retarded have long been regarded as dumping grounds for persons who are despised by society.[109] It is relatively easy for the judicial mind, once freed from the shackles of the hands-off doctrine, to imagine abuses taking place in these dark places; the same is not true for foster care. When children are taken from their parents out of an expressed concern for their welfare and, following removal, placed in a seemingly normal home for care by civilians who have volunteered for the job, one is not automatically concerned. The supervision of the placement is done not by wardens or jailers, but by social workers, members of the epitome of a helping profession.[110] It is hard to grasp the idea that here, too, abuses can occur, and that when they do, they are largely unchecked by the state.

Flowing from the idea that only good intentions are at work in the foster care field is the corollary notion that decisions with regard to foster care require a type of skill that is not appropriately the subject of judicial review. After all, the job of a foster care agency involves child rearing, a discipline whose complexity has generated scores of theories and occupied the attention of numerous scholars. It may have been this thought that motivated the Supreme Court, in a case involving the due process rights of a foster child and a foster parent to remain together, to declare that foster care administration involves "issues of unusual delicacy . . . where professional judgments regarding desirable procedures are constantly and rapidly changing."[111]

Third, in addition to the courts' reluctance to entertain right-to-safety cases, litigators do not seem to press claims to safety in foster care with the same vigor that they exert in the prison and mental health fields. Fewer public interest lawyers work in the foster care field than in the other fields where this issue has been litigated,[112] and the few that are in the field have primarily chosen to concentrate on other pressing issues that foster care administration raises, including questions of permanency planning and preventive services, often to the exclusion of right-to-safety concerns. Success in a right-to-safety case will not provide a permanent home for the children, only a safer placement while they remain in temporary care.[113] Thus, the dearth of lawyers pursuing the issue and the reluctance of the courts to entertain the claims have combined to create a barrier between foster children and the constitutional promise of safe custodial conditions. It is now necessary to consider whether any principled reasons exist that might render the right to safety inapplicable to foster children.

Withholding the Right to Safety

There are two possible explanations for denying a constitutional right to safety to foster children while providing it to other groups or persons cared for by the state. First, children in foster family care are not institutionalized. Second, foster children come into state care voluntarily. Does either of these proposed differences provide a principled basis for a determination that foster children are not eligible for the constitutional protection of the right to safety?

Custody Without Institutionalization

Children in foster family care do not reside in large, communal custodial settings like prisons or mental institutions.[114] Moreover, because of their age, children in foster care would be under the control of an adult whether or not they were placed in foster care. In this sense, children in foster care differ from institutionalized adults, who, but for their confinement, would be free to do what they wished and live where they pleased.

These factors were important to the Supreme Court in *Lehman v. Lycoming County Children's Services Agency*,[115] which held that a foster child was not in "custody" for purposes of the habeas corpus jurisdiction of the federal court. Without reaching the merits, the Court held that habeas corpus did not lie because the children "are not prisoners . . . [who] suffer any restrictions imposed by a state criminal justice system."[116]

This reasoning is misplaced. Foster children, like prisoners, rely on the state for shelter, clothing, food, and freedom from physical abuse or neglect. Although they may not be held in large institutional settings, they are just as dependent on the state for their needs as are prisoners. This similarity is not diminished because the state chooses to act through private agents in the foster care context. Surely, if the state maintained a group home for children on state property, providing two adults per child, it would be most difficult to distinguish the children's situation from that of prisoners. In that circumstance, the state, having institutionalized the children, would presumably be compelled to comply with the constitutional requirements, including the right to safety, applicable to institutionalized persons generally.[117] Regardless of the locus of confinement, the sole purpose of the state's intervention into the children's lives is protection.[118] Both the rationale for foster care placement and the dependence on the state emphasize the absurdity of excluding foster children from the constitutional protection from harm merely because they are not institutionalized in the traditional way.[119]

Voluntary Placement and the Right to Safety

The overwhelming majority of foster care placements are voluntary, meaning that the child's parents have consented to a placement.[120] Consent to foster care occurs when physical or mental illness, economic problems, or other family crises make it impossible for parents—particularly single mothers—to provide a stable home life for their children.[121] Often the consensual placement follows a state-sponsored investigation into deteriorating home conditions caused by these pressures. At other times, a parent may seek government help.[122]

The decision by the Supreme Court in *Youngberg* can be understood as supporting the notion that the distinction between voluntary and involuntary institutionalization is significant. In no fewer than eleven places in the majority opinion, Justice Powell stated that the due process right to safety that the Court was recognizing for the first time applied to the involuntarily committed.[123] Given the emphasis by the Court on the involuntary nature of the confinement, one must ask whether the entitlement to safety in foster care should depend on, or be influenced by, the voluntary nature of most foster care placements. For three reasons, it should not.

First, characterizing foster care placements as voluntary is highly questionable; certainly they are not voluntary for the person under care. The children themselves have no more choice about placement than an involuntarily committed prisoner or mental patient. And even for the foster child's parent, the choice is largely illusory as well. Many parents reluctantly agree to relinquish custody temporarily in the face of a clear inability to care for their child by themselves.[124] This is particularly true of impecunious parents, who "have little choice but to submit to state-supervised child care when family crises strike."[125]

Parents in this predicament must either consent to the placement, retaining some chance of having the child returned later, or refuse consent and face the prospect of losing a state-sponsored child protection proceeding in the local family court, and thereby significantly diminishing the possibility of retaining parental rights.[126] Even when the consent is genuine, it cannot reasonably be understood as a voluntary decision to expose a child to unsafe conditions. Indeed, such a decision would constitute child abuse as that term is defined in most state laws.[127]

The second reason that the constitutional right to safety should not depend upon the voluntariness of the placement is that the right, as even the *Youngberg* court appears to have recognized, is too basic to depend upon that factor alone. The Supreme Court's reasoning in *Youngberg* itself, notwithstanding its repeated use of the term "involuntarily committed," suggests that the right to safety encompasses the voluntarily as well as the involuntarily confined.

Third, the right to safety must apply to voluntary admissions because of the established constitutional principle that a state must administer constitutionally even those services that it only provides on a voluntary basis.[128] Similar treatment by the Supreme Court of the state provision of education illustrates this principle. The Supreme Court has repeatedly held that a state cannot be compelled to establish a system of free education for its citizens.[129] However, the Court has also held that once it elects to provide one, it must administer that system in conformity with constitutional commands.[130] Similarly, although there is no recognized affirmative constitutional right to the provision of foster care,[131] the state, having chosen to provide the service, is obligated to administer it constitutionally.[132]

A Remedy for Violence in Foster Care

It is well established that for every right there should be a corresponding remedy.[133] It is particularly important to find an effective remedy for violence in foster care. Without the basic right to safety, the dignity of foster children and their ability to develop into mature, functioning adults are diminished. This section canvasses the available remedies for violence in foster care, and demonstrates that the structural injunction, not the damage action, offers the only effective remedy.

Damage Actions

Abused foster children are increasingly turning to state damage actions for compensation for the injuries they have suffered. Some of the suits that have survived pretrial dismissal[134] reveal a formidable array of state tort law barriers to ultimate success. Foremost among these is the common law doctrine of sovereign immunity. In its purest form, the doctrine bars a suit against a state agency providing a governmental service.[135] Suits are permitted in the doctrine's more modern version, but only if the plaintiff can show that the governmental activity sued upon is ministerial rather than discretionary.[136] The theory of this distinction is that the state ought to be free to carry on its wide-ranging activities unimpeded by the risk of liability for decisions that involve its discretionary, policy-making functions.[137]

In jurisdictions that recognize the modern sovereign immunity doctrine, a key issue in a suit brought by an abused foster child is whether or not an agency's actions involved discretionary decision-making. If the court finds that they did, sovereign immunity bars the suit regardless of the agency's negligence. The courts that have examined the issue have split on whether the conditions of foster care placement involve this judicially protected discretion. Several jurisdictions have held that there is no sovereign immunity[138] because there is no discretion involved in the foster care supervision process. Others, however, have applied sovereign immunity.[139] These courts, pointing to the "delicate and complex judgments" required of foster care agencies,[140] and alluding to foster care as an altruistic governmental service[141] entitled to a high degree of judicial deference, have shielded agencies from "hindsight scrutiny by the courts."[142]

Even in jurisdictions that do not accord sovereign immunity to foster care agencies, however, recovery is difficult. The agency may escape liability by shifting its portion of the blame for the injury to the foster parents.[143] Having done so, it is then able to avoid responsibility for the injury under the doctrine of respondeat superior, on the ground that foster parents are not employees of the state.[144]

In addition, in several jurisdictions foster parents are immune from suit for negligent supervision of their foster children[145] on the theory that foster parents stand in the place of permanent parents and therefore are entitled to the same family immunity.[146] If this "loco parentis"[147] doctrine of parental immunity is applied, no judgment can be awarded for negligence against foster parents for their failure to maintain a safe home. Even if the parental immunity doctrine is not invoked, however, the chance of a recovery remains slight. Foster parents, normally drawn from the ranks of moderate-income families, are often judgment-proof,[148] and as they are not considered state employees, the states do not indemnify them for judgments entered against them.[149]

Suits under state law against individual, state-employed caseworkers, while theoretically possible in states without sovereign immunity doctrines, are also unlikely to succeed because state-employed caseworkers are generally judgment-proof.[150] Federal civil rights damage actions are unavailing as well, because the Supreme Court has approved several imposing barriers to recovery in actions that charge violations of federal constitutional rights,[151] or "constitutional torts."[152]

Individual damage actions, even if available, are not useful mechanisms for obtaining reform. They tend to focus attention, myopically, on individual culpability for past actions instead of on detection and correction of institutional deficiencies that contribute to the maltreatment of foster children. By its nature, a claim for damages examines past wrongs. It seeks to compensate for an injury that has already occurred.[153] By contrast, an equitable action for an injunction seeks to prevent harm from occurring in the first instance.[154] Because an individual damage action is concerned with the culpability of the assigned caseworker or foster parent for the abuse suffered by the child, it diverts attention from the real culprit: the state's failure to fund and maintain an adequate foster care system.

With the real problem obscured, several undesirable results follow. The first is to shift blame for the danger to children onto overworked caseworkers or poorly selected and ill-trained foster parents.[155] Such charges are often unfair, since these people often lack the support or environment to do an acceptable job. Furthermore, this shift of focus diverts desperately needed funds from structural reform to individual payments that change nothing in the system.

Second, the fear of liability may influence qualified people who might otherwise be attracted to this form of public service to seek other kinds of work. Those who do enter or remain in the field may engage in what has been called "defensive social work,"[156] a term referring to practices followed because of a desire to avoid liability rather than to advance the interests of the children.[157] Thus, individual damage actions are not useful mechanisms for obtaining the structural reform that is needed to ensure the right to safety in foster care. Examination of the structural injunction, undertaken in the next section, demonstrates its superiority as a form of relief in the foster care area.

The Structural Injunction

Structural injunctions grant broad, detailed relief as a remedy to constitutional violations in the operation of government-run services. The structural injunction focuses prospectively on changing organizational behavior.[158] Beginning with *Brown v. Board of Education*,[159] and coming to maturity in later school desegregation cases, the structural injunction has since been used by federal courts in a wide variety of civil rights contexts.[160] Structural injunctions remain highly controversial. The criticism most often uttered in opposition to this form of relief is that "courts lack the expertise and administrative capacity necessary to improve"[161] large bureaucratic governmental systems such as the foster care system.

No doubt there are serious impediments to effective implementation of a decree calling for safe treatment of foster children. Implementation may require substantial restructuring of a large, bureaucratic institution. Reform will require piercing the institutional veil, for unless the will to change is transmitted to the caseworkers who select and supervise the foster homes, and to the foster parents themselves, the right to safety will be a chimera.[162] Moreover, organizational and psychological change alone will be insufficient. Safety will come only at a price. Increased appropriations will be needed to hire and train more and better-qualified caseworkers and foster parents and to provide support services for foster parents and children.[163]

The only remedy that holds significant promise of accomplishing this feat is a structural injunction. Of course, the benefits are not felt overnight; change is often measured by "inches and centimeters" rather than "leaps and bounds."[164] The cases involving prison violence exemplify the successful use of structural injunctions.[165] Similar results have been obtained in the implementation of structural injunctions dealing with other concerns. Prison systems in general have been reshaped,[166] and institutions for the mentally ill and the mentally retarded have been drastically altered.[167] Moreover, the available evidence on cases that have addressed educational issues indicates that compliance with judicially ordered reform is obtainable.[168] In all these areas, the initial recalcitrance of defendants to obey the decree was overcome by patient yet persistent efforts by courts and by plaintiffs' attorneys.

The Search for a Forum

Both federal and state courts have jurisdiction to entertain right-to-safety cases.[169] This section discusses the superiority of federal courts as a forum for right-to-safety cases and explains why two abstention doctrines that operate to close federal courts to some claims—the domestic relations exception and the *Younger v. Harris* doctrine—are not applicable to right-to-safety cases.

The Superiority of Federal Courts

Since the passage of the Fourteenth Amendment and the Civil Rights Act of 1871, federal courts have been seen as the "fundamental protectors of . . . federal rights."[170] The primary basis for confidence in the federal courts in this role is the protection provided by the Article III requirement of lifetime appointment for federal judges.[171] Since state judges often lack this electoral independence,[172] they are subject to political pressures that dilute their ability to order and supervise reform of state institutions, such as the foster care system.[173] In contrast to a case where a single individual is raising a single constitutional issue, the judge in a foster care reform case is asked to oversee the fundamental restructuring of a major social service system in order to guarantee an entire class essential constitutional rights.

There are other reasons why federal courts provide a superior forum for foster care right-to-safety cases. First, because federal judges spend the bulk of their time adjudicating federal claims, they have much greater familiarity with federal constitutional problems.[174] Second, federal judges tend to have what Professor Burt Neuborne terms a "psychological set"[175] that disposes them to be more receptive to constitutional claims. They are "heirs of a tradition of constitutional enforcement."[176]

This is not to say that state judges are uniformly unable to handle foster care reform cases competently. However, given the added obstacles that state judges must overcome to achieve the results required, foster care reform cases belong in federal court.[177] The following section examines whether either of two major abstention doctrines would prevent the federal courts from examining such cases.

Abstention in Right-to-Safety Cases

In *Younger v. Harris*,[178] the Supreme Court gave new life to an abstention doctrine applicable to civil rights cases.[179] The *Younger* doctrine is an exception to the general duty of federal courts to enforce federal law and "fearlessly protect"[180] federal constitutional rights from encroachment by state officials.[181] *Younger* instructs district courts to refrain from adjudicating properly presented federal constitutional issues when the relief sought would result in halting a state criminal proceeding, unless plaintiffs can demonstrate "extraordinary circumstances."[182] The Supreme Court has steadily enlarged the boundaries of this highly controversial doctrine by holding that the underlying policies dictate restraining federal involvement not only when state criminal proceedings are pending, but also during civil proceedings in which the state is a party in its "sovereign capacity."[183] To permit federal jurisdiction in such cases is considered undesirable because it would seem to imply that the state judiciary is unable or unwilling to enforce federal rights.[184] The doctrine's boundaries were enlarged in *Moore v. Sims*,[185] in which a sharply divided Court applied the *Younger* abstention doctrine to state child protection proceedings.

Although *Moore v. Sims* concerned an attempt by parents to regain custody of their children, which they lost when they were suspected of child abuse, courts have since interpreted the decision as requiring the application of the *Younger* principle to all family court proceedings.[186] While one must therefore ask whether the *Younger* doctrine applies or should apply to foster child right-to-safety cases, an examination of the policies underlying the doctrine reveals that the answer is no. The *Younger* doctrine developed as a response to special cases where the state's interest in enforcement of its own laws outweighs the strong federal interest in the federal court enforcement of federal constitutional rights.[187] In right-to-safety cases, the important constitutional rights at stake outweigh any possible interference with the state's law enforcement interests. In such a context, the balance tips against *Younger* abstention because the predicate for the doctrine's applicability is missing.

When a federal court changes the *procedures* to be used in a state proceeding by, for example, ordering the appointment of counsel in a support order proceeding,[188] it comes dangerously close to intruding on the overriding state interest in conducting its own judicial proceedings. *Younger* is designed, in part, to avoid federal displacement of the state court "in supervising the conduct of trials in state court."[189] The effect of a federal injunction that alters a state procedure is to transfer control of the case from a judge in one system to a judge in another system. Such a transfer can create the same type of confusion and inefficiency as would an injunction against the state proceeding itself.

Equitable relief in right-to-safety cases does not pose these dangers. A federal court order to improve a foster care system in no way interferes with the local family court process. It neither dictates the procedures that the state court should follow nor limits the range of disposition alternatives that the state judge may consider. The overriding purpose of a family court foster care proceeding is to determine whether or not foster care placement is necessary, and, if it is, to determine when and by what means it should be terminated. That purpose is not disturbed by a right-to-safety injunction. The state's interest in the integrity of its own proceedings, therefore, is not compromised by federal injunctive relief protecting the safety of foster children.

Lower federal courts confronting *Younger* issues in family court and foster care matters have applied the doctrine in a manner consistent with this analysis. Thus, cases seeking to enjoin the use of certain family court procedures have been dismissed,[190] but the courts have refused to apply *Younger* where, as in a right-to-safety case, the plaintiff does not seek to enjoin the state proceeding or to interfere with family court proceedings.[191]

There are two additional reasons why *Younger* should not relegate right-to-safety cases to the state courts. First, *Younger* does not apply when there is no adequate remedy in the state court proceeding or when the plaintiff is suffering great, immediate, and irreparable harm.[192] In the right-to-safety context, both exceptions to *Younger* usually apply. First, a single family court judge, in a single case, is unlikely to have either the perspective or the authority to fashion relief that will improve the quality of the foster care system. Second, foster children do suffer great, immediate, and irreparable harm when their right to safety is violated. Violations of the right to safety cannot be rectified or minimized by subsequent review. When safety is at stake, every moment counts. Life itself may be at stake—certainly, health and emotional well-being are. With the potential damage so great, the *Younger* rationale for delay is not persuasive.

The Domestic Relations Exception in Right-to-Safety Cases

"Poorly defined and unevenly applied,"[193] the domestic relations exception is a judge-made doctrine that permits federal courts to decline to exercise diversity jurisdiction when to do so might embroil them in family disputes. In its most extreme expression of the concept, the Supreme Court described the doctrine as impelled by the notion that "[t]he whole subject of the domestic relations of husband and wife, parent and child, belongs to the laws of the States and not to the laws of the United States."[194]

Several rationales have been offered for the doctrine, which constitutes a major restriction of federal jurisdiction. It has been said that the domestic relations exception is justified by the strong state interest in family law matters, by the state courts' superior competence in divorce and custody cases,[195] and by a fear of the possibility of incompatible decrees in divorce and child custody cases involving continuing judicial supervision.[196]

The doctrine is generally confined to diversity jurisdiction cases, where, absent the doctrine, a state law claim could be brought in federal court solely because the parties reside in different states. On occasion, however, federal courts have declined to adjudicate claims involving domestic disputes even when they are otherwise properly brought under the federal question jurisdiction of the federal courts.[197] A recent panel opinion of the Eleventh Circuit suggested that the domestic relations doctrine might apply in a right-to-safety case.[198] But the doctrine, which has dubious credentials in any setting,[199] has no place in right-to-safety cases.

After *Erie Railroad v. Tompkins*,[200] a federal court's only substantive concern in most diversity cases is to apply state law in an even-handed manner.[201] In that limited context, the domestic relations exception, despite its questionable pedigree, serves reasonably well. Unlike tort or contract matters, family law enforcement is generally entrusted to a specialized tribunal,[202] and family law cases often involve emotional matters of unique state concern.[203]

The balance, however, changes significantly when the litigation is brought to vindicate federal rights. No longer must the court weigh the relative importance of an impartial federal forum for the adjudication of a pure state law claim against the disruption to the state system caused by the provision of the alternative forum. In right-to-safety cases, the clash is between the overriding duty of federal courts to enforce and uphold constitutional rights and the state's interest in having its courts hear these cases.

Thus, since there are no genuine obstacles to the provision of a federal forum for the vindication of a foster child's federally secured constitutional right to safety, and since a structural injunction granted by a federal court is the preferred remedy, we now turn to guidelines for fashioning and administering the appropriate injunctive relief if foster care systems are to be made safe.

Guidelines for Effective Structural Injunctions

Unfortunately, a precise recipe for success in obtaining implementation of complex injunctive decrees does not exist.[204] This is certainly true for foster care. Important lessons emerge from the extensive experience in closely related fields about what the court and the parties involved in the case must do to increase the chances that a structural decree will be effective.[205] Four guidelines derived from those cases would, if followed, materially increase the probability of successfully implementing a structural injunction that protects the right to safety in foster care while preserving the independence and integrity of the court.

A Specific Decree

The decree itself must be detailed and specific. It is not enough to declare that the plaintiff foster children have the right to be protected from harm; the court must specify what the foster care system must do to effectuate the right. A concrete decree focuses the parties and the court on the deficiencies in the system that caused the problem. Decrees should be quantitative and precise and should provide specific tasks, possibly along with timetables for achieving them. If nonobjective standards and goals are provided, intermediate, objective standards should also be outlined.[206] *G.L. v. Zumwalt* is a model of this type of decree.[207]

The *G.L.* decree dealt with fifteen aspects of the problem, including caseworker caseloads, foster parent compensation, medical and dental examinations, selection and supervision of foster homes, and investigations of suspected instances of foster parent abuse and neglect. For each topic, the decree provides standards for gauging the defendants' performance.

While a court must avoid excessive detail that will enmesh it in the minutiae of child-care management, it is important that its order not be too general to provide effective relief. A decree that prescribes specific standards for the defendants to meet saves the court and the parties from later time-consuming and frustrating disputes about what constitutes compliance.[208] A court formulating a decree has the opportunity to seek the input of the defendants. Used wisely, the defendants' participation in the decree formulation process can be beneficial. By incorporating defendants' suggestions, the court encourages voluntarism and cooperation, and also becomes more fully informed about the practical consequences of its decree; by encouraging the defendants' participation, it helps blunt the criticism that the judiciary lacks the information needed to formulate feasible remedies for systemic constitutional injuries.

The Need for Monitoring

Institutional judgments are not self-executing. Child welfare agencies have been resistant to reform, and, if the past is any guide, merely hortatory court orders may be treated no more seriously than other calls for change. An institutional injunction case cannot end at final judgment.

Therefore, in addition to its substantive provisions, the decree must provide for monitoring the defendants' performance. Monitoring allows the court and the parties to determine the extent to which defendants have implemented the decree.[209] Moreover, it forces the defendants to confront their obligation to change the system to comply with the decree. Unless defendants deliberately abdicate all responsibility, monitoring educates them about the system that they are responsible for running.

Several methods are utilized by the courts to monitor decrees. One is for the court merely to retain jurisdiction, leaving plaintiffs' counsel solely responsible for monitoring. This method is generally coupled with provision for the plaintiffs' counsel to have access to the institutional records, documents and other relevant materials in the defendants' possession.[210] In addition, most courts require the defendants to submit regular reports detailing the progress of implementation.[211]

The general consensus is, however, that this alone is not an effective method of implementation.[212] Illustrating its ineffectiveness is *Mills v. Board of Education of the District of Columbia*.[213] In *Mills*, the court ordered the Board of Education to provide suitable education for the handicapped. Over the next three years, the plaintiffs were unsuccessful in obtaining compliance.[214] As a result, the court, on motion of the plaintiffs, appointed a special master.[215] A special master may have a broad range of powers, including fact-finding, reporting, making recommendations, negotiating disputes between the parties, acting as an arbitrator, and in some cases issuing orders binding the parties.[216] Although controversial, the use of masters in institutional reform cases has been considered "highly effective" by some commentators.[217]

A third method of monitoring used by the courts, and one somewhat less intrusive than a master, is the appointment of a monitor. In contrast to the role of a master, a monitor's powers are usually more limited. In a typical case the monitor serves as the court's "eyes and ears during the implementation process,"[218] but is not vested with direct responsibility for implementation.[219]

The Role of the District Judge

The district judge must be actively involved to ensure successful implementation of a structural injunction. By relying upon counsel and, if appropriate, court-appointed monitoring adjuncts, the court can avoid the appearance of administrative involvement, which has been criticized by opponents of structural injunctions. Activity should not be confused with partisanship. The court need not shed the mantle of independence and become identified as a partisan powerbroker in order to be effectively involved. The key to success here is not that the judge identifies with one side or the other—of course she should not—but that the court not end its involvement merely because a judgment has been entered.

A court's clearly communicated willingness to use its powers to enforce its decree is paramount. Without this, the natural reluctance of defendants to comply is reinforced. Of all the variables associated with institutional compliance with structural injunctions, this is the one that appears to be predictive.

The Need for Flexibility

Finally, the decree must be flexible so that unanticipated consequences can be dealt with through modification of its terms. Any attempt, whether judicial, legislative or executive, to reform an institution as complex as a modern social services bureaucracy is likely to produce unintended consequences.[220] The decree in *G.L. v. Zumwalt*, for example, limited the number of children permitted in any single foster home to six[221] because of concern that overcrowded foster homes were more likely to become centers of maltreatment than foster homes that were not overcrowded. While in the abstract this provision seems sensible,[222] in practice it produced difficulty.

Several excellent foster homes were caring for more than six *G.L.* class members when the decree was entered. In order to comply with the literal language of the decree, defendants would have had to remove children doing well in their homes. The disruption and anxiety for these children would have outweighed any benefit that they might have gained from being sent to smaller foster families. The Federal Rules of Civil Procedure provide a mechanism by which an injunction can be modified when it is not having its intended effect.[223] In *G.L.* this was not necessary, as plaintiffs' counsel agreed to permit the children to remain in these homes so long as no others were sent to them until they had shrunk, by attrition, to the required size.[224] The court and parties must always be ready to modify the decree to avoid detrimental, unintended consequences.[225]

These general guidelines do not begin to answer the many specific questions that any serious effort at implementation of a right-to-safety decree will present.[226] They do serve, however, to identify at least the major tasks that must be attended to if implementation is to be achieved. If these tasks are undertaken, given the effectiveness of structural decrees in other settings, there is reason to be hopeful that a federal court can achieve its function of ensuring that the constitutional right to safety is provided to foster children.

Conclusion

The time has come to recognize that foster children have a right to safety while in foster care. Foster care is intended to be a temporary refuge for children whose parents cannot care for them. But, in practice, more often than has been acknowledged by many observers, foster care is not safe. Abuse and neglect of foster children occur at levels that far exceed in quantity and magnitude what a reasonably run system of care should produce. State-countenanced mistreatment of innocent children has serious ramifications for society. The infliction of harm on children who have suffered the trauma of parental default retards or even eliminates their potential for normal development. However, the political process has proven to be ineffective in alleviating this problem. Foster children, drawn largely from the disadvantaged and from minority groups, simply do not have the access or influence to move the executive or legislative branches of government to increase the funding needed to bring about change. As a practical matter, the courts must become involved if foster care is to function as it is intended.

The basis for judicial involvement is clear. The right to safety has deep roots in

American jurisprudential thought. During the past two decades, federal courts have developed and implemented the right for every group of persons held under state custody other than foster children. Ironically, foster children are the one group with the most to gain from recognition of this fundamental right.

This chapter demonstrates that it is not possible to construct a logical distinction between foster children and other groups that have been afforded the benefits of the right to safety. To make the right to safety effective, a court must be able to fashion prospective relief with the flexibility to take into account the wide range of factors that can stimulate the organizational change needed. Experience with right-to-safety cases for other groups shows that only the structural injunction provides the court with these tools. Federal courts have historically served as the forum for the protection of citizens' constitutional rights from abridgment by the state. Therefore, they are the preferred forum for foster care right-to-safety cases. Reform of foster care will not come easily or quickly, but if the guidelines offered in this article for courts and parties are followed, experience from other structural injunction cases demonstrates that federal courts have it in their power to make foster care, at last, the haven it was always intended to be.

NOTES

1. G.L. v. Zumwalt, 564 F. Supp. 1030 (W.D. Mo. 1983) (cited in D. Caplovitz & L. Genevie, Foster Children in Jackson County, Missouri: A Statistical Analysis of Files Maintained by the Division of Family Services 86–87, case 5.2 (July 21, 1982) (unpublished report on file with author)).

2. The child was experiencing constant diarrhea and had not been toilet-trained. In addition, she was so emotionally deprived that, although she was three-and-one-half, she had not been taught how to kiss. Caplovitz & Genevie, Statistical Analysis, *supra* note 1, at 87.

3. *Id.* at 87, case 5.3.

4. *Id.* at 89, case 5.6.

5. Gil, Institutional Abuse of Children in Out-of-Home Care, 3 Child & Youth Services 7, 10 (1981).

6. Foster family care is distinguished from institutional care and adoption in that "the foster family care is designed to be temporary and to offer the child care in a family setting." A. Kadushin, Child Welfare Services 425 (1967). In this chapter the term "foster care" is used to refer to foster family care arrangements.

Once it is determined that a child can no longer remain in her original home, state law usually places the child in the custody of the state or local department of child welfare. R. Horowitz & H. Davidson, Legal Rights of Children 358 (1984). The child welfare agency normally selects and licenses adults to serve as foster parents. *Id.* at 361–65. The foster family then often enters into a contractual arrangement with the agency that requires the family to care for the child under the agency's direction and supervision. *Id.* A typical foster family consists of a middle-aged, working- or lower-middle-class couple who own their own home and have agreed to undertake the responsibility of foster care parenting out of either a need for extra cash or an altruistic desire to help needy children. Mnookin, Foster Care—In Whose Best Interest?, 43 Harv. Educ. Rev. 599, 610 (1973); A. Gruber, Children in Foster Care: Destitute, Neglected, Betrayed 151–74 (1978); T. Festinger, No One Ever Asked Us: A Proscript to Foster Care 270–71 (1983).

7. For the years 1977 to 1983, estimates have varied from 273,913 to 502,000. T. Tatara, Characteristics of Children in Substitute and Adoptive Care: A Statistical Summary of the VCIS National Child Welfare Data Base 30, table 2 (1985). In 1983, the latest year for which data were available when this chapter was written, the American Public Welfare Association (APWA) estimated that 447,000 children were served by the nation's foster care system. *Id.* at 32, table 3. Of that number, 69.5 percent were sent to foster family homes, while the remainder resided in group homes or institutions. *Id.* at 62. *See also* F. Kavaler & M. Swire, Foster-Child Health Care 1 (1983); Children's Defense Fund, Children without Homes: An Examination of Public Responsibility to Children in Out-of-Home Care 2 (1978); Lowry, Derring-Do in the 1980s: Child Welfare Impact Litigation after the Warrren Years, 20 Fam. L.Q. 255, 275 (1986).

8. Besharov, Foster Care Reform: Two Books for Practitioners (Book Review), 18 Fam. L.Q. 247 (1984). Three major reasons have been offered to explain the expansion in the use of foster care. R. Mnookin, In the Interest of Children: Advocacy, Law Reform, and Public Policy 69 (1985) (decrease in use of institutions for abandoned and neglected children); Besharov, The Misuse of Foster Care: When the Desire to Help Children Outruns the Ability to Improve Parental Functioning, 20 Fam. L.Q. 213, 215 (1986) (increase in births to young single mothers unable to raise their children); Besharov, Child Protection: Past Progress, Present Problems, and Future Directions, 17 Fam. L.Q. 151, 153–55 (1983) (increase in child abuse and neglect reporting systems). Almost eight times as many children are reported to state officials as suspected victims of abuse or neglect as were reported in 1960. *Id.* at 151. Still, it is likely that many children who ought to be in substitute care are not, either because their cases are not reported or because of the failure of the child welfare system to respond to legitimate pleas for protection of endangered children. *Id.* at 161 (estimates 50,000 cases of observable injuries not reported in 1979).

It is also likely, however, that some children go into foster care unnecessarily. Children's Defense Fund, Children without Homes, *supra* note 7, at 15–18 (lack of family services). Mnookin, In Whose Best Interest?, *supra* note 6, at 619–20 (vagueness of statutes permits class, race, and lifestyle biases to affect decisions).

9. *See* Bureau of the Census, U.S. Department of Commerce, Statistical Abstract of the United States 174, chart 307 (107th ed. 1987) (503,601 state and federal prisoners). *Id.* at 171, chart 301 (223,551 held in jails). *Id.* at 100, chart 159 (220,700 mental health inpatients). *Id.* at 171, chart 299 (51,402 juveniles in public custody, 34,112 in private custody). *Id.* at 99, chart 158 (132,235 in state facilities for the mentally retarded).

10. Two other articles offer arguments for a foster child's right to safety. *See* Donella, Safe Foster Care: A Constitutional Mandate, 19 Fam. L.Q. 79 (1985); Comment, Child Abuse in Foster Homes: A Rationale for Pursuing Causes of Actions [sic] against the Placement Agency, 28 St. Louis U.L.J. 975 (1984).

11. *See, e.g.,* G.L. v. Zumwalt, 564 F. Supp. 1030 (W.D. Mo. 1983) (consent decree); L.J. v. Massinga, 838 F.2d 118 (4th Cir. 1988), *cert. denied,* 488 U.S. 1018 (1989). These decisions indicate the possibility that other courts soon will be required to determine for the first time whether it is appropriate to assert jurisdiction to fashion structural injunctive decrees for the protection of foster children. *See infra* note 104.

12. *See* Comment, Beyond the Ken of Courts: A Critique of Judicial Refusal to Review the Complaints of Convicts, 72 Yale L.J. 506 (1963).

13. Zeigler, Federal Court Reform of State Criminal Justice Systems: A Reassessment of the Younger Doctrine from a Modern Perspective, 19 U.C. Davis L. Rev. 31, 56 (1985) (citing cases).

14. *See, e.g.,* A. Neier, Only Judgment: The Limits of Litigation in Social Change 170–71 (1982).

15. Wolff v. McDonnell, 418 U.S. 539, 555–56 (1974). Professor Zeigler dates the demise of the hands-off doctrine a decade earlier, to Cooper v. Pate, 378 U.S. 546 (1964). *See* Zeigler, Federal Court Reform, *supra* note 13.

16. *See, e.g.,* Pugh v. Locke, 406 F. Supp. 318 (M.D. Ala. 1976), *modified sub nom.* Newman v. Alabama, 559 F.2d 283 (5th Cir. 1977), *rev'd in part sub nom.* Alabama v. Pugh, 438 U.S. 781 (1978) (prison); Morgan v. Sproat, 432 F. Supp. 1130 (S.D. Miss. 1977) (juvenile detention facility); Wyatt v. Stickney, 325 F. Supp. 781 (M.D. Ala. 1971), *modified sub nom.* Wyatt v. Aderholt, 503 F.2d 1305 (5th Cir. 1974) (mental hospital); New York State Ass'n for Retarded Children v. Rockefeller, 357 F. Supp. 752 (E.D.N.Y. 1973) (institution for the mentally retarded); Hamilton v. Schiro, 338 F. Supp. 1016 (E.D. La. 1970) (prison).

17. Child Welfare League of America, Standards for Foster Family Services 8 (1975); Musewicz, The Failure of Foster Care: Federal Statutory Reform and the Child's Right to Permanence, 54 S. Cal. L. Rev. 633, 637 (1981).

18. A. Gruber, Betrayed, *supra* note 6, at 182; Caplovitz & Genevie, Statistical Analysis, *supra* note 1, at 37, table 2.3; P. Ryan, Analyzing Abuse in Family Foster Care: Final Report 59 (1987).

19. Ryan, Analyzing Abuse, *supra* note 18, at 59 and authorities cited therein; Vera Institute of Justice, Foster Home Child Protection 31–32 (Feb. 1981) (unpublished report) (children who were abused in foster care were three times as likely to have entered foster care because of parental abuse than children who were not abused); Caplovitz & Genevie, Statistical Analysis, *supra* note 1, at 100 (children with severe emotional, intellectual, or physical difficulties tended to be at higher risk of abuse or neglect).

20. Vera Institute of Justice, Foster Protection, *supra* note 19, at 43. *See also* P. Ryan & E. McFadden, National Foster Care Education Project: Preventing Abuse in Family Foster Care 11, 14 (1986).

21. Vera Institute of Justice, Foster Protection, *supra* note 19, at 8–9 (use of belts, switches, electric cords, dog leashes, bread boards, and broomsticks).

22. *See* Vonner v. State Dep't of Pub. Welfare, 273 So. 2d 252 (La. 1973) (foster child beaten to death); Caplovitz & Genevie, Statistical Analysis, *supra* note 1, at 94–95, case 5.14 (child killed by foster mother's boyfriend); Vera Institute of Justice, Foster Protection, *supra* note 19, at v (foster child beaten to death by his foster mother).

23. B. Warren & G. Bardwell, G.L. v. Zumwalt, Case Record Monitoring, April 11, 1983 through June 30, 1984: Final Report 52–54 (Apr. 24, 1985) (unpublished report on file with author) (children forced to stand in the center of a room for up to thirteen and one-half hours at a time, made to use a tin can for a toilet, locked in a basement, toilet-trained by being forced to stand with their pants over their heads); Caplovitz & Genevie, Statistical Analysis, *supra* note 1, at 88, case 5.4.

24. Caplovitz & Genevie, Statistical Analysis, *supra* note 1, at 64 (children received only two meals a day and were bitten by bedbugs); Vera Institute of Justice, Foster Protection, *supra* note 19, at 13–14 (children smelled of "urine and vomit" and were "continually hungry").

25. Ryan, Analyzing Abuse, *supra* note 18, at 60. An additional factor accounting for the higher level of sexual abuse in foster care is that a large number of foster children were sexually abused in the past. *Id.* at 105. *See also* Warren & Bardwell, Case Record, *supra* note 23, at 53–54, case 549.

26. *See supra* note 6 and accompanying text.

27. Warren & Bardwell, Case Record, *supra* note 23, at 54, 64, cases 549, 536, 660 (citing cases in which foster parents have called child a "dummy," said, "I feel sorry for you," and talked negatively about the child's mother).

28. *See* Mnookin, In Whose Best Interest?, *supra* note 6, at 632.

29. Vera Institute of Justice, Foster Protection, *supra* note 19, at 63–64 (49 abused children per 1,000 in general population and 77 per 1,000 for children in foster family care).

30. The number of complaints ranged from 3 per 1,000 homes to 67 per 1,000 homes. Substantiated abuse complaints ranged from 1.2 per 1,000 to 27 per 1,000. Ryan & McFadden, Education Project, *supra* note 20, at 11. According to the U.S. Department of Health and Human Services, the rate of maltreatment of children in 1978 for those thirty-four states reporting on the subject was 2.55 per 1,000. Department of Health and Human Services, National Analysis of Official Child Neglect and Abuse Reporting 10–11, table 2 (1978).

Unfortunately, the reported statistics on foster family abuse studies are not widely known. Comment, Pursuing Actions, *supra* note 10, at 976 ("Statistics indicate that the percentage of abused children who suffer at the hands of foster parents is 'miniscule [*sic*],' a mere 0.3%") (quoting Note, The Challenge of Child Abuse Cases: A Practical Approach, 9 J. Legis. 127, 139 (1982)). The statistic that only 0.3 percent of all reported abuse cases involve foster parents is not terribly illuminating for several reasons. First, it represents only the raw number of substantiated abuse cases involving foster children, without comparison to the number of foster parents generally. Therefore, it does not supply the relationship between the number of foster parents and those who are abusive, a figure that is relevant where, as here, one is interested in knowing the risk of abuse to any given foster child. Obviously, the overwhelming majority of American children are not cared for in foster homes.

Second, the percentage does not disclose how many foster children were abused by foster parents. Since multiple placements are not rare, see *infra* note 34 and accompanying text, and since many foster homes are not closed despite reports of abuse and neglect, see *supra* notes 1, 5, and 8 and accompanying text, it is reasonable to assume that there is a greater than one-to-one relationship between abusing foster parents and abused foster children.

Third, the report deals with only substantiated cases of foster parent abuse and neglect. This statistic does not include children who are harmed by "program" abuse. *See infra* note 31 and accompanying text.

31. Gil, Institutional Abuse, *supra* note 5, at 10.

32. *Id.*

33. D. Fanshel & E. Shinn, Children in Foster Care: A Longitudinal Investigation 137 (1978).

34. *See* Caplovitz & Genevie, Statistical Analysis, *supra* note 1, at 20–24; Children's Defense Fund, Children without Homes, *supra* note 7, at 41; Gruber, Betrayed, *supra* note 6, at 67–68.

35. *See, e.g.,* Vera Institute of Justice, Foster Protection, *supra* note 19, at vi (reporting that 28 percent of victims of foster family abuse had been in three or more foster homes as compared with only 13 percent of foster children generally).

36. Child Welfare League of America, Standards, *supra* note 17, at § 3.10.

37. F. Kavaler & M. Swire, Foster Health, *supra* note 7. The authors undertook an extensive independent evaluation of the physical condition of 668 New York City foster children. *See also* Gruber, Betrayed, *supra* note 6, at 73 (Massachusetts); Caplovitz & Genevie, Statistical Analysis, *supra* note 1, at 35–37 (Kansas City).

38. Kavaler & Swire, Foster Health, *supra* note 7, at 149.

39. *Id.* at 143. These findings have been confirmed. *See, e.g.,* Caplovitz & Genevie, Statistical Analysis, *supra* note 1, at 41–43.

40. Kavaler & Swire, Foster Health, *supra* note 7, at 142.

41. *Id.* at 146.

42. *Id.*

43. *See also* Caplovitz & Genevie, Statistical Analysis, *supra* note 1, at 38; Gruber, Betrayed, *supra* note 6, at 89, 183.

44. *See* Child Welfare League of America, Standards, *supra* note 17; American Public Welfare Association, Standards for Foster Family Systems for Public Agencies (1975). *See also* Cavara & Ogran, Protocol to Investigate Child Abuse in Foster Care, 7 Child Abuse & Neglect 287, 293 (1983); Ryan, Analyzing Abuse, *supra* note 18, at 7; Vera Institute of Justice, Foster Protection, *supra* note 19, at 33–34.

45. *See, e.g.,* American Public Welfare Association, Family Systems, *supra* note 44, at 55–56; Child Welfare League of America, Standards, *supra* note 17, at § 4.16; Vera Institute for Justice, Foster Protection, *supra* note 19, at 33.

46. Foster children are not easy to handle, because often they have been sexually or physically abused in the past. They present their caretakers with patterns of behavior that are extremely upsetting and provocative to persons not prepared to cope with them. Compliance with professionally recognized standards would require the availability of training programs for foster parents. Child Welfare League of America, Standards, *supra* note 17, at § 4.4.

47. The failure of a foster care agency seriously to consider prior to placement whether a particular child should live with a particular set of foster parents is often the direct cause of the maltreatment of foster children. Child Welfare League of America, Standards, *supra* note 17, at § 3.9. *See also* Vera Institute of Justice, Foster Protection, *supra* note 19, at 36–37.

48. *See, e.g.,* American Public Welfare Association, Family Systems, *supra* note 44, at 64; Child Welfare League of America, Standards, *supra* note 17, at § 4.4; Ryan,

Analyzing Abuse, supra note 18, at 105–106, recommendations 17–19; Vera Institute of Justice, Protection of Children in Foster Family Care: A Guide for Social Workers (Mar. 10, 1982) (unpublished manuscript).

49. Child Welfare League of America, Standards, *supra* note 17, at 4.27. The Child Welfare League standards require that the agency maintain personal contact with the child once a month for the first year, after which personal contact every other month may be sufficient. *Id.* at § 4.28. Regular supervision is also stressed in the literature of foster family abuse and neglect. *See, e.g.,* American Public Welfare Association, Family Systems, *supra* note 44, at 65; Ryan, Analyzing Abuse, *supra* note 18, at 103, recommendation 11; Vera Institute of Justice, Foster Protection, *supra* note 19, at 39–42.

50. Ryan, Analyzing Abuse, *supra* note 18, at 59–60.

51. Child Welfare League of America, Standards, *supra* note 17, at § 4.7.

52. Vera Institute of Justice, Protection of Children, *supra* note 48, at 17–20 (condoning corporal punishment raises the risk of severe injury to foster children, who are, in addition, more likely to interpret it as rejection, reinforcing their poor self-image).

53. Gil, Institutional Abuse, *supra* note 5, at 8. *See also* Ryan, Analyzing Abuse, *supra* note 18, at 107–108, recommendation 22.

54. *See, e.g.,* Gruber, Betrayed, *supra* note 6, at 9 (1930 White House conference marking establishment of national foster care program); Kadushin, Welfare Services, *supra* note 6, at 411 (citing Lewis, Long-Time and Temporary Placement of Children, in Selected Papers in Casework 40 (1951) (by the 1950s foster care was failing to fulfill its purpose)); H. Mass & R. Engler, Jr., Children in Need of Parents (1959).

55. Children's Defense Fund, Children without Homes, *supra* note 7; National Commission on Children in Need of Parents, Who Knows? Who Cares? Forgotten Children in Foster Care (1979); Gruber, Betrayed, *supra* note 6 (Massachusetts foster care system).

56. Children's Defense Fund, Children without Homes, *supra* note 7, at xiii.

57. National Commission on Children in Need of Parents, Who Knows, *supra* note 55, at 4.

58. *Id.* at 5.

59. *Id.* at 6.

60. Lowry, Impact Litigation, *supra* note 7, at 257.

61. National Commission on Children in Need of Parents, Who Knows, *supra* note 55, at 21. *See also* Gruber, Betrayed, *supra* note 6, at 172.

62. Lowry, Impact Litigation, *supra* note 7, at 274.

63. Mnookin, In Whose Best Interest?, *supra* note 6, at 607 and sources cited therein; Kavaler & Swire, Foster Health, *supra* note 7, at 47. *See* Lowry, Impact Litigation, *supra* note 7, at 257.

64. National Commission on Children in Need of Parents, Who Knows, *supra* note 55, at 25; Children's Defense Fund, Children Without Homes, *supra* note 7, at 49–52; Lowry, Impact Litigation, *supra* note 7, at 257.

65. *See, e.g.,* Player v. Alabama Dep't of Pensions & Security, 400 F. Supp. 249, 255 (M.D. Ala. 1975), *aff'd,* 536 F.2d 1385 (5th Cir. 1976) (finding black children in the Alabama foster care system were not given equal treatment in referrals to specialized placements); Wilder v. Bernstein, 645 F. Supp. 1292 (S.D.N.Y. 1986) (consent decree designed to ensure that all children, regardless of race or religion, are served by the New York City foster care system on a "first come, first served" basis). *See also* Children's Defense Fund, Children without Homes, *supra* note 7, at 49–54.

66. Caplovitz & Genevie, Statistical Analysis, *supra* note 1, at 99–100, table 5.5 (black children are more likely to be abused or neglected in foster care).

67. A. English, Foster Care Reform: Strategies for Legal Services Advocates to Reduce the Need for Foster Care and Improve the Foster Care System 4 (1981).

68. *See infra* note 75 and accompanying text for a discussion of the historical roots of the right to safety.

69. Professor Mnookin has observed that children as a group may not qualify for special protection as a discrete and insular minority because of the "multitude of potential and part-time spokesmen [*sic*] for children." Mnookin, In the Interest, *supra* note 8, at 41. Whatever may be said of children generally, however, foster children are a discrete and insular minority, especially where a claim for which they have no obvious allies is concerned.

70. Mnookin, In the Interest, *supra* note 8, at 31.

71. Prince v. Massachusetts, 321 U.S. 158 (1944).

72. *Id.* at 168–69 (upholding law that prohibited children from selling magazines in a public place).

73. New York v. Ferber, 458 U.S. 747 (1982) (upholding New York law prohibiting knowing promotion of sexual performance by children even if it is not obscene); H.L. v. Matheson, 450 U.S. 398 (1981) (upholding notification and consultation barriers to the exercise of the right to an abortion for an immature minor that would be unconstitutional if applied to an adult); Ginsberg v. New York, 390 U.S. 629, *reh'g denied*, 391 U.S. 971 (1968) (upholding criminal statute prohibiting sale to minors of material that would not be obscene if sold to adults).

Taken together, these decisions establish a right unique to children to be protected from "endangering surroundings and influences." S. Davis & M. Schwartz, Children's Rights and the Law 73 (1987).

74. 457 U.S. 307, 324 (1982). While there were two concurrences in addition to the majority opinion in *Youngberg*, the Court did not divide on this issue. *See infra* text accompanying note 95.

75. *See* Calvin's Case, [1608] 4 Co. Rep. 1 (K.B.) (Cooke, C.J.); 1 W. Blackstone, Commentaries on the Laws of England ¶ 129 (W. Draper Lewis ed. 1902); T. Hobbes, Leviathan (1651). This conception of the centrality of the right of protection has not changed in modern times. *See, e.g.,* O. W. Holmes, Natural Law, in Collected Legal Papers 310, 312 (1920); Miranda v. Arizona, 384 U.S. 436 (1966) (White, J., dissenting); W. Burger, Annual Report to the American Bar Association 2 (Feb. 8, 1981) *reprinted* in 67 A.B.A. J. 290 (1981). For a thorough account of the historical underpinnings of the right to safety and its roots, see Willing, Protection by Law Enforcement: The Emerging Constitutional Right, 35 Rutgers L. Rev. 1, 22–54 (1982).

76. Wolff v. McDonnell, 418 U.S. 539, 555–56 (1973).

77. New York State Ass'n for Retarded Children v. Rockefeller, 357 F. Supp. 752, 758 (E.D.N.Y. 1973). *See* New York State Ass'n for Retarded Children v. Carey,

393 F. Supp. 715 (E.D.N.Y. 1975) (consent decree encompassing protection from harm caused by physical injury as well as from conditions causing the deterioration, or preventing the development, of an individual's capacities), *modification denied*, 551 F. Supp. 1165 (E.D.N.Y. 1982), *aff'd in part and rev'd in part*, 706 F.2d 956 (2d Cir.), *cert. denied*, 464 U.S. 915 (1983). *See also* D. Rothman & S. Rothman, The Willowbrook Wars (1984).

78. *See, e.g.*, Society for Good Will to Retarded Children v. Cuomo, 737 F.2d 1239 (2d Cir. 1984); Ass'n for Retarded Citizens v. Olson, 561 F. Supp. 473 (D.N.D. 1982), *aff'd*, 713 F.2d 1384 (8th Cir. 1983); Welsch v. Likins, 373 F. Supp. 487 (D. Minn. 1974), *aff'd in part and vacated and remanded in part*, 550 F.2d 1122 (8th Cir. 1977).

79. Santana v. Collazo, 533 F. Supp. 966 (D.P.R. 1982), *aff'd in part and vacated and remanded in part*, 714 F.2d 1172 (1st Cir. 1983), *cert. denied*, 466 U.S. 974 (1984); Pena v. New York State Div. for Youth, 419 F. Supp. 203 (S.D.N.Y. 1976), *aff'd*, 708 F.2d 877 (2d Cir. 1983); Martarella v. Kelley, 349 F. Supp. 575 (S.D.N.Y. 1972).

80. City of Revere v. Massachusetts Gen. Hosp., 463 U.S. 239, 245 (1983).

81. Duran v. Elrod, 760 F.2d 756 (7th Cir. 1985); Jones v. Diamond, 636 F.2d 1364 (5th Cir. 1981).

82. *See, e.g.*, Harlow v. Fitzgerald, 457 U.S. 800 (1982) (the Court rejected the previous standard, which permitted a finding of liability based on proof that the official acted in bad faith. Instead, the Court held that the individual must prove that her clearly established constitutional right was violated by the defendant). Given the uncertainty as to the standard governing the right to safety, this is a difficult burden indeed. Harper v. Cserr, 544 F.2d 1121, 1124 (1st Cir. 1976). *But see* Gann v. Schramm, 606 F. Supp. 1442 (D. Del. 1985) (official immunity denied where officials at state mental hospital violated the well-known constitutional right to a safe environment for those involuntarily committed to mental institutions).

83. Rone v. Fireman, 473 F. Supp. 92, 132 (N.D. Ohio 1979) (physical improvements in the facility to provide an appropriate environment for the mentally retarded).

84. Woe v. Cuomo, 638 F. Supp. 1506, 1517 (E.D.N.Y. 1986) (enjoining additional patients from being admitted to the Bronx Psychiatric Center); New York State Ass'n for Retarded Children v. Carey, 393 F. Supp. 715, 717 (E.D.N.Y. 1975) (requiring sharp reduction in the population of Willowbrook to a capacity of 250 beds or less).

85. *See, e.g.*, New York State Ass'n for Retarded Children v. Rockefeller, 357 F. Supp. 752, 769 (E.D.N.Y. 1973).

86. *Id.* at 768 (consent decree increased staffing and training provision). *See also* Rone v. Fireman, 473 F. Supp. 92, 133–34 (N.D. Ohio 1979).

87. In the Willowbrook case, the consent decree mandated individually designed instruction for residents. New York State Ass'n for Retarded Children v. Carey, 596 F.2d 27, 31 (2d Cir. 1979) (programs to include education, physical therapy, and speech pathology and audiology services). *See also* Ass'n for Retarded Citizens v. Olson, 561 F. Supp. 473, 494 (D.N.D. 1982), *aff'd*, 713 F.2d 1384 (8th Cir. 1983).

88. *See, e.g.*, Rhem v. Malcolm, 377 F. Supp. 995 (S.D.N.Y. 1974), *aff'd*, 507 F.2d

333 (2d Cir. 1974); Inmates of Suffolk County Jail v. Eisenstadt, 360 F. Supp. 676, 689–90 (D. Mass. 1973) (Charles Street Jail deemed unfit for failing to meet a standard of "basic humanity toward men" and ordered replaced).

89. Ingraham v. Wright, 430 U.S. 651, 664 (1977) (the Eighth Amendment was "designed to protect those convicted of crimes").

90. Some states base the institutionalization on the *parens patriae* theory. *Parens patriae* refers to the inherent power of a state to "provid[e] care to its citizens who are unable . . . to care for themselves." Addington v. Texas, 441 U.S. 418, 426 (1979). *See, e.g.,* Welsch v. Likins, 373 F. Supp. 487, 496 (D. Minn. 1974), *aff'd in part and vacated and remanded in part,* 550 F.2d 1122 (8th Cir. 1977) (the court cited approvingly the language of the doctrine, but did not explicitly mention *parens patriae*). For a history of the *parens patriae* theory, see Custer, The Origins of the Doctrine of Parens Patriae, 27 Emory L.J. 195 (1978); Rendleman, Parens Patriae: From Chancery to the Juvenile Court, 23 S.C. L. Rev. 205 (1971). The Supreme Court has imposed constitutional limits on the doctrine by holding that when the state exercises this power, it must take steps to ensure that the exercise bears some relationship to its purpose. Jackson v. Indiana, 406 U.S. 715 (1972).

91. Halderman v. Pennhurst State Sch. & Hosp., 446 F. Supp. 1295 (E.D. Pa. 1977), *aff'd in part and rev'd in part,* 612 F.2d 84 (3d Cir. 1979) (en banc), *rev'd on other grounds,* 451 U.S. 1 (1980).

92. 457 U.S. 307 (1982).

93. *Id.* at 310.

94. *Id.* at 311.

95. *Id.* at 324.

96. *Id.* at 315–16.

97. *Id.* at 321–22.

98. *Id.*

99. *Id.* at 322.

100. *Id.* at 310.

101. *Id.* at 319–20.

102. 791 F.2d 881 (11th Cir. 1986), *aff'd in part and rev'd in part on reh'g,* 818 F.2d 791 (11th Cir. 1987) (en banc).

103. 791 F.2d at 884. The opinion made no mention of *Youngberg*. Indeed, it referred to the "deliberate indifference" standard, which the Supreme Court in *Youngberg* specifically rejected as insufficient for persons not convicted of crime. 457 U.S. at 312 n.11. In Atchley v. County of DuPage, 638 F. Supp. 1237 (N.D. Ill. 1986), and Gibson v. Merced County Dep't of Human Resources, 799 F.2d 582 (9th Cir. 1986), two other right-to-safety claims were rejected.

104. Taylor v. Ledbetter, 818 F.2d 791, 795 (11th Cir. 1987) (en banc). In addition to the en banc opinion in *Taylor*, two cases granting relief to foster children indicate that the pendulum may now be swinging in the direction of recognition of the constitutional right to safety of children in foster care. *See* Doe v. New York City Dep't of Social Servs., 670 F. Supp. 1145 (S.D.N.Y. 1987); L.J. v. Massinga, 838 F.2d 118 (4th Cir. 1988), *cert. denied,* 488 U.S. 1018 (1989).

105. Brooks v. Richardson, 478 F. Supp. 793 (S.D.N.Y. 1979).

106. 649 F.2d 134 (2d Cir. 1981), *cert. denied,* 464 U.S. 864 (1983) (*Doe I*) and 709 F.2d 782, *cert. denied,* 464 U.S. 844 (1983) (*Doe II*).

107. For a graphic description of the facts, see Doe v. New York City Dep't of Social Servs., 649 F.2d 134, 137–40 (2d Cir. 1981), *cert. denied*, 464 U.S. 864 (1983).

108. The *Doe* court observed that where the child is placed in a foster home, there is a tendency "to respect the foster family's autonomy and integrity [and to] . . . minimize intrusiveness, given its goals of approximating a normal family environment for foster children." 649 F.2d at 142.

109. *See* Halderman v. Pennhurst State Sch. & Hosp., 446 F. Supp. 1295, 1299 (E.D. Pa. 1977) (quoting W. Wolfensberger, The Origin and Nature of Our Institutional Models 3 (1975)), *aff'd in part and rev'd in part*, 612 F.2d 84 (3d Cir. 1979) (en banc), *rev'd on other grounds*, 451 U.S. 1 (1980).

110. *See* Wyman v. James, 400 U.S. 309, 322–23 (1971); H. Ginott, Between Parent and Child 215–16 (1965).

111. Smith v. Organization of Foster Families for Equality & Reform (OFFER), 431 U.S. 816, 855 (1977).

112. In 1980, there were approximately 700 public interest lawyers working in 117 public interest law centers. Mnookin, In the Interest, *supra* note 8, at 45. Fewer than 7 percent of these lawyers concern themselves with children's issues, a number smaller than a "medium-sized law firm in Denver, Colorado." *Id.* at 49.

113. *See supra* notes 105–107 and accompanying text, and *infra* note 158 and accompanying text.

114. *See supra* note 6 and accompanying text.

115. 458 U.S. 502 (1982).

116. *Id.* at 510.

117. *See, e.g.,* Youngberg v. Romeo, 457 U.S. 307, 317 (1982) ("[w]hen a person is institutionalized—and wholly dependent on the state . . . [there is] a duty to provide certain services").

118. *See, e.g.,* Conn. Gen. Stat. Ann., § 17–38a (West 1987) ("The public policy of [the] state is: To protect children whose health and welfare may be adversely affected through injury and neglect; to strengthen the family and to make the home safe for children by enhancing parental capacity for good child care; to provide a temporary or permanent nurturing and safe environment for children when necessary"); Mass. Gen. Laws Ann. ch. 119 § 1 (West 1987); N.Y. Soc. Serv. Law § 395 (McKinney 1983) (a public welfare district shall be responsible for the welfare of children residing or found in its territory who are in need of public assistance, support, and protection); Fla. Stat. Ann. § 409.145 (West 1986). *See also supra* note 17 and accompanying text. Courts have expressed this purpose as well. *See, e.g.,* Brooks v. Richardson, 478 F. Supp. 793, 795–96 (S.D.N.Y. 1979).

119. *Lehman*'s discussion of the liberty implications of foster family placement is inapposite to a right-to-safety analysis for another reason: *Lehman* dealt solely with a question of statutory, not constitutional, construction.

120. *See* Areen, Intervention Between Parent and Child: A Reappraisal of the State's Role in Child Neglect and Abuse Cases, 63 Geo. L.J. 887, 921–22 (1975) (as many as 50 percent voluntary placements); Gruber, Betrayed, *supra* note 6, at 138 (studies from New York and elsewhere estimate the percentage of voluntary placements between 50 and 90 percent; in Massachusetts, 58.8 percent of the placements are voluntary); Mnookin, In Whose Best Interest?, *supra* note 6, at 601;

Information Services, Characteristics of Children in Foster Care, New York City Reports, table 11 (1976).

121. Smith v. OFFER, 431 U.S. 816, 824 (1977).

122. Kadushin, Welfare Services, *supra* note 6, at 316. Voluntary placement in foster care is usually a two-part process. Initially parents and a local social service official enter a voluntary placement agreement (VPA), which sets forth the terms and conditions of a child's care and transfers the custody of the child from the parent to the authorized agency.

If a child will be in custody for more than thirty days, the social service official must obtain judicial approval of the VPA. The judge must be shown that the parents voluntarily and knowingly entered the VPA, that they were unable to provide adequate care at home, and that the child's best interests would be promoted by placement in foster care. Joyner v. Dumpson, 712 F.2d 770, 773 (2d Cir. 1983); Smith v. OFFER, 431 U.S. 816, 824 n.9 (1977).

123. 457 U.S. at 310, 312, 313, 314, 315, 316, 318, 321, 322.

124. *See supra* notes 121–22 and accompanying text.

125. Smith v. OFFER, 431 U.S. at 834. *See also* Ass'n for Retarded Citizens v. Olson, 561 F. Supp. 473, 484 (D.N.D. 1982), *aff'd*, 713 F.2d 1384 (8th Cir. 1983).

126. Mnookin, In Whose Best Interest?, *supra* note 6, at 601. *See also* Children's Defense Fund, Children without Homes, *supra* note 7, at 18.

127. Such treatment would, for example, constitute neglect under New Jersey law: "Neglect of a child shall consist in any of the following acts, by anyone having the custody or control of the child: . . . failure to do or permit to be done any act necessary for the child's physical or moral well-being." N.J. Stat. Ann. § 9:6-1 (West 1976). *See also, e.g.,* Mass. Gen. Laws Ann. ch. 119 § 1 (West 1958); Conn. Gen. Stat. § 17-38a (West 1975). Federal standards also suggest that exposure to unsafe conditions constitutes abuse or neglect. Placing a child in such conditions, for example, falls within the definition of child abuse and neglect given in the Child Abuse Prevention and Treatment Act: "[C]hild abuse and neglect means the physical or mental injury, sexual abuse or exploitation, negligent treatment, or maltreatment of a child under the age of eighteen . . . by a person who is responsible for the child's welfare under circumstances which indicate that the child's health or welfare is harmed or threatened thereby." 42 U.S.C. § 5102 (1982). This act and other federal child protection acts are discussed in D. Besharov, The Abused and Neglected Child: Multi-Disciplinary Court Practice 11–33 (1978).

128. *See* Perry v. Sindermann, 408 U.S. 593, 597 (1972). This principle has been relied upon in several cases dealing with voluntary and involuntary confinement. *See, e.g., Youngberg*, 457 U.S. at 315–16; Society for Good Will to Retarded Children v. Cuomo, 737 F.2d at 1245–46.

129. San Antonio Indep. Sch. Dist. v. Rodriguez, 411 U.S. 1, 29–39 (1973), and cases cited therein.

130. Goss v. Lopez, 419 U.S. 565 (1975).

131. *See* Child v. Beame, 412 F. Supp. 593, 602 (S.D.N.Y. 1976).

132. *See* Society for Good Will to Retarded Children v. Cuomo, 737 F.2d 1239, 1246 (2d Cir. 1984). Indeed, most state foster care laws do not even discuss distinctions between voluntary and involuntary placement when dealing with the

level of care to which the foster child is entitled. *See, e.g.*, N.Y. Soc. Serv. Law §§ 358a, 372a, 372c (Consol. 1978); Minn. Stat. Ann. § 257.071 (West 1982); Ohio Rev. Code Ann. § 3107.02 (Baldwin 1987); N.J. Stat. Ann. § 30.4C (West 1981); Mass. Gen. Laws Ann., ch. 119, § 23 (West 1969).

133. *See* Marbury v. Madison, 5 U.S. (1 Cranch) 137, 163 (1803) (the laws of the United States furnish remedies for the violation of vested legal rights).

134. *See, e.g.*, Mayberry v. Pryor, 352 N.W.2d 322 (Mich. Ct. App. 1984), *rev'd*, 374 N.W.2d 683 (Mich. 1985) (summary judgment in favor of foster parents reversed); Zink v. Dep't of Health and Rehabilitative Servs., 496 So. 2d 996 (Fla. App. 1986) (summary judgment in favor of the defendant reversed).

135. Osborn v. Bank of the United States, 22 U.S. (9 Wheat.) 738 (1824).

136. *See, e.g.*, Koepf v. County of York, 251 N.W.2d 866 (Neb. 1977). Despite important variations, all states retain immunity from suits that result from discretionary governmental activities. The variations are as follows: a few states retain total immunity from suit; some still preclude suits by individuals in courts, but have created administrative agencies that have the authority to decide claims against the state; others have consented judicially to suits in only a very limited class of cases. Most states, however, allow suits for nondiscretionary activities that cause injury. Prosser & Keeton on the Law of Torts § 131, at 1044 (W. Keeton et al. eds, 5th ed. 1984) [hereinafter Prosser & Keeton, Torts].

137. Prosser & Keeton, Torts, *supra* note 136, § 131, at 1044.

138. *See, e.g., Koepf*, 251 N.W.2d at 866; National Bank of South Dakota v. Leir, 325 N.W.2d 845 (S.D. 1982).

139. Brown v. Phillips, 342 S.E.2d 786 (Ga. Ct. App. 1986); Walker v. State, 428 N.Y.S.2d 188 (N.Y. Fam. Ct. 1980); Pickett v. Washington County, 572 P.2d 1070 (Or. Ct. App. 1977); Jiminez v. County of Santa Cruz, 116 Cal. Rptr. 878 (Cal. Ct. App. 1974).

140. *Pickett*, 572 P.2d at 1074.

141. *Id.*

142. *Id.*

143. *See, e.g.*, Blanca v. Nassau County, 480 N.Y.S.2d 747 (1984), *aff'd sub nom.* Blanca C. by Carmen M. v. Nassau County, 481 N.E.2d 545 (N.Y. 1985); Parker v. St. Christopher's Home, 431 N.Y.S. 2d 110 (1980).

144. *See, e.g.*, New Jersey Property-Liability Ins. Guar. Ass'n v. State, 446 A.2d 189 (1982), *rev'd*, 477 A.2d 826, *cert. denied*, 491 A.2d 691 (N.J. 1984); Kern v. Steele County, 322 N.W.2d 187 (Minn. 1982).

145. Brown v. Phillips, 342 S.E.2d 786 (Ga. Ct. App. 1986); Goller v. White, 122 N.W.2d 193 (Wis. 1963).

146. *In re* Diane P., 424 A.2d 178 (N.H. 1980); Rutkauski v. Wasko, 143 N.Y.S.2d 1 (1955); Hush v. Devilbiss Co., 259 N.W.2d 170 (Mich. Ct. App. 1977); Thomas v. Inmon, 594 S.W.2d 853 (Ark. 1980).

147. "Loco parentis" refers to a person "who intentionally accepts the rights and duties of natural parenthood with respect to a child not his own." *In re* Diane P., 424 A.2d 178 (N.H. 1980) (citing Niewiadomski v. United States, 159 F.2d 683, 686 (6th Cir. 1947), *cert. denied*, 331 U.S. 850 (1947)).

148. *See* Cathey v. Bernard, 467 So. 2d 9, 10 (La. App. 1985).

149. New Jersey Property-Liability Ins. Guar. Ass'n v. State, 446 A.2d 189 (N.J. Super.), *rev'd*, 477 A.2d 826 (N.J. Super.), *cert. denied*, 491 A.2d 691 (N.J. 1984).

150. Note, A Damages Remedy for Abuses by Child Protection Workers, 90 Yale L.J. 681, 695 (1981).

151. For a discussion of the various barriers to recovery for constitutional tort actions, see Spurrier, Federal Constitutional Rights: Priceless or Worthless? Awards or Money Damages Under Section 1983, 20 Tulsa L.J. 1, 26 (1984).

152. "Constitutional torts" is the term used by Christina Whitman to describe such damage actions. Whitman, Constitutional Torts, 79 Mich. L. Rev. 5, 7 (1980).

153. See Restatement (Second) of Torts § 821(B)(i) (1979); P. Schuck, Suing Governments 15 (1983).

154. See Restatement (Second) of Torts § 821(B)(i) (1979); Rothstein v. Wyman, 467 F.2d 226, 241 (2d Cir. 1972); Schuck, Suing Governments, *supra* note 153, at 15–16.

155. See D. Besharov, The Vulnerable Social Worker 15, 65, 133.

156. *Id.* at 138. *Cf.* Whitman, Constitutional Torts, *supra* note 152, at 53.

157. See D. Besharov, Vulnerable Social Worker, *supra* note 155, at 136–38.

158. Robertson, Surviving Incarceration: Constitutional Protection from Inmate Violence, 35 Drake L. Rev. 101, 146 (1985–86), and authorities cited therein.

159. 347 U.S. 483 (1954), 349 U.S. 294 (1955). *Brown* has been frequently mentioned as the progenitor of all modern structural injunction cases. *See, e.g.,* Rudenstine, Judicially Ordered Social Reform, 59 S. Cal. L. Rev. 451 (1986); Rosenberg & Phillips, Institutionalization of Conflict in the Reform of Schools: A Case Study of Court Implementation of the PARC Decree, 57 Ind. L.J. 425 (1982).

160. *See, e.g.,* Levy v. Urbach, 651 F.2d 1278 (9th Cir. 1981) (institution for treatment of persons suffering from leprosy); French v. Owens, 538 F. Supp. 910 (S.D. Ind. 1982) (prisons); Rhem v. Malcolm, 377 F. Supp. 995 (S.D.N.Y. 1977), *aff'd,* 507 F.2d 333 (2d Cir. 1974) (jails); Morgan v. Sproat, 432 F. Supp. 1130 (S.D. Miss. 1977) (juvenile detention facility); Welsch v. Likins, 373 F. Supp. 487 (D. Minn. 1974), *aff'd in part and vacated and remanded in part,* 550 F.2d 1122 (8th Cir. 1977) (mental institution); New York State Ass'n for Retarded Children v. Rockefeller, 357 F. Supp. 752 (E.D.N.Y. 1973) (institution for the mentally retarded); Pennsylvania Ass'n for Retarded Children v. Pennsylvania, 334 F. Supp. 1257 (E.D. Pa. 1971), *adopted,* 343 F. Supp. 279 (E.D. Pa. 1972) (special education).

161. Comment, Confronting the Conditions of Confinement: An Expanded Role for Courts in Prison Reform, 12 Harv. C.R.–C.L. L. Rev. 367, 388 (1977).

162. *See supra* notes 155–56 and accompanying text.

163. *See also* Zeigler, Federal Court Reform, *supra* note 13, at 40–42 (review of the authority that holds that inadequate resources cannot be used as an excuse to avoid compliance with constitutionally guaranteed rights).

164. Rebell, Implementation of Court Mandates Concerning Special Education: The Problems and the Potential, 10 J.L. & Educ. 335, 355 (1981). *See also* Note, The *Wyatt* Case: Implementation of a Judicial Decree Ordering Institutional Change, 84 Yale L.J. 1338, 1356 (1975).

165. A decree seeking to reduce prison violence is, if anything, more difficult to implement than one concerned with foster parent abuse and neglect. Prisons are typically populated with adults who have demonstrated a proclivity for extreme violence. Robertson, Surviving Incarceration, *supra* note 158, at 106. If significant results can be obtained in that inherently volatile environment, then positive change should be possible in the more benign setting of foster family care. Although it is true that the state has less control over what happens in a civilian

foster home than in the highly regimented setting of a prison, ample means are available for the control of violence in foster care. *See supra* notes 44–53 and accompanying text. If these safeguards are followed, there is every reason to believe that foster care mistreatment can be greatly minimized with less effort than would be required to achieve safety in prisons.

166. *See generally* M. Harris & D. Spiller, After Decision: Implementation of Judicial Decrees in Correctional Settings (1977).

167. *See* Rothman & Rothman, Willowbrook, *supra* note 77 (successful implementation of the Willowbrook remedial decree resulted in the community placement of half of the facility's residents; it also brought about positive changes in the state's policy regarding the care of retarded persons).

168. M. Rebell & A. Block, Educational Policy Making and the Courts 65 (1982) (compliance achieved in most of forty-one randomly selected education decrees not involving desegregation). The results of school desegregation decrees are less clear. *Compare* U.S. Civil Rights Commission, Fulfilling the Letter and Spirit of the Law: Desegregation of the Nation's Schools, Letter of Transmittal (1976) (communities in which desegregation proceeds without major incident far outnumber those like Boston and Louisville) *with* H. Kalodner & J. Fishman, Limits of Justice: The Court's Role in School Desegregation (1978) (case studies of several school desegregation cases where the level of compliance was minimal). The spotty results in school desegregation cases may be explained by their high visibility and the tremendous amount of opposition desegregation orders inspire.

169. Maine v. Thiboutot, 448 U.S. 1, 11 (1980) (section 1983 actions may be brought in the state courts). *See also* Martinez v. California, 444 U.S. 277, 283 n.7 (1980); M. Schwartz & J. Kirklin, Section 1983 Litigation: Claims, Defenses and Fees 15 (1986).

170. M. Redish, Federal Jurisdiction: Tensions in the Allocation of Judicial Power 1 (1980).

171. U.S. Const. art. III, § 1 ("The judges . . . shall hold their offices during good behavior"). *See also* Neuborne, The Myth of Parity, 90 Harv. L. Rev. 1105, 1127–28 (1977) (removal only by impeachment means maximum insulation from majority pressures).

172. State judges are ordinarily elected for a fixed term. *See generally* Neuborne, Myth of Parity, *supra* note 171, at 1122.

173. *Id.* at 1127–28 and authorities cited therein.

174. M. Redish, Federal Jursidiction, *supra* note 170, at 2. Another reason that the federal courts seem better suited to address the right-to-safety cases is that the workload of state judges is much greater than that of their federal colleagues. Neuborne, Myth of Parity, *supra* note 171, at 1122.

175. Neuborne, Myth of Parity, *supra* note 171, at 1124.

176. *Id.*

177. It has been argued that there is empirical support for the notion of parity between federal and state courts. Solimine & Walker, Constitutional Litigation in Federal and State Courts: An Empirical Analysis of Judicial Parity, 10 Hastings Const. L.Q. 213 (1983). The data from that study, however, do not support the conclusion that state courts are as competent to handle class action right-to-safety claims for structural injunctive relief as are federal courts. The data were drawn

from reported decisions without apparent differentiation between individual and class claims, or between established and as-yet-unestablished rights. *Id.* at 238. Individual adjudications of established rights differ from the class claims of previously unrecognized rights pertinent to the problem of foster care abuse. In such uncharted waters, the sympathy, independence, and expertise of federal judges is especially important. Whitman, Constitutional Torts, *supra* note 153, at 24 n.114. In addition, some authors report that federal courts uphold federal claims in a greater percentage of cases than do state courts. Solimine & Walker, Judicial Parity, *supra*, at 240, table II; *see also* Doernberg, There's No Reason for It; It's Just Our Policy: Why the Well-Pleaded Complaint Rule Sabotages the Purposes of Federal Question Jurisdiction, 38 Hastings L.J. 597, 647–50 (1987); Mishkin, The Federal "Question" in the District Courts, 53 Colum. L. Rev. 157, 168 (1953).

178. 401 U.S. 37 (1971).

179. The abstention doctrine now commonly associated with *Younger* traces its roots back to *In re* Sawyer, 124 U.S. 200 (1888).

180. Parker v. Turner, 626 F.2d 1, 6 (6th Cir. 1980).

181. Mitchum v. Foster, 407 U.S. 225, 242 (1972); Morial v. Judiciary Comm. of Louisiana, 565 F.2d 295, 298–99 (5th Cir. 1977), *cert. denied*, 435 U.S. 1013 (1978).

182. *Younger*, 401 U.S. at 53.

183. Trainor v. Hernandez, 431 U.S. 434, 444 (1977).

184. *See* Huffman v. Pursue, Ltd., 420 U.S. 592, 604 (1975), *reh'g denied*, 421 U.S. 971 (1975); Juidice v. Vail, 430 U.S. 327 (1977).

185. 442 U.S. 415 (1979).

186. *Id.* at 425, 430. District courts have based their opinions on a broad understanding of *Moore*. *See, e.g.*, Brown v. Jones, 473 F. Supp. 439, 443–46 (N.D. Tex. 1979).

187. Trainor v. Hernandez, 431 U.S. 434, 444 (1977); Juidice v. Vail, 430 U.S. 327, 334–35 (1977).

188. Parker v. Turner, 626 F.2d 1 (6th Cir. 1980).

189. New Jersey v. Chesmard, 555 F.2d at 68 (3d Cir. 1977).

190. *See, e.g.*, L.H. v. Jamieson, 643 F.2d 1351 (9th Cir. 1981); J.P. v. DeSanti, 653 F.2d 1080 (6th Cir. 1981); Haag v. Cuyahoga County, 619 F. Supp. 262 (N.D. Ohio 1985); Brown v. Jones, 473 F. Supp. 439 (N.D. Tex. 1979).

191. *See, e.g.*, L.H. v. Jamieson, 643 F.2d 1351, 1354 (9th Cir. 1981); A.T. v. County of Cook, 613 F. Supp. 775, 778 (N.D. Ill. 1985).

192. *Younger*, 401 U.S. at 45.

193. Atwood, Domestic Relations Cases in Federal Court: Toward a Principled Exercise of Jurisdiction, 35 Hastings L.J. 571, 573 (1984).

194. *In re* Burrus, 136 U.S. 586, 593–94 (1890).

195. *See, e.g.*, Buechold v. Ortiz, 401 F.2d 371, 373 (9th Cir. 1968); Phillips, Nizer, Benjamin, Krim and Ballon v. Rosenstiel, 490 F.2d 509, 516 (2d Cir. 1973) (quoting C. Wright, Federal Courts 84 (2d ed. 1970)).

196. *See, e.g.*, Lloyd v. Loeffler, 694 F.2d 489, 493 (7th Cir. 1982) (recognizing that "the exercise of federal jurisdiction will create a potential for inconsistent decrees"); Sutter v. Pitts, 639 F.2d 842, 844 (1st Cir. 1981) ("there is an obvious likelihood of incompatible state and federal decrees").

197. *See, e.g.*, Peterson v. Babbitt, 708 F.2d 465, 466 (9th Cir. 1983) ("[t]here is no subject matter jurisdiction over these types of domestic disputes"); Zak v. Pilla, 698 F.2d 800, 801 (6th Cir. 1982) (even a valid claim under 42 U.S.C. § 1983 should be "dismissed by a federal district court for lack of jurisdiction"). *But see* Franks v. Smith, 717 F.2d 183, 185 (5th Cir. 1983) ("[t]he mere fact that a claimed violation of constitutional rights arises in a domestic relations context does not bar review of those constitutional issues"). The Supreme Court has not expressly stated that the domestic relations exception does not apply to cases brought under federal question jurisdiction. However, the Court has not invoked this exception in cases challenging the constitutionality of a child's placement or treatment in foster care. *See, e.g.,* Moore v. Sims, 442 U.S. 415 (1979); Smith v. OFFER, 431 U.S. 816 (1977).

198. Taylor v. Ledbetter, 791 F.2d 881, 884 (11th Cir. 1986), *aff'd in part and rev'd in part on reh'g,* 818 F.2d 791 (11th Cir. 1987) (en banc).

199. *See* Atwood, Domestic Relations, *supra* note 193; Comment, Federal Jurisdiction and the Domestic Relations Exception: A Search for Parameters, 31 UCLA L. Rev. 843 (1984); Note, The Domestic Relations Exception to Diversity Jurisdiction: A Re-Evaluation, 24 B.C. L. Rev. 661 (1983). Much of the criticism of the exception (which originated from dicta in two Supreme Court opinions) questions whether it is justified. Critics have also condemned its inconsistent application.

Although authorities debate whether the exception should be redefined or abolished, most agree that it should not extend to cases brought under federal question jurisdiction. An extension of this sort would preclude federal courts from deciding important constitutional issues that were intended to be within their jurisdiction. Comment, Federal Jurisdiction, *supra*, at 882–83.

200. 304 U.S. 64 (1938).

201. *Id.* at 71.

202. H. Clark, The Law of Domestic Relations in the United States 284 (1968); Armstrong v. Armstrong, 508 F.2d 348, 350 (1st Cir. 1974).

203. An example is the *Baby "M"* case, involving surrogate parenting arrangements. *In re* Baby "M", 525 A.2d 1128 (N.J. Super. Ct. Ch. Div. 1987), *aff'd in part and rev'd in part,* 537 A.2d 1227 (N.J. Super. Ct. 1988), *on remand,* 542 A.2d 52 (N.J. Super. Ct. Ch. Div. 1988).

204. Lowry, Impact Litigation, *supra* note 7, at 280.

205. There is a growing literature, primarily in the form of case studies, on the effect of structural injunctions. *See, e.g.,* Alpert, Prison Reform by Judicial Decree: The Unintended Consequences of Ruiz v. Estelle, 9 Just. Sys. J. 291 (1984); Champagne & Hass, The Impact of Johnson v. Avery on Prison Administration, 43 Tenn. L. Rev. 275 (1976); Mnookin, In the Interest, *supra* note 8; Rothman & Rothman, Willowbrook, *supra* note 77, at 66–89.

206. Lottman, Enforcement of Judicial Decrees: Now Comes the Hard Part, 1 Mental Disability L. Rep. 69, 74 (1976); Note, Domestic Relations Exception, *supra* note 199, at 457.

207. The district court in that case published the consent decree that it approved because of the "assistance this case may render other courts considering similar questions." G.L. v. Zumwalt, 564 F. Supp. 1030, 1030 (W.D. Mo. 1983).

208. Harris & Spiller, After Decision, *supra* note 166, at 189.

209. Note, Implementation Problems in Institutional Reform Litigation, 91 Harv.

L. Rev. 428, 463 (1977); Special Project, The Remedial Process in Institutional Reform Litigation, 78 Colum. L. Rev. 784, 824–37 (1978).

210. This device has been used frequently as an adjunct to the retention of jurisdiction. *See, e.g.,* G.L. v. Zumwalt, 564 F. Supp. 1030, 1042 (W.D. Mo. 1983).

211. Rothman & Rothman, Willowbrook, *supra* note 77, at 356–57.

212. Note, Implementation Problems, *supra* note 209, at 441. This method typically leaves enforcement up to an overworked plaintiffs' counsel, whose lack of time and financial backing can hamper the enforcement effort. Lottman, Enforcement of Decrees, *supra* note 206, at 70.

213. 348 F. Supp. 866 (D.D.C. 1972).

214. Rebell, Implementation of Mandates, *supra* note 164, at 337–38.

215. *Id.* at 338.

216. Nathan, The Use of Masters in Institutional Reform Litigation, 10 Toledo L. Rev. 419, 421 (1979). Schwimmer v. United States, 232 F.2d 855, 865 (8th Cir.), *cert. denied,* 352 U.S. 833 (1956) (quoting *ex parte* Peterson, 253 U.S. 300, 312 (1920)). *See generally* Kaufman, Masters in the Federal Courts: Rule 53, 58 Colum. L. Rev. 452 (1958).

217. Nathan, Use of Masters, *supra* note 216, at 421; Special Project, Remedial Process, *supra* note 209, at 835.

218. Note, The *Wyatt* Case, *supra* note 164, at 1360.

219. *Id.* at 1361.

220. Note, The Modification of Consent Decrees in Institutional Reform Litigation, 99 Harv. L. Rev. 1020, 1033 (1986). *See also* Horowitz, Decreeing Organizational Change: Judicial Supervision of Public Institutions, 1983 Duke L.J. 1265, 1305; Wyatt v. Stickney, 325 F. Supp. 781 (M.D. Ala. 1971), *modified sub nom.* Wyatt v. Aderholt, 503 F.2d 1305 (5th Cir. 1974).

221. *G.L.,* 564 F. Supp. at 1036.

222. *See supra* note 51 and accompanying text.

223. Fed. R. Civ. P. 60(b)(5) & (6); C. Wright, The Law of Federal Courts § 52, at 661 (4th ed. 1983). As early as 1932, Justice Cardozo stated that a "continuing decree of injunction directed to events to come" should be understood to be "subject always to adaptation as events may shape the need." United States v. Swift & Co., 286 U.S. 106, 114 (1932). *See also* Jost, From Swift to Stotts and Beyond: Modification of Injunctions in the Federal Courts, 64 Tex. L. Rev. 1101 (1986).

224. *See* Letter from plaintiffs' counsel to defendants, dated Feb. 3, 1984, at 4 (on file with author).

225. Examples of court-ordered modifications of structural injunctions include New York State Ass'n for Retarded Children v. Carey, 393 F. Supp. 715 (E.D.N.Y. 1975), *modification denied,* 551 F. Supp. 1165 (E.D.N.Y. 1982), *aff'd in part and rev'd in part,* 706 F.2d 956 (2d Cir. 1983), *cert. denied,* 464 U.S. 915 (1983); Goldsby v. Carnes, 365 F. Supp. 395 (W.D. Mo. 1973), *modified,* 429 F. Supp. 370 (W.D. Mo. 1977).

226. *See supra* notes 162–64 and accompanying text.

CHAPTER TWELVE

Making It Work: Implementation of Court Orders Requiring Restructuring of State Executive Branch Agencies

Chris Hansen

MICHAEL MUSHLIN'S article on the right to safety in foster care,[1] Chapter 11 in this volume, was an early and thoughtful discussion of systemic foster care reform litigation. Since its publication, many more foster care class actions have been filed and thus much more is now known about such cases. This chapter first places that litigation in a historical and theoretical context. It then addresses the evidence that has been developed since Professor Mushlin's article concerning the effectiveness of that litigation in forcing significant improvements in foster care systems. Many of those suits, seeking systemic reform in foster care and in other areas, have utilized a variety of techniques to ensure implementation of the court orders. The chapter finally discusses the effectiveness of these techniques.

History of Institutional Reform Litigation

The authority of state and national executive branches of government has grown dramatically over the last century. There are now many executive branch agencies that take legal and physical custody of groups of individuals. Corrections agencies take custody of prisoners in prisons and jails; mental retardation agencies take custody of mentally retarded children and adults; mental health agencies take custody of those people said to be mentally ill; juvenile delinquency agencies take custody of children accused of crime; and foster care agencies take custody of children abused or neglected by their parents. Other executive branch agencies, such as school boards and welfare agencies, while not assuming formal custody, exercise extensive control over groups of individuals.

The growth in executive authority has been inevitably accompanied by abuses of that authority.[2] Some of those abuses have been purposeful and directed at individuals; such abuses are generally remedied by individual suits for damages.[3] Other abuses have been policy judgments remedied by challenges to the policy in question. In some instances, undoing those broad policy judgments requires substantial restructuring of the agency. For example, many school districts segregated their schools on the basis of race. Undoing the effects of that policy judgment has been a major focus of the courts and indeed of society for almost forty years.[4] In yet other instances, the abuses of authority by executive branch agencies have been a result of grossly inadequate management and funding. Thus, for example, state officials in many states have allowed prisons and jails to deteriorate to a level that is indisputably inhumane.[5] States have also built and maintained institutions for mentally retarded children and adults that shocked the consciences of even the most skeptical observers.[6]

Historically, those offended by such conditions first attempted to remedy them through lobbying the legislature or executive branch agencies and publicizing the abuses. When those efforts failed, in part due to the powerlessness of the people in state custody, reformers turned to the judicial branch. Lawyers began to build on the lessons learned in the school desegregation litigation and to seek judicial redress in the form of injunctions requiring comprehensive reform of the agency involved. Probably because prisoners are both the most articulate of the various groups over which executive branch officials maintain custody and the group most accustomed to defining their situation in legal terms, comprehensive reform litigation initially spread beyond school desegregation into prisons and jails.[7] In the last twenty years, however, it has spread further into challenges to mental health[8] and mental retardation[9] agencies. Most recently, the litigation has focused anew on school finance and equity disparities and school adequacy,[10] and included school treatment of handicapped students[11] and conditions in foster care agencies.[12]

Both academics and conscientious state officials have questioned the legitimacy of this litigation.[13] The critics have argued that it impermissibly thrusts the judiciary into matters at the heart of both legislative and executive authority,[14] usurping legislative authority to decide that spending should be increased to improve roads rather than prisons, and circumscribing the discretionary policy judgments that are at the heart of executive authority.

Some of these criticisms have a superficial appeal. For example, the litigation has unquestionably affected state spending priorities. However, states need not establish agencies to protect mentally retarded people or abused and neglected children. The growth and success of litigation against such agencies reflect a collective judgment that if a state takes total control of an individual, particularly an individual who, due to age or disability, is unable to protect herself, the state may not force him or her to live in inhumane and harmful conditions. It is difficult to maintain the theoretical objections to litigation when other reform efforts have failed and:

- Black children are required to attend segregated and inferior schools.[15]
- Mentally retarded children are crammed fifty or more into small enclosures encrusted with feces and urine, where they are provided no clothing, toys, or books, and given nothing to do but listen to the din of a television placed above their heads, where two or three physically handicapped children are piled on top of each other in unpadded, eighteen-inch-wide "cripple carts," and where only one staff person, if any, is assigned to supervise.[16]
- An eleven-year-old boy, Kevin E., after entering foster care as a normal infant and spending his whole life in foster care, became so damaged that "[h]e told hospital staff that he hated himself and he climbed into a trash can and asked to be thrown away."[17]
- A prison for 1,200 people has no doctor, no dentist, and no psychiatrist, though it has many inmates with serious contagious diseases and serious mental health problems. No emergency medical care is available, and as many as 90 percent of the prison security force consists of inmate guards ("armed trusties").[18]

Some of the critics of this litigation have argued that however compelling the facts, there is no evidence that the litigation can be successful in remedying the very difficult administrative and financial problems that lead to those facts. The ineffectiveness of the litigation, it is argued, reduces the authority of the courts.[19] This criticism is susceptible to empirical inquiry.

The Effectiveness of Child Welfare Reform Litigation

Some of the litigation seeking comprehensive reform of executive branch agencies has been subjected to an extensive evaluation. For example, there is a large body of scholarly work on the effectiveness of school desegregation litigation, utilizing a wide variety of measures.[20] Most studies of the effectiveness of other types of litigation have been limited to individual case studies.[21]

Litigation to force comprehensive reform of foster care systems is among the newest forms of this litigation, so that evidence of its effectiveness remains tentative. Since Professor Mushlin's article, there has been growing evidence that the litigation is having a significant impact on foster care in this country.

A number of class action cases have been filed around the country in order to enforce the protections afforded foster children by both federal law and the Constitution. As of mid-1992, cases have been settled or decided in Massachusetts,[22] Maryland,[23] Connecticut,[24] the District of Columbia,[25] Kansas City,[26] New Mexico,[27] Alabama,[28] Louisiana,[29] Los Angeles,[30] Illinois,[31] Cincinnati,[32] and Arkansas.[33] Cases are pending in New York,[34] Philadelphia,[35] Florida,[36] Indiana,[37] Kansas,[38] and New Hampshire.[39]

In five cases the judgment was issued sufficiently long ago that some conclusions can be drawn about the effectiveness of the case. In Louisville, Kentucky,[40] a neglect petition was brought against the local office of the state Cabinet for

Human Resources for neglecting children who had been placed in the Cabinet's custody and for whom the Cabinet had determined adoption was appropriate. Petitioners argued that the state was not taking minimally adequate steps to accomplish the goal it had set for itself. In 1981, the state agreed to a court-ordered judgment intended to reform the adoption process in Louisville. The court order listed each of the steps that must be taken to free a child for adoption and find him or her an adoptive home, and it specified a time period within which each step should be accomplished. In 1989, the case was closed when Kentucky achieved full and lasting compliance with the consent decree. Kentucky was so pleased with the systems it had put in place to achieve compliance that it voluntarily expanded those systems throughout the state.[41]

In Massachusetts, prior to the filing of *Lynch v. King*, case plans detailing the goals for the child and the family, and the services needed to achieve those goals, were often not done and not reviewed. Some cases were not assigned to a worker for long periods. Caseloads were excessive.[42] The court ordered significant reform.[43] Today, caseworkers are assigned promptly, and no cases are unassigned. Caseloads remain low, within the court-ordered limits. Case plans are developed and reviewed periodically.[44]

In Kansas City, prior to the consent decree in *G.L.*, 14 percent of children had no contact with their caseworker in a year's time, and only 19 percent had ten or more contacts in a year. Now, most children see their caseworker in the foster home twice a month. Prior to the consent decree, 87 percent received no annual medical examination. Now, Missouri has set up an extensive medical services system, providing for periodic examinations and necessary treatment that is monitored by medical case managers. Prior to the consent decree, only 30 percent of all children had written case plans, and 55 percent had plans of long-term foster care. Today, permanency planning conferences with genuine permanency goals are held on a timely basis for virtually every child. Prior to the consent decree, 97 percent of all foster parents had received no training. Today, although training rates are still inadequate, all foster parents receive preservice training, 87 percent have received thirty hours of training in abuse and neglect, and 45 percent have received ten hours of annual training.[45]

In New Mexico, there was no training for caseworkers when *Joseph A.* was filed. In 1987, as a result of the suit, preservice and annual training became available to all workers. The number of social workers has increased by forty-nine and the number of supervisors by six. Without a computerized tracking system, the New Mexico Department of Human Services did not even know the number of children in its care. A system now exists that not only tracks children but provides "ticklers" for important planning events. A new Quality Assurance Program measures the quality of casework and planning. Average length of time in state custody has dropped from four-and-one-half years before trial to one-and-one-half years as of 1988. Adoptive placements increased from 52 in 1983 to 261 in 1988.[46]

After *L.J.*, a Maryland case, caseloads were substantially reduced in Baltimore

City, where more than half the state's foster children reside. In addition, case-workers assigned to foster children placed with relatives have had caseloads reduced from as many as ninety children to thirty-three, and children in relative homes now receive all the protections and services given to other foster children. Several hundred new foster homes for disabled children were created and the board rates increased. As a result, since early 1991, after years of many foster parents leaving the system, Maryland has had a large net increase in foster homes. Children now receive initial medical examinations, and each child has a medical care record, which is also provided to foster parents. Maryland had abandoned an intensive family services program designed to prevent unnecessary foster care placement, but reinstated it as a result of the court order.[47]

In cases that have been decided more recently, there is also evidence of substantial initial improvement. After *Juan F.*, Connecticut established a state-of-the-art training academy. With the technical assistance provided by the experts on a monitoring panel, the state developed a series of comprehensive policy and practice manuals to guide individual social workers. At a time when Connecticut's budget problems were at their worst, the child welfare system was virtually the only part of state government that received increased funding. Approximately a hundred new social workers were hired, and child welfare was the only agency of the state that did not experience layoffs.[48]

After the judgment in *LaShawn A.* was issued, the District of Columbia began, with the help of the Center for the Study of Social Policy, to show improvement. The District created specialized family preservation units. By August 1992, there had been a net increase in child welfare staff of seventy-five. A plan providing all current workers with eighty hours of preservice training was created.[49]

After *Angela R.*, the Arkansas legislature, in extraordinary session, committed the state to increase foster care funding by $15.3 million in the first year and an additional $45–55 million in the following two years in order to settle that case.[50]

After *B.H.*, at a time of extremely tight budgets, Illinois increased its budget for child welfare by $100 million in the first year after the judgment, an increase of about 20 percent. The requested increase for the second year was for an additional $70 million. Additional social worker positions were authorized, and the state wrote new contracts or expanded existing contracts to increase the range of services available to children and families.[51]

Another Illinois case, *Norman v. Johnson*,[52] enforcing the requirement of federal law that a state make "reasonable efforts" to prevent foster care placement and preserve the family, caused an extensive revision of state policies and procedures and resulted in the creation of several new statewide preventive services, including a $1.8 million cash assistance program and a housing advocacy program. Change has been so dramatic that the court-ordered monitors have described Illinois as being at the "forefront of good child welfare programs."[53]

After *R.C.*, Alabama committed itself to an increase of between $3 and $6 million in fiscal year 1993 for child welfare. Six counties were chosen as sites for restructuring the child welfare system to increase preventive services. Those counties each experienced a one-third increase in staff, created flexible funding mechanisms for preventive services, and hired a respected outside consultant to assist them in revamping the system toward a greater emphasis on preventive services.[54]

Even after *Del A.*, in which the district court ruled against the plaintiffs,[55] Louisiana developed an extensive reform plan as a direct result of the lawsuit. That plan provided for a large number of changes in both policies and procedures.[56] The legislature funded that plan by appropriating an additional $8 million for child welfare at a time when the state was cutting other budget areas.

This evidence must be considered with caution. Indeed, there is no consensus on the criteria that should be used to measure success in these cases. The ultimate measure of a successful foster care system is whether it protects children and preserves families. However, the available ways of measuring those factors, such as the average length of time a child stays in care, are crude and, at best, inadequate. Thus, a declining average length of time in care may reflect families being reunited inappropriately, at the expense of children's safety. More sophisticated "outcome measures" do not exist.

The evidence discussed in this section would more appropriately be described as evidence of improvement in the prerequisites for a successful foster care system. For example, a better-funded foster care system is not necessarily a more effective one. An inadequately funded system, however, is likely to be ineffective. Similarly, a foster care system that provides minimal procedures—such as reviewing each child's case frequently to assess the agency's goal for that child and to ensure that the means to achieve that goal are in place—may be going through the motions or may be diverting attention from more important problems. For example, Kentucky is following the procedures required by In re *P.* on a timely basis, but there are as yet no data on the effect of that compliance on the actual number of children being adopted. Failure to review periodically the child's needs, however, increases the likelihood that the child will fail to receive needed services.

All of this evidence is anecdotal, and none of it is based on comparison of the system at issue with a control system. There is no way to be certain that the reforms were caused by the litigation or would not have taken place without it. It is also possible that other reforms, either more or less effective, would have occurred.

Despite these caveats, people on all sides of foster care reform litigation often describe it as having precipitated significant reform. The limited evidence available, cited above, supports the conclusion that litigation generated advances in child welfare.

The Effectiveness of Techniques Used in Implementation

All agencies—school boards, departments of corrections, departments of mental health or mental retardation, foster care agencies, and others—present remarkably similar problems when comprehensive reform is attempted through the courts. However, just as there has been little research or literature on the effectiveness of litigation in general, very little research or literature has used the lessons learned in each type of suit (for example, prison litigation, school litigation, foster care litigation) to identify those factors that increase the likelihood that the litigation will be effective. However, some interesting questions can be defined and some tentative conclusions can be drawn.

The earliest decisions that must be made have to do with the nature of the decree. Modern management theory suggests that the ideal decree would be one that sets broad goals and leaves wide discretion for those responsible for their implementation to determine the methods by which those goals will be achieved.[57] According to this theory, creativity and energy are unleashed when people are freed from tight regulatory restrictions.

If this approach were to be applied to litigation, the court orders would be brief, setting broad goals. For example, a court order in a mental retardation case might require normalization—an increase in the ability of the affected people to move into normal living and working situations. In a foster care case, the decree might require permanency—an increase in the number of families that are preserved and reunited and the number of children promptly adopted. The foster care decree might also require that children in foster homes be kept safe. The method by which those successes are achieved would be left to the discretion of the relevant executive branch officials. Such an approach would also minimize the degree to which the judicial branch of government intrudes into executive branch decision making. The court could concern itself with the easier and more traditional task of defining the right or goal to be achieved, and avoid the much more difficult and nontraditional task of developing methods to ensure its achievement.

However, the common wisdom among litigators is that the decree should be as specific as possible.[58] The broad outcome measures, such as normalization for mentally retarded people or permanency for foster children, were recognized by state officials as their goals long before these cases were filed, but, as plaintiffs' successes suggest, state officials have not been able to implement them.

Further, the less specific the decree, the more cluttered the postdecree implementation phase will be with disputes over the meaning of the decree or the appropriate measures of compliance. Unless there is an agreed-upon method of measuring "normalization" or "permanency," the parties are likely to have to retry the case repeatedly in endless efforts to define those terms further. It makes more sense to provide specific definitions at the outset, which inevitably requires detailed decrees, so that the implementation phase can focus on compliance rather than definition.

Broad-goal management theory may well be applicable only when management itself is seeking to lead an organization to reform. Perhaps different principles need to be developed when the reforms are being forced on management from the outside. It may also be that this management theory is less applicable when, compared with measures such as profit per share or the cleanliness of streets, the "outcomes" lack easy measurement.

As yet, there is no way to reconcile management effectiveness research with the experiential wisdom of litigators in these cases. However, litigators are trying new models in an effort to maximize the effectiveness of the litigation. These models give different weights to different factors, including the detail to be found in the decree, the technical assistance given to management, and the fewer restrictions found in private enterprise, to see if variance in any of those factors will increase the effectiveness of reform. For example, the theorists of government management[59] often argue that there are restrictions, such as civil service or bureaucracy, that are inherent in government but not found in private enterprise. In the Willowbrook case,[60] both government officials and nonprofit providers blamed noncompliance in part on the restrictions inherent in governmental organization. The parties agreed to "privatize" several of the buildings at Willowbrook to determine whether a private, nonprofit agency with a proven track record of effective service could do a better job than government. The detailed decree remained, but the agency was able to try to implement it without government-imposed restrictions. In that case, the private agency proved no more effective than government.

In *LaShawn A.*, the District of Columbia foster care case, the consent decree provides that the respected Center for the Study of Social Policy will assist the District government in developing methods by which the decree's detailed standards and procedures can be achieved. This approach combines a detailed decree with assistance from a respected agency with management expertise. In *Juan F.*, the consent decree provides for three agreed-upon individuals to develop detailed procedures that must be followed by the Connecticut foster care agency. This approach rejects the management concepts of "ownership" and "flexibility" in favor of prompt application of proven expertise. In neither case is there yet sufficient experience with the model to determine its effectiveness.

Whatever the nature of the decree, postdecree monitoring is inevitable. To the extent possible, that monitoring should be done in a manner calculated to minimize disputes about the accuracy of the results. In both *G.L.* and the Willowbrook case, the parties were able to agree upon monitoring standards and methodologies that called, in part, for measuring compliance through reading a random sample of case records. That reading was done jointly by representatives of both the states and the court's monitoring body. Although this monitoring has not eliminated disputes about the facts, it has minimized them. It has also largely freed plaintiffs' counsel from the extremely time-consuming and expensive task of gathering statistical information about compliance.

A common technique for maximizing the effectiveness of comprehensive reform decrees is the appointment by the court of a person or body with some authority over the implementation process. In some cases, individuals have been appointed as masters or monitors.[61] In other cases, panels or committees have been appointed.[62] These appointed individuals or groups have sometimes been limited to gathering information about compliance.[63] Others have been given authority to make presumptively binding recommendations of steps necessary to achieve compliance.[64] They may be experts in the area of the litigation,[65] or lawyers or community leaders.[66] Groups appointed for this purpose have sometimes included both legal and substantive experts.[67] The limited data available suggest that none of these differences are of any real significance in maximizing the implementation of the decree. What matters is that the individual or body is bright, energetic, and most of all determined; nothing else seems to be of consequence.[68]

Compliance will not automatically follow after a decree is entered and a monitoring system is established and operating. In virtually all of the cases seeking comprehensive reform, the implementation phase is protracted. The traditional techniques used by courts to ensure compliance with their decrees—contempt orders followed by fines or imprisonment—are remarkably ill-suited to the task of forcing an executive branch agency to comply with a complex court order.

In developing techniques to force compliance, the first step is to identify the reasons for noncompliance. There are three common reasons: incompetence, inattentiveness, and intransigence. Each calls for different responsive techniques.

Probably the most common reason for noncompliance is incompetence. Plaintiffs' counsel have responded to incompetence by seeking, cooperatively if possible, to bring outside expertise into the system to train executive branch officials in the skills necessary to achieve compliance.[69] One of the interesting side effects of litigation is that forcing the agency to adopt standards by which to measure success provides a means for identifying and rewarding staff members who are competent and identifying and ultimately driving out those who are not. Thus, for example, the much criticized *Gary W.* litigation[70] forced creation of a cadre of highly competent state employees. When the state's appalling foster care system was sued, the state was able to take those *Gary W.* employees and move them to the foster care system, which immediately began to show significant improvement. If agency management is sincerely interested in reform, technical assistance and personnel changes can have a dramatic effect.[71]

Often, the problems in these systems can be traced to the inattentiveness of high state officials and/or the legislature. Some of the systems, like foster care, are largely invisible as a result of considerations of confidentiality. Few have politically powerful constituencies. Many do not maintain even the most obvious and rudimentary management information systems. For example, the District of Columbia foster care system, when sued, was not able to provide a reliable list of the children in its custody.

The filing of a suit seeking comprehensive reform is often sufficient to dramatically increase the visibility of the problems in an agency. Prejudgment discovery and postjudgment monitoring can provide extensive evidence of the problems. Because it is largely statistical in nature, this evidence can be widely disseminated. The attentiveness of an active plaintiffs' counsel and an active judge can virtually guarantee the attentiveness of executive and legislative officials.[72]

The third and by far the most difficult problem in implementation of these decrees is executive branch officials who are simply intransigent. Thus, many school officials around the country have stalled full compliance with *Brown*'s desegregation mandate for almost forty years.[73] Many of the cases, including *Brown* itself, are still open. So are many of the older mental retardation cases—such as the Willowbrook case, filed in 1972. Only one foster care case, In re *P.,* has ever been closed, and some have taken on legendary status as a result of lack of progress.[74]

So far, no effective techniques have been developed that would allow plaintiffs' counsel to overcome intransigent executive officials and force compliance in the absence of an active and determined judge.[75] A determined judge, prodded by determined plaintiffs' counsel, and utilizing a combination of threats and patience, can overcome state intransigence.[76] Alternative means to overcome intransigent officials are badly needed.

In short, there is now substantial evidence that the courts can be used to force comprehensive reform on executive branch agencies. As plaintiffs' counsel and the courts become more sophisticated in this litigation, its effectiveness may increase.

NOTES

Note: This chapter does not necessarily reflect the views of the American Civil Liberties Union.

1. *See* Mushlin, Unsafe Havens: The Case for Constitutional Protection of Foster Children from Abuse and Neglect, 23 Harv. C.R.–C.L. L. Rev. 199 (1988) (original publication).

2. "Power tends to corrupt and absolute power corrupts absolutely." Letter from Lord Acton to Bishop Mandell Creighton, Apr. 3, 1887, in The Oxford Dictionary of Quotations (3d ed. 1979).

3. *See, e.g.,* Halperin v. Kissinger, 424 F. Supp. 838 (D.D.C. 1976), *rev'd,* 606 F.2d 1192 (D.C. Cir. 1979), *aff'd in part and cert. dismissed in part,* 452 U.S. 713 (1981).

4. *See* Brown v. Board of Educ., 347 U.S. 483 (1954). A recent desegregation case is Freeman v. Pitts, 112 S. Ct. 1430 (1992). *Brown* itself remains an open, active case. *See* Brown v. Board of Educ., 892 F.2d 851 (10th Cir. 1989), *vacated,* 112 S. Ct. 1657 (1992), *reinstated on remand,* 978 F.2d 585 (10th Cir. 1992).

5. *See, e.g.,* Holt v. Sarver, 309 F. Supp. 362 (E.D. Ark. 1970), *aff'd,* 442 F.2d 304 (8th Cir. 1971).

6. *See, e.g.,* New York State Ass'n for Retarded Children v. Carey, 393 F. Supp. 715 (E.D.N.Y. 1975), 409 F. Supp. 606 (E.D.N.Y. 1976), 438 F. Supp. 440 (E.D.N.Y. 1977), 456 F. Supp. 85 (E.D.N.Y. 1978), 466 F. Supp. 479 (E.D.N.Y. 1978), *aff'd,* 612 F.2d 644 (2d Cir. 1979), 466 F. Supp. 487 (E.D.N.Y. 1979), 492 F. Supp. 1099 (E.D.N.Y. 1980), 492 F. Supp. 1110 (E.D.N.Y. 1980), *rev'd,* 631 F.2d 162 (2d Cir. 1980), 596 F.2d 27 (2d Cir. 1979), *cert. denied,* 444 U.S. 836 (1979), 551 F. Supp. 1165 (E.D.N.Y. 1982), *aff'd in part and rev'd in part,* 706 F.2d 956 (2d Cir. 1983), *cert. denied,* 464 U.S. 915 (1983).

This case is known as the Willowbrook case because it began as a challenge to conditions in a mental retardation institution then known as the Willowbrook State School.

7. *See* Mushlin, Unsafe Havens, *supra* note 1, at 219–20; *see also* notes 75–76 to Chapter 11 in this volume with accompanying text.

8. *See* Mushlin, Unsafe Havens, *supra* note 1, at 221–23.

9. *See id.*

10. *See, e.g.,* Charlet v. Legislature of the State of Louisiana, No. 379–560 (Division D, 19th La. Judicial District Court, East Baton Rouge Parish filed Mar. 24, 1992); Harper v. Hunt, Civ. 91-0188-R (Montgomery Co., Ala. Circuit Court filed 1991); McSuic, The Use of Education Clauses in School Reform Litigation, 28 Harv. J. on Legis. 307 (1991).

11. *See, e.g.,* Mills v. Board of Educ., 348 F. Supp. 866 (D.D.C. 1972); Pennsylvania Ass'n for Retarded Children v. Commonwealth, 343 F. Supp. 279 (E.D. Pa. 1972). *See also* 20 U.S.C. §§ 1400–1485 (1988) (concerning education of the handicapped).

12. *See* cases cited *infra* notes 22–40.

13. *See* Mushlin, Unsafe Havens, *supra* note 1, at 251–56; *see also* notes 158–68 to Chapter 11 with accompanying text.

14. *See* Mushlin, Unsafe Havens, *supra* note 1, at 252–53.

15. *See* R. Kluger, Simple Justice (1975).

16. *See, e.g.,* Hansen, Willowbrook, 9 Mental Retardation 6 (1977).

17. LaShawn A. v. Dixon, 762 F. Supp. 959, 985 (D.D.C. 1991). *See also* Mushlin, Unsafe Havens, *supra* note 1, at 199–200, 204–209; notes 1–5, 18–43 to Chapter 11 with accompanying text.

18. *See* Finney v. Arkansas Board of Corrections, 505 F.2d 194, 202–204 (8th Cir. 1974).

19. *See* Mushlin, Unsafe Havens, *supra* note 1, at 253; *see also* notes 161–63 to Chapter 11 with accompanying text.

20. *See, e.g.,* W. Hawley et al., Strategies for Effective Desegregation: Lessons from the Research (1983); Crain & Mahard, How Desegregation Orders May Improve Minority Academic Achievement, 16 Harv. C.R.–C.L. L. Rev. 693 (1982); Symposium, Courts, Social Science, and School Desegregation, 39 Law & Contemp. Probs. (1975).

21. *See, e.g.,* R. Mnookin, In the Interest of Children: Advocacy, Law Reform, and Public Policy (1985) (children's rights cases); D. Rothman and S. Rothman, The Willowbrook Wars (1984) (mental retardation case); L. Yackle, Reform and Regret: The Story of Federal Judicial Involvement in the Alabama Prison System (1989) (prison case); Hansen, Willowbrook, 10 Soc. Pol'y 41 (1979) (mental retardation case); Mushlin et al., Court-Ordered Foster Family Case Reform: A Case Study, 65 Child Welfare 141 (1986) (foster care). *See also* P. Cooper, Hard Judicial Choices: Federal District Court Judges and State and Local Officials (1988). There are also a number of individual case studies of school desegregation cases. *See, e.g.,* P. Dimond, Beyond Busing: Inside the Challenge to Urban Segregation (1985); D. Monti, A Semblance of Justice: St. Louis Desegregation and Order in Urban America (1985); R. Pride & J. Woodard, Burden of Busing: The Politics of Desegregation in Nashville, Tennessee (1985).

22. *See* Lynch v. King, 550 F. Supp. 325 (D. Mass. 1982), *aff'd*, 719 F.2d 504 (1st Cir. 1983).

23. *See* L.J. v. Massinga, 838 F.2d 118 (4th Cir. 1988), *cert. denied*, 488 U.S. 1018 (1989).
24. *See* Juan F. v. O'Neill, No. H 89 859 (Conn. 1991) (consent decree).
25. *See* LaShawn A. v. Dixon, 762 F. Supp. 959 (D.D.C. 1991).
26. *See* G.L. v. Zumwalt, 564 F. Supp. 1030 (W.D. Mo. 1983).
27. *See* Joseph A. v. New Mexico Dep't of Human Servs., 575 F. Supp. 346 (D.N.M. 1982).
28. *See* R.C. v. Hornsby, Civ. Act. No. 88-D-1170-N (M.D. Ala. Apr. 19, 1989) (consent decree approved June 11, 1991).
29. *See* Del A. v. Edwards, Civ. Act. No. 86-0801 (E.D. La. Mar. 2, 1988) (motion to dismiss), *aff'd*, 855 F.2d 1148 (5th Cir. 1988), *reh'g granted*, 862 F.2d 1107 (5th Cir. 1988), *appeal dismissed*, 867 F.2d 842 (5th Cir. 1989).
30. *See* Timothy J. v. Chaffee, Case No. 001128 (Cal. Super. Ct., Los Angeles Co. filed August 26, 1988).
31. *See* B.H. v. Johnson, 715 F. Supp. 1387 (N.D. Ill. 1989) (consent decree entered 1991).
32. *See* Roe v. Staples, No. C-1-83-1704 (S.D. Ohio 1986) (consent decree).
33. *See* Angela R. v. Clinton, No. LR-C-91–415 (E.D. Ark. 1992) (consent decree).
34. *See, e.g.,* Grant v. Cuomo, 130 A.D.2d 154 (N.Y. App. Div. 1987), *aff'd*, 73 N.Y.2d 820 (1988); Martin A. v. Gross, 524 N.Y.S.2d 75 (N.Y. Sup. Ct. 1987), *aff'd*, 153 A.D.2d 812 (N.Y. App. Div. 1989).
35. *See* Baby Neal v. Casey, No. 90–2343 (E.D. Pa. filed 1990).
36. *See* M.E. v. Chiles, No. 90–1008 (S.D. Fla. 1990); Children A–F v. Chiles, No. 90–2416 (S.D. Fla. 1990).
37. *See* B.M. v. Magnant, No. IP891054 (S.D. Ind. filed Sept. 29, 1989).
38. *See* Sheila A. v. Hayden, N. 89–CV–33 (Kan. Dist. Ct., Shawnee Co., amended compl. filed Feb. 1990).
39. *See* Eric L. v. Bird, No. 91–376–D (N.H. filed 1991).
40. *See In Re* Michael and Michele P., 7 Fam. Law Rep. 2722.
41. The court-appointed monitor in *In re* P. testified concerning that case during a contempt hearing in G.L. v. Zumwalt, 564 F. Supp. 1030 (W.D. Mo. 1983). On January 30, 1992, she testified to the facts cited in the text.
42. *See* Lynch v. King, 550 F. Supp. 325, 336 (D. Mass. 1982), *aff'd*, 719 F.2d 504 (1st Cir. 1983).
43. *See id.* at 355–57.
44. Interview with plaintiffs' counsel (June 1992).
45. *Compare* D. Caplovitz & L. Genevie, Foster Children in Jackson County, Missouri (July 21, 1982) (on file with author) *with* Foster Care Consent Decree Committee, Report of Compliance (Jan. 1992) (on file with author).
46. Andrea Poole, Compliance Monitor, Federal Consent Decree Compliance Report, Second Quarter, 1988.
47. Interview with plaintiffs' counsel (June 1992).
48. Interview with Dr. Theodore J. Stein, one of the three members of the court-appointed monitoring body (June 1992).
49. Center for the Study of Social Policy, Quarterly Progress Report (June 30, 1992) (on file with author).
50. Interview with plaintiffs' counsel (June 1992).

51. Interview with plaintiffs' counsel (June 1992).

52. 739 F. Supp. 1182 (N.D. Ill. 1990).

53. Interview with plaintiffs' counsel in *B.H.* (June 1992).

54. Interview with plaintiffs' counsel (June 1992).

55. *See* Del A. v. Roemer, 777 F. Supp. 1297 (E.D. La. 1991).

56. *See id.* at 1302.

57. *See, e.g.,* D. Osborne & T. Gaebler, Reinventing Government (1992); T. Peters & R. Waterman, In Search of Excellence (1982).

58. *See* Mushlin, Unsafe Havens, *supra* note 1, at 272–73; *see also* notes 206–208 to Chapter 11 with accompanying text.

59. *See* Osborne & Gaebler, Reinventing Government, *supra* note 57.

60. *See supra* note 6.

61. *See, e.g.,* Gary W. v. Louisiana, 437 F. Supp. 1209, 1225 (E.D. La. 1976).

62. *See, e.g.,* G.L. v. Zumwalt, 731 F. Supp. 365 (W.D. Mo. 1990); New York State Ass'n for Retarded Children v. Carey, 466 F. Supp. 487 (E.D.N.Y.), *aff'd,* 612 F.2d 644 (2d Cir. 1979).

63. *See* Joseph A. v. New Mexico Dep't of Human Servs., 575 F. Supp. 346 (D.N.M. 1983).

64. *See, e.g.,* New York State Ass'n for Retarded Children v. Carey, 612 F.2d 644 (2d Cir. 1979).

65. *See, e.g.,* Palmiagiano v. DiPrete, 737 F. Supp. 1257 (D.R.I. 1990).

66. *See, e.g.,* Wyatt v. Stickney, 344 F. Supp. 387, 392–93, 407 (M.D. Ala. 1972).

67. *See* Gary W. v. Louisiana, 437 F. Supp. 1209 (E.D. La. 1976). In Juan F. v. O'Neill, No. H 89 859 (Conn. 1991), the panel consists of two experts and a federal judge.

68. There was a radical difference in the progress made in implementing the Willowbrook decision after the demise of the panel. *See* New York State Ass'n for Retarded Children v. Carey, 492 F. Supp. 1110 (E.D.N.Y.), *rev'd,* 631 F.2d 162 (2d Cir. 1980). Although a master was subsequently appointed (*see Carey,* 551 F. Supp. 1165 (E.D.N.Y. 1982), *aff'd in pertinent part,* 706 F.2d 956 (2d Cir. 1983)), the master proved much less determined to force compliance and progress slowed radically.

69. The most noteworthy recent examples of this are in *LaShawn A.* and *Juan F. See supra* notes 25–26 and accompanying text.

70. *See* Gary W. v. Louisiana, 437 F. Supp. 1209 (E.D. La. 1976).

71. *See* Rothman & Rothman, Willowbrook, *supra* note 21.

72. *See* Mushlin, Unsafe Havens, *supra* note 1, at 271–72, 276–77; *see also* notes 219–20 to Chapter 11 with accompanying text.

73. *See, e.g.,* Freeman v. Pitts, 112 S.Ct. 1430 (1992) (finding that black children still receive separate and unequal education in DeKalb County, Georgia).

74. *See, e.g.,* Wilder v. Bernstein, 645 F. Supp. 1292 (S.D.N.Y. 1986), *aff'd,* 848 F.2d 1338 (2d Cir. 1988) (a case in which the author has been involved).

75. *See* Mushlin, Unsafe Havens, *supra* note 1, at 276–77; *see also* notes 219–20 Chapter 11 with accompanying text.

76. *See* Gary W. v. Louisiana, 437 F. Supp. 1209 (E.D. La. 1976); J. Peltason, 58 Lonely Men (1971); Rothman & Rothman, Willowbrook, *supra* note 21.

CHAPTER THIRTEEN

Protection of Foster Children: A Constitutional Duty Anchored in a State's Choices?

Brenda L. Kelley

THIS CHAPTER examines a state's public policy decision to provide programs of child protection and foster care in light of the subsequent constitutional liability that may flow from such choices. This liability may result from lawsuits filed on behalf of foster children and arguing that states have an affirmative duty to protect foster children from abuse and neglect under the due process clause of the Fourteenth Amendment. We shall review in detail the legal basis for these lawsuits and discuss the scope of the duty that might be imposed on the states under this litigation. The various standards and factors that are used to determine whether a violation of the duty occurred will be dissected and evaluated. The legal background will then be put in context from the perspective of a child welfare system administrator, emphasizing the difficulties and limitations under which state child welfare agencies must labor.

We begin our examination of the potential grounds for a claim by children in foster care to protection from harm with the evolution of federal court decisions addressing the liberty interest of distinct classes of citizens based on their disability, physical place of confinement, or status.[1] Challenges to confinement claiming constitutionally protected liberty interests have been presented in the context of both the fact and duration of confinement[2] as well as the nature of confinement in terms of freedom from cruel and unusual punishment, personal safety and freedom from restraint, and the physical location of confinement.[3] The right to communication also emerges as a protected constitutional right and as an interrelated safeguard inherent in the promotion of personal safety and security.[4] Two Supreme Court decisions, *Youngberg v. Romeo*[5] and *DeShaney v. Winnebago County*

Department of Social Services,[6] are very important in this context. This chapter examines whether *Youngberg* and *DeShaney* may be interpreted as offering support for extension of a constitutionally mandated personal safety interest to foster children or as providing a basis for speculation on the scope of such interest. I argue for a prudent and balanced application of these decisions to foster children, taking present realities into account, and list safeguards that state child welfare systems should put in place to prevent harm to foster children.

The Substantive Liberty Interest Claim to Personal Safety

Youngberg

Nicholas Romeo was a profoundly retarded thirty-three-year-old resident of a Pennsylvania facility serving individuals with functional limitations due to mental retardation. He had been cared for at home by his parents until his father's death left his mother unable to care for him or control his aggressive behavior. While confined in state care, he suffered numerous injuries both through his own violent behavior and through other residents' reactions to him. During the course of treatment for a broken arm, a physician ordered the use of soft restraints for his protection and the protection of other residents in the hospital. A behavior management program had been designed to reduce his aggressive behavior, but it was not implemented because of his mother's objections. Nonetheless concerned about his injuries, Nicholas Romeo's mother sued the institution on his behalf, claiming that her son had constitutional rights to safety and freedom from physical restraints. In its review of the circumstances in *Youngberg v. Romeo*, the Supreme Court granted the petition for certiorari due primarily to the importance of the question presented as it related to the administration of state institutions for the mentally retarded.

An obstacle to drawing foster children under the historically defined circumstances of confinement that warrant constitutional protection lies in the obvious inability of young minor children to exercise independence and liberty even if they were not confined. A close analogy is Nicholas Romeo's lack of real opportunity to exercise his protected liberty interest had it been made available to him.[7] Some courts had seemed to suggest in other decisions that when individuals not capable of exercising a true liberty interest in being free of state custody are involuntarily committed to a state institution, the state's provision of basic necessities, "for which the residents have no other source, forms an adequate basis for some state-imposed restriction on their liberty."[8]

Youngberg established that state control of individuals unable to live on their own because of their incapacity or lack of capable family triggers a commensurate state duty to provide reasonably safe conditions and basic care in terms of food, clothing, shelter, and medical services. The *Youngberg* Court noted that satisfaction of procedural due process requirements in order to allow infringement of the individual's liberty interest in freedom (i.e., institutionalization by the state) does not extinguish any other substantive liberty interests of the confined individual. The Court found that the right to personal security constitutes a "historic liberty interest" and held that "that right is not extinguished by lawful confinement."[9] The Court reasoned that since there is a constitutional prohibition against confining convicted criminals in unsafe conditions, it must therefore, be unconstitutional to confine involuntarily committed individuals in unsafe conditions, when, unlike criminals, they are not the subjects of state-imposed punishment.

Nicholas Romeo was an adult incapacitated by severe mental retardation and lawfully confined in an institution in order to protect him and others from his violent, aggressive behavior. Are his circumstances similar enough to those of foster children to support extension of the *Youngberg* protections to them? As in *Youngberg*, foster children are placed in state custody pursuant to certain procedural due process safeguards. They are incapacitated by both their minority and lack of responsible family. The state also acts affirmatively in its *parens patriae* role as continuing custodian pursuant to a judicial order.[10] Finding that constitutionally protected interests in reasonable care and safety do not disappear upon institutionalization, the Court also elaborated the ways in which Romeo's retardation imposed limitations on his ability to exercise independently his interest in freedom. Similarly, through either incapacity or minority, children do not have a real expectation of the independent exercise of freedom. They are limited by their inability to live on their own and provide for their basic daily needs. Both mentally retarded individuals and foster children in state custody for provision of care, then, are totally dependent on the state.

The *Youngberg* Court, recognizing the duty to provide certain essentials of care to the institutionalized, noted this departure from the general principle that a state has no constitutional obligation to provide substantive services to its citizens. The Court placed its emphasis on the individual's lack of real opportunity to exercise an interest in freedom and total dependence on the state for daily care. The Court held that it is the *physical control* of the person, not the type of care setting or incapacitating factor, that triggers the constitutional duty. In fact, the Court spoke of these factors only as postcommitment interests.

DeShaney

Joshua DeShaney was a four-year-old child who suffered severe brain damage due to repeated head injuries inflicted over an extended period of time. Randy DeShaney, his father and custodian pursuant to a divorce judgment, was convicted of child abuse. Winnebago County social services employees had received a report from Randy DeShaney's second wife that DeShaney was hitting Joshua hard enough to leave marks on him. Subsequent to this report, Joshua received on three separate occasions hospital treatment for injuries that medical personnel reported as suspicious. The caseworker noted in monthly visits to the home suspicious injuries to Joshua's head and his lack of school enrollment, as well as her personal suspicion of child abuse in the home.

Joshua's mother petitioned the Court for a finding that the state had a duty to protect Joshua and sought damages related to his injuries. In *DeShaney*, the Supreme Court granted the petition for certiorari primarily because of the inconsistent approaches taken by the lower courts in determining when, if ever, a state's failure to provide an individual with adequate protective services is violative of due process rights. The Court also recognized the importance of the issue to the administration of state and local governments.

The *DeShaney* Court denied Joshua's claim to state protection, basing its holding on the general principle that a state has no constitutional duty to provide services to its citizens. The Court further held that the intent of the due process clause of the Fourteenth Amendment was to limit state power and protect the people from state action. Combining these two principles, the *DeShaney* Court found Joshua's injuries to have been caused by his father, a private actor, and not by the state, and emphasized that the state's conduct did not create the danger or render Joshua more vulnerable to it.

DeShaney specifically rejects the assertion that the state's mere knowledge of a child's circumstances and its expression of an intention to protect through receipt and investigation of child abuse complaints create a special relationship with a child, thereby triggering an affirmative state duty. The Court speaks of certain limited circumstances in which the Constitution creates for the state duties of care and protection with regard to particular individuals. It reviews, for example, the holding in the *Estelle* case requiring medical care to be provided to prisoners, based on the fact that their deprivation of freedom by the state prevents them from seeking care on their own. The Court then reviewed *Youngberg* and acknowledged its extension of the *Estelle* doctrine beyond the prison setting. In speaking of *Estelle* and *Youngberg*, the Court in *DeShaney* states: "Taken together, they stand only for the proposition that when the State takes a person into its custody and holds him there against his will, the Constitution imposes upon it a corresponding duty to assume some responsibility for his safety and general well-being."[11]

The *DeShaney* Court traces the triggering of the state duty to the point where the state imposes a limitation on the individual's freedom to act on his own behalf "through incarceration, institutionalization, or other similar restraint of personal liberty."[12] It appears, then, that the Court in *DeShaney* opened the door for foster children to claim entitlement to these postcommitment substantive liberty interest protections by concluding, "In *Youngberg v. Romeo we extended this analysis beyond the Eighth Amendment setting,* holding that the substantive component of the Fourteenth Amendment's Due Process Clause requires the State to provide involuntarily committed mental patients *with such services as are necessary to ensure their 'reasonable safety' from themselves and others.*"[13]

Indeed, the Court specifically suggested that its holding might have been different had Joshua incurred his injuries while in state custody. In a footnote the Court commented, "Had the State by the affirmative exercise of its power removed Joshua from free society and placed him in a foster home operated by its agents, we might have a situation sufficiently analogous to incarceration or institutionalization to give rise to an affirmative duty to protect."[14] The Court noted that two U.S. Courts of Appeals had relied on *Youngberg* and *Estelle*[15] as authority for their recognition of a state duty to protect foster children from mistreatment.[16] The *DeShaney* Court, through its use of the language "or other similar restraint of personal liberty" and its acknowledgment of state involvement in foster care custodial arrangements, explicitly envisions situations of state custody, other than the prison and institutional settings, as falling within the purview of a constitutionally protected personal safety interest.

The Scope of Expectation of Personal Safety

In *Youngberg*, the Court addressed the right to personal security in terms of a right not to be confined in unsafe conditions. The duty to provide the essentials of daily life, including adequate food, shelter, clothing, and medical care, is stated quite clearly. However, in the area of safety and freedom from bodily restraint, the Court notes that these interests are not absolute. The scope of protection is formulated thus: "The question then is not simply whether a liberty interest has been infringed but whether the extent or nature of the restraint or lack of absolute safety is such as to violate due process."[17] The Court notes that some restraint may be necessary in order to protect residents from violence or as part of a training program.

The need for freedom of movement by the residents within an institution, however, conflicts with the potential for dangerous situations caused by such freedom. The Court therefore requires as the appropriate test for determining due process violations *balancing* "the liberty of the individual" against "the demands of organized society."[18] One aspect of this balancing in past cases involved the state's asserted reasons for restraining the individual's liberty. The *Youngberg* Court held that there must exist some rational relation between the nature and duration of commitment and its purpose.[19] The state's purpose in confining Nicholas Romeo, for example, "was to provide reasonable care and safety, conditions not available to him outside of an institution."[20] The Court found that a protected interest in conditions of reasonable care and safety "would comport fully with the purpose of respondent's confinement."[21]

This analysis is applicable to an examination of the special interest in protection that foster children may claim by virtue of their being in foster care as a result of the state's exercise of its *parens patriae* authority. This interest is separate and distinct from the state's duty to provide the essentials of care.

States elect to administer a foster care program to achieve two primary goals: the protection of children from parental/guardian abuse and neglect and the assumption of responsibility for a child in the absence of or abandonment by a parent. The state's role in each instance involves an exercise of its *parens patriae* authority to care for children and offer them protection from generalized risk in society, as would any parent. Thus, it is important to discern how and in what context the child entered the foster care system. Foster children generally enter state custody either through a formal adjudication transferring custody from the child's parent or guardian or through voluntary agreement between the agency and the parent or guardian.[22] In the first type of case, the state acts on an existing family unit through its child protection system. All fifty states have reporting statutes authorizing receipt of and investigation of reports of abuse and neglect.[23]

The federal courts have generally been supportive of the state's interest in protecting children at risk of abuse and neglect when such state actions were challenged as infringements of protected Fourteenth and Fourth Amendment family privacy/integrity interests and due process rights.[24] From the time a child is placed in state custody, separate from parental custody and control, up to the time the child is returned home or parental rights are terminated, the state continues to exercise its *parens patriae* power to protect the child from risk of harm. The specific types of harm from which children may be protected by state intervention can be found in the state's child abuse/neglect reporting statute and the state juvenile code governing adjudications of children in need of state care.[25]

The Supreme Court in *Parham v. J.R.* suggested that children have liberty interests in freedom from confinement, but recognized that, absent child abuse or neglect, parents or guardians were to be afforded the presumption that they were acting in their children's best interest.[26] Inherent in that decision was a recognition of the parental right to rear one's children. It would seem logical, then, that if state intervention in the family unit is authorized for the purpose of protecting the child from harm, then that state's interest and purpose in protection would follow that child into foster care placement, whatever that placement might be (that is, a foster home or treatment facility).[27] The state would then have a minimal duty to protect the child from the types of harm that precipitated placement and were present in his or her family, as well as a general duty to prevent the child's exposure to the types of harm enumerated in the state child abuse law and juvenile code.

The Court in *Youngberg* recognized that the state's purpose in offering care to Nicholas Romeo was the protection of himself and others. For foster children, the state's purpose is to protect the child from certain identified risks, but for which the child could have remained at home in his own family. When applied to the foster care setting, the *Jackson v. Indiana* standard, which states that "the nature and duration of commitment must bear some reasonable relationship to the purpose for which the individual is committed,"[28] helps to emphasize the fundamental reason for providing a state system of alternative care for children. Moreover, the Adoption Assistance and Child Welfare Act of 1980[29] specifies that although reasonable efforts should be made to avoid placing children in foster care, placement becomes desirable when the child is in danger. The act also underscores the notion that foster care was not designed to afford children better custodial care than they might have received at home.[30]

What guidance, then, does the *DeShaney* decision provide in this respect? The *DeShaney* Court found that the interest in personal safety "requires the State to provide involuntarily committed mental patients with such services as are necessary to ensure their 'reasonable safety' from themselves and others."[31] The Court, in a footnote, refers back to *Youngberg* and adds a proviso: "Even in this situation, we have recognized that the State has considerable discretion in determining the nature and scope of the responsibility."[32] Elsewhere, the Court also observes that "the protections of the Due Process Clause, both substantive and procedural, may be triggered when the State, *by the affirmative acts of its agents,* subjects an involuntarily confined individual to deprivations of liberty *which are not among those generally authorized by his confinement.*"[33] Thus, since the authority for confinement of foster children other than those placed by voluntary parental agreement is protection from danger, which allows the infringement of their interest in being a part of their natural family, it seems that a claim based on a *Youngberg–DeShaney* analysis could arise through abuse and neglect of the child or deprivation of basic necessities.

Even in the case of care provided pursuant to a voluntary parental placement agreement, *Youngberg* and *Deshaney* suggest that the state still has some duty to protect the child. However, the scope of this duty does not encompass an expectation of absolute safety. Instead, it is the expectation that a state, in choosing to offer services not constitutionally mandated, will not provide those services in such a manner as to deprive its citizens of the due process protection of freedom from abuse.

Determining Whether a State Violated Its Duty

An initial rereading of *DeShaney* seems to suggest that the Court was poised to extend to foster children a more expanded constitutionally protected spectrum of substantive interests than recognized for Nicholas Romeo in *Youngberg*. However, upon closer examination of these two decisions and several intervening Circuit Court decisions cited by the Supreme Court in *DeShaney*, it appears that the message is more one of "perhaps, but . . . "

The Supreme Court adopted in *Youngberg* an "exercise of professional judgment" standard to measure a state's conduct in these situations. This standard prevailed over other suggestions, such as "compelling necessity," 'substantial necessity," and "prevailing professional judgment." The Court held that "the Constitution only requires that the courts make certain that professional judgment was exercised. It is not appropriate for the courts to specify which of several professionally acceptable choices should have been made."[34] The Court, in its decision, rejected the *Estelle* "deliberate indifference" standard, which had been applied in relation to medical care in a prison setting. The Court held that persons who are involuntarily committed under noncriminal law are entitled to more considerate treatment and conditions of confinement than criminals, for whom punishment is a permissible element of confinement.

The *DeShaney* Court found no state duty to protect its citizens from "private violence, *or other mishaps not attributable to the conduct of its employees.*"[35] The Court then affirmed the lower court's holding that the causal connection between state conduct and Joshua's injuries was too attenuated to make out a constitutional deprivation.[36] The Court also cited a Seventh Circuit case, *Archie v. City of Racine*, involving the failure of a municipal emergency services dispatcher to send out a medical rescue unit following two calls for assistance.[37] The facts of *Archie* are similar to the *DeShaney* facts in that the injured party was not under state control at the time of injury. In *Archie*, the Seventh Circuit explored the intent of the due process clause to prevent abuse of power, analyzed the dispatcher's actions in relation to the physical causes of the death of the person on whose behalf the calls for assistance had been made, and discussed the proper relationship between the Constitution and state law. The *Archie* court then concluded that the due process clause does not forbid deprivations of liberty that stem from mere or gross negligence. The standard was instead set at the level of deliberate, unauthorized acts, and the court in applying that standard found that the dispatcher's actions, while grossly negligent, were not intentional. The court proceeded to discuss reckless conduct under constitutional law in terms of the standard applied in criminal law, which defines a reckless act as one reflecting complete indifference to risk or an act so dangerous that the defendant's knowledge of its danger can be inferred. The final issue that the Seventh Circuit addressed in *Archie* related to the situation in which the state is the *initiator* and strips away the individual's "avenues of self-help."[38] The cases cited by the court involve prison settings and use the deliberate indifference standard from *Estelle* and *Youngberg* with respect to the requirement of humane medical care. The court proposes "jettisoning" the special relationship language and substituting the following principle: "[W]hen the state puts a person in danger, the due process clause requires the state to protect him to the extent of ameliorating the incremental risk."[39] The Seventh Circuit concluded its opinion by emphasizing the choices that governmental entities must make as choices that belong in the political, not the judicial, branch of government.

Sounding much like the Seventh Circuit in *Archie*, the *Deshaney* Court found that "[w]hile the State may have been aware of the dangers that Joshua faced in the free world, it played no part in their creation, nor did it do anything to render him any more vulnerable to them."[40]

What do these cases suggest for foster children and state agencies charged with their care? The Supreme Court's reliance on the Seventh Circuit's *Archie* analysis suggests that this decision sets approved parameters on actionable deprivation under the due process clause. The Court recognizes the potential for a claim in a special relationship but has cautioned that even in such a situation, limitations on the scope of the interest exist. The Court, although relying on

Youngberg for the extension of personal safety protection beyond the prison setting, thus appears to disregard the professional judgment standard of *Youngberg*. The Court's silence on this issue could be attributed to the belief that discussion of this issue was irrelevant, as it was unnecessary to reach the actor's state of mind.[41] The Court's discussion, however, seems to point back to the pre-*Youngberg* standard of deliberate indifference.

In addition, the *DeShaney* Court commented in a footnote on two circuit court decisions involving physical and sexual abuse of children in foster care: *Doe v. New York City Department of Social Services*[42] and *Taylor ex rel. Walker v. Ledbetter*.[43] Both cases held that states may be liable for failing to protect children in foster homes from mistreatment at the hands of their foster parents. The Supreme Court expressed no view on the validity of these holdings.

The *Taylor* decision merits further consideration. The *Taylor* court acknowledged two earlier Supreme Court decisions[44] and held deliberate indifference to be a threshold requirement in order to maintain a lawsuit on behalf of the foster children. The court added a second requirement that "the failure [of the state] to act must have been a substantial factor" leading to the deprivation.[45] The *Taylor* court cited *Youngberg* for the recognition of a substantive interest in personal safety and for the extension of the protection to the foster care setting. According to the court's analysis, the child's physical safety was a primary objective of the foster home placement. The court acknowledged that a balancing of the interests of the child and of the state was required to determine whether the child's rights were infringed. In order to prevail in a deprivation claim under the *Taylor* standard, a child must show "actual knowledge of abuse or that agency personnel deliberately failed to learn what was occurring in the foster home."[46]

The *Taylor* court found that government officials may be held liable if they exhibit "deliberate indifference to a known injury, a known risk, or a specific duty and their failure to perform the duty or act to ameliorate the risk of injury was a proximate cause of plaintiff's deprivation of rights under the Constitution."[47] The court cautioned that its holding did not mean that "incidental injuries or *infrequent* acts of abuse" rise to the level actionable in a section 1983 action (i.e., an action under 42 U.S.C. § 1983) and employed deliberate indifference to the child's welfare as the relevant standard.[48] The *Taylor* court also acknowledges the Eleventh Circuit's reliance on the special relationship theory to find the child's right to protection and the state's corresponding duty.

Three Eleventh Circuit judges joined in an opinion concurring in part and dissenting in part in *Taylor*, noting, as did the Supreme Court in *DeShaney*, the special tensions inherent in child protection and foster care cases. The judges noted that simultaneous duties exist to preserve children in families and accord some recognition of family privacy and normalcy, while maintaining vigilance to protect children who may be at risk because of abuse and neglect. In this dissenting opinion, the judges propose a three-pronged test. First, they point to the requirement of a *causal relationship* between the state conduct and the deprivation.[49] Second, these judges require a custodial or *special relationship* in which the state exposes the individual to danger. Third, they require a display of *deliberate indifference* by the state.

Given the delicate balancing of interests required of the state to maintain stable, family-like placements within a foster family's home while ensuring the child's protection, I fully agree with the three Eleventh Circuit judges, who seem to disagree more with the majority's application of substantive due process principles to the circumstances at hand than to the principles per se. Their application of the substantive liberty interest claim to freedom from abuse and neglect to the facts in *Taylor* is the best statement yet of the post-*Youngberg* interest and is consistent with the *DeShaney* Court's cautious approach to the scope of the due process interest.

In summary, the three-pronged test enunciated by the dissenters in *Taylor* provides the appropriate overlay for establishing deprivation of a foster child's constitutionally protected liberty interest in personal safety, reflecting the spirit of the *DeShaney* balance between restraint on expansion of liability and protection of interests of a constitutional magnitude.

Foster Care Litigation in Context

A Dose of Reality

After an exploration of the legal issues involved in foster care litigation, it is critical to examine these issues from a real-life day-to-day perspective within a child welfare system. The standards suggested by the *Taylor* dissenters become very significant when one is confronted with the current status of states' child protection and foster care programs. Stresses in today's child welfare system must be considered in formulating appropriate liability standards. These include:

The adequacy of the financial base for child welfare programs
The impact of liability and litigation on decision making in child welfare practice and a state's ability to recruit and retain career staff and foster parents in child welfare programs
The lack of uniform standards for defining actionable abuse and neglect
The lack of data and research needed to understand the proper scope and mix of preventive interventions, to define the long-term effectiveness of various models for risk assessment, and to predict future harmful behavior toward children.

The years 1990 and 1991 marked the publication of reports by the Children's Defense Fund, the Child Welfare League of America, the American Public Welfare Association, the North American Council on Adoptable Children, and the U.S. Department of Health and Human Services, as well as reams of Congressional testimony documenting the ongoing crisis in child welfare systems in this country. Those reports, along with the Children's Defense Fund's annual reports, establish that the financing provided at the federal, state, and local levels is woefully inadequate, not only for the number of children and families coming in contact with state child welfare systems, but also for the basic human needs of these children and families. Since states have embraced the "reasonable-efforts" provisions of the Adoption Assistance and Child Welfare Act of 1980,[50] only children in situations of great danger—those whose safety, even with services, is in question—are coming into foster care. As a result, these children often have suffered severe physical or emotional trauma that demands intensive, and thus expensive, ameliorative care and treatment.

Congress and state legislatures make resource-allocation decisions through the political process, as so aptly described by the Seventh Circuit in *Archie*. Unfortunately for all, the needs of children and families in this country far exceed what has been allocated to meet those needs. Child welfare administrators, in turn, must prioritize those resources and allocate them across the three core programs present in each state's child welfare system: child protection, foster care, and adoption. In making those decisions, it is absolutely critical that the public, the state legislatures, the executive branch, and courts exercising juvenile jurisdiction understand what constitutional minima mean in providing care and treatment for children in foster care. With the number of allegations of abuse or neglect rising each year and approximately 15 percent of those cases nationally resulting in foster care placement, states that choose to offer a child protection plan must know and understand the nature of the duty to protect foster children. And if this duty could reach the level of constitutional protection for Kathy Taylor but not for Joshua DeShaney, the implications for the reallocation of a state's very limited child welfare resources should be fairly clear.

As a matter of public policy, it seems cruelly hypocritical to pour more of those limited funds into documenting abuse and neglect through child protection investigation systems and then have even fewer resources to meet the identified needs of the families and children. What are we accomplishing in the name of child protection? Investigations and intervention in family life hold out the expectation that something will be done if needed to improve the family's situation. Reading even one of the Children's Defense Fund's annual reports and then examining states' child protection/family services budgets for the same period will quickly expose any such expectation as misguided. This nation and individual states are facing budgetary deficits of proportions unfathomable to the ordinary citizen. States' child welfare systems are expected each year to serve more and more families and children with fewer and fewer dollars. Small rays of federal relief in the form of increased Head Start and Maternal and Child Health funds are insufficient. States are validating neglect complaints in poor families in numbers consistent with the percentage of children living in poverty, while low-cost housing, financial and medical assistance, and substance abuse treatment programs are short-changed.

Without an adequate financial response and commitment to this national epidemic, states must choose, as *Archie* described so vividly, what components of its traditional child welfare system will be funded. As a result, administrators must make tough choices among equally compelling and competing needs across the spectrum of child protection, foster care, and adoption. To read *DeShaney* and cases such as *Doe* and *Taylor* together is to undermine legally a systems approach to child welfare services. At a time when fiscally driven state policy prohibits deficit expenditures, state administrators are being forced to choose among and ration resources for investigating growing numbers of reports of alleged abuse or neglect of children in their own homes; providing for appropriate care and treatment for victims of abuse or neglect; providing prevention or reunification services to avoid or reduce time in foster care; providing appropriate care and treatment for foster children; recruiting, screening, training, and supporting foster and adoptive families; and effecting and supporting adoptive placements for foster children who cannot return home. Child welfare systems are expected to carry out these serious responsibilities with increasingly less experienced staff (as a result of high turnover rates) serving more and more children and families needing help with daily survival in the face of reduced or inflation-ravaged federal and state budgets.

Is it critical for foster children to have a constitutional personal safety interest, not absolute, but reasonable within the limits of what is humanly known in a given child's situation and within the knowledge base of child welfare practice? Absolutely. Is it critical for first-line workers, supervisors, foster parents, policymakers, and administrators to know and understand the parameters of that child's constitutionally protected interest in personal safety? Absolutely. In the litigious climate that has developed in this country, which has extended to child welfare systems, actors in a state system should understand that in protecting a child they are inherently and incidentally protecting themselves. To the extent that fear of making a mistake and being the subject of litigation is a deterrent in the recruitment and retention of child welfare staff and foster parents, an acceptance of the three elements enunciated by the dissenting justices in *Taylor* should neutralize some anxiety about the countless decisions made in the course of a day in child welfare practice.

Finally, each state has its own definitions of abuse and neglect for purposes of reporting and investigation. There is no clear, uniform, nationally defined line marking off the maltreatment of children. When it comes to describing a constitutionally protected interest in personal safety for children in foster care, this lack of a uniform definition is troubling. It is difficult to relate the *Taylor* majority's use of the terms "incidental injuries and infrequent abuse" to definitions contained in a state child abuse/neglect statute. The dissent's use of "harm or danger" is clearer and seems to describe the kinds of actions or omissions that would, in the child's own home, result in removal. Reasonable efforts, which by their nature involve some risk, could be made to sustain the foster family placement, just as they are made before transferring a child from the natural family to a foster family setting.

Safeguards Against Abuse and Neglect

Traditional child protection responses provide systemic safeguards for the foster care population to the same extent that they are offered to the general population.

It is unclear how effective criminal record and abuse registry checks have been in the prevention of child abuse in relation to the cost of securing checks on every employee and foster/adoptive parent. Given the increase in child sexual abuse allegations and criminal convictions for sexually related crimes involving children, and the increase in child fatalities, it is important to continue such checks until more data are available on the cost effectiveness of this prevention measure.

One key safeguard is systemwide preservice and ongoing training and orientation for workers, supervisors, and foster parents that emphasizes protection of foster children from harm and the mandate to report any evidence that a child is at risk. It cannot be assumed that this basic premise is understood. It must be expressed and recognized as a *value* held within the system.

Annual reevaluation of foster homes and regular visits with children should be a part of the monitoring of the system of care. An additional effective safeguard is the appointment by courts of Court Appointed Special Advocates (CASA volunteers) to provide individual monitoring and support for a child in foster care. CASA volunteers may be one of the most effective (in terms of outcome and cost) but least available systemwide resources for children in state custody.

Protection of individual children from specific harm necessarily depends on knowledge of some existing or potential danger. In this sense children in foster family care are similarly situated to children who are living with parents or relatives and are alleged to be in danger. The policy and procedures utilized in child protection investigations involving foster children should certainly be no *less* stringent than those utilized in the investigation of children living in their own homes.

The standard for assessing state actors' conduct after a deprivation-of-personal-safety claim should be a fact-based determination not dissimilar to the fact-finding and decision making utilized in child protection investigations to assess parental conduct. Participation and involvement in causing children harm or exposing them to harm, or passively acquiescing to conditions of known harm or risk, are critical elements in assessing parental culpability. The three elements the *Taylor* dissenters required to establish a constitutional deprivation of personal safety do not appear to be significantly different from the analysis used by child protection systems to assess parental conduct. They ensure fact-based, rather than speculative, scrutiny.

Corrective action plans and followup are critical when an allegation is validated and the child remains in the home. The potential conflict of interest when the child protection arm of the child welfare agency investigates allegations in homes utilized by the foster care arm can be minimized by providing state criminal penalties for failure to report and attempts to obstruct an investigation. Joint investigation of serious cases with law enforcement and reporting procedures requiring a review of all valid cases by the local district attorney would provide checks and balances external to the child welfare system.

No system has yet been devised that predicts risk and parental behavior with certainty. A number of good risk-assessment models have been developed, but no national model for uniform use. Consensus has been reached in the field of practice on some high-risk indicators, but national child fatality statistics involving prior or active child protection cases confirm that almost twenty years after passage of the federal Child Abuse Prevention and Treatment Act of 1974, an empirically based, outcome-proven method of targeting adults who will harm children has yet to be devised. And key to knowing the real incidence and character of child maltreatment in this country is the establishment of a national system to collect such data from all states and provide feedback analysis to them. Such data are needed to evaluate the effectiveness of interventions, not only in terms of accountability for fiscal resources, but in terms of human costs as well. States would be expected to finance linking their systems to a national data collection effort.

Finally, until more research is available to identify the factors that contribute to the successful reunification of children with their families with no subsequent abuse or neglect, there will be uncertainty about the long-term risk reduction promised by the various available treatment and prevention models. Given this uncertainty, the *Taylor* three-pronged analysis is critical in its emphasis on direct causation and deliberate indifference.

In summary, certain safeguards should be put into place that recognize the *Youngberg* court's valid concern for more considerate treatment of individuals under state control. For state systems incorporating these practices, standards of deliberate indifference, causal connection, and endangerment should not create excessive concern, as the *Youngberg* court noted, about potential liability for every decision made during the course of the day. States should require the following minimum practices to reduce unknown risks:

1. Screening of employees and foster parents against state criminal records and child abuse/neglect registries
2. An absolute ban on the use of corporal punishment for foster children in any placement setting
3. Mandatory preservice training for employees and foster parents regarding the mission of the agency, and mandatory reporting of suspicions of abuse and neglect
4. Prompt reporting of any allegation of abuse or neglect involving foster children, and investigation of allegations in accordance with standard child protection policy[51]
5. A corrective action plan for any validated abuse/neglect complaint in which a child is not removed from the placement
6. Criminal sanctions for obstruction of any child protection investigation and failure to report abuse or neglect
7. Medical care and treatment decisions based on professional judgment
8. Access to communication and freedom of movement for children, with restrictions imposed only by a qualified professional
9. Medical evaluation on child's entry into care and annual medical update thereafter
10. Mandatory visits with and observations of the child in foster care
11. Annual reevaluation and recertification of foster care placement settings.

Conclusion

This nation's desire to protect vulnerable children from harm, is reflected in child abuse/neglect reporting and investigation statutes in every state. As a result, states incur the responsibility and duty to provide reasonable protection for children who are removed from their family homes through state intervention. The *DeShaney* decision makes clear that a state's decision to offer a program of child protection, reporting, and investigation is not constitutionally mandated. However, the *DeShaney* decision, coupled with *Youngberg*, clearly signals that a state's voluntary choice to offer programs of services to its vulnerable citizens can have constitutional consequences.

These decisions take on greater significance as increasing demands for services in state voluntary programs result in increasing numbers of citizens accorded constitutional protection. With declining revenues, states must make difficult fiscal decisions about the scope of services to be made available in response to competing demands. *DeShaney* suggests legal parameters that are similar to the characterizations used to prioritize funding in the political process: discretionary versus nondiscretionary choices. Basically, from a constitutional perspective, a state has the choice to offer a program of child protection services and determine the scope of that program. However, once the state acts to remove children from their families to protect them from a known danger, the state may not elect to expose those children to harm or danger, notwithstanding its resource limits.

The child's right to be free from known danger or risk is not an absolute guarantee of safety, for how do we distinguish a potentially abusive foster parent from the undetected "madman" of general society?[52] The standards set for finding that the state violated its duty must recognize the delicate balance required between the interest of protecting a child isolated within the control of a family and the respect accorded to family life and family preservation. Thus, children have a constitutionally protected expectation that they will not be placed in danger by the state; that the state will not be a substantial factor in causing them harm; and that they will not be a victim of the state's deliberate indifference to known harm or danger.

NOTES

1. *See generally* Besharov, Malpractice in Child Placement: Civil Liability for Inadequate Foster Care Services, 63 Child Welfare 195 (1984); Donnella, Safe Foster Care: A Constitutional Mandate, 19 Fam. L.Q. 79 (1985); Grimm, Case Worker and Agency Liability in Child Welfare Cases, in Children and the Law 41 (1988) (providing a historical review of cases in other settings, with discussion of application of these holdings to foster care and emerging grounds for liability).
2. *See* Parham v. J.R., 442 U.S. 584 (1979); Duchesne v. Sugarman, 566 F.2d 817 (2d Cir. 1977); Brooks v. Richardson, 478 F. Supp. 793 (S.D.N.Y. 1979); Cameron

v. Montgomery County Child Welfare Serv., 471 F. Supp. 761 (E.D. Pa. 1979)(dealing with the fact of confinement). Cases that involve the duration of confinement include Donaldson v. O'Connor, 493 F.2d 507 (5th Cir. 1974), *vacated and remanded,* 422 U.S. 563 (1975); *Duchesne,* 566 F.2d 817; *Brooks,* 478 F. Supp. 793.

3. For a history of challenges to conditions of confinement, see generally Wyatt v. Stickney, 325 F. Supp. 781 (M.D. Ala. 1971); Wyatt v. Aderholt, 503 F.2d 1305 (5th Cir. 1974); Gary W. v. Louisiana, 437 F. Supp. 1209 (E.D. La. 1976); Estelle v. Gamble, 429 U.S. 97 (1976); Ingraham v. Wright, 430 U.S. 651 (1977); Brooks v. Richardson, 478 F. Supp. 793 (S.D.N.Y. 1979); Doe v. New York City Dep't of Social Serv., 649 F.2d 134 (2d Cir. 1981), *cert. denied,* 464 U.S. 864 (1983); Santana v. Collazo, 533 F. Supp. 966 (D.P.R. 1982), *aff'd in relevant part,* 714 F.2d 1172 (1st Cir. 1983), *cert. denied,* 466 U.S. 974 (1984); Rogers v. Okin, 478 F. Supp. 1342 (D. Mass. 1979), *modified,* 634 F.2d 650 (1st Cir. 1980), *vacated,* 457 U.S. 291 (1982); Youngberg v. Romeo, 457 U.S. 307 (1982); *see also* Garrity v. Gallen, 522 F. Supp. 171 (D.N.H. 1981) (challenging the conditions and place of confinement).

4. *Gary W.,* 437 F. Supp. at 1224.

5. 457 U.S. 307 (1982).

6. 489 U.S. 189 (1989).

7. *Youngberg,* 457 U.S. at 317–18.

8. *Compare* Garrity v. Gallen, 522 F. Supp. 171, 239 (D.N.H. 1981) (discussing involuntarily confined individuals who have no real opportunity to exercise interest in freedom) *with* O'Connor v. Donaldson, 422 U.S. 563 (1975)(dealing with an involuntarily confined individual who could exercise interest in freedom through available friends and family).

9. *Youngberg,* 457 U.S. at 315.

10. *Compare* Duchesne v. Sugarman, 566 F.2d 817 (2d Cir. 1977) *with* Brooks v. Richardson, 478 F. Supp. 793 (S.D.N.Y. 1979) (involving procedural due process challenges to continued custody of children in foster care). It is assumed throughout for purposes of brevity that procedural due process in initial custody and continuing custody is met through a state's juvenile procedures for emergency custody, adjudication, disposition, and periodic review. If these are defective, there may be separate procedural due process or equal protection challenges available related to the fact of or duration of confinement in foster care.

11. DeShaney v. Winnebago County Dep't of Social Servs., 489 U.S. 189, 199–200 (1989).

12. *Id.* at 200.

13. *Id.* at 199 (citation omitted) (footnote omitted) (emphasis added).

14. *Id.* at 201 n.9.

15. 429 U.S. 97 (1976).

16. *Deshaney,* 489 U.S. at 200 n.9.

17. *Youngberg,* 457 U.S. at 320.

18. *Id.*

19. *Id.* at 320 n. 27, citing Jackson v. Indiana, 406 U.S. 715 (1972). *See also* Garrity v. Gallen, 522 F. Supp. 171 (D.N.H. 1991) (applying the *Jackson* standard for evaluation of deprivation of liberty interests for individuals confined by the state).

20. *Youngberg,* 457 U.S. at 320 n. 27.

21. *Id.* at 324.

22. Potential liability arising from voluntary placement is omitted from this discussion, since the focus here is on confinement flowing from affirmative state intervention in an intact family unit.

23. *See* National Commission on Child Welfare and Family Preservation, Factbook On Public Child Welfare Services and Staff 7 (1990); Meriwether, Child Abuse Reporting Laws: Time for a Change, 20 Fam. L.Q. 142 (1986).

24. *See* Austin v. Borel, 830 F.2d. 1356 (5th Cir. 1987); Stem v. Ahearn, 908 F.2d 1 (5th Cir. 1990); Hodorowski v. Ray, 844 F.2d 1210 (5th Cir. 1988); E.Z. v. Coler, 603 F. Supp. 1546 (N.D. Ill. 1985); Cameron v. Montgomery County Child Welfare Serv., 471 F. Supp. 761 (E.D. Pa. 1979); *see also* DeShaney v. Winnebago County Dep't of Social Servs., 489 U.S. 189 (1989) (explaining the state interest in protecting children at risk of abuse).

25. See Meriwether, Child Abuse Reporting Laws, *supra* note 23, at 143–44 (giving examples of state child abuse/neglect statutes); 1991 La. Sess. Law Serv. 603, 606, 666 (West) (an example of a state juvenile code for finding children in need of care).

26. *See* Parham v. J.R., 442 U.S. 584 (1975).

27. *See* Gary W. v. Louisiana, 437 F. Supp. 1219 (E.D. La. 1976).

28. 406 U.S. 715, 738 (1972).

29. 42 U.S.C. §§ 670–679a (1988).

30. *See* M. Allen et al., A Guide to the Adoption Assistance Act of 1980, in Foster Children in the Courts 588–90 (M. Hardin ed., 1983). For more background on custodial care, see Gary W. v. Louisiana, 437 F. Supp. 1209, 1216–17 (E.D. La. 1976). For a discussion of parens patriae power, see generally Developments in the Law: The Constitution and the Family, 93 Harv. L. Rev. 1156, 1198–1202 n.27 (1980) (citing Quilloin v. Walcott, 434 U.S. 246, 255 (1978)).

31. *DeShaney*, 489 U.S. at 199.

32. *Id.* at 200 n.7.

33. *Id.* at 200–201 n.8 (emphasis added).

34. *Youngberg*, 457 U.S. at 321.

35. *DeShaney*, 489 U.S. at 198 (emphasis added).

36. *Id.* at 194 (noting that the circuit court's decision was based primarily on the earlier case of Martinez v. California, 444 U.S. 277, 285 (1980)).

The Court also notes the Seventh Circuit's failure to deal with the issue of the state of mind "necessary to make out a due process claim" following the decisions in Daniels v. Williams, 474 U.S. 327 (1986), and Davidson v.Cannon, 474 U.S. 344 (1986). *See DeShaney*, 489 U.S. at 189. The *DeShaney* Court returns to the state of mind factor in two footnotes, but concludes, as did the Seventh Circuit, that it is unnecessary to deal with the issue, as there is no basis for a constitutional claim to protection in the *DeShaney* circumstances. *See id.* at 202 n.10.

37. 847 F.2d 1211 (7th Cir. 1988).

38. *Id.* at 1222.

39. *Id.* at 1223.

40. *DeShaney*, 489 U.S. at 200.

41. *See supra* note 36.

42. 649 F.2d 134 (2d Cir. 1981). The case was in process in the Second Circuit, using a deliberate indifference standard, while the Supreme Court was deciding

Youngberg using exercise of professional judgment, not deliberate indifference, as the appropriate standard to assess deprivation of liberty interests in personal safety.

43. 818 F.2d 791 (11th Cir. 1987). The case was decided prior to *DeShaney*. The Supreme Court rendered its decision in *DeShaney* in February 1989 and denied certiorari in both *Archie* and *Taylor* on March 6, 1989.

44. *See* Daniels v. Williams, 474 U.S. 327 (1986); Davidson v. Cannon, 474 U.S. 344 (1986).

45. *Taylor*, 818 F.2d at 794.

46. *Id.* at 796.

47. *Id.* at 797.

48. *Id.* (emphasis added). Presumably, the court meant infrequent child care deficiencies and not acts of abuse. Otherwise, it is difficult to understand frequency of abuse as a factor, given that in *DeShaney* repeated acts led to severe, irreversible injury, whereas in *Taylor* one violent episode of abuse apparently had the same result.

49. *See id.* at 817. The dissenting judges relied here on Martinez v. California, 444 U.S. 277 (1980) to buttress their conclusion.

50. 42 U.S.C. § 671(a)(15) (1988) states that "in each case, reasonable efforts will be made (A) prior to the placement of a child in foster care, to prevent or eliminate the need for removal of the child from his home, and (B) to make it possible for the child to return to his home."

51. *See generally* Besharov, The Misuse of Foster Care: When the Desire to Help Children Outruns the Ability to Improve Parental Functioning, 20 Fam. L.Q. 213, 217–219 (1986); R. Barth & M. Berry, A Decade Later: Outcomes of Permanency Planning in the First Ten Years 9, 12, 15–17 (North American Council on Adoptable Children ed., Aug. 1990) (discussing the incidence of abuse in foster care).

52. *See* Bowers v. DeVito, 686 F.2d 616 (7th Cir. 1982).

■ CHAPTER FOURTEEN

Homeless Families: Do They Have a Right to Integrity?

Donna Mascari Baker

THE INCREASING NUMBER of homeless families in the United States is a fairly recent social problem, part of the diversification of the homeless population. Although the various subsets of this population are alike in many ways, they differ in the causes of their homelessness and in the needs that must be met to permit recovery.[1]

Advocates for the homeless have urged the courts to recognize a right to shelter. They have met with success only in states whose constitutions and statutory provisions guarantee such a right. In California, for instance, litigation in the lower courts continues to define the parameters of a California Supreme Court decision guaranteeing support of "all incompetent poor, indigent persons, and those incapacitated by age, disease, or accident."[2] So far, the decisions have not only established a right to shelter but also have taken the first steps toward mandating some standards for the quality of the shelter provided.

The homeless can generally be divided into four broad categories: (1) chronically homeless single males or females; (2) the deinstitutionalized mentally ill; (3) the chemically dependent; and (4) the "new poor." This chapter focuses on the homeless family, a subcategory within the "new poor." The dearth of material on the homeless family indicates that it is a recent phenomenon, and attempts to remedy the homeless crisis have neither considered the particular needs of families nor recognized that a long-term solution to their problems requires a specialized

Originally published in 35 UCLA L. Rev. 159. Copyright 1987, The Regents of the University of California. All Rights Reserved. Reprinted in redacted form with permission.

response to those needs. Current attempts to remedy the crisis are inadequate and often violate the families' constitutional rights to autonomy and privacy.

A long-term solution to the problems of the homeless family requires a multifaceted approach. Emergency relief in the form of shelter, food, medical assistance, and psychological counseling is the most immediate need. To establish economic self-sufficiency, support, including job training and employment search assistance, is required. Low-cost housing, the ultimate necessity, is becoming a very scarce commodity.

This chapter is inspired by the problems facing homeless families as they struggle to regain their self-sufficiency. The struggle is critical because their homelessness need not become a chronic condition if effective emergency support is given. I shall first explore homelessness in general, its causes, and the results of litigation in this area. Because many of the characteristics of the general homeless population also apply to the homeless family, this section is intended to give a background against which the unique characteristics of the homeless family may later be considered. I next present the characteristics of the homeless family and critique the effect on such families of current responses to the homeless problem. Particular attention is given to New York and California, primary sources of research and litigation concerning the homeless. Finally, I offer proposals geared toward enabling homeless families to regain self-sufficiency.

Homelessness in the United States

A Growing Social Problem

The problem of homelessness affects nearly every part of the United States.[3] Its magnitude is rapidly increasing as more people find themselves unable to secure adequate and stable housing. Emergency shelter providers in Los Angeles report a doubling or a tripling of the demand for shelter since 1980.[4] Estimates of the homeless population nationwide range from 250,000 to 3,000,000 people, depending on the agency conducting the research.[5] The estimates of homeless persons in California in 1984 ranged from 55,000 to 90,000.[6] That same year, the Department of Housing and Urban Development (HUD) identified Los Angeles as having the largest population of homeless persons in the country.[7] Its estimate was between 31,300 and 33,800, excluding runaway youths.[8]

As the numbers increase, so does the variety of homeless populations. Traditionally, the homeless person was single, male, and chronically homeless. He could be found almost exclusively in the local skid row. The demographic characteristics of the homeless population have changed radically, however. Ever-increasing numbers of homeless families, women with children, battered women, seniors, youths, mentally ill people, and substance abusers can be found in cities, suburbs, and rural areas.[9] Although the causes of their homelessness differ, they share the basic trauma of lack of shelter.

If the basic need of shelter is not met quickly, homelessness can become chronic, affecting an individual's physical and emotional well-being. Many of the physical and emotional problems that afflict these displaced persons are immediate by-products of homelessness.[10] "[H]omelessness is a crisis that would confuse and disorient even the healthiest person or family,"[11] and research shows that it causes confusion and cognitive dissonance.[12] Once this disorientation occurs, others, including other homeless people who still maintain a semblance of mental health, shun the individual, thereby leading to further disorientation.[13] Homelessness affects physical health as well. As one study states, "[T]he homeless have greater medical needs and less access to health care than the population at large because of the stress of living without safe shelter and nutritional food."[14] The nutrition-related illnesses afflicting the homeless typically include heart and respiratory diseases and ulcerated legs.[15]

Homeless people face legal problems as well. Vagrancy laws continue to threaten them with criminal sanctions despite U.S. Supreme Court rulings declaring many such statutes unconstitutionally vague.[16] Thus, homeless people find themselves in an impossible situation: Emergency shelter is scarce, and the law prohibits living in a car, park, or another public area.

Emergency shelter is the most immediate need of the homeless. Research on the availability of emergency shelters generally focuses on two areas: the number of shelter beds available compared with the demand and the quality of care provided. Most available research has centered on Los Angeles County and New York City.

In Los Angeles, the United Way concluded that "the number of available beds and food services is disproportionately lower than even the most conservative census of the number of homeless people."[17] Less than 5 percent of the county's homeless who seek emergency shelter receive it.[18] The few shelter programs that exist are unevenly distributed geographically, leaving some areas without a program.[19] The programs are primarily funded through private sources, which frequently cover only a small portion of a month's expenses.[20] Two-thirds of the programs are run by religious organizations,[21] and the majority of these require participation in their religious services as a prerequisite to receiving aid.[22] Many of the shelter "beds" provided in Los Angeles are not beds at all, but rather floors or church benches.[23] Living conditions are often overcrowded to the point of being unsafe.[24]

Orange County, which is adjacent to Los Angeles County and one of the wealthiest counties in the country, is no exception. In 1986 the Orange County Coalition for the Homeless found that of the 3,169 people who sought shelter (1,176 of them children in families), only 12 percent received shelter from the agencies participating in the survey.[25] This trend is consistent with national patterns.[26]

New York City is one of the few cities to guarantee a right to shelter,[27] so that the concern there has shifted from the number of shelter beds provided to the quality of shelter care. Emergency shelters in New York are operated predominantly under private auspices, and few professionally trained people are directly involved in staffing them.[28] As a result, "[i]nvestigators have found several shelters to be in substantial violation of fire and food handling codes, and have inadequate toilet facilities, overcrowding, and inadequate staffing and security."[29] Thus, even when the law mandates that emergency shelter be provided, the services available are not adequate to fulfill the needs that go beyond a bed and a roof over one's head.

Paradoxically, stopgap solutions may *add* to the problem of chronic homelessness if they are implemented without consideration of long-term solutions. Emergency shelter offers immediate protection from the threats of street life. It is also a necessary first step in an overall program aimed at helping homeless people regain self-sufficiency. Advocates for the homeless suggest a three-tiered approach to the homeless problem: (1) short-term emergency shelter; (2) transitional or intermediate services; and (3) long-term permanent housing.[30] All three are needed for an effective and long-term solution. Presently, few programs provide supportive services, such as employment assistance or medical care, that go beyond the first tier of simply providing a roof for three to seven nights.[31] Thus, "[i]t may be that homelessness is a permanent and insoluble problem, but such a hypothesis cannot be tested while existing public and private welfare policies preclude there being enough adequate service delivery for the homeless population."[32]

As the homeless population increases and the current approaches to the problem continue to be used, certain trends will emerge. First, the diversity of that population will steadily increase, thereby creating more complex problems when dealing with the issue of homelessness.[33] Second, an "unnatural selection process [will] take effect in public shelters."[34] Young, able-bodied people of sound mind will take the places of the disabled, elderly, mentally ill, or fearful homeless. The alternatives for these less capable individuals are the streets or overcrowded private shelters. Finally, the emergency shelter will become a "permanent home."[35] The employment skills of many of these homeless individuals are rapidly becoming obsolete, creating and fostering a cycle that frustrates an individual's or family's attempt to regain independence and self-reliance. Some commentators predict "a swell of discontent and demoralization . . . the equal of which has not been seen for fifty years."[36]

Causes

The recent recession, the rise in unemployment, current welfare policies, and the severe shortage of affordable housing have all played significant parts in the increase and diversification of the homeless population. Although homelessness is the culmination of a series of factors on both individual and societal levels, its distinctive characteristic is the inability to secure stable and permanent housing.[37] Homelessness has a fairly common pattern of genesis. Prior to being homeless, the individual or family was able to maintain permanent housing through a low-paying job or public assistance. Then a crisis, such as a job loss, illness, a late welfare check, or being the victim of a crime, precipitated eviction and homelessness, often for the first time in their lives. Once homeless, it becomes nearly impossible to secure the necessary resources to acquire other housing while struggling for daily subsistence on the streets.[38] If more affordable housing, jobs, or welfare were available, the individual or family could overcome the temporary crisis and remain housed, but three converging trends in unemployment, welfare, and housing prevent this.

Unemployment

In 1978, the proportion of people living in poverty began to increase sharply. By April 1986, 15 percent of the U.S. population lived below the poverty line.[39] This eight-year period reflects the first steady increase in the poverty rate since 1959.[40] Closely linked to the poverty rate is the unemployment rate.[41] Today, researchers have tied the rise in homelessness to the rise in unemployment, which is attributed to the economic stagnation caused by the series of recessions and rising inflation of the 1970s and 1980s.[42] Once an individual is unemployed, a return to the labor force usually means a reduction in wages or hours, due to the recent restructuring of the labor force from an industrial economy to one that requires more technical knowledge and skill.[43] The problem then becomes self-perpetuating: Once one is unemployed and homeless, it becomes impossible to secure adequate housing. Even if one finds new employment, the reduction in salary frustrates the search for housing; and without shelter, it is extremely difficult to hold down a job.

Welfare Policies

Welfare policies at all levels of government have had a tremendous impact on the extent of homelessness. Before the late 1970s, increased government assistance offset the rising unemployment and poverty rates.[44] Recent changes are most evident at the federal level, where the Reagan administration's large-scale restrictions and cutbacks in federal benefit programs eliminated thousands from welfare eligibility.[45] More than 34,000 families in California have had their benefits under Aid to Families with Dependent Children (AFDC) eliminated, and over one million people in the United States have lost their eligibility for food stamps.[46] These federal cutbacks put pressure on state and local governments to deal with the crisis.

Under California law, the counties must provide relief to the poor, but it is up to the individual county to determine the amount and type of aid to be given.[47] The result is that the amount of aid given, the eligibility requirements, and the procedures for obtaining aid vary drastically from county to county.[48] The critical problem, however, is that no county provides an adequate level of relief according to studies of what is necessary to subsist there, particularly when it comes to housing.[49]

Housing Policies

Skyrocketing housing costs, the loss of thousands of units of low-cost housing, and major cuts in federal housing programs are among the foremost causes of homelessness in the United States.[50] In 1968 a study done for the Johnson administration estimated that six million units were needed to meet the housing needs of low-income people. Fewer than half of these units were ever built.[51] In 1978 the California Department of Housing and Community Development estimated that there were "almost twice as many low-income renter households as there were rental units at an affordable price range."[52] The alternative for many low-income people is to live in housing that does not meet federal and local standards. HUD figures for 1979 to 1983 reveal that approximately two million people nationwide live in substandard housing.[53]

Urban renewal continues to deplete the already low stock of low-income housing. Between 1970 and 1980 approximately one million single-room-occupancy (SRO) units were destroyed or converted.[54] Los Angeles recently enacted an earthquake ordinance that may eliminate 17,000 SRO units.[55] Brad Paul, of the Marketing Planning Coalition in San Francisco, testified before the California legislature that "in California there are 86,000 low-cost hotel rooms housing at least one person per room and 80,000 low-cost rooms and 100,000 trailer spaces housing at least two people per unit, which may be destroyed to make room for office buildings, businesses, or more expensive housing."[56] The result is that nearly a half-million Californians could soon be without housing.[57]

Recent recessions and welfare policies undermine people's ability to pay for adequate housing. In California, 1.5 million families pay 60 percent of their income for rent, leaving them an average of $150 a month for food, clothing, and other necessities.[58] The high cost of living in California makes it impossible for those receiving some public assistance to secure and maintain adequate housing.[59] The waiting lists for publicly subsidized housing range from four to twenty years.[60] HUD regulations regarding eligibility for subsidized housing merely add to the problem.[61]

Judicial Responses

The U.S. Constitution does not guarantee a right to shelter.[62] Absent a constitutional mandate, guaranteed access to adequate housing is a legislative matter rather than a judicial function.[63] In *Koster v. Webb*,[64] the federal district court of New York noted that while there is no federal constitutional right to shelter or income supplementation, state governments are free to make such guarantees. Once a state voluntarily provides emergency shelter, it may be obligated to continue to do so.[65]

Litigation establishing a right to shelter generally focuses on guarantees provided by state constitutions and statutes. *Callahan v. Carey*[66] is the landmark case establishing a right to shelter on such a theory. Citing the New York constitution, New York social service laws, and the New York City Administrative Code, the *Callahan* court held that the homeless were entitled to "board and lodging."[67] The court entered a consent decree guaranteeing that shelter would be provided to all eligible applicants and that public shelters would adhere to minimum quality standards.[68] *Callahan* also addressed the quality of shelter that the City of New York was required to provide. The decree specified the size of the beds and type of linens; the attendant-to-resident ratio; the mandatory provision of lockers and laundry services; residents' right to come and go as they please at reasonable hours; group recreation; mandatory mail and telephone service; and limits on the capacity of each shelter.[69] If hotels are used, the residents' safety must be assured, guards must be posted at particular hotels, and a minimum amount of space must be provided for each person.[70] When the only available emergency shelter is far from the referring agency, transportation must be provided to a homeless person who otherwise would be unable to gain access.[71]

Similarly, the West Virginia Supreme Court used the state's adult protve service law to guarantee housing. The court reasoned that a homeless adult was within the statutory definition of an "incapacitated adult."[72] It then said that, because the statutes required that all incapacitated adults be provided with shelter, by implication homeless persons must also be given shelter.[73] In New Jersey, a court required Atlantic City officials to provide emergency shelter and immediate assistance to the homeless pursuant to the state's welfare laws.[74] All these cases demonstrate the effective use of existing state law to guarantee shelter for homeless people.[75]

The California Supreme Court, in *Mooney v. Pickett*,[76] interpreted California's welfare laws as imposing a mandatory duty upon all counties to support "all incompetent, poor, indigent persons, and those incapacitated by age, disease, or accident."[77] Each county's discretion in carrying out these statutory mandates is limited.[78] The court rejected the excuse that a county cannot afford to provide such support.[79]

Lower courts continue to define the parameters of this decision. In *Boehm v. Superior Court*,[80] the court held that the welfare code required counties to provide recipients with an amount adequate for the necessities of life, which include food, clothing, housing, utilities, transportation, and medical care.[81] Omission of a monetary grant for any of these needs must be justified by a demonstration that the services are otherwise available to recipients of general relief.[82]

The California Court of Appeals in *Boehm* construed the California Supreme Court, in *County of Los Angeles v. Workers' Compensation Appeals Board*,[83] as recognizing that the "[c]ourts play an important role in assuring that the provisions of the public welfare laws are liberally interpreted and actively enforced."[84] The California Supreme Court also recognized that the courts have a second function motivated by a

> public policy [that] prompts the efforts of the state to preserve the self-reliance of its citizens, even if at extra expense. . . . The state recognizes that many of its citizens are indigent, but it still wishes them to be independent. The relief legislation was enacted with that purpose in view. . . . The evolution of public welfare has been from public "charity" toward social justice. Courts should facilitate such development by an enlightened and liberal interpretation of all welfare laws.[85]

In Los Angeles County, there has been litigation challenging the county's general relief shelter allowance,[86] application processes that require extensive identification before shelter is provided,[87] and the quality of shelter provided by welfare hotels.[88] All of the actions are based on the state's statutory guarantees of the support necessary for minimum subsistence. The cases then challenge whether counties are adequately carrying out the intent of these constitutional and statutory provisions.

In Los Angeles, the petitioners in *Paris v. Los Angeles County Board of Supervisors* challenged the failure of welfare hotels to provide minimal heating (68 degrees Fahrenheit) between 6 p.m. and 6 a.m.[89] A temporary restraining order was issued requiring such relief.[90] This litigation expanded into a challenge of "illegal and wasteful expenditures of taxpayer funds in the form of payment to owners of uninhabitable voucher hotels whose hotels violate the county [building codes]."[91] The plaintiffs challenged the county's expenditures for uninhabitable rentals, asserting that such actions were wasteful and therefore illegal.[92] They claimed that California's implied warranty of habitability applies without limitation to shelters and welfare hotels.[93] While there are no California cases directly on point, the provision for reasonable levels of safety seems implicit in the California constitution.[94] At a minimum, government officials may not place individuals in unsafe environments.

It appears that California's constitution and welfare laws entitle the homeless to shelter that, at a minimum, does not breach the implied warranty of habitability. By implication, they also are entitled to shelter that is safe and does not endanger their health. The policy behind welfare laws argues for shelter or aid, or both, that fosters independence and self-reliance. Scarcity of funds is not an adequate excuse for failing to carry out these laws.[95]

Yet, as the previous discussion suggests, the homeless are not receiving these entitlements. The demand for shelter beds greatly outweighs the supply. The welfare system does not provide adequate financial relief, and there are significant difficulties in obtaining what relief it does provide. When shelter is available, it usually does not meet minimum quality standards and is in an unhealthy and unsafe environment.

Homeless Families in the United States

Unique Problems

Despite the country's recent economic growth, a "trend towards increased inequality in the distribution of income has lessened the positive impact of economic growth on families with the lowest incomes."[96] So it is not surprising that, during this period of growth, the character of homelessness in the United States has shifted from an isolated problem among a small percentage of single adults to a growing crisis among families. Although homelessness is not a new social problem, its impact on American families is recent and represents "the culmination of many social problems which have not been adequately dealt with over the years by federal, state, local housing and social welfare policies."[97]

The phenomenon of the homeless family shocks many people because the family unit is traditionally seen as the source of economic well-being. Families are generally less likely to be poor than single adults.[98] Reports of the scale and seeming longevity of the problem raise grave concerns not only for the families involved, but also for society in general, which depends on the family for basic socialization and stability.[99]

Few studies have examined homeless families. Until recently, it was "implicitly assumed that [homeless persons] either are childless or no longer have significant ties to any children they may have had."[100] Homeless families, however, make up the fastest-growing segment of the nation's homeless population.[101] They now represent 28 percent of the homeless in the United States.[102] The trend is nationwide.[103] In New York, a 1984 study found that half of the 20,200 homeless people who sought shelter were parents with children.[104] In Massachusetts, 75 percent of the homeless population are parents with children.[105]

These statistics offer only an introduction to the problem because the homeless population is so elusive. Families who live in parks, cars, or campsites are not represented in the statistics derived from studies limited to people who sought shelter from either a welfare agency or private social service agency.[106] Families who "double up" with others, thereby creating additional problems, such as overcrowding, are another elusive homeless group. The New York City Housing Authority estimated that about 17,000 families were "doubled-up" in the public housing units. Since there is an express city policy against this practice, city officials estimated that it was even more widespread in the private sector.[107] The demand for affordable public housing far outstrips the supply of such units. For example, there is a waiting list of over 164,000 families for public housing in New York City.[108] In California there are 642,000 more low-income families than available low-income housing units.[109] Without access to this housing, many families are forced onto the streets. There are no definitive statistical studies on homeless families in Los Angeles, though there have been recent exploratory studies.[110]

Homelessness affects the physical and emotional health of children in families just as it affects other homeless populations. "[E]ven a short period of homelessness places severe stress on a family and each of its members."[111] In a study of homeless children living in shelters with their families, most of the children over the age of five stated that they had suicidal thoughts. Furthermore, "[o]ne-third of the children scored so high on the Children's Depression Scale as to qualify as presumptive evidence of clinical depression and over one-half scored at a level to require further clinical evaluation for depression."[112] Of the children under the age of five, one-third manifested lags in two or more areas of development (gross motor skills, fine motor skills, language, and personal and social development).[113]

It is apparent that children suffer from the extremely stressful situation of being homeless. These children manifest symptoms of dire psychological distress. The most common symptoms are associated with severe anxiety and depression. Moreover, a greatly disproportionate number of homeless children are failing to develop normally in several important ways. The parents in homeless families also bear the marks of desperate existence. They most commonly suffer from severe depression and anxiety. There are reasons to fear that homelessness is causing severe permanent psychological injuries to the children.[114]

Pregnant women and infants under the age of one are particularly hard-hit by the experience of homelessness. A New York study concluded that more than half the pregnant women living in welfare hotels received minimal or no prenatal care.[115] They were often housed in barrack shelters, "where the danger of exposure to disease, including rubella, is high."[116] Women in their ninth month of pregnancy were found sleeping on the floors of welfare offices.[117] Infants born to homeless mothers begin life adversely affected by their mothers' homelessness. Many of the infants born to homeless mothers in New York City weigh less than five pounds at birth.[118]

> [T]he proportion of low birth weight babies born to mothers living in welfare hotels [in New York City] is more than twice as high as the city as a whole. These children are likely to suffer from mental retardation, cerebral palsy, seizures and other irreversible development disorders. Further, the infant mortality rate is high among the babies of homeless, pregnant women.[119]

The seriousness of the problem is not alleviated by the minimal shelter afforded by a welfare hotel.

The study found that "[h]omeless families with newborn infants continue to be denied emergency shelter and other life sustaining needs by New York City's welfare bureaucracy."[120] Eight hundred homeless infants were found to be without sufficient food, cribs, health care, and diapers.[121] In a random survey of fifty homeless families, three infant deaths were reported;[122] this figure represents a 6 percent mortality rate and is significantly higher than the 1.5 percent infant mortality rate for New York City.[123] First Deputy Mayor Stanley Brezenoff ordered city agencies to stop referring families with infants to the city's barrack shelters because of the serious health hazards the shelters posed, but these directives have been routinely ignored.[124] For many homeless women, the only viable alternative to the barrack shelters is sleeping on the floor of a welfare office.[125]

Similar studies do not exist for other parts of the United States. Because New York City has the most extensive shelter system in the country, the inference can be drawn that such health problems exist on an even more critical level elsewhere.

Cutbacks in public assistance are devastating to families. Once family members lose their benefits and become homeless, "case workers must assess the potential for child abuse or neglect resulting from the new situation."[126] In one study, 13 percent of the families had children taken away by child protection services while they were homeless.[127] Because a family is no longer eligible for AFDC benefits if there are no children in the home, the elimination of these resources poses the dilemma of how to secure a home so the children can be returned.[128] The fear of such an event inhibits many eligible people from applying for AFDC benefits in the first place.[129]

The few shelters that exist provide little relief for homeless families. Homeless families are often turned away from existing shelters because few of them house families, and even fewer house two-parent families.[130] In Los Angeles as of 1986, 730 of the 3,542 shelter beds available were designated specifically for families.[131] Because most shelters restrict occupancy to single men, single women, or battered women with children under the age of thirteen,[132] families must often split up in order to find shelter. Similarly, children are voluntarily put into foster homes so that they and their parent(s) can secure shelter.[133]

Even when beds are available for families, few shelters specialize in care for homeless families; thus, families with children are often surrounded by the mentally ill or chemically dependent.[134] The shelters mostly resemble dormitories or barracks, offering the family no privacy. Families with funds for minimal shelter often find themselves in "welfare hotels." These hotels are "notorious for their roving populations of prostitutes and drug addicts, and are paid $1,800 a month by the city [New York] to put up each family."[135]

Furthermore, most shelters provide only a place to sleep at night and then for less than a week. Consequently, homeless families must often drift from shelter to shelter.[136]

Constitutional Protection for a Family's Desire to Remain Intact

A homeless family's inability to remain intact implicates constitutional principles that concern the family in general. I suggest that constitutional principles give a nuclear family a fundamental right to remain intact.

One commentator has suggested that:

> [a] point "as important as it is easy to overlook" is that "the family unit does not simply co-exist with our constitutional system" but "is an integral part of it," for our political system is superimposed on and presupposes a social system of family units, not just of isolated individuals. No assumption more deeply underlies our society.[137]

Lawrence Tribe, however, has refined this analysis, stating that the

> "exercises of familial rights and responsibilities" . . . prove to be *individual* powers to resist governmental determination of who shall be born, with whom one shall live, and what values shall be transmitted. . . . *But the embedding of a choice within a close human relationship or network of relationships should always be regarded as significantly increasing the burden of justifying for those who make the choice illegal or visit it with some deprivation.*[138]

The Supreme Court recognizes that decisions related to the bearing and rearing of children concern a liberty interest protected by the Constitution.[139] The Court's definition of family extends to biological relationships outside the context of marriage[140] but does not include a fundamental right of unrelated persons to live together.[141]

With regard to bearing children, the Supreme Court has invalidated laws restricting the ability to conceive children[142] and interfering with a person's choice to have children.[143] The Court began protecting parents' child-rearing decisions by holding that parents have the right to determine what language their children will speak,[144] what school they will attend,[145] and whether their children should be committed to a mental institution.[146] There also have been decisions protecting the freedom to marry[147] and divorce.[148] While this collection of rights creates a presumption in favor of family autonomy, it does not provide an absolute guarantee against state interference.[149]

In essence, the Supreme Court has recognized a "private realm of family life," stating that "[i]t is cardinal with us that the custody, care and nurture of the child reside first in the parents, whose primary function and freedom include preparation for obligations the state can neither supply nor hinder."[150] Furthermore, "the importance of the familial relationship, to the individuals involved and to the society, stems from the emotional attachments that derive from the intimacy of daily association,and from the role it plays in promoting a way of life."[151] Thus, a family's constitutional right is abridged when the State "attempt[s] to force the breakup of a natural family, over the objections of the parents and their children, without some showing of unfitness and for the sole reason that to do so was thought to be in the children's best interest."[152]

While the implication of the Supreme Court decisions is that the "private realm of family life" is fundamental and includes the right of a family to remain intact, a majority of the Court has never specifically so held. However, three concurring Justices in *Griswold v. Connecticut*[153] emphasized that the traditional relation of the family is "as old and as fundamental as our entire civilization."[154] In addition, Justice Harlan, dissenting in *Poe v. Ullman*,[155] stated that "the integrity of that [family] life is something so fundamental that it has been found to draw to its protection the principles of more than one explicitly granted Constitutional right."[156]

Moore v. City of East Cleveland[157] dealt with the right of an extended family to live together. The plurality decision stated that "the Constitution protects the sanctity of the family precisely because the institution of the family is deeply rooted in this Nation's history and tradition."[158] Thus, whenever "the government intrudes on choices concerning family living arrangements, this Court must examine carefully the importance of the governmental interests advanced and the extent to which they are served by the challenged regulation."[159] The plurality did not specify the level of judicial review it used in reaching its decisions but did state that the "usual judicial deference to the legislature is inappropriate."[160] As a result, it is not entirely clear whether an extended family has a fundamental right to live together, warranting strict scrutiny, or a right that is significant, triggering an intermediate level of review. It is conceivable, however, that the Court would characterize the right of a nuclear family to live together as fundamental, thereby warranting strict scrutiny, since considerable discussion in *Moore* centered on whether an extended family should be afforded the same constitutional consideration as a "traditional" or "nuclear family."[161]

The recognition of a family's fundamental right to autonomy and integrity will "serve three distinct interests . . . : that of the parents in achieving fulfillment through childbearing; that of the child in being raised by those whose affection and intimate familiarity makes them best suited to the task; and that of society as a whole in diversity and pluralism."[162] Yet even if the Court fails to recognize this fundamental status, familial integrity will at a minimum trigger an intermediate level of scrutiny.

Guaranteed Shelter and a Family's Right to Integrity

Although the Constitution guarantees various rights, it does not obligate government to fund the exercise of these rights.[163] Once a state decides to provide certain benefits, however, the distribution of these benefits is subject to constitutional limitations.[164]

[The Supreme Court] has consistently held that the state cannot refuse to extend benefits on a forbidden basis, even if this refusal creates no governmental obstacles to the exercise of a right, and leaves those affected with the same range of choice that they would have had if government provided no benefits at all.[165]

The previous section suggests that the right of a family to remain intact is a fundamental right.[166] Thus, if states provide a right to shelter, they must do so in a way that allows the homeless family to remain intact. The states' practices in this regard warrant strict scrutiny because they concern the administration of benefits, not the funding and encouragement of the right.

Whether the appropriate analysis is based on equal protection or due process, the direct intrusion or burdening of a fundamental right warrants strict scrutiny.[167] Thus, when government action burdens the exercise of a fundamental right, it can only be justified by a compelling state interest.[168] In the context of this discussion, a state's failure to house a homeless family as an intact unit, once a shelter entitlement is given, can only be justified by a compelling state interest.

Several possible governmental interests are at stake in shelter programs. The first state interest involved is preserving the programs' financial integrity. In establishing a shelter system, some extra expense may be incurred in ensuring that the system provides for intact families. Funds may have to be redirected from other programs in order to house homeless families. Because the guarantee of shelter is a recent and isolated phenomenon, complete shelter systems have not been implemented that can test these assertions. It has been demonstrated, however, that it is more economical to house an intact family than to provide child protective services for a single child.[169] This particular fact raises doubts that a shelter program that did not keep the family unit intact could satisfy the "close fit" requirement that government rules be "substantially related to achievement of . . . [the] objectives" intended by the rules.[170] Even if some financial burden could be demonstrated, the Court has held that the saving on welfare costs does not justify an abridgment of a fundamental right.[171]

A second possible state interest is a paternalistic concern for the interests of homeless children. The state may argue that it is in the homeless child's best interest to be housed separately from the parent(s). This assertion is difficult to evaluate because it can involve cultural and class bias. The Supreme Court has recognized that the middle-class backgrounds of social workers and judges can result in evaluations that discriminate against poor families.[172] On the other hand, the psychological trauma caused by separation is well documented.[173] The Supreme Court, however, has determined that these factors cannot be the sole considerations before allowing the breakup of a family unit.[174]

Other factors in strict scrutiny analysis include whether the state intended to cause the breakup of homeless families and whether the breakup amounts to a total deprivation of the right to family integrity. Although the issue of intent is central to discrimination cases, it is not integral to an equal protection or due process analysis in the instant case. Whatever the intent, the state is not free to disregard the consequences of its action.[175]

Regarding the issue of family integrity, the Court has drawn a distinction between absolute and relative deprivations.[176] While homeless families can theoretically reunite once they have gained sufficient financial resources, the states' practices create a total deprivation for the period of homelessness and work against the "emotional attachments that derive from the intimacy of daily association."[177] This is not a case of "mere differences in *relative levels* of support,"[178] but rather is a total deprivation of an aspect of life that the Court has held essential.

The "step-by-step" doctrine is similar to the absolute/relative deprivation analysis. According to this jurisprudential rule, a state need not alleviate all social problems when it attempts to remedy one specific problem.[179] The present discussion does not present a proper arena for the application of the *step-by-step* rule, however. It involves not a related problem but rather a distinct problem arising from the direct implementation of a specific social program.

The application of strict scrutiny is "strict in theory and usually fatal in fact."[180] If strict scrutiny is applied to the breakup of homeless families, as I suggest here, states that have already conferred a shelter entitlement would be obligated to provide shelter that keeps families intact. The application of strict scrutiny is dependent, however, on the determination that the right to family integrity is fundamental.

Entitlement to Welfare Relief and the Right to Shelter as an Intact Unit

The previous section suggested that if a state gives an entitlement to shelter, a homeless family must then be given shelter in a way that protects its integrity.

This section explores the state's allocation of welfare funds when the legislature mandates that the allocation reflect minimum standards of adequate care.

A state's provision of adequate levels of relief to indigent families is critical to homeless families. The level of relief provided can directly affect the homeless family's ability to recover from homelessness and become self-sufficient. More importantly, adequate levels of welfare relief affect the homeless family's ability to remain intact.

California's welfare system is one that requires the relief to meet minimum standards.[181] In *Vaessen v. Woods*,[182] the California Supreme Court addressed the state's administration of the federal AFDC program. California participates in the federal program, which is designed to provide financial support to families with dependent children so that the children may remain in their homes.[183] The court held that the grant level should reflect "minimum basic standards of adequate care,"[184] which, presumably, would include shelter. Thus, if shelter provision is included in the aid, the entitlement would include a familial right to be housed together.[185] In addition, as the *Hansen v. McMahon* and *In re P.L. & E.*[186] cases suggest, it is less expensive to support an intact family than to provide foster care for individual children away from their parents. Assuming this is true, then adequate levels of state aid that provide for the necessities of life intrude less on the family's protected rights if families are housed as a unit. As one commentator has noted, "In some contexts, substantial government expenditures have been required to avoid burdening important individual rights; however, the [U.S.] Supreme Court has not enunciated a general theory of when protection of the public fisc will outweigh such rights."[187]

Poverty and Findings of Child Abuse

A similar analysis is appropriate in child abuse determinations. Findings of child abuse are another problem facing homeless families. In California, for example, up until January 1, 1987, homelessness per se qualified as child abuse and provided sufficient grounds to commence dependency hearings.[188] Although the law has changed in California, that will not assuage the fear of many homeless parents or prevent undetected actions by individual welfare officials.

While the California legislature is to be commended for its action in this regard, the question remains whether such a statute or practice can withstand judicial scrutiny. The Supreme Court has recognized this issue but has never directly ruled on the question. For example, in *Smith v. Organization of Foster Families for Equality and Reform*,[189] the Court recognized that the social class of the parents often affects a court's interpretation regarding the scope of family autonomy.[190] The Court observed that neglect findings are overwhelmingly made with respect to poor families by judges and social workers,[191] and further observed that despite the long tradition of family autonomy, a "number of states allow a finding of neglect to be based upon the financial inability—not unwillingness—of the parents to provide for the child."[192]

If, as I suggest in this chapter, family integrity is a fundamental right, then the practices just described must be justified by a compelling state interest. The discussion in the previous section suggests that no such compelling state interest exists.[193] Poverty and homelessness, therefore, may not be the sole criteria for separating children from their parents.

Judicial Protection of Family Autonomy Based on Statutory Interpretation

The few cases that suggest that a homeless family has an entitlement to shelter that allows it to remain intact as a family, like other homeless litigation, rely on statutory interpretation rather than a constitutional violation of the right to family integrity. Litigation in Los Angeles challenged the California Department of Social Services' (DSS) practice of excluding homeless children in the company of their parents from shelter care.[194] In *Hansen v. McMahon*,[195] the Los Angeles Superior Court granted a preliminary injunction nullifying the department's procedural policies that defined "emergency shelter care in a manner more restrictive than Welfare and Institutions Code sections 16501 and 16504.1 so as to exclude homeless children, regardless of whether the homeless children remain with their parent(s), guardian(s) or caretaker(s)."[196] Prior to the injunction, the department's Emergency Response Program provided emergency shelter to "neglected, abused, or exploited" children only after they had been removed from their parents.[197] The court held that homeless children fell within the definition of "neglected" because they did not have the care and protection necessary for their health and development.[198] Therefore, they were eligible for the emergency shelter care available under the Emergency Response Program.[199] The court further held that because it was unnecessary to remove the children from their families to protect their safety, the department's practice of mandating the child's removal as a prerequisite to his or her receiving emergency shelter violated the legislative intent behind the statutory provisions.[200] Because DSS's practice was more restrictive than the statutes authorizing the program, the court ordered the practice stopped. The plaintiffs also pointed out that the $140 per night spent to shelter a homeless child in the county's children's facility could be better spent providing shelter for the entire family, in addition to protecting the family's autonomy.[201]

The California Court of Appeals affirmed the *Hansen* decision.[202] The court held that the DSS definition of emergency shelter care—one that excluded homeless children who were part of a homeless family unit—was inconsistent with the legislature's directives.[203] In reaching its conclusion, the court stated that both the federal and the state legislatures considered the preservation of the family unit to be of paramount importance. The court also underscored the extremely detrimental effect on children of separation from their family. In similar litigation in the District of Columbia, a woman sued, alleging that her family remained separated solely because of the lack of affordable housing.[204] She also claimed that the "government had the duty, authority and ability to remedy the situation because the District's Family Division had the authority to order any other public agency of the District to provide any service the Family Division deemed necessary and that was within that other agency's legal authority."[205] The court seemed to agree, holding that the $1,000 per month being spent to keep the children in foster care could better be used in providing permanent housing for the entire family.[206]

In New York, the courts extended the *Callahan* decision to give homeless families an entitlement to emergency shelter.[207] The court also held that it has the power to set and enforce minimum standards of habitability.[208] In providing shelter, the Department of Social Services now mandates that "[a]s far as possible families shall be kept together, they shall not be separated for reasons of poverty alone, and they shall be provided services to maintain and strengthen family life."[209]

What Is Needed

Homeless families are a significant component of the homeless population. They have unique characteristics that should be taken into account when implementing programs for the homeless. These unique characteristics include their capacity to recover from homelessness, their right to family autonomy, and the need to protect their children from unsafe and unsuitable environments. In order to help homeless families effectively, specialized services are required that meet these particular needs without burdening their right to family autonomy.

In California, the state appears to be required to provide relief that is adequate for the necessities of life, meets minimum quality standards, is safe, protects privacy, and fosters self-reliance and independence. In the case of homeless families, the relief must protect family integrity and autonomy. This is true for New York and other states as well.

The most immediate need is emergency shelter, with transportation provided when necessary. More shelter beds are needed to meet the tremendous demand. At a minimum, emergency shelter for homeless families should house the family members together in an environment that is safe and healthy, particularly for the children. Location of family shelters is critical, and consideration must be given to the surrounding social environment and any health hazards that exist there. Skid row environments are dangerous for families and inappropriate sites for their shelter.

Adequate nutrition is another critical need. Children, adults, pregnant women, and nursing mothers have different nutritional requirements that should be met in order to ensure their health. In addition, medical attention is needed by most homeless family members, particularly pregnant women and infants.

Laws that discriminate against or harass homeless families must continue to be abolished. Even more subtle, though, are the practices of individual government or administrative officials, which often go undetected. Government officials, administrative clerks, and judges should confront biases regarding child rearing that originate from their own particular economic background when making determinations on dependency, custody, and child abuse. These biases should not infringe upon the constitutional rights of homeless families.

Beyond these minimal requirements, other considerations will maximize the benefits a shelter program can provide homeless families as they work toward self-sufficiency. For instance, the physical layout of a family shelter is important. Small, community-based shelters that provide individualized housing units provide a healthy environment and protect the family's privacy and autonomy. Each family member should have a bed (or crib) and a minimum amount of additional space. The *Callahan* litigation offers an appropriate guide.

Emergency family shelters also need to provide long-term, twenty-four-hour accommodations. Emergency shelter for a minimum of three months allows the family to stabilize itself with the help of supportive services, and then to secure sufficient monetary resources to acquire permanent shelter. Twenty-four-hour living arrangements are necessary so that families are not forced to fight for their subsistence during the day. Life on the streets during the day is terribly difficult for the homeless family.

Supportive services are necessary to ensure the recovery of the homeless family: psychological counseling, for both parents and children; job training, employment assistance, or both for the parents. Remedial schooling is necessary to overcome the learning handicaps children already have experienced, although educational problems will be alleviated by the mere fact that they are in more stable environments and are able to attend school more regularly. Child care will allow parents the time to work and provide children with adequate supervision. All these services should be provided either by the shelter on site or through a direct link from the shelter to offsite providers. This link must consist of more than mere information and referral; it must allow homeless families direct access to these services.

Finally, permanent housing is an essential component of a long-term solution to the homeless problem. To focus solely on temporary solutions, particularly when dealing with homeless families, disregards their capacity to recover from the crisis they are experiencing. These stopgap measures will lead only to a proliferation of other social problems. Low-cost permanent housing is a preventive measure, protecting families from the emotional, medical, and financial devastations that result from homelessness. Cases such as *Hansen* suggest that it is more cost-effective to house a family together than to house a child separately. In time there may be more empirical evidence to suggest that a comprehensive program for homeless families, such as the one suggested, is more cost-effective than letting the problems run their course or burgeon into even more massive social problems.

Few of these problems can be solved solely by the courts. Comprehensive legislation that is attuned to the current research, and that addresses both short-term and long-term solutions to the crisis, is sorely needed. Cooperation between federal, state, and county governments is also essential for effective relief.

Conclusion

One problem for the homeless family is that emergency shelter is most often unavailable because of the scarcity of shelter beds. Another problem is that the available shelter does not accommodate their unique needs and thereby perpetuates their homelessness, a status that by all indications is not a chronic condition for these families. Emergency shelter is an important but temporary solution; long-term solutions require a multifaceted approach, including emergency relief, transitional assistance to return to self-sufficiency, and low-cost housing, so that emergency shelters do not become "permanent homes" and homeless families can regain their independence.

Recognition of the right to shelter and setting quality standards for the shelter provided are important first steps. A second important step is the recognition of the family's fundamental right to autonomy and consideration of this right when providing relief. Although the federal government has been slow to take these steps, a few states, California and New York included, have begun the process. Advocates for the homeless have used states' constitutions and statutory provisions to force the recognition of these rights that are so essential to ensuring that homeless families will receive adequate relief.

NOTES

Acknowledgments: I would like to thank Professor Robert Goldstein for his assistance during the writing of this chapter. I am especially grateful to Jean Forbath, Scott Mather, and others affiliated with the Orange Coast Interfaith Shelter for their support and guidance during my tenure there, and to the Sisters of St. Joseph of Orange who subsidized my work there. This chapter is dedicated to my parents, Dr. and Mrs. Anthony Mascari.

1. Stoner, Analysis of Public and Private Sector Provisions for Homeless People, 17 Soc. Sci. Rev. 3, 3–4 (1984).

2. Mooney v. Pickett, 483 P.2d 1231 (Cal. 1971); *see also* Robbins v. Superior Court of Sacramento County, 695 P.2d 695 (Cal. 1985) (in-kind benefits program, which precluded cash grants to single and employable persons, infringed upon constitutional rights to privacy); Vaessen v. Woods, 677 P.2d 1183 (Cal. 1984) (income tax refunds are not to be considered income for the purposes of reducing AFDC benefits), *cert. denied*, 470 U.S. 1049 (1985); Boehm v. Superior Court of Merced County, 178 Cal. App. 3d 494 (1986) (general assistance benefits must provide for the necessities of life, including minimum subsistence levels of clothing, transportation, and medical care); City and County of San Francisco v. Superior Court of San Francisco County, 57 Cal. App. 3d 44, 47 (1976) (claim that county cannot afford to provide the necessities of life to welfare recipients is unavailing; taxpayer "burdens were not so grievous as to permit indigents, in the midst of plenty, to go hungry, cold and naked, without fault") (citations omitted).

3. Cuomo, 1933/1983—Never Again: A Report to the National Governors' Association Task Force on the Homeless (1983), *found in* Homelessness in America II: Hearings before the House Subcommittee on Housing and Community Development of the Committee on Banking, Finance and Urban Affairs, 98th Cong., 1st Sess. 354, 373 (1984) [hereinafter Homelessness II]. The definition of "homeless" generally includes people who have no stable residence, no place where they can sleep and receive mail.

4. R. Ropers & M. Robertson, Basic Shelter Research Project 16 (1984).

5. An exact census of the homeless population is impossible because of the nature of that population. For example, the homeless are not simply those who occupy emergency shelters. They are also people who sleep on park benches, under bridges, in campgrounds, in cars, in a friend's garage, or on a relative's living room floor. Arguably, they also include those who are forced to live in motels because they cannot afford permanent housing, although people in this situation are not included in the numbers given below.

The National Conference of Mayors estimates the number of homeless people to be between 2 million and 3 million. Jones, Youngsters Share Plight of Homeless, L.A. Times, May 19, 1987, at 1. The Department of Housing and Urban Development (HUD), on the other hand, estimates the number to be between 250,000 and 350,000. Department of Housing and Urban Development, A Report to the Secretary on the Homeless and Emergency Shelters, *cited in* Community for Creative Non-Violence v. Pierce, 814 F.2d 663, 664–65 (D.C. Cir. 1987). In the litigation that ensued over the HUD report, Judge Mikva of the Court of Appeals for the District of Columbia recognized the difficulties that HUD's underestimation posed for homeless advocates. *Id.* at 673. *See also* Werner, Homelessness: A Litigation Roundup, 18 Clearinghouse Rev. 1255, 1265–66 (1985) (discussion of challenges to HUD's estimate). *See generally* J. Erickson & C. Wilhelm, Housing the Homeless 127–64 (1986) (four chapters devoted to the role of numbers in the homeless problem); Langdon & Kass, Homelessness in America: Looking for the Right to Shelter, 19 Colum. J.L. & Soc. Probs. 305, 308–10 (1985). For a discussion of the "hidden homeless" *see* Erickson & Wilhelm, *supra.*

6. Homelessness II, *supra* note 3, at 946; *see also* Background Paper for the Hearings on the Homeless: The Role of the State, Joint Hearing of the [California] Assembly Human Services Committee and Senate Health and Human Services Committee (1985) [hereinafter Background Paper].

7. Ropers & Robertson, Basic Shelter, *supra* note 4, at 5 (footnote omitted).

8. *Id.* (footnote omitted); *see also* McMillan, Foundation Laid at "Campground" for the Homeless, L.A. Times, June 28, 1987, § 2, at 1; Oltman, No "Emergency," County Homeless Help Barred, L.A. Daily J., Jan. 7, 1987, at 20; Los Angeles in Lead as Needs of the Homeless Increase, L.A. Daily J., Dec. 19, 1986, § 2, at 1.

9. Langdon & Kass, Homelessness in America, *supra* note 5, at 308.

10. The following discussion suggests that the state of being homeless creates physical and emotional problems for individuals who had a reasonable semblance of mental health before becoming homeless. The problems of the deinstitutionalized mentally ill are beyond the scope of this chapter.

11. Kaufman, Homelessness: A Comprehensive Policy Approach, 17 Soc. Sci. Rev. 21, 23 (1984); *see also* Stoner, Analysis of Provisions, *supra* note 1, at 4.

12. P. Brickner et al., Health Care of Homeless People 179–222 (1985).

13. Stoner, Analysis of Provisions, *supra* note 1, at 18.

14. Background Paper, *supra* note 6, at 22.

15. *Id.; see also* Hansen v. McMahon, No. CA 000 974 (L.A. Super. Ct. May 19, 1986), *aff'd,* 193 Cal. App. 3d 283, 238 Cal. Rptr. 232 (1987) (declaration of Mary Smith, Supervisor of the Homeless Health Care at Venice Family Clinic in Los Angeles).

16. Note, Building a House of Legal Rights: A Plea for the Homeless, 59 St. John's L. Rev. 530, 539–40 (1985).

17. Stoner, Analysis of Provisions, *supra* note 1, at 5.

18. Ropers & Robertson, Basic Shelter, *supra* note 4, at 35.

19. Stoner, Analysis of Provisions, *supra* note 1, at 5.

20. *Id.*

21. *Id.*

22. Werner, On the Streets: Homelessness Causes and Solutions, 17 Clearing-house Rev. 11, 14 (1984) (footnote omitted); Department of Housing and Community Development Emergency Shelter Program, California Homeless Shelter Provider Directory 10–26 (1986) [hereinafter California Directory].

23. Ropers & Robertson, Basic Shelter, *supra* note 4, at 11.

24. Werner, On the Streets, *supra* note 22, at 14–15.

25. B. Lovell, Report of the Orange County Coalition for the Homeless 1 (1985) (Orange County Coalition for the Homeless, P.O. Box 888, Balboa, Calif., 92661) (see appendix of the report for a description of the Orange County homeless as to education, sex, years of residence in the county, educational background, work experience, and race); *see also* Homelessness II, *supra* note 3, at 283 ("Most of the newly homeless in Orange County, it is reported, are better educated, more likely to have been recently employed, more likely to be female with children, and less likely to be alcoholic, transients, or 'flower children'").

26. Stoner, Analysis of Provisions, *supra* note 1, at 5.

27. Callahan v. Carey, No. 42582/79 (N.Y. Sup. Ct. Aug. 26, 1981) (consent decree), *found in* Community Service Society of New York, One Year Later: The Homeless Poor in New York City, app. I (1982) (Community Service Society of New York, 105 East 22d Street, New York, N.Y. 10010). *See generally* Erickson & Wilhelm, Housing the Homeless, *supra* note 5, at 26–36, 82–105 (discussion of New York's homeless population).

28. Stoner, Analysis of Provisions, *supra* note 1, at 5.

29. *Id. See generally* Wright v. City of Roanoke Redev. & Hous. Auth., 479 U.S. 418 (1987) (nation's low-income housing residents have standing to sue over federal housing law violations).

30. Werner, On the Streets, *supra* note 22, at 15. *See generally* Erickson & Wilhelm, Housing the Homeless, *supra* note 5, at 97–99 (suggesting that effective solutions for the "economic only" cases must be specialized to that group and must prevent dependency).

31. *See* California Directory, *supra* note 22.

32. Stoner, Analysis of Provisions, *supra* note 1, at 3.

33. Homelessness II, *supra* note 3, at 516.

34. *Id.*

35. *Id.*

36. *Id.* at 517.

37. K. Hooper & J. Hamberg, The Making of America's Homeless from Skid Row to New Poor 1945–1984, at 64 (1984) (pub. by Community Service Society of New York, *supra* note 27); *see also* Erickson & Wilhelm, Housing the Homeless, *supra* note 5, at 106–12 (discussion of unemployment, lack of low-income housing, federal public housing policies, and welfare policies).

38. K. Clary & D. Venezio, Exploratory Study of Homeless Families: Socio-Economic Factors Leading to Homelessness 98–99 (1986) (Master of Social Welfare thesis, UCLA); K. Young-McChesney, Homeless Women and Their Children (Feb. 1985) (unpublished manuscript); *see also* Homelessness II, *supra* note 3, at 951.

39. Shipp, Poverty: Trends, Causes and Cures, 7 Cong. Res. Serv. Rev. 6 (1986).

40. *Id.* at 7.

41. Homelessness II, *supra* note 3, at 387.

42. Clary & Venezio, Exploratory Study of Homeless Families, *supra* note 38, at 9–10 (footnotes omitted).

43. *Id.* at 10–11.

44. *Id.* at 22.

45. Homelessness II, *supra* note 3, at 955. An example of such a cutback is the U.S. Supreme Court decision allowing the federal Food Stamp Program to consider the degree of relationship in households in determining eligibility. Lyng v. Castillo, 477 U.S. 635 (1986).

46. Hooper & Hamberg, The Making of America's Homeless, *supra* note 37, at 46 (footnotes omitted).

47. The statute reads as follows:

> Every county and every city and county shall relieve and support all incompetent, poor, indigent persons, and those incapacitated by age, disease, or accident, lawfully resident therein, when such persons are not supported and relieved by their relatives or friends, by their own means, or by state hospitals or other state or private institutions.

Cal. Welf. & Inst. Code § 17000 (Deering 1986).

The program varies with the different counties. In 1987 the highest general relief (GR) grant was $357 per month in Santa Barbara County; the lowest, in San Bernadino County, was $98.40. Los Angeles County recently raised its grant to $248 per month; Orange County's is $240 per month. These figures are grant levels for one adult.

48. Background Paper, *supra* note 6, at 79 (discussion of the Emergency Aid Program grants within the AFDC program); Stoner, Analysis of Provisions, *supra* note 1, at 4–5 (unresponsiveness of welfare workers in providing emergency aid, difficulties in securing aid caused by lack of an address); Background Paper, *supra* note 6, at 21 (difficulties caused by lack of address and identification).

49. Homelessness II, *supra* note 3, at 955; Dombrink, Survey of Orange County Hotel and Motel Room Rates (1985), *found in* Lovell, Report of the Orange County Coalition, *supra* note 25.

50. Homelessness II, *supra* note 3, at 951; *see* Ropers & Robertson, Basic Shelter, *supra* note 4, at 14; *see also* Background Paper, *supra* note 6, at 2. *See generally* Erickson & Wilhelm, Housing the Homeless, *supra* note 5, at 315–21 (discussion of federal housing programs and their impact on homelessness).

51. Alter, Homeless in America, Newsweek, Jan. 2, 1984, at 22; *see also* Hombs, Social Recognition of the Homeless: Policies in Indifference, 31 Wash. U. J. Urb. & Contemp. L. 143 (1987).

> The National Housing Law Project estimates that 500,000 low-rent units are lost annually. This occurs not only through demolition, but also through

abandonment, conversion, arson, and outright unaffordability. Federal assistance has dropped drastically for low-cost units. In fiscal year 1985, low-income housing assistance funds were at a low of ten billion dollars, down from a high of thirty-one billion dollars in 1981.

Id. at 144 (footnotes omitted). *See generally* Children's Defense Fund, A Children's Defense Budget 116–18 (1987) (the federal government budget has consistently increased housing assistance to the middle class and decreased aid to the most needy).

A comprehensive examination of the habitability of the available low-cost housing units is beyond the scope of this chapter. For a description of living conditions in some of New York City's low-income housing, see Robbins & Newfield, New York's 10 Worst Landlords, Village Voice, Aug. 18, 1987, at 12.

52. Homelessness II, *supra* note 3, at 951.

53. Alter, Homeless in America, *supra* note 51, at 23; *see* Talbot v. Romney, 334 F. Supp. 1074 (S.D.N.Y. 1971) (no legally protectable right to housing in buildings condemned for urban renewal); Celis, Crumbling Projects: Public-Housing Units Are Rapidly Decaying, Causing Many to Close, Wall St. J., Dec. 15, 1986, at 1.

54. Alter, Homeless in America, *supra* note 51, at 23. "At the same time, inexpensive rentals are being lost through 'urban renewal' projects and economic development. Between 1970 and 1980, San Francisco lost 10,000 rooms in low-cost hotels. In San Diego, the loss was approximately 2,000 while Los Angeles lost 17,000 rooms." Background Paper, *supra* note 6, at 11 (footnotes omitted). *See generally* Asian Americans for Equality v. Koch, 514 N.Y.S. 2d 939 (N.Y. App. Div. 1987) *aff'd*, 531 N.Y.S. 2d 782 (N.Y. 1988) (upholding redevelopment project despite dissent's concern about its impact on the homeless); Barton, Housing Revitalization and Development, 5 Pub. L. Forum 99 (1986); Hartman, An Urban Planner's Perspective on Displacement Urban Revitalization, 5 Pub. L. Forum 85 (1986).

55. Background Paper, *supra* note 6, at 11.

56. *Id.*

57. *Id.* Some cities and counties are attempting to combat this trend. In California, the County of Orange and City of Irvine "specify that all newly zoned housing developments must include at least 10% low-cost housing units. The City of Irvine recently required an additional 10% very low-cost units in its Family Mortgage Revenue Bond Program." Homelessness II, *supra* note 3, at 286–87.

58. Background Paper, *supra* note 6, at 2. Families can find themselves in low-income motels, paying $125 per week rent, because of their inability to find permanent, affordable housing. *Id.* at 26; *see also* Ropers & Robertson, Basic Shelter, *supra* note 4, at 14.

59. Families also face the problem of saving up first and last months' rent on an AFDC check. P. Mcgerigle & A. Lauriat, More Than Shelter: A Community Response to Homelessness 142 (1983). Some landlords are reluctant to rent to them:

They just don't want children. Even a mother with a single child is difficult to place. Finding housing for a woman with four or five children . . . takes a miracle. . . . Some landlords made no secret of the fact that they chose only "appropriate" tenants and that the "inappropriate" included woman receiving AFDC, black or Hispanic families, and, often, any families including young children.

Id. at 143. During the 1970s, median rent increased twice as fast as income while construction of low-income housing came to a virtual standstill. Alter, Homeless in America, *supra* note 51, at 22.

60. Alter, Homeless in America, *supra* note 51, at 23. Other commentators state that the waiting period is from six to twelve months (Stockton and San Joaquin counties, California). Background Paper, *supra* note 6, at 27.

61. The restrictions on publicly subsidized housing often disqualify families even if they meet the financial eligibility requirements. For example, federal law requires no more than two children of the same sex per bedroom. This poses an overwhelming obstacle to families of more than two children. Homeless advocates suggest that relaxing these requirements would help alleviate part of the overall problem. Homelessness II, *supra* note 3, at 288.

The California legislature removed some of the restrictions that Section 8 of the U.S. Housing Act of 1937 (42 U.S.C. § 1437(f)) places on public housing in its own allocation of housing funds in the 1986 session. The legislature found these restrictions "substantially in excess of those required for a decent, healthy, and safe residential unit." Cal. Health & Safety Code § 52080(a)(4) (West 1987 Supp.).

62. Lindsey v. Normet, 405 U.S. 56 (1972).

63. Langdon & Kass, Homelessness in America, *supra* note 5, at 323–24 (appendix listing which of the fifty states have constitutions and/or state statutes supporting a right to shelter); Comment, Homelessness: The Policy and the Law, 16 Urb. Law. 317, 323–29 (1984) (discussing Callahan v. Carey and the right to shelter).

64. 598 F. Supp. 1134 (E.D.N.Y. 1983).

65. *Id.; see* Good, Freedom from Want: The Failure of United States Courts to Protect Subsistence Rights, 6 Hum. Rts. Q. 335 (1984). *Compare* Robbins v. Reagan, 780 F.2d 37, 49 (D.C. Cir. 1985) (ruling that closure of government shelter was not "arbitrary or capricious" and upholding district court ruling that government must provide interim shelter while renovations are completed) *and* Williams v. Barry, 708 F.2d 789, 793 (D.C. Cir. 1983) (holding that the Fifth Amendment due process clause required notice of the planned closing of men's shelters and an opportunity to present written comments but not an oral hearing) *with* Goldberg v. Kelly, 397 U.S. 254 (1970) (due process requires that welfare recipients be afforded an evidentiary hearing prior to termination of benefits).

66. Callahan v. Carey, No. 42582/79 (N.Y. Sup. Ct. Aug. 26, 1981).

67. *Id.*

68. *Id.* at 3–6, apps. A & B; *see also* Jones v. Berman, 332 N.E.2d 303, 309–10, (N.Y. 1975).

69. Callahan v. Carey, No. 42582/79 at 3–6 (N.Y. Sup. Ct. Aug. 26, 1981); *see* Seawall Assoc. v. City of New York, 34 Misc. 2d 187 (N.Y. Sup. Ct. 1986) (holding that Local Law 22—mandating that private owners of SRO buildings maintain units in habitable condition, rehabilitate vacant units, and rent at state-authorized prices—violated owners' due process rights); Dep't of Hous. Preservation & Dev. v. Cohen, 489 N.Y.S.2d 979, 983 (N.Y. Civ. Ct. 1985) (rejecting agency's argument that economic feasibility precluded making repairs on SRO hotels) ("A vacate order issued to insure the safety of the tenants and others should not be used as a pretext for permanently reducing the housing stock"); City of New York v. Blum, 121 Misc. 2d 982 (N.Y. Sup. Ct. 1983) (ruling that Department of Social Services may deny men's shelter reimbursement for violating rules and regulations); Artis v. City of New York, 133 Misc. 2d 629, 638 (N.Y. Civ. Ct. 1986) (holding city to same regulations as private landlords in maintaining habitable shelter) ("The conditions of the building qualify them as slums. The City has become the landlord of the last resort for the homeless and others. These cases show that it has also become the slumlord of last resort."); *see also* Perez v. Boston Hous. Auth., 400 N.E.2d 1231 (Mass. 1980) (holding that Boston Housing Authority must maintain premises in habitable conditions as private landlords must, and establishing receivership to allocate funds to provide habitable housing).

70. *Callahan*, No. 42582/79 at 7–9.

71. *Id.* at 9–11. *But see* Jiminez v. Gross, 121 A.D.2d 382 (N.Y. App. Div. 1986) (refusing to impose a requirement that local commissioner always reimburse homeless person for whatever moving expenses are incurred in transferring to various shelters).

72. Hodge v. Ginsberg, 303 S.E.2d 245 (W. Va. 1983).

73. *Id.* at 249–50.

74. Werner, Homelessness, *supra* note 5, at 1257.

75. Once the right to shelter is established, the next step has been to protect this right from arbitrary cessation of shelter and other benefits. *Id.* at 1260–62.

76. Mooney v. Pickett, 483 P.2d 1231 (Cal. 1971).

77. *Id.* at 1235 (quoting Cal. Welf. & Inst. Code § 17000 (Deering 1986)).

78. *Id.* at 1237. During the 1986 session, the California legislature passed AB 3368, Ch. 1146 (filed Sept. 25, 1986), which allotted $5 million to assist counties that were unable to provide basic welfare and justice programs because of severe lack of funds.

79. Robbins v. Superior Court of Sacramento County, 695 P.2d 695 (Cal. 1985); Boehm v. Superior Court, 178 Cal. App. 3d 494, *modified*, 179 Cal. App. 3d 524 (1986); City and County of San Francisco v. Superior Court of San Francisco County, 57 Cal. 3d 44 (1976).

80. Boehm v. Superior Court, 178 Cal. App. 3d 494, *modified*, 179 Cal. App. 3d 524 (1986).

81. *Id.* at 502 (footnotes omitted).

82. *Id.* at 503.

83. 637 P.2d 681 (Cal. 1981).

84. *Boehm*, 178 Cal. App. 3d at 500 (footnotes omitted).

85. *Id.* at 500–501.

86. Blair v. Los Angeles County Board of Supervisors, No. C568184 (L.A. Super. Ct. July 11, 1986) (denying injunction); Ross v. Los Angeles County Board of Supervisors, No. C501603 (L.A. Super. Ct. Aug. 16, 1986) (holding grant of eight dollars for shelter to recipients of general relief arbitrary and granting preliminary injunction, hearing pending).

87. Eisenheim v. County of Los Angeles, No. C479453 (L.A. Super. Ct. Dec. 20, 1984) (enjoining the county from requiring extensive identification and delaying the issuance of shelter vouchers).

88. Paris v. Los Angeles County Board of Supervisors, No. C523361 (L.A. Super. Ct. Nov. 20, 1984) (ordering a minimum of 68 degrees Fahrenheit from six in the evening to six in the morning). Subsequent action in the case challenges the issuance of any shelter vouchers to hotels that violate county regulations and ordinances in regard to health and safety, *citing* Cal. Uniform Hous. Code § 1211, 1982, ch. 7; L.A. City Code § 11.20.140 b10; L.A. Municipal Code § 91.4902–31; L.A. Health & Safety Code Title 11; L.A. County Department of Social Services Handbook for Emergency Housing.

89. Paris v. Los Angeles County Board of Supervisors, No. C523361 (L.A. Super. Ct. Nov. 20, 1984).

The Los Angeles County Counsel DeWitt Clinton issued an opinion stating that Los Angeles County's general relief program satisfied the requirements set forth by Mooney v. Pickett. He asserted, however, that the City of Los Angeles has "the statutory authority and a corresponding duty to alleviate homelessness by increasing the amount of available low-income housing through zoning, density allowances and redevelopment." Guccione, Opinion Holds County Meets Law on Homeless, L.A. Daily J., Aug. 31, 1987, § 2, at 1.

90. *Paris*, No. C523361.

91. *Id.*

92. *Id.* (citing Cal. Civ. Proc. Code § 256(a) (West 1982)).

93. *See* Green v. Superior Court, 517 P.2d 1168 (Cal. 1974) (en banc) (warranty of habitability is implied by law in California residential leases; breach of the warranty is accepted as a defense in an unlawful detainer action).

94. "All people are by nature free and independent and have inalienable rights. Among these are enjoying and defending life and liberty, acquiring, possessing, and protecting property, and pursuing and obtaining safety, happiness, and privacy." Cal. Const. art. I, § 1.

95. The conflict between judicial holdings and legislative responsibility for allocations of funds is beyond the scope of this chapter.

96. Cahill, The Distribution of Income among Families with Children, 1968–1984, 7 Cong. Res. Serv. Rev. 15 (1986). "The number of poor children under eighteen years of age rose from 12.2 million in 1981 to 13.5 million in 1982 and their poverty rate rose from 19.8 percent to 21.7 percent." Los Angeles RoundTable for Children, Profile of the Children of Los Angeles County 20 (1984). "In 1980, nineteen percent of Los Angeles County's children or 388,155 boys and girls live in homes where income was below the poverty level compared to 14.2 percent in 1970." *Id.* at 15. The poverty level for a family of four in 1982 was $9,862. *Id.* at 19. *See generally* American Public Welfare Association & National Council of State Human Service Administrators, Investing in Poor Families and Their Children: A Matter Of Commitment (1987) (one in four children in the United States live in poverty; suggests a family investment program to reduce poverty among families); Los Angeles RoundTable for Children, The Children's Budget of Los Angeles County Government (1986); M. Kimmich, America's Children: Who Cares? Growing Needs and Declining Assistance in the Reagan Era (1985).

97. Kaufman, Homelessness: A Comprehensive Policy Approach, *supra* note 11, at 21.

98. *Id.*; *see also* Clary & Venezio, Exploratory Study of Homeless Families, *supra* note 38, at 7–9 (noting the minimal role that the deinstitutionalization of the mentally ill plays in causing the homelessness of families). For a history of homelessness in the United States, see Erickson & Wilhelm, Housing the Homeless, *supra* note 5, at xx–xxv; Hooper & Hamberg, The Making of America's Homeless, *supra* note 37; Ropers & Robertson, Basic Shelter, *supra* note 4, at 3–5; Cuomo, Never Again, *supra* note 3.

99. Clary & Venezio, Exploratory Study of Homeless Families, *supra* note 38, at 7 (footnote omitted).

100. Crystal, Homeless Men and Homeless Women: The Gender Gap, 17 Soc. Sci. Rev. 2, 5 (1984).

101. Karlen, Homeless Kids: Forgotten Faces, Newsweek, Jan. 6, 1986, at 20.

102. Jones, Youngsters Share Plight, *supra* note 5, at 1 (500,000 of the nation's homeless are children, with over 20,000 of them in California and 10,000 in Los Angeles).

103. According to the U.S. Conference of Mayors:

> The number of families requesting emergency shelter during the last two years increased, by an average of 31 percent, in all but one of the 29 survey cities. That one city said the number of [*sic*] requesting shelter had remained the same. In no city has there been a decrease in requests for emergency shelter by families. Families represent just over one-third of the homeless population across the survey cities. Well over two-thirds of the homeless families are headed by a single parent; 30 percent are headed by two parents.

U.S. Conference of Mayors, A Status Report on Homeless Families in America's Cities 1 (1987) [hereinafter Homeless Families]; *see also* Karlen, Homeless Kids, *supra* note 101, at 20. *See generally* Crystal, Homeless Men and Homeless Women, *supra* note 100, at 5; Clary & Venezio, Exploratory Study of Homeless Families, *supra* note 38, at 2.

For a series of profiles of homeless families, see Homeless Families, *supra*, at 13–19; Jones, Youngsters Share Plight, *supra* note 5; King, A Family Down and Out, Newsweek, Jan. 12, 1987, at 44 ("We're beginning to raise a generation of kids in the streets. That has dire consequences for the future" (quoting Ellen Bassuk, M.D., associate professor of psychiatry at Harvard Medical School)).

104. Karlen, Homeless Kids, *supra* note 101, at 20.

105. *Id. See generally* Ropers & Robertson, Basic Shelter, *supra* note 4, at 84–85; Cuomo, Never Again, *supra* note 3.

106. Homelessness II, *supra* note 3, at 282; *see* Jones, Youngsters Share Plight, *supra* note 5, at 1 ("[homeless] youngsters are invisible to most people").

107. Children, Youth, & Families 1983, A Year End Report on the Activities of the House Select Committee on Children, Youth, & Families, 98th Cong., 2d Sess. 60 (1984) [hereinafter Children, Youth, & Families].

108. *Id.*

109. Background Paper, *supra* note 6, at 2.

110. *See, e.g.*, Clary & Venezio, Exploratory Study of Homeless Families, *supra* note 38.

111. Hansen v. McMahon, No. CA 000 974 (L.A. Super. Ct. May 19, 1986) (quoting declaration of Ellen Bassuk, M.D., associate professor of psychiatry at Harvard Medical School); *see also* declarations of Dr. Joanne Jubelier, psychiatrist, and Dr. Richard Barth, University of California, Berkeley. *Id.*

112. *Id.* at 4 (declaration of Dr. Bassuk).

113. *Id.* at 4–5; *see also* Hansen v. McMahon, 193 Cal. App. 3d 283, 295 (1987),

citing Delgado v. Freeport Pub. Sch. Dist., 131 Misc. 2d 102 (N.Y. Sup. Ct. 1986) (noting that homeless children miss school more often); Homeless Families, *supra* note 103, at 9 (homeless children experience a number of school-related problems, including unstable attendance, truancy, dropping out, learning problems, and stigmatization).

114. *Hansen*, No. CA 000 974, at 5–6 (declaration of Dr. Bassuk).

115. New York Coalition for the Homeless, A Crying Shame—Official Abuse and Neglect of Homeless Infants 6 (1985) (citing New York Department of Health, Birth Outcomes Among Homeless Women Residing in Hotels, 1982–1983, in 3 City Health Information No. 29 (1984)).

116. *Id.* at 8.

117. *Id.* at 9.

118. *Id.* at 12 (app. B gives a summary of nutritional patterns for families living in a welfare hotel).

119. *Id.* at 2.

120. *Id.* at 1 (footnote omitted).

121. *Id.* (footnote omitted).

122. *Id.*

123. Public Health Service, U.S. Department of Health & Human Services II (A), Vital Statistics of the United States 11 (1981).

124. New York Coalition for the Homeless, A Crying Shame, *supra* note 115, at 1.

125. *Id.* at 2. For a general discussion of child health in Los Angeles, see Los Angeles RoundTable for Children, Profile, *supra* note 96, at 33–37.

126. Stoner, Analysis of Provisions, *supra* note 1, at 60–61.

127. *Id.*

128. The resulting cycle may be described as follows:

[T]he loss of AFDC eligibility follows the loss of custody. In the absence of appropriate assistance, parents in these circumstances become even less able to afford adequate housing than they were prior to the loss of their children. Consequently, what is intended to be temporary foster care due to the family's inability to secure housing, has been known to result in the permanent separation of parent from child.

Hansen v. McMahon, 193 Cal. App. 3d 283, 294 (1987).

129. Clary & Venezio, Exploratory Study of Homeless Families, *supra* note 38, at 60–61; interview with Debra Little, attorney, Orange County Legal Aid (Sept. 8, 1986); interview with Donna Venezio, author of Exploratory Study, *supra* note 38 (Sept. 9, 1986); Homelessness II, *supra* note 3, at 57–58 (footnote omitted).

130. Clary & Venezio, Exploratory Study of Homeless Families, *supra* note 38, at 51; *see also* Homeless Families, *supra* note 103, at 25, 25–28 ("On average, 30 percent of the demand by families for emergency shelter" goes unmet).

131. California Directory, *supra* note 22. *See generally* Clary & Venezio, Exploratory Study of Homeless Families, *supra* note 38, at 85.

132. California Directory, *supra* note 22.

Thirty-five percent [of women interviewed] had children living with relatives, seven percent with other informal caretakers, while 26% had children in foster care or institutional placement. Children had seldom been released for adoption; children had been adopted in only two cases, less than two percent.

Many of the interviews indicated substantial ongoing involvement by the clients with their children, despite the current inability to live with and care for them. Sixty-four percent of those with children under 18 stated they had last taken care of their children within the past two years. Fifty-eight percent stated they were currently maintaining contact with all their children, and another six percent were currently in contact with one or more children but not all of them. Sixty-six percent said they plan to rejoin their children, and another 10 percent saw this as a "possibility."

Crystal, Homeless Men and Homeless Women, *supra* note 100, at 5; *see also* Hansen v. McMahon, 193 Cal. App. 3d 283, 288 (1987) ("growing concern that the expenditure of these funds [42 U.S.C. § 606 (a) (1)—funds for abused and neglected children] was resulting in the warehousing of children in foster homes and in the break-up of families"); *In re* Cheryl E., 161 Cal. App. 3d 587, 594–95, (1984) (indigent mother signed a relinquishment-for-adoption form, in large part, because of her inability to secure adequate shelter for her infant daughter); Homeless Families, *supra* note 103, at 24–25; Jones, Youngsters Share Plight, *supra* note 5, at 25 ("Ironically, one problem for homeless children comes from an institution created to help them—the shelters. The rules often drive children and parent apart.").

133. Children, Youth, & Families, *supra* note 107, at 61. *See generally* Clary & Venezio, Exploratory Study of Homeless Families, *supra* note 38, at 14 (footnote omitted).

134. Clary & Venezio, Exploratory Study of Homeless Families, *supra* note 38, at 85; *see also* Morris & Mahardige, Need, Politics Send Homeless to Shelter Said Unsanitary, L.A. Daily J., Jan. 16, 1987, § 2, at 1.

135. Karlen, Homeless Kids, *supra* note 101, at 20; *cf.* Morris, Shootings Seen as Just One More Way to Die on Skid Row, L.A. Daily J., Oct. 10, 1986, § 2, at 1.

136. Ropers & Robertson, Basic Shelter, *supra* note 4, at 53–54; *see also* California Directory, *supra* note 22. Homeless families are often restricted both in the hours during the day they may spend at the shelter and in the number of days the shelter will allow them to stay. Families have inadequate alternatives when they are required to leave the shelter during the day. Homeless Families, *supra* note 103, at 29–31.

137. L. Tribe, American Constitutional Law § 15–21 (1977) (quoting Heyman & Barzelay, The Forest and the Trees: Roe v. Wade and Its Critics, 53 B.U. L. Rev., 765, 772–73 (1973)).

138. *Id.* (quoting Runyon v. McCrary, 427 U.S. 160, 178 (1976)) (emphasis in original).

139. *Id.*

140. Smith v. Organization of Foster Families for Equality and Reform, 431 U.S. 816 (1977) (stating in dictum that protection of "family" is not limited to blood relationships); Moore v. City of East Cleveland, 431 U.S. 494 (1977) (invalidating ordinance excluding extended families from residence); U.S. Department of Agriculture v. Moreno, 413 U.S. 528 (1973) (no rational basis for Food Stamp Act provision excluding households containing unrelated persons); Eisenstadt v. Baird, 405 U.S. 438 (1972) (invalidating statute that prohibited distribution of contraceptive materials to nonmarried individuals); Stanley v. Illinois, 405 U.S. 645, 651

(1972) ("Nor has the [Constitution] refused to recognize those family relationships unlegitimized by a marriage ceremony").

141. *Cf.* Belle Terre v. Boraas, 416 U.S. 1 (1974) (no fundamental right of unrelated individuals to live together); Bowers v. Hardwick, 474 U.S. 943 (1986) (no fundamental right to sodomy).

142. Skinner v. Oklahoma, 316 U.S. 535 (1942) (invalidating sterilization requirement for all felons).

143. Griswold v. Connecticut, 381 U.S. 479 (1965) (invalidating statute prohibiting sale of contraceptives to married persons); *Eisenstadt*, 405 U.S. at 438; Roe v. Wade, 410 U.S. 113 (1973) (state may not interfere with a woman's choice to have an abortion).

144. Meyer v. Nebraska, 262 U.S. 390 (1923).

145. Pierce v. Society of Sisters, 268 U.S. 510 (1925).

146. Parham v. J.R., 442 U.S. 584 (1979); Halderman v. Pennhurst State Sch. & Hosp., 707 F.2d 702 (3d Cir. 1983) (parents have a substantial constitutional right to direct the upbringing of their children, and this right must be afforded sufficient consideration in commitment proceedings).

147. Zablocki v. Redhail, 434 U.S. 374 (1978) (invalidating law that banned fathers with unmet support obligations from remarrying); Loving v. Virginia, 388 U.S. 1 (1967) (invalidating law against racial intermarriage). *But see* Reynolds v. United States, 98 U.S. 145 (1878) (upholding prohibition on polygamy).

148. Boddie v. Connecticut, 401 U.S. 371 (1970) (state cannot require indigents to pay a court fee for divorce proceedings).

149. Tribe, American Constitutional Law, *supra* note 137, § 15-21 (citing Runyon v. McCrary, 427 U.S. 160 (1976) (outlawing segregation does not violate parents' rights); Baker v. Owen, 423 U.S. 907 (1976) (parental approval of corporal punishment in school is not constitutionally required); Planned Parenthood v. Danforth, 428 U.S. 52 (1976) (rejecting absolute parental veto over a minor's abortion)).

150. Prince v. Massachusetts, 321 U.S. 158, 166 (1944) (citation omitted).

151. Wisconsin v. Yoder, 406 U.S. 205, 231–32 (1972).

152. Quilloin v. Walcott, 434 U.S. 246, 255 (1978) (citation omitted).

153. 381 U.S. 479 (1965).

154. *Id.* at 496.

155. 367 U.S. 497 (1961).

156. *Id.* at 551–52.

157. 431 U.S. 494 (1977).

158. *Id.* at 504 (footnote omitted).

159. *Id.* at 499.

160. *Id.*

161. *Id.* at 500–501, 504–12, 532–40, 550–52.

162. Note, Developments in the Law: The Constitution and the Family, 93 Harv. L. Rev. 1156, 1353 (1980).

163. Harris v. McRae, 448 U.S. 297 (1980) (state receiving federal Medicaid funds is not obligated to pay for medically necessary abortions); Maher v. Roe, 432 U.S. 464 (1977) (state's choice to fund indigent's childbirth costs does not obligate it to fund elective abortions).

164. Cox, Foreword: Freedom of Expression in the Burger Court, 94 Harv. L. Rev. 75, 99 (1980) (footnotes omitted).

165. *Id.* at 100 (footnotes omitted).

166. *See supra* notes 137–62 and accompanying text.

167. Cox, Foreword, *supra* note 164, at 100; Goodpaster, The Constitution and Fundamental Rights, 15 Ariz. L. Rev. 479, 503–505 (1973).

168. Tribe, American Constitutional Law, *supra* note 137, § 16-7, at 1002.

169. Note, Developments in the Law; *supra* note 162, at 1321 (footnotes omitted).

170. Tribe, American Constitutional Law, *supra* note 137, § 16-30 (quoting Craig v. Boren, 429 U.S. 190, 197 (1976) (intermediate level of review)).

171. Shapiro v. Thompson, 394 U.S. 618, 633 (1969) (one-year residency requirement for welfare benefits is unconstitutional) (footnote omitted).

172. Smith v. Organization of Foster Families for Equality and Reform, 431 U.S. 816, 834–35 n.36 (1977).

173. Note, Developments in the Law, *supra* note 162, at 1329 (footnotes omitted) (referring to joint custody considerations and the necessity of positive contact between a child and both parents).

174. Quilloin v. Walcott, 434 U.S. 246, 255 (1978).

175. G. Gunther, Cases and Materials on Constitutional Law, 588–89 (1985); Tribe, American Constitutional Law, *supra* note 137, at § 16-17.

176. Plyler v. Doe, 457 U.S. 202 (1982) (statute denying free education to undocumented alien children violated equal protection). Tribe, American Constitutional Law, *supra* note 137, § 16-9, at 1005 (citing San Antonio Indep. Sch. Dist. v. Rodriguez, 411 U.S. 1 (1973) (holding school financing scheme that afforded different levels of funding for various schools constitutional)).

177. Smith v. Organization of Foster Families for Equality and Reform, 431 U.S. 816, 844 (1977).

178. Tribe, American Constitutional Law, *supra* note 137, at § 16-9.

179. Railway Express Agency v. New York, 336 U.S. 106 (1949) (holding New York traffic regulation constitutional even though it failed to address all related traffic problems).

There is a line of cases that stand for the proposition that the *indirect* effects a particular government aid program has on indigent families do not warrant heightened scrutiny. The Supreme Court, in each of the cases, held that no fundamental freedoms were affected and, therefore, the rational basis test was the appropriate standard.

In Bowen v. Gilliard, 107 S. Ct. 3008 (1987), the Supreme Court applied the rational basis test to the Deficit Reduction Act of 1984 (DEFRA). The act amended the AFDC program and requires families to include in their aid application and subsequent reports all children living in the same house. The purpose of the DEFRA was to reduce aid payments to families in which one or more children were receiving support payments from other sources. Prior to this, the listing of such children was optional. The Court held that the possibility "[t]hat some families may decide to modify their living arrangements in order to avoid the effect of the amendment, does not transform the amendment into an act whose design and direct effect is to 'intrud[e] on choices concerning family living arrangements.'" *Id.* at 3017 (quoting Moore v. City of East Cleveland, 431 U.S. 494, 499 (1977)).

In Lyng v. Castillo, 477 U.S. 635 (1986), the Court rejected a constitutional challenge to a provision in the federal Food Stamp Program that determines eligibility and benefit levels on a "household" rather than on an individual basis. The provision treated parents, children, and siblings who lived together as a single household differently than groups of more distant relatives and unrelated persons. In effect, intact families received less aid than the other groups. The Court applied the rational basis test because "the statutory classification [did] not 'directly and substantially' interfere with family living arrangements and thereby burden a fundamental right." *Id.* at 635 (citation omitted).

Finally, in Dandridge v. Williams, 397 U.S. 471 (1970), the Court upheld a Maryland AFDC provision that imposed a maximum limit on the amount of aid a family could receive. The provision's effect was to provide most families with aid based on their need and size. A $250 ceiling, however, was imposed no matter how large the family's size or need was. As in the above-mentioned cases, the Court held that in "the area of economics and social welfare, a State does not violate the Equal Protection Clause merely because the classifications made by its laws are imperfect. If the classification has some 'reasonable basis,' it does not offend the Constitution." *Id.* at 485.

> For here we deal with state regulation in the social and economic field, not affecting freedoms guaranteed by the Bill of Rights, and claimed to violate the Fourteenth Amendment only because the regulation results in some disparity in grants of welfare payments to the largest AFDC families. For this Court to approve the invalidation of state economic or social regulation as "overreaching" would be far too reminiscent of an era when the Court thought the Fourteenth Amendment gave it power to strike down state laws "because they may be unwise, improvident, or out of harmony with a particular school of thought."

Id. at 484 (quoting Williamson v. Lee Optical Co., 348 U.S. 483, 488 (1955)).

180. Tribe, American Constitutional Law, *supra* note 137, § 16-6, at 100 (footnote omitted) (citing Gunther, The Supreme Court, 1971 Term—Foreword: In Search of Evolving Doctrine on a Changing Court: A Model for a Newer Equal Protection, 86 Harv. L. Rev. 1, 8 (1972)).

181. *See supra* notes 76–85 and accompanying text.

182. 677 P.2d 1183 (Cal. 1984), *cert. denied,* 470 U.S. 1049 (1985).

183. *Id.* at 1187 (citations omitted).

184. *Id.* (citations omitted) (quoting County of Alameda v. Carleson, 488 P.2d 953, 961 n.14 (Cal. 1971), *appeal dismissed,* 406 U.S. 913 (1972)) (emphasis in original).

185. *See supra* notes 80–82 and accompanying text. The rights of a homeless family become less clear if there is no state guarantee of shelter or minimum levels of aid. An analogy might be made to Plyler v. Doe, 457 U.S. 202 (1982), where the Supreme Court ruled that even though public education was not a right guaranteed by the Constitution, the denial of free public education to undocumented alien children violated equal protection. The *Plyler* Court distinguished San Antonio Ind. Sch. Dist. v. Rodriguez, 411 U.S. 1 (1973) on the basis that the deprivation in *Plyler* was total, whereas in *Rodriguez* the alleged constitutional violation was merely a difference in funding levels of education and therefore did not qualify for constitutional scrutiny. In order for the analogy to hold, however, the Court must first recognize shelter and welfare benefits as having the same level of importance as public education. This seems doubtful, given the specific language in *Plyler* and *Rodriguez* distinguishing education from other social welfare programs.

186. *See infra* notes 195–209 and accompanying text.

187. Note, Developments in the Law, *supra* note 162, at 1322; *see also* Committee to Defend Reproductive Rights v. Myers, 625 P.2d 779 (Cal. 1981) (excluding Medi-Cal funds for elective abortions is unconstitutional); O'Neil, Unconstitutional Conditions: Welfare Benefits with Strings Attached, 54 Cal. L. Rev. 443 (1966); Good, Freedom from Want, *supra* note 65.

188. Cal. Wel. & Inst. Code § 300(b) (West 1984) (prior to amendment effective Jan. 1, 1987).

189. 431 U.S. 816 (1977).

190. *Id.* at 835 n.36 and accompanying text; *see also* text accompanying note 161.

191. Note, Developments in the Law, *supra* note 162, at 1318 n.60.

192. *Id.* at 1321–22; *see also* Karlen, Homeless Kids, *supra* note 101, at 20; Hansen v. McMahon, No. CA 000 974 (L.A. Super. Ct. May 19, 1986) (declarations of Beverly Conadera, Howard Wade, and Jenny Rhode); Cal. Wel. & Inst. Code § 300(b) (West 1984) (before amendment effective Jan. 1, 1987).

193. *See supra* notes 169–74 and accompanying text.

194. Hansen v. McMahon, 193 Cal. App. 3d 283 (1987).

195. *Hansen,* No. CA 000 974.

196. *Id.* at 3.

197. *Hansen,* No. CA 000 974 (L.A. Super. Ct. May 19, 1986) (plaintiff's and defendant's briefs).

198. *Id.*

199. *Id.*

200. *Id.*

201. *Id. See generally* J. Haugaard & B. Hokanson, Measuring the Cost-Effectiveness of Family-Based Services and Out-of-Home Care (1983).

202. Hansen v. McMahon, 193 Cal. App. 3d 283 (1987).

203. *Id.*

204. *In re* P. L. & E., No. N79 (D.C. Super. Ct. Apr. 12, 1982), *cited in* Werner, Homelessness, *supra* note 5, at 1266–67.

205. Werner, Homelessness, *supra* note 5, at 1267.

206. *Id.; see also* Maticka v. City of Atlantic City, 524 A.2d 416 (N.J. Super. Ct. 1987) (New Jersey has an obligation to shelter homeless families; until there is a hearing to determine the actual effect of the ninety-day limitation of shelter benefits, there will be no termination of benefits). *See generally* Coker v. Bowen, Civ. No. 86-2448 (D.D.C. 1986), *cited in* Blodgett, America's Homeless, A.B.A. J., Jan. 1, 1987, at 19 (alleging that twenty-five states participating in the Emergency Assistance to Families Program are required, but have failed, to provide either emergency shelter, assistance payments for shelter, or assistance in securing shelter).

207. McCain v. Koch, 70 N.Y.2d 109 (1987).

The New York Court of Appeals reversed the lower court holding that setting minimum habitability standards was outside the boundaries of judicial discretion. *Id. See also* McCain v. Koch, 117 A.D.2d 198, 216 (N.Y. App. Div. 1986):

> [T]he failure of the Legislature to [set minimum shelter standards] . . . is discouraging, saddening, and disheartening. When thousands of children are

put at risk in their physical and mental health, and subject to inevitable emotional scarring, because of the failure of City and State officials to provide emergency shelter for them which meets minimum standards of decency and habitability, it is time for the Court of Appeals to reexamine and, hopefully, change its prior holdings in this area.

208. N.Y. Soc. Serv. L. § 131(3) (McKinney 1983), *quoted in* Chackles, Sheltering the Homeless: Judicial Enforcement of Governmental Duties to the Poor, 31 Wash. U. J. Urb. & Contemp. L. 155, 177 (1987). *See also* Adams v. Cuevas, 68 N.Y.2d 188 (1986) (invalidating the Homeless Family Initiative, which required that homeless families be housed in enclosed sleeping areas rather than current barracks facilities, because the initiative did not conform to funding requirements); Lamboy v. Gross, 126 A.D.2d 265 (N.Y. App. Div. 1987) (placing a family in an emergency assistance unit—welfare offices open all night, weekends, and holidays—is a violation of applicable regulations); Slade v. Koch, 135 Misc. 2d 283 (N.Y. Sup. Ct. 1987) (placing pregnant women and children under six years of age in barracks-style mass shelters causes irreparable harm and therefore should be enjoined); Rodriguez v. Westco Realty Co., 133 Misc. 2d 283 (N.Y. Civ. Ct. 1986) (holding that homeless families have rights to have their apartments repaired by private owners); Goodwin v. Gleidman, 119 Misc. 2d 538 (N.Y. Sup. Ct. 1983) (enjoining the Department of Housing Preservation from terminating shelter benefits of homeless families that refused to move into apartments in buildings with up to three immediate hazardous violations).

209. N.Y. Soc. Serv. L. § 131(3) (McKinney 1983).

CHAPTER FIFTEEN

Combating Family Homelessness to Protect Children

Steven Banks

WHEN IT COMES to social policy, the old adage "the more things change the more they remain the same" may well be viewed as trite until the day comes when we are forced to realize that years of neglect of pressing social problems have caused irreparable harm to a generation of children and to the body politic.

Writing a century ago in an effort to rouse the nation to action, Jacob Riis exposed in grim detail the conditions in New York City's decrepit tenement housing for the poor, and chronicled the destructive impact of those conditions on human lives:

> Long ago it was said that "one half of the world does not know how the other half lives." That was true then. It did not know because it did not care. The half that was on top cared little for the struggles, and less for the fate of those who were underneath, so long as it was able to hold them there and keep its own seat. There came a time when the discomfort and crowding below were so great, and the consequent upheavals so violent, that it was no longer an easy thing to do, and then the upper half fell to inquiring what was the matter. Information on the subject has been accumulating rapidly since and the whole world has had its hands full answering for its old ignorance.[1]

Were Riis among us today, he would no doubt be struck by the similarities between the living conditions that he described in *How the Other Half Lives* and the New York City family shelter system. He would be struck particularly by the impact of the shelter system on children, about whom he observed: "[B]e it remembered, these children with the training they receive—or do not receive—with the instincts they inherit and absorb in their growing up, are to be future rulers if our theory of government is worth anything."[2]

In a law review article reproduced in Chapter 14 of this volume, Donna Mascari Baker argues that federal constitutional law principles protect family integrity and that government is obligated to provide adequate emergency shelter and related services, including housing assistance, to homeless families in order to vindicate this right to family integrity. To support this position, the article describes in some detail the primary causes of family homelessness—unemployment, inadequate public assistance levels, efforts to reduce or terminate public assistance benefits, and the lack of affordable housing—and the adverse impact of homelessness on children and family functioning.

Conditions confronting homeless families in New York City continue to cause irreparable harm to a generation of children made to live literally for days in city offices, and indefinitely in squalid welfare hotels and shelters. Riis's observations resonate with the voices of today's homeless children in the New York City family shelter system:

> It's strange, but I really like when the lights go off in the movies because then I'm no longer a "homeless kid." I'm just a person watching the movie like everyone else.
>
> A lot of the children at the hotel believe that they are "hotel kids." They've been told by so many people for so long that they are not important, that they live up to what is expected of them. It gets so some children have no dreams and live in a nightmare because they believe that they are "hotel kids." It's worse than being in jail. In jail you can see the bars and you know when you're getting out. In the hotel you can't see the bars because they're inside of you and you don't know when you're getting out.[3]

Consider too the impact of homelessness on young Janet May Patterson, who recounted the following experience in a welfare hotel for homeless families in court papers:

1. I am seven years old.
2. I know the difference between right and wrong. I know that telling a lie is wrong. I am telling the truth in this paper.
3. This paper is being read to me. I read a little bit, but not well.
4. The Carter Hotel is a bad place.
5. Last week or so I saw three men on the eighth floor. Each of the men stuck a needle in his arm. Then the men put the needles in their pockets.
6. I was scared and took the elevator back to my floor.[4]

In this chapter I attempt to paint a picture of the conditions of the homeless, using New York City as an example. I then discuss the need for action and draw attention to litigation intended to address the problem and grounded in state, as opposed to federal, law.

Homeless Families in New York City

In New York City, where court orders require the provision of shelter to homeless families with children,[5] more than 5,400 families, including some 9,500 children, were languishing in the city's family shelter system in 1992.[6] The average length of stay in the shelter system is six months, and some 2,000 families have been in the shelter system for more than six months.[7] Some 1,100 of the families in the shelter system, including more than 1,700 children, are consigned to welfare hotels,[8] despite the fact that every major report on the problems of homeless families over the past five years has condemned such facilities and called for closure plans.[9]

Family homelessness contributes to a wide range of social and medical problems that are extraordinarily costly to government and society in general, let alone to the children and adults who are affected directly. For example, lack of adequate prenatal care and poor nutrition among pregnant homeless women leads to low birth weight and infant mortality rates that surpass even those of some poor developing nations.[10] The impact of homelessness and displacement from their community is particularly severe on children, who typically suffer disruption of their education when their families are rendered homeless.[11] The stress and trauma of homelessness in many cases can lead to family breakup as well.[12]

Evidence submitted in *McCain v. Koch* and related litigation in New York State courts on behalf of homeless families with children presents a grim picture. Over the past two years, hundreds of children and their families have been regularly denied shelter, and have then been left to spend the night in city welfare offices, sleeping on filthy public floors, hard plastic chairs, desks, or table tops. There is no place to bathe or wash infants. Sinks and toilets in the limited bathroom facilities in these city offices have been frequently stopped up or caked with vomit, feces, and urine from overuse. Consequently, bathroom floors have often been filthy with vomit, feces, and urine. Roach and mouse infestation is noticeable. In many cases, families have remained in welfare offices for additional hours because transportation to shelter placements has not been provided in a timely fashion.[13]

Spending the night in city offices under these conditions—often on a repeated basis—poses obvious health risks to homeless families, including pregnant women, infants, and children and adults with special medical needs.[14] Children and adults are exhausted, disoriented, and vulnerable to disease. Children's school attendance and performance are affected by such experiences.

Conditions in the city's barracks-style shelters are equally inappropriate for children.[15] As the *McCain* court found in a decision regarding placement in "overnight" beds in barracks-style family shelters:

The conditions in these shelters as described in the various affidavits submitted are horrendous. Families with young children sleep on canvas cots or mattresses placed one next to the other so that there is no walking space. Cribs are unavailable. Family members have been forced to share beds in violation of 18 N.Y.C.R.R. § 900.12(e)(3). Blankets, pillows, soap and towels are often unavailable. Residents, awakened each morning, are required to pack their belongings and remain in the shelter all day in anticipation of a lawful placement.

Shuffling families with children between short term placements results in nutritional deprivation and exhaustion and contributes both to physical ill health and emotional instability. Children cannot go to school, medical appointments are missed and special nutritional needs go unmet.

Infectious diseases spread easily among members of this particularly vulnerable population because of use of shared bathrooms, cots placed so close that they are separated by less than one foot from those of other families, and noisy situations interfering with sleep. There have been instances of outbreaks of communicable illnesses and illnesses warranting hospitalizations for as much as several weeks.[16]

There have been repeated outbreaks of chicken pox and measles in these shelters. Sheltering families in barracks-style facilities costs more than keeping them in welfare hotels: For example, the cost of sheltering a family at the city's Auburn barracks-style family shelter is well in excess of $100 per night.[17]

Meanwhile, evidence submitted in the *McCain* litigation documents the extreme health risks to homeless families with children resulting from welfare hotel placements. Some noncompliant hotels now in use in New York City lack cooking facilities, window guards, beds and cribs for each family member, and tables and chairs for schoolwork and eating meals. Harm caused by chipping, peeling lead paint and roach and vermin infestation is also documented; instances of prostitution and crime in these hotels are detailed in affidavits from families.

As the court found in *McCain*:

The resumption of use of commercial hotels for homeless families presents numerous problems. First, this Court has already ordered that the Hamilton Place Hotel not be used because of code violations involving broken windows, window guards, electrical problems and peeling lead paint.

Second, several hotels enforce a policy that families may not remain in a hotel for more than twenty-eight days in order to avoid creating statutory tenancies. Consequently, families in these hotels are evicted after short stays and may be allowed back into the hotel only after a hiatus of one or two nights. It is axiomatic that such policies substantially increase instability in an already unstable population.

Third, affidavits submitted by the fifty-nine families disclose that hotels, despite claims to the contrary, do not regularly provide the basic furniture necessary for daily living for families—cribs for infants, tables and chairs or separate beds for each family member as required by 18 N.Y.C.R.R. § 353.3(g)(4) and (6). Door and window locks are often broken in violation of 18 N.Y.C.R.R. § 352.3(g)(8), making tenants feel unsafe, and unsavory activities continue in other parts of the hotels. . . . Finally . . . the absence of cooking facilities presents serious problems for families with young children.[18]

Lack of cooking facilities has profound health consequences for homeless children and adults, particularly pregnant women:

All of the parents at the Cross Bronx, for example, reported that because of the lack of cooking facilities, they use hot tap water to try to clean bottles and plastic nipples that they use for formula for their infants. This technique, however, is not adequate. Normally children under the age of six or seven months are exposed gradually to bacteria so that their ability to resist infection is developed gradually without risking overwhelming infection. Because it is impossible to thoroughly sterilize bottles and plastic nipples with hot tap water, children under the six to seven month range who are fed formula from these bottles and nipples will receive large doses of bacteria with every feeding. This results in premature and precipitous bacterial colonization of the intestine which can cause severe diarrhea. Dehydration and, in extreme cases, even death are potential outcomes. . . . Lack of cooking facilities for older children and adults also pose health risks. Retrospective studies of undernourished populations tell us that prenatal nutritional deprivation and early childhood malnutrition are correlated with long-term impairment of cognitive functioning. Chronically deficient diet due to limitations on food storage in hotel rooms also places children at nutritional and long-term health risk. . . . The adverse impact of poor nutrition on adults and children cannot be overemphasized. Chronic low level nutritional deficiencies can lead to borderline functional capacity. Ability to learn in school, ability to fight infections, and ability to perform in general and cope with normal tasks of daily living are all affected by ongoing nutritional deficiency. Lack of ability to cook and provide meals in hotel placements . . . are serious matters with long term health and developmental consequences. Damage can result from even short-term deprivations.[19]

Not only are the conditions in these hotels and "overnight" shelters inadequate, but the "short-stay" nature of placements and the remote location of some of the facilities disrupt education and continuity of medical care. Shuttled between "overnight" shelter placements and short-stay hotels, children and parents often literally do not know whether they are coming or going.

Hope for the Future

Against this bleak backdrop, in New York and elsewhere legal strategies are emerging to prevent and ameliorate family homelessness. As Florence Roisman of the National Housing Law Project has observed:

A right to housing is emerging in the United States. It is rooted not primarily in federal constitutional doctrine but rather in *state* lawmaking and *state* court litigation involving *state* constitutions and state statutes. The right is often grounded on state laws focused not on housing in particular but on public assistance and child welfare. Often the right begins with the right to shelter, and then is expanded into a right to have housing provided by the government.[20]

In New York City, for example, as a result of orders issued in the *McCain* litigation requiring the provision of safe, suitable, and adequate emergency housing, assistance, and services, the state and local government have developed permanent housing production, rehabilitation, subsidy, and priority referral programs for homeless families with children.[21] Furthermore, in response to contempt proceedings based upon its failure to provide shelter to families in accordance with court orders, the city agreed as part of a remedial compliance plan to implement a family homelessness prevention program. This program includes $12 million in annual government funding for the provision of legal services to avert evictions and correct the inadequate housing conditions that typically result in homelessness.[22] Aside from preventing families from losing their permanent housing and sparing them the trauma of homelessness, a New York State study has found that this type of preventive program saves government four dollars in averted shelter costs for every dollar spent.[23]

Likewise, a number of state courts have now ruled that public assistance benefit amounts, which are set by each individual state, should bear some reasonable relationship to rent levels so that families with children can maintain permanent housing and avert entry into the shelter system.[24] Given the direct relationship between a lack of sufficient income to retain or obtain permanent housing and family homelessness, favorable judicial decisions in this area can be a major breakthrough in efforts to prevent homelessness, and in so doing preserve family integrity.[25]

Equally critical is an increase in the supply of housing that is affordable to poor families, through some combination of increased availability of housing subsidies with protections for long-term occupancy and housing quality standards, rehabilitation of existing units, and new construction. Family homelessness is in large part the product of a failure during the past decade, at the federal, state, and local levels, to allocate sufficient resources for housing for low-income families, particularly those living at or below the federal poverty level. Increasing the supply of affordable permanent housing is therefore the indispensable ingredient in solving this national tragedy. While some have argued that homeless families need services as much as housing, this debate is reminiscent of arguments over how many angels can dance on the head of a pin. Arguing whether a particular homeless family, or any number of families, may need services in addition to housing ignores the defining feature of family homelessness: Homeless families with children need a roof over their heads.

At the same time, simply substituting more physically adequate shelter space for welfare hotel and barracks-style shelters will not fully address the family homelessness crisis either. Children in better shelters are no less marginalized and displaced than homeless children in other, less adequate facilities, and their education can be equally disrupted; even relocation to a more desirable shelter can have a disruptive effect. Without a sufficient supply of permanent housing, families end up staying in shelters for longer and longer periods, at great public expense.[26] As the New York City Commission on the Homeless chaired by Andrew Cuomo concluded recently, "The success of transitional housing is, by definition, dependent on the existence of permanent housing to which people can be transitioned."[27]

Although the events of the past decade have caused irreparable harm to homeless families with children, the continuing crisis can be solved by greater prevention efforts, including providing families with public assistance benefit levels that are reasonably related to housing costs, and allocating sufficient permanent housing resources to meet the needs of homeless families with children. Without such efforts the current crisis will continue unabated. The long-term consequences of not addressing these urgent needs of homeless families will, in the words of Jonathan Kozol, result in the creation of a "diseased, distorted, under-educated and malnourished generation of small children who, without dramatic intervention on a scale for which the nation seems entirely unprepared, will grow into the certainty of unemployable adulthood."[28]

In the long run, the social costs of producing a lost generation of children—which include the resulting increased costs for criminal and juvenile justice, medical care, and special education programs—will far exceed the costs of a comprehensive homelessness prevention and permanent housing program to end the crisis of family homelessness.

NOTES

1. J. Riis, How the Other Half Lives (1890).
2. *Id*. at 134.
3. J. Berck, No Place to Be: Voices of Homeless Children 105 (1992).
4. Affidavit of Janet May Patterson, dated Mar. 19, 1984, submitted in McCain v. Koch, now known as McCain v. Dinkins, No. 41023/83 (N.Y. Sup. Ct.).
5. *See* McCain v. Koch, 502 N.Y.S.2d 720 (N.Y. App. Div. 1986), *rev'd on other grounds*, 511 N.E.2d 62 (N.Y. 1987); *see also* Lamboy v. Gross, 513 N.Y.S.2d 393 (N.Y. App. Div. 1987), *aff'g* 493 N.Y.S.2d 709 (N.Y. Sup. Ct. 1985).
6. *See* New York City Human Resources Administration, Adult Services Agency, Crisis Intervention Services, Mid-Month Census: Emergency Housing Services for Homeless Families (Oct. 15, 1992) (on file with author) [hereinafter Mid-Month Census].
7. *See* New York City Human Resources Administration, Adult Services Agency, Crisis Intervention Services, Monthly Report: Emergency Housing Services for Homeless Families (Sept. 1992) (on file with author).

8. *See* Mid-Month Census, *supra* note 6.

9. *See, e.g.,* Report of the New York City Commission on the Homeless, The Way Home: A New Direction in Social Policy (Feb. 1992) (commission appointed by Mayor David N. Dinkins and chaired by Andrew Cuomo) [hereinafter The Way Home]; Report of the Manhattan Borough President's Task Force on Housing for Homeless Families, A Shelter Is Not a Home (Mar. 1987) (by the Office of the Manhattan Borough President, New York City, commission appointed by then Manhattan Borough President David N. Dinkins); Mayor's Advisory Task Force on Homelessness, Toward a Comprehensive Policy on Homelessness (Feb. 1987) (commission appointed by then Mayor Edward I. Koch); Report of the Select Committee for the Homeless of the New York City Council, Report on the Homeless Crisis (Nov. 1986). In addition to these major government studies calling for an end to the use of welfare hotels, in August 1988 New York City made a commitment to the U.S. Congress to cease use of welfare hotels within two years. *See* Testimony of Mayor Edward I. Koch before the New York City House of Representatives Delegation Field Hearing, Aug. 1, 1988. Subsequently, the city entered into a consent decree in McCain v. Koch to end use of noncompliant welfare hotels by August 1, 1990. *See* McCain v. Koch, Stipulation of Partial Settlement and Enforcement Order (June 1, 1990) (on file with author).

10. *See* Institute of Medicine, Homelessness, Health, and Human Needs (1988).

11. *See, e.g.,* Y. Rafferty, And Miles to Go . . .: Barriers to Academic Achievement and Innovative Strategies for the Delivery of Educational Services to Homeless Children (Nov. 1991) (report by the Advocates for Children of New York, Inc., on file with author); Y. Rafferty, Learning in Limbo: The Educational Deprivation of Homeless Children (Sept. 1989) (report by the Advocates for Children of New York, Inc., on file with author).

12. *See, e.g.,* A. Dehavenon, No Room at the Inn: An Interim Report with Recommendations on Homeless Families with Children Requesting Shelter at New York City's Emergency Assistance Units in 1991 (Dec. 1991) (on file with author); A. Dehavenon & K. Benker, The Tyranny of Indifference: A Study of Hunger, Homelessness, Poor Health and Family Dismemberment in 1,325 New York City Households with Children in 1989–1990 (Oct. 1990) (on file with author).

13. Longstanding court orders prohibit consigning families to stay overnight in city welfare offices, but New York City has already been found in civil contempt once for such practices. *See* McCain v. Koch, N.Y.L.J., Jan. 10, 1991, at 25 (N.Y. Sup. Ct.).

14. *See* Lamboy v. Gross, 513 N.Y.S.2d 393, 397 (N.Y. App. Div. 1987).

15. Conditions in barracks-style family shelters are acknowledged to be harmful to children. A local ordinance enacted by the New York City Council in 1990 requires the city to phase out use of barracks-style family shelters and develop new shelters with self-contained living units, including individual bathrooms and cooking facilities, for each family. As a result of this ordinance, in combination with *McCain* and related litigation, the city is in the process of ending use of barracks shelters for families. However, the city has failed to adhere to the closure deadlines for these facilities established by local law, and, as of October 1992, more than 150 families, including nearly 200 children, were still living in barracks-style shelter space.

16. McCain v. Koch, N.Y.L.J., March 26, 1991, at 24 (N.Y. Sup. Ct.).

17. *See* Citizens Committee for Children, Children in Storage: Families in New York City's Barracks-Style Shelters (Nov. 1988).

18. McCain v. Koch, N.Y.L.J., Jan. 10, 1991, at 24 (N.Y. Sup. Ct.).

19. Affirmation of Saundra Shepherd, M.D., dated October 30, 1990, submitted in McCain v. Koch (on file with author). Dr. Shepherd, who died in 1992, earned her masters degree in molecular biology from Hunter College and her medical degree from the Yale Medical School. She was a member of the American Academy of Pediatrics and the director of clinical training for the program in social medicine at the Albert Einstein School of Medicine.

20. F. Roisman, Establishing a Right to Housing: An Advocate's Guide (Aug. 1991) (report of the National Support Center for Low Income Housing, Washington, D.C., on file with author) (emphasis added).

21. *See, e.g.,* McCain v. Koch, Stipulation of Partial Settlement and Enforcement Order (June 1, 1990); *see also* McCain v. Koch, N.Y.L.J., Sept. 22, 1989, at 22 (N.Y. Sup. Ct.) (court orders procedures for referring homeless families from a noncompliant welfare hotel to, at the family's option, either permanent or alternative temporary housing).

22. *See* City Defendants' Nov. 26, 1992 *McCain* Plan for Coming into Compliance with the June 1, 1990 Stipulation and Enforcement Order (on file with author).

23. *See* New York State Department of Social Services, The Homelessness Prevention Program Outcomes and Effectiveness (Mar. 1991).

24. *See, e.g.,* Jiggetts v. Grinker, 553 N.E.2d 570 (N.Y. 1990); *In re* Petitions for Rulemaking, 566 A.2d 1154 (N.J. 1989), *aff'g* 538 A.2d 1302 (N.J. Super. Ct. App. Div. 1988); Massachusetts Coalition for the Homeless v. Secretary of Human Servs., 511 N.E.2d 603 (Mass. 1987).

25. Aid to Families with Dependent Children (AFDC) is the basic federal and state income support program for poor families with children. However, benefit levels are so low that families in receipt of AFDC are literally on the brink of homelessness. According to the Children's Defense Fund, median state AFDC benefits "fell by 39 percent between 1970 and 1990 after adjusting for inflation, and in no state do they now reach the inadequate federal poverty level." L. Mihaly, Homeless Families: Failed Policies and Young Victims 14 (Jan. 1991) (report by the Children's Defense Fund, Washington, D.C.). Indeed, in thirty-three states, the average metropolitan-area Fair Market Rent established by the U.S. Department of Housing and Urban Development as the prevailing cost of renting housing is greater than the *entire* AFDC grant for poor families. *See* C. Dolbeare, Out of Reach: Why Everyday People Can't Find Affordable Housing, at table 3 (Feb. 1990) (report by the Low Income Housing Information Service, Washington, D.C.).

26. In New York City, the average cost of adequate shelter placements in facilities operated by either not-for-profit organizations or the city itself is approximately $3,000 per month. *See* The Way Home, *supra* note 9. With the average length of stay in the family shelter system at six months and more than 2,000 families currently languishing in the shelter system for more than six months, the cost of keeping families in temporary shelter rather than providing permanent housing for them is extraordinary. Half of these costs are generally borne by the federal

government, one quarter by state government, and one quarter by local city funds. The U.S. Department of Health and Human Services has been unwilling to permit the federal share of these payments—$1,500 per month—to be redirected to provide permanent housing. Although state and local government are free to do so, neither has redirected its $750 share of these payments to provide permanent housing for families on a systemic basis.

27. The Way Home, *supra* note 9, at 88.
28. J. Kozol, Rachel and Her Children (1988).

CHAPTER SIXTEEN

Do the Poor Have a Right to Family Integrity?

Stephen Wizner

THE SUPREME COURT has recognized a right to family integrity that encompasses the autonomy and responsibility of adults in marriage and other family relationships, such as procreation and child rearing, and includes the right of children to the care and companionship of their parents.[1] Except where necessary to enforce criminal laws, deter domestic violence, or protect children from parental abuse or neglect,[2] the Court has read the Constitution to insulate families from state intrusion.

Implicit in the Court's understanding of the right to family integrity is the idea that family integrity is best achieved and protected when the state stays out of family life and parental decision making. Thus, the Court has not understood the Constitution generally to empower the state to intervene in the family, even for beneficent reasons, or to obligate the state to assist families in maintaining their integrity, even when such assistance is needed.

The increasing numbers of poor families in the United States residing in congregate shelters and welfare hotels, doubled up with relatives or friends, living in parks or automobiles, and even sleeping on the floors of welfare offices or in the streets, have demonstrated dramatically the destructive impact of poverty on the family life of the poor. Widespread unemployment, low wages for unskilled labor, inadequate welfare benefits, increasing housing costs, and a shortage of affordable housing have all contributed to the housing crisis for poor families.

The Supreme Court has not interpreted the Constitution to guarantee the poor a right to shelter, or, for that matter, any of the other necessities of life. In *Lindsey v. Normet*[3] the Court refused to recognize a right to shelter, stating that "the Constitution does not provide judicial remedies for every social and economic ill."[4] Further, the Court in *Lavine v. Milne*[5] asserted that "[w]elfare benefits are not a fundamental right, and neither the State nor Federal Government is under any sort of constitutional obligation to guarantee minimum levels of support."[6] If the Court is correct in its interpretation of the Constitution, then it would be constitutionally permissible for a state to provide no assistance at all to its indigent citizens.[7]

If poor families have no right to shelter, or to public assistance in an amount sufficient to enable them to meet their basic needs, what does this say about the right to family integrity? Consider a statute that allows a determination that parents have neglected their children, and authorizes removal of the children from their parents' custody, based upon the parents' financial inability (not their unwillingness) to provide for them: "A 'neglected child' is one who lives in an environment or under circumstances injurious to his or her well-being, or who lacks adequate food, clothing or shelter."[8]

Surely the state, in the proper exercise of its *parens patriae* powers, may act to protect children by requiring their parents to feed, clothe, and shelter them. But if it is constitutional for the state to require parents to provide proper care for their children, should not the family's constitutional right to family integrity obligate the state, in the case of parents who are willing but unable because of poverty to provide such care, to assist the parents in carrying out their parental obligations?

Donna Mascari Baker argues in Chapter 14 that the constitutional right to family integrity requires the government, when it provides shelter for homeless families, to do so in a manner that enables the family to remain intact.[9] Her argument is directed to the administration of welfare programs, not the obligation to establish and fund them. But if there truly is a constitutional right to family integrity, the Constitution should be read to obligate government to fund the exercise of that right by those whose poverty jeopardizes their family integrity.

A Right to Shelter

Prevailing constitutional theory does not support a right of families to state assistance for the protection of family integrity. The most that can be claimed with confidence is that once a state decides to provide certain benefits, such as emergency housing for homeless families, the distribution of those benefits is subject to some constitutional limitations, such as procedural fairness,[10] rational eligibility requirements,[11] and rough equity in the distribution of benefits to eligible families.[12]

Although the Supreme Court has repeatedly upheld the right to family integrity, a right not explicitly provided in the Constitution, it has not interpreted the Constitution to obligate government to fund the exercise of that right. As a result, advocates for the poor have had to frame their claims and arguments narrowly, basing them on existing entitlement programs, or state constitutional or statutory provisions that can be read to impose affirmative obligations on local government to provide assistance to the needy.[13] These efforts have met with limited success in addressing the problem of homelessness.

In *Jiggets v. Grinker*,[14] the culmination of over twelve years of litigation by advocates for the homeless, the New York Court of Appeals held that state law required the provision of shelter allowances to recipients of Aid to Families with Dependent Children (AFDC) in an amount "reasonably related" to actual housing costs. On the other hand, in *Savage v. Aaronson*,[15] the Connecticut Supreme Court upheld a durational limit on emergency housing assistance for homeless families in the face of a challenge based on state AFDC and child welfare laws. Even if the plaintiffs had prevailed in *Savage*, their "victory" would have assured them only the right to remain in welfare motels or other temporary emergency housing for an extended period of time.[16]

Although *Jiggets* and *Savage* represent opposing judicial responses to advocates' claims of a right to shelter for homeless families, they coexist within a narrow range of legal claims. While advocates have achieved limited success in improving living conditions in temporary shelters,[17] in establishing a claim to minimally adequate welfare housing allowances,[18] and in compelling the development of social services for homeless families,[19] none of this litigation has even come close to establishing a right to housing for homeless families that protects their right to family integrity.[20] Advocates have been unable to obtain a constitutional ruling articulating a right to housing, a normative statement that could have political impact and could rally the homeless and their advocates.[21]

Poverty and Family Integrity

In the world confronting poor people today, vacancy rates for affordable housing are at a historic low, rents are rising, and welfare benefits (and wages) have failed to keep pace with increasing housing costs.[22] As a consequence, increasing numbers of poor families find themselves unable to afford housing and are joining the ranks of the homeless.

Homelessness is a symptom of poverty. To ask whether homeless families have a right to integrity, therefore, is to ask whether poor families have a right to integrity, and if so, to define that right. For, while it is true that homelessness can have a devastating effect on a family, other symptoms of poverty—poor nutrition, inadequate health care, inferior education, wretched living conditions, and the social and psychological effects of economic deprivation—can also pose formidable challenges to the ability of parents (and children) to maintain a stable and healthy family life.

There is an obvious correlation between poverty and poor nutrition, housing, and health care. Perhaps less obvious is the fact that the physical deprivation, psychological stress, and feeling of hopelessness that are consequences of poverty can lead to a variety of individual and family problems that endanger family integrity, such as substance abuse, absent parents, and child neglect. These problems are exacerbated when a family is without a home. In his Chicago study, Peter Rossi found significantly higher levels of depression and demoralization among the homeless than in the rest of the population.[23]

Children especially suffer from homelessness. Both physical and emotional health is affected. Children born into conditions of extreme poverty often suffer the physical effects of their mothers' poor nutrition, ill-health, and inadequate prenatal care. Many experience depression and developmental delays. All are exposed to the health hazards and harmful social conditions of shelter life.[24]

Under these circumstances the right to family integrity is not protected by mere state nonintervention. In order to remain intact, many poor families need both financial assistance and social services. Some may require highly dependent living arrangements, while others need basic or occasional support services, such as crisis intervention, social casework, psychological counselling, job training, or other rehabilitative services, and child care. Those whose wages or welfare benefits are too low to enable them to afford market rents require rent subsidies or public housing.

The causes of poverty and homelessness, and their destructive impact on family integrity, will not be addressed—at least in the short run—by the inaction of government. Economic recession, inflation, unemployment, the failure of wages and welfare benefits to keep pace with an increased cost of living, and a shortage of affordable housing are economic conditions that affect the poor most harshly because the poor are least able to overcome or avoid these obstacles.

The accepted view of the right to family integrity protected by the Constitution is that it is a right to noninterference by the state in family matters absent some compelling state interest in preventing criminal conduct[25] or protecting children from harm at the hands of their parents.[26] The Supreme Court has repeatedly held that the Constitution protects family integrity:

> The rights to conceive and to raise one's children have been deemed "essential," *Meyer v. Nebraska*, 262 U.S. 390, 399 (1923), "basic civil rights of man," *Skinner v. Oklahoma*, 316 U.S. 535, 541 (1942), and "[r]ights far more precious . . . than property rights," *May v. Anderson*, 345 U.S. 528, 533 (1953). "It is cardinal with us that the custody, care and nurture of the child reside first in the parents, whose primary function and freedom include preparation for obligations the state can neither supply nor hinder." *Prince v. Massachusetts*, 321 U.S. 158, 166 (1944). The integrity of the family unit has found protection in the Due Process Clause of the Fourteenth Amendment, *Meyer v. Nebraska, supra*, at 399, the Equal Protection Clause of the Fourteenth Amendment, *Skinner v. Oklahoma, supra*, at 541, and the Ninth Amendment, *Griswold v. Connecticut*, 381 U.S. 479, 496 (1965) (Goldberg, J., concurring).[27]

The Court's consistent recognition of the rights of family privacy and parental autonomy, and of the liberty interests of parents and children in living together, and its use of words such as "essential," "basic," "precious," and "primary" in characterizing family relationships, imply that the Court views family integrity as a fundamental right that may not be abridged by the state absent compelling reasons.[28]

The right against intrusion by the state in family matters, however, provides small comfort to a family too poor to afford the benefits of family integrity. Parents who because of poverty are unable to assure their children a safe and healthy environment, good education, and economic opportunity, not to speak of a roof over their heads, may experience an erosion of family integrity without any active interference by the state. For such families protection of the right to family integrity requires affirmative assistance by government in the form of financial aid and social services.

Maintaining the analytical distinction between noninterference and affirmative assistance by the state in the protection of family integrity is attractive in the abstract. In theory, the idea that a government of limited powers should not be involved in family life and should be precluded from intruding upon family privacy and autonomy, even for arguably beneficent reasons, has a superficial allure. At first glance, family integrity appears to be respected when the state stays out of the business of providing assistance to, and as a consequence exercising control over, family life.

However, poor parents may be unable, through no particular fault of their own, to provide their children with adequate food, clothing, and shelter. Such children may be deemed "neglected" under state law and subject to removal from their parents' custody.[29] Homeless parents may find themselves in congregate shelters where their children are exposed to an environment injurious to the children's welfare but outside the parent's control. Such children may also be found to be neglected or "uncared for" under state law and may face removal from their parents' custody.[30]

In practice, the state already is unavoidably and quite properly involved in both regulating and assisting families in certain limited realms. For example, the state requires parents to send their children to school and provides universal public education to enable every family to do so. The state requires parents to provide food, clothing, shelter, and medical care to their children, and provides welfare and other public assistance benefits to those families that are too poor to afford them. The state prohibits families from violating criminal laws,[31] and intervenes when parents mistreat or neglect their children.[32]

While it is true that a fundamental component of a right to family integrity is noninterference by the state in family life, it is equally true that protection of family integrity often requires affirmative state assistance, particularly when families are unable, because of poverty, to meet their basic needs.

Homelessness and Constitutional Theory

Homeless and other extremely poor families present a challenge to constitutional theory. If the state can intervene in the family and remove children who are neglected as a result of their parents' financial inability to provide for them, then a lack of state assistance can lead to state interference, through no fault of the parents, and contrary to the interests of the children.

A constitutional theory that equates a right to family integrity with both non-interference *and* nonassistance by the state is insufficient to protect that right. Adequate state assistance to a poor family that enables the family to remain intact actually prevents state interference in the family in the form of neglect proceedings and removal of "neglected" children.

A constitutional theory that would protect the right of the poor to family integrity must, therefore, incorporate both a right to state noninterference and a right to state assistance. If poverty alone is not a constitutionally permissible basis for the state to remove children from their families, then the Constitution should be read to impose an obligation on the state to provide adequate assistance to the family to prevent state action that would violate family integrity.

In other contexts, the Supreme Court has mandated the expenditure of public funds to prevent burdening or violating individual rights. For example, the Court has struck down durational residency requirements for the receipt of public assistance in order to uphold the right to travel,[33] has required the funding of remedial educational programs ancillary to school segregation,[34] and has ordered states to pay unemployment compensation benefits to individuals who are terminated from employment for refusal to work on the Sabbath.[35]

The Court has not held that protection of the substantive due process right to family integrity obligates the state to expend funds to enable families to remain intact. However, when the state imposes obligations upon parents to provide for their children in particular ways, it is unconstitutional for the state to break up families that lack the financial means to meet those obligations. And if the state enforces those parental obligations, the Constitution should require the state to provide parents with the means—welfare assistance, social services, job training, employment, child care, affordable housing—to enable them to comply.

The restrictive interpretation the Supreme Court has given to the Constitution in the social welfare area, placing government assistance to the poor in the same category as economic regulation, has produced decisions such as *Dandridge v. Williams*[36] and *Lavine v. Milne.*[37] These rulings permit a state to decide how to allocate social welfare programs for the poor, or not to provide any programs at all.

The Constitution limits the powers of government to interfere in the lives of citizens or to burden the exercise of their rights. It requires government to operate in a manner that guarantees due process and equal protection of the law to all citizens. It acknowledges the existence of rights not specifically provided in the text of the Constitution, especially in the family area.[38] The Court has obligated the government to expend public funds to protect the exercise of individual rights.[39] Therefore, the Constitution should be interpreted to obligate the government to provide minimum subsistence to poor families whose poverty is the result of economic conditions.[40]

Conclusion

Neither the language of the Constitution nor the society it envisions requires that the Constitution be interpreted to deny the poor a right to assistance from the government in exercising basic rights. The Supreme Court has repeatedly recognized a fundamental right to family integrity that is protected by and transcends the Constitution. There is a compelling public interest in encouraging and protecting family integrity. Constitutional theory must encompass not only a right of families to remain intact, but an obligation of government to provide necessary assistance to families to enable them to exercise that right. If the government does not assist families as they struggle to remain intact, the right to family integrity will remain illusive.

NOTES

1. *See infra* note 27 and accompanying text.
2. *See infra* notes 25–26, 31–32, and accompanying text.
3. 405 U.S. 56 (1972).
4. *Id.* at 74.
5. 424 U.S. 577 (1976).
6. *Id.* at 584 n.9.
7. Indeed, some states have recently terminated welfare programs for individuals who do not qualify for aid under one of the federally subsidized categorical assistance programs.
8. Many states have adopted such statutes. *See, e.g.,* Ill. Ann. Stat. ch. 37, para. 802–3 (Smith-Hurd 1990); Conn. Gen. Stat. Ann. § 46b-120 (West Supp. 1992); N.C. Gen. Stat. § 7A-517(21) (1990). *See also infra* notes 29–30 and accompanying text; *see generally* Note, Developments in the Law: The Constitution and the Family, 93 Harv. L. Rev. 1156, 1321 (1980); Mascari, Homeless Families: Do They Have a Right to Integrity?, 35 UCLA L. Rev. 159, 196 (1987), reprinted as Chapter 14 in this volume.
9. *See* Chapter 14.
10. *See* Goldberg v. Kelly, 397 U.S. 254 (1970).
11. *See* Shapiro v. Thompson, 394 U.S. 618 (1969); King v. Smith, 392 U.S. 309 (1968).
12. *See* Dandridge v. Williams, 397 U.S. 471 (1970); Lyng v. Castillo, 477 U.S. 635 (1986).
13. *See* Chapter 14.
14. 553 N.E.2d 570 (N.Y. 1990).
15. 571 A.2d 696 (Conn. 1990).
16. For discussions of the *Savage* litigation, see Gilkerson, Poverty Law Narratives: The Critical Practice and Theory of Receiving and Translating Client Stories, 43 Hastings L.J. 861, 926–43 (1992); Slye, Community Institution Building: A Response to the Limits of Litigation in Addressing the Problem of Homelessness, 36

Vill. L. Rev. 1035, 1037–54 (1991); Solomon, The Clinical Experience: A Case Analysis, 22 Seton Hall L. Rev. 1250 (1992); Wizner, Homelessness: Advocacy and Social Policy, 45 Miami L. Rev. 387 (1991).

17. *See, e.g.,* McCain v. Koch, 511 N.E.2d 62 (N.Y. 1987) (establishing minimum standards for shelters housing families with children).

18. *See, e.g., Jiggets,* 553 N.E.2d at 570; Massachusetts Coalition for the Homeless v. Secretary of Human Servs., 511 N.E.2d 603 (Mass. 1987).

19. *See* Martin A. v. Gross, 546 N.Y.S.2d 75 (N.Y. App. Div. 1989), *appeal dismissed sub nom.* Consentino v. Perales, 551 N.E.2d 603 (N.Y. 1990).

20. For a critical view of the usefulness of litigation in solving the homelessness problem, see Slye, Community Institution Building, *supra* note 16, at 1037–54 (noting the failure of litigation to address long-term structural problems that cause homelessness). *Cf.* Roisman, Establishing a Right to Housing: An Advocate's Guide (parts I–III), 20 Housing L. Bull. 39 (1990) (discussing state and local laws creating a right to shelter); *id.* at 65 (discussing litigation involving state AFDC programs); *id.* at 107 (discussing assertion of right to housing under child welfare and foster care statutes). For a discussion of the use of child welfare laws to address the problem of homelessness, see Bussiere, Advocates for Homeless Families Look to Child Welfare System, Youth L. News, Sept.–Oct. 1989, at 1.

21. *See* Slye, Community Institution Building, *supra* note 16, at 1053–54.

22. *See* sources cited in Wizner, Homelessness, *supra* note 16, at 389 n. 15, 16; Slye, Community Institution Building, *supra* note 16, at 1046–48.

23. *See* P. Rossi, Down and Out in America: The Origins of Homelessness and Extreme Poverty 149 (1989).

24. *See* Chapter 14.

25. *See* Reynolds v. United States, 98 U.S. 145 (1878).

26. *See* Quilloin v. Walcott, 434 U.S. 246 (1978).

27. Stanley v. Illinois, 405 U.S. 645, 651–52 (1972). *See also* Smith v. Organization of Foster Families for Equality and Reform, 431 U.S. 816, 843–45 (1977); Lassiter v. Dep't of Social Servs., 452 U.S. 18, 27 (1981); Santosky v. Kramer, 455 U.S. 745, 753, 758–59 (1982).

28. See Chapter 14.

29. One commentator has noted that "[a] number of states allow a finding of neglect to be based upon the financial inability—not the unwillingness—of the parents to provide for the child." Note, Developments in the Law, *supra* note 8, at 1321. *See, e.g.,* Ill. Ann. Stat. ch. 37, para. 802–3 (Smith-Hurd 1990) ("Those who are neglected include . . . any minor under 18 years of age whose parent . . . does not provide the . . . care necessary for his or her well-being, including adequate food, clothing and shelter").

30. *See, e.g.,* Conn. Gen. Stat. Ann. § 46b-120 (West Supp. 1992) ("[A] child or youth may be found 'neglected' who . . . is being permitted to live under . . . circumstances . . . . injurious to his well-being, . . . a child or youth may be found 'uncared for' who is homeless"); N.C. Gen. Stat. § 7A-517(21) (1990) (defining a "[n]eglected juvenile" as one "who lives in an environment injurious to his welfare").

31. *See* Reynolds v. United States, 98 U.S. at 145.

32. *See Quilloin,* 434 U.S. at 236; *Lassiter,* 452 U.S. at 18; *Santosky,* 455 U.S. at 745.

33. *See* Shapiro v. Thompson, 394 U.S. 618 (1969).

34. *See, e.g.,* Milliken v. Bradley, 402 F. Supp. 1096 (E.D. Mich. 1975), *aff'd,* 433 U.S. 267 (1977).

35. *See* Sherbert v. Verner, 374 U.S. 398 (1963).

36. 397 U.S. 471 (1970) (holding that it is constitutional to provide the same amount of welfare benefits to small and large families).

37. 424 U.S. 577 (1976) (finding no constitutional obligation to provide minimum level of subsistence).

38. *See, e.g.* Roe v. Wade, 410 U.S. 113 (1973); Wisconsin v. Yoder, 406 U.S. 205 (1972); Griswold v. Connecticut, 381 U.S. 479 (1965); Pierce v. Society of Sisters, 268 U.S. 510 (1925); Meyer v. Nebraska, 262 U.S. 390 (1923).

39. *See, e.g., Shapiro,* 394 U.S. at 618; *Milliken,* 402 F. Supp. at 1096; *Sherbert,* 374 U.S. at 398.

40., Amar, Some Thoughts on Minimal Entitlements and the Thirteenth Amendment, 55 Alb. L. Rev. 643 (1992); Amar, Forty Acres and a Mule: A Republican Theory of Minimal Entitlements, 13 Harv. J.L. & Pub. Pol'y 37 (1990); Edelman, Mandated Minimum Income, Judge Posner, and the Destruction of the Rule of Law, 55 Alb. L. Rev. 633 (1992); Grey, Are Some Interests Obligatory? Relations to Entitlements and Unenumerated Rights, 55 Alb. L. Rev. 653 (1992).

■ PART III

Children and School

■ CHAPTER SEVENTEEN

A New Legal Duty for Urban Public Schools: Effective Education in Basic Skills

Gershon M. Ratner

FOR MANY YEARS, urban public schools nationwide have failed to provide effective education in basic skills to huge numbers of students, especially the poor and racial minorities. This widespread failure produces severe political, economic, social, and military costs, as well as profound injuries to the affected children. Despite these adverse effects, a thoughtful commentator argued in 1973 that schools could not be held legally responsible for inadequate education because no showing had been made that schools could effectively educate such students, let alone that effective schools shared common characteristics that ineffective schools might be required to adopt. If schools could not succeed, this commentator argued, it would be pointless and irrational to impose a legal duty to do so.[1]

Although this analysis was sound when it was offered, in this chapter I contend that more recent educational research now requires a recognition of the legal responsibility of public schools. In the last two decades, two critical findings have been widely accepted in the educational community. First, some urban schools serving large percentages of poor and minority students do successfully educate the vast majority of their students in basic skills. Second, effective schools share certain common educational characteristics. Further, these characteristics are peculiarly within the power of schools to create. Given the demonstrated capacity of schools to succeed, public policy no longer provides any justification for excusing their failure. Any school's adoption of the characteristics of success is likely to

Adapted from an article published originally in 63 Texas Law Review 777–864 (1985). Copyright 1985 by the Texas Law Review Association. Reprinted by permission.

result in significantly higher student achievement. The interests of society in success are too great to allow schools to refuse to institute these changes.

But public policy is not self-enforcing. For its requirements to be enforceable, they must be given the power of law. It is not sufficient to rely on public opinion to induce the necessary changes. The popular will is too fickle to be a reliable basis for major institutional reform. Nor is it sufficient to rely on public employees to institute the needed improvements voluntarily. Pressures of interest groups, fear of change, force of habit, and the natural reluctance to cede power conspire against what must be done.

The law can rise to this challenge. When old legal doctrines are applied to new facts, new legal duties often arise. A hundred years ago, for example, the duty to exercise reasonable care did not require doctors to prescribe antibiotics to patients suffering from serious bacterial infections, because antibiotics did not exist; today the duty has expanded, so that failure to offer such treatment normally would constitute clear negligence.

So it is here. What duties the principles of "thorough and efficient" education, due process, federal and state equal protection, and negligence impose on school districts must be determined in light of the contemporary state of educational knowledge. Although as recently as 1973 it would have been excusable for urban public schools to fail to educate one half or more of their students, because it was not known to be possible to do otherwise, it is no longer rational for schools to perform so poorly. It is my central task in this chapter to show that when existing sources of law are applied to these new facts, a new legal duty emerges: the duty to educate effectively. The duty requires every urban public school to educate the vast majority of its students in basic skills,[2] regardless of the proportions of poor and minority students, or at least to introduce into the school the proven characteristics of success.

The first part of this chapter establishes the factual premises on which the legal duty rests. These include the significance of the development of basic skills to the purposes of American public education, the injuries to individuals and to society from the schools' failure to ensure such education, and the magnitude of the current failure. I also describe the success some schools already achieve and the common characteristics of effective schools. Finally, I rebut some of the most common arguments against recognizing a duty to educate adequately in basic skills.

The second part elaborates on how the legal duty to educate derives independently from five legal sources: state constitutions, Fourteenth Amendment due process rights, federal and state equal protection clauses, and common law negligence doctrine. I then briefly describe how the duty can be enforced by courts.

The chapter concludes that when new factual developments are joined to existing legal doctrines, a new legal duty to educate is born. It remains for local school boards, administrators, and teachers in ineffective schools to incorporate the practices of effective schools. School parents, interested citizens, and the media should demand that schools make the necessary changes. Finally, the courts must be available to articulate and enforce the legal duty whenever voluntary improvement is not forthcoming.

Factual Premises

The Purposes of Public Education

The fundamental purpose of American public schools is to teach the basic skills of reading, writing, and arithmetic. The recognition that teaching basic skills is the central mission of the public schools dates at least to the beginning of the Republic: "Historically, the function of the public schools has been viewed as training in the three R's."[3] Recent case law suggests that this understanding of the key goal of the public schools has continued to this day. The major reasons for the historical emphasis on education in basic skills are beyond dispute. Such education is essential to preserve the political and economic foundations of our society. In addition, it has become a prerequisite to the nation's self-defense. To accomplish these purposes, schools must do more than provide teachers and classrooms; they must actually educate students.

Dimensions of the Problem

Grade Equivalents and Median Scores

Before examining the dimensions of urban school failure, it is important to understand both the measure of achievement—grade equivalents on standardized tests—and the inadequacy of the median or mean achievement figures that are commonly announced by the news media and have become the currency of public debate. Most school systems administer nationally standardized, norm-referenced tests to measure student achievement in basic skills.[4] Under these standards, a school system or a single school would be regarded as statistically average if half of its children were at or above the norm and the other half at or below it.[5]

Examining only these average achievement figures might lead one to believe that the children are being educated adequately if a system's or a school's mean or median scores equal or exceed the national norm, especially if the scores had previously been far below the norm. But mean or median scores are extremely misleading; they do not reflect how far the below-average performers were below the norm, or what percentage of those children were seriously below.[6] Thus, it is necessary to look beyond mean or median achievement and determine the percentage of students significantly below the norm and how far below they are.

Failure

For many years, urban[7] public schools[8] nationwide have failed to educate millions of their students adequately[9] in basic skills. The problem is dramatically illustrated by New York City's public school system, the country's largest.

In 1981, approximately one out of four New York City students in grades two through eight was at least one year below grade level in reading and mathematics. In some grades, one out of three students was at least one year below grade level; by seventh grade, one out of every two students was at least a year below grade level in mathematics. More ominously, significant percentages of students systemwide were two years or more below grade level: one out of five seventh and eighth grade students was two years or more below grade level in reading, and one out of three seventh grade students in math.[10] In absolute numbers, there were 106,000 students in grades two through eight who were one year or more below grade level in reading. Even more seriously, 42,000 of these students were two years or more below grade level.[11]

New York's failure is not unique. Examination of three school systems—those of New York, Houston, and Philadelphia—varying in size and in the racial, ethnic, and income composition of their student bodies, reveals four key features of inadequate education in basic skills in urban public schools. First, high percentages of students in many schools fall severely below grade level in basic skills. Second, as students advance from second to eighth grade, increasingly larger percentages fall farther and farther behind grade level. Third, disproportionately large percentages of these inadequately educated students are poor and racial/ethnic minorities, particularly black and Hispanic. Fourth, high rates of student failure are by no means distributed evenly throughout all schools in a system. Failure to educate sizable proportions of students is concentrated in particular, readily identifiable schools, generally ones serving large percentages of poor and minority children.[12]

Excuses for Failure and Counterarguments

How does society justify its continuing failure to educate millions of poor and minority children in basic skills? Four answers have been given. First, some argue that it cannot be done. Public schools cannot successfully teach poor and minority students basic skills because serious deficiencies in their home and family backgrounds or intelligence make them incapable of learning. This view is often expressed as: "The fault is not the schools'; it's the kids'." Second, even if individual schools are occasionally successful, there are no known characteristics of such schools that unsuccessful schools can adopt so as to become effective. Third, even if common characteristics exist, they are not replicable. Fourth, because poor children typically come from intellectually and socially deprived families, they require expensive additional school personnel for whom the federal, state, and local governments supposedly have failed to provide the funds.

The short answer to these proffered justifications for failure is that they are false. Effective education of the poor *is* possible. Successful schools *do* have important characteristics in common.[13] These characteristics *are* capable of being replicated. And success *is* affordable. The proof that public schools can educate the vast majority of their students in basic skills is that many have already done so. Enough public schools serving sizable populations of poor and minority students in enough different locations nationwide have successfully taught the vast majority of these students basic skills within existing budgets, and the evidence of common characteristics and replicability is so strong that the purported justifications for failure are no longer defensible.

Effective Schools

Although many urban schools serving predominantly poor and minority students fail to educate effectively, others succeed. Achievement data from New York, Houston, and Philadelphia demonstrate that in a number of schools serving a large proportion of poor (40–100 percent) and minority (10–100 percent) children, the vast majority of the students in each grade perform no more than one year below grade level in basic skills.

A national standard can be extracted from the remarkably similar success rates of the most effective New York, Houston, and Philadelphia schools serving large percentages of poor and minority students. No more than 20 percent of the students in any grade from two through six were one year or more below grade level in reading, mathematics, or composite basic skills, and no more than 10 percent were two or more years below. This 20/10 percent standard will serve throughout this chapter as the appropriate measure of effectiveness.

Thus, the first purported justification for society's failure to educate effectively the vast majority of students in urban elementary schools, including poor and minority children, is false. The claim that it cannot be done is refuted by the fact that it has been done.

Common Characteristics of Successful Schools

The second purported justification—the absence of common characteristics of successful schools—fares no better than the first. Since 1971, a substantial quantity of educational research has been undertaken to identify characteristics of urban public schools that successfully educate their students,[14] including poor and minority students, in basic skills.[15] Although scholars apply a variety of labels to the characteristics, attribute varying degrees of importance to each, and do not agree on every characteristic, they generally agree that five characteristics are commonly present among successful schools. Indeed, the five-part scheme developed by the late Ronald Edmonds of Michigan State University is "becoming the new catechism of urban school improvement."[16] Professor Edmonds identified the characteristics as follows:

> (1) the principal's leadership and attention to the quality of instruction; (2) a pervasive and broadly understood instructional focus; (3) an orderly, safe climate conducive to teaching and learning; (4) teacher behaviors that convey the expectation that all students are expected to obtain at least minimum mastery; and (5) the use of measures of pupil achievement as the basis for program evaluation.[17]

Instructional leadership includes setting "a tone of order and purpose for the school as a whole," "build[ing] commitment for specific academic goals," and guiding teachers toward achieving those goals.[18] Principals who exercise instructional leadership "spend most of their time out in the school—usually in the classrooms. They are constantly engaged in identifying and diagnosing instructional problems,"[19] and they suggest to teachers "alternative ways to teach that particular content."[20] A "broadly understood instructional focus" means that the principal and teachers agree that the chief mission of the school is to educate children in basic skills.[21] To exhibit an orderly, safe climate, the school must avoid tangible evidence of institutional neglect and must consistently enforce clear and generally accepted disciplinary standards. This requirement extends both to the physical plant, which must be well maintained, and to proper supervision of students. As Edmonds notes, "One of the reasons effective schools are relatively quiet is that all teachers take responsibility for all students, all the time, everywhere in the school."[22]

The fourth characteristic of effective schools—teacher behaviors that convey the expectation that all students will learn—appears to be the most significant of the five. School personnel's expectations "determine [the] . . . appropriateness and intensity of instruction" and thus directly affect the level of student achievement. The most seminal insight that Edmonds gained from his extensive study of effective and ineffective schools is that "poor and minority children *can* learn and *will* learn if adults believe in them."[23] Although teachers may convey their expectations by tone of voice, mode of discipline, or other means, Edmonds has emphasized the need for teachers to call on children randomly, without regard to race, social class, or sex. When teachers call disproportionately on the children who "they predict are most likely to know the answers" (generally white, middle-class children), the other "[c]hildren who sit in those classes day after day without being asked to participate eventually decide the teacher doesn't expect them to know as much."[24] They stop doing their homework, and the teacher's expectation of their failure becomes a self-fulfilling prophecy.

Finally, evaluating programs through measures of pupil achievement means that successful schools regularly administer standardized tests on basic skills, rely on the results as an indicator of whether students are being educated, and adjust instruction accordingly. Edmonds stresses that educators must inform the students and their parents accurately about the students' performance on these tests. Schools must stop saying that students are progressing satisfactorily when they are not; such misrepresentations only camouflage educational defects.

Judges, legislators, and administrators can rely on the effective schools research. The research findings are generally agreed upon in the academic community,[25] supported by common sense,[26] and have been implemented with success in a number of school districts.[27] Because the research has not determined the relative importance of the individual characteristics, however, it is essential that they be implemented together rather than piecemeal.

Schools' Power to Implement

The third supposed justification for failure, that it is beyond schools' power to institute the common characteristics of success, is no more valid than the first two. None of the five relevant characteristics is unattainable;[28] all are within school district control.[29] First, by carefully selecting, training, and, if necessary, replacing their principals, school districts can ensure that principals provide support and leadership to staff on instructional matters. Second, school administrators and teachers can clearly define the goals of their schools, giving priority to basic skills. Third, school personnel are uniquely able to establish and enforce clear and generally accepted disciplinary standards and procedures and to maintain property carefully. Fourth, schools, through hiring, training, rewarding, and disciplining teachers, can ensure that teachers convey to their students the expectation that all will master basic skills. Finally, the schools can easily administer standardized tests at regular intervals and adjust their instructional efforts in light of the results. Thus, given the nature of the five characteristics, the defense of inability to implement them is unavailing.

In fact, approximately 585 school districts nationwide have initiated school improvement programs implementing the effective schools research, including approximately 82 of 396 urban districts. Two of the oldest and most developed programs are in New York and Milwaukee.

Beginning in the fall of 1979, the school systems in both cities implemented the characteristics of success in participating schools. Both programs have produced substantial improvements in student achievement. In New York, during the course of three school years, the percentage of students reading two years or more below grade level was cut significantly in twenty-eight of the twenty-nine schools for which data are available, with reductions of more than 50 percent in approximately three-quarters of the schools. By spring of 1982, approximately two-thirds of the schools had 5 percent or fewer students two years or more below grade level, and in none of the remaining schools were more than 13 percent of the students that far below. The percentage of students reading from one to two years below grade level was also reduced in approximately five-sixths of the schools, with reductions of 25 to 70 percent in two-thirds of the twenty-nine schools. In Milwaukee, the percentage of third grade students who scored in the average or high-achievement category, as defined by the city, rose from approximately 57 to 80 percent in math, and from approximately 52 to 65 percent in reading in the course of two years. The percentage of fifth grade students who scored in the average or high-achievement category rose during the same period from approximately 40 to 75 percent in math and from 37 to 55 percent in reading.

The Cost of Success

The argument that successful education of poor children is unaffordable hinges on two factual premises: Success requires unusually high per pupil expenditures, and school districts cannot acquire the necessary additional funds. Neither premise of this fourth justification for failure can be sustained.

First, research studies contain "no evidence that school district or school or project expenditures are related to school outcome measures."[30] Although there is widespread scholarly agreement on the core common characteristics of successful urban schools, abnormally high funding is not even included in these characteristics, let alone recognized as a prerequisite to success.

Second, even if unusually high levels of funding were required for success, it has not been shown that the additional funding required is beyond the reach of urban school districts. The cost of supplementary personnel, staff training, and related programs in successful urban public schools "is dwarfed in most instances by traditional expenditures."[31] Further, school districts already receive substantial outside funding for the education of low-income students; through Title I of the Elementary and Secondary Education Act, the federal government provides more than $3 billion per year to school districts for that purpose. These considerations, in conjunction with the success at existing funding levels of many schools serving large percentages of poor and minority students in cities as diverse as New York, Houston, and Philadelphia, render the defense of insufficient funds meritless.

Arguments against Recognizing the Duty

Because society's interest in educating its children in basic skills is so strong, it is unlikely that anyone in our democracy would argue publicly that schools should intentionally deprive some students of this knowledge.[32] The crucial question, therefore, is not whether children *should* be effectively educated, but whether it is *possible* to do so. If it were not possible to educate the vast majority of students, the law could not reasonably impose a duty to do so. But if the task can be accomplished, absent some immense and overriding harm to the public, public policy demands that it must be. No such harm exists. Capacity requires performance.

Administrative Burden

Some school systems may argue that a duty to educate will impose an unbearable administrative burden on them. They will face the difficult task of changing some of their attitudes, methods, and personnel. Schools may have to change their instructional procedures so as to increase their expectations for student achievement, spend more classroom time emphasizing basic skills, and provide strict but fair discipline. They may have to incorporate success in teaching basic skills into criteria for hiring, training, rewarding, and disciplining principals and teachers. Finally, schools may have to improve maintenance of their physical plants.

These changes may be painful for school board members, administrators, and teachers, but the public as a whole has no legitimate interest in preventing such "harm." To the contrary, the public has an immense interest in seeing that such burdens are imposed. These changes must take place for the public schools to discharge their responsibility effectively.

Experimentation

Schools may argue that imposing a legal duty to educate children adequately in basic skills would stifle experimentation with new educational methods. This argument is invalid. Without a duty to educate effectively, the schools have been free to perpetuate ineffective attitudes and practices, refusing to change in the face of continuing failure. Recognition of a duty to educate, far from stifling experimentation, would encourage it by compelling changes in methods and attitudes.

Moreover, even if enforcement of the duty should reduce educational experimentation, there is no reason to think that the reduction would be important. Any harm it caused could not offset the public interests that favor recognizing the duty. The tail of experimentation cannot be allowed to wag the dog of effective education. Experimentation cannot come at the expense of denying adequate education, the goal it is supposed to serve.

Financial Liability

Schools may argue that the potential financial liability of school districts for breach of the duty to educate outweighs the interests favoring recognition. This argument fails because its basic premise—that the duty necessarily entails a damage remedy for its breach—is false: Recognition of the duty is not contingent upon allowing damages. The duty's principal purpose is to ensure that school administrators and teachers educate effectively. Although a damage remedy may be desirable both to compensate injured students and to deter continuation of ineffective practices, equitable remedies will be much more direct and efficacious in eliminating substandard education for the large class of deprived students. Moreover, equitable remedies do not pose any significant threat to the public treasury. Equitable remedies, without damages, will suffice to enforce the duty advocated in this chapter.

Whatever the source of the duty to educate effectively, legislatures or courts can ensure that its breach would yield only equitable remedies. Congress could limit remedies for violation of the federal equal protection and due process duties to declaratory judgments and injunctions rectifying inadequate education.[33] State legislatures could similarly restrict remedies for violation of state constitutional and common law duties, either by preserving sovereign immunity or by other means. Finally, state courts could limit the negligence cause of action to equitable remedies.

Inability to Program Implementation Precisely

Schools may argue that courts should not recognize the duty to educate effectively because implementation of the five characteristics of success cannot be precisely programmed in advance, requires exercise of judgment, and is difficult to accomplish. But the law does not shrink from imposing important duties merely because their accomplishment is difficult or requires the exercise of skill and judgment. Perhaps the most notable example is the Supreme Court's order that southern states desegregate their public schools with all deliberate speed. The law also requires state governments to provide welfare and Medicaid benefits with reasonable promptness, despite the extensive regulation, coordination of large staffs over hundreds of miles, and complex computerization that may be necessary.

Similarly, Congress has ordered all governments owning waste water treatment plants to reduce the discharge of pollutants from sewage and other sources to certain federally specified levels on a fixed time schedule, despite managerial and technological difficulties. Finally, the law compels local housing authorities to maintain public housing in compliance with state sanitary codes, although limited funds and rampant mismanagement may make this task difficult.

The principle that the law may impose difficult obligations without being able to prescribe implementation guidelines for each regulated activity has likewise been applied to the private sector. Congress ordered auto manufacturers to reduce the volume of toxic particles emitted from car exhausts even though it knew that the necessary technology was not then available. Similarly, industrial manufacturers are required to reduce the discharge of pollutants from their factories to federally established standards embodying the "best available technology economically achievable," even though this may demand imagination and impose heavy technological burdens on them, and industrial manufacturers have been ordered to reduce levels of hazardous air pollution. Thus, the mere fact that the steps for success cannot be precisely programmed in advance and success guaranteed in every instance is not a valid basis for refusing to recognize a duty.

Legal Sources of the Duty to Educate

The preceding discussion demonstrates that urban public schools can provide an effective education in basic skills to the vast majority of their students, including poor and minority students, and that public policy supports recognizing a duty to do so. The recent trend in the law and the views of commentators strongly reinforce this idea. Indeed, in recent decades, cases and statutes have already imposed on states the duty to educate adequately those students who are not English-speaking, are racially segregated, and are physically or mentally handicapped. Providing a duty to educate all children is merely a logical progression of the law. Likewise, numerous commentators have endorsed a legal duty to educate all students effectively, at least to the extent of requiring schools to exercise reasonable care. The remaining task is to show that application of prevailing constitutional and common law doctrines to the new facts about effective schools produces the new legal duty as a matter of law.

It has been widely noted that the Supreme Court has shifted the focus of constitutional adjudication of individual rights away from the Court's prior heavy dependence on federal law and federal courts toward greater reliance on state law and state courts. In so doing, the Court in effect encouraged state courts to read their own constitutions and laws to provide greater protections than those contained in the U.S. Constitution. The state courts have responded; indeed, the courts that have already found a general duty to educate effectively in basic skills have been state courts relying on state constitutions, rather than federal courts invoking federal law.

State Constitutional Education Provisions

Types of Provisions

The most direct sources of the duty to educate are state constitutions. Unlike the Federal Constitution, the constitutions of forty-eight of the fifty states provide explicit protection for education. The states created the public school systems and have plenary power over them. Indeed, as the Supreme Court has said, "Providing public schools ranks at the very apex of the function of a State."[34]

Specific education provisions generally fall into one of four basic groups. Provisions in the first group contain only general language and are exemplified by the Connecticut constitution: "There shall always be free public elementary and secondary schools in the state."[35] Provisions in the second group emphasize the quality of public education, as illustrated by the New Jersey constitution: "The Legislature shall provide for the maintenance and support of a thorough and efficient system of free public schools for the instruction of all the children in this State between the ages of five and eighteen years."[36] Provisions in the third group contain a stronger and more specific education mandate than those in the first and second groups. Typical is the Rhode Island constitution, which requires the legislature "to promote public schools and to adopt all means which they may deem necessary and proper to secure . . . the advantages . . . of education."[37] Provisions in the fourth group mandate the strongest commitment to education. This group is exemplified by the Washington constitution: "It is the paramount duty of the state to make ample provision for the education of all children residing within its borders."[38]

All four categories impose duties on the state to provide some form of public education. Even the weakest provision compels states to maintain free public schools. For example, the Connecticut constitution states, "There *shall* always be free public elementary and secondary schools in the state. The general assembly *shall* implement this principle by appropriate legislation."[39] The Washington Supreme Court, in construing the paramount duty clause of the Washington constitution, has stated that the provision "does not merely seek to broadly declare policy, explain goals, or designate objectives to be accomplished. It is declarative of a constitutionally imposed *duty*."[40]

Principles of Interpretation

Because it is clear that the states have a duty to provide education, the only significant question is what standards the state constitutions require public education to meet. The education provisions of state constitutions, like many important federal constitutional provisions, are extremely vague. Constitutional interpretation requires a court to put meat on the bare bones of the constitutional language.

In interpreting state constitutions and laws, the state supreme courts are the ultimate arbiters. Thus, the state courts are free to interpret these provisions as expansively as they see fit, as long as the interpretation does not contravene federal constitutional or statutory provisions. In light of the Court's deference to state laws, many commentators have called on state courts to protect individual rights more fully under state constitutions. The invitation has not fallen on deaf ears. In many areas of the law—criminal procedure, land use, and education financing, for example—state courts have found greater protection for individual rights under state constitutions than currently exists under the Federal Constitution.

There are compelling reasons for state courts to construe their constitutions expansively when considering whether to recognize a duty to educate in basic skills. Not only is the provision of public education probably the most important state function, but the particular educational interest at issue here—basic skills—goes to the heart of the states' educational responsibility. Although many state courts have properly given searching review to attacks on unequal school finance schemes brought under state constitutions, here there is even greater reason for close scrutiny. Increasing per pupil expenditures has no necessary connection to improving the quality of education. By contrast, recognition of the right to adequate education would directly improve the quality of education in basic skills, the most important objective of public education. Further, school finance challenges thrust the state courts into the difficult position of having to invalidate state statutes if they wish to vindicate plaintiffs' claims. Here the courts will have no such burden. State statutes pose no obstacle to recognizing the right to adequate education in basic skills; to the contrary, many statutes provide additional legal support for doing so. The state courts will merely be construing explicit language in their constitutions to clarify school officials' most basic educational obligations.

Finally, a reading of state constitutions that acknowledges the right to adequate education is supported by a vital principle of constitutional interpretation. A constitution must be interpreted in light of the importance to contemporary society of the interests seeking protection, not their importance at the time the particular provision was adopted. As the Supreme Court stated in construing the Fourteenth Amendment in *Brown v. Board of Education*,[41] "[W]e cannot turn the clock back to 1868 when the Amendment was adopted, or even to 1896 when *Plessy v. Ferguson* was written. We must consider public education in the light of its full development and its present place in American life throughout the Nation."[42]

Cases

We have identified four kinds of education provisions in state constitutions. Each one can and should be construed to require, at a minimum, that states provide an adequate education in basic skills. Indeed, that is how state supreme courts have interpreted provisions in two of the four categories. In *Pauley v. Kelly*,[43] a school finance case, the West Virginia Supreme Court interpreted a constitutional provision of the second kind, which required the legislature to provide a "thorough and efficient" system of schools. Indeed, the court held that the state constitution required the government to go far beyond effectively educating students in basic skills. It defined a "thorough and efficient" system as follows: "It develops, as best the state of education expertise allows, the minds, bodies and social morality of its charges to prepare them for useful and happy occupations, recreation and citizenship, and does so economically."[44]

The mandate to provide thorough and efficient education requires that schools take certain steps to ensure that knowledge and skills are effectively transmitted. As the *Pauley* court concluded, "Implicit[ly] [required by the constitutional provision] are supportive services: (1) good physical facilities, instructional materials and personnel; (2) careful state and local supervision to prevent waste and to monitor pupil, teacher and administrative competency."[45]

Pauley surpasses any reported decision in identifying the nature and content of public education mandated by a state constitution. The opinion recognizes many of the theses of this chapter. First, the court recognized that the meaning of the "thorough and efficient" clause was so vague that it was incumbent on the court to give it content. Second, the court interpreted the clause so as to effectuate its underlying purposes. Third, the court interpreted these purposes broadly in light of the contemporary role and importance of education. Fourth, the court established the duty to educate not principally in terms of providing input, such as physical facilities, materials, and personnel, but more critically in terms of output, requiring the state to educate every child in certain skills.[46]

In fact, the court established a more far-reaching output standard than is advocated here. Under *Pauley*, the state not only must ensure that all children are educated to a minimum level of adequacy, but also must ensure the "development in every child to his or her capacity."[47] Most importantly, the court recognized that schools cannot be allowed to close their eyes to the successful educational strategies used by other schools. Indeed, the court held that the schools must adopt the most effective educational practices known anywhere—that is, they must develop the students "as best the state of education expertise allows."[48] This is the most critical prong of *Pauley* because, as applied to the facts here, it directly requires ineffective schools to adopt the characteristics of success. Finally, the court recognized that education in basic skills is not sufficient by itself to constitute a thorough and efficient education. But it reaffirmed the central importance of effectively educating all children in basic skills by listing literacy and math skills first on the list of constitutionally required educational elements.[49]

In *Seattle School District No. 1 v. Washington*,[50] another school finance case, the Washington Supreme Court construed the state constitution's "paramount duty" provision.[51] The Washington court interpreted this category 4 clause essentially as *Pauley* interpreted West Virginia's category 2 clause. The court noted that "[t]he constitutional right to have the State 'make ample provision for the education of all [resident] children' would be hollow indeed if the possessor of the right could not compete adequately in our open political system, in the labor market, or in the marketplace of ideas."[52] Referring to the skills necessary for an individual to compete in these areas, the court concluded: "[W]e hold that . . . the effective teaching and opportunities for learning these essential skills make up the *mini-*

mum of the education that is constitutionally required."[53] Two aspects of this holding are noteworthy.

First, like the *Pauley* court, the Washington court defined the constitutional duty to educate exclusively in terms of accomplishing the aims of education: to enable individuals to participate adequately in our democratic political system, to hold jobs and be economically self-supporting, to think, and to debate ideas. The court refused to allow the state to satisfy its educational obligation merely by providing educational inputs, such as school facilities and teachers. Instead, the constitutional right to education demands that the state actually educate the student to such a level that the student can "compete adequately" in the specified undertakings. The school must provide not only teaching and an opportunity to learn, but "*effective* teaching and opportunities for learning."[54]

Second, although the court did not specifically articulate a duty to educate students in basic skills, the obligation to do so is implicit in its holding. The state cannot enable students to compete adequately in the political, economic, and intellectual spheres unless it has first adequately educated them in basic skills.

The approach used in *Pauley* and *Seattle* to interpret education provisions in categories 2 and 4 is equally applicable to provisions in categories 1 and 3. Indeed, while category 2 provisions typically require "thorough and efficient" education, those in category 3 normally add an extra mandate—either in clauses requiring states to use "all suitable means" to accomplish this objective,[55] or in preambles that stress the relationship between education and the exercise of basic rights[56] or make direct commitments to the equalization of educational opportunity.[57] These additional provisions make recognition of the duty even more compelling in category 3 clauses than in category 2 clauses.

Category 1 provisions, construed in light of their purpose, produce the same result. Their essence is that the state must "always [provide] free public elementary and secondary schools."[58] The same fundamental public policies that underlie the specific provisions of clauses in categories 2, 3, and 4 also underlie a more general constitutional mandate to provide free public schools. Absent evidence to the contrary, it must be assumed that free public schools have been constitutionally compelled so that students will receive at least the minimum education necessary to satisfy society's political and economic needs. Once this purpose is recognized, the analysis leading to the duty to provide effective education in basic skills flows exactly as in *Pauley* and *Seattle*.

In short, all four categories of provisions may legitimately be interpreted to establish a duty to educate effectively in basic skills. Although the language of the provisions is so vague that no single interpretation is mandated, compelling principles of constitutional interpretation and public policy require such a construction. This duty is not satisfied when 20 to 70 percent of the students in some grades are one year or more below grade level and 10 to 45 percent are two years or more below grade level in basic skills, and the schools refuse to adopt measures (the characteristics of success) that are likely to improve their students' education. Indeed, refusal runs directly afoul of the *Pauley* principle mandating adoption of the most effective educational practices known.

Fourteenth Amendment Due Process Claims

The fundamental premise underlying the due process claim[59] is that compulsory education deprives students of constitutionally protected liberties—freedom from physical confinement, freedom of association, freedom to travel, and the right to privacy. For such extensive governmental deprivations of personal liberty over a prolonged period to be rational, they must at least serve the basic purpose for which they were imposed: adequately educating children in basic skills.

Compulsory Education and Liberty

States began enacting compulsory school attendance laws in the second half of the nineteenth century; by 1918 such laws were in effect in all states. Few dispute that the states have a sufficiently important interest to justify compulsory attendance laws. Mastery of the basic skills by the members of society is essential to the political, economic, and military strength of the country.

But it must be remembered, however important compulsory school attendance laws are, that they are compulsory: They put the full power of the state, including criminal punishment, behind compelling students to spend approximately six hours a day, five days a week, thirty-six weeks a year, for ten to twelve years, in school buildings, subjected to numerous requirements imposed by teachers and administrators. State-mandated school attendance laws deprive students of their basic liberty interests in freedom of movement[60] and freedom of association.

The Requirements of Substantive Due Process

Substantive due process[61] requires that any state action that deprives a person of liberty or property must, at a minimum, be rational—that is, reasonably related to some legitimate governmental objective. Once the individual shows that the state has deprived him or her of a protected interest, the state has the burden of identifying the legitimate governmental objective that its conduct allegedly serves.

In *Jackson v. Indiana*,[62] the Supreme Court applied this general substantive due process doctrine to a criminal defendant who had been involuntarily and indefinitely committed to a state mental institution before trial, "solely on account of his incapacity to proceed to trial."[63] The Court held: "At the least, due process requires that the nature and duration of commitment bear some reasonable relation to the purpose for which the individual is committed."[64]

Under the *Jackson* principle, the nature of the education that students are provided must be rationally related to the purpose for which they are compelled to attend school. The fundamental purpose of state compulsory attendance laws is "to *insure the education* of all children."[65] The principal content of education is academic knowledge, of which basic skills are the heart. Under the *Jackson* principle, therefore, compulsory education is not reasonably related to its purposes unless schools provide adequate education in basic skills.[66] It is not rational for schools to educate so ineffectively that more than 20 percent of their students are one year or more below grade level in reading or mathematics and more than 10 percent are two years or more below, while refusing to adopt the characteristics of success.

Fourteenth Amendment Equal Protection Claims

The Supreme Court has articulated three tests for determining whether governmental conduct satisfies Fourteenth Amendment equal protection requirements.[67] The first test, frequently referred to as strict scrutiny, applies whenever the challenged discrimination intentionally impinges on a fundamental right or is based on a suspect classification. Strict scrutiny prohibits a difference in treatment unless it is necessary to achieve a compelling government interest. The second, or intermediate, test so far has been applied to differences in treatment based on gender, illegitimacy, and illegal alien status. The test prohibits a difference in treatment unless it is substantially related to achieving an important governmental interest. The least demanding test prohibits governmental discrimination unless the difference in treatment is rationally related to a legitimate state interest. The theme unifying the three tests is that "all persons similarly situated shall be treated alike."[68]

Under any of these tests, a school system's knowing failure to educate effectively a disproportionately large number of poor and minority students in some of its schools, while effectively educating similarly situated students in other schools, violates the equal protection clause unless the system adopts the characteristics of success.

Strict Scrutiny

The Supreme Court has held that plaintiffs seeking to invoke strict scrutiny on the basis of a suspect classification or interference with a fundamental right must prove that the government acted with discriminatory purpose. This requirement would have to be satisfied to warrant strict scrutiny of equal protection claims based on race, poverty,[69] or discrete and insular minority status.

The factors a court may consider in determining the existence of discriminatory purpose include: (1) the extent to which the action or inaction has a disparate impact on particular groups; (2) whether the disparate impact was known or foreseeable; (3) whether the agency had a legal duty to mitigate the impact; (4) whether the disparate impact was avoidable; (5) whether the agency took action to avoid the impact; and (6) whether the agency had legitimate nondiscriminatory reasons for its actions or inaction. Although there is no fixed minimum number or combination of elements a court must find to make a valid inference of discriminatory purpose, these six factors combined appear to be sufficient.

The class of inadequately educated poor and minority students should be able to prove at least a prima facie case of intent to discriminate on the basis of wealth or race on the part of any urban school district that continues to operate ineffective schools without instituting the characteristics of success. The plaintiff class can prove disparate impact by contrasting the high percentages of students below grade level in basic skills in some schools in a given district with the low percentages in other schools in the same district. They can show disparate impact on the basis of wealth by contrasting the high rates of failure in schools that have large populations of poor students with the low failure rates in schools serving predominantly middle-income students. To show that the disparate impact was known or foreseeable, plaintiffs can prove that the school district had been failing for years to educate effectively large numbers of students in certain schools, that the school officials knew that the average family income of students in these schools was low compared with the family incomes of students in schools in which most students succeeded, and that they knew that students in ineffective schools were disproportionately minority, while predominantly white schools were successful.

Plaintiffs can show that the district has continued the same educational practices that have failed in the past and that predictably will continue to fail, perpetuating inferior education. Plaintiffs can rely on state constitutional education provisions to establish that schools have a legal duty to educate all of their students. They can introduce the substantial research on the characteristics of effective schools to demonstrate the availability of another course of action that predictably would reduce or eliminate schools' disparate effectiveness, and they can show that the district has failed to institute some or all of the five characteristics. Finally, plaintiffs can prove that none of the potentially plausible justifications for failure to institute successful practices is valid.

A school district may try to defeat this threshold proof of discriminatory purpose by proving that its refusal to institute effective practices is based not on a desire to perpetuate inadequate education for poor or minority students, but, for example, on the fear of upsetting school staff and their unions. It may point to the existence of successful schools in the district with high percentages of poor and minority students as proof that it lacks discriminatory intent. The court will have to determine whether the district's explanation is sufficiently persuasive to rebut the plaintiff's prima facie case of purposeful discrimination on the basis of a suspect classification. If a court finds purposeful discrimination on this basis, it will apply strict scrutiny to the equal protection claim.

Inadequate education has been shown to affect adversely a suspect class (low-income students) and a suspect subclass (low-income minority students). Accordingly, the challenged educational practices can be sustained only if necessary to achieve a compelling state interest. Few, if any, school districts could prove that their failure to educate effectively the vast majority of students in some schools while successfully educating the vast majority of students in others serves a compelling state purpose. Neither avoiding administrative burdens nor saving money constitutes such a purpose. Nor can hostility to poor or minority children or a desire to reduce social or economic competition justify discrimination against these students.

The only obviously compelling justification for the discrimination is impossibility. If a school district proves that it has done everything within its power to educate the vast majority of students in all its schools but has failed for reasons beyond its control, the failure should not violate equal protection even under strict scrutiny. To establish this defense, however, the district must prove that it has already implemented the five characteristics of successful schools and has failed to provide effective education nonetheless.[70]

Even if some compelling interest other than impossibility can be established, the discrimination will still fail under strict scrutiny unless the current high rate of student failure is the least drastic means available to accomplish the interest. It is virtually inconceivable that a district will be able to prove that it has tailored its educational practices to minimize student failure unless it has already adopted the characteristics of success.

Intermediate Test

Even if strict scrutiny were not applied, the Supreme Court's decision in *Plyler v. Doe*[71] supports review under the intermediate test. The plaintiffs in *Plyler* were alien school-age children who had been brought into the United States illegally by their parents. Plaintiffs challenged a Texas statute[72] that denied the local school districts state educational aid for children of illegal aliens while providing such aid for children of citizens and legal resident aliens. The children also challenged a local school district rule that required illegal alien children, but not others, to pay tuition of $1,000 per year.[73] Because the plaintiff children were too poor to pay tuition, the challenged policies in effect deprived them entirely of a public education.[74]

In determining the equal protection standard to apply, the Court determined that strict scrutiny was not appropriate because education generally is not a fundamental right,[75] and "[u]ndocumented aliens cannot be treated as a suspect class because their presence in this country in violation of federal law is not a 'constitutional irrelevancy.'"[76] Rather, the Court held that the discriminatory denial of state-subsidized public education must be judged by the intermediate standard of review;[77] the defendants must show that the discriminatory policies furthered a substantial government interest.[78]

The *Plyler* Court appeared to rest its decision to apply an intermediate, rather than rational basis, test on at least three factors. First, the plaintiff class was discriminated against because of a disabling status over which its members had no control;[79] they were in the country illegally because of their parents' conduct, which they were powerless to affect. Such a class is entitled to special solicitude under the equal protection clause because "legislation directing the onus of a parent's misconduct against his children does not comport with fundamental conceptions of justice."[80] Second, the challenged discrimination would produce extremely severe and longlasting injuries to the members of the plaintiff class.[81] Finally, the discrimination resulted in profound "costs to the Nation."[82] By denying the plaintiff class an education, the discrimination precluded the plaintiffs from developing essential intellectual, political, cultural, and social skills, depriving the country of the contributions they could make "to the progress of our

Nation."[83] These factors apply with equal strength to the class of inadequately educated poor and minority students.

The Court rejected each of the defendants' proffered justifications for their exclusionary policy. Two of those justifications are particularly pertinent here. First, the Court gave little weight to the defendants' interest in saving school funds to provide a better education for citizens and legal aliens, because the record did not establish that exclusion of alien children was "likely to improve the overall quality of education in the State."[84] Moreover, because the illegal alien children have the same "educational cost and need"[85] for education as legal alien children, saving funds by itself was not a legitimate basis for distinguishing between members of a group who were otherwise similarly situated.

Second, the Court rejected the contention that there was a substantial basis for the discrimination because illegal aliens are less likely than citizens or legal aliens "to put their education to productive social or political use within the State."[86] This argument failed both because there was no record to support it and because of a cost-benefit assessment: "[W]hatever savings might be achieved by denying these children an education, they are wholly insubstantial in light of the costs involved to these children, the State, and the Nation."[87]

Because the defendants' justifications could not withstand intermediate scrutiny, the Court invalidated both the state's refusal to fund the education of illegal aliens and the locality's failure to provide them free education. *Plyler* strongly supports the claim developed here in three critical respects. First, the Supreme Court held that provision of public education to some children, while denying it to others similarly situated as to educational need and cost, violates equal protection in at least one context.[88] Second, the Court invalidated this discriminatory denial of education even without applying strict scrutiny. Finally, the opinion strongly implies that, because of the critical importance of basic education to our political, economic, cultural, and social institutions, and because of the serious injuries to individuals and society from illiteracy, all discriminatory denials of adequate education should be scrutinized under a stricter standard than the rational basis test.

The discriminatory denial of adequate education in basic skills to students in different schools within the same district can no more be sustained under the intermediate test than could the denial of free public education to illegal alien children in *Plyler*. Once the plaintiffs establish a prima facie case of disparate treatment, the defendant school officials bear the burden of proving both that the unequal treatment in fact furthers the particular government interests claimed and that these interests are substantial. Under *Plyler*, the interest in saving money and analogous administrative interests are not substantial justification for discrimination.

Rational Basis Test

Finally, the discriminatory denial of adequate education in basic skills to poor children cannot withstand an equal protection challenge even under the rational basis test. To survive that scrutiny, the state must show that its "distinction . . .

rationally furthers a legitimate state purpose."[89] A school district cannot show that a legitimate state purpose is furthered by denying adequate education to large percentages of poor and minority children in some schools while providing it to the vast majority of students in other schools. As the Supreme Court stated in *Plyler*, there is a "presumption that denial of education to innocent children is not a rational response to legitimate state concerns."[90] It is no more rational to deprive children in some schools of an adequate education while providing it to children in other schools than it is to deprive some children of free education entirely. Insofar as there is a meaningful difference between the two situations, it is in the severity of the injury, not the rationality of the deprivation.

School districts might offer at least four purportedly rational justifications for their failure. First, they might assert their interest in conserving resources. But discriminatory denial of adequate education does not further any legitimate interest in saving funds. As *Plyler* held, "[A] concern for the preservation of resources standing alone can hardly justify the classification used in allocating those resources. . . . The State must do more than justify its classification with a concise expression of an intention to discriminate."[91] Thus, although saving money is a valid state objective, a desire to save money is not, by itself, a legitimate basis for discriminating between persons who are similarly situated in pertinent respects. For discrimination to be permissible, the state must identify a relevant distinguishing characteristic of the class against which it discriminates; this school districts cannot do. In any case, the discrimination here does not serve the school districts' interest in saving funds. Effective education is not dependent on higher expenditures. It is no more costly to operate schools with the five characteristics than without them. Thus, even if inadequately educated children were situated differently than other children with respect to their need for, or ability to acquire, basic skills, the discrimination could not be justified as furthering a state interest in saving money.

Second, a school district might invoke its interest in preserving administrative stability. A district might argue that it has a legitimate interest in allowing educational disparities to continue in order to avoid the potential opposition of unions and staff and the burden of implementing major changes in personnel, curriculum, attitudes, facility maintenance, or other aspects of operations. But this interest is no more a legitimate basis for discriminatorily denying benefits to certain persons than is the interest in saving government funds. Neither the level of government expenditures nor the form of government administration is an end in itself; both are merely means to discharge certain legal obligations that the citizens have imposed. A state may have a legitimate interest in preserving its established methods of administration, as admittedly it has a valid interest in preserving its funds. But that interest alone cannot justify denying to some individuals governmental benefits that are provided to others similarly situated.[92]

Third, school districts might argue that the discriminatory denial of adequate education is rationally related to their interest in preserving local autonomy, an interest recognized in *San Antonio Independent School District v. Rodriguez*.[93] But unlike *Rodriguez*, the claim here does not challenge a state's interest in permitting separate localities to set different expenditure levels. Rather, the adequate education claim challenges only each locality's failure to educate its own students. A locality's interest in operating its own schools is no more a legitimate basis for discriminating among similarly situated students than is its interest in saving money or avoiding administrative burdens.

Finally, school districts might argue that their interest in educational experimentation justifies the discrimination. But perpetuation of attitudes and behaviors that have failed in the past does not constitute experimentation. Moreover, the state has no legitimate interest in experimentation that inflicts profound injuries on large numbers of students.

In short, the knowing discriminatory denial of adequate education to students in certain schools has no rational basis. Perpetuating low expectations, inattention to basic skills, weak instructional leadership, and other failings cannot be justified, particularly when some schools in a district educate effectively all but 5 to 10 percent of their students while others fail to educate 50 to 60 percent or more. Unless a district can prove that it has continued to fail despite instituting the characteristics of success, or that it was impossible to implement these characteristics, the discrimination must fail under the rational basis test.

State Constitutional Equal Protection Provisions

As strong as the arguments may be that discriminatory denial of adequate education violates federal equal protection rights, arguments founded on the counterpart state clauses are even stronger. The state interest in effectively educating the vast majority of students is even more compelling than the federal interest, and, under Supreme Court principles, it is extremely important for state courts to protect state constitutional rights.

State equal protection analysis begins with the recognition of two basic facts. First, almost every state constitution contains a provision similar to the federal equal protection clause.[94] Second, state courts are empowered to construe their own equal protection provisions independently of the Supreme Court's construction of the federal clause.

In interpreting state equal protection clauses, most state courts have chosen to apply the same rational basis and strict scrutiny tests that the Supreme Court applies when interpreting the federal clause. The states generally have adopted the federal criteria of fundamental right and suspect classification as the basis for strict scrutiny. But application of those criteria to state constitutions leads to even more expansive protection of the right to effective education, because that right is a fundamental right under many state constitutions, even though it is not fundamental under the Federal Constitution.

Criteria for Assessing Fundamentality

Explicit or implicit guarantee in state constitutions. Some state courts apply the federal "explicitly or implicitly guaranteed by the Constitution" test for determining what rights are fundamental under the respective state's constitution.[95] When state courts apply this test to education, however, they usually reach a result opposite from the federal courts. The reason for the difference is simple: Although the federal constitution does not explicitly protect education, virtually all state constitutions do. Under this test, therefore, education is a fundamental right under state equal protection clauses.[96]

Nonfederal criteria. Other states have chosen not to rely exclusively on the federal test for fundamentality and have identified at least two additional tests: the overall importance of the right to the state, and the nexus between the right and other constitutional rights.

State courts have recognized that education is a right of extreme importance to the states. In *Horton v. Meskill*,[97] the Connecticut Supreme Court focused on three factors in addition to the explicit protection of education in the Connecticut constitution: the lengthy history of the state's interest in education, education's regulation by state statute, and its compulsoriness. All these factors, the court held, supported the court's conclusion that in Connecticut any infringement of the right to education must be strictly scrutinized.

In *Serrano v. Priest (Serrano I)*,[98] the California Supreme Court relied on five factors in considering the fundamentality of education: the large number of persons affected by it, the long period of time it directly affects residents, the significance of its effect on residents, its critical importance to economic prosperity and social stability, and its mandatoriness. Based on these measures of importance, the court concluded, "We are convinced that the distinctive and priceless function of education in our society warrants, indeed compels, our treating it as a 'fundamental interest' [under the California constitution]."[99]

State courts are free, of course, to consider factors other than those relied upon in *Horton* and *Serrano I*. Regardless of the factors considered or the weight given them, the result of the judicial calculus seems inescapable. What the Supreme Court noted almost forty years ago remains equally true now: "Today, education is perhaps the most important function of state and local governments."[100] Under the overall importance test, therefore, education must be regarded as fundamental.[101]

The second nonfederal criterion state courts have applied for assessing fundamentality involves the nexus to other constitutionally protected rights. Indeed, this was a major criterion for the California Supreme Court in *Serrano I*:

> The analogy between education and voting is . . . direct: both are crucial to participation in, and the functioning of, a democracy. Voting has been regarded as a fundamental right because it is 'preservative of other basic civil and political rights[.]' . . . At a minimum, education makes more meaningful the casting of a ballot. More significantly, it is likely to provide the

understanding of, and the interest in, public issues which are the spur to involvement in other civic and political activities.[102]

The nexus approach to fundamentality gains additional support from the U.S. Supreme Court's decision in *San Antonio Independent School District v. Rodriguez.* The plaintiffs argued that education should be regarded as a fundamental right implicitly protected by the Federal Constitution because it is a prerequisite to meaningful discharge of First Amendment rights and the right to vote. The Court rejected the notion that the entire field of education is implicitly protected by the Federal Constitution, relying on its prior holdings that neither welfare nor housing enjoys such protection.[103]

Significantly, however, the Court left open the possibility that the Constitution protects students' narrow interest in an adequate education in basic skills. The Court said, "Even if it were conceded that some identifiable quantum of education is a constitutionally protected prerequisite to the meaningful exercise of either [free speech or voting rights], we have no indication that the present levels of educational expenditures in Texas provide an education that falls short."[104]

Several commentators have read the Court's hypothetical concession to indicate that a minimum education is a fundamental interest. Although the Court's decision in *Plyler v. Doe* appears to foreclose this possibility under the Federal Constitution, the *Rodriguez* formulation of the issue suggests compelling reasons for recognizing such a right under state constitutions. The rights freely to express views in political matters and to vote in governmental elections are central to a democracy. An adequate education in basic skills is crucial to a citizen's ability to exercise these rights meaningfully.

In short, regardless of which criterion is applied—explicit or implicit guarantee in the constitution, overall importance to the state, or nexus to other constitutionally protected rights—the result should be the same. Under state equal protection clauses, education should be regarded as a fundamental right.

Application of Strict Scrutiny

Having established that education is a fundamental right, the remainder of the state equal protection analysis parallels that of federal equal protection. Because education is a fundamental right, most state courts should apply strict scrutiny to alleged discriminations. Moreover, because the class of low-income students and the subclass of low-income minority students are suspect classes, state courts should subject discrimination to strict scrutiny whether or not education is regarded as a fundamental right. The denial of adequate education to large percentages of students in some schools while providing it to the vast majority of students in other schools and refusing to adopt the characteristics of success serves no compelling government interest; therefore, it is unconstitutional under strict scrutiny. Even if the challenged discrimination were not entitled to strict scrutiny under state equal protection clauses, it would still fail under the intermediate test because it is not substantially related to an important government interest and under the rational basis test because it is not rationally related to a legitimate state interest.

Common Law Negligence: Educational Malpractice

The legitimate power of the judiciary to create new law approaches its zenith in determining whether any particular conduct constitutes negligence. Negligence means a breach of a noncontractual legal duty to exercise reasonable care.[105] In deciding whether any class of individuals should owe a legally enforceable duty of care to another, the taproot must be public policy. The state appellate courts that have considered whether to recognize a tort for educational negligence or malpractice have acknowledged that the decision must be based on policy considerations.[106]

When public policy favors recognizing a new common law tort duty, it is the courts' role to respond favorably. The common law is characterized by its ability to impose new legal responsibilities when warranted by changing social conditions and values. As the Supreme Court found in *Hurtado v. California*, "[F]lexibility and capacity for growth is the peculiar boast and excellence of the common law."[107] If public policy factors favor recognition of a duty to educate adequately in basic skills, the new duty must be recognized.

Public Policy

Favorable policies. Strong public policies favor recognizing that teachers and school administrators have a duty to exercise reasonable care in educating students in basic skills. The factual foundation for the duty has already been laid. Effective education in basic skills is essential to the political, economic, and military well-being of society and to the welfare of its individual members. Withholding education causes severe economic, psychological, and political injuries to the deprived students. Schools can educate the vast majority of their students effectively, yet many schools fail to do so.

Given these considerations, recognition of the tort would serve public policy in several respects. First, it would deter negligent teaching and hiring and encourage school systems "to take appropriate steps to insure at least basic intellectual development."[108] Second, recognition would subject educators to the same duty of care that other professionals and skilled craftsmen must already assume. No valid basis exists for excluding educators from legal standards of care to which other professionals have long been held. Finally, imposition of the duty is necessary to eliminate another anomaly in the law. Educators are liable for their negligence when it results in physical injury to their students, but are immune when they fail to exercise reasonable care in discharging their central educational responsibility: teaching basic skills. If this distinction made sense in the past, when the severity of educational injuries may not have been recognized or when it might legitimately have been assumed that failing to learn was the student's fault, it is no longer valid.

Counterarguments. Three principal public policy arguments have been invoked against recognizing educational malpractice as a tort: It would cost too much in damages, produce a flood of litigation, and improperly interfere with school board discretion. These arguments are without merit. First, because the duty described here contemplates only equitable remedies, the cost of damages is not a valid ground for opposing the duty.

In refusing to recognize a tort duty to educate effectively, the court in *Peter W. v. San Francisco Unified School District*[109] expressed fear that such a duty would produce a flood of litigation. But this concern too is premised on the availability of damages. Once the damage remedy is removed, there is no greater risk of a flood of litigation under this theory than under any of the other legal theories.

Finally, in *Donohue v. Copiague Union Free School District*,[110] the New York Court of Appeals refused to recognize a claim for educational malpractice, stating that it would constitute unwarranted judicial intrusion on the administrative responsibilities of school officials. But the court's concern is misplaced. It is immaterial that the tort necessarily will involve judicial review of conduct by school administrative agencies with whom state law lodges responsibility for administering the schools. All governmental functions are entrusted by constitution or statute to some governmental agency. Whenever the judiciary reviews government action, it reviews the action of an agency. School agencies are not and should not be immune. To the contrary, courts already review many aspects of school administration, including desegregation, finance, curriculum, personnel practices, and discipline.

Further, any concern with intruding on the schools' discretion is mitigated by the fact that the courts would not be reviewing the administration of schools that adequately educate the vast majority of their students. The courts will intervene in school operations only where the administrative system has broken down to such an extent that it has seriously injured many students. Moreover, schools can minimize judicial involvement by framing the remedies in large part themselves through proposed remedial plans. Thus, judicial reluctance to review school administrators' inadequate discharge of their most basic function is not a substantial justification for refusing to recognize the tort.

Common Law Criteria

For a claim to satisfy the traditional requirements of common law negligence, it must be possible to define a duty of care, establish what conduct constitutes breach of the duty, prove that the breach proximately caused an injury, and show that the injury is of a type traditionally compensable by tort law. The tort duty described here satisfies all of these elements.

Duty of care. Traditional negligence law provides an appropriate definition of an educator's duty of care: to use the care that a reasonable and prudent educator would use under similar circumstances. Because the jobs of schoolteacher and administrator call for special skills and knowledge, under basic negligence principles the reasonable educator will be expected "to possess a standard minimum of special knowledge and ability."[111] As suggested in *Donohue*, the duty of care for educators will be essentially the same as that already applied to doctors, lawyers, accountants, and other professionals.[112] The central mandate of the overall reasonable care requirement for the purposes of the duty discussed here is the duty to make use of known and available alternative approaches when it is plain that existing practices are unsuccessful.

This duty is already well established in the law of negligence. When a school fails to educate a large percentage of students in basic skills, reasonable care requires it to adopt alternative, proven methods of instruction. In no sense is refusal to adopt them under these circumstances supported by "commonsense notions of reasonableness."[113]

Breach of duty. Breach of the duty of care may be shown by establishing that defendants have failed to use known and available educational alternatives in an effort to rectify known educational failings. Plaintiffs will show that the defendant school system is unsuccessful in educating students in one or more specified schools. Plaintiffs will prove that there are widely known and available educational practices—the five characteristics of success—that exemplify effective schools and that, if adopted, are likely to lead to significant improvement. Plaintiffs will establish breach by showing that the defendant system has failed to adopt the effective practices.

Causation. Causation will be defined and proven as in any other negligence action. The school's conduct would be the cause of the students' inadequate learning if it was a material element and a substantial factor in bringing it about.

The cumulative proof leading to an inference of causation may be made as follows. First, plaintiff students will establish that the school system regards them as educable. Had the system not thought so, it would have identified the plaintiffs as students with special educational needs (e.g., as mentally retarded) and educated them accordingly.[114] Second, plaintiffs will show, by their scores on tests administered by defendants, that the relevant class of students in their schools is not being adequately educated in basic skills. Third, they will show that other schools are successful in educating groups of students with comparable economic and racial characteristics. Fourth, they will introduce research findings that effective schools typically share the five characteristics of success. Fifth, plaintiffs will show that the defendants have failed to adopt those five characteristics. Finally, plaintiffs will prove that if their schools had developed the characteristics of success, the students' achievement would likely have been greater than it was.

These facts will establish a prima facie case that defendants' failure to employ appropriate educational methods was a substantial factor in the students' failure to learn. The burden will shift to the school district to rebut this showing. A school may rebut causation in at least two ways. First, it might prove that some characteristics of the plaintiff class so distinguish it from apparently comparable groups of students that it is not reasonable to infer that plaintiffs can be educated adequately. Second, a school might prove that certain characteristics of successful schools or their localities make it unreasonable to assume that approaches successful there will work in the defendant system. Given the basic similarity of low-income and minority students as a group nationwide, the large number of successful schools in varying geographic and political environments, and the broad range of economic and racial mixes of students in those schools, it is unlikely that defendants would be able to overcome plaintiffs' prima facie proof of causation.

Once the plaintiff class has shown that the defendants' conduct was in fact a cause of their injury, the question of whether the conduct is a proximate cause of the injury is essentially a question of law and public policy, not of fact. Compelling public policies support recognition of liability here. Even if the requirement that liability be limited to foreseeable risks were applied as part of proximate cause, rather than in initially defining the scope of the duty, the result remains the same. It is plainly foreseeable that if a school persists in the same kinds of educational behavior that have failed in the past, it will cause the very educational injuries of which the plaintiffs complain. In this situation, the school's misfeasance and nonfeasance are both a cause-in-fact and a proximate cause of plaintiffs' injuries.

Injury. Students who are negligently deprived of an adequate education in basic skills suffer economic and psychological injury, both of which are traditionally cognizable in tort. Economically, their functional illiteracy will cause them disproportionate unemployment or underemployment, with a corresponding loss of income. Psychologically, defendants' conduct causes mental distress, humiliation, and pain and suffering. These injuries, which would be sufficient for a damage award, support injunctive relief as well.

Judicial Enforcement

For an obligation to be judicially enforceable, it must be possible to define the duty, prove breach, and provide an appropriate judicial remedy. The duty arising from the legal theories discussed above satisfies all three criteria. First, the duty is easily defined. Based on the levels of success achieved in New York, Houston, and Philadelphia, no school should allow more than 20 percent of its students in any grade from two through six to fall one year or more below grade level, or more than 10 percent of its students to fall two years or more below grade level, in reading, mathematics, or composite basic skills.[115] If a school fails to satisfy this standard, it must adopt the characteristics of success.

Whether a school has committed a prima facie breach of this duty can be proven by determining the percentages of students in each grade who perform at the requisite levels on standardized tests the school already administers. If the school does not satisfy the achievement standard, the plaintiff can establish prima facie breach by showing that the school has not adopted the characteristics of success. A school's argument that it was impossible to adopt them creates an issue of fact susceptible to traditional forms of proof. Both defendants and plaintiffs can rely not only on local school personnel but also on other expert witnesses.

The courts must assess the evidence and determine the facts as they do in every other case of disputed facts. As Merle McClung notes, "The objection that evaluation of the adequacy of education is beyond the expertise of courts is not convincing because 'courts are routinely called upon to evaluate conflicting expert opinions and to resolve technical controversies in areas outside judicial expertise.'"[116]

A court can order a defendant found in violation to prepare and submit a plan indicating the kinds of educational changes it proposes. This practice has become common in school desegregation cases. Similarly, as in both desegregation and mental health cases, the court can draw on experts, including administrators and teachers from successful schools and scholars who have studied those schools, to gain insight into the reasonableness of the defendant's plan. If necessary, a court has inherent power to appoint experts to assist it in developing its own plan. Normally, it should not be necessary for a court to enter detailed orders regulating implementation of the court-ordered plan. Responsibility and concomitant discretion in achieving compliance should presumptively remain with the schools. As in any case involving institutional reform, devising effective orders to change organizational behavior in specified ways poses definite problems. But courts have successfully ordered the improvement of care in state mental hospitals and the desegregation of schools; they are equally capable of enforcing the duty involved here.

Conclusion

This chapter applies traditional tools of legal analysis to new facts; effective public schools exist and share important common characteristics within school districts' control that, if adopted by ineffective schools, are likely to lead to improvement in students' acquisition of basic skills. It shows that each of five established sources of law, when applied to these facts, produces a new legal duty to educate effectively. The duty requires every urban public school to educate the vast majority of its students, regardless of race or income, to the national standards of adequacy already achieved by many schools, or else to adopt the five common characteristics of effective schools.[117] The practical question becomes: What must be done now to implement the duty?

The greatest need is to galvanize the will of society toward this objective. People must not only come to believe in the possibility of success but commit themselves to its achievement. The widespread assumption that the failure of poor and minority students in urban public schools is inevitable must be overcome. From governors to local school officials, from state and federal education officials to civic leaders, from businesses to teachers' unions, from the media to the President—the message that must go out across the country and be institutionalized in the schools is that from now on poor and minority urban elementary school students are expected to succeed.

Furthermore, every urban public school system needs to review and publish regularly its most recent student achievement data on reading and mathematics for each elementary school. Each system must report separately the percentages of students in each grade who are one year or more and two years or more below grade level in either subject.[118] Any urban public school in which more than 20 percent of the students in any grade are one year or more below grade, or more than 10 percent are two years or more below grade, in reading or mathematics, is prima facie in violation of the school district's legal duty to educate effectively. Schools with that many students so far behind must be examined further.

School districts must determine whether each school presumptively in violation has adopted the five characteristics of success. This assessment can be accomplished through a systematic, formal evaluation using research instruments developed for this purpose.

Every school that has not incorporated each element of success needs to develop a plan to do so. Schools should develop their plans with the maximum participation of teachers, both to make each plan reflect the school's strengths as well as problems and to maximize teachers' commitment to the plan's success. The plans should focus on matters over which the local schools have control and should provide, to the extent possible, modest additional funding for administrative implementation, including staff support and training. If implementation substantially increases students' performance, the plans should be followed; if not, both the plans and their implementation should be reanalyzed. If individual principals or teachers are, after appropriate counseling and training, unwilling or unable to implement the characteristics, they must be replaced. School districts must make appropriate changes to ensure that children achieve at the requisite level unless they can show that they have implemented the characteristics of success for a substantial period of time and are still failing.

If repeated efforts by organizations, businesses, politicians, the media, parents, and other interested persons fail to persuade certain schools to adopt the characteristics of success, the courts may be invoked, but only as a last resort. Major class action litigation is time-consuming and expensive. In addition, because plaintiffs will be asking the courts to recognize new legal duties, the chances of success are unpredictable. By comparison, voluntary cooperation by school districts and individual school personnel, if attainable, is likely to produce faster and more certain educational improvements. Thus, local groups should use the legal duty to increase their bargaining power in negotiating institutional reform.

The first cases will inevitably become critical precedents. It is imperative, therefore, that the earliest lawsuits be brought only in circumstances in which the students are likely to win. Suits should be limited to situations in which: (1) very high percentages of the students are severely below grade level (e.g., 50 to 70 percent one year or more below grade level, and 30 to 45 percent two or more below); (2) the schools have dramatically failed to adopt the characteristics of success; (3) plaintiffs have made diligent efforts to persuade the school district to adopt them, including a full presentation of the research findings on effective schools; and (4) the school district has refused to change its operations.

Finally, plaintiffs must select the best forum. The most positive judicial developments in this area so far have been under state constitutional law. Early cases, therefore, should be brought in state courts invoking such laws, preferably in jurisdictions already shown to be sympathetic to similar claims. Federal claims in federal courts and negligence claims in state courts should await later development.

What is asked from the courts is simply that they be open to new facts, apply the law fairly to those facts in light of contemporary public policy, and not shrink from the legal and remedial consequences. This is an instance in which, as Justice Brandeis observed, "[I]f we would guide by the light of reason, we must let our minds be bold."[119] It remains for the public to demand implementation of the duty, the schools to undertake it, and the courts to enforce it.

NOTES

1. Yudof, Equal Educational Opportunity and the Courts, 51 Tex. L. Rev. 411, 418, 422, 430 (1973).

2. This chapter focuses only on the approximately 90 percent of all public school children who are not so physically, intellectually, or emotionally handicapped as to require special education. Future references to the "plaintiff class" and "all children" refer only to this nonhandicapped class.

3. Kirp et al., Legal Reform of Special Education: Empirical Studies and Procedural Proposals, 62 Cal. L. Rev. 40, 48 (1974); McClung, Do Handicapped Children Have a Legal Right to a Minimally Adequate Education? 3 J.L. & Educ. 153, 156 (1974).

4. Standardized tests are used here as the basis for measuring student achievement in basic skills because they are designed for that purpose, are reasonably reliable, are widely administered in public schools nationwide, and provide a uniform and objective standard for comparing the achievement of students in different schools. They are used because they are the only available measures that meet these criteria, not because they are perceived as perfect.

5. Because the norm for each grade level on any particular test merely represents a fixed number of correct answers, there is no inherent reason why 75 or 100 percent of the students taking the test could not score at or above the norm.

6. Thus, a school's mean achievement will be at or above the norm as long as 50 percent of its students achieve at or above grade level; the other 50 percent may be one month below grade level or three years below.

7. The problem of inadequate education in basic skills is not limited to urban areas. But the heaviest concentration of failing students is in the cities. And it is predominantly successful urban public schools and their characteristics that have been identified. Urban schools are the focus of this chapter.

8. The emphasis here on the failings of pre–high school education should not be taken to imply that high schools do any better; to the contrary, they commonly do worse. Higher percentages of students typically fall more years below grade level in urban public high schools than they do in eighth grade and below. In Philadelphia in 1982, for example, the percentage of students falling one to three years below grade level in basic skills ran from 7 percent in grade two to 20 percent in grade eight; these figures rose to 29 percent three years or more below in grade ten, and 34 percent four years or more below in grade twelve. Office of Research, Planning and Evaluation, Division of Testing Services, 1981–1982 Philadelphia City-Wide Testing Program 11, 14, 15 (1982). This chapter, however, is limited to pre–high school education because only at that level has research identified effective schools and their characteristics sufficiently to warrant recognizing a legal requirement to educate effectively. Preliminary research suggests that successful high schools have similar characteristics in common.

9. A student's educational achievement in basic skills in grades one through eight is generally regarded by the educational community as inadequate if it falls one year or more below grade level in reading or mathematics as measured by nationally standardized tests. Nevertheless, because some may consider this standard too demanding, figures are also presented for the percentages of students two years or more below grade level. Achievement at that level is unquestionably inadequate.

It is widely agreed that one needs basic skills at the eighth-grade level (at least) to discharge the political, economic, and military responsibilities for which education is required. Some cases support recognition of ninth, tenth, or even twelfth grade as the minimum level of achievement.

10. If one looks only at the median achievement systemwide, a far more positive picture emerges: In 1981, the median achievement in reading in grades two through eight citywide was *at or above* the national norm. *See* New York City Board of Education, School Profiles 1980–1981, New York City Public Schools A (1982).

11. Extrapolating from the New York figures, it may be estimated that, at any given time, approximately 1,374,000 urban public school students nationwide in grades two through eight are one year or more below grade level in reading, and that 528,000 of these students are two years or more below. *See id.*

12. Although many school districts do not publish data for student achievement, income, and racial/ethnic composition in the format and detail necessary for this analysis, the information that is available indicates that these four characteristics of failure are typical of urban schools nationwide. New York, Houston, and Philadelphia were selected as examples solely because they publish the requisite data.

13. For several reasons, the proper unit for analysis is the effective school, rather than the effective teacher or the effective school district. First, to show that the public school system can effectively educate poor and minority students, it is necessary to identify a level of the system at which repeated success has been demonstrated. Second, most of the educational research that identifies the common characteristics of effective educational entities has been done at the school level. *See*

Purkey & Smith, Too Soon to Cheer? Synthesis of Research on Effective Schools, Educ. Leadership, Dec. 1982, at 64 (summarizing literature). Finally, although many teachers undoubtedly are effective in teaching poor children basic skills, the success of individual teachers does not establish the necessary institutional accountability.

14. This effective schools research is entirely distinct from the research reported *supra*, under "Effective Schools," describing successful schools in New York, Houston, and Philadelphia. The research from those cities did not seek, and is not offered, to identify the characteristics of successful schools, but to establish an achievable standard of effectiveness.

15. James Coleman has recanted his suggestion that schools cannot effectively educate the poor because learning correlates with socioeconomic status and family background rather than quality of schooling; *see* J. Coleman et al., Equality of Educational Opportunity Survey (1966). As Coleman has acknowledged, his earlier research went awry in part because it examined the effects of the wrong school factors. *See* Fiske, Studies Dispute View That Schools Cannot Overcome Effect of Poverty, N.Y. Times, Dec. 26, 1979, at B12.

16. Brandt, Overview—The New Catechism for School Effectiveness, Educ. Leadership, Dec. 1982, at 3.

17. Edmonds, Programs of School Improvement: An Overview, Educ. Leadership, Dec. 1982, at 4.

18. Mackenzie, Research for School Improvement: An Appraisal of Some Recent Trends, Educ. Researcher, Apr. 1983, at 11.

19. On School Improvement: A Conversation with Ronald Edmonds, Educ. Leadership, Dec. 1982, at 13 [hereinafter Edmonds Interview].

20. *Id.*

21. *Id.*

22. *Id.* at 13–14.

23. Brandt, Overview, *supra* note 16, at 3 (emphasis in original).

24. Edmonds Interview, *supra* note 19, at 14.

25. *See* Mackenzie, Research for School Improvement, *supra* note 18, at 7.

26. *See, e.g.,* Educational Research Service, Effective Schools: A Summary of Research 57 (1983); Purkey & Smith, Effective Schools: A Review, Elementary Sch. J., Mar. 1983, at 427.

27. *Compare generally* Elson, Suing to Make Schools Effective, or How to Make a Bad Situation Worse: A Response to Ratner, 63 Tex. L. Rev. 889 (1985), *with* Ratner, Rebuttal of Elson, 63 Tex. L. Rev. 919 (1985).

28. It is possible to imagine certain characteristics that schools would be powerless to emulate. If it had been found, for example, that successful schools commonly are staffed entirely by teachers with at least thirty years teaching experience or that such schools commonly have at least 5,000 square feet of floor space per pupil, schools might legitimately argue that, at least in the foreseeable future, they could not adopt these characteristics.

29. "[T]he consensus of the experts was that there is nothing magical about the existence of high-achieving urban schools. Exceptionality results from explicit improvement efforts, efforts that could be implemented in other urban schools." Lotto, Evidence from Experts, in Why Do Some Urban Schools Succeed? 199 (Phi

Delta Kappa ed., 1980). Of course, to say that schools have the power to implement the characteristics of success is not to say that doing so is easy. "[C]hanging schools is a complicated, frustrating, and often idiosyncratic process that entails changing people's behaviors, motivations, and attitudes." *Id.* at 200.

30. Clark, An Analysis of Research, Development, and Evaluation Reports on Exceptional Urban Elementary Schools, in Why Do Some Schools Succeed?, *supra* note 29, at 181.

31. *Id.* at 182.

32. Of course, many people may feel threatened by the prospect that the underclass of poor and minority children may become educated. Some may fear competition for jobs, housing, and income. Others may oppose adequate education for all out of racial prejudice, or the desire to feel socially superior to a less educated group. *See generally* Hentoff, The Integrationist, New Yorker, Aug. 23, 1982, at 37, 38–39 (profiling Dr. Kenneth B. Clark and his work to improve education of poor and minority students). Dr. Clark concludes that society perpetuates inadequate education for poor and minority children because it does not value them. *See id.* at 39.

33. In fact, various federal statutes have been interpreted this way, allowing equitable relief but barring damages. *See* Transamerica Mortgage Advisors v. Lewis, 444 U.S. 11, 19, 24 (1979) (Investment Advisers Act of 1940); Marvin H. v. Austin Indep. Sch. Dist., 714 F.2d 1348, 1356 (5th Cir. 1983) (Education for All Handicapped Children Act).

34. Wisconsin v. Yoder, 406 U.S. 205, 213 (1972).

35. Conn. Const. art. VIII, § 1. Other provisions in this category include Alaska Const. art. VII, § 1; Ariz. Const. art. XI, §1; Hawaii Const. art. IX, § 1; Kan. Const. art. VI, § 1; La. Const. art. VIII, § 1; Neb. Const. art. VII, § 1; N.M Const. art. XII, § 1; N.Y. Const. art. XI, § 1; N.C. Const. art. IX, § 2; Okla. Const. art. XIII, § 1; S.C. Const. art. XI, § 3; Utah Const. art. X, § 1; Vt. Const. ch. 2, § 68.

36. N.J. Const. art. VIII, § 4. Other provisions in this category include Ark. Const. art. XIV, § 1; Colo. Const. art. IX, § 2; Del. Const. art. X, § 1; Fla. Const. art. IX, § 1; Idaho Const. art. IX, § 1; Ky. Const. § 183; Md. Const. art. VIII, § 1; Minn. Const. art. XIII, § 1; Mont. Const. art. X, § 1; N.D. Const. art. VIII, § 1; Ohio Const. art. VI, § 3; Or. Const. art. VIII, § 3; Pa. Const. art. III, § 14; Tenn. Const. art. XI, § 12; Tex. Const. art. VII, § 1; Va. Const. art. VIII, § 1; W. Va. Const. art. XII, § 1; Wis. Const. art. X, § 3. This type of provision is discussed at length and subcategorized in Pauley v. Kelly, 255 S.E.2d 859, 864–77 (W. Va. 1979).

37. R.I. Const. art. XII, § 1. Other provisions in this category include Cal. Const. art. IX, § 1; Ind. Const. art. VIII, § 1; Iowa Const. art. 9 2d, § 2; Mass. Const. pt. 2, ch. 5, § 2; Nev. Const. art. XI, § 2; S.D. Const. art. VIII, § 1; Wyo. Const. art. VII, § 1.

38. Wash. Const. art. IX, § 1. Other provisions that explicitly characterize education as a fundamental or primary state duty include Ga. Const. art. VIII, § 1; Ill. Const. art. X, § 1; Me. Const. art. 8, § 1; Mich. Const. art. VIII, § 2; Mo. Const. art. 9, § 1(a); N.H. Const. pt. 2, art. 83.

39. Conn. Const. art. VIII, § 1 (emphasis added). Similarly, New York's constitution provides: "The legislature *shall* provide for the maintenance and support of a system of free common schools, wherein all the children of this state may be educated." N.Y. Const. art. XI, § 1 (emphasis added).

40. Seattle Sch. Dist. No. 1 v. Washington, 585 P.2d 71, 85 (Wash. 1978) (en banc) (emphasis in original); *see* Robinson v. Cahill (*Robinson I*), 303 A.2d 273, 291 (N.J. 1973) (construing a "thorough and efficient" education clause and holding that the "ultimate responsibility for a thorough and efficient education" is on the state), *cert. denied*, 414 U.S. 976 (1973).

41. 347 U.S. 483 (1954).

42. *Id.* at 492–93.

43. 255 S.E.2d 859 (W. Va. 1979).

44. *Id.* at 877.

45. *Id.*

46. *See id.* at 874–78.

47. *Id.* at 877.

48. *Id.*

49. *See id.*

50. 585 P.2d 71 (Wash. 1978) (en banc).

51. Wash. Const. art. IX, § 1.

52. 585 P.2d at 94–95 (brackets in original).

53. *Id.* at 95 (emphasis in original).

54. *Id.* (emphasis added).

55. *E.g.*, Cal. Const. art. IX, § 1; Ind. Const. art. VIII, § 1; Nev. Const. art. XI, § 2.

56. *See, e.g.*, Ark. Const. art. XIV, § 1; Cal. Const. art. IX, § 1.

57. *See, e.g.*, Mass. Const. pt. 2, ch. 5, § 2; Tenn. Const. art. XI, § 12.

58. Conn. Const. art. VIII, § 1; *cf.* Horton v. Meskill, 376 A.2d 359 (Conn. 1977) (construing clause in context of school financing disparity).

59. Substantive due process came to an end with West Coast Hotel Co. v. Parrish, 300 U.S. 379 (1937), and generally remained in disfavor until Roe v. Wade, 410 U.S. 113 (1973). *See generally* Tribe, Foreword: Toward a Model of Rules in the Due Process of Life and Law, 87 Harv. L. Rev. 2–15 (1973) (comparing substantive due process in the early part of the century with *Roe*).

60. The Supreme Court's decision in Ingraham v. Wright, 430 U.S. 651 (1977), supports the claim that compulsory school attendance infringes a protected liberty interest. In *Ingraham*, the Court held that schoolchildren's interest in not having public school officials subject them to corporal punishment for their misconduct was a liberty interest protected by the Fourteenth Amendment. *Id.* at 673–74. The Court so held without regard to whether corporal punishment was beneficial to children in general or in particular instances. It found that a liberty interest existed even though the interest was being invoked only for children and even though at common law teachers had a privilege "to inflict reasonable corporal punishment on children in their care." *Id.* at 674.

Children's interest in not being subjected to governmentally imposed physical confinement in school buildings for massive periods of time seems equally worthy of recognition as a protected liberty interest. A parallel governmental mandate compelling adults to live or work in a particular building six hours a day for ten to twelve years undoubtedly would be regarded as a deprivation of a protected liberty. *Cf.* O'Connor v. Donaldson, 422 U.S. 563, 575 (1975) (finding no constitutional basis for confining mentally ill if they can live safely in freedom without danger to others). Under *Ingraham,* children have enforceable liberty interests just as adults do. *See Ingraham,* 430 U.S. at 674; *see also* Tinker v. Des Moines Indep. Community Sch. Dist., 393 U.S. 503, 506 (1969) (holding that constitutional protections do not stop because the beneficiaries are children who have stepped inside the schoolhouse door).

Children's interest in avoiding state-imposed physical confinement is even greater from a legal and historical perspective than their interest in avoiding corporal punishment. Unlike corporal punishment, the interest in avoiding physical confinement was never circumscribed by the common law; compulsory attendance was a creature of state statute. Because children retain a liberty interest in avoiding corporal punishment even though the common law explicitly authorized it, a fortiori they retain a liberty interest in avoiding state-imposed school attendance to which they were not even subject at common law.

61. At the outset, it must be made clear that the due process claims do not seek to invalidate state compulsory attendance laws. To the contrary, the claims are premised on the existence of such laws and presume their legality.

Although there is a theoretical risk that states may repeal their compulsory attendance laws if courts find that the laws give rise to a duty to educate adequately, this is unlikely to occur. Compulsory school attendance laws are deeply embedded in the social and political fabric of the United States. These laws are so important, the claim to adequate education so legitimate, and the burden of providing the education so manageable that state governments are not likely to repeal them merely to avoid the obligation. Indeed, even in response to mandatory racial desegregation of the schools, only three states (Mississippi, South Carolina, and Virginia) repealed their compulsory attendance laws. *See* Project, Education and the Law: State Interests and Individual Rights, 74 Mich. L. Rev. 1373, 1383 n.43 (1976). The attendance laws were subsequently reenacted and remain in effect today in all three states.

62. 406 U.S. 715 (1972).

63. *Id.* at 738.

64. *Id.*

65. McClung, Do Handicapped Children Have a Legal Right, *supra* note 3, at 171 (emphasis in original).

66. *See, e.g.,* Dimond, The Constitutional Right to Education: The Quiet Revolution, 24 Hastings L.J. 1087, 1123 (1973). Put dramatically, "[A]bsent minimally adequate education, the school is transformed into a penitentiary where one can be held in custodial confinement eight hours a day from age six to sixteen." McClung, Do Handicapped Children Have a Legal Right, *supra* note 3, at 166. The California Supreme Court agrees: " A child of the poor assigned willy nilly to an inferior school takes on the complexion of a prisoner, complete with a minimum sentence of 12 years." Serrano v. Priest (*Serrano I*), 487 P.2d 1241, 1259 (Cal. 1971) (en banc) (quoting Coons et al., Educational Opportunity: A Workable Constitutional Test for State Financial Structures, 57 Cal. L. Rev. 305, 388 (1969)), *cert. denied,* 432 U.S. 907 (1977).

67. Although the state constitutional equal protection claim may be even stronger than its federal counterpart, there are several reasons for beginning the discussion with federal equal protection. First, although the Supreme Court has considered federal equal protection challenges to other aspects of public schooling, such as exclusion of alien children, racial segregation, and unequal school financing, it has never considered the precise legal and factual questions raised by discrimination in basic education involved here. The logic of related decisions, however, suggests that the Court should respond favorably.

Second, because federal equal protection doctrine is generally used by state courts as a guide in interpreting parallel state constitutional provisions, it is most efficient to analyze federal equal protection first. Indeed, the federal analysis demonstrates not only the powerful reasons for recognizing the federal claim, but also how state courts may construe their own constitutions to recognize the state claim, regardless of how the Supreme Court might ultimately rule on the federal claim.

Third, because federal equal protection doctrine is more developed than its state counterparts, analysis of federal doctrine allows the most comprehensive consideration of the issues.

68. Plyler v. Doe, 457 U.S. 202, 216 (1982).

69. Although the Supreme Court noted in San Antonio Indep. Sch. Dist. v. Rodriguez, 411 U.S. 1 (1973), that it had "never heretofore held that wealth discrimination alone provides an adequate basis for invoking strict scrutiny," *id.* at 29, it suggested that the plaintiff class might be considered suspect on the grounds of wealth if it consisted of a "definable category of 'poor' people," *id.* at 25, and the challenged conduct caused them "absolute deprivation" of education. *Id.* at 20.

To meet the first criterion, plaintiffs must show that the challenged conduct "operates to the peculiar disadvantage of any class fairly definable as indigent, or as composed of persons whose incomes are beneath any designated poverty level." *Id.* at 22–23. Although prior wealth discrimination cases had involved plaintiffs too poor to pay for certain services, the Court made clear that plaintiffs can show wealth discrimination simply by proving that the class discriminated against consists of poor persons.

Although the Court characterized the requisite degree of injury as "absolute deprivation of education," it implicitly defined education as adequate education. This interpretation of the Court's language is supported by common sense and by analogous Supreme Court cases guaranteeing criminal defendants the right to effective assistance of counsel, adequate transcripts on appeal, and competent psychiatrists. Thus, the plaintiff's burden is to prove absolute deprivation of adequate education. Conversely, a defendant cannot defeat a demonstration of "absolute deprivation" simply by showing that it offers students some, albeit inadequate, education.

70. A school district may argue that special local conditions make approaches used successfully in other schools inapplicable to that district, or that it is impossible for the district even to implement the characteristics of success. The first argument is implausible because there is no reason to believe that the characteristics of success, which typify many effective schools in various environments, are less applicable in one district serving such students than in another. The second hypothetical argument is even less plausible because the effective practices are peculiarly within the power of school districts to implement. *See supra,* under "Schools' Power to Implement."

71. 457 U.S. 202 (1982).

72. Tex. Educ. Code Ann. § 21.031 (West Supp. 1981) (current version at Tex. Educ. Code Ann. § 21.031 (West Supp. 1985)).

73. *See* Doe v. Plyler, 628 F.2d 448, 450 (5th Cir. 1980), *aff'd,* 457 U.S. 202 (1982).

74. *See* Doe v. Plyler, 458 F. Supp. 569, 580–81 (E.D. Tex. 1978), *aff'd,* 628 F.2d 448 (5th Cir. 1980), *aff'd,* 457 U.S. 202 (1982).

75. *See Plyler,* 457 U.S. at 223 (citing *Rodriguez,* 411 U.S. at 28–39). Even though the interest in education generally, including such matters as school athletic and breakfast programs and personnel practices, is not fundamental, a court logically could find that interests in some specific educational functions are fundamental. Indeed, this narrower approach to assessing fundamentality was used in *Rodriguez* along with the broader analysis of the general interest in education. The Court found that four considerations militated against holding that the specific interest in equal school financing invoked in *Rodriguez* was fundamental. First, the plaintiffs failed to prove that unequal expenditures produced unequal educational quality. *Rodriguez,* 411 U.S. at 23–24. Second, the plaintiffs directly challenged state tax law, an area of traditional judicial deference. *Id.* at 40–41. Third, vindicating the plaintiffs' claim would have had serious consequences for federalism because it would have resulted in the invalidation of virtually all states' school finance laws. *Id.* at 44. Finally, because the challenged statute reduced expenditure disparities, it was a positive reform that did not prejudice the free exercise of constitutional rights. *Id.* at 39.

None of these negative considerations applies to the claim described in this chapter. Unequal educational quality is the heart of the claim here. State tax laws are not challenged. No serious federalism concerns are implicated, since relief does not necessitate invalidating state laws, but merely local practices. And the claim contests not a reformatory act, but a school district's failure to discharge its essential educational responsibility. Thus, *Rodriguez* is distinguishable. A court could find that a citizen's specific interest in adequate education in basic skills is a fundamental right, even while an interest in education generally is not.

76. *Id.; see Plyler* at 219 n.19.

77. *See id.* at 217–18 & n.16; *accord id.* at 238 n.2, 239 n.3 (Powell, J., concurring).

78. *See id.* at 224, 226. Although *Plyler* apparently foreclosed the possibility left open in *Rodriguez* that individuals have a fundamental right to a limited quantum of education (*see Plyler,* 457 U.S. at 223 ("Nor is education a fundamental right", *but see supra* note 75), the *Plyler* Court emphasized that education is a vital prerequisite to meaningful participation in a democratic form of government. *See* 457 U.S. at 221–23. This was the principal basis for distinguishing education from "other forms of social welfare legislation," *id.* at 221, and justifying a higher level of equal protection scrutiny, *see id.* at 223–24. Thus, *Plyler* may be read to have adopted the *Rodriguez* hypothetical that an "identifiable quantum of education is a constitutionally protected prerequisite to the meaningful exercise of [speech and voting] right[s]," *Rodriguez,* 411 U.S. at 36, but the degree of constitutional protection is intermediate scrutiny, not the strict scrutiny applied to fundamental rights.

79. *See* 457 U.S. at 219–20.

80. *Id.* at 220.

81. *See id.* at 222; *id.* at 234–35 (Blackmun, J., concurring).

82. *Id.* at 224.

83. *Id.* at 223; *see id.* at 220 n.20.

84. *Id.* at 229.

85. *Id.*

86. *Id.* at 230.

87. *Id.*

88. This holding reflects an attitude much broader than the facts of *Plyler*, as may be inferred from the Court's statement that there is a "presumption that denial of education to innocent children is not a rational response to legitimate state concerns." *Id.* at 224 n.21; *see id.* at 234 (Blackmun, J., concurring) ("[W]hen the State provides an education to some and denies it to others, it immediately and inevitably creates class distinctions of a type fundamentally inconsistent with [the] purposes . . . of the Equal Protection Clause"). It is constitutionally irrelevant that *Plyler* involved a total denial of free public education while the claim here is denial of adequate education. *See* note 69 *supra*.

89. Zobel v. Williams, 457 U.S. 55, 60 (1982); *accord* Williams v. Vermont, 105 S. Ct. 2465, 2472 (1985); Schweiker v. Wilson, 450 U.S. 221, 230, 235 (1981).

90. 457 U.S. at 224 n.21.

91. *Id.* at 227; *accord id.* at 249 (Burger, C.J., dissenting on other grounds) ("Of course such fiscal concerns alone could not justify . . . an arbitrary and irrational denial of benefits to a particular group of persons").

92. To accept these interests as legitimate justifications for discrimination between persons similarly situated would validate a vast proportion of all governmental discrimination and eviscerate the goals of equal protection. In considering the state's argument that excluding illegal aliens from free public school was justified by the state's interest in decreasing its costs, the Fifth Circuit held that to accept this contention would mean that cost by itself could justify exclusion of "any group of people from any government program that requires funding. This is clearly not the case." Doe v. Plyler, 628 F.2d 448, 459 (5th Cir. 1980), *aff'd*, 457 U.S. 202 (1982).

93. 411 U.S. 1, 54–55 (1973).

94. *See* Diamond, Education Law, 29 Syracuse L. Rev. 103, 133 (1978); *see generally* Williams, Equality Guarantees in State Constitutional Law, 63 Tex. L. Rev. 1195 (1985).

95. *See* San Antonio Indep. Sch. Dist. v. Rodriguez, 411 U.S. 1, 33–34 (1973).

96. *See, e.g.,* Horton v. Meskill, 376 A.2d 359, 372–73 (Conn. 1977); Pauley v. Kelly, 255 S.E.2d 859, 878 (W. Va. 1979). *But cf. In re* Levy, 345 N.E.2d 556, 588–89 (N.Y. 1976) (holding that education is not a fundamental right under Federal Constitution, without identifying whether claim adjudicated is federal or state equal protection), *appeal dismissed sub nom.* Levy v. City of New York, 429 U.S. 805 (1976).

97. 376 A.2d 359 (Conn. 1977).

98. 487 P.2d 1241 (Cal. 1971) (en banc), *cert. denied*, 432 U.S. 907 (1977).

99. 487 P.2d 1241, 1258, (Cal. 1971) (en banc), *cert. denied*, 432 U.S. 907 (1977). In Serrano v. Priest (*Serrano II*), 557 P.2d 929, 951 (Cal. 1976) (en banc), *cert. denied*,

432 U.S. 907 (1977), the court reaffirmed that education is fundamental under the California equal protection law, notwithstanding the intervening decision in *Rodriguez* holding education not fundamental under the federal equal protection clause.

100. Plyler v. Doe, 457 U.S. 202, 222 (1982) (quoting Brown v. Board of Educ., 347 U.S. 483, 493 (1954)).

101. The Supreme Court has commonly defined rights at a high level of generality for purposes of assessing their fundamentality under federal equal protection. However, state courts remain free to define rights narrowly for purposes of assessing fundamentality under state constitutions. Specifically, state courts can legitimately define the right at issue here as the right to adequate education in basic skills, distinguishing it from the broader right to education in all skills and from other types of education claims, such as the right to equal school financing. So defined, the right's importance is even greater than that of education overall, because basic skills are at the core of the education that states are required to provide.

102. 487 P.2d at 1258.

103. *See* 411 U.S. 1, 37 (1973) (citing Lindsey v. Normet, 405 U.S. 56 (1972) (housing); Dandridge v. Williams, 397 U.S. 471 (1970) (welfare)).

104. 411 U.S. at 36. Because the Court found that Texas provided enough funds for adequate education, it never reached the question whether a right to sufficient education to meaningfully discharge First Amendment and voting rights is constitutionally guaranteed.

105. *See generally* W. Keeton et al., Prosser and Keeton on the Law of Torts, § 30, at 164 (5th ed. 1984).

106. *See, e.g.,* D.S.W. v. Fairbanks N. Star Borough Sch. Dist., 628 P.2d 554, 555–56 (Alaska 1981); Peter W. v. San Francisco Unified Sch. Dist., 60 Cal. App. 3d 814, 822, 131 Cal. Rptr. 854, 859 (1976); Hunter v. Board of Educ., 439 A.2d 582, 584–86 (Md. 1982); Donohue v. Copiague Union Free Sch. Dist., 391 N.E.2d 1352, 1354 (N.Y. 1979).

107. 110 U.S. 516, 530 (1884).

108. Comment, The Rights of Children: A Trust Model, 46 Fordham L. Rev. 669, 711 (1978).

109. 60 Cal. App. 3d 814, 131 Cal. Rptr. 854 (1976).

110. 391 N.E.2d 1352 (N.Y. 1979).

111. Prosser & Keeton, *supra* note 105, § 32, at 185.

112. 391 N.E.2d at 1353.

113. Elson, Suing to Make Schools Effective, *supra* note 27, at 891 n.6.

114. Although a school system might try to prove that particular members of a large class have been misclassified and are not educable to the adequacy standard, it is virtually impossible that the system could make such a showing as to the class as a whole. If a system attempted such a showing, the plaintiffs should be able to rebut it by proving that the members of the class learned at a satisfactory rate in the earliest elementary grades and that they could not have done so without the requisite intellectual capacity.

115. While it seems highly unlikely that the percentages of success will be significantly different in effective schools in other cities, if significant differences were proven, the benchmark percentages could easily be adjusted to reflect a different general standard.

116. McClung, Do Handicapped Children Have a Legal Right, *supra* note 3, at 166 (quoting Case Comment, *Wyatt v. Stickney* and the Right of Civilly Committed Mental Patients to Adequate Treatment, 86 Harv. L. Rev. 1282, 1297 (1973)).

117. Significantly, the duty does not impose strict liability. In effect, it requires only that schools exercise reasonable care in educating their students. If a school fails to educate successfully a large percentage of its students in basic skills, it must adopt an alternative approach—the five characteristics of success—that has succeeded elsewhere. What the court held in Rettig v. Kent City Sch. Dist., 539 F. Supp. 768 (W.D. Ohio 1981), in the context of schools' responsibilities toward the handicapped is equally applicable to regular students: School systems have "an obligation to keep abreast of changing educational strategies and implement them where success may be demonstrated." *Id.* at 777.

118. If urban school districts do not publish such data on a regular basis, they must be induced to do so. If necessary, Congress or the state legislature should enact statutes requiring disclosure of the information. Similarly, if parents and other interested parties do not already have a right of access to the schools, laws must be passed to create the right. It is essential that school operations be open to observation so that any school's implementation of the characteristics of success (or its failure to do so) can be monitored.

119. Jay Burns Baking Co. v. Bryan, 264 U.S. 504, 520 (1924) (Brandeis & Holmes, JJ., dissenting).

CHAPTER EIGHTEEN

New Educational Standards and the Right to Quality Education

Paul Weckstein

New standards for what schools should teach and students should learn are at the heart of current education reform efforts. Recently, reform has focused on the emergence of new educational standards under authority of state statutes. Such standards, however, can also form the basis for other types of legal claims to quality education. This chapter describes these other claims—under the state constitutional provisions for education, federal statutes (Chapter 1 of the Vocational Education Act, the Individuals with Disabilities in Education Act, and the Civil Rights Acts), and the Fourteenth Amendment—and how they may be strengthened by the emergence of the new state statutory standards for education. This chapter also examines the legal implications of these educational standards for students entering the workplace.

Raising educational standards alone, in the absence of better programs for allowing students to reach the standards and better jobs that use and compensate the skills called for by those standards, will only add new barriers for disadvantaged students and workers. On the other hand, these new educational standards can help us bridge the gap between our ideal of a society that develops, uses, and values its human talent and our reality of waste and inequality. We can challenge the inequalities that leave many schools with resources that are inadequate to meet the new standards. We can challenge the programs and curricula that are not designed to teach students how to master the skills and knowledge identified by the new standards. And, finally, we can challenge the employers whose jobs and workplace organization fail to utilize and adequately compensate those skills and that knowledge. Through combined reforms in education and the workplace, these efforts can seek to utilize more fully the talents of our youth.

State Statutory Standards for Educational Content

New state educational standards have been appearing either directly in statutory language or in administrative mandates issued under authority of state statute.[1] Examples include graduation and promotion standards that encompass certain skills or bodies of knowledge, curriculum standards, school quality standards, and skill statements that form the basis for developing new modes of student assessment. These are often framed in the form of educational content or outcomes—implicit or explicit new definitions of skills or curricula that students should master. Sometimes there are also new process and resource standards.

Whether these educational standards are directly enforceable as a matter of state statutory law requires particularized analysis of both the specific mandates and the background of state law on private causes of action. Regardless of their direct enforceability, these emerging educational standards issued under state statutory authority can be central to a greatly invigorated role for both state constitutional law and federal statutory law, as discussed below.

Other Bases for Enforcing Quality-Education Standards

State Constitutional Doctrines

An argument for students' rights to high-quality education can be founded on the education clauses that appear in almost all state constitutions, often in terms of a duty to provide a thorough and efficient system of education in the state.[2] These clauses help explain the continued liveliness of state court activity concerning claims that financial inequalities among school districts are unconstitutional, long after the window for casting such claims in federal constitutional law all but closed.[3] Such education clauses have also been invoked, in a manner that supports a state constitutional right to education, in cases challenging the charging of school fees to parents and students for educational services central to that education.[4]

The important point here is that these education clauses, together with the school finance case law and the emerging state educational standards, may have a vital role in establishing and defining a substantive *state constitutional right to education* that goes beyond the issues of school finance and fees.

In some of the finance and fee cases, the focus has been on a direct substantive right to education under the education clause itself. In other cases, the presence of the education clause has been used to establish a standard of strict scrutiny of inequalities under the state's equal protection clause, in contrast to the U.S. Supreme Court's more restrained review under the federal equal protection clause, based upon the absence of explicit reference to education in the U.S. Constitution.[5]

Many of these cases establish education as a fundamental state right, and then move directly to a determination that gross levels of school finance inequality cannot survive the high standards for judging state interference with fundamental rights, whether under the education clause itself or under the equal protection clause.

Other cases, however, provide important additional guidance in defining education standards. For example, the court in *Pauley v. Kelly*[6] found it necessary to identify the elements of the state constitutional mandate for a "thorough and efficient" system of education, in order to determine whether the state's system of finance deprived students in the low-wealth districts of such education. It therefore used masters to help it first define, in quite elaborate detail, standards for such things as curriculum, instruction, and facilities necessary for a thorough and efficient education and then analyze the extent to which the low-wealth districts failed to meet those standards.

The job for which the court in *Pauley* sought masters' help—defining the contours and elements of the state constitutional right to education—can now in many states be assigned in part to the educational standards emerging under authority of state statute. The fact that students in certain schools, or certain tracks within a school, are not receiving an education that meets standards that the state itself has said are appropriate for all students is certainly relevant to whether the mandate for a thorough and efficient system of education has been achieved, or whether the qualitative differences in education meet the high standards of scrutiny under the state equal protection clause.

Federal Statutory Doctrines and Mandates

Chapter 1

Low-achieving students whose education program does not effectively teach the "basic and more advanced skills that all children are expected to master"[7] may claim a violation of Chapter 1.[8] Chapter 1 (known as "Title I" prior to 1981) is the largest federal education program, totaling $6.7 billion in fiscal year 1992. Funds go to school districts based on numbers of low-income children, and then are used in certain schools for extra services to improve the basic achievement of the lowest-achieving students, regardless of income.

In 1988, a new quality focus was added to the program, after evaluations showed only modest impact and an overemphasis on rote learning and drill.[9] The law now requires that school districts identify "desired outcomes," which must be stated in terms of the "basic and more advanced skills that all children are expected to master."[10] Schools that fail to make substantial progress toward those outcomes on an annual basis must then develop school improvement plans designed to achieve those outcomes, incorporating "those program changes which have the greatest likelihood of improving the performance" of low-achieving students.[11] Likewise, regardless of the school's overall progress, it must focus additional attention on those individual Chapter 1 students who do not annually make substantial progress toward the desired outcomes—that is, toward mastery of the basic and advanced skills that all students are expected to master.[12]

While there might be reasonable dispute about how to define "substantial progress,"[13] the problems and failures of implementation have been far more basic. Few school districts have defined their desired outcomes in the required terms at all;[14] instead, they have commonly defined them in terms of minimal gains on a norm-referenced, standardized achievement test—most frequently in terms of one Normal Curve Equivalent (NCE) gain per year.[15] Such educational standards are not stated in terms of "skills" at all, let alone those that all children should master. Further, the standardized, multiple-choice tests used often cannot reasonably claim to measure "more advanced skills," as defined in the act. Even were this not the case, a gain of one NCE per year means that the students with the most academic difficulty, who are the prime focus of the act, will never even approach mastery of the skills within their academic lifetimes.

The problems in setting educational standards and evaluating progress are compounded by models of delivering educational services that also make it difficult for Chapter 1 students to master the full range of skills expected for all students.[16] For example, students may be pulled out of their regular classes for special Chapter 1 instruction, which is often not aimed at helping them master the same curriculum taught to the other students. They may be placed in "regular" classes that are in fact low tracks, which also fail to incorporate effectively the curriculum and skills taught to other students. These practices arguably violate other statutory mandates as well, such as a requirement to "allocate time and resources for frequent and regular coordination" between the Chapter 1 curriculum and the regular instructional program.[17] The legislative history notes that this coordination is a two-way requirement that includes efforts to identify practices in the regular program, such as tracking, which may be frustrating achievement of the desired skills.[18]

State educational standards should often play a key role in determining the desired outcomes under Chapter 1. If the state (or the local district) has, in a different context, already set forth some of the basic and advanced skills that all children are expected to master (for example, in a list of minimum competencies), then the local outcomes for Chapter 1 must at least incorporate these. Yet, in most states with such educational standards, local desired outcomes have been set without any reference to already articulated skills and skill levels.[19]

Vocational Education

New quality standards have also been added to federal vocational education law.[20] Again, state education standards can play a vital role in this area.

Key requirements for vocational education now focus on whether programs:

(1) integrate academic and vocational education and provide strong student development and use of basic and advanced problem-solving and academic skills (including math, reading, writing, science, and social studies) in the vocational setting, so that vocational programs do not form a separate, academically inferior track;

(2) provide students with strong experience in and understanding of all

aspects of the industry they are preparing to enter, including planning, finance, management, technical and production skills, principles of technology, labor, community issues, and health, safety, and environment, instead of trying to predict exactly what jobs future workers will have and exactly what skills will be required for those jobs, and then providing only rote training for that narrow definition; and

(3) provide access and the supplemental services needed for success to students who are members of special populations, including those who are economically disadvantaged, academically disadvantaged, limited-English-proficient, disabled, single parents and displaced homemakers, or seeking to enter fields not traditional for their sex.

These three sets of conditions are the constants in state planning requirements[21] and in the annual local program evaluations, based upon state performance standards, that trigger a program improvement process similar to that prescribed in Chapter 1.[22] Further, recipients are annually required to review programs, with full and informed participation of special populations, to identify and adopt strategies to overcome any barriers resulting in lower rates of access to or success in such programs for special populations.[23] States must also develop effective procedures by which students, parents, teachers, and area residents can participate in state and local program decisions and make expedited appeals.[24]

The new law opens up a range of possibilities for low-income students and communities, including ways to meet the mandates through involving youths in community development projects, where they assess their community and then plan, start, and run enterprises to address unmet community needs.[25] Major inadequacies in understanding and implementing the new provisions have been identified.[26] In seeking remedies, advocates should not ignore the interplay, once again, between state academic educational standards and federal mandates concerning academic skills for vocational education students. The key question should be whether these students are receiving effective academic instruction that meets the state educational standards applicable to all students.

Education of Students with Disabilities

Few aspects of education have received more attention from advocates than the laws governing "special education," the education of disabled students. Both the rights to a free, appropriate public education in the least restrictive environment under the Individuals with Disabilities in Education Act (IDEA)[27] and the parallel and complementary rights to nondiscriminatory education under section 504 of the Rehabilitation Act of 1973[28] are involved. From the perspective of an emerging quality standard, however, it is increasingly clear that these struggles can be cast in terms of the laws' requirements that students with disabilities be helped to master the core curriculum prescribed for all students.

Much of the programing for students with disabilities is based upon assumptions, usually both unstated and unproven, that they cannot master the full range of skills expected of other students.[29] For example, individualized education plans

(IEPs), which must be developed by staff and parents based upon thorough assessment of individual needs, are often not directed to assisting the students to overcome barriers to their mastery of skills taught in the mainstream curriculum, but instead are built around a set of lower expectations. Similarly, when students with disabilities are "mainstreamed" into regular classes, those "regular" classes are often (as with Chapter 1 students) low-track groupings that are not aimed at teaching the full range of academic skills. These two practices appear to be in direct conflict with the requirements of laws concerning nondiscrimination, least restrictive environment, and appropriate education—except in those cases where it can be clearly demonstrated through an objective, professional evaluation process that the student is so severely disabled that, even with appropriate assistance, he or she is unable to master those skills and that curriculum.

Here again, independent state and local educational standards for what students should learn, know, or be able to do are highly relevant. These federal laws should be seen as barring educational practices that provide disabled students with lesser opportunities to meet those standards.

Students with Limited English Proficiency

Students with limited English proficiency (LEP) are entitled to affirmative steps designed to overcome the barriers to learning caused by that limitation, both under Title VI of the 1964 Civil Rights Act[30] and under the Equal Educational Opportunities Act of 1974.[31]

Under the case law related to these two statutes, a three-part, quality-oriented test has emerged for evaluating the sufficiency of language programs for LEP students.[32] First, the program must be based upon an educational theory or approach that has the support of at least some experts. Second, steps must be taken to implement that approach effectively. Third, after a legitimate trial period, the program must either be shown to work or be modified to accomplish that end.

The similarity of this standard to those for Chapter 1 students and for students with disabilities should be noted. Further, the independent emergence of new state and local educational standards for what all students should know and be able to do should strengthen and add precision to this legal standard. Programs for LEP students can be assessed in terms of whether they are designed to teach, have the resources to teach, and over time are in fact successful in teaching those skills and that knowledge.

Civil Rights Laws and Academic Tracking

The Civil Rights Acts protect students against discrimination by recipients of federal aid on the basis of race and national origin,[33] sex,[34] or disability.[35] Central to these acts is protection against assumptions, differences in treatment, or practices with disparate impact, when those assumptions, treatment differences, or practices have not been sufficiently justified.[36]

The common practice of creating tracks for students within the regular program, based upon purported differences in "ability," illustrates the connection between these civil rights laws and the increased focus on higher student achievement standards. These tracks can take the form of separate classes within a school, separate but relatively permanent groupings within a single classroom (e.g., the "hawks" and the "pigeons"), or separate schools (e.g., certain magnet or admission-through-examination schools). In the low tracks, students typically receive a watered-down curriculum, which is taught at a slower rate, and in which teachers' expectations for students are often more focused on good behavior than on academic mastery or intellectual inquiry.[37] As a result, these students fall further and further behind their peers.

Where, as often happens, racial minorities are overrepresented in the low tracks, the relevant legal inquiry focuses on the relationship between the nature of the education in those tracks and the student selection methods. If the program in the low tracks is enriched and accelerated, so that students selected are helped to catch up and achieve academic mastery, the relevant inquiry would be largely limited to whether the students selected are those who can and do benefit from this arrangement—those who need extra help in reaching the standards set for all.[38] On the other hand, when the low tracks are based upon lowered expectations and a curriculum that moves more slowly and does not teach the same range of skills and knowledge taught to other students, then the practice can be justified as nondiscriminatory only if it can be clearly demonstrated that the selection mechanisms identify only those students who are simply, and permanently, incapable of mastering or benefiting from the curriculum made available to others. The grades, teacher recommendations, tests, and other methods typically used to select students for low tracks cannot meet that standard—except, again, for students with the most severe mental disabilities, who constitute only a negligible portion of the enrollment in low-track regular classes.

Federal Constitutional Standards

While many of the claims above, relying on state law and federal statutory law, may render federal constitutional claims unnecessary, arguments under the equal protection and due process clauses of the Federal Constitution could be made, using a similar mode of analysis.

Equal Protection

First, unjustified assumptions about selected student groups' ability to learn, which emerge when the content of their actual educational programs is compared with academic standards stated for all students, may satisfy the requirement of showing discriminatory intent in order to establish a suspect classification meriting strict scrutiny under the equal protection clause (in contrast to the effects standard under federal civil rights laws and some state equal protection clauses).[39] Discriminatory intent requirements would also be satisfied by showing that students' current placement in inferior programs with weaker curricula is in part the result of *prior* intentional discrimination, such as the students' prior attendance in an intentionally segregated system.[40]

Second, regardless of intent, one can demonstrate that providing some students, and denying others, skills and knowledge affects the ability to exercise other constitutional rights of citizenship, such as voting. The Court in *San Antonio Independent School District v. Rodriguez* left at least partially open this avenue for asserting that some forms of educational inequality could burden fundamental rights and trigger heightened equal protection scrutiny.[41] The statements and debates concerning the adoption of higher academic standards are at least an indication of new social and governmental consensus about the skills and knowledge needed for effective exercise of fundamental rights.[42]

Third, placement of students in programs that, by their very nature and content, cannot result in mastery of the state-articulated goals of education, without a rational basis for determining that these students are incapable of achieving those goals, may justify an equal protection claim even under restrained, rational relationship review.

Due Process

Placement by the state in a program that is not designed to provide the skills that the state has articulated as the purpose of compulsory education could be viewed as a deprivation of liberty without due process of law, analogous to the right-to-treatment cases.[43] Here again, success would appear to depend upon a clear contrast between state achievement standards and the content of the program.

Probably the most important federal constitutional claim, however, rests upon a different due process analysis. It is fundamentally unfair to condition educational decisions of great importance for students on their mastery of educational content that they have not had an adequate opportunity to learn. Thus, the court in *Debra P. v. Turlington* held that Florida could not require passage of a minimum competency test for high school graduation until a sufficient period had passed for students to be aware of the new standards and for schools to realign their curricula and instruction, so that it was a fair test of what in fact was taught.[44] While the remedial focus in *Debra P.* was on overturning diploma denials, remedies could also focus directly on ensuring that students received an education adequate to master the standards.

This approach, while very powerful, has one condition. It only works where the education system seeks to impose a serious penalty (such as diploma denial) on the student who fails to master the new standards. The other statutory and constitutional claims described above are in this sense more intrinsic—the right to education that they posit can be asserted regardless of whether the state imposes additional punishment for failure to obtain it.

Claims and Remedies: Input, Process, or Outcome?

In general, the claims above differ significantly from earlier arguments for educational malpractice in that they do not focus primarily on a specific set of professionally determined practices on one side, or a specific educational outcome on the other. Instead, their primary focus is most often upon required process, but the process is outcome-oriented and input-sensitive.

For example, under Chapter 1, it is *not* a violation per se to fail to produce the requisite level of student achievement. It *is* a violation to fail to take the requisite steps designed to achieve that level, such as identifying the basic and advanced skills all children are expected to master, aligning the program with those skills, devoting resources of sufficient size, scope, and quality toward that end, and evaluating the program on that basis. It is also a violation to fail to take the requisite steps toward improvement when the evaluation shows that the desired results have not been achieved.

The distinctions here, however, should not be overdrawn. Chapter 1 also requires, for example, that program improvement plans for schools that are not succeeding must incorporate those changes that have the greatest likelihood of improving performance.[45] More specifically still, certain bodies of practice may eventually become incorporated into legal standards. For example, the professional standards recently issued by the National Council of Teachers of Mathematics[46] have gained widespread support, and, aside from the possibility that they may achieve a professional status similar to the accepted standards of good practice in medicine, such teaching standards may someday be directly incorporated into formal state educational standards.

The fact that process is what ultimately seems enforceable (along with equalization of inputs, taking into account differing needs) highlights the need to ensure that the process is participatory. Chapter 1, the Perkins Vocational Act, IDEA, and, more effectively, Head Start require the involvement of parents, students, teachers, or community members in decision making.[47] These requirements, often treated cavalierly, instead need to be seriously implemented, as well as improved and extended, as an important adjunct to other forms of monitoring and enforcement. Currently, there are practical and political limits on substantive enforcement by higher state or federal agencies. Further, an emerging, more sophisticated consensus about the desired skills (higher-order, active thinking and decision-making skills), about the nature of human learning and development (the student as active learner and explorer), and about the nature of successful school change and restructuring (including the establishment of an active and intentional learning community of teachers and students) also poses limits on mechanical notions of enforcement.

In the face of these limits on top-down enforcement, those at the local level who have a stake in positive educational outcomes—particularly the parents and students—must be empowered, in terms of both authority and information, to help decide the desired outcomes, see that the mandated processes are followed, and seek remedies when they are not. This is particularly important in the context of a society and community where the education professionals may not fully reflect the cultural breadth and diversity of their clients.

Educational Standards and the Workplace

The current focus on new educational standards poses both a major opportunity and a major danger for the rights of, and indeed the fates of, young people. Far too few jobs fit the fantasy of a high-skill, high-wage economy waiting to employ the talents of a well-educated populace.[48] The interaction between historical inequalities and an economy that provides only limited slots for full use of that talent is evident in the fact that, among full-time workers, female college graduates earn less than males with only high school diplomas, female high school graduates earn less than males with only eight years of elementary school education, and the unemployment rate for black high school graduates is higher than the rate for white high school dropouts.[49]

The huge shortage of jobs in our current economy that fully utilize, or reward, the higher skills we want our schools to teach poses both a dilemma and an opportunity. Reducing educational standards to the low skill levels demanded by the bulk of jobs currently available would compound the injury of wasted careers with the matching injury of minimal education. On the other hand, allowing employers to use higher educational certification standards, such as heightened graduation requirements, for hiring or promotion, when their jobs do not in fact demand those skills, would be a direct violation of Title VII of the 1964 Civil Rights Act,[50] which bans employment discrimination.[51]

From this point of view, however, civil rights law can and must be seen as an engine of economic growth and recovery, not an obstacle. It tells employers that the problems of the economy cannot be blamed on students and workers, or shifted to the schools, as inadequate as the schools may be. It tells them that pretending to have a high-skills workplace, and screening out people on that basis, is not enough. Instead, they must actually have a high-skills workplace where the development we want our schools to foster is utilized and valued. Making employers demonstrate that they have such a workplace as a condition of partnership with the schools, whether for student work placements or the use of educational certification requirements, is both consistent with existing law and a significant stimulus for eliminating the waste of human talent that limits our society.

Conclusion

Whether the movement toward higher standards for schools fulfills our fears or our hopes is linked to whether the notion of rights becomes central to the change process. Students must be seen as having rights to an educational program that is effectively designed to achieve those standards, to well-designed attention when the program is not working, and, along with their parents, to a role in the process by which these outcomes are determined.[52] The basis for those rights appears in our emerging law, but they will not be realized without active advocacy.

NOTES

1. *See, e.g.,* Council of Chief State School Officers, Higher Learning for All (1990). *See also* National Council on Education Standards and Testing, Raising Standards for American Education: A Report to Congress, the Secretary of Education, the National Education Goals Panel, and the American People (1992).

2. *See* McUsic, The Use of Education Clauses in School Finance Reform Litigation, 28 Harv. J. on Legis. 307 (1991); Paul Minorini, Chapter 19 in this volume.

3. *Compare* Edgewood Indep. Sch. Dist. v. Kirby, 777 S.W.2d 391 (Tex. 1989), *with* San Antonio Indep. Sch. Dist. v. Rodriguez, 411 U.S. 1 (1973), *reh'g denied*, 411 U.S. 959 (1973). *See also* Serrano v. Priest, 487 P.2d 1241 (Cal. 1971), *cert. denied*, 432 U.S. 907 (1977); Rose v. Council for Better Educ., 790 S.W.2d 186 (Ky. 1989); Helena Elementary Sch. Dist. No. 1 v. Montana, 769 P.2d 684 (Mont. 1989); Abbott v. Burke, 575 A.2d 359 (N.J. 1990).

4. *See, e.g.,* Hartzell v. Connell, 679 P.2d 35 (Cal. 1984).

5. Fiscal inequalities have also been subject to state equal protection challenges based upon the establishment of a suspect class or the absence of a rational relationship between the finance system and the state's legitimate goals, but these avenues are less directly relevant to the focus in this chapter on establishment of a right to education.

6. 255 S.E.2d 859 (W. Va. 1979). *See also* Rose v. Council for Better Educ., 790 S.W.2d 186 (Ky. 1989).

7. 20 U.S.C. § 2722(b) (1988).

8. Chapter 1 of Title I of the Elementary and Secondary Education Act of 1965, 20 U.S.C. §§ 2701–2854 (1988).

9. According to evaluators:

> [M]ost Chapter 1 elementary reading and mathematics projects provided students with few opportunities to engage in higher order skills. In reading, for example, students were taught phonics and vocabulary and taught to read words or sentences. They were rarely asked to read paragraphs or stories or to construe meaning from text. In mathematics, students practiced computation skills and seldom applied mathematics facts to solving problems.

Office of Educational Research and Improvement, U.S. Department of Education, National Assessment of Chapter 1: The Current Operation of the Chapter 1 Program 86 (1987). *See also* 20 U.S.C. § 2801(b)(1988); S. Rep. No. 122, 100th Cong., 1st Sess. 110–12 (1987); H.R. Rep. No. 95, 100th Cong., 1st Sess. 24–25 (1987).

10. 20 U.S.C. § 2722(b) (1988).

11. 20 U.S.C. § 2731(b)(1)(A) (1988).

12. *See* 20 U.S.C. § 2731(f) (1988).

13. The legislative history indicates that "substantial progress" means enough progress each year to close the gap and achieve mastery of the mainstream skills by the end of three years. *See* 134 Cong. Rec. S4383 (daily ed. Apr. 20, 1988) (statement of Sen. Simon).

14. *See* Center for Law and Education, Training and Resource Materials on Quality Education: Schools, Communities and Law 233–47 (1991); B. Turnbull et al., State Administration of the Amended Chapter 1 Program (1990) (prepared for the U.S. Department of Education).

15. In part this has happened because of a confusion by administrators between two separate standards set out in the act, either of which is sufficient by itself to trigger the need for a program improvement plan—failure to make substantial progress toward meeting the desired outcomes, and failure to show improvement in aggregate performance. *See* 20 U.S.C. § 2731(b)(1) (1988). While one NCE might constitute an appropriate standard for showing some improvement in aggregate performance, it does not indicate substantial progress toward meeting the desired outcomes, stated in terms of the basic and advanced skills all students are expected to master.

16. *See* Low Achievers Can Catch Up: Chapter 1 Expects More of Schools, 7 Harvard Educ. Letter 1–4 (Jan./Feb. 1991).

17. 20 U.S.C. § 2722(c)(3) (1988).

18. *See* H.R. Rep. No. 95, 100th Cong., 1st Sess. 25 (1987); 134 Cong. Rec. H1821 (daily ed. Apr. 19, 1988) (statement of Rep. Hayes).

19. Concerning the enforceability of Chapter 1 requirements in court, see Valdez v. Grover, 563 F. Supp. 129 (W.D. Wis. 1983); Nicholson v. Pittenger, 364 F. Supp. 669 (E.D. Pa. 1973). *Nicholson* is also significant in that, even before the new program quality requirements, it found Title I violations by the state for, *inter alia*, continuing to approve, without substantial modification, local programs that evaluations had shown to be ineffective. *Nicholson* relies on the requirement, still present in the statute, for programs of "sufficient size, scope, and quality." 20 U.S.C. § 2722(c)(1) (1988).

20. The Carl D. Perkins Vocational and Applied Technology Education Act Amendments of 1990, Pub. L. No. 101-392, § 1(a), 104 Stat. 753 (1990), rewrote the provisions governing approximately one billion dollars in federal vocational education aid, 20 U.S.C. § 2301, and indirectly affects several times that amount in state and local funding for vocational programs receiving federal aid.

21. *See* 20 U.S.C. §§ 2323(a)(3)(B), (b)(1)–(3) (1988); 2326(a), 2328 (Supp. II 1990).

22. *See* 20 U.S.C. § 2327 (Supp. II 1990).

23. *See* 20 U.S.C. § 2327(a)(1)(A) (Supp. II 1990).

24. *See* 20 U.S.C. § 2328(d) (Supp. II 1990).

25. For a fuller discussion of the law, program options, and advocacy strategies, see Center for Law and Education, Vocational Education: A New Opportunity for Educational and Community Change, Newsnotes no. 43 (Dec. 1991), special issue on vocational education.

26. *See, e.g.,* Center for Law and Education, Problems in Implementing the Perkins Act: Preliminary Report Concerning State Plans (1991) (on file with author).

27. 20 U.S.C. §§ 1400–1485 (1988), formerly the Education of the Handicapped Act.

28. 29 U.S.C. § 794 (1988).

29. *See* D. Lipsky & A. Gartner, Beyond Separate Education: Quality Education for All (1989).

30. 42 U.S.C. § 2000d (1988). *See* Lau v. Nichols, 414 U.S. 563 (1974).

31. 20 U.S.C. §§ 1703(f), 1706 (1988).

32. The leading case in the development of this standard is Castaneda v. Pickard, 648 F.2d 989 (5th Cir. 1981).

33. Title VI of the 1964 Civil Rights Act, 42 U.S.C. § 2000d (1988).

34. Title IX of the Education Amendments of 1972, 20 U.S.C. § 1681 (1988).

35. Section 504 of the Rehabilitation Act of 1973, 29 U.S.C. § 794 (1988).

36. The Title VI regulations barring unjustified practices that, despite being facially neutral, have racially disparate impact were upheld in Guardians Ass'n v. Civil Service Comm'n, 463 U.S. 582 (1983). *See also* Larry P. v. Riles, 793 F.2d 969 (9th Cir. 1986) (applying the standard to use of IQ tests in California schools).

37. *See, e.g.,* J. Oakes, Keeping Track: How Schools Structure Inequality (1985).

38. *See* McNeal v. Tate, 508 F.2d 1017 (5th Cir. 1975); Georgia Conference of Branches of NAACP v. State of Georgia, 775 F.2d 1403 (11th Cir. 1985). *See also* Larry P. v. Riles, 793 F.2d 969 (9th Cir. 1986).

39. *See* Washington v. Davis, 426 U.S. 229 (1976).

40. *See* Debra P. v. Turlington, 474 F. Supp. 244, 254–57 (M.D. Fla. 1979), *modified,* 644 F.2d 397 (5th Cir. 1981).

41. *See* 411 U.S. 1, 37 (1973).

42. *See, e.g.,* National Council on Education Standards and Testing, Raising Standards for American Education, *supra* note 1; Secretary's Commission on Achieving Necessary Skills, What Work Requires of Schools: A SCANS Report for America 2000 (1991); U.S. Department of Education, America 2000: An Education Strategy Sourcebook (1991).

43. *See, e.g.,* Nelson v. Heyne, 491 F.2d 352 (7th Cir. 1974), *cert. denied,* 417 U.S. 976 (1974); Wyatt v. Aderholt, 503 F.2d 1305 (5th Cir. 1974).

44. *See* Debra P. v. Turlington, 474 F. Supp. at 266–67, 644 F.2d at 403–407.

45. 20 U.S.C. § 2731(b)(1)(A) (1988).

46. *See* Curriculum and Evaluation Standards for School Mathematics (1989); Professional Standards for Teaching Mathematics (1991).

47. 42 U.S.C. § 9837(b) (1988); 45 C.F.R. Part 1304, Subpart E (Parent Involvement Objectives and Performance Standards) and Appendix B (Head Start Policy Manual: The Parents).

48. *See* Commission on the Skills of the American Workforce, National Center on Education and the Economy, America's Choice: High Skills or Low Wages! (1990); L. Mishel & R. Teixeira, The Myth of the Coming Labor Shortage: Jobs, Skills, and Incomes of America's Workforce 2000 (1991).

49. *See* National Center for Education Statistics, Digest of Education Statistics (1988); J. Wetzel, American Youth: A Statistical Snapshot (1989).

50. 42 U.S.C. § 2000e (1988).

51. *See* Griggs v. Duke Power Co., 401 U.S. 424 (1971); Civil Rights Act of 1991, Pub. L. No. 102-166, 105 Stat. 1071 (1991), codifying the *Griggs* line of cases and overturning the contrasting decision in Wards Cove Packing Co. v. Atonio, 490 U.S. 642 (1989).

52. *See* Pressman, Twenty-Three Years of Education Advocacy: Progress, Lessons, and Future Challenges, 26 Clearinghouse Rev. 10, 20 (1992):

> Will government, at appropriate levels: (i) identify broad curricula which all (or substantially all) students should master; (ii) develop methods to insure their delivery in the classroom to *all* students; (iii) provide local districts the resources needed to address the needs of their particular student populations; (iv) address the concomitants of poverty affecting increasing numbers of students; and (v) create an opportunity structure in society, with enough good jobs, evidencing to increasing numbers of students that strong school achievement will have rewards?

CHAPTER NINETEEN

Avoiding the Limitations of the Texas and New Jersey School Finance Remedies with an Educational Adequacy Theory of School Reform

Paul Minorini

LAWSUITS CHALLENGING state school financing schemes are pending in about half the states around the country.[1] Typically, students and parents residing in under-funded school districts have brought such school finance cases in state court, challenging the state's system of financing public education under either the state constitution's equal protection clause, its education clause, or both.[2]

These suits generally involve one of two related claims. The first, commonly referred to as a "funding equity" claim, alleges that the state's system of funding public schools results in constitutionally impermissible disparities in per pupil expenditures between school districts. The second, commonly referred to as an "educational adequacy" claim, alleges that some schools in the state fail to provide students with a constitutionally guaranteed minimum level of education. To date, no court has decided a case based exclusively on an adequacy theory.[3] However, issues of educational adequacy are often raised in funding equity suits to illustrate the negative effects inadequate funding may have on educational opportunities and student achievement.

The surge in school finance litigation in the 1990s follows a period in the late 1980s marked by significant plaintiffs' victories in funding equity cases in Texas,[4] Kentucky,[5] and New Jersey.[6] These recent victories indicate that school finance litigation will play a critical role in education reform in the years to come.

The effectiveness of that role, however, must be questioned in light of the political and public responses to judicially ordered remedies in New Jersey and Texas.

In this chapter I use those responses to illustrate the limitations of school finance reforms based on a funding equity theory. I then outline a model for an educational adequacy claim and recount how a lawsuit in Alabama applied such a model. Finally, I describe how a suit based on an educational adequacy theory can avoid the limitations that have plagued the Texas and New Jersey reform efforts.

Limitations of the Texas and New Jersey School Finance Remedies

Public and Political Responses—Texas

In *Edgewood Independent School District v. Kirby*, the Texas Supreme Court held that the Texas system of financing public schools violated the state constitution's mandate that the state establish and maintain an "efficient" system of public education to provide for the "general diffusion of knowledge."[7] Holding that disparities in educational expenditures have a "real and meaningful impact on the educational opportunity offered students,"[8] the court in *Edgewood* ordered the Texas legislature to establish a new educational funding system by May 1990.

While the court in *Edgewood* acknowledged a relationship between educational expenditures and the quality of educational opportunities provided in a particular school, it did not interpret the "general diffusion of knowledge" clause of the Texas constitution as requiring schools to provide a certain minimum level of education. Rather, the court held generally that "the present system . . . provides not for a diffusion that is general, but for one that is limited and unbalanced. The resultant inequalities are thus directly contrary to the constitutional vision of efficiency."[9] The court limited its holding and remedial order to funding equity issues.

After nearly a year of public and political turmoil, on April 11, 1991, the Texas legislature passed a school finance plan that the trial court accepted.[10] Under the plan, referred to by some as the "Robin Hood" plan, school districts with high property values were to shift money to districts with low property values within newly created "county-based education taxing districts."[11] This plan sparked fierce opposition from the high-property-value districts, which stood to lose significant funding for their schools under the new scheme. These wealthier districts filed a lawsuit challenging the plan, resulting on January 30, 1992, in the Texas Supreme Court's declaring that the county-based education taxing districts were unconstitutional.[12] The court gave the legislature until June 1, 1993, to devise a new school funding plan consistent with all of the court's previous orders,[13] and allowed the state to continue to collect taxes under the "Robin Hood" plan until that time.

This decision immediately sparked hostile reactions from both the general public and the legislature. Some legislators proposed a state constitutional amendment restricting the Texas Supreme Court's power to review laws relating to the state's public school system.[14] The amendment would have applied a presumption of constitutionality to such laws if there was "any evidence that the statute rationally furthers a legitimate state interest," thereby effectively allowing the legislature to control school financing plans free of court interference. In addition, some private citizens filed a lawsuit challenging the legality of continuing to administer a tax that the Texas Supreme Court had declared unconstitutional.

The battle over school finance equity in Texas illustrates the limitations of a remedy based on a funding equity theory. That battle is clearly not over. The important question, however, is how much longer students will continue to receive substandard educations in underfunded schools, while the legislature and public fight it out.

Public and Political Responses—New Jersey

The school finance remedy in the New Jersey case also illustrates the limitations of the funding equity theory. In *Abbott v. Burke*, plaintiffs representing four of New Jersey's poorest school districts claimed that the state's school finance system violated the New Jersey constitution's guarantee of a "thorough and efficient" system of public education.[15] In 1990 the New Jersey Supreme Court ruled that the state's public school financing system was indeed unconstitutional as applied to the poorer urban districts, because the education delivered in those schools was neither thorough nor efficient. The court found that "under the present system . . . the poorer the district and the greater its need, the less money [is] available, and the worse the education" that it can provide.[16] While *Abbott* discussed the substantive inadequacies of educational opportunities provided to students in New Jersey's poorer school districts,[17] its remedial order merely required that the legislature amend the New Jersey school finance scheme to eliminate the funding disparities between poor and wealthy school districts.[18]

Abbott has sparked years of turmoil and infighting in New Jersey's political and educational systems. To comply with the court's mandate, the New Jersey legislature passed, and the governor signed into law, the Quality Education Act ("QEA I") in July 1990. The QEA I allocated an additional $1.1 billion to the state's public school system, with much of this money aiding the poorest urban districts.[19]

Before the 1991–92 school year began, however, voter outrage over increases in state sales and income taxes created intense political pressure and maneuvering that resulted in a new legislative program called the Quality Education Act II ("QEA II").[20] The QEA II redirected $360 million of the funds designated for educational programs under the QEA I to municipal property tax relief.[21] In addition, the QEA II placed substantial spending caps on many school districts.[22]

In response to the QEA II's passage, the *Abbott* plaintiffs filed another lawsuit challenging the constitutionality of the QEA II in light of the decision in *Abbott*. This new suit claims in part that the QEA II actually widened the spending disparities between poor urban and wealthy suburban schools. As in Texas, the battle over school finance reform in New Jersey will most likely continue to rage well into the future.

Limitations of Funding Equity Remedies

The practical limitations of funding equity remedies are illustrated by the legislative and public hostility inspired by the courts' orders in New Jersey and Texas. In both cases the remedial orders were limited strictly to equalizing school funding. In neither case did the court require that the schools receiving additional money under revised school funding packages use it specifically to improve the educational opportunities available to students in underfunded districts. In both *Edgewood* and *Abbott,* the courts' involvement will end when the legislatures finally passes school finance plans that satisfy the courts' notions of funding equity. This limited role stops far short of ensuring that the educational opportunities offered to students in deficient schools will improve.

A second limitation of funding equity remedies is the political difficulty of gaining public support for the tax adjustments required to equalize school funding. Such remedies focus the public's attention on equalizing dollars spent per pupil. This emphasis results in the public perception that revenues raised from increased taxes are simply shifting resources; taking money away from the rich and giving it to the poor. The increased dollars are not directly tied to any new or innovative educational programs that would offer the promise of children receiving better educations. If the increased dollars were tied to such programs, the public would at least have a sense that their money was "buying something" whose success or failure they could measure by evaluating student performance over time.

Educational Adequacy Claims

A Model for an Adequacy
Theory of School Reform

An educational adequacy theory of school reform focuses directly on the lack of educational opportunities in one or more plaintiff school districts. Such a suit alleges that students in those districts are not receiving an adequate education, as measured by state-defined or other contemporary educational standards, and as guaranteed by the education clause of the state constitution. The injury that an adequacy claim seeks to remedy, therefore, is the unconstitutionally inadequate education available in certain school districts. In most instances, the inadequacy results from a combination of the special needs of schoolchildren attending those schools and the lack of educational resources to meet those needs. A remedy in a successful adequacy case would require that the state make available sufficient resources to support programs and improvements in the plaintiff school districts specifically designed to address the inadequacies and to meet the educational needs of students residing there.

An educational adequacy model of school reform involves several steps. The first is to define a constitutional standard for a minimum level of education. Such a definition can be based on the state constitution's language and legislative history, as well as on regulations—promulgated by the legislature and the state education agency—that set substantive educational standards for all schools. State board of education standards are an appropriate measure of the constitutionally required minimum level of education because in most states the state constitution charges the state legislature with the responsibility of establishing and administering the school system, and the state legislature in turn often delegates that constitutional responsibility to the state board of education. One type of educational standard might require schools to provide students with minimum educational opportunities (input standards). Other standards might set minimum levels of educational achievement for students leaving the schools, such as minimum performance levels on standardized achievement tests (output standards).

Both types of standards are essential to an educational adequacy theory. First, plaintiffs must evaluate the educational resources available in their schools, such as science laboratory facilities, course offerings, instructional materials, staff, library resources, and other input measures, and compare them with the state standards. Plaintiffs must also examine educational achievements of students throughout the state. Such an evaluation can rely, for example, on standardized test scores, tests of reading and writing skills, and statewide dropout, promotion, attendance, and graduation rates. These measures would indicate what basic skills students leaving the school system actually possess. Plaintiffs must then compare the actual educational achievements of students in deficient schools with the standard of educational achievement mandated by the constitution and state standards.

If deficiencies exist in the educational achievements of students in some schools and in the educational opportunities offered there, then the court could find a constitutional violation and attempt to fashion an appropriate remedy. Such a remedy, while necessarily involving additional funding, could direct the state generally to improve the substantive education offered to students throughout the state. The court could also suggest programmatic remedies that would address specific educational deficiencies. For instance, it could direct the state to fund and implement a dropout prevention program to address a high dropout rates in particular schools within the system. The court's role in supervising the education offered to students schools would not end until schools began to provide constitutionally adequate educational opportunities to students that allow them to attain constitutionally adequate levels of educational proficiency.

The Alabama Suit: An Example of an Adequacy Claim

A school reform suit filed in Alabama, *Harper v. Hunt*, relied primarily on an educational adequacy model similar to the one outlined above, in conjunction with a traditional funding equity theory.[23] The plaintiffs were more than thirty parents and students from four of the state's poorest school districts. The lawsuit sought a ruling that the Alabama constitution contains a right to an adequate level of education and that such an education is not being provided under the state's inadequate and unequal system of school financing.

The Alabama suit was unique because it relied primarily on an educational adequacy theory. The plaintiffs alleged that the state was failing to provide students in some poor schools with the opportunity to receive a minimally adequate education required by the Alabama constitution. Relying in part on the legislative history of the state constitution's education clause,[24] the plaintiffs argued that every student is constitutionally entitled to an education that will "qualify him for the responsible duties of life."[25] In addition to the constitutional basis for the adequacy claim, the Alabama plaintiffs relied on the state's statutory and regulatory framework. Plaintiffs pointed to the state board of education's achievement standards to define the constitutionally mandated minimum level of education all students must receive.[26]

Measured by both input and output standards, Alabama's education system is particularly in need of the reforms that could result from a lawsuit of this kind. Alabama ranks next to last in the nation in per capita expenditures for public schools, spending only 65 percent of the national average. Moreover, that money is not equitably distributed. The school system with the most money available in 1987–88, for instance, spent $4,335.00 per enrollee, while the school system with the least spent $1,912.63.[27] Many schools also lack adequate textbooks, science laboratories, guidance counselors, school librarians, or school buses.[28] Such deficiencies in educational resources keep the schools from providing the educational opportunities that would enable students to attain constitutionally mandated minimum levels of educational achievement. In addition, student performances on standardized tests in Alabama, although an imperfect measure of achievement, confirm that many are receiving an inadequate level of education.

On March 31, 1993, a state trial court in Alabama declared Alabama's entire public school system unconstitutional under the state's education and equal protection clauses, which the court found guaranteed both an adequate and an equitable public education to every schoolchild in the state, including children with disabilities. The court noted pervasive disparities in funding throughout the state, resulting in a school system that fell dramatically short of allocating educational opportunities fairly or equitably. The disparities in educational opportunities were reflected in school facilities, curriculum, instructional materials and supplies, staff, and extracurricular activities. The court concluded that "the quality of educational opportunities available to a child in the public schools of Alabama depends upon the fortuitous circumstances of where that child happens to reside and attend school—a situation that the Governor himself, according to his own testimony, cannot condone."

The court also found that the education provided in Alabama's public schools was constitutionally inadequate. Many Alabama schools fell far below the state's own standards of educational adequacy in facilities, curriculum, staffing, textbooks, supplies and equipment, and transportation. In addition, the court held that Alabama schools failed to provide a minimally adequate education in an absolute sense. The court cited unacceptably high dropout rates and students' unpreparedness for college or the workforce as evidence that students were not receiving adequate educations measured by any standard.

The plaintiffs' victory in Alabama, the first case to rely extensively on an educational adequacy claim, could spark educational adequacy lawsuits in other states around the country. Even in states where previous funding equity claims have failed, well-defined state education standards could allow plaintiffs to file a suit alleging that the education offered in some or all of the state's schools is constitutionally inadequate.

How an Educational Adequacy Theory Avoids the Limitations of a Funding Equity Suit

An educational adequacy model of school reform, such as the one employed in Alabama, avoids the remedial limitations of a funding equity claim. It allows the court to order increases in funding as a vehicle to improving educational opportunities and student achievement levels, rather than simply treating additional funding as an end in itself. In contrast to funding equity suits, under an adequacy theory the court's involvement in education reform would not end simply when underfunded school districts receive more money. The state would need to provide more educational opportunities and improve student achievement levels to rid itself of the court's supervision. The adequacy model allows courts to supervise the schools' use of additional funding, and to ensure that the state takes responsibility for improving the educational achievement of students in deficient schools.

Some would argue that sustained court involvement is a bad thing. However, in some circumstances such involvement is necessary to ensure that any remedy is both effective and efficient, and that children get an education that gives them the skills necessary to participate in society as educated and productive members.

An adequacy claim also would make it easier for a legislature to gain the support of the general public for any tax adjustments required to fund the remedy. Politicians could directly tie increased funding to enacting specific educational programs, and the success or failure of those programs could be measured in terms of student achievements. The public could hold the legislature accountable for how any additional funding was spent by evaluating whether schools were providing students with greater educational opportunities and improving achievement levels.

However, it is important for the courts, public, and legislatures to realize that education reforms will not result immediately in increased student achievement. Such reforms take time. They must eliminate all vestiges of the previously deficient education system before there will be measurable improvements in students' performance.

The court's decision in *Rose v. Council for Better Education*,[29] and the Kentucky legislature and public's response to the court's remedial order in that case, demonstrates that an adequacy-based theory of school reform avoids the remedial limitations of a funding equity claim. *Rose*, while originally based on a funding equity theory, resulted in the broadest remedy in a school finance case to date. The court declared that the entire system of public schools in Kentucky failed to provide for a constitutionally mandated "efficient" system of common schools.[30] It ordered the Kentucky legislature not only to correct the funding disparities between rich and poor districts, but also to create a new education system that provided adequate and equal educational opportunities for all students.[31] Beyond providing general guidelines as to what constituted an "efficient" system of education, the court left the task of designing a specific plan for reform to the legislature.

Because *Rose* reached far beyond equal funding and required an overhaul of the entire system of education, it resembles the type of remedy that would result from an adequacy claim. Given this similarity, it is interesting to note that when the Kentucky legislature increased taxes to fund the education reform packages it designed in response to the court's order, it did not meet the fierce public opposition encountered by the Texas and New Jersey legislatures. The ease with which the Kentucky legislature and public responded to the court's order most likely is due to the nature of the reforms the legislature implemented. In April 1990, the legislature passed the Kentucky Education Reform Act,[32] which, through a series of innovative and specific reform programs, fundamentally changed the way educational services are delivered to students in Kentucky. Any increased taxes were tied directly to specific new educational programs with a built-in system of accountability. People in the state generally have been supportive of these programmatic education reforms.

The lesson to be learned from Kentucky is that programmatic remedies, the type that would result from a case based on an adequacy theory, are more likely to receive the public and political support they need to be effective.

Conclusion

While the Texas and New Jersey legislatures struggle to comply with the courts' remedial orders without alienating the public that elects them and pays for school reforms, children continue to receive constitutionally deficient and unequal educations. Judging from the experiences in Texas and New Jersey, an educational adequacy theory of school reform may promise a brighter future for such children. The programmatic remedies offered by such a model will not only more directly improve the quality of education offered to students, but they will also be more acceptable to the public and legislatures. If the Alabama adequacy-based claim is ultimately successful, students there may not need to wait years for an education that meets constitutional standards, as students in New Jersey and Texas have.

NOTES

1. During the summer of 1993, litigation was pending at the trial stage in the states listed below. In some instances, the plaintiffs lost a previous case in the state supreme court, but further complaints have been filed. Where that occurred, the prior decision is also mentioned. Arizona: Roosevelt Elementary Sch. Dist. 66 v. Bishop (1991), prior decision in Shofstall v. Hollins, 515 P.2d 590 (1973); Idaho: Frazier v. Idaho (1990), prior decision in Thompson v. Engleking, 537 P.2d 635 (1975); Kansas: Mock v. Kansas (1989), Unified Sch. Dist. 259 v. Kansas (1991), Hancock v. Stephan (1991), Newton Unified Sch. Dist. 373 v. Kansas (1990); Louisiana: Charlet v. Louisiana (1992); Massachusetts: Webby v. Dukakis (1988), and Murdoch v. Weld (1990); New York: Reform Educ. Financing Inequities Today (REFIT) v. Cuomo (1991), prior decision in Board of Educ. v. Nyquist, 578 N.Y.S.2d 969 (1987); Ohio: Howard v. Walter, 1992 Ohio App. LEXIS 4223 (Ohio Ct. App. Aug. 20, 1992), and Thompson v. Ohio (1991), prior decision in Board of Educ. v. Walter, 390 N.E.2d 813 (1979); Oklahoma: Fair Sch. Financing Council of Oklahoma v. Oklahoma, 746 P.2d 1135 (Okla. 1987); Pennsylvania: Pennsylvania Ass'n of Rural and Small Schs. v. Casey (1992), prior decision in Danson v. Casey, 613 A.2d 1198 (Pa. 1987); Rhode Island: City of Pawtucket v. Sundlun (1992); South Dakota: Bezdichek v. South Dakota (1991).

Plaintiffs won at the trial court level, but an appeal is either pending or expected in the following states—Minnesota: Skeen v. Minnesota (1990); Missouri: The Committee v. Missouri, and Lee's Summit P.S.U. v. Missouri (1990); North Dakota: Bismarck Public Schools v. North Dakota (1993). Plaintiffs won at the trial court level and no appeal is expected in Alabama: Harper v. Hunt (1991), and Alabama Coalition for Equity v. Hunt (1990).

Plaintiffs lost at the trial court stage, but an appeal was filed in the following states—Alaska: Matanuska-Susitna Borough v. Alaska (1989); Illinois: The Committee v. Edgar (1990); Nebraska: Gould v. Orr (1990); New Hampshire: Claremont v. Gregg (1991).

In five states the plaintiffs won at the state supreme court level, but further compliance litigation has been filed—California: Serrano v. Priest, 569 P.2d 1303 (Cal. 1977); Connecticut: Sheff v. O'Neill (1992); New Jersey: Abbott v. Burke, 575 A.2d 359 (N.J. 1990); Washington: Seattle Sch. Dist. No. 1 v. Washington, 585 P.2d 71 (Wash. 1978); West Virginia: Pauley v. Kelly, 255 S.E.2d 859 (W. Va. 1979).

2. For a discussion of school finance cases that have been based on state constitutional equal protection grounds and/or education clauses, *see* McUsic, The Use of Education Clauses in School Finance Reform Litigation, 28 Harv. J. on Legis. 307 (1991).

3. A March 31, 1993, Alabama trial court decision for the plaintiffs found that Alabama's public education system was unconstitutional, under both a funding equity *and* an educational adequacy theory.

4. Edgewood Indep. Sch. Dist. v. Kirby, 777 S.W.2d 391 (Tex. 1989), *aff'd on other grounds*, 804 S.W.2d 491 (Tex. 1991), *later proceeding*, Carrollton-Farmers Branch Indep. Sch. Dist. v. Edgewood Indep. Sch. Dist., 826 S.W.2d 489 (Tex. 1992).

5. Rose v. Council for Better Educ., 790 S.W.2d 186 (Ky. 1989).

6. Abbott v. Burke, 575 A.2d 359 (N.J. 1990).

7. *Edgewood*, 777 S.W.2d at 397 (1989) (citing Tex. Const. art. VII, § 1).

8. *Id*. at 393.

9. *Id*. at 396.

10. *See* Key Events in School Finance Case, Houston Post, Jan. 31, 1992, at A10.

11. *See* Educational Testing Service, The State of Inequality, at 20 (1991).

12. Carrollton-Farmers Branch Sch. Dist. v. Edgewood Indep. Sch. Dist., 826 S.W.2d 489 (Tex. 1992).

13. *Id*.

14. West, Amendment on School Finance Gaining Ground, Houston Post, Feb. 2, 1992, at C3.

15. Abbott v. Burke, 575 A.2d 359, 363 (N.J. 1990) (citing N.J. Const., art. VIII, § 4 (1947)).

16. *Id*.

17. *Id*. at 394–400.

18. *Id*. at 408.

19. *See* Educational Testing Service, State of Inequality, *supra* note 11, at 22.

20. *Id*.

21. *Id*.

22. *Id*.

23. Harper v. Hunt, No. Civ-91-0117-R (Cir. Ct. Montgomery Co., Ala. filed Jan. 18, 1991).

24. *Id*. at 18 (citing Ala. Const. art. XIV, § 256).

25. *Id*. at 18–19 (citing Opening Statement of John B. Knox, president of Constitutional Convention of 1901, *in* Official Proceedings of the 1901 Convention, at 15).

26. *Id*. at 20–27 (citing Ala. Admin. Code rr. 290-010-010, 290-090-020).

27. *Id*.

28. *Id*. at 27–33.

29. 790 S.W.2d 186 (Ky. 1989).

30. *Id*. at 215.

31. *Id*.

32. *See* Legislative Research Commission, A Guide to the Kentucky Education Reform Act of 1990 (April 1990); Commonwealth of Kentucky, Tracking Our Schools: Strategies for Achieving Education Goals, Kentucky's First Annual Report to the President (1991).

■ CHAPTER TWENTY

Hazelwood School District and the Role of First Amendment Institutions

Bruce C. Hafen

THE SUPREME COURT'S 5 to 3 decision in *Hazelwood School District v. Kuhlmeier*,[1] which authorizes educators to supervise the content of an official high school newspaper, is probably the most significant free speech case involving public school students since the Court decided *Tinker v. Des Moines Independent Community School District*[2] almost twenty-five years ago, holding that schools could not prohibit students from wearing black armbands protesting the Vietnam war. *Hazelwood* is interesting not only because it marks the Court's first application of First Amendment principles to public school newspapers, but because the case creates a category of student speech subject to school supervision: "school-sponsored expressive activities."[3] I wish to suggest that, rather than weakening the Court's commitment to the constitutional rights of students, *Hazelwood* seeks to strengthen students' fundamental interest in the underlying principles of free expression: the right to develop their own educated capacity for self-expression.

This decision reinforcing the institutional authority of schools also reflects the Court's developing perspective on the general role of First Amendment institutions.[4] The *Hazelwood* Court rejected students' claims to individual freedom of expression in favor of educators' broad authority to define and supervise the educational mission of public schools both in and out of the classroom. Clarifying doubts about the breadth of its rationale in a 1986 student assembly speech case[5] and resolving some of the uncertainty arising from its fractured opinions in a 1982

Reprinted with permission in redacted form from Bruce C. Hafen, Hazelwood School District *and the Role of First Amendment Institutions*, 1988 Duke L.J. 685.

library-book–banning case,[6] the Court strengthened schools' right to institutional discretion whenever educational activities are involved. *Hazelwood's* deferential approach in an area where limitations on expression have become highly suspect—newspapers—reflects the Court's emerging recognition of the affirmative role of certain intermediate institutions in First Amendment theory.

The Court's new emphasis on First Amendment institutions seems to arise not merely from the speech-related associational interests of individual members in a group, but also from an understanding that First Amendment institutions qua institutions can sustain conditions that nourish such values as those associated with religion and expression. Significantly, this understanding follows a turbulent generation in which critics opposed to all forms of institutional authority expressed a profound anti-institutional skepticism in the name of individual rights.[7] But not all institutional influences undermine individual rights. Indeed, as the Court is beginning to note, personal rights may take ongoing sustenance from certain forms of institutional nurturing.

Thus, *Hazelwood* contrasts sharply with what seemed during the 1960s and 1970s to be a long-term and probably irreversible trend: the expansion of individual rights in derogation of all forms of institutional authority, including the discretion of schools and other public and private agencies involved with children.[8] Because *Hazelwood* reflects the Court's new emphasis on First Amendment institutions, it deserves attention even beyond its impact on student speech per se.

The Student Expression Cases

The Court first protected student expression in 1969, in the *Tinker* case. In most school speech cases since then, lower courts generally assumed that *Tinker* established a constitutional presumption against limitations on student expression—rebuttable only upon a showing of material (usually physical) disruption of schoolwork or clear invasions of the rights of others. Until *Hazelwood* the presence of education-related interests in extracurricular affairs typically did not overcome this presumption.

Although after *Tinker* the Supreme Court continued to address other issues raised in the public school context,[9] the Court did not hear another school speech case until *Board of Education v. Pico*[10] in 1982. But *Pico* by no means suggested that the Court was suspicious of a school board's discretionary judgments on most educational matters. A three-Justice plurality found that students have a "right to receive information and ideas"[11] that prevents the arbitrary or suppressive removal of library books, but the plurality still acknowledged a school board's right to remove books that the board finds "pervasively vulgar" or otherwise lacking in "educational suitability."[12] Those subjective limits went well beyond *Tinker's* concerns with disruption and harm, arguably anticipating *Hazelwood's* general deference in situations implicating educational judgments in or out of the classroom.

Bethel School District No. 403 v. Fraser,[13] in 1986, marked a potentially significant departure from *Tinker,* with the Court painting the school's educational domain in broad strokes, even resurrecting the in loco parentis doctrine[14] to reaffirm the place of public schools in teaching basic values within and beyond the classroom. *Fraser* could be read more narrowly, because it dealt with vulgar and offensive (even if not obscene) expression by a student directed toward a captive audience of minors. *Hazelwood* makes clear, however, that *Fraser* rested on a more substantial foundation, making it an important transitional case that signaled the Court's willingness to read *Tinker* more narrowly than many lower courts had read it.

Hazelwood and the Limits of *Tinker*

Spectrum was the official school newspaper produced by students in a journalism class at Hazelwood High School, near St. Louis. The paper had a reputation for addressing controversial topics, but in May 1983 the principal found certain of *Spectrum*'s stories on teenage pregnancy and divorce inappropriately sensitive and personal, and deleted the pages containing the stories.[15] The student authors filed suit, claiming infringement of their First Amendment rights, and eventually won on appeal to the Eighth Circuit.[16] The court held that *Spectrum* was a public forum[17] and applied the standards established in *Tinker.* Because the court of appeals found no factual justification for the principal to forecast either a disruption or possible tort liability, it saw no basis for distinguishing the *Tinker* presumptions favoring student speech.[18]

In an opinion by Justice White, the Supreme Court found that the high school had not designated *Spectrum* as a public forum[19] and held that educators have presumptive control over "school-sponsored publications, theatrical productions, and other expressive activities" whenever such activities are faculty-supervised and involve a school's educational mission in a way that implies school sponsorship.[20] The Court thus read *Fraser* broadly as a case that turned not only on the vulgarity of the speech in question, but also on the school's sponsorship of the assembly in which the speech occurred. Students' First Amendment rights will outweigh educators' decisions not when a speech lacks vulgarity, but "only when the [educator's] decision . . . has no valid educational purpose."[21] By creating such a category of education-related speech, the opinion limits *Tinker* to "personal expression that happens to occur on the school premises."[22]

When the Court applied the "valid educational purpose" standard to the *Hazelwood* facts, it required only a rational basis for the principal's actions. The Court found that the principal "could reasonably" have based some of his decisions on educational considerations, such as whether the student writers had mastered the journalism class curriculum on the treatment of controversial issues, whether student editorial decisions had satisfied journalistic standards, or whether the material was appropriate for *Spectrum*'s high-school-age readers.[23] Other decisions by the principal were commonsense judgment calls, such as assessing the likelihood that the stories would offend the families they described and judging whether time allowed changes in the stories before the publication deadline.[24]

The Court's analysis suggests that the *Hazelwood* standard involves two stages of inquiry: Courts must first ask whether the student expression at issue occurs in a context that implicates the school's educational mission and must then ask whether the educator's decision has a rational—but not necessarily an explicitly educational—basis. Satisfying the first requirement demands the presence of an education-related activity—an activity, in or out of the classroom, that is "supervised by faculty members and designed to impart particular knowledge or skills to student participants and audiences,"[25] or an activity that "students, parents, and members of the public might reasonably perceive to bear the imprimatur of the school."[26] The presence of such an activity removes the limited but real presumption favoring student speech under *Tinker*—a presumption that continues to apply to personal expression not involving educational activities—and creates at least some presumption favoring the school's discretion. This presumption requires a student who challenges an educator's decision within the educational sphere to prove that the decision lacked any reasonable basis.

Unfortunately, the majority was not entirely consistent in explaining how this standard should be applied. Although Justice White spoke generally of reasonableness, he defined the standard in this way: "It is only when the decision to censor . . . student expression has no valid *educational* purpose that the First Amendment" requires judicial intervention.[27] Elsewhere he stated that a school's editorial control is justified "so long as [educators'] actions are reasonably related to legitimate pedagogical concerns."[28] A literal application of this language could require an "educational"—not just a reasonable—justification for each decision that limits student expression, even if the decision occurs in connection with a school-supervised activity. However, the larger context of *Hazelwood* suggests the appropriateness of a less demanding rational basis standard.

Justice White, for example, consistently used a general reasonableness test in evaluating the decisions of Hazelwood High's principal, never asking whether any of those decisions had an explicit educational purpose. The test did not require the principal to cite educational objectives to justify his concern about invading some students' privacy, his belief that the parents mentioned in the stories should have an opportunity to respond, his decision that time allowed no rewrites of the questionable stories, or his judgment that the paper's timely publication required pulling certain nonoffending stories.[29]

Moreover, the Court's prior public forum cases had already created a reasonableness standard for decisions denying adult speakers access to nonpublic forums,[30] and the limited maturity of students ordinarily gives public schools greater discretion than other state agencies.

This deferential approach finds support in Justice White's wide-ranging rationale for regarding educational activity as a sphere requiring special treatment: "[T]he education of the Nation's youth is primarily the responsibility of parents, teachers, and state and local school officials, and not of federal judges."[31] The opinion gave three reasons why courts should defer to public school officials within the realm of educational activities: (1) to maximize the educational or "teaching" value of the activity, (2) to protect immature student audiences, and (3) to avoid erroneous attribution of school sponsorship.[32] The first of these reasons (and, more remotely, the third) arguably applies to educational institutions at any level, but the second and third especially concern the effect of institutional sponsorship on the teaching of social and other norms to public-school-age children.

Taken together, these three factors indicate the Court's concern with strengthening the overall institutional authority of public schools in recognition of the compelling need to educate the nation's children more successfully, both in academic skills and in citizenship. Deferring to school officials within a broadly defined educational context may seem to have a chilling effect on student expression, but too much deference to student expression can have an equally chilling effect on the exercise of authority that successful education frequently requires. On balance, even an emphasis on students' First Amendment interests calls for a general choice favoring the best educational outcome.

Hazelwood echoes the Court's highly deferential treatment of institutional academic freedom in *Regents of the University of Michigan v. Ewing*, which upheld a faculty committee's judgment of a university student's unfitness for continued enrollment.[33] Whom, then, does the First Amendment protect in a public school, and against what forms of intrusion? Because we typically think about rights of expression only in individual terms, and because a school is technically an agency of the state, the school as an institution—or the principal representing the institution—may not seem a proper candidate for constitutional protection. For example, courts such as the Eighth Circuit assume that the school newspaper enterprise implicates only students' rights of expression.

The root question, which the typical First Amendment model fails to address, is how to organize and operate schools in order to maximize their overall contribution to the values and purposes of the First Amendment. *Hazelwood* regards that issue as a matter of educational policy, not constitutional law; therefore, it gives presumptive responsibility for such inquiries to the educational system rather than the judiciary. Thus, the school's principal and faculty supervise all educational activities to ensure that their school will educate successfully, and not merely because they are "publishers." In that sense, the institution of a school, like that of a newspaper corporation, is protected by the First Amendment. The First Amendment's interest in promoting sound educational policies protects schools from second-guessing by the courts when educational issues are at stake. As the next section explores, this basic stance advances rather than obstructs the achievement of the goals of our system of free expression.

Schools as First Amendment Institutions

It has been argued persuasively[34] that First Amendment theory should act primarily to limit the exercise of schools' discretion, in order to protect children against the risks of indoctrination and to teach them the value of participatory democracy and personal autonomy. This approach would also enable them to learn both literally and symbolically that the purpose of the Bill of Rights is to limit state authority.

However, judicial intervention intended to limit abuses of discretion by educators does not necessarily lead to meaningful autonomy for students, who may need protection against the harmful consequences of their own decisions as much as protection against abuses by school personnel. That fact about children lies at the base of our legal system's concept of the status of minors.

Arguments that stress students' rights of expression also presuppose that children have the rational capacity necessary for meaningful participation in the political process and the marketplace of ideas. But because "a child . . . is not possessed of that full capacity for individual choice which is the presupposition of First Amendment guarantees,"[35] children do not enjoy the most fundamental of democratic rights, the right to vote. Moreover, because children lack the capacity to evaluate the meaning of apparent state sponsorship, the establishment clause forbids public prayer in schools—even while it permits public prayer in a legislative chamber.[36] The *Hazelwood* dissenters overlooked the mature capacity issue, arguing instead that a published disclaimer of official sponsorship could overcome the majority's fears about erroneous attribution of school sponsorship to ideas expressed in a school newspaper.[37] Query whether a similar public disclaimer before a group classroom prayer would overcome any appearance of school endorsement.[38]

Beyond the difficulties created by children's lack of mature capacity, the idea that the First Amendment exists only to constrain state or institutional action overlooks (and indeed interferes with) the affirmative contributions that schools and other institutions can make in fulfilling the amendment's purposes. A child's most fundamental interest in First Amendment values may be in developing the capacity for self-expression and the capacity to enjoy meaningful personal autonomy. "[F]reedom of expression has two meanings: (1) freedom *from* restraints on expression and (2) freedom *for* expression—that is, having the capacity for self-expression."[39] Until children have developed this freedom "for expression," their freedom "from restraints on expression" has only limited value. Thus, a child's "right" to an effective education directly involves both the personal and the social interests that underlie the First Amendment.

Even accepting the need for effective education, however, children arguably will best develop their faculties if they are protected against adult authority. That was a major premise of the 1960s reform era, a period symbolized by anti-authoritarian protests on college campuses and by popular childhood education theories that challenged the need for adult authority.[40] One well-known theory, for example, began with the view that a child is "innately wise and realistic. If left to himself without adult suggestion of any kind, he will develop as far as he is capable of developing."[41] Empirical evidence accumulated since the reform era, however, forcefully demonstrates that the widespread reduction of institutional authority in public schools over the past generation is statistically correlated with the recently publicized declines in the academic achievement of American students. Indeed, most studies assessing that period agree: "You don't replace something with nothing. Of course, that was exactly what the educational reform of the sixties was doing."[42]

Whatever one makes of this evidence, the question whether authoritarian or antiauthoritarian approaches will best develop the minds and expressive powers of children is more a matter of educational philosophy and practice than of constitutional law. For that reason alone, First Amendment theories applied by courts largely on the basis of antiauthoritarian assumptions are at best a clumsy and limited means of ensuring optimal educational development, whether the goal is an understanding of democratic values or a mastery of basic intellectual skills. Thus, one of *Hazelwood*'s major contributions is its reaffirmation of schools' institutional role—and their accountability to the public for fulfilling it responsibly—in nurturing the underlying values of the First Amendment.

A school is not just another bureaucratic arm of the state, but an institution that mediates between the individual and the megastructures of contemporary government. Partly because of this function, parental influence over and local control of the schools have been major themes in the nation's educational history.[43] From this vantage point, the schools' primary purpose is to contribute affirmatively to the development of the American system of free expression. To achieve that goal, schools must interact with students in ways unique among all forms of interaction between the state and individuals: supervising, directing, forbearing, all according to personalized educational judgments about the needs and circumstances of each child.

In *Hazelwood*, the Supreme Court recognized the schools' distinctive institutional role as a potential source of support for, not always interference with, First Amendment values. To gain a sense of the historic significance of this development, consider some of the origins of the assumption that First Amendment protections are primarily a matter of individual rights.

The highly visible individualism of the past twenty or thirty years is but a noisy extension of such slow-moving but definite historical currents as the movement from group-oriented status to individual-oriented contract[44] and the concept of "history as the decline of community."[45] Thus, individualistic assumptions regarding First Amendment interests have direct antecedents in Western history. The Reformation led by Martin Luther was, at its theological as well as its political core, a rejection of institutional religious authority. Even more significantly for our American assumptions about the meaning of "religion" in the First Amendment, the dominant Protestant consciousness of our founding era emphasized a direct, two-way relationship between the individual and God, as opposed to the emphasis on institutional and community authority in the Catholic and Jewish traditions.[46] In addition, the notion of academic freedom had an individualistic flavor when imported from Germany in the late nineteenth and early twentieth centuries, especially in its American version, which stressed the interest of individual faculty members in "protecting [their] academic job[s]" against intrusion by lay boards of trustees.[47] Constitutional protection for academic freedom also developed as an individual matter; the Court applied the political speech theories that grew out of the 1950s anticommunism cases to the early academic freedom cases.[48]

Institutional interests hardly needed emphasis in First Amendment theory when these developments were taking place. Despite the slowly growing intellectual force of the individualistic theories, longstanding and customary patterns of institutional authority dictated an attitude of judicial deference toward established institutions until well past 1950. Indeed, the Supreme Court hardly took an interest in freedom of speech as an individual right until World War I, and from that time until the 1960s, the generally developing protection for individual expression simply chipped away at the proinstitutional status quo.[49]

During the 1960s and 1970s, however, the traditional hegemony of institutions declined dramatically, and the pendulum of constitutional history swung away from the relatively uncritical assumptions favoring institutional authority toward powerfully articulated individual protections. It could have been predicted that this pendulum would at some point hit the individualistic extreme and reverse course. During the last few years we have begun to sense the limits of unrestrained individualism and its toll on community and institutional continuity, especially with respect to mediating institutions.

Contemporary studies report Americans' deep concern "that this individualism may have grown cancerous," and may be undermining the influence of such institutions as family, church, and local community in ways that threaten "the survival of freedom itself."[50] Similarly, a thoughtful comparison of American and European approaches to the reform of abortion and divorce laws[51] finds that, despite some basic common assumptions, the American approach has become so individualistic and unbalanced that it has severed the connections between personal values and social values that European approaches have retained.[52]

In 1830, Alexis de Tocqueville foresaw the risks of democracy's tendency to encourage an acquisitive and destructive individualism, but he also believed that the commitment of Americans to "free [i.e., mediating] institutions" would "combat the effects of individualism."[53] Thus, for Tocqueville, the "intellectual and moral associations" in American life—of which the local school is a classic example—were so important that "[n]othing . . . more deserves attention."[54] Closer to our own time, Robert Nisbet echoed Tocqueville's theme with his argument that the institutional strength of mediating structures provides a crucial protection against totalitarianism. The totalitarian cannot succeed until "the social contexts of privacy—family, church, association—have been atomized. The political enslavement of man requires the emancipation of man from all the [intermediate] authorities and memberships . . . that serve . . . to insulate the individual from external political power."[55] Nisbet warned that reducing the authority of mediating institutions creates exactly the kind of "spiritual and cultural vacuum" that "the totalitarian must have for the realization of his design."[56]

American public schools were originally established as an extension of the private, local, mediating sphere, receiving from parents a delegation of authority to teach not only intellectual matters, but also the skills and values that allow individuals to resist domination by the state. That was the Jeffersonian ideal. In more modern times, the place of public schools in our cultural and political structure has become less clear, perhaps in part because the schools were called upon to perform a leading role in fulfilling the urgent need to desegregate American society. One unintended consequence of requiring schools to serve as political agents of the state may be that their normal institutional authority can appear to threaten individual liberties in the same way that any potent governmental bureaucracy does. Partly for this reason, the role of public schools today can be a source of tension and confusion, erupting in conflicts between parents and schools, local communities and state governments, state interests and federal interests, and individuals and the state.

The *Hazelwood* case reminds us, however, that the idea of in loco parentis as an educational premise is not only not dead, but can become a needed means of protecting the right of children to develop their capacity for meaningful expression—if the schools in fact respond to this constructive reinforcement of their authority. It is as though the Court needed the perspective furnished by a time of excessive individualism to see that First Amendment institutions such as schools and churches are not always an impediment to individual rights, but can be a vital means of fostering long-term personal liberty: "Solicitude for a church's [or a school's] ability to [engage in its own self-definition] reflects the idea that furtherance of the autonomy of religious [or educational] organizations often furthers individual religious [and other First Amendment] freedom[s] as well."[57]

The First Amendment embodies values that are the carriers of meaning for individuals and the sources of social and political continuity for society. Those values can and should guard the institutional interests that sustain and nurture individual development. The First Amendment must therefore protect not only individual writers, but newspapers; not only religious persons, but churches; not only individual students and teachers, but schools. These "intellectual and moral associations" form a crucial part of the constitutional structure, for they help teach the peculiar and sometimes paradoxical blend of liberty and duty that sustains both individual freedom and the entire culture from one generation to the next.

NOTES

1. 484 U.S. 260 (1988).
2. 393 U.S. 503 (1969).
3. *Hazelwood*, 484 U.S. at 273.
4. I have elsewhere more fully described the role of "mediating institutions," which can nurture constitutional values by enabling personal development and by providing a buffer against state intrusion. *See* Hafen, Developing Student Expression through Institutional Authority: Public Schools as Mediating Structures, 48

Ohio St. L.J. 663 (1987). That article's theory of public schools as First Amendment institutions provides some of the conceptual framework for this chapter.

5. Bethel Sch. Dist. No. 403 v. Fraser, 478 U.S. 675 (1986).

6. Board of Educ. v. Pico, 457 U.S. 853 (1982).

7. The student rights movement exemplifies this era. *See* Hafen, Developing Student Expression, *supra* note 4, at 677–81.

8. I have summarized applications of this trend to policies involving children in Hafen, Exploring Test Cases in Child Advocacy, 100 Harv. L. Rev. 435 (1986) (reviewing R. Mnookin, In the Interest of Children: Advocacy, Law Reform, and Public Policy (1985)).

9. *See, e.g.,* New Jersey v. T.L.O., 469 U.S. 325 (1985) (Fourth Amendment search and seizure); Goss v. Lopez, 419 U.S. 565 (1975) (procedural due process).

10. 457 U.S. 853 (1982).

11. *Id.* at 867 (quoting Stanley v. Georgia, 394 U.S. 557, 564 (1969)).

12. *Id.* at 871.

13. 478 U.S. 675 (1986).

14. *See id.* at 683.

15. *Hazelwood,* 484 U.S. at 262–64.

16. Kuhlmeier v. Hazelwood Sch. Dist., 795 F.2d 1368 (8th Cir. 1986), *rev'd,* 484 U.S. 260 (1988).

17. *Id.* at 1372.

18. *Id.* at 1375–76.

19. *See Hazelwood,* 484 U.S. at 265–69.

20. *See id.* at 269–73

21. *Id.* at 273.

22. *Id.* at 270.

23. *Id.* at 274–75.

24. *Id.*

25. *Id.* at 271.

26. *Id.*

27. *Id.* at 273 (emphasis added).

28. *Id.*

29. *See id.* at 274–75.

30. *See, e.g.,* Perry Educ. Ass'n v. Perry Local Educators' Ass'n, 460 U.S. 37 (1983).

31. *Hazelwood,* 484 U.S. at 273.

32. *See id.* at 272.

33. 474 U.S. 214 (1985).

34. *See, e.g., Hazelwood,* 484 U.S. at 277–82 (Brennan, J., dissenting); Levin, Educating Youth for Citizenship: The Conflict between Authority and Individual Rights in the Public School, 95 Yale L.J. 1647, 1662–67 (1986); van Geel, The Search for the Constitutional Limits on Government Authority to Inculcate Youth, 62 Tex. L. Rev. 197, 237 (1983).

35. Tinker v. Des Moines Indep. Community Sch. Dist., 393 U.S. 503, 515 (1969) (Stewart, J., concurring) (quoting Ginsberg v. New York, 390 U.S. 629, 649–50 (1968)); *see also* J. Mill, On Liberty 13 (C. Shields ed., 1956) ("It is, perhaps, hardly necessary to say that [the marketplace of ideas] doctrine is meant to apply only to human beings in the maturity of their faculties. We are not speaking of children. . . ."); sources cited in Hafen, Developing Student Expression, *supra* note 4, at 702–709.

36. *Compare* Wallace v. Jaffree, 472 U.S. 38 (1985) (state statute authorizing period of silence in public schools for meditation or silent prayer violates establishment clause) *with* Marsh v. Chambers, 463 U.S. 783 (1983) (state legislature's practice of opening each session with prayer led by state-paid chaplain does not violate establishment clause).

37. *See Hazelwood*, 484 U.S. at 289 (Brennan, J., dissenting).

38. *See* Stone v. Graham, 449 U.S. 39 (1980), which held that the establishment clause was violated when copies of the Ten Commandments were placed on the walls of public classrooms in Kentucky, even though the posted copies contained "[i]n small print below the last commandment" a notation indicating that the "secular application of the Ten Commandments is clearly seen in its adoption as the fundamental legal code of Western Civilization and the Common Law of the United States." *Id.* at 39 & n.1.

39. Hafen, Developing Student Expression, *supra* note 4, at 666.

40. *See id.* at 677–81.

41. A. Neill, Summerhill: A Radical Approach to Child Rearing 4 (1960).

42. A. Bloom, The Closing of the American Mind 320 (1987). For summaries of research reported by James Coleman, Gerald Grant, and Diane Ravitch, among others, as well as the recommendations of such groups as the National Commission on Excellence in Education (which authored *A Nation at Risk*), see Hafen, Developing Student Expression, *supra* note 4, at 677–95.

43. *See generally* Hafen, Developing Student Expression, *supra* note 4.

44. *See* H. Maine, Ancient Law 163–65 (F. Pollock ed., 1963) (relations between persons no longer defined by family but by free agreement among individuals).

45. *See* R. Nisbet, The Quest for Community 75–98 (1953).

46. The influence of Protestant conceptions in Western civilization shifted the focus in religion from the visible to the invisible church: "the individual man of faith replaced the corporate Church as the repository of divine guidance." *Id.* at 243; *see* Tushnet, The Constitution of Religion, 18 Conn. L. Rev. 701, 731 (1986).

47. R. Hofstadter & W. Metzger, The Development of Academic Freedom in the United States 398 (1955). In fact, however, it was the institutional academic freedom of the nineteenth-century German universities that vitalized the concept of a university as a place defined primarily as a community of free inquiry. Institutional leaders of these universities were elected by their faculty colleagues, not appointed by lay trustees, as was the typical case in America. This difference accounts for much of the increased emphasis on the individual faculty member advocated by such organizations as the American Association of University Professors in the early 1900s. *Id.* at 396–400.

48. *See, e.g.,* Keyishian v. Board of Regents, 385 U.S. 598 (1967) (state plan designed to remove "subversive" employees violated First Amendment); Sweezy v. New Hampshire, 354 U.S. 234 (1957) (contempt conviction of college professors for refusal to answer questions concerning content of lectures violated academic freedom and right to political expression).

49. The historical development of academic freedom in the United States after 1900 illustrates this pattern. Note the progression of the essays in The Constitutional Status of Academic Freedom (W. Metzger ed., 1977).

50. R. Bellah et al., Habits of the Heart, at vii (1985).

51. *See* M. Glendon, Abortion and Divorce in Western Law (1987).

52. In contrast to the American experience:

> Continental legal systems have imagined the human person as a free, self-determining individual, but also as a being defined in part through his relations with others. The individual is envisioned, more than in our legal system, as situated within family and community; rights are viewed as inseparable from corresponding responsibilities; and . . . [p]ersonal values are regarded as higher than social values, but as rooted in them.

See id. at 133.

53. A. de Tocqueville, Democracy in America 509 (J. Mayer ed., 1966).

54. *Id.* at 517.

55. Nisbet, The Quest for Community, *supra* note 45, at 202.

56. *Id.* at 203.

57. Corporation of the Presiding Bishop v. Amos, 483 U.S. 327, 342 (1987) (Brennan, J., concurring).

CHAPTER TWENTY-ONE

From Consistency to Confusion: The Aftermath of *Hazelwood School District v. Kuhlmeier*

Mark Goodman

In 1988, a comment written for the *University of Virginia Law Review* warned:

> [T]he failure of the Court in *Hazelwood* to provide definitive guidelines as to what is and is not protected by the Constitution may significantly restrict the content of school newspapers. Educators, armed with the broad discretion allotted to them by *Hazelwood*, may limit school newspapers to mundane matters and cause students to ignore important, though controversial, issues."[1]

Several years and countless censorship incidents later, the accuracy of this commentator's prediction can hardly be questioned. Student publications and surveys of high school journalism teachers indicate that the Supreme Court decision in *Hazelwood School District v. Kuhlmeier*[2] upholding the right of school officials to exercise extensive censorship control over many school-sponsored student publications has been a blight on the world of scholastic journalism.[3]

From the perspective of many, high school censorship has increased since *Hazelwood*. More publication advisers report efforts by school officials to censor,[4] and more students call on legal resources for help with their censorship problems.[5] The topics school officials have attempted to expunge from student publications indicate a motivation to avoid sometimes unpleasant realities. Stories about a shooting of a student,[6] a tennis coach overcharging team members for court fees and pocketing the money,[7] student drug abuse,[8] burglary in the school,[9] racially motivated fighting in a school cafeteria,[10] teacher contract negotiations,[11] and candidates for a school board election[12] are just a few of the many that have been censored since the Supreme Court decision in *Hazelwood*.

Even more troubling, those working directly with high school journalists are persuaded that the attitudes of students toward their own press freedom have changed. One 1989 survey reported that more than 41 percent of the high school teachers who advise student publications believe students are becoming more accepting of *Hazelwood*'s restrictions with the passage of time.[13]

Justice Brennan's stinging dissent in *Hazelwood* expressed the philosophical basis for the outrage of the opinion's critics. Brennan objected that "[i]nstead of 'teach[ing] children to respect the diversity of ideas that is fundamental to the American system,'" and teaching "'that our Constitution is a living reality, not parchment preserved under glass,' . . . the Court today 'teach[es] youth to discount important principles of our government as mere platitudes.'"[14]

On a more practical level, however, was the *Hazelwood* decision worth it? Did the Supreme Court make life easier for beleaguered school administrators or settle uncertain questions of law for student journalists and their advisers? On the contrary, *Hazelwood* added new levels of complication to the issue of student press freedom that continue to leave participants unclear about their rights.

Contrary to the perception of some commentators, the Supreme Court's *Hazelwood* decision did not arise amid a "divergence of opinion"[15] among the courts regarding the rights of high school students working on school-sponsored publications. Since the Supreme Court's *Tinker v. Des Moines Independent Community School District* decision in 1969,[16] a uniform standard had been applied to all situations in which school officials attempted to censor school-sponsored student publications, whether they were curricular or extracurricular.

It was in the *Tinker* majority opinion that Justice Fortas drafted the memorable phrase: "It can hardly be argued that either students or teachers shed their constitutional rights to freedom of speech or expression at the schoolhouse gate."[17] In *Tinker*, public junior high and high school students in Des Moines had been suspended from school for wearing black armbands in protest against United States involvement in Vietnam. The students and their parents went to court claiming infringement of their First and Fourteenth Amendment rights; the Supreme Court ultimately agreed with them.

The Court declared: "Students in school as well as out of school are 'persons' under our Constitution. . . . [They are] possessed of fundamental rights which the State must respect. . . . In our system, students . . . may not be confined to the expression of those sentiments that are officially approved."[18] In holding that absent a showing of "material and substantial interference with schoolwork or discipline," a school could not curtail the free expression rights of its students, the *Tinker* Court set a standard that was soon adopted as a gauge for determining when censorship by school officials would be permitted.[19]

Although *Tinker* did not involve a student publication, the decision was immediately recognized as a landmark. Within months of the decision, a case involving censorship of a school-sponsored high school newspaper came before a federal court in New York. In *Zucker v. Panitz*,[20] the principal of New Rochelle High School had directed the student editor of the *Huguenot Herald* not to run an advertisement submitted by a student group that opposed the war in Vietnam.[21] The student advertisers and editors argued that their free expression rights were being infringed. Based on the recent *Tinker* ruling, the district court in *Zucker* found the students' claim valid, concluding that "[t]he rationale of *Tinker* carries beyond the facts in that case."[22]

The *Zucker* case directly confronted what some nineteen years later was to become the central issue in the *Hazelwood* case. Should censorship of a student newspaper be treated differently from censorship of a black armband because the student newspaper is school-sponsored? New Rochelle school officials answered yes. They described the student newspaper as a "'beneficial educational device' developed as part of the curriculum and intended to inure primarily to the benefit of those who compile, edit and publish it."[23] As such, the school maintained that it should be permitted to take those steps it deemed appropriate to preserve the educational nature of the publication.[24] The students argued that an important purpose of the newspaper was "'to provide a forum for the dissemination of ideas and information by and to the students of [the high school].'"[25]

When the same debate reached the Supreme Court in 1987 in the *Hazelwood* case, it would be dealt with under public forum analysis the Court had developed to apply to expressive activity on state-owned property.[26] Is a school-sponsored high school newspaper a public forum for expression of student viewpoints and opinions and thus entitled to extensive First Amendment protection, the Court would ask, or is it merely a curricular device where student expression can be curtailed as administrators see fit? The *Zucker* court, for example, had held that the *Huguenot Herald* at New Rochelle High School was clearly a public forum. After looking at the content of the publication, the court concluded that "the school paper appears to have been open to free expression of ideas in the news and editorial columns as well as in letters to the editor."[27] The court further noted that the newspaper's "function as an educational device surely could not be served" if its contents were as devoid of controversial topics as the school suggested.[28] "[T]he teaching of journalism includes dissemination of such ideas. Such a school paper is truly an educational device," the court reasoned.[29]

Zucker was the first step in what were to be nineteen years of uniform development on the subject of school-sponsored student newspapers. Courts from around the country were confronted with cases involving censorship of high-school- and college-sponsored student publications. These courts did not uniformly rely on the public forum analysis as a method for determining the level of protection student publications were entitled to; many did not even mention it.[30] But all the courts consistently found that school officials could not censor students unless the school could meet the *Tinker* standard.[31]

The Fourth Circuit's 1977 *Gambino v. Fairfax County School Board*[32] decision offered the clearest enunciation of forum analysis applied to a student publication. In that case, the student newspaper at Hayfield High School in Fairfax County, Virginia, planned to run an informational story on birth control. Most of the students on the newspaper staff were enrolled in a journalism class and received credit for their work. Through an informal survey of their peers, the student editors of the newspaper discovered that many students who were sexually active took no precautions to avoid pregnancy. Thus, editors Gina Gambino and Laura Boyd prepared a piece that provided information about the forms of birth control available at the time and their relative rates of effectiveness. Their school principal balked, claiming the story would be in violation of a school policy that prohibited sex education in the school.

The school claimed that the student newspaper was merely an "in-house organ of the school system, funded and sponsored by the [Fairfax County School] Board" and thus could not be considered a public forum.[33] The courts disagreed. After considering that the newpaper was "conceived, established, and operated as a conduit for student expression on a whole variety of topics,"[34] both the district court and the Fourth Circuit agreed that *The Farm News* at Hayfield High School was established as a public forum for student expression.[35] The courts noted that "[t]he extent of state involvement in providing funding and facilities for The Farm News does not determine whether First Amendment rights are applicable."[36] The Fourth Circuit concluded: "[A]ccordingly, the general power of the Board to regulate course content does not apply."[37]

No court in the years after *Tinker* and before *Hazelwood* disagreed with the notion expressed in *Gambino* and *Zucker* that a high school student newspaper, even if school-sponsored and produced as part of a journalism class, was presumed to be a forum for student expression. School officials would therefore be allowed to censor that publication only if they could demonstrate that the *Tinker* standard of material and substantial disruption had been met.[38] Between 1969 and 1988, when *Tinker* was the law of the land, there was never an indication that schools were suffering as a result.[39]

The decision the Supreme Court reached in *Hazelwood* ignored the nineteen years of post-*Tinker* case law. Rather than following the useful *Tinker* standard, the five-member majority of the Court found that *Tinker* did not apply in this context. The Court skirted a settled method for dealing with student press censorship cases and proceeded to unsettle the law.

In the eyes of the majority, the practice at Hazelwood had been for the adviser to exercise complete editorial control over the student newspaper;[40] the Court therefore maintained that school policy did not indicate an intention to create a forum where students could exercise their own editorial discretion.[41] Based on this determination and the fact that *Spectrum* was a school-sponsored curricular program, the majority held that the student newspaper was not a forum for student expression.

In this non-forum, school officials would be allowed to censor when they could demonstrate that their censorship was "reasonably related to legitimate pedagogical concerns."[42] The Supreme Court further declared that only when the censorship has "no valid educational purpose" should courts act to protect student rights.[43] This new standard, while still leaving the burden of justifying censorship on school officials, gave the Hazelwood administrators much more authority to censor than they would have had under the *Tinker* standard. The *Hazelwood* decision suggested an attitude of deference by the Court to decisions made by a school as to what was educationally inappropriate and warranted removal from a student publication.[44]

The Supreme Court in *Hazelwood* did not, however, neatly replace the *Tinker* standard with a new one. It failed to explicitly overrule any of the lower court decisions such as *Gambino* and *Zucker*. Instead, it found that the particular circumstances of the student newspaper at Hazelwood East High School did not establish *Spectrum* as a forum.[45] The Court left open the possibility that student newspapers at other schools in other contexts might still be considered forums for student expression, even though they were school-sponsored and tied to a journalism class. If in fact a publication is determined "in substance to be a free speech forum,"[46] it seems the *Tinker* standard would still apply.

Thus the Supreme Court replaced the uniformly applied *Tinker* standard with two tiers of constitutional protection for high school publications. School officials can now censor student publications that *are* forums only if they can demonstrate material and substantial disruption, as mandated by *Tinker*.[47] But for those school-sponsored student publications that are not forums, the new "legitimate pedagogical concerns" standard sets the limitation on censorship.

The Court's decision suggested that the presumption of forum status that seemed implicit in cases like *Gambino* and *Zucker* would no longer be appropriate. Rather, a school-sponsored publication would be presumptively *not* a forum. But the determination of forum status remains far from simple. The Court made clear that the determination could only be made on a case by case basis, by looking at the particular circumstances of the individual student publication in question. School-sponsored student publications will be forums if school officials have " 'by policy or practice' " made them such.[48]

The Supreme Court majority found the policy and practice at Hazelwood East High School regarding *Spectrum* not to have established a forum. But at those schools where a student publication runs advertising or letters to the editor and student editors are given the authority to make decisions about what material will go in the newspaper, and especially at those schools that have already established their publications as forums by written policy, the *Tinker* standard is still the rule. In fact, it would be entirely possible that a different forum status could attach to different publications at the same school if there was evidence that they had been operated with differing amounts of faculty or administrative control.[49]

In practice, many student publications across the country would still be considered forums entitled to *Tinker*-level protection, even after *Hazelwood*, for one simple reason: The classroom teachers of journalism and publications advisers operate them that way.

One suprisingly unheralded fact about the *Hazelwood* litigation was that, from the outset, journalism educators from around the country sided firmly with the students in the case. The two national groups of high school journalism advisers and teachers, the Journalism Education Association and the Columbia Scholastic

Press Advisers Association, as well as organizations such as the Quill and Scroll Society, the International Honorary Society for high school journalists; the National Scholastic Press Association (sponsor of the largest national workshops and conventions for student journalists), and the Southern Interscholastic Press Association (the nation's largest regional organization for student journalists) filed a friend-of-the-court brief before the Supreme Court in opposition to the censorship by the *Hazelwood* school district.[50] Even the state organization of journalism teachers in Missouri, which included five advisers of student publications in the Hazelwood School District at the time, supported the students in the case.[51]

The membership and constituencies of these organizations included tens of thousands of high school journalism teachers and publications advisers who joined with college-level journalism educators and the Student Press Law Center in the brief. As teachers and advisers, they declared that they "affirmatively reject the censorship control the Hazelwood School District requests and assure the Court that such censorship plays no role in the maintenance of order in our classrooms, but in fact makes impossible the teaching of journalism and is inimical to a quality educational environment."[52] As journalism educators, they voiced their alarm "about the lessons that schools such as Hazelwood East High School, through their casual censorship, are teaching tomorrow's citizens about the importance of the First Amendment in our democracy."[53]

The *Hazelwood* decision was a blow to many journalism teachers and advisers,[54] but few were willing to give up their commitment to high-quality journalism education. Even if school administrators ignore their responsibility for inculcating in students an appreciation for our Constitution and the democratic values of free expression and press freedom, many teachers will not. A school principal might find it useful to encourage students to blindly accept the administration's view of the world, but many teachers will not stop encouraging students to think critically.

Many teachers continue to operate the student publications they advise just as they did before the decision, giving student editors and reporters expert guidance on the practice of responsible journalism but ultimately leaving to students all the content decisions. Consequently, their student publications remain forums and are thus unaffected by *Hazelwood*.

The difficulty of determining forum status clearly makes the question of student press rights more complicated after *Hazelwood*. Moreover, widespread dissatisfaction with the decision has prompted a flurry of state legislation to rectify the damage the Supreme Court has done; such ad hoc state solutions have further muddied the waters.

Within days of the *Hazelwood* decision, the scholastic journalism community focused on California's long-ignored law protecting the free press rights of high school students.[55] After the Supreme Court's ruling, the law took on dramatic new significance. Because of the statute, "California public school students still enjoy substantial 'freedom of the press' despite the recent U.S. Supreme Court decision to the contrary," stated State Superintendent of Public Instruction Bill Honig.[56]

With California as an example, the drive began to establish more states as *Hazelwood*-free zones. In July 1988, Massachusetts became the first state to enact such post-*Hazelwood* protections for student expression. This Massachusetts law declares that students' rights to free expression shall not be abridged except in situations where "disruption or disorder within the school" results, a clear reference to the *Tinker* standard the Court rejected in *Hazelwood*.[57] Since 1988 Iowa, Colorado, and Kansas have joined California and Massachusetts in enacting student free expression protections into law.[58] Although the wording of each state law differs, each provides students with greater protections than they have under the Supreme Court's interpretation of the First Amendment in *Hazelwood*, and each uses a substantial disruption threshold, adopted from *Tinker*, as the primary limitation on students' rights.

Hazelwood has therefore done anything but provide uniformity. Before 1988, the straightforward *Tinker* standard made clear what school officials could censor. Now, to avoid conflict with the First Amendment, censors must determine whether student publications are public forums for student expression or non-forums, a determination that may require a detailed inquiry into the operation of each publication. In addition, they must evaluate the status of free expression law in their state.[59] Ultimately, many schools may decide it is simply too complicated to stifle student publications with *Hazelwood*-inspired controls.

Regrettably, administrative confusion and fear of legislative interference appear the most likely inhibitors of censorship by school officials. It is a sad comment on the state of secondary education that few schools can be counted on to protect student press freedom because of their commitment to educate young people for life in this democracy where free expression is cherished.

NOTES

1. Smith, Comment, High School Newspapers and the Public Forum Doctrine: *Hazelwood School District v. Kuhlmeier*, 74 Va. L. Rev. 843, 860–61 (1988).
2. 484 U.S. 260 (1988).
3. *See* Herr, Papers Struggle against Censorship, Student Journalist (Michigan Interscholastic Press Ass'n, East Lansing, Mich.), Apr. 28, 1989, at 31 (reporting that a survey of student newspapers indicated that "22 percent had been censored after *Hazelwood*, compared with 11 percent prior to *Hazelwood*"); Kovas, The Impact of *Hazelwood* in the State of Indiana, 65 Quill & Scroll 4, 7 (Feb./Mar. 1991) (noting that the advisers of scholastic journalism programs surveyed throughout Indiana "strongly agreed that their newspaper staffs are less likely to publish controversial or sensitive stories as a result of *Hazelwood*").
4. *See* J. W. Click & L. Kopenhaver, Opinions of Principals and Newspaper Advisers toward Student Press Freedom and Advisers' Responsibilities Following *Hazelwood v. Kuhlmeier*, paper presented to the Secondary Education Division, Association for Education in Journalism and Mass Communication 1–2 (Aug. 1990)

(on file with author); *see also* Patten, High School Confidential: The Alarming After-math of the *Hazelwood* Decision, Colum. Journalism Rev., Sept./Oct. 1990, at 8, 10.

5. In 1988, the Student Press Law Center (SPLC) received 548 requests for legal assistance. By 1992, the number of requests for help had increased to 1,364.

6. *See* Principal Censors Story; Editors Resign in Protest, SPLC Rep. (Student Press Law Center, Washington, D.C.), Fall 1991, at 8; Madison, Wisconsin, Newsl. on Intell. Freedom (Am. Library Ass'n, Chicago, Ill.), Sept. 1991, at 158–59.

7. *See* Principal Foils Investigative Reporting: Story Exposing Coach's Overcharg-ing of Students Is Censored, SPLC Rep. (Student Press Law Center, Washington, D.C.), Winter 1990–91, at 17.

8. *See* Peyser, Censored: Drug Article Yanked from Bronx Prep-School Paper, N.Y. Post, May 2, 1991, at 3.

9. *See* Newspaper Staff Pressured by Board, SPLC Rep. (Student Press Law Cen-ter, Washington, D.C.), Fall 1990, at 15.

10. *See* Principal Censors Story, *supra* note 6, at 8–9.

11. *See* Montana Adviser Wins Fight; Defeats Prior Review Policy, SPLC Rep. (Student Press Law Center, Washington, D.C.), Fall 1990, at 27.

12. *See* Principal Steers Paper Away from 'Politics,' SPLC Rep. (Student Press Law Center, Washington, D.C.), Winter 1990–91, at 12.

13. *See* Patten, High School Confidential, *supra* note 4, at 10.

14. Hazelwood Sch. Dist. v. Kuhlmeier, 484 U.S. 260, 290–91 (1988) (Brennan, J., dissenting) (citations omitted).

15. Smith, Comment, *supra* note 1, at 849.

16. 393 U.S. 503 (1969).

17. *Id.* at 506.

18. *Id.* at 511.

19. *See id.*

20. 299 F. Supp. 102 (S.D.N.Y. 1969).

21. *See id.* at 103.

22. *Id.* at 105.

23. *Id.* at 103.

24. *See id.*

25. *Id.*

26. *See Hazelwood*, 484 U.S. at 267–70 (1988).

27. *Zucker*, 299 F. Supp. at 105.

28. *Id.* at 103.

29. *Id.*

30. *See, e.g.,* Trachtman v. Anker, 563 F.2d 512 (2d Cir. 1977); Joyner v. Whiting, 477 F.2d 456 (4th Cir. 1973); Bazaar v. Fortune, 476 F.2d 570, *aff'd per curiam en banc*, 489 F.2d 225 (5th Cir. 1973); Reineke v. Cobb County Sch. Dist., 484 F. Supp. 1252 (N.D. Ga. 1980); Frasca v. Andrews, 463 F. Supp. 1043 (E.D.N.Y. 1979); Bayer v. Kinzler, 383 F. Supp. 1164 (E.D.N.Y. 1974), *aff'd without opinion*, 515 F.2d 504 (2d Cir. 1975); Trujillo v. Love, 322 F. Supp. 1266 (D. Colo. 1971); Antonelli v. Hammond, 308 F. Supp. 1329 (D. Mass. 1970); Korn v. Elkins, 317 F. Supp. 138 (D. Md. 1970); Panarella v. Birenbaum, 327 N.Y.S.2d 755 (N.Y. App. Div. 1971), *aff'd*, 296 N.E.2d 238 (N.Y. 1973).

31. *See, e.g., Trachtman,* 563 F.2d at 516; *Joyner,* 477 F.2d at 461; *Bazaar,* 476 F.2d at 573; *Reineke,* 484 F. Supp. at 1256–58; *Frasca,* 463 F. Supp. at 1049; *Bayer,* 383 F. Supp. at 1165–66; *Trujillo,* 322 F. Supp. at 1270; *Korn,* 317 F. Supp. at 143 n.5; *Antonelli,* 308 F. Supp. at 1336–37; *Panarella,* 296 N.E.2d at 242.

Even the cases the Smith Comment cites as having distinguished between curricular and noncurricular publications stated that *Tinker* was the standard for school censorship of student expression in school-sponsored publications. *See* Smith, Comment, *supra* note 1, at 848 n.41; Nicholson v. Board of Educ., 682 F.2d 858, 863 n.3 (1982); Gambino v. Fairfax County Sch. Board, 564 F.2d 157 (4th Cir. 1977).

The *Nicholson* court permitted prepublication review of student-written articles by the school's principal where the principal "often expressed his disapproval but never denied publication or censored the submitted piece." 682 F.2d at 861. The court found that it "was not faced with a situation where school officials prohibited or censored a student publication." *Id.* at 863 n.3. The court noted that "[s]ince scholastic newspapers fall within the ambit of the first amendment, outright prohibition or censorship would require a strong showing on the part of the school administrators that publication of the forbidden materials would 'materially and substantially interfere with the requirements of appropriate discipline in the operation of the school.'" *Id.* (quoting Tinker v. Des Moines Indep. Community Sch. Dist., 393 U.S. 503, 509 (1969)).

In *Gambino,* the Fourth Circuit explicitly endorsed the district court's ruling, which had "found that the newspaper was established as a public forum for student expression, and therefore is subject to first amendment protection." *Gambino,* 564 F.2d at 158. Significantly, the district court had relied on Fourth Circuit case law that explicitly applied the *Tinker* standard. Gambino v. Fairfax County Sch. Board, 429 F. Supp. 731, 736 (E.D. Va. 1977).

32. 429 F. Supp. 731 (E.D. Va.), *aff'd per curiam,* 564 F.2d 157 (4th Cir. 1977).

33. 564 F.2d at 157–58; *see also* 429 F. Supp. at 734.

34. 429 F. Supp. at 735.

35. *See* 564 F.2d at 158; 429 F. Supp. at 736.

36. 564 F.2d at 158 (endorsing the district court's findings and reasoning); 429 F. Supp. at 734.

37. 564 F.2d at 158.

38. Courts have generally held that a showing by school officials that material in a student publication is libelous or legally obscene would be sufficient to satisfy the *Tinker* standard. *See, e.g.,* Nitzberg v. Parks, 525 F.2d 378 (4th Cir. 1975); Shanley v. Northeast Indep. Sch. Dist., 462 F.2d 960 (5th Cir. 1972); Frasca v. Andrews, 463 F. Supp. 1043 (E.D.N.Y. 1979).

39. As one national study reported, "[w]here a free, vigorous student press does exist, there is a healthy ferment of ideas and opinions, with no indication of disruption or negative side effects on the educational experience of the school." Captive Voices, The Report of the Commission of Inquiry into High School Journalism, at 49 (J. Nelson ed., 1974).

40. *See* Hazelwood Sch. Dist. v. Kuhlmeier, 484 U.S. 260, 268–70 (1988). Significantly, the adviser himself disagreed with this finding. Kuhlmeier v. Hazelwood Sch. Dist., 795 F.2d 1368, 1372 (8th Cir. 1986).

41. *See Hazelwood,* 484 U.S. at 270. The dissenters found that the policies indicated the exact opposite. *Id.* at 277 (Brennan, J., dissenting).

42. *Id*. at 273.

43. *Id*.

44. Examples the Court gave of topics that could be censored under the *Hazelwood* standard included "the existence of Santa Claus in an elementary school setting," "the particulars of teenage sexual activity in a high school setting," material that might "associate the school with any position other than neutrality on matters of political controversy," and "speech that might reasonably be perceived to advocate drug or alcohol use, irresponsible sex, or conduct otherwise inconsistent with the 'shared values of a civilized social order.'" *Id*. at 272 (quoting Bethel Sch. Dist. No. 403 v. Fraser, 478 U.S. 675, 683 (1986)).

45. *See supra* text accompanying notes 33–35.

46. *Gambino*, 429 F. Supp. at 734 (E.D. Va. 1977).

47. "Underground," alternative, or other non-school-sponsored publications were not affected by *Hazelwood* and would be entitled to this level of protection as well. And at least one federal court decision has suggested that school-sponsored publications produced as extracurricular activities may be exempt from *Hazelwood*. Romano v. Harrington, 725 F. Supp. 687, 689–90 (E.D.N.Y. 1989).

48. *Hazelwood*, 484 U.S. at 267 (quoting Perry Educ. Ass'n v. Perry Local Educators' Ass'n, 460 U.S. 37, 47 (1983)).

49. Planned Parenthood v. Clark County Sch. Dist., 941 F.2d 817, 821–24 (9th Cir. 1991), gives weight to the notion that the method of operation of a particular student publication will determine its forum status.

50. *See* Amicus Curiae Brief of Student Press Law Center, *Hazelwood*, No. 86–836.

51. *See id*.

52. *Id*. at 4.

53. *Id*.

54. In a statement issued on January 16, 1988, the Secondary Education Division of the Association for Education in Journalism and Mass Communication stated that it "deplore[d]" the Supreme Court decision, explaining that "[t]his decision ignores the value of a vibrant student press and encourages a repressive school environment." Statement in Response to the Supreme Court's Decision in *Hazelwood v. Kuhlmeier* (Secondary Education Division, Association for Education in Journalism and Mass Communication, Knoxville, Tenn.), Jan. 16, 1988 (on file with author).

55. *See* Cal. Educ. Code § 48907 (West Supp. 1992).

56. News Release (California State Department of Education, Sacramento, Cal.), Mar. 18, 1988 (on file with author).

57. Mass. Ann. Laws ch. 71, § 82 (Law Co-op. 1992).

58. *See* Iowa Code § 280.22 (West Supp. 1992); Colo. Rev. Stat. § 22-1-120 (Supp. 1991); Kan. Stat. Ann. §§ 72.1504–1506 (Supp. 1992).

59. Significantly, state constitutions may provide additional protection for student free expression rights. In a 1991 case, a New Jersey court stated that the state constitution provided broader protection than did the First Amendment after the *Hazelwood* holding. Desilets v. Clearview Regional Board of Educ., No. C-23-90, 14–15 (N.J. Super. Ct. Law Div. May 7, 1991), *aff'd on other grounds*, 630 A.2d 333 (N.J. Super. Ct. App. Div. 1993). The case is currently pending before the state supreme court.

CHAPTER TWENTY-TWO

Student Speech Rights: The True Meaning of *Hazelwood School District v. Kuhlmeier*

Jay Worona

MUCH HAS BEEN written about *Hazelwood School District v. Kuhlmeier*[1] and whether this decision serves to undercut the protected First Amendment free speech rights of students in our public schools.[2] Critics have joined their voices with Justices Brennan, Marshall, and Blackmun, whose *Hazelwood* dissent declared, "Instead of 'teach[ing] children to respect the diversity of ideas that is fundamental to the American system,' . . . the [majority opinion] 'teach[es] youth to discount important principles of our government as mere platitudes.'"[3] However, the dissenters' viewpoint, and that of those who join them, is based upon the assumption that the constitutional rights of students to engage in *personal* expression were at issue in *Hazelwood*, and that, therefore, the "material disruption" standard set forth by the Supreme Court in *Tinker v. Des Moines Independent Community School District*[4] was applicable.[5]

In *Tinker*, the Supreme Court was faced with the issue of whether a school district could prevent students from wearing black armbands on school premises in protest against the Vietnam war. The Court upheld the students' right to do so, recognizing that students do not "shed their constitutional rights to freedom of speech or expression at the schoolhouse gate,"[6] and noting that the record did not support a finding that allowing students to exercise this form of personal expression would substantially disrupt or materially interfere with school activities.[7]

The "material disruption" standard was, however, inapplicable in *Hazelwood* and similar settings. The *Hazelwood* Court was faced, not with the issue of a student's right to *personal* expression, but rather with the right of a school district to control its own curriculum and *school-sponsored* student speech.[8] The Court rejected the proposition that a school district's refusal to lend its name and resources to the dissemination of student expression was tantamount to the unconstitutional punishment of student expression. This chapter presents the perspective of those who counsel school boards as they constantly grapple with student speech issues. In it I argue that the Supreme Court's *Hazelwood* decision was appropriate because, when a school sponsors educational speech, it has the right to guide such student expression according to the school's educational mission.

The *Hazelwood* Litigation

The Facts

It is necessary to understand the very specific facts upon which the Supreme Court based its *Hazelwood* decision in order to comprehend why the First Amendment free speech rights of students were not trampled on by this case.

Hazelwood concerned a decision by a high school principal to delete two full pages of a newspaper published by journalism students at Hazelwood East High School in Hazelwood, Missouri. One of the articles concerned three students' experiences with pregnancy, and the other discussed the impact of divorce on children and students' thoughts on their parents' divorces. When the student authors met with the principal to discuss the deletions, the principal informed them that the stories were inappropriate, personal, sensitive, and unsuitable.[9]

The newspaper was produced by members of a journalism class taught by a faculty member, and its staff was essentially restricted to members of that class. A grade and academic credit were granted upon completion. The school's curriculum guide described the class as a "laboratory situation" through which students could gain practical experience.[10] The faculty member followed a curriculum guide, and a textbook was used in the class.[11] School board policy required that all school-sponsored publications be developed within the adopted curriculum.

The Decisions of the Lower Courts

Eventually, three staff members of the paper filed a civil rights lawsuit in which they claimed that their First Amendment free speech rights were violated. The U.S. District Court for the Eastern District of Missouri found that the newspaper was part of the school curriculum and had not been established by the school district as a public forum.[12] Based on this reasoning, the district court held that school officials were entitled to "a great deal of discretion."[13]

On appeal, the U.S. Court of Appeals for the Eighth Circuit reversed the district court's decision, holding that the newspaper was a public forum because it was "intended to be operated as a conduit for student viewpoints."[14] That the students selected the staff members, determined the articles to be written, and decided the content of the articles led the circuit court to this conclusion.

The Eighth Circuit found that the newspaper was "a forum in which the school encouraged students to express their views to the entire student body freely, and students commonly did so."[15] The court further noted that the newspaper had in the past published stories dealing with such topics as student use of drugs and alcohol, religious cults, and runaways.[16] The court therefore concluded that the paper was not simply part of the school curriculum but a public forum for student expression.

Assessing the principal's justification for censorship, the circuit court held that school officials are justified in limiting student speech "only when publication of that speech could result in tort liability for the school."[17] The court concluded that "because no tort action could have been maintained against Hazelwood East, school officials were not justified in censoring the two articles."[18]

Shortcomings of the Circuit Court's Decision

The Eighth Circuit holding forced school officials to choose between a possible civil rights lawsuit by student journalists and potential liability through an invasion of privacy lawsuit by individuals alleging injury from publication of articles in student newspapers.[19] School officials are not lawyers, nor are they commercial journalists who work with counsel on a daily basis.[20] Generally, school districts do not contemplate submitting the contents of their student newspaper to an attorney for review. Requiring districts to consult counsel regarding individual articles to determine whether a court would find tort liability would be both expensive and time-consuming.

Furthermore, educators have a duty to guide high school students in making responsible decisions, whether in a journalism class or in any other subject. The circuit decision gave educators less authority than the student editor of the newspaper. It treated school newspapers as private newspapers published in the community, notwithstanding the fact that even private newspapers have editors whose duties include deciding which reporter's stories or portions of such stories to print. Therefore, on petition for a writ of certiorari, the looming issue for the Supreme Court was who determines the content of school newspapers that are printed and sold to students and the public under the aegis of school systems.

The Supreme Court Decision

On writ of certiorari, the U.S. Supreme Court reversed the circuit court's decision and upheld the school district's actions.[21] The Court noted that "the First Amendment rights of students in the public schools 'are not automatically coextensive with the rights of adults in other settings.' . . . A school need not tolerate student speech that is inconsistent with its 'basic educational mission.' "[22]

Citing its earlier decision in *Bethel School District No. 403 v. Fraser*,[23] the Court further noted that "a student could be disciplined for delivering a speech that was sexually explicit, but not legally obscene at an official school assembly, because the school was entitled to disassociate itself from the speech in a manner that would demonstrate to others that such vulgarity is wholly inconsistent with the 'fundamental values' of public school education."[24] The Court recalled that it had recognized in *Fraser* that "[t]he determination of what manner of speech in the classroom or in school assembly is inappropriate properly rests with the school board . . . rather than with the federal courts."[25]

Rejecting the applicability of *Tinker* to the *Hazelwood* case, the Court reasoned that

the standard articulated for determining when a school may punish student expression need not be the standard for determining when a school may refuse to lend its name and resources to the dissemination of student expression. Instead, we hold that educators do not offend the First Amendment by exercising editorial control over the style and content of student speech in *school-sponsored expressive activities* so long as their actions are reasonably related to legitimate pedagogical concerns.[26]

Thus, the Court reaffirmed its position in *Fraser* that school districts require and should be afforded great deference when refusing to sponsor student speech that counters their educational mission.

The *Hazelwood* Decision: Appropriate Policy

Rather than trampling on the rights of students to *personal* expression under the First Amendment, *Hazelwood* upholds the right of school districts to set high standards for student speech that is disseminated under their auspices, and to refuse to disseminate student speech that does not meet those standards. The Hazelwood school district had decided that it would not lend its name and resources to the dissemination of student expression, in a school-sponsored publication, which it found ran contrary to its own educational mission.

The Supreme Court accepted the school's decision, noting that "[o]therwise, the schools would be unduly constrained from fulfilling their role as 'a principal instrument in awakening the child to cultural values, in preparing him for later professional training, and in helping him to adjust normally to his environment.'"[27] Furthermore, the Court reasoned that "[e]ducators are entitled to exercise greater control over [school-sponsored] student expression to assure that . . . the views of the individual speaker are not erroneously attributed to the school."[28]

On the issue of whether a school-sponsored student newspaper is a public forum, the Court, distinguishing public schools from other traditional public forums, found that public school facilities may be deemed public forums "only if school authorities have 'by policy or by practice' opened those facilities 'for indiscriminate use by the general public' or by some segment of the public, such as student organizations."[29]

The Court concluded that the Hazelwood School District had not offered the newspaper for indiscriminate use by students, but had instead intended that the newspaper serve "as a supervised learning experience for journalism students."[30] Therefore, school officials could "regulate the contents of *Spectrum* in any reasonable manner."[31]

If the courts were to hold that all school-sponsored newspapers were public forums, school districts would not be able to realize their educational mission. Individuals who disagree with the Supreme Court's decision may be correct in asserting that student writings of which adults disapprove are simply indicative of adolescent behavior. However, such commentators are incorrect in asserting that, as a result, the school district must be mandated to pay for, promote, and distribute to the children of the district written material that runs contrary to its own educational mission. If this were so, school districts would be forced to support and allow the distribution to its students of all types of student speech, no matter how vulgar or inappropriate, so long as the words accurately depict whatever the writer is trying to describe.

The responsibility of school boards to shape school-sponsored activities has also been recognized by the U.S. district court for Vermont in the context of a school board's refusal to sponsor a particular play for the annual school performance.[32] In upholding the school district's action, this court held that "the students' rights to free expression must give way to the board's responsibility for the well-being of the larger student body that would be affected by production of the play."[33]

Conclusion

The *Hazelwood* decision conclusively stands for the proposition that a public school district may delete from a school publication certain student speech that the school determines to be inconsistent with its basic educational mission. When a district's actions are in fact reasonably related to legitimate pedagogical concerns, constitutional rights of free speech are not violated.

Tinker's "material disruption" standard is not relevant when school-sponsored publications are at issue. In such instances, "the standard articulated . . . for determining when a school may punish student *[personal]* expression need not also be the standard for determining when a school may refuse to lend its name and resources to the dissemination of student expression."[34]

If the Supreme Court had required school districts to utilize *Tinker*'s "material disruption" test or the tort liability test articulated by the Eighth Circuit Court of Appeals in *Hazelwood*, the ability of school districts to structure and run their educational programs, as they are statutorily authorized and required to do, would have been seriously impeded.

NOTES

1. 484 U.S. 260 (1988).

2. *See, e.g.*, Schimmel, Censorship of School-Sponsored Publications: An Analysis of *Hazelwood v. Kuhlmeier*, 45 Educ. L. Rep. 941 (1988); Morris, Censoring the

School Newspaper, 45 Educ. L. Rep. 1 (1988); Smith, Comment, High School Newspapers and the Public Forum Doctrine: *Hazelwood School District v. Kuhlmeier*, 74 Va. L. Rev. 843 (1988).

3. 484 U.S. at 291–92 (Brennan, J., dissenting) (citations omitted); *see also* Smith, Comment, *supra* note 2, at 843.

4. 393 U.S. 503 (1969).

5. *See Hazelwood*, 484 U.S. at 277–91 (Brennan, J., dissenting); Smith, Comment, *supra* note 2, at 843.

6. 393 U.S. at 506.

7. *Id.* at 509.

8. 484 U.S. at 262.

9. *Id.* at 263–64.

10. *Id.* at 268.

11. Kuhlmeier v. Hazelwood Sch. Dist., 795 F.2d 1368, 1372 (8th Cir. 1986).

12. Kuhlmeier v. Hazelwood Sch. Dist., 607 F. Supp 1450, 1465 (E.D. Mo. 1985).

13. *Id.* at 1467.

14. 795 F.2d at 1372.

15. *Id.* at 1373.

16. *Id.* at 1372.

17. *Id.* at 1376.

18. *Id.*

19. *See id.* at 1378 (Wollman, J., dissenting).

20. *Id.*

21. 484 U.S. 260 (1988).

22. 484 U.S. at 266 (citations omitted).

23. 478 U.S. 675 (1986).

24. 484 U.S. at 266–67 (citations omitted).

25. *Id.* at 267 (citations omitted).

26. *Id.* at 272–73 (footnotes omitted) (emphasis added).

27. *Id.* at 272 (quoting Brown v. Board of Educ., 347 U.S. 483, 493 (1954)).

28. *Id.* at 271.

29. *Id.* at 267 (quoting Perry Educ. Ass'n v. Perry Local Educators' Ass'n, 460 U.S. 37 (1983)).

30. *Id.* at 270.

31. *Id.* (citation omitted).

32. Bell v. U-32 Board of Educ., 630 F. Supp. 939 (D. Vt. 1986). The play in question was entitled "Runaways" and "focuse[d] on the emotions and reflections of several child runaways concerning the problems at home from which they fled and the problems they face alone in the city." *Id.* at 941.

33. *Id.* at 945.

34. 484 U.S. at 272–73.

■ PART IV

Children and Health Policy

■ CHAPTER TWENTY-THREE

Paying for Children's Medical Care: Interaction between Family Law and Health Care Cost Containment

Walter J. Wadlington

IN ADDITION TO the difficulties that new cost-containment measures will present for health care institutions and practices generally, our system for delivering medical care to children may face special problems that we are only beginning to recognize. Choices about resource allocation may be limited by political and legal restraints largely beyond the control of planners trying to focus on the most effective distribution of health care dollars. In the current political climate, increased emphasis is being placed on enforcing private child support obligations in order to reduce governmental costs, while at the same time there is increased conflict over the respective roles of parents and state in deciding what constitutes appropriate or required medical care for children.

This chapter is the result of an exploration of possible ways in which family law and legal rules regarding children and their rights may interact with cost-containment measures directed toward children's health care. Such interaction might limit workable alternatives by producing family destabilization and other unwanted results, or it might help promote better health care for children. Some findings do little more than confirm the bleakness of the current picture; others seem to suggest a need to alter our approach if we are to provide adequate health care for children in accordance with widely held societal values in a time of diminishing resources.

Adapted and reprinted with permission from 36 Case Wes. L. Rev. 1190 (1986). Copyright 1986 by the Case Western Reserve Law Review.

Some Distinctive Problems and Needs

Although assertions that children have a basic "right" to adequate health care are not uncommon, such statements at this time are best categorized as exercises in political rhetoric. It is ironic that despite long and vocal public affirmation of over-riding interest in the protection and nurture of children, the United States is virtually the only industrialized nation with no family allowance programs.[1] Some consider it anomalous that Medicare, our first major venture into a broad national health care system, focused not on young children but on the elderly. In recent years, the latter group has increased in size while the former has decreased. Because the elderly are especially likely to require highly cost-intensive services, attempts to institute a broad social insurance scheme for children may thus be all the more difficult.[2]

Although many children today receive medical assistance through government programs such as Medicaid or Supplemental Security Income (SSI), those programs focus on population groups with the greatest financial need—persons eligible for public assistance under a program such as Aid to Families with Dependent Children (AFDC) or close enough to that eligibility line to be deemed "medically needy." Further, these public assistance programs are already under attack from many quarters, and the services they provide vary from one state to another. Other categorical assistance programs and various private philanthropic efforts may aid some children who have specific medical needs, but such a fragmented system can hardly be regarded as the embodiment of a "right" to medical care.[3]

Budgetary constraints are not new to those involved in trying to expand children's health care.[4] Financial cuts hamper existing programs and preclude the development of new ones, moving us farther from the goal of assuring health care to children on the basis of medical need, regardless of family economic status. Nevertheless, barring major changes in political priorities, it seems unrealistic to expect significant expansion of government funding in the near future. In fact, some existing Medicaid coverage may be in jeopardy. Under most predictable scenarios, private insurance and family contributions are likely to be of increasing importance. Each of these sources, however, has built-in limitations on its effectiveness in a time of cost cutting, since many families with young children stand low on the economic ladder.

At a time when private employers seek to pare their health care insurance contributions (a significant part of employee fringe benefit packages), their interests might best be served by maintaining health coverage for their employees while decreasing coverage of other family members, including children. Even without such an extreme approach, other measures such as increasing employee deductibles may have a harsh impact on children's medical care. Although cost-sharing measures could be structured so as to minimize or avoid such a result, it must be recognized that children will not be sitting at contract negotiating tables or in underwriters' offices when those decisions are made. This concern highlights a central problem: Too often there is no effective mechanism for raising the concerns and protecting the interests of children in policy determinations that will have great impact on them.[5]

In considering where cuts might be made in children's health care costs, it is important to recognize that with a few major exceptions, such as neonatal intensive care, pediatrics has not involved, until recently, either the commitment to routine use of expensive technology or the potential for excessive hospitalization that has characterized the practice of many other specialties. Although highly regarded in their communities, pediatricians often command smaller fees than other major specialists. These factors suggest that there may be fewer areas where funding cuts might be made without immediate, noticeable effects on patient care.

The economic well-being of many families is vulnerable to even modest increases in medical costs. With the prospect of new specialty procedures and greater use of expensive technology, many families who traditionally have paid for their children's basic medical care without governmental help are uneasy. Significant reductions in insurance coverage could exacerbate their worries.

Weighing Potential Impact on Families: The Significance of Family Law

Recent legal consideration of children's medical care has focused chiefly on state intervention to protect defective neonates or seriously ill children whose parents refuse to permit or provide traditional medical treatment because of personal or religious views.[6] Courts in those cases usually have not explained what, if any, consideration was given to who should pay for such treatment or care. One might speculate that many were "test" cases involving difficult constitutional issues that needed resolution before cost-allocation problems could be faced.[7] In this judicial vacuum, courts may have assumed that someone was prepared to foot the bill, and thereby ignored the cost issue. Perhaps no one gave serious thought to the relationship between health care policy or resource allocation and legal rules involving family governance and children's rights. Whatever the reason, legal and practical developments make it almost inevitable that financial factors will increasingly crop up in legal disputes regarding medical care for children. These include an increased emphasis on enforcing private support obligations, a broader definition of medical neglect, and intensified financial pressures from the state. Already some cases have involved children in state custody with no parents available. In such instances courts have not been reluctant to find a state duty of support under doctrines such as *parens patriae* or in loco parentis.[8]

Obvious legal implications of new developments in medical practice have been ignored in the past.[9] There may now be sufficient recognition of the need to consider legal issues as well as ethical, scientific, and economic factors if we are to introduce health care reforms that will function effectively without unduly threatening existing institutions. Legal changes may obviate many such concerns, but we need to anticipate the problems and take the necessary steps before crises arise.

Defining Parental Duties to Provide Health Care

One might assume that most questions regarding the legal duty of parents to pay for their children's medical care and the means for enforcing such an obligation were answered long ago. This is not the case. Worse yet, new questions now are being raised in a time of changing views about the rights of children and the state's role in health care decisions regarding them. This situation may be analogized to the uncertain scope of an older child's capacity to consent to medical care, an area of much confusion today.[10] More than providing an analogy, the manner in which we resolve some important issues regarding children's capacity to give, and parental authority to withhold, consent may affect the determination of who must pay for children's medical care.

Much of our law governing support duties has developed through cases involving parents who were separated or divorced. One explanation for this is that restrictions on intrafamily legal actions prevented children from suing their parents, and thus it was in the context of a custodial parent's action against an absent (perhaps divorced) parent that the issue most often reached the courts. Exceptions to this tendency are those cases involving parents who refused consent to necessary medical procedures (particularly in the face of life-threatening circumstances), and cases where parental failure to provide a minimal level of support so jeopardized a child's welfare that removal from the home and perhaps even criminal prosecution were considered appropriate. Changes in this process may now occur as a result of modern moves toward abolishing procedural rules that have prevented legal actions by minors against their parents.[11]

Equitable and Statutory Responses to Inadequate Common Law Remedies

A melange of statutory, equitable, and common law approaches have been used to seek reimbursement from parents of children to whom medical care has been extended. At common law a parent was considered to have a natural but not necessarily legal duty to support a child.[12] This meant that the duty could not be enforced through legal action. As recently as 1953, the Supreme Court of New Jersey confronted this problem in a physician's action against the parents of a child whom he had treated for a broken foot.[13] The child had been taken to a doctor by the father of one of her friends, and in the ensuing months the parents had seen their child on crutches and knew that she had received medical treatment. They refused to pay for it, however, because they had not contracted with the physician for the care. Taking notice of the common law view that a parent's obligation was only moral rather than legal in such an instance, the court elected to follow the approach developed through equity, under which a parent could be held liable for necessities supplied to a child in an emergency or when there was an inference that the parents had accepted them. The decision, now regarded as a landmark, illustrates the surprising recentness of the establishment of a clear, nonstatutory parental duty to provide needed medical care for a child.[14]

State statutes specifically requiring parents to support their minor children are now widespread.[15] Generally, they do not abrogate existing common law support duties, but they do provide a means for permitting exercise of extraordinary judicial enforcement measures such as the contempt power. Because of constitutional concerns about sex discrimination, many legislatures have amended their statutes to restate the duty created as being owed by both parents.[16]

Equitable (or judicially established) support duties and statutory provisions on nonsupport may be gauged by different standards with respect to the required level of maintenance. The statutory duty often assumes a basic minimum level of support. Under the nonstatutory duty, there may be greater latitude for subjective appraisal and determination based on a particular parent's ability to maintain a support level higher than that required under the nonsupport statute.[17]

Laws on Child Abuse and Neglect

Another group of statutes must be considered in addressing issues of parental responsibility to provide medical assistance. Generally described as abuse and neglect statutes, these laws impose upon parents the duty to provide certain basic needs to their children on pain of criminal prosecution, temporary removal of children from the home, or even peremptory severance of parental rights.

In the popular view, perhaps, abuse and neglect statutes apply to extreme cases of failure to provide minimal sustenance or of intentional acts causing physical injury. In fact, a typical statutory definition of a "dependent or neglected child" is one whose parent or guardian "fails or refuses to provide proper or necessary subsistence, education, medical care, or any other care necessary for his health, guidance, or well-being."[18] Under such definitions, the concept of "medical neglect" has gained increasing recognition.

Minors are regarded as legally incompetent for many purposes, including the authorization of medical care for themselves.[19] Thus, a physician who performs an invasive procedure on a child in a nonemergency situation without parental consent is theoretically vulnerable to a tort action for battery.[20] Children once were considered virtually to be the property of their parents, and thus state intervention in order to override a parental decision concerning a child's medical care might have been viewed as just short of heresy at the turn of this century.[21] Given the state of medicine at the time, this principle may have been of little practical importance;[22] clearly, it is of legitimate concern today. Modern law has developed a concept of medical neglect largely through cases involving parental refusal to authorize specific medical procedures considered necessary or desirable for their children.

Changes in the rules affording virtually absolute parental authority came slowly at first, with courts willing to protect children against life-threatening conditions while retaining respect for parental decision-making autonomy in most other instances.[23] Eventually, some courts began to display a willingness to overrule parental decisions when the threat to quality of life was deemed sufficiently grave, even though there was no prognosis of imminent death.[24] Older minors may now consent to some procedures as a result of either special statutory authorization or what is described as the "mature minor" rule.[25] But for very young children, and even for older adolescents in cases involving elective procedures, the concept of medical neglect is of considerable importance as a means of ensuring that parents obtain needed medical care for their children.

Federal standards for care of defective neonates. A detailed review of the actions and assertions of the Department of Health and Human Services (HHS) in the saga of the Babies Doe would extend beyond the scope of this chapter. It is important, however, to understand that after two sets of administrative regulations faltered in the face of formidable legal obstacles,[26] a third approach was taken by Congress in the enactment of the Child Abuse Amendments of 1984.[27] These amendments require that states wishing to qualify for federal assistance in developing and enforcing child abuse and neglect prevention and treatment programs must establish certain procedures or programs "for the purpose of responding to the reporting of medical neglect (including instances of withholding of medically indicated treatment from disabled infants with life threatening conditions . . .)."[28] The amendments include detailed elaboration on the types of programs required and redefine "child abuse and neglect" so as to place special emphasis on the meaning of "withholding of medically indicated treatment."[29] This approach was further amplified in the third set of Baby Doe Regulations published in April 1985 under the direction of the congressional amendment.[30]

State laws addressing the measures that must be taken in dealing with defective neonates vary substantially. Louisiana's initial statutory response[31] was one of the most explicit and inclusive. In addition to prohibiting denial of nutrients or treatment, the statute provided a way in which parents might surrender their child to the state Department of Human Resources or another licensed adoption agency if they refused to consent to treatment, without necessarily terminating their financial responsibility for medical expenses.[32] In 1992, however, the latter provision was changed to allow relinquishment without that requirement.[33]

Federal involvement in expanding the concept of medical neglect has occurred largely in the context of withholding treatment or life support systems from defective neonates, an area of considerable polarization of personal and medical views. From the standpoint of this chapter, however, it is important to note two factors that extend the impact of federal involvement beyond the poignant problems of defective neonates. One is the more than symbolic reinforcement of the concept of medical neglect as a basis for state intervention. The other is the unwillingness, despite the elaborate administrative regulations and legislation, to face such issues as who will pay for the most expensive child care and treatment. In 1982 and 1984, Congress directed HHS to study ways to fund the care and treatment of such infants independently of Medicaid.[34]

Child abuse reporting statutes. An important component of the scheme for protecting children against abuse and neglect is the modern system of mandatory reporting laws. Statutory proposals of this type were enacted in record time and on an unusually wide scale by legislatures beginning in the 1960s. They require physicians and other health care providers[35] to inform a governmental agency about cases of suspected child abuse that come to their professional attention. By this time, many of the original statutes have gone through several stages of revision and expansion. Although the drafters of the original versions may not have fully anticipated or intended it, health care professionals have used these statutes to report cases of medical neglect.

New Teeth for an Old Enforcement Process

Attempts to enforce private child and family support obligations in order to lessen economic burdens on state public assistance programs are by no means new. In 1950, a time when family law was characterized by lack of uniformity and could realistically have been described as a major bastion of states' rights, a uniform law known as the Uniform Reciprocal Enforcement of Support Act (URESA) was published.[36] Soon afterward it was widely adopted by state legislatures for the avowed purpose of simplifying enforcement of private support obligations across state lines. Even after subsequent revisions, many critics considered the act to be an ineffective collection mechanism because it relied largely on its *in terrorem* effect.[37] This concern began dissipating after the adoption of the Child Support and Establishment of Paternity Amendments to the Social Security Act in 1974 and 1975.[38] These amendments set minimum standards with which state programs must comply in order to remain eligible for federal cost sharing, and provided for inauguration of programs such as a parent-locator service utilizing Social Security numbers, waiver of sovereign immunity by the United States with regard to child support payments due from federal employees, and certification by the secretary of HHS to the federal courts of certain support enforcement actions without respect to the amount in controversy.[39]

Even more effective measures were introduced in response to the Child Support Enforcement Amendments of 1984 (CSEA).[40] Again, states are required to enact certain provisions in order to maintain continued federal participation in the funding of public assistance programs. The mandated provisions for collecting overdue support obligations include simplified and speedy withholding from wages, deductions from tax refunds, requiring an absent parent to give security, and establishing liens against real or personal property.[41] Some states provide that support payments made by the parent of a child on public assistance be paid directly to the public agency responsible for child support enforcement, with only the amount in excess of the public grant being remitted to the obligee.[42]

These provisions, combined with the earlier ones (including URESA), unquestionably establish a far more organized means for enforcing private support obligations, including those for medical assistance. The reason for them is economic—to shift state expenditures for child or family support to private obligors. Although cutting the costs of medical assistance may not have been perceived as a primary goal, it was recognized as one area in which state expenditures could be reduced.

Children's Financial Responsibility
for Their Own Medical Care

Determining whether children will be obligated to pay for their own medical care raises new and old legal issues. The old ones stem from traditional common law limitations on minors' contractual capacity, discussed earlier in the context of children's longstanding incapacity to consent to medical treatment. The new ones reflect the trend toward granting increased personal autonomy to minors in response to what is sometimes labeled (or mislabeled) the "children's rights" movement.

At common law, minors were largely incompetent to execute binding contracts of any sort, and this rule remains widespread. In its strictest version, a minor can disaffirm a contract for the purchase of an item not classifiable as a necessity without incurring any liability for use, depreciation, damage, or other diminution in property value following the purchase.[43] A recent Wisconsin Supreme Court case[44] indicates how the rule can affect an obligation to pay for medical services. An unmarried minor was hospitalized for the birth of a child. Medicaid paid only that part of the bill directly related to the infant's care, so the hospital sought reimbursement for the remainder of the bill from the minor patient and the infant's father, who had married the mother after she left the hospital. A claim against the mother's father was dismissed on the procedural basis of failure to obtain service of process. The appeals court affirmed dismissal of the claim against the minor patient on the ground that even though hospital care could be regarded as a necessity in this instance, there was no showing that she had expressly or impliedly agreed to make payment after she attained her majority. The court indicated that the duty to pay could have been imposed on the patient's father[45] if he had been properly before the court. The court eventually rationalized a way to hold the patient's new husband liable (based on his paternity), even though payment was a premarital obligation of the mother.

Clearly, rules allowing minors to disaffirm their contracts still retain considerable vitality. They are now under attack, however, as part of the trend toward earlier recognition of minors' capacity to act for themselves, either generally or with regard to such specific matters as medical treatment. The latter area is where the most significant developments have occurred, and it is of special moment for this analysis. As noted earlier, parental consent historically has been required for medical treatment of children except in emergencies.[46] In response to problems that might flow from parental consent requirements in situations where some minors are reluctant to consult or confide in their parents, state legislatures have adopted statutes permitting minors to consent to medical treatment for themselves in certain enumerated cases,[47] among them alcohol and substance abuse, crisis mental health counseling, family planning, pregnancy,[48] and treatment for certain contagious diseases. As a matter of policy, these laws reflect the substantial degree of change (some might say breakdown) that has taken place in the modern family. The selection of particular medical conditions for which minors can independently consent to treatment obviously was rooted in expediency and the fear that otherwise children might not obtain timely medical care, thereby exacerbating drug-related problems, spreading contagious disease, increasing unwanted pregnancies, or postponing prenatal care.

These minor consent statutes have created two sets of problems. One group stems from the failure to define the permissible and required scope of communication between physicians and the parents of their minor patients who consent in accordance with the statutes. The other concerns liability for medical treatment. The IJA/ABA *Standards Relating to Rights of Minors,* an important contemporary statement of goals and a blueprint for legislative reform, affirms the basic duty of parents to be liable to persons providing medical treatment to their children "if the parent consents to such services, or if the services are provided under emergency circumstances."[49] However, the standards express the view that a minor who consents to medical treatment under a special enabling statute should also be financially liable for such services and should not disaffirm any such obligation because of minority.[50] In what many consider a well-meaning but impractical attempt to balance the minor patient's right to privacy and the problem of securing payment, the standards propose that insurance coverage should be payable under any policy in which the minor is a beneficiary, even though the child rather than the parent has consented to the treatment.[51] However, no private or public health insurer should inform the parent or policyholder that such a claim has been filed unless the treating physician has previously notified the parent. Anyone who has dealt with billing procedures of either Blue Cross or most private health insurers is bound to feel skeptical about the workability of the last part of the proposal, but it reflects the trend toward greater recognition of the personal rights of minors.

Some newer statutes specify not only that a minor cannot disaffirm a contract for medical care that was received, but also that the parent, guardian, or spouse of such a minor has no liability to pay for such care in the absence of a specific agreement to do so.[52] What if some parents refused to consent to treatment (or chose to have their minor children consent) in order to avoid financial responsibility? Might such conduct be construed as constituting abuse or neglect, or does the statute provide a tacit exception under the circumstances?[53]

Ending or Replacing Parental Rights and Duties

Increased concern about defining the rights and duties that flow between children and parents without regard to the gender or marital status of the latter has been part of what some describe as the "constitutionalization" of family law in recent years. This has been accompanied by questions about what procedural requirements are necessary if a state wishes to terminate parental rights.[54] These developments have also affected existing procedures for adoption, through which a new "legal" parent may be substituted for a biological parent. Once used in ancient societies to accomplish some of the same goals for which the modern will was developed,[55] adoption could in the future become important as a means for shifting responsibility for children's medical needs, either voluntarily or involuntarily.

Adoption

Through the mechanism of adoption, an existing parent–child relationship is terminated and a new parent is substituted to assume all the legal rights and duties of parenthood. Though not an indigenous American legal institution,[56] adoption has been reshaped by our legal system over the past century as a special means for providing homes and families for minor children who have no living parents or whose parents are unwilling or incapable of caring for them. Today this country has no effective, widespread system of long-term child-care institutions. Orphanages began to disappear or change focus many years ago and were replaced by a system of foster care and adoptive placement institutions operated by public agencies and state-licensed private organizations. By mid-century, most adoption laws had been refined to provide for judicial involvement and screening of the potential adopters and their homes by some responsible agency (at least in the case of nonrelative adoptions) before a final decree. Some states placed narrow limits on "private placements" for adoption involving previously unrelated parties, thus increasing the importance of the agency placement process.

For many years demand for adoptable children has exceeded supply, often by a substantial margin.[57] Once this imbalance was probably affected by the prevailing emphasis on placements of healthy children immediately after birth. During that period specific criteria, some of which would be at best of questionable legal validity today, were used by some agencies to establish adopter eligibility. Such requirements as a low age ceiling, no prior divorces, or conformity with certain social or religious standards severely limited the pool of persons who might adopt through agency placements.

In recent years social, legal, and economic changes[58] have further reduced the number of normal, healthy infants available for adoption, while the demand for adoptable children has increased, causing the demise of some placement agencies, shifts in the major function of others, and the expansion of efforts to include children with "special needs" in the adoption pool. That label generally extends to several well-defined groups of children who once were considered difficult to place and, as a result, largely remained outside the adoption process. Older children, members of a larger sibling group needing placement together, children of minority racial or ethnic origins, and children with mental or physical handicaps or special medical demands are typically regarded as having special needs.

Although they may not constitute the largest number of "hard-to-place" children, this chapter addresses only the problems of handicapped and medically needy children. Locating prospective adoptive parents who are able to cope with children's handicaps or severe medical needs presents one problem. Providing services and funding poses another.

Subsidized adoption. Subsidized adoption, a special procedure for facilitating adoption of children with special needs, has achieved wide legislative enactment since New York passed the first enabling statute about two decades ago.[59] It opened to mixed reviews, probably because of both insufficient understanding of what it was designed to do and skepticism about governmental willingness to provide adequate funding.[60] One commentator noted the irony of this reception: "In a society in which two of the most cherished values are children and money, it is surprising that a proposal holding promise of both has met with much resistance."[61] The reference to saving money as well as children derives from a comparison of long-term foster care with legal adoption by parents who want the child. Subsidized adoption costs the state less than foster care,[62] and adoption is generally perceived as psychologically superior to serial foster homes.

Subsidized adoption received an enormous boost with Congressional passage of the Adoption Assistance and Child Welfare Act of 1980.[63] Prior to 1980, federal funds were available for assisting foster care but not for adoption. This provided a disincentive for state placement of "special needs" children for adoption under subsidy. The 1980 law extended the scope of federal financial assistance to subsidized adoption. Each state must now provide such adoption assistance in order to qualify for participation in the federal AFDC program.[64] Children eligible for the federal subsidy contribution must have "special needs" and qualify for AFDC or SSI benefits.[65] The amount of governmental assistance can vary according to the adoptive parents' circumstances and the child's needs, although federal assistance cannot exceed what the child would have received from that source if the child had been placed in foster care.[66]

Children eligible for federally assisted subsidized adoption programs also are eligible for Medicaid because they are deemed to be dependent children and AFDC recipients. Problems have arisen, however, in some interstate placements or in situations in which a family has moved to another state after completing a subsidized adoption. Although the state in which the subsidy adoption agreement[67] was made can simply send the basic payments to the client's out-of-state address, third-party providers in one state may be reluctant to accept another state's Medicaid card for reasons ranging from a concern about extra paperwork and payment delays to the possibility that some services may not be covered under the other state's program. A key feature of the federal act is its intended reliance on interstate compacts to remedy such problems in our mobile society. Suggested language for an Interstate Compact on Adoption and Medical Assistance, developed by the American Public Welfare Association under a HHS grant and published in 1983, addresses the problem by providing for issuance of identification for medical assistance in the state where the child resides. It also suggests a formula under which the state of adoption would pay for services it normally would cover if such costs are not included under the program of the state of the child's residence. Enabling legislation that would allow appropriate agencies to enter into such compacts has been adopted by only a small number of states thus far, although HHS has issued instructions on the level of required compliance with medical assistance reimbursement across state lines even if a state has not entered into such a compact.[68]

In summary, developments in the area of subsidized adoption have focused on the goal of providing stable families for children with handicaps or special medical needs, as opposed to relegating them to long-term foster care that could involve a series of homes where emotional and developmental requirements may not be met. Although statistical information is sparse, there is some indication that children with special medical handicaps or needs are becoming an increasingly larger portion of those served by this program. However, as cost-containment pressures increase, needed expansion may be in a precarious condition because of the dependency on Medicaid eligibility and further problems of interstate enforcement and inconsistency of services.

There is a legitimate concern that subsidized adoption has been viewed too much as a cost-containment mechanism, although many obviously have supported it as an alternative to further expansion of what is regarded as a deeply troubled foster care system. The promise of cost reduction may not be fully justifiable if the program is to accomplish its "child-saving" goal effectively in cases where the special needs are medical.

Some ask whether children may enter the adoption process rather than remain in foster care when they are in foster care in the first place largely because of the financial inadequacies of parents who might function satisfactorily if the subsidized adoption funding were instead given to them. This question may deserve serious policy consideration, but it should not be assumed that channeling funding to the natural parents would resolve all the cases in which subsidized adoption of children with special medical needs is being attempted. For example, the requirement that a child must be eligible for AFDC can serve to limit the use of subsidized adoption by financially capable parents trying to avoid future responsibility for the medical costs of a child with a permanent or long-term handicap.

Voluntary adoptive placement to obtain medical insurance. Without reliable data one can only speculate about what is occurring or might occur as medical costs increase and parents feel incapable of coping with the needs of their children. In that speculative vein, consider the possibility that some parents might voluntarily relinquish their children for adoption by someone with adequate medical insurance. If the adopter is a close relative, perhaps even a member of the same extended household, the adoption could be considered as taking place entirely for the purpose of securing insurance benefits. Modern laws typically provide for facilitating private placements between close relatives through such means as eliminating the number of judicial proceedings involved or deemphasizing certain review procedures.

Although data documenting the extent of this practice are insufficient, a West Virginia Supreme Court opinion,[69] well known in family law for its explication of the "primary caretaker" doctrine as the criterion for determining child custody, substantiates and acknowledges its existence. The mother of an infant with a chronic respiratory infection requiring hospitalization and "considerable medical attention" agreed to allow her own grandparents to adopt the child, who then qualified for coverage under the grandfather's hospitalization and medical insurance.[70] Before the child's birth the mother had separated from the father, to whom she was not married, and returned to live with her grandparents. Although the father had not been supporting the child, he opposed the grandparents' petition for adoption and sought custody. A key issue before the court was whether the mother's consent to the adoption constituted abandonment, thereby making her an unfit parent. The court found that there had been no abandonment under the circumstances, but rather that the mother had "mobilized all of the resources at her command, namely the solicitous regard of her grandparents, in the interest of this child and that she went to extraordinary lengths to provide for him adequate medical attention and financial support."[71] The court also noted that "it is well recognized that mothers in penurious circumstances often resort to adoption in order to make the child eligible for social security or union welfare benefits, all of which significantly enhance the child's opportunities in life."[72]

Even though one can only speculate about the extent to which adoption is used to enroll a child for medical coverage, the ease with which this can be accomplished and the pressures that may dictate its use must be recognized. It is not among the traditional purposes for which adoption was developed, but qualifying a child for medical coverage is a new need that is in some ways comparable to factors considered by unwed mothers several decades ago when deciding whether to relinquish children for adoption in order to afford them better opportunities in life.

Voluntary relinquishment for adoption to end parental duties. Some parents seek to end financial obligations for a child through consenting to private adoption by a specific person or relinquishment to an adoptive placement agency.[73] The former instance is illustrated by the noncustodial parent who, though required to pay for child support, has little or no meaningful relationship with the child and therefore consents to adoption by a stepparent.[74] The latter is exemplified by the mother who does not wish to bear the extra economic and social burdens that can fall on a single parent and thus relinquishes her child to an agency.[75] In the past, both types of cases have usually involved a normal, healthy child. A scenario of growing concern today involves a parental desire to relinquish a child with irremediable defects or medical problems likely to be remediable only at the cost of draining all of the parents' assets. This is by no means farfetched. It echoes the theme of a celebrated case of the late 1940s in which a father had killed his child in what would generally be described as an act of euthanasia.[76] The issue before the court was whether the father, who in an earlier proceeding had been convicted of manslaughter and placed on probation, was of "good moral character" for purposes of becoming a U.S. citizen through naturalization. The court's remarks indicated its assumption that the father's motive was the nurture of his other four children, "which was being compromised by the burden imposed upon him in the care of the fifth."[77] Had the alternative been relinquishment to the state or adoption, one wonders whether the outcome would have been different.

In assessing the likelihood that this could become a serious problem, one should understand that parents may owe a legal duty of support to their incapacitated children if the incapacity continues past majority.[78] Although many states have statutory provisions that formally provide for voluntary relinquishment of parental rights, such laws were probably enacted in order to provide a means for avoiding costly and time-consuming court proceedings in instances where less than adequate parents would at least acquiesce in the termination of their rights. That these provisions might, in the absence of further legislative direction, be construed as establishing a "right" to relinquish a child because of special medical needs seems questionable—particularly in a time when states are concerned about shouldering medical costs.

A more likely course would be for the state to remove the child from the home while seeking continued support from the parents. As noted earlier, Louisiana once had a provision stating that parents who refuse to consent to care and treatment of a child under that state's particular "Baby Doe"–style enactment "shall at all times be free to execute a voluntary act of surrender" to a state or other adoptive placement agency.[79] The statute also provided, however:

> All medical expenses incurred by the Department of Health and Human Resources on behalf of the child shall be reimbursed by the parent or parents of the child, provided they have not been declared financially needy. No medical insurer of the parent or parents of a child who would have otherwise been liable for such medical expenses may deny liability to the insured solely because of the parent's or parents' desire to withhold medical or surgical treatment for their child.[80]

The statute further provided that the agency to which the child is relinquished shall immediately provide treatment and "make every effort" to find an adoptive home.[81] It made no reference to the potential long-term medical obligation of the relinquishing parents. However, the "financially needy" limitation on required reimbursement could conceivably be construed to deal with the problem of a child ineligible for federal subsidized adoption assistance by virtue of not being qualified for AFDC.[82]

Congress has authorized the secretary of HHS to make grants to states to help with the establishment, operation, or implementation of "programs to help in obtaining or coordinating necessary services, including social and health services and financial assistance for families with disabled infants with life-threatening conditions, *and those services necessary to facilitate adoptive placement of such infants who have been relinquished for adoption.*"[83]

Involuntary Termination of Parental Rights

Adoption serves to shift parental rights, but it requires either the consent of existing parents or formal termination of their legal rights as parents. Termination of parental rights can be based on incapacity or unwillingness to care for a child's medical needs, though such peremptory action is taken only in extreme cases.[84] Such cases are distinguishable from situations in which the state intervenes to overrule a specific parental decision about medical care. The latter situation, though known as medical neglect, is viewed by some courts as involving little, if any, moral culpability on the part of the nonconsenting parent.[85]

One might ask why parental rights should be terminated for failure or unwillingness to provide medical care. The action might free a child for adoptive placement with parents who will extend such care,[86] but many such children will be difficult to place for adoption because of their medical needs. Some children might qualify for subsidized adoption that could include Medicaid coverage. If they do not, the state simply may be relieving the natural parents of further financial responsibility through the termination procedure. Those interested in child protection would say that termination should be predicated on parental incapacity or misconduct, whether or not an adoptive placement is likely to take place.[87] State agencies, however, will be reluctant to take steps likely to result in greater cost to the state if an adoptive placement is uncertain.[88]

The Tort System and Children's Health Care Costs

The impact on children's health care costs of professional liability under tort law could be increasingly significant, though projections are difficult to quantify. Costs of medical services might be expected to escalate because of defensive medical practice and increases in liability exposure and insurance premiums. Is children's health care more vulnerable to cost increases than other areas of medical practice? Once again, special legal and practical concerns should be considered.

Until recently, practitioners in the children's health care field (other than those with narrowly defined specialties) usually were not cast into the more expensive professional liability categories occupied by surgeons, anesthesiologists, and orthopedists. This is still the case for family and general pediatric practice, though not for neonatology and obstetrics.[89] The increase in the number and severity of claims associated with birth-related procedures has become of special concern, and attention is being focused on the degree to which this increase is affecting delivery of services.[90] Some health care professionals are limiting their obstetrical practice, and nurse midwives, in particular, find it hard to obtain liability insurance coverage at a cost that would allow them to continue practice. Because many nurse practitioners and midwives have historically served lower-income mothers, the impact will fall most heavily on those least able to afford to see a physician.

Among the explanations given for the liability crisis in obstetrics are inadequate practices and risk management, increased specialization, and new technology coupled with a time lag in adequate training for its use. If these are indeed significant contributing factors, one might postulate that similar developments could occur in pediatric practice. Increasing demands for expertise in areas such as genetic screening and counseling provide illustrations, though whether such practices will settle into the domain of pediatrics rather than another specialty is uncertain.

One special factor in children's actions under tort law is the extended time period during which such actions can be commenced. In many states a statute of limitations will not begin to toll until a child reaches majority, generally age eighteen.[91] Some states have reduced this time period, but not all such modifications have survived constitutional attacks based on their limited applicability to medical malpractice cases.[92] It is difficult to assess the effect on physicians' costs of this extended period, but uncertainty is often identified as the cause of inflated liability insurance rates. Although the passage of time and the staleness of evidence may make defense of a case more difficult, they also make it harder for plaintiffs to meet their burden of proof. Perhaps a more important concern is the difficulty, in a period of dynamically changing medical practice, of reconstructing the prevailing standard of care that existed a decade or two earlier but is now rejected because of increased technology, new drugs, or greater experience.

There is also concern about new causes of action that raise the specter of unusually high damage awards. Prime examples are the actions described (or misdescribed) as wrongful pregnancy and wrongful life. The former refers to an action by the parent of a defective child based on physician negligence before the child's birth, while the latter is an action by the child himself or herself. Considerable criticism of both actions has arisen because of what might best be described as their ethical and philosophical underpinnings—namely, that they are based on failure to afford a parent the opportunity to choose abortion over childbirth. The conceptual problem is especially troubling in the case of an action by a child, who in essence seeks damages for having been born. Despite these theoretical difficulties, wrongful pregnancy or birth actions have been recognized by courts in numerous states,[93] while wrongful life actions have been recognized by courts in three jurisdictions.[94] States that have recognized such actions—especially the suit for wrongful life—have tended to restrict the scope of recoverable damages, including extraordinary medical care but excluding pain and suffering or impairment of childhood.[95] Critics have suggested that limiting recovery primarily to medical expenses in effect warps the tort system by providing a mechanism for assuring payment for expensive medical care that otherwise might be either a devastating burden to parents or a charge to the state, if not both. It is significant that the legislature of one state where a cause of action for wrongful life was judicially recognized has adopted a statute providing that "[n]o cause of action arises against a parent of a child based upon the claim that the child should not have been conceived or, if conceived, should not have been allowed to have been born alive."[96]

Another special liability problem that pediatricians may have to face stems from the uncertainty concerning their duty or discretion to communicate with parents of their minor patients, discussed earlier in a different context.[97] The issue raised by this problem is whether revealing such information about the child's medical treatment can be used as the basis for a tort action based on breach of the duty to maintain confidentiality.[98] A further concern is what standard a physician must follow in obtaining informed consent from a minor whose comprehension may be limited because of age.[99] Because all of these problems create uncertainty, they may have a substantial impact on insurance rates.

Family Law and Cost Restraints: Some Conjectural Assessments

Major governmental assistance for medical care is now geared to children in the neediest families. Family law generally formulates more universally applicable duties, though some of its processes (such as those imposing criminal sanctions for nonsupport) may be used most often against parents with the least ability to pay. Both family law support provisions and Medicaid, through their strong but differing relationships to public assistance programs such as AFDC, often have the greatest impact on children of broken families. In Medicaid the issue is eligibility, while in family law the concern is with minimizing state payments by enforcing support obligations against absent parents.

Key family law doctrines that require parents to provide medical care (especially those provisions dealing with medical neglect) are geared toward intervention primarily in extreme cases, such as failure to provide necessary care or refusal to consent to treatment when a child is at serious risk. Cases involving defective neonates or children in need of an immediate procedure such as blood transfusion to avoid death are good examples.

While the law now recognizes the right to recovery from parents for necessities extended to their children, the definition of "necessary" medical care is not always clear. Increased recognition of the capacity of an older child to consent to some important medical procedures without parental concurrence may have come at the expense of diluting parental financial responsibility.

At a time when both government assistance and private insurance coverage may be diminishing, the financial burden on parents for children's medical care is likely to increase. Other factors, such as the demise of historical patterns of cost shifting through the rise of health maintenance and preferred provider organizations, may increase the financial burden for some families more than might have been anticipated. Increased technology and specialization in the child-care field, plus expanding costs from such ancillary areas as professional liability exposure, could compound the problem. At the same time, new and powerful support enforcement mechanisms, not necessarily adopted with medical care in mind but certainly covering it, will make it easier to collect child support from parents through procedures such as garnishment of wages, posting of security bonds, and liens against property.

It would be helpful if basic family law rules would reinforce provision for health care needs through private sources where governmental assistance is least likely. Unfortunately, the legal and funding systems do not complement each other in this manner. Neither basic preventive care needs nor the catastrophic needs of children in families with previously sufficient means are adequately addressed under most governmental programs. Prevention does not fit well into the private system either, though private systems are now geared to ensure that children's catastrophic needs are met.

The picture is not an attractive one: Just as older persons may divorce to achieve eligibility for medical assistance, or may seek to divest themselves of assets to qualify for assistance before the most devastating stage of Alzheimer's disease develops, we may see parents trying to shift the economic burden of children with exceptional medical needs by relinquishing parental rights or through adoption. This is not necessarily something that we can expect to witness only with the very poor. A family that does not qualify for public assistance but has inadequate health insurance could be hit the hardest and thus might be most likely to react in such a manner.

More desirable alternatives are politically difficult if not untenable at this time. Some form of "medical family allowance" might eventually lessen the cost of Medicaid by focusing on preventive care. Consideration also should be given to developing a system of children's health care that would be nearly universal in eligibility and "expandable" in its coverage. Other measures would protect against financial ruin from catastrophic events, or provide transitional health care coverage for young adults shortly after minority and before they have entered the labor force. Such a "bridge" approach would be designed to reach a large population that loses parental insurance coverage at a time when opportunities for substitute coverage can be very limited. Reorientation of private health insurance coverage to focus more adequately on minors' needs might be undertaken now with less political opposition than most of the suggestions made above.

Imaginative programs such as subsidized adoption should be further refined, with their development emphasizing both services to the children involved and potential cost savings. Innovative new programs should be encouraged, but with awareness of their potential impact on families and not simply of their potential for saving money.

Finally, current family law rules regarding children's medical care should be carefully reevaluated and clearly restated. Such a formulation should try to balance the interests of all parties involved, and should include some statement of the role that cost concerns play in determinations of what care is appropriate under the circumstances.

PAYING FOR CHILDREN'S MEDICAL CARE: UPDATE

The movement toward expanded access to health care has gained momentum since the preceding chapter was written, with special interest in the large group of currently uninsured children.[100] Many states now extend coverage to "medically needy" families whose incomes and assets are too high to qualify them for AFDC benefits, and there has been some expansion of coverage for prenatal care and for very young children.[101] A new development that seems noteworthy because it was not addressed earlier is the movement toward compensating certain severely impaired newborns through "selective" no-fault schemes. Limited undertakings of this sort are now operational in Virginia and Florida, and legislatures in New York and North Carolina have considered proposals for significantly expanded schemes.

Such compensation schemes were introduced in response to concerns that many obstetricians and family practitioners might stop delivering babies, leaving rural and inner-city locations with limited or no access to obstetrical services.[102] That fear was generated in Virginia because of insurer decisions to limit underwriting or raise malpractice premiums unless some type of relief could be provided from the highest claims on behalf of newborns. Virginia's 1987 statute thus can be considered another response to the insurance-generated malpractice crisis of the 1980s.[103] Florida's statutory provision was part of a broader package of tort reforms aimed at medical malpractice concerns generally.

The Virginia law[104] and the Florida law patterned after it focus on infants sustaining certain severe injuries during delivery. They provide the exclusive remedy against participating providers[105] for infants falling within the definition of each act unless the injury was willfully or intentionally caused.[106] The Virginia act defines "birth-related neurological injury" so narrowly[107] that only one claim has been paid since the program's inception. Florida's law has a somewhat less restrictive definition of birth-related neurological injury,[108] but neither program in its present form is likely to provide medical care and other benefits for more than a very limited number of defective neonates. It must, however, be recognized that the avowed purpose of the acts was to ensure the continued availability of malpractice insurance[109] rather than to provide expanded access to health care for children.

Variations on the selective no-fault theme considered during the 1992 legislative sessions in New York and North Carolina would have extended medical care to a much larger number of defective infants. The North Carolina proposal would have covered all of the 150 to 200 children born annually in the state with cerebral palsy.[110] The New York statute would have provided the exclusive remedy for an "impairment," defined in the proposed legislation as "any injury, sickness, disease or bodily harm of a newborn occurring during gestation, labor, delivery or within seventy-two hours of delivery, excluding death and excluding injuries that, to a reasonable degree of medical certainty, generically cannot be caused by a negligent act or omission of a health care provider."[111] Benefits under the proposed act would largely have covered necessary medical or custodial care not paid for through any private insurance, public program, or tort awards or settlements. Noneconomic losses would not have been covered.

Reasons given in support of expanded coverage for impaired neonates include ensuring access to care; concern about defensive medicine, inconsistency of awards, and the sometimes tenuous relationship between awards and fault; the protracted nature of the tort process; and the fact that under the tort system many impaired newborns are not compensated either because they cannot establish fault or because their injury is not severe enough to make legal representation financially feasible.[112]

Even though the existing statutes and those under consideration were designed primarily to deal with malpractice issues, the approach is of special interest in the context of paying for children's health care because such schemes can provide costly medical care for some children who previously would not have received reimbursement through the tort system or perhaps through any existing insurance or compensation scheme. The proposed North Carolina and New York statutes would have substantially expanded the population of included infants, though their coverage would not have been generous. Significantly, an integral part of the Virginia scheme is the absolute requirement that each participating physician and hospital agree to provide obstetric care to indigent patients under a plan to be approved by the Virginia commissioner of health.[113]

NOTES

1. Family allowances may be described as regular cash payments to families with children. *See* Social Security Administration, U.S. Department of Health and Human Services, Social Security Programs throughout the World 1983, Research Report No. 59, at xxv (1984).

2. Another obstacle, of course, is our traditional approach to financing social insurance schemes, which bases eligibility on participation in the workforce.

3. *See generally* Cluff, Chronic Disability of Infants and Children, 38 J. Chronic Disease 113 (1985); Strauss, The Arms Race and Children in Fiscal Year 1985, 75 Pediatrics 1149 (1985).

4. For an excellent review of these cost problems, see Blendon, Paying for Medical Care for Children: A Continuing Financial Dilemma, 29 Advances in Pediatrics 229 (1982).

5. This problem can extend to judicial decisions as well. Among the most noteworthy of such examples is Stanley v. Illinois, 405 U.S. 645 (1972), a case involving a state's denial of a fitness hearing to the father of illegitimate children upon the mother's death. Although seemingly unintended, the language of the court's decision created havoc in the process of adoptive placement, and its impact is still felt. *See also* Lehr v. Robertson, 463 U.S. 248 (1983) (a custody case in which the court seemed more interested in whether procedural requirements were followed than in ensuring subjective determination of the best interests of the child).

6. *See, e.g., In re* Hofbauer, 393 N.E.2d 1009 (N.Y. 1979); Custody of a Minor, 379 N.E.2d 1053 (Mass. 1978); Custody of a Minor (No. 3), 393 N.E.2d 836 (Mass. 1979) (the Chad Green cases).

7. Among such pioneering cases dealing with the confrontation between parents and the state (or the medical establishment) were State v. Perricone, 181 A.2d 751 (N.J. 1962) (blood transfusion); People *ex rel.* Wallace v. Labrenz, 104 N.E.2d 769 (Ill. 1952); Custody of a Minor, 379 N.E.2d 1053 (Mass. 1978), 393 N.E.2d 836 (Mass. 1979); and *In re* Hofbauer, 393 N.E.2d 1009 (N.Y. 1979).

8. *See, e.g., In re* Tanner, 549 P.2d 703 (Utah 1976) (ordering a state's division of family services to pay for orthodontia needed by a child whose mother was dead and whose father had disappeared). *See also In re* Karwath, 199 N.W.2d 147 (Iowa 1972) (court ordered removal of tonsils at state expense over father's religious objections).

9. One obvious instance is the field of artificial conception. *See* Wadlington, Artificial Conception: The Challenge for Family Law, 69 Va. L. Rev. 465 (1983).

10. For further discussion see A. Holder, Legal Issues in Pediatric and Adolescent Medicine (2d ed. 1985); Bennett, Allocation of Child Medical Care Decision Making Authority: A Suggested Interest Analysis, 62 Va. L. Rev. 285 (1976); IJA/ABA Juvenile Justice Standards Project, Standards Relating to Rights of Minors, Part IV: Medical Care (1980); Goldstein, Medical Care for the Child at Risk: On State Supervention of Parental Autonomy, Chapter 26 in this volume; Wadlington, Minors and Health Care: The Age of Medical Consent, 11 Osgoode Hall L.J. 115 (1973).

11. Even when the rule against initiating such an action has been relaxed, courts may for some time be unwilling to permit children actually to sue their parents for support, on the theory that other provisions, such as the abuse and neglect laws, have been designed to deal with support problems. *Cf.* Burnette v. Wahl, 588 P.2d 1105 (Or. 1978) (children's damage actions for failure to perform parental duties not allowed).

12. This belief is reflected in the statements of Sir William Blackstone, an eighteenth-century commentator who in recent years has occasionally been cited or quoted on the general subject of parent and child relationships in a strange or misguided fashion. *See* 1 W. Blackstone, Commentaries on the Laws of England *434.

13. Greenspan v. Slate, 97 A.2d 390 (N.J. 1953).

14. Ironically, in 1983 the *Greenspan* holding was used by a court of another state to support its decision that the owner of five Great Dane dogs seized by a humane society was required to pay for the animals' support while they were in protective custody. *See* Biggerstaff v. Vanderburgh Humane Soc., 453 N.E.2d 363 (Ind. App. 1983).

It is interesting to note that the New York Society for Prevention of Cruelty to Children (the first SPCC) was founded in 1875, a year after the Society for the Prevention of Cruelty to Animals (SPCA) had assisted in the rescue of a maltreated child. The SPCA was founded in 1866. *See* 6 Dictionary Am. Hist. 331 (1976).

15. *See, e.g.,* Va. Code § 20-61 (1983). *See also* H. Krause, Child Support in America (1981).

16. *See, e.g.,* Va. Code § 20-61 (1983).

17. In such jurisdictions, one might expect to find the nonsupport statutes used particularly in cases involving the neediest portion of the population—those more likely to be eligible for public assistance and Medicaid.

18. Colo. Rev. Stat. § 19-1-103(20)(d) (1983).

19. *See* W. Wadlington et al., Cases and Materials on Children in the Legal System (1983); W. Wadlington, Consent to Medical Care for Minors: The Legal Framework, in Children's Competence to Consent 57 (G. Melton et al. eds., 1983) [hereinafter cited as Competence to Consent]; Batey, Rights of Adolescents, 23 Wm. & Mary L. Rev. 363 (1982).

20. Battery can be defined as the unauthorized and unprivileged invasion of another person's protected bodily interest. *See* Restatement (Second) of Torts §§ 13–20 (1965).

21. The 1912 case of Tony Tuttendario, 21 P. Dist. 561 (Q.S. Phil.), a seven-year-old boy with rickets, provides an example of this attitude. When the child's doctors recommended surgery and his mother refused to consent, an agent of the SPCC attempted to obtain a judicial commitment that would allow the substitute custodian to authorize the procedure. In rejecting such a challenge to parental authority, the court explained, "We have not yet adopted as public policy the Spartan rule that children belong, not to their parents, but to the state. As the law stands, the parents forfeit their natural right of guardianship only in cases where they have shown their unfitness by reason of moral depravity." *Id.* at 563.

22. The court in *Tuttendario* noted that in 1912 there remained in medicine "a residuum of the unknown . . . which scientists, by a necessary law for the development of science, disregard, but which parents, in their natural love for their children, regard with apprehension and terror." *Id.*

23. *Compare* People *ex rel.* Wallace v. Labrenz, 104 N.E.2d 769 (Ill. 1952) (judicially authorizing blood transfusion for a child in the face of religiously based parental objection) *with In re* Seiferth, 127 N.E.2d 820 (N.Y. 1955) (no intervention to overrule parental refusal to consent to surgery for correcting cleft palate) *and In re* Hudson, 126 P.2d 765 (Wash. 1942) (no intervention followiong parental refusal to permit amputation of oversized arm posing strains on body systems).

24. Probably the best-known illustration of this is *In re* Sampson, 65 Misc. 2d 658 (Fam. Ct. Ulster Cty. 1970), *aff'd*, 278 N.E.2d 918 (N.Y. 1972). Over a mother's religious objection, the courts appointed a guardian with authority to consent to essentially corrective surgery for a child whose face was grossly deformed due to neurofibromatosis. Because the objectionable growth was clinically benign and the proposed surgical intervention was substantial, one might analyze the case as one in which the operation was essentially cosmetic in purpose but potentially life-threatening in nature. The trial court explained one basis for appointing the guardian:

> I am persuaded that if this court is to meet its responsibilities to this boy it can neither shift the responsibility onto his shoulders nor can it permit his mother's religious beliefs to stand in the way of attaining through corrective surgery whatever chance he may have for a normal, happy existence, which . . . is difficult of attainment under the most propitious circumstances, but will unquestionably be impossible if the disfigurement is not corrected.

65 Misc. 2d at 674. Not all courts have agreed with the New York court's rationale in *Sampson*. For an opposing view, see *In re* Green, 292 A.2d 387 (Pa. 1972), *aff'd*, 307 A.2d 279 (Pa. 1973).

25. For further discussion of the development of the mature minor rule, see Wadlington, Minors and Health Care, *supra* note 10, at 117–20. Special statutes authorizing children to consent to their own medical care in limited instances are discussed *infra* at notes 47–53 and accompanying text.

26. *See* American Academy of Pediatrics v. Heckler, 561 F. Supp. 395 (D.D.C. 1983); United States v. Univ. Hosp. of State Univ. of New York, 729 F.2d 144 (2d Cir. 1984). In Bowen v. American Hosp. Ass'n, 476 U.S. 610 (1986), the Supreme Court held that the HHS regulations were not authorized by § 504 of the 1973 Rehabilitation Act.

27. 42 U.S.C. §§ 5101-5105 (1982 & Supp. II 1984).

28. 42 U.S.C. § 5103(b)(2)(k) (Supp. II 1984).

29. *Id.*

30. 50 Fed. Reg. 14,878 (1985).

31. La. Rev. Stat. § 40:1299.36.1 (West Supp. 1985).

32. *See id.* at § 1299.36.2.A. Physicians also are required to report parental refusal to consent to treatment and are protected from liability if they provide medical care when delay would be life-threatening. *Id.* at § 40:1299.36.2.B. For further discussion of the question of who must pay after such a relinquishment, see *infra* notes 63–98 and accompanying text.

33. La. Civ. Code Ann. Art 1559 (1992).

34. *See* 42 U.S.C. § 5103 (1982 & Supp. II 1984).

35. Some people outside the health care system, such as teachers, social workers, and probation officers, may also be required to report. Other persons who are not required to report may be given an incentive to do so through providing immunity from liability for reporting. *See, e.g.,* Va. Code §§ 63.1-248.3, 63.1-248.4 (1983).

36. 9 U.L.A. 747 (1979).

37. Major reasons for this were the problem of locating peripatetic or intentionally elusive obligors and the lack of incentives for officials in a responding state to process petitions promptly.

38. Child Support & Enforcement Amendments of 1974, 42 U.S.C. §§ 651-60 (Supp. II 1974); Amendments Relating to Social Security Act, Pub. L. No. 94-88, 89 Stat. 433 (1975).

39. For a more thorough discussion of these federal provisions, see Krause, Child Support in America, *supra* note 15, at 281.

40. 42 U.S.C. § 666 (Supp. 1985).

41. *See id.* States are expected to honor requests for withholding that come from other jurisdictions. A Model Interstate Withholding Act has been developed by the ABA National Legal Resource Center for Child Advocacy and Protection in cooperation with the National Conference of State Legislatures. *See* U.S. Department of Health and Human Services, Office of Child Support Enforcement, Model Interstate Income Withholding Act with Comments (1984).

42. *See, e.g.,* Minn. Stat. Ann. § 518.551 (West Supp. 1986).

43. Halbman v. Lemke, 298 N.W.2d 562 (Wis. 1980), is the case widely cited to epitomize this dilemma in today's world.

44. Madison Gen. Hosp. v. Haack, 369 N.W.2d 663 (Wis. 1985).

45. In addition to providing new enforcement mechanisms, some states have extended the statutory support duty among family members. Under an act adopted in Wisconsin during 1985 (1985 Wisconsin Act 56), the minor mother's parents might be required to support the minor's children during their minority. *See* Wis. Stat. § 49.19(4)(a) (West Supp. 1986).

46. For more complete discussion of the issues, see Competence to Consent, *supra* note 19, at 57.

47. *See id.* at 61. For an example of such a minor consent statute, see Va. Code § 54-325.2 (Supp. 1985).

48. A minor's consent to abortion, however, typically is dealt with in a separate statutory provision.

49. IJA/ABA Juvenile Justice Standards Project, Standards Relating to Rights of Minors, *supra* note 10, at 59.

50. *Id.* at 61.

51. *Id.*

52. *See, e.g.,* Mont. Code Ann. § 41-1-404 (1985).

53. Refusal might not be perceived as a problem with regard to elective procedures.

54. *See, e.g.,* Santosky v. Kramer, 455 U.S. 745 (1982) ("Before a state may sever completely and irrevocably the rights of parents in their natural child, due process requires that the state support its allegations by at least clear and convincing evidence"); Lassiter v. Dep't of Social Serv., 452 U.S. 18 (1981) ("The Constitution does not require the appointment of counsel for indigent parents in every parental status determination proceeding. The decision whether due process calls for the appointment of counsel is to be answered in the first instance by the trial court, subject to appellate review").

55. *See* Huard, The Law of Adoption: Ancient and Modern, 9 Vand. L. Rev. 743 (1956).

56. For further discussion of the development of American adoption law, see Presser, The Historical Background of the American Law of Adoption, 11 J. Fam. L. 443 (1971); Wadlington, Minimum Age Difference as a Requisite for Adoption, 1966 Duke L.J. 392.

57. Exact figures relating to adoption are difficult to determine today because of a lack of centralized statistical reporting. For a view of the general dimensions, see Plumez, Adoption: Where Have All the Babies Gone? N.Y. Times, Apr. 13, 1980, § 6 (Magazine), at 34.

58. These changes include legal access to abortion and contraceptive information and devices; changes in social and legal positions on legitimacy; greater economic access to child-care assistance for single mothers who previously might have relinquished their children for adoption; the desire of many unwed fathers for custody of their children; and the development of better mechanisms for proving paternity and fixing and enforcing paternal support duties.

59. All states now have some provision for adoption assistance. For a general discussion of the various approaches, see Hardy, Adoption of Children with Special Needs: A National Perspective, 39 Am. Psychologist 901 (1984).

60. For example, the original California statute included a three-year limitation period on payments. This limitation was increased to five years in 1975 and finally removed in 1982 with respect to payments starting after that date. *See* Cal. Welf. & Inst. Code § 16120(b) (1975 & West Supp. 1986).

61. Watson, Subsidized Adoption: A Crucial Investment, 51 Child Welfare 220–24 (1972).

62. One cost advantage of subsidized adoption is that it obviates the need for ongoing state monitoring and supervision of foster placements.

63. 42 U.S.C. §§ 620–28 and §§ 670–76 (1982). For a detailed review of this act and its subsequent administration, see Bussiere, Federal Adoption Assistance for Children with Special Needs, 19 Clearinghouse Rev. 587 (1985).

64. 42 U.S.C. § 602(a)(20) (1982).

65. *Id.* at § 673(a)(1).

66. *Id.* at § 673(a)(2).

67. The written subsidy or adoption assistance agreement is a key part of the individualized approach to subsidized adoption. For discussion of matters that should be addressed in negotiating such an agreement, see Bussiere, Federal Adoption Assistance, *supra* note 63, at 587, 590–91.

68. For a critique and overview of the model compact, see *id.* at 594.

69. Garska v. McCoy, 278 S.E.2d 357 (W. Va. 1981).

70. The grandfather, with whom the granddaughter and her child were residing, was a retired coal miner with liberal medical benefits. *Id.* at 359.

71. *Id.* at 364.

72. *Id.*

73. Relinquishment might also be made to a private individual in some states. However, this is less likely to carry the same degree of finality that often is accorded the agency placement.

74. Although there is an increasing tendency to impose child support duties on a stepparent who is married to and living with the custodial legal parent, usually these duties are secondary to the duties of the noncustodial natural parent and will end on dissolution of the marriage between the stepparent and the custodial parent unless the stepparent has adopted the child or continues to enjoy a special in loco parentis relationship. *See, e.g.,* Mo. Rev. Stat. § 453.400 (Supp. 1986); Washington Statewide Organization of Stepparents v. Smith, 536 P.2d 1202 (Wash. 1975).

75. Another variation of this can be the case of a child born to a married woman when her husband is not the parent. While once there would have been a strong, often unchallengeable, presumption of the husband's paternity, this scenario is increasing in complexity today through the erosion or disappearance of older rules barring husband and wife from testifying if it would affect their child's legitimacy, as well as the increased recognition of the standing of the biological father to assert paternity.

76. Repouille v. United States, 165 F.2d 152 (2d Cir. 1947).

77. *Id.* at 152.

78. *See* H. Clark, The Law of Domestic Relations in the United States 505 (1968); Elkins v. Elkins, 553 S.W.2d 34 (Ark. 1977) (upholding a judicial decree that obligated the father to continue child support payments as long as the dyslexic child was attending college); Commonwealth v. Shepard, 188 S.E.2d 99 (Va. 1972) (holding the estate of an incompetent mother liable for maintaining her son, who lived in a mental hospital); Va. Code Ann. § 20-61 (1983).

79. La. Rev. Stat. Ann. § 40:1299.36.2 (A) (West 1984). *See supra* notes 31–32 and accompanying text.

80. La. Rev. Stat. Ann. § 40:1299.35.2 (West 1984).

81. *Id.*

82. *See supra* notes 73–76 and accompanying text.

83. 42 U.S.C. § 5106a (Supp. 1992) (emphasis added).

84. *In re* M.L.G., 317 S.E.2d 881 (Ga. App. 1984) illustrates the type of case in which parental rights have been terminated because of physical or mental inability to meet a child's special medical needs. The child in question had been born without a sacrum, resulting in paralysis of her bladder that required maintenance of an ileostomy bag after a cutaneous vesicotomy. The parents were separated, and the child had been placed in foster care by court order. The father, an alcoholic, had a history of beating the wife and on one occasion had knocked the child from a couch, causing her stoma to bleed. He was unemployed, lived alone in a trailer, was delinquent in child support payments, and had indicated to a caseworker that he felt it inappropriate for him to have to change his nine-year-old daughter's ileostomy bag. The mother also had a record of excessive drinking and failure to maintain a sanitary living environment or even to bathe the child during the period when she was with her for weekend visits. On one occasion she applied a plastic sandwich bag to the ileostomy rather than the appropriate medical bag.

85. For example, in *In re* Sampson, 65 Misc. 2d 658 (Fam. Ct. Ulster Cty. 1970), *aff'd*, 278 N.E.2d 918 (N.Y. 1972), the court overruled a mother's refusal to consent to corrective surgery for her son, but nevertheless stated that the adjudication "in no way imports a finding that the mother failed in her duty to her child in any other respect." 65 Misc. 2d at 676.

86. Though it may be only peripheral to the current inquiry because of its key focus on costs, note should be taken of the increasing willingness of some courts to consider the concept of "psychological parenthood" as a factor in determining child custody independent of a blood relationship of parent and child. The cases regarding the guardianship of Phillip B. provide a possibly relevant example. A fourteen-year-old boy with Down's syndrome was institutionalized by his parents soon after birth. Subsequently a legal controversy developed over whether a guardian should be appointed to authorize a cardiac catheterization. The court held that the state had not met its burden of establishing a clear and convincing reason. *In re* Phillip B., 92 Cal. App. 3d 796, 803 (1979). Subsequently, two volunteer workers at the institution where the child resided were successful in petitioning to become his guardian on the basis of having become his psychological parents. The court explained that "*[i]t is the emotional abandonment of Phillip, not his institutionalization, which inevitably has created the unusual circumstancs which led to the award of limited custody to respondents.*" Guardianship of Phillip B., 139 Cal. App. 3d 407, 424 (1983) (emphasis in original).

87. For a different point of view, see Garrison, Why Terminate Parental Rights? 35 Stan. L. Rev. 423 (1983).

88. The cost may be increased in some cases by a difficult and time-consuming legal procedure.

89. Some family practitioners deliver babies, which can increase their professional liability insurance costs. The greatest liability risk is generally considered to be associated with practices related to birth.

90. Possible reasons for the increase in claims range from the vagaries of the tort system to inadequate medical risk management. With regard to the latter, *see*

Julian, Investigation of Obstetric Malpractice Closed Claims: Profile of Events, 2 Am. J. Perinatology 320 (1985).

91. For an illustration of such a provision for extension, see Va. Code § 8.01-229 (1984).

92. *See, e.g.,* Sax v. Votteler, 648 S.W.2d 661 (Tex. 1983); Schwan v. Riverside Methodist Hosp., 452 N.E.2d 1337 (Ohio 1983). Some states have upheld the validity of legislation shortening statutes of limitations even when applied to children. *See, e.g.,* Rohrabaugh v. Wagner, 413 N.E.2d 891 (Ind. 1980); Reese v. Rankin Fite Memorial Hosp., 403 So. 2d 158 (Ala. 1981). It should be recognized that changing a statute of limitations may not affect outstanding claims under the construction announced by some courts. *See, e.g.,* Goodman v. St. Louis Children's Hosp., 687 S.W.2d 889 (Mo. 1985) (en banc).

93. *See, e.g.,* Schroeder v. Perkel, 432 A.2d 834 (N.J. 1981).

94. *See* Procanik v. Cillo, 478 A.2d 755 (N.J. 1984); Harbeson v. Parke-Davis, Inc., 656 P.2d 483 (Wash. 1983); Turpin v. Sortini, 643 P.2d 954 (Cal. 1982).

95. The cases also indicate that recovery for these expenses can only be awarded once. In Procanik v. Cillo, 478 A.2d 755 (N.J. 1984), the court recognized that the child's right of action was independent rather than derivative from that of the parents, whose action had already been barred by the statute of limitations.

96. Cal. Civ. Code § 43.6 (West 1982). The statute further provides that "[t]he failure or refusal of a parent to prevent the live birth of his or her child shall not be a defense in any action against a third party, nor shall the failure or refusal be considered in awarding damages in any such action."

97. *See supra* notes 47–49 and accompanying text.

98. For further elaboration of the nature of this duty, see Horne v. Patton, 287 So. 2d 824 (Ala. 1974). In a somewhat unusual variation, in Humphers v. Interstate Bank, 696 P.2d 527 (Or. 1985), a physician was alleged to have written a false letter about exposure to diethylstilbestrol (DES) to help an adopted child locate her natural mother (the plaintiff in the action). The court held that the mother had an action for breach of confidentiality but not for invasion of privacy.

99. *See* Competence to Consent, *supra* note 19, at 64.

100. *See, e.g.,* Harvey, A Proposal to Provide Health Insurance to All Children and All Pregnant Women, 323 New Eng. J. Med. 1216 (1990).

101. For a general discussion of these developments, see Chapter 24 in this volume.

102. For background on adoption of the Virginia Birth Related Neurological Injury Compensation Act, see Epstein, Market and Regulatory Approaches to Medical Malpractice: The Virginia Obstetrical No-Fault Statute, 74 Va. L. Rev. 1451, 1464 (1988); O'Connell, Pragmatic Constraints on Market Approaches: A Response to Professor Epstein, 74 Va. L. Rev. 1475 (1988). For a general discussion of the original version of the act, see White, Note, Innovative Tort Reform for an Endangered Specialty, 74 Va. L. Rev. 1487 (1988).

103. For further discussion, see Bovbjerg, Legislation on Medical Malpractice: Further Developments and a Preliminary Report Card, 22 U.C. Davis L. Rev. 499, 503 (1989); Wadlington, Legal Responses to Patient Injury: A Future Agenda for Research and Reform, L. & Contemp. Probs., Spring 1991, at 199.

104. *See* Va. Code Ann. §§ 38.2-000–5021 (Michie 1990).

105. Participation in the Virginia scheme by physicians who deliver babies and hospitals in which delivery takes place is voluntary but requires an annual fee for the physician and payments based on the number of deliveries each year in the hospital. Payment is triggered by a claim of "birth-related neurological injury" in a delivery by a "participating physician" or in a "participating hospital." Va. Code Ann. § 38.2-5001 (Michie 1990). Under the act as amended in 1990, if only one entity (hospital or physician) had elected to participate in the program at the time of the injury, a tort action against the nonparticipant can be instituted, but its filing will constitute an election not to pursue recovery under the act. If recovery under the act is elected, the program can be subrogated to any malpractice action against the nonparticipating physician or hospital.

106. With regard to a participant under the act, the qualifying infant's legal relief consists of payment for medical, rehabilitative, and residential expenses not reimbursable through any other state program or private insurance; reasonable expenses incurred in filing a claim (including attorney's fees); and loss of earnings from age eighteen through sixty-five, which are conclusively presumed to be "fifty percent of the average weekly wage in the Commonwealth of workers in the private, nonfarm sector." Va. Code Ann. § 38.2-5009 (Michie 1990).

It should be noted that Virginia has a recovery "cap" for medical malpractice cases of one million dollars, including both economic and noneconomic losses. *See* Va. Code Ann. § 8.01-581.15 (Michie 1992). The constitutionality of that provision was upheld in Etheridge v. Medical Center Hosps., 376 S.E.2d 525 (Va. 1989). It also includes punitive damages, though it is possible that in some instances there may be independent actions by parent and child, with each subject separately to the damage ceiling. *See* Bulala v. Boyd, 389 S.E.2d 670 (Va. 1989).

107. The definition is:

> injury to the brain or spinal cord of an infant caused by the deprivation of oxygen or mechanical injury occurring in the course of labor, delivery or resuscitation in the immediate post-delivery period in a hospital which renders the infant permanently motorically disabled and (i) developmentally disabled or (ii) for infants sufficiently developed to be cognitively evaluated, cognitively disabled.

Va. Code Ann. § 38.2-5001 (Michie 1990). The act further requires that the disability must cause the infant "to be permanently in need of assistance in all activities of daily living," and it extends only to live births and excludes "disability or death caused by genetic or congenital abnormality, degenerative neurological disease, or maternal substance abuse." *Id.*

108. Under the Florida act such injury is defined as:

> injury to the brain or spinal cord of a live infant weighing at least 2,500 grams at birth caused by oxygen deprivation or mechanical injury occurring in the course of labor, delivery, or resuscitation in the immediate post-delivery period in a hospital, which renders the infant permanently and substantially mentally and physically impaired. This definition shall apply to live births only and shall not include disability or death caused by genetic or congenital abnormality.

Fla. Stat. ch. 706.302(2) (1991).

109. This was made clear by courts upholding the constitutionality of the financing mechanisms of the two acts. *See* King v. Virginia Birth-Related Neurological Injury Compensation Program, 410 S.E.2d 656 (Va. 1991); Coy v. Florida Birth-Related Neurological Injury Compensation Plan, 595 So. 2d 943 (Fla. 1992).

110. *See* Bobbitt et al., North Carolina's Proposed Birth-Related Neurological Impairment Act: A Provocative Alternative, 26 Wake Forest L. Rev. 837, 859 (1991).

111. N.Y. Senate Bill 471 (1991–92 Regular Session).

112. These are described in the Memorandum Supporting the New York Governor's Bill (1991) (on file with author).

113. *See* Va. Code Ann. § 38.2-5001 (Michie 1990).

CHAPTER TWENTY-FOUR

Expanding Health Care for Children

Alice Sardell
Harvey Catchen

THE CONTEMPORARY discussion of the consequences of health care cost-containment initiatives for family law and children's rights must be understood within the context of the changing nature of family life in America within the past few decades. One political response to some of these changes, at the federal level, has been an expansion of child health rights. In this chapter we first discuss recent economic and social changes in family structure. We then trace the political process that resulted in the expansion of Medicaid eligibility for pregnant women and children during the 1980s. We argue that although a consensus exists that primary and preventive care for children is very cost-effective, the past decade has seen only incremental changes in access to health care through expansion of Medicaid eligibility.

Family Structure and the Status of Children

The Economic and Social Transformation of Families

The past few decades have witnessed dramatic changes in the economic status and social structure of American families. Since 1970 the number of high-paying manufacturing jobs in the United States has declined while the number of low-

Adapted from Alice Sardell, "Child Health Policy in the U.S.: The Paradox of Consensus," *Journal of Health Politics, Policy and Law* 15:2 (1990), copyright Duke University Press. Subsequently included in *Health Policy and the Disadvantaged* edited by Lawrence D. Brown, 1991, copyright Duke University Press. Reprinted with permission of the publisher.

paying service-sector jobs has increased. Many of these service-sector jobs pay salaries at or slightly above the minimum wage. Between 1973 and 1989 the median hourly wage of males twenty-five and over declined by almost one-fifth (19 percent); for males under age twenty-five, the decline in hourly wage was almost one-third (29 percent). Although the minimum wage was increased to $4.25 per hour in April 1991, its buying power has declined significantly in the past decade. In 1979 the minimum wage provided a family of three with a yearly income slightly higher than the federal poverty level. In 1991 the yearly income for a family of three with a single wage earner earning the minimum wage was $8,844, or only 84 percent of the federal poverty level of $10,560.[1] The number of children living in poverty has increased by 21 percent in the past decade.[2] Women in increasing numbers have entered the labor force to compensate for the declining earning power of their husbands and as primary wage earners of single-parent families.[3] Between 1970 and 1988 the proportion of women with children under eighteen in the labor force increased from 40 percent to 65 percent.[4] In 1990 over half (53 percent) of all women who gave birth were in the labor force.[5] Three out of every four mothers of school-age children in 1992 were employed.[6]

The structure of American families has also changed. One out of every two first marriages ends in divorce, and six out of every ten second marriages also fail.[7] The size of the American family is declining. The average number of births per woman decreased from 3.7 in the mid-1950s to 1.8 in the mid-1970s. In recent years there has been only a slight increase in births.[8] The 1950s image, as depicted in popular television shows such as "Father Knows Best" and "Leave It to Beaver," of the typical American family as a married couple and their dependent children has become less and less representative of family life. In 1970 married couples with children under the age of eighteen constituted 40 percent of all households.[9] By 1991 only one-quarter (26 percent) of all households consisted of married couples with children under eighteen. In 1991 almost three out of ten (29 percent) women who gave birth were not married.[10] The percentage of unmarried teenage mothers (81 percent) in the late 1980s was double the percentage of unmarried teenage mothers (43 percent) in the late 1960s.[11]

Child Health and Family Value

In the United States the obligation of society to provide income security to persons sixty-five years old and above is a widely held value. Americans also believe that the nuclear family is the foundation of society. In the 1992 presidential election, both Republican and Democratic candidates attempted to portray themselves as the staunchest supporter of family values. Yet if we measure commitment to the nuclear family in terms of the amount of governmental support provided to families raising children, the United States is the "least family-oriented society in the civilized world."[12] All other industrialized nations provide tax-free child allowances for each child in every family. The benefit varies from country to country but usually amounts to 5 to 10 percent of the median wage for one child. Families with more children usually receive higher benefit levels. The allowance does not cover all of the costs of caring for a child but dramatically improves the quality of life for poor children. It is usually a fixed amount that all families receive regardless of income. Like Social Security in the United States, child allowances are popular in every society that has such a benefit.[13]

In addition to the child allowance, most industrialized nations also provide housing allowances, universal health insurance, day care, and child support programs. Poor families with children receive housing allowances to pay rent, property taxes, or other costs associated with home ownership. The allowance is usually based upon family size, income, and housing costs. Sweden has the most generous housing subsidy program, covering more than one-third of all families. In France about one-fourth of all families receive some subsidy. Many countries have guaranteed child support programs. When divorced parents do not provide child support or provide it irregularly, public agencies will advance support payments and then pursue the delinquent parent to recover the monies advanced to the family.[14] This enables many single-parent families to maintain a stable family life, since government child support payments are provided on a regular basis.

Traditionally in the United States, the family has been viewed as an autonomous unit for raising children. Thus, public support was provided only to handicapped children or to children who lacked a family unit to care for them.[15] The Child Welfare League of America, the oldest advocacy group for children, focused on the need for foster care and adoption services.[16] The benefit that covers the largest number of U.S. families is the mortgage interest deduction on income tax returns. This benefit allows many families to live out the American dream of home ownership and provide opportunities for their children. However, the mortgage interest deduction is available to anyone who owns a home, whether or not they are raising children. The benefits of this deduction are limited primarily to middle- and upper-class families; the poor who rent apartments receive no similar benefit. In addition, the United States allows taxpayers an exemption for each child, but this benefit also is unavailable to many poor people who pay little or no taxes. In contrast, the primary programs that do help poor children (Aid to Families with Dependent Children and Medicaid) are provided only when families meet strict eligibility requirements and endure a complex bureaucratic process.

The Health of Children

Child health is an area in which the paradoxes of American health policy are very clear. We provide excellent, high-technology, specialized services to those with acute conditions, but we neglect the social factors that increase medical risk. The United States ranks first in the world in its ability to save the lives of premature and very small infants, yet it is thirtieth in the proportion of babies born with low birth weight (LBW).[17] There has been no significant decline in the percentage of LBW babies in the past decade. This lack of progress has been attributed to a failure to provide adequate prenatal care to poor pregnant women.[18]

In terms of infant mortality (death between birth and age one year), the U.S. rate was the highest of twenty-three industrial nations. In 1991 an average of 8.9 out of every 1,000 infants under one year of age died.[19] The rate for black infants was approximately twice the white rate.[20] According to the National Commission to Prevent Infant Mortality, if infant deaths continue at the current rate, the number of infants who will die between 1988 and 2000 is greater than the total number of battlefield deaths of Americans in World War I, World War II, Korea, and Vietnam combined.[21] The vast majority of these deaths are thought to be preventable through adequate low-cost prenatal care.

A major public health achievement of the United States in the post–World War II period was the immunization of children against many childhood diseases such as polio, measles, mumps, rubella, and pertussis (whooping cough). In 1954, there were 57,000 cases of polio; by 1984, only 4 cases were reported. Vaccination rates for young children in the United States have declined since 1980, while the incidence of major childhood illnesses has increased. In the late 1980s epidemics of preventable childhood diseases began to reemerge. In 1989, 18,000 cases of measles and 41 deaths were reported, the highest number of cases since 1978. In 1990, 25,000 cases and 60 deaths were reported. The United States also experienced outbreaks of other preventable diseases, including mumps and pertussis.[22] The administration of child health programs within the federal government involves a vast labyrinth of overlapping bureaucracies. More than 356 health programs are administered by sixteen different agencies to provide services to children. Access to most programs is based upon meeting specific eligibility criteria such as disease, age, family income, or geographic location. Children with complex clinical conditions may require care from several programs. Such families are often unable to negotiate the bureaucratic maze without the help of trained social service staff. Other children who require care do not receive it if they fail to meet specific categorical criteria.[23]

The effective communication of this kind of data, along with the argument that the rate of infant mortality and childhood illness and disability could be reduced, produced a consensus among policy-makers in the mid-1980s that action had to be taken to improve the health of American children. One consequence of that consensus was a series of legislative provisions that have expanded eligibility for Medicaid and separated it from eligibility for Aid to Families with Dependent Children (AFDC), to which it had been linked since Medicaid's inception.

The Expansion of Medicaid Eligibility in the 1980s

In 1979 a report by the U.S. surgeon general called the reduction of infant mortality a "fundamental national goal."[24] During the 1980s the Reagan administration began a series of initiatives to restructure the relationship between the federal and state governments. These initiatives, called the "New Federalism," resulted in reduced allocation of resources for the health and welfare of the poor. Medicaid funding for maternal and child health and nutrition programs were reduced just as unemployment and economic recession increased the need for such services in the early 1980s. Stories about increases in the numbers of poor pregnant women and malnourished and sick children were widely reported in the media. The infant mortality rate for some inner cities, it was claimed, resembled that of third world nations.

Thus, in 1983, House and Senate Democrats began to work on expanding eligibility for Medicaid. At the same time, officials in southern states, where infant mortality was highest, became interested in new initiatives in maternal and child health. This interest was stimulated in part by the work of the Children's Defense Fund (CDF) and other child advocacy groups at the state level.[25]

CDF is an advocacy organization that has worked since 1972 to put child rearing on the political agenda and expand the safety net for children. "CDF's goal is to make it unacceptable to allow any child in the United States to grow up homeless, hungry, sick, uncared for, unsafe, undereducated, or without hope for the future. CDF is working to create a nation in which the web of family, community, private sector, and government supports for children are so tightly woven that no child can slip through."[26]

Although the movement toward this goal has thus far consisted of incremental steps in various areas of child welfare, children's issues have achieved mainstream status on the American political agenda. CDF's primary message is that child rearing in the United States must be "socialized" in the same way that old age has been. Child support should be viewed as the responsibility of the whole society[27] for reasons of self-interest as well as altruism. CDF argues that the future productivity of the American workforce and the future tax base necessary to support social insurance programs depends on our current investment in American children. The CDF was a central actor in the expansion of Medicaid described below. Its carefully documented reports on the increasing poverty of American children, and the inability of many pregnant woman and children to get access to health care, received extensive Congressional and media attention. CDF was also instrumental in creating coalitions of interest groups and members of Congress supportive of the expansion of Medicaid eligibility. By the mid-1980s, CDF was one of the most respected and influential advocacy groups in Washington, "a formidable public interest lobby."[28]

The February 1983 vote to establish the Select Committee on Children, Youth and Families in the House of Representatives was a significant step in focusing public attention and Congressional action on children's issues. The large affirmative vote, coming after years of effort by Representative George Miller of California, reflected the forces that would put children's issues on the governmental agenda. Congress was responding to reports about the impact of cuts in social programs on families, to a voting bloc of women concerned about these issues, and to the mobilization of a policy community of interest groups and liberal members of Congress.[29] The committee held a series of hearings in various parts of the country on the relationship between LBW and access to prenatal care.[30]

During 1984, the CDF and the Food Research and Action Center issued studies on the state of child health in the United States that received wide publicity and Congressional attention. The CDF documented a large increase in poor children as well as an increase in the proportion of women receiving late or no prenatal care. At the same time, the Southern Governors Association appointed a Task Force on Infant Mortality, which in 1985 recommended that states have the option to provide Medicaid to pregnant women and children with family incomes below the federal poverty level.[31]

In 1984 legislation enacted as part of the Deficit Reduction Act mandated that states provide Medicaid for all pregnant women and children under age five with family incomes meeting the eligibility criteria for AFDC, even if they were in families that did not meet other AFDC criteria.[32] This action "decoupled" Medicaid from AFDC. A broad coalition of groups had worked to enact this legislation, including the CDF, the American Academy of Pediatrics, the March of Dimes, the National Association of Community Health Centers, the Association of Maternal and Child Health Programs, the Catholic Conference, and the National Governors Association. Conservative, right-to-life members of Congress and some corporate business leaders also were supportive.[33] The CDF and the Catholic Conference, along with key Congressional staff, had previously negotiated a separation of child health issues from the abortion issue.[34]

Subsequent expansions of Medicaid eligibility were enacted as part of the budget reconciliation process. New provisions were initially state options and in later legislation became federally mandated. In some ways the budget reconciliation process has been helpful to child health advocates. Reconciliation rules limit the number of amendments that can be offered on a budget bill, and in a very large piece of legislation, such as the budget bills, controversial provisions have less time to be considered and therefore are often accepted.[35]

The next set of Medicaid reforms were provisions of the 1986 and 1987 Omnibus Budget Reconciliation Acts. The 1986 act allowed states to disregard assets in deciding Medicaid eligibility for pregnant women and for children under age five, and to grant automatic eligibility to pregnant women while their applications were being processed and for sixty days after they gave birth. It also allowed states to provide Medicaid coverage for children up to age eight in families with incomes between the AFDC eligibility level and the federal poverty level. The 1987 act allowed states to cover all pregnant women and infants with family incomes up to 185 percent of the poverty level. In 1988, as part of the Medicare Catastrophic Coverage Act, Congress mandated that by 1990 state Medicaid programs cover all pregnant women and infants whose family incomes do not exceed 100 percent of the federal poverty level. This legislation did not have a great impact, because thirty states had already expanded eligibility to cover pregnant women and infants with family incomes up to 100 percent of the poverty level. Ten other states covered pregnant women and children whose family incomes are above that level.[36] These expansions in eligibility were again supported by a broad coalition of state officials, child advocacy and women's groups, and members of Congress.[37]

The Budget Reconciliation Acts of 1990 and 1991 included further expansions of Medicaid coverage for pregnant women and children. In the 1990 act, coverage was extended to pregnant women and children to age six who lived in families with incomes less than 133 percent of the poverty level. The next year Congress mandated that all poor children up to age nineteen be covered by Medicaid by the year 2002, beginning with six-year-olds.[38] This legislation was enacted in spite of opposition from the National Governors Association and the Bush administration, but with the support of children's advocacy groups, physicians' groups, hospitals, insurers' associations, and other business groups. The health insurers, business groups, and institutional providers who were members of this coalition viewed the expansion of Medicaid as a way to reduce the amount of uncompensated care by decreasing the number of uninsured children.[39]

Framing the Issue: Viewing Children as Good

The way an issue is defined or "framed" in public discourse is critical to the nature of activity on the issue, the type of groups that become involved, and the specific policies that are proposed.[40] Child advocates have framed the issues of reducing infant mortality and improving children's health as consensual rather than conflictual, thus making proposals acceptable to diverse policy constituencies and the general public.

Five themes and strategies dominate the discussion: (1) infant mortality and many childhood illnesses and disabilities are preventable through known treatment modalities; (2) preventive services are cost-efficient, avoiding large future health care costs; (3) investment in young children is an investment in the future of the U.S. economy; (4) children and babies are innocents who are not responsible for their poverty, and (5) talking about their health avoids focusing on the adult poor, a category of persons not usually viewed favorably by the population at large.[41] These themes are reflected in many governmental and nongovernmental reports, and in public officials' pronouncements on the condition of children in the last decade of the twentieth century.

Three influential "second-generation" government-sponsored studies on child health are a 1988 report of the Congressional Office of Technology Assessment (OTA), a report by the National Commission to Prevent Infant Mortality issued in August 1988, and a report by the National Commission on Children in 1991.[42] Maternal and child health issues have also been discussed by private-sector organizations concerned with public policy.[43]

The consensus within the health policy community is that prenatal care improves the outcome of pregnancy, especially in populations at high risk. Demographically, high-risk pregnant women are likely to be young, black or Hispanic, unmarried, and poor.[44] OTA reviewed fifty-five studies that examine the relationship between infant mortality and prenatal care and found that LBW and neonatal mortality can be reduced if mothers have early, "comprehensive" prenatal care.[45]

The report of the Ford Foundation Project on Social Welfare and the American Future states that "bringing a healthy baby into the world is something *we know how to do,* but too often in America we fail to do it."[46] The National Commission to Prevent Infant Mortality is explicit in framing infant mortality as a solvable problem, in contrast to other policy issues: "Unlike other social problems, where cause and effect can blend together to obscure solutions, we know what we can do to halt the tragedy of infant mortality.[47]

The argument that reducing infant mortality and improving children's health can save health care dollars gained much attention as the result of a 1985 study by the Institute of Medicine. That report compared LBW rates to infant mortality and disability rates and argued that investing in prenatal care would save large sums of money that would have to be spent on neonatal intensive care and other services for disabled children. Every dollar spent for prenatal care for high-risk women could save $3.38 in neonatal health costs.[48]

The cost-effectiveness of preventive interventions in terms of overall spending for health and social services was a major argument for children's programs at the state level in the mid-1980s. Governors Michael N. Castle of Delaware, a Republican, and Martha Layne Collins of Kentucky, a Democrat, co-chaired a National Governors Association "campaign" on children's programs. Governor Castle stated that "investing in young children is like compound interest—the benefits in reduced costs to society accrue year after year." Governor Collins declared: "Early childhood programs cost money and sometimes a lot of it. But crime costs more, overcrowded prisons cost more, welfare costs more and undereducation costs more."[49] This is still a central theme in current policy discussions of maternal and child health services.

OTA analyzed the cost-effectiveness of a policy of Medicaid eligibility for all pregnant women with incomes below the federal poverty level and concluded that the additional prenatal care would be more than paid for by savings in hospitalization and other health care services associated with the birth of LBW infants. OTA also calculated that childhood immunizations are cost-effective in these terms. There were not enough data to draw conclusions about the cost-effectiveness of other forms of well-child care.[50]

The National Commission to Prevent Infant Mortality uses OTA data to make the argument that providing health services to pregnant women and children will save money: $400 spent on prenatal care saves between $14,000 and $30,000 in health costs for the care of a LBW baby during his or her lifetime.[51] Similarly, the Committee for Economic Development's *Children in Need* presents a chart of cost-effective programs for children, including the Women Infants and Children Program (WIC), prenatal care, Medicaid, childhood immunizations, and educational programs. For example, every dollar spent on childhood immunization saved ten dollars in later medical costs. Such economic arguments were a major reason for the popularity of infant mortality initiatives in the 101st Congress, a Congress in which children's issues had high visibility.

Argument 3, as noted above, is that maternal and child health services are an investment in the future American workforce. The National Commission to Prevent Infant Mortality argues that if our infant mortality rate were reduced to that of Japan (the nation with the lowest rate in the world), the additional 20,000 children who would survive each year would contribute $10 billion to the economy as workers.[52] A Ford Foundation report similarly argues that "[w]e ought to invest in human capital with the same entrepreneurial spirit and concern for long-range payoffs that venture capitalists bring to investments in new enterprises."[53] The report describes a severe "employment crisis" for business and a crisis in our political institutions if there is not widespread reform of our educational institutions and family support services.

Finally, the issue of health care for children fits comfortably into the American value system. Children are innocent in two ways. First, they are malleable, "fixable" as adults may not be. They are, in a sense, a "new frontier" where we as a society can begin again and succeed in solving the social problems that frustrate us. As Governor Collins of Kentucky observed, "It is easier to build successful children than repair men and women."[54]

Children are also innocent because they have not chosen to do things that many in the population would consider antisocial: taking illegal drugs, having children without being married, or receiving public assistance. Even those with an individualistic view of the origins of social problems such as poverty and drug addiction can see children as the victims of adults' actions. Research conducted for the Democratic Party in the fall of 1987 found far more support for social and economic programs that benefit children that for those that assist adults.[55] Focusing on children, as Marion Wright Edelman recognized when she founded the CDF in 1973, is probably the most comfortable way for Americans to deal with issues of class and race.

The Limitations of Medicaid Expansions

While the Medicaid reforms of the 1980s and early 1990s have reduced the financial barriers to health care for numbers of poor pregnant women, infants, and children, these populations still face major obstacles. For example, the final report of the National Commission on Children estimated that 21 percent of families with incomes below the poverty level and one-quarter of those with incomes between 100 percent and 150 percent of the poverty level remain uncovered.[56]

Furthermore, while the recent Medicaid expansions dealt with eligibility and enrollment, they did not address health care resources and delivery—a perennial flaw of Medicaid policy. Several factors have limited the number of providers available to care for low-income pregnant women in the United States. Two of these are the geographic maldistribution of specialists and the increasingly high malpractice insurance rates for obstetrical practices, which have led many obstetrician/gynecologists to stop providing prenatal and childbirth services. In the United States, the number of certified nurse midwives, an occupational group that has had great success in working with both low- and middle-income pregnant women, is extremely small (2,600 in 1988).[57] "In some U.S. communities, particularly those with poor populations and no teaching or public facilities, obstetrical care may be disappearing entirely."[58]

In areas with enough obstetricians, many physicians do not accept uninsured women or women on Medicaid as patients. Such women may require care that is more complicated and time-consuming than the care needed by privately insured women, but Medicaid fees are far below the charges usually paid to private specialists (and far below the reimbursement provided by Medicare for equivalent services to the elderly). Physicians also find Medicaid paperwork and reimbursement delays burdensome, and many physicians believe that malpractice claims are substantially higher within the Medicaid population. For all of these reasons, many obstetricians (44 percent in a 1983 survey) will not treat women receiving Medicaid.[59]

With limited access to the private sector, low-income pregnant women are likely to seek prenatal care at publicly funded clinics. The demand for such services has been increasing, and the waiting time for prenatal appointments is long. One study of public health and nonprofit hospital clinics quoted by a committee of the Institute of Medicine complains that "a woman has to call for an appointment before she gets pregnant to get an appointment before the end of the first trimester."[60]

Primary-care clinics are reimbursed for services in only one-third of the states, and an additional one-third receive reimbursement only for some services provided. Outreach, health education, and counseling services provided by nonphysicians are not generally covered by Medicaid.[61] Community health centers, which were originally established to provide the type of community-based and comprehensive, yet individualized, care that experts now agree is necessary to reduce infant mortality and childhood illness in high-risk populations, had their funding reduced during the 1980s.

Clinics funded by the maternal and child health block grants serve only a small proportion of uninsured pregnant women and children. A 1986 CDF survey of the agencies of all fifty states and the District of Columbia that were responsible for maternal and child health programs found a lack of service relative to need in four areas: outpatient prenatal care, inpatient maternity care, and outpatient and inpatient pediatric care.[62]

Child Health Policy and Health Care Politics

Reducing the infant mortality rate and improving access to care for poor women and children became major issues on the health policy agenda during the 1980s. Congress responded with incremental reform in the form of expansions of Medicaid eligibility. While a policy community concerned with the health of children discusses universal access to care and the kind of outreach programs found in other industrialized democracies, Congressional initiatives in this direction have thus far been limited. The future of maternal and child health policy is not clear.

We are now in a new phase of agenda building and policy formation in which the central question is what should be done about child health beyond making more people eligible for Medicaid. One set of proposals calls for increasing employer and/or government financing of maternal and child health services. Another emphasizes the role of lifestyle and the physical and social environment in the birth and growth of healthy children. Yet, unlike those who argued in the 1970s that the "limits of medicine" implied that there should be less health care,[63] those concerned with child health today would define health care more broadly. The National Institute of Medicine, the National Commission to Prevent Infant Mortality, and the National Commission on Children all recommend providing services to address the social factors that impact on health status—nutrition counseling, substance abuse treatment, parenting education, and so on. In this model of health services, medical care is tightly integrated with educational and social services.

This model for improving the health of mothers and children is not new—it goes back to the child welfare movement of the Progressive era. Some of the health policy community returned to it in the mid-1960s when federal community and migrant health centers were initially funded,[64] and it is being discussed today by those concerned with child health issues.

Policy formulation will now, however, be more complicated and problematic than it was when Medicaid expansion was the issue in the mid-1980s. Some of the current proposals involve major changes in the financing and structure of the entire health system. Their implementation would force policy-makers to confront the broader issue of the nation's investment in "human capital" at a time when there is more concern about trade and budget deficits. As these issues emerge, the "consensus" about child health may begin to unravel.

Conclusion

The future of U.S. child health policy depends on the larger question of how policy-makers resolve the tension between concern with federal budget deficits and long-term investment in the social infrastructure of American society. American economic, fiscal, and social policies together face a watershed. Incremental policy change on behalf of children has been popular because children's health problems appear to be solvable in a way that other social crises do not. There is, however, a fundamental flaw in this type of analysis: It ignores the complicated web of economic and social forces that produce LBW babies and sick and disabled children.

Children live in families and in communities. To become a society that produces healthy children, we must develop a comprehensive family policy such as those that exist in European countries. Such a policy would provide comprehensive economic, housing, health, child care, and social services to enable all American families to live out the American dream.

NOTES

1. *See* Children's Defense Fund, The State of America's Children 1991, at 24 (1991).
2. *See* National Commission to Prevent Infant Mortality, Troubling Trends Persist: Shortchanging America's Next Generation 17 (1992).
3. *See* R. Fosler et al., Demographic Change and the American Future 115 (1990).
4. *See* Children's Defense Fund, The State of America's Children, *supra* note 1, at 37–38.
5. *See* Pear, Larger Number of New Mothers Unmarried, N.Y. Times, Dec. 4, 1991, at A20.
6. *See* Barringer, New Census Data Reveal Redistribution of Poverty, N.Y. Times, May 29, 1992, at A15.
7. *See* Rosewater, Child and Family Trends: Beyond the Numbers, 37 Proc. Acad. Pol. Sci. 4, 5 (1989).
8. *See* National Commission on Children, Beyond Rhetoric: A New American Agenda for Children and Families 16 (1991).
9. *See* Married with Children: The Waning Icon, N.Y. Times, Aug. 23, 1992, at E2.
10. *See id.*
11. *See* Pear, Larger Number, *supra* note 5, at A20.
12. Brazleton, Why Is America Failing Its Children? N.Y. Times, Sept. 9, 1990, § 6 (Magazine), at 41, 50.
13. *See* Kamerman & Kahn, The Possibilities for Child and Family Policy: A Cross-National Perspective, 37 Proc. Acad. Pol. Sci. 84, 91 (1989).
14. *See id.* at 92–97.
15. *See* G. Y. Steiner, The Children's Cause 1 (1976).
16. *See id.* at 145–46.
17. *See* L. B. Schorr, Within Our Reach: Breaking the Cycle of Disadvantage 66 (1988). Low birth weight is defined as less than 2,500 grams or 5.5 pounds. It is an important risk factor for neonatal and postneonatal infant mortality, for morbidity during the first year of life, and for mental and physical disability later. *See* Starfield, Motherhood and Apple Pie: The Effectiveness of Medical Care for Children, 63 Milbank Memorial Fund Q. 523, 525 (1985); Pear, U.S. Reports Rise in Low-Weight Births, N.Y. Times, Apr. 22, 1992, at A18.
18. *See* National Commission to Prevent Infant Mortality, Troubling Trends, *supra* note 2, at 10.
19. *See* Pear, U.S. Reports Rise, *supra* note 17, at A18.
20. *See* Office of Technology Assessment, Healthy Children: Investing in the Future 38 (1988).
21. *See* National Commission to Prevent Infant Mortality, Death before Life: The Tragedy of Infant Mortality 8 (1988).
22. *See* National Commission to Prevent Infant Mortality, Troubling Trends, *supra* note 2, at 33–34.

23. *See* Harvey, Toward a National Health Care Policy, 264 JAMA 252 (1990).

24. Office of Technology Assessment, Healthy Children, *supra* note 20, at 5 (quoting the report).

25. *See* S. Rosenbaum, Lives in the Balance 23 (Sept. 1, 1988) (unpublished manuscript, on file with author).

26. J. Weill, Child Advocacy in the U.S.: The Work of the Children's Defense Fund 1 (1990).

27. *See* Edelman & Weill, Status of Children in the 1980's, 17 Colum. Hum. Rts. L. Rev. 139, 141–44 (1986).

28. J. Berry, The Interest Group Society 96 (2d ed. 1989).

29. *See* Now a Select Committee for Families, N.Y. Times, Feb. 23, 1983, at A18.

30. *See* Kosterlitz, Concern about Children, 18 Nat'l J. 2255 (1986).

31. *See* Rosenbaum, Lives in the Balance, *supra* note 25, at 26, 27, 30–31, 36.

32. *See* Reconciliation Dominates Policy-Making Process, Cong. Q. Wkly. Rep., Apr. 29, 1989, at 965.

33. *See* Rosenbaum, Lives in the Balance, *supra* note 25, at 32–33.

34. *See id.* at 28.

35. *See* Kosterlitz, Watch Out for Waxman, 21 Nat'l J. 577, 580 (1989).

36. *See* Rosenbaum, Update on Maternal and Child Health Developments: Memorandum to State Primary Care Associations and Health Centers, Health Policy Seminar Series, 1988, at 17–28 (National Ass'n of Community Health Centers, Inc.) (an annual policy handbook distributed at the organization's annual meeting) (on file with author).

37. *See* Rosenbaum, Lives in the Balance, *supra* note 25, at 34–39.

38. *See* 46 Cong. Q. Almanac 569 (1991).

39. *See* Pear, Deficit or No Deficit, Unlikely Allies Bring about Expansion in Medicaid, N.Y. Times, Nov. 4, 1990, § 1, at 24.

40. *See* R. Cobb & C. Elder, Participation in American Politics: The Dynamics of Agenda-Building (1972); B. Nelson, Making an Issue of Child Abuse (1984); E. E. Schattschneider, The Semisovereign People (1960).

41. *See* M. Katz, The Undeserving Poor: From the War on Poverty to the War on Welfare (1989).

42. The OTA study evaluates the cost-effectiveness of strategies to improve children's health. The National Commission to Prevent Infant Mortality was created by Congress in 1986 to analyze public policies related to the health of infants and women of reproductive age. The bipartisan National Commission on Children was established to develop broad policy recommendations to improve the quality of life for children and their families.

43. Two such discussions can be found in Research and Policy Committee of the Committee for Economic Development, Children in Need: Investment Strategies for the Educationally Disadvantaged (1987), and Ford Foundation Project on Social Welfare and the American Future, The Common Good: Social Welfare and the American Future (1989).

44. *See* Committee to Study Outreach for Prenatal Care, Institute of Medicine, Prenatal Care: Reaching Mothers, Reaching Infants 2–4 (National Academy Press 1988).

45. *See* Office of Technology Assessment, Healthy Children, *supra* note 20, at 9.

46. *See* Ford Foundation, Social Welfare, *supra* note 43, at 12 (emphasis added).

47. *See* National Commission to Prevent Infant Mortality, Death before Life, *supra* note 21, at 10.

48. *See* Kosterlitz, Concern about Children, *supra* note 30, at 2257.

49. *See* Children's Agenda Making Headway in States, 18 Nat'l J. 2849 (1986) (quoting Governors Castle and Collins).

50. *See* Office of Technology Assessment, Healthy Children, *supra* note 20, at 9–10, 13–14.

51. *See* National Commission to Prevent Infant Mortality, Death before Life, *supra* note 21, at 9.

52. *See id.* at 10.

53. Ford Foundation, Social Welfare, *supra* note 43, at 46.

54. Children's Agenda, *supra* note 49, at 2849.

55. *See* Dionne, Children Emerge as Issue for Democrats, N.Y. Times, Sept. 27, 1987, §1, at 36.

56. *See* National Commission on Children, Beyond Rhetoric, *supra* note 8, at 136.

57. *See* Committee to Study Outreach For Prenatal Care, Prenatal Care, *supra* note 44, at 66–69.

58. *Id.* at 69.

59. *See id.* at 66–69.

60. *Id.* at 66.

61. *See* Rosenbaum, Lives in the Balance, *supra* note 25, at 45.

62. Rosenbaum et al., Maternal and Child Health Services for Medically Indigent Children and Pregnant Women, 26 Medical Care 321 (1988).

63. *See* Knowles, The Responsibility of the Individual, 106 Daedalus 57, 57–58 (1977).

64. *See* A. Sardell, The U.S. Experiment in Social Medicine: The Community Health Center Program 1965–1986 (1988).

CHAPTER TWENTY-FIVE

Universal Access to Health Care for Children

Judith Cohen Dolins, Jenifer D. C. Cartland,
James G. Pawelski, Beth K. Yudkowsky

ALTHOUGH PROVIDING medical care to children may be of intrinsic value to society, public policy traditionally has not reflected that value. Only with the introduction of the Clinton administration's health care reform plan in 1993 did the federal government begin to consider seriously any kind of comprehensive policy for the delivery of children's health services. The need for change was readily apparent. At the time of the plan's introduction, only poor children through the Medicaid program and children whose needs were compatible with state Title V services (Maternal and Child Health Block Grant Program) or other special government programs (e.g., Medicare's renal dialysis program) were entitled to government assistance.

Children, unfortunately, often have been the least able to cope with the hardships that result from weaknesses in our health care delivery system. By the late 1980s, precipitously rising medical costs forced cuts in government programs for children,[1] pressed private employers to drop coverage for their employees' dependents,[2] and prohibited parents from purchasing their own coverage,[3] thereby rendering 12 million children without health insurance coverage.[4] In addition, many insured children have not had coverage that adequately meets their health care needs. Many private indemnity insurance plans do not cover preventive care, which includes highly cost-effective immunizations and screening for debilitating diseases. For example, only half of these plans provide well-baby care.[5]

Children also have been more likely than individuals in any other age group to live in poverty. In 1990, fully 20 percent of children lived in families with incomes below the federal poverty line.[6] Poor children are more likely than others both to need health care services and to be uninsured.[7] But, as we will demonstrate, the financial burden of securing health care services is no longer a problem of just the poor. The rise in health care costs has made it difficult for middle-class families to meet this responsibility. While the average family income increased 88 percent between 1980 and 1991, the average amount spent by families on health care has increased 147 percent.[8] Finally, a recent study suggests that increasing numbers of middle-income children are relying on local public health departments to receive their immunizations without charge because the costs of immunizations in private settings have become prohibitive for their parents.[9]

Lack of insurance for over 37 million Americans and the publicly perceived need to control soaring health care costs precipitated the public debate on health care reform. The country's focus on reforming the health care system further creates an opportunity to provide all children with health insurance coverage. As a nation we must realize that children's health and well-being are moral imperatives, not luxuries. Developed nations that spend less on health services than the United States provide higher levels of equity in the provision of health services to children.[10] But even if we do not accept the moral imperative to provide health insurance coverage for all children, the social and economic well-being of our nation will be weakened by allowing our children to grow without the support that they need to develop into healthy, contributing adults.

In this chapter, we first examine the factors that warranted the onset of children's health care reform in the United States and demonstrate that if our health care system were allowed to develop incrementally with little concern for equity, access to health care for our children would continue to deteriorate. Second, we examine how children fare under the most prominent health care delivery models. We contend that only a program that provides universal coverage and comprehensive health services can adequately guarantee children the health care services they need to grow into productive members of society.

Financing Children's Health Care

Although most children in the United States have health insurance that pays a portion of their health care expenses, estimates prior to the introduction of reform initiatives in the early 1990s were that approximately 12 million children twenty-one years of age or younger were without health insurance. They represented roughly one-third of the total number of uninsured Americans. The number of uninsured children grew throughout the 1980s; from 1977 to 1988 the percentage of uninsured children rose from 12.7 percent to 17.8 percent.[11]

Lack of health insurance has not been a problem for children of low-income families alone. In 1990, nearly 40 percent of uninsured children lived in two-parent families where at least one parent was employed full-time.[12] Even when employers offer health insurance, parents frequently cannot afford it. For example, one union found that although their employers offered health insurance coverage, up to 48 percent of its members could not afford the premiums that the employers required.[13] The continuing erosion of employer-based health insurance contributed to the increase in the number of uninsured middle-income children as well. In 1987, 6.6 percent of middle-income children were uninsured; in 1989 that rate rose to 7.9 percent—an increase of 700,000 children in only two years.[14]

Moreover, even if children have health insurance coverage, it often does not cover the services that children need. In 1984, approximately 26 percent of non-elderly Americans who had insurance were *under*insured:[15] Frequently, health insurance does not cover essential services such as preventive health care and immunizations. Still other families have health insurance coverage that requires expensive cost sharing, making many benefits unaffordable.

The government traditionally has provided some assistance to parents who are willing but financially unable to provide needed medical services for their children. Children in families receiving cash assistance also have been eligible for the Medicaid program, while those from low-income families have qualified for Title V services, the Children With Special Needs Program, and other aid. Finally, if a child from a low-income family has no health insurance coverage, the parents have had the option to take him or her to a public hospital or community clinic.[16] Federal, state, and local governments usually have underwritten the cost of this care.

Another impetus for reform has been the phenomenon of cost shifting. As the number of uninsured and underinsured children increases, the burden of paying for children's care has been transferred, indirectly, to other users of health services.[17] Parents of children lacking insurance coverage often have had to resort to expensive hospital emergency rooms, even though they cannot afford to pay for the child's care. Hospitals make up for this uncompensated care by shifting costs to their insured patients. "Cost shifting" has been one of the prime reasons for the increase in employers' insurance premiums in the past decade.[18] Employers, in turn, compensate by requiring employees to take on more of the premium cost,[19] or, most problematically, dropping dependent coverage altogether.[20] Without systemic change, the pressure between rising health insurance costs and the efforts to contain the cost of delivering services could only increase, with the net result being more uninsured children.

In many respects, then, the debate over how to extend insurance coverage to uninsured and underinsured children has been driven by a desire to contain costs. Policy-makers are realizing that it is less expensive to pay for children's care on the front end than to wait until children are very sick and require more expensive care. The best way to do this, many observers maintain, is to ensure, first, that all children have insurance and, second, that the insurance covers preventive and primary care that can be delivered in a primary-care setting, such as physicians' offices and clinics, rather than a hospital.[21]

In response to the political pressure to control costs, both federal and state governments took steps in the latter half of the 1980s to provide more low-income children with insurance coverage. This commitment took the form of three types of legislative reforms.

The first type of reform expands the Medicaid program, a state-administered program, jointly funded by the federal and state governments, that provides health insurance coverage to the most economically disadvantaged children. Between 1986 and 1990, Congress enacted five major laws that incrementally expanded pregnant women's and children's eligibility for Medicaid and the scope of benefits offered. Upon implementation of the last of these acts in July 1991, all children younger than six years and pregnant women with family incomes up to 133 percent of the federal poverty level became eligible for Medicaid. In addition, state Medicaid programs are mandated to phase in, one year at a time, all children born after September 1, 1983, with family incomes below 100 percent of the federal poverty level. Thus, all children through age eighteen who live in families with incomes at or below the federal poverty line will have Medicaid coverage by the year 2002. As of 1990, 810,000 children have been added to the Medicaid program as a result of these expansions.[22]

State and local governments have also responded to the plight of uninsured and underinsured children. Colorado, Maine, Minnesota, New York, Vermont, and Wisconsin have established special state-subsidized children's primary health insurance programs. They target children whose families are "too rich" for Medicaid but cannot afford private insurance.

The final type of state initiative targets the problem of underinsured children. The District of Columbia and eleven states (California, Connecticut, Florida, Hawaii, Iowa, Maryland, Massachusetts, Minnesota, Montana, Ohio, and Rhode Island) enacted insurance mandates in the late 1980s and early 1990s that require all private health insurance companies to cover preventive care for children, including health supervision visits, routine immunizations, and laboratory tests. However, the fact that federal law prohibits states from regulating self-insured employers compromises the effectiveness of these statutes.

Despite these attempts by both the federal and state governments to help parents secure health insurance coverage for children, the number of uninsured and underinsured children has continued to increase throughout the early 1990s. The group of "unable" parents has expanded to include a significant number traditionally considered to be "prudent" caretakers of their children.[23] Health care costs have risen at a rate that exceeds the financial capability of middle-income families. In 1980 the average health payment made by families was $1,742.[24] By 1991, the average payment had risen to $4,296. Although the Medicaid expansions and other governmental programs were expected to stem the tide of uninsured children, such incremental approaches have been unable to keep pace with the plethora of threats to children's insurance coverage. Systemic reform is a necessary component of any effort to dissolve the connection between rising costs and increasing numbers of uninsured children.

How Children Fare under Different Health Care Financing Systems

The many shortcomings in our nation's health care system as it existed at the start of the 1990s made reform inevitable.[25] As discussed above, middle-class families have felt the squeeze of rising health care costs. Nonpoor children were 35 percent more likely to be uninsured in 1987 than in 1977.[26] And while many commentators argue that it is businesses that have paid more for health care, data show that families have been paying a larger proportion of this nation's expanding health care bill while business's share has been decreasing.[27] Furthermore, the attempts of the federal and state governments to halt the effects of rising health care costs for families have centered exclusively on low-income families. Once health care costs became an issue for middle-income families, the federal government's efforts to reform the system took on a new urgency. A survey of voters found that health care was the second most important issue in the 1992 presidential election, the first being the economy.[28]

Reforms aimed at relieving middle-income families have a profound impact on health insurance coverage for children. Typically, most children have relied on the coverage that their parents receive through employment.[29] However, an employer is much more likely to pay a substantial portion of the coverage for employees than for their dependents.[30] Dependent coverage can be expensive, averaging $269 per month in 1989.[31] Parents may find this too difficult to shoulder and may decide to purchase insurance only for themselves. Hence, any policies that are focused on making it easier for families to purchase health insurance will have a disproportionate effect on children because parents need more help with coverage for their children than for themselves.

While a health care financing system can take many shapes, we argue that the most efficacious program necessarily must provide universal coverage and comprehensive services to alleviate the inequities and cost inefficiencies created by having a large uninsured population. Only by providing health insurance to all children can health care costs begin to be contained. Universal insurance eliminates the need for cost shifting and its dual consequences of higher premium costs and more uninsured children.

Five basic models of health care financing dominated reform discussions in the early 1990s. Each has a different effect on children. The first three are designed to provide universal coverage—health insurance for all Americans. The fourth provides "virtual" universality; the last does not have universality as its goal. We discuss them in the order of the magnitude of change each would hold for the system as it exists in the early 1990s. Many reform proposals contain elements of more than one of these models.

The Single-Payer Model

The first model is known as the single-payer plan. Generally imitative of the Canadian health financing system, proposals that fall into this category provide basic insurance coverage for all persons through a government-run and government-financed insurance plan. Such a plan is operated either by the federal government or, as is the case with Canada, by a lesser subdivision, such as a state or province. This system is generally financed through income or other taxes. Commercial insurance companies are prohibited from offering coverage that overlaps with the coverage provided by the government; they can offer only supplemental coverage.

The Public Utility Model

One variation on the single-payer model can be thought of as the "public utility" model. Plans that fall into this subcategory borrow heavily from the traditional provision of utility services in the United States. Under a public utility model, each geographic area, such as a state or county, establishes a contractual relationship with one or a few private insurers. All persons living within that area are covered by this insurance. The community, then, has a certain degree of control over the comprehensiveness of the services being offered and the price of the premiums.

The chief differences between the broader single-payer model and the public utility model are, first, the treatment of commercial insurance companies and, second, the level of government that is most likely to implement and administer the plan. Both systems have a similar effect on children's health coverage: All children are covered by health insurance. The single-payer model, though, implies a universality of benefits and premiums, as well as coverage. Hence, from state to state, children are likely to have very similar financial access to health services, although the benefits included in the insurance package may not be comprehensive. The public utility model provides less uniform coverage. In some geographic areas, children may be covered for preventive services; in others, they may not. Furthermore, each geographic area decides which families need the most support for premium and co-payments. Hence, the public utility model allows for a great deal of variation in children's coverage between geographic areas. Although it fits into the American view of the equitable distribution of resources better than the more centralized single-payer model, the public utility model can leave children in certain areas with notably less comprehensive health care coverage than children in other areas.

The Play or Pay Model

The third model is termed "play or pay." Under this scenario, employers are the primary providers of health insurance and are required either to provide health insurance coverage for their employees or to pay a tax that would be used to fund a public insurance pool from which their employees could purchase insurance. However, as long as insurance is tied to employment, there are bound to be gaps in coverage. In order to ensure universal coverage, the play or pay plan must make an effort to close these gaps.

Children are more likely to be covered by health insurance under a play or pay plan than under the kind of piecemeal coverage that has characterized health care delivery to children in the United States for so long. In 1990, 40 percent of uninsured children had at least one parent who was employed, and such children will gain coverage under the plan.[32] A strong play or pay system can fill the gaps for children in households that are not linked to the job market. To do so, the "pay" option needs to be constructed so that all of these children are able to obtain coverage from the public insurance pool. A sliding scale of payments is necessary to guarantee affordability. The American Academy of Pediatrics' Children First Proposal is one example of such a plan. In addition, this proposal guarantees a comprehensive benefit package for children regardless of whether they get their insurance from their parent's employer or the state-administered pool. Many play or pay proposals require that insurers offer a minimum benefit package. Such packages vary considerably in scope, from "bare-bones" to very comprehensive coverage. Employers, while being required to offer certain basic services, can choose whether to offer additional benefits. If the basic service package does not include the essential services that children need, such as preventive care, the variability between employers means that not all children will have coverage for routine services such as immunizations.

Managed Competition Model

The fourth model is referred to as managed competition. Under this market-based model, health care plans compete for subscribers on the basis of price, quality, and benefits rather than risks.[33]

Central to the managed competition model is an entity to create collective buying power among insurance purchasers (that is, employers, public agencies, individuals) so that they can bargain effectively for the best prices available. These purchasing cooperatives also provide consumers with information, allowing them to compare the prices of various plans. Coupled with the purchasing cooperatives, employers are mandated to buy coverage for their employees and their dependents. Unemployed persons receive government subsidies with which to purchase the insurance premium. If the subsidies are insufficient, universal coverage will not be achieved for low-income families.

The managed competition model relies on a government requirement that all health plans offer a minimum package of benefits. Herein lies a possible shortcoming for children; if needed services such as speech and physical therapies for children with chronic diseases are not included in the benefit package, coverage may be available but only at additional expense to the family. Depending on financial circumstances, a family may have to forgo the additional coverage and ultimately the needed services.

Tax Incentives

The final reform model changes the tax code. Families are given a tax deduction or credit for purchasing health insurance. The size of the tax deduction is crucial: If it is too high, tax revenues decline, forcing increases in the tax rate to make up for the loss; if too low, the tax deduction does not adequately offset families' health care costs. Furthermore, low-income families generally do not pay enough tax to take full advantage of the tax deduction. Therefore, a tax credit needs to be included in this model to assist low-income families. In addition, this model does not guarantee insurance coverage. Consumers have the responsibility of applying for the deduction or credit.

Children's coverage may expand as a result of tax incentives. However, many commentators believe that the change is insignificant because these proposals do not tend to offer enough relief to make a difference for most families.[34] Large numbers of children are likely to remain uninsured, and the benefits for which insured children have coverage are unlikely to improve. However, coupled with a much expanded public insurance system, tax incentives targeted at the middle class can play an important role in providing universal coverage for children.

The Role of Cost Containment

Any efficient health care delivery system must incorporate strong cost-containment measures in order to ensure that the national health care system does not grow beyond the economy's capacity to support it.[35] Virtually all of these cost-containment efforts curtail access to or the comprehensiveness of health care services. Four cost-containment strategies frequently mentioned in health financing reform proposals are global budgeting, the rationing of services, managed care, and outcomes research. Each mechanism will be discussed in terms of its effect on the comprehensiveness of services offered to children.

Global Budgeting

A global budgeting strategy, in which the government sets a total amount of money that can be spent on health care services at either the state or the federal level (or both), has the greatest potential to contain costs. Some proposals incorporating global budgeting tie yearly increases in the overall health care budget to increases in the gross national product.[36] A government entity negotiates payment rates with various providers and health professionals. The objective is to force the system to become more efficient by limiting the budget to a fixed amount.

Curbing the overall health care budget this way is likely to force competition for scarce resources between children and other health care constituencies. Historically, children have not fared well when competing against other age groups for limited social and health service dollars.[37] Hence, the effects of global budgeting may offset any improvement in children's access that these reform proposals would hope to achieve.

Rationing Services

The second cost-containment mechanism involves the rationing of services. Although none of the most prominent delivery models speak directly of "rationing," systems that incorporate aspects of either the single-payer or the public utility model suggest that costs might be contained by restricting access to high-risk, high-cost, or overutilized services. Many of these systems would employ national, state, or local boards with the explicit power to reduce the availability of certain services. The philosophical assumption underlying the rationing approach holds that rationing services is morally preferable to rationing insurance coverage (that is, restricting the access of persons to health services because they do not have health insurance).[38]

The effect of a rationing strategy on children's access to health services depends on which benefits are covered. For example, if preventive and primary-care services were not covered, the comprehensiveness of children's services would not be significantly changed; indeed, it is these services to which underinsured children traditionally have not had access. Very expensive services (for example, organ transplants), which only a small proportion of children use, are more likely to be excluded from coverage under a rationing strategy. Although most children will get the services that they need, children with special needs may be more vulnerable because services that they need are more likely to be excluded from coverage.

Managed Care

A third cost-containment strategy involves the use of managed care. This approach incorporates the use of a primary-care physician as a gatekeeper to other types of care. Health maintenance organizations (HMOs), preferred provider organizations (PPOs), and their hybrids operate on this principle. Recent research, however, has shown that, according to employers, managed care has not kept costs down.[39] In the most frequently implemented form, managed care appears as ineffective at controlling costs as traditional payment systems. Furthermore, researchers question how well managed-care systems serve certain subgroups of the population, such as children.[40] Because managed-care insurers contract primarily with adult specialist providers in order to benefit from economies of scale, pediatric specialists are underrepresented and thus somewhat inaccessible in managed-care systems. This means that parents may be forced to leave the managed-care system to seek more appropriate and inevitably more expensive care for their children. Additionally, there is a constant risk that "gate keeping" may become a subtle form of rationing as expensive treatments and diagnostic tests, as well as referrals to specialists, are dispensed with or delayed.

Outcomes Research

Outcomes research evaluates the effectiveness of medical procedures with the hope of increasing the quality of care. Many believe that it can also unearth ineffective and expensive procedures that can be replaced with more effective and inexpensive ones.[41] Some universal insurance proposals explicitly include arrangements for continued funding for this type of research for the primary purpose of containing costs. Outcomes research as an approach to cost-containment is incremental by nature and therefore unsatisfactory to those advocates who believe the problem of increasing cost is entrenched in the structure of our health care system.[42] As in rationing and managed-care efforts, children may be denied access to certain services—in this case those which outcomes research has determined are not cost-effective.

There is no shortage of ideas when it comes to saving costs under a health insurance system that provides universal coverage. However, the cost-saving devices that are implemented must ensure that savings are accrued by families as well as by the insuring bodies. Whatever the nature of the delivery system, gaps in services available to children are inevitable. The extent of these gaps determines in part the level of middle-class satisfaction and, hence, the system's success. At some point, a form of rationing or managed-care system will be implemented in the United States, and therefore certain services will not be covered by the reformed health care system. Under such a system, the majority of children should have enhanced access to health services, and families' cost burdens should be relieved to some extent. However, some children, particularly those with special needs, will continue to face access barriers because of the cost to their families of providing uncovered services. While this latter group may be in the minority, unaddressed concerns will ensure that cost containment will continue to be a political issue—even given a system that extends coverage to all children.

Conclusion

Starting in the mid-1980s, government at both the state and federal levels attempted to address the health care access problems of uninsured children. As children from middle-class families swelled the ranks of the uninsured in the early 1990s, pressure increased on politicians to have government play a more proactive role in providing access to health services.

Five models of health care delivery that can expand coverage for children have been examined; each has profoundly different effects on children. Moreover, the cost-containment mechanisms that the models employ likely compromise the comprehensiveness of benefits for children.

We argue that universal coverage and access to comprehensive services for children are the two necessary components of a reformed system, and we judge reform models and cost-containment measures by how well they meet these two objectives. Much of children's health care is routine, and a large portion of it is predictable.[43] But this characterization does not mean that even middle-class parents can finance their children's health care without help. Whether reform is motivated by concerns over equity or economic efficiency, the twin goals of universality and comprehensiveness must be kept clearly in focus.

NOTES

Note: Opinions expressed are those of the authors and do not necessarily reflect the views of the American Academy of Pediatrics.
1. *See* Sardell, Child Health Policy in the U.S.: The Paradox of Consensus, 15 J. Health Pol. Pol'y & L. 271, 279–80 (1990); *see also* Chapter 24 in this volume.

2. *See* U.S. Congress, Congressional Research Service, Health Insurance and the Uninsured: Background Data and Analysis 66 (1988).

3. *See* National Commission on Children, Beyond Rhetoric: A New American Agenda for Children and Families 135–36 (1991).

4. Children under age eighteen are overrepresented among the uninsured; they make up 29 percent of the total number of uninsured Americans and only 25 percent of the total population. Tabulated from J. Foley, Employee Benefit Research Institute, Uninsured in the United States: The Nonelderly Population without Health Insurance 21, 70 (1991).

5. *See* Gabel et al., Employer-Sponsored Health Insurance, 1989, 9 Health Aff. 161, 167 (1990).

6. *See* Foley, Uninsured in the United States, *supra* note 4, at 63.

7. *See id.*

8. *See* Carveth, Health Spending: The Growing Threat to the Family Budget, Med. Benefits, Jan. 15, 1992, at 1.

9. *See* Schulte et al., Changing Immunization Referral Patterns among Pediatricians and Family Practice Physicians, Dallas County, Texas, 1988, 87 Pediatrics 204, 206 (1991).

10. *See* Schieber et al., Health Care Systems in Twenty-Four Countries, 10 Health Aff. 22 (1991).

11. *See* Cunningham & Monheit, Insuring the Children: A Decade of Change, 9 Health Aff. 76, 80 (1990).

12. *See* Foley, Uninsured in the United States, *supra* note 4, at 63.

13. *See* The Crisis in Health Insurance, 1990 Consumer Rep. 533, 534.

14. *See* Cartland & Yudkowsky, State Estimates of Uninsured Children, 12 Health Aff. 144, 146 (1993).

15. *See* Friedman, The Uninsured: From Dilemma to Crisis, 265 JAMA 2491, 2491–92 (1991).

16. *See* B. Bloom, U.S. Department of Health and Human Services, National Center for Health Statistics, Health Insurance and Medical Care: Health of Our Nation's Children, Advance Data from Vital and Health Statistics, Oct. 1, 1990, at 4.

17. *See* National Commission on Children, Beyond Rhetoric, *supra* note 3, at 138.

18. *See* Johnson & Aquilina, The Cost-Shifting Issue, 1 Health Aff. 101, 103 (1982).

19. *See* Gabel et al., Employer-Sponsored Health Insurance, *supra* note 5, at 165.

20. *See* National Commission on Children, Beyond Rhetoric, *supra* note 3, at 136.

21. *See* Sardell, Child Health Policy in the U.S., *supra* note 1, at 288–91.

22. *See* Cartland, Expansions Bring 800,000 Children into Medicaid, 8 Child Health Financing Rep. 4 (Fall 1991).

23. *See* Powers, Justice and the Market for Health Insurance, 1 Kennedy Inst. Ethics J. 307, 309 (1991).

24. *See* Carveth, Health Spending, *supra* note 8, at 2.

25. *See* Reinhardt, Breaking American Health Policy Gridlock, 10 Health Aff. 96, 101 (1991).

26. Tabulated from Cunningham & Monheit, Insuring the Children, *supra* note 11, at 83.

27. *See* Levit et al., Health Spending and Ability to Pay: Business, Individuals, and Government, 10 Health Care Financing Rev. 1, 6 (1989).

28. *See* Survey Shows Widespread Public Concern about Health Insurance Coverage and Costs, Kaiser Family Foundation, Apr. 8, 1992, at 1.

29. *See* Including Children and Pregnant Women in Health Care Reform 5 (S. S. Brown ed., 1992).

30. *See* 1989 Hay/Huggins Benefits Report, Med. Benefits, Nov. 30, 1989, at 3.

31. *See* Gabel et al., Employer-Sponsored Health Insurance, *supra* note 5, at 166.

32. Tabulated from Foley, Uninsured in the United States, *supra* note 4, at 70.

33. *See* Enthoven & Kronick, A Consumer-Choice Health Plan for the 1990s, 329 New Eng. J. Med. 29 (1989).

34. *See* Tax Credits: A Paradise with Snakes, Med. & Health Perspectives, Apr. 6, 1992, at 1.

35. *See* W. McNerney, The Control of Health Care Costs in the United States in the Context of Health Insurance Policies, in The Public and Private Mix for Health: The Relevance and Effects of Change 331, 334–35 (G. McLachlan & A. Maynard eds., 1984).

36. *See, e.g.,* J. Reichard, Insuring the Uninsured: A Guide to the Proposals and the Players 20 (1992).

37. *See* Benjamin et al., Intergenerational Equity and Public Spending, 88 Pediatrics 75 (1991).

38. *See, e.g.,* L. Churchhill, Rationing Health Care in America: Perceptions and Principles of Justice 5–19 (1987).

39. *See* 1989 Managed Care Survey, Med. Benefits, Nov. 30, 1989, at 1–2.

40. *See* Cartland & Yudkowsky, Barriers to Pediatric Referral in Managed Care Systems, 89 Pediatrics 183, 187 (1992).

41. *See* L. Brown, Competition and the New Accountability: From Market Incentives to Medical Outcomes, paper presented at the Symposium on Competitive Health Policy Reforms: An Appraisal and Prognostication 22–23 (1991)(on file with author).

42. *See, e.g., id.,* at 23–26.

43. *See, e.g.,* Brown, Including Children, *supra* note 29, at 15–17.

■ CHAPTER TWENTY-SIX

Medical Care for the Child at Risk: On State Supervention of Parental Autonomy

Joseph Goldstein

> Of all tyrannies a tyranny sincerely exercised for the good of its victims
> may be the most oppressive. . . . [T]hose who torment us for our own
> good will torment us without end for they do so with the approval of
> their own conscience.[1]

To BE A *child* is to be at risk, dependent, and without capacity or authority to decide what is "best" for oneself.

To be an *adult* is to be a risk-taker, independent, and with capacity and authority to decide and to do what is "best" for oneself.

To be an *adult who is a parent* is to be presumed in law to have the capacity, authority, and responsibility to determine and to do what is good for one's children.

The law is designed to assure for each child an opportunity to meet and master the developmental crises on the way to adulthood—to that critical age when he or she is presumed by the state to be qualified to determine what is "best" for oneself. As Jeremy Bentham observed not so long ago in 1840:

> The feebleness of infancy demands a continual protection. Everything
> must be done for an imperfect being, which as yet does nothing for itself.
> The complete development of its physical powers takes many years; that of
> its intellectual faculties is still slower. At a certain age, it has already
> strength and passions, without experience enough to regulate them. Too

---

Reprinted by permission of The Yale Law Journal Company and Fred B. Rothman & Company from The Yale Law Journal, Vol. 86, pp. 645–670.

sensitive to present impulses, too negligent of the future, such a being must be kept under an authority more immediate than that of the laws.[2]

That "more immediate" authority is parental authority. Thus, society's law, in accord with nature's law, seeks to assure for each child permanent membership in a family with at least one and preferably two caretaking adults.[3] The law, reflecting Bentham's view, has a strong presumption in favor of parental authority free of coercive intrusion by agents of the state. Indeed, it is a function of law to protect family privacy as a means of safeguarding parental autonomy in child rearing. At the same time the law attempts to safeguard each child's entitlement to autonomous parents who care and who feel responsible and who can be held accountable for continually meeting the child's ever-changing physical and psychological needs.

Like all authority, however, parental authority may be abused. Family privacy may become a cover for exploiting the inherent inequality between adult and child. Thus children, who by definition are both physically and psychologically at risk, may sometimes be placed at further risk by the adult "caretakers" who are presumed to be essential to their well-being.

This chapter explores the role of law in protecting children from parental exploitation and protecting parents and children within a family from state exploitation in the provision or denial of medical care. The goal is to determine the extent to which the law should supervene, not only the right and obligation of parents to decide what medical attention should or should not be provided for their children, but also the reciprocal right of children to have their parents assume responsibility for making such decisions. This quest incorporates two questions about empowering the state to breach its commitment to family privacy and to parental autonomy: (1) What circumstances, if any, should constitute *probable cause* for the state to intrude on family privacy by investigating parental decisions about a child's health and medical care needs? and (2) What must such an investigation find in order to *justify* the abridgment of parental autonomy by substituting the state's judgment for that of the parents? Although both of these questions are important, this chapter focuses on the second question, for it presents the ultimate dilemma: *When* should the state itself become the "parent"?

This question of primary focus arises in two quite distinct forms. The first, on which this chapter does not dwell, takes the form of *generally applicable* societal judgments that no parents shall have a choice, for example, with regard to having their children vaccinated against smallpox. Such legislative infringements of parental autonomy are without regard to any specific individual parent's wishes. They are perceived as a "reasonable and proper exercise of police power" in furtherance of compelling state interests—for example, to safeguard society generally from a smallpox epidemic.[4]

The second form of intrusion, and the one on which this chapter does dwell, is less precisely defined. It concerns case by case determinations that turn on whether the state should supervise or supervene individual parental judgments concerning health care for their children. The authority for state intervention is found in often vague and imprecise neglect, abuse, and delinquency statutes, as well as in administrative and judicial decisions that some children under certain circumstances are entitled to obtain or to reject medical care without regard to or against their parents' wishes. In an effort to tease out some tentative guides for fixing limits to intrusions on parental autonomy and family privacy, a series of cases will be examined that involve (1) a choice between life and death for "normally" formed and "malformed" newborn infants; (2) a choice between life and death for a teenager; (3) non-life-threatening choices for young children and teenagers; and (4) two interrelated life-threatening and non-life-threatening choices concerning a transplant from a well child to a dying sibling.

Presumptions of Parental Autonomy and Family Privacy

The cases are analyzed in terms of the strong presumptions in our legal system in favor of parental autonomy and family privacy and *against* coercive state intervention. The law presumes the capacity and recognizes the authority of adults to parent their children in accord with their own individual beliefs, preferences, and lifestyles. It does not establish rules for child rearing to accord with some particular religious or scientific ideal. It requires only that parents meet *minimal* standards of child care *negatively* set in neglect, abuse, and abandonment statutes and *affirmatively* set in provisions such as those obligating parents to send their children to school, to keep them out of the labor market, and to have them vaccinated against smallpox. In accord with fundamental notions of liberty, the law thus presumes that parents, as adults, are qualified to decide how to meet the needs of their children until these children themselves become adults presumed competent to decide what is in their own and their children's interests.[5]

The right to family privacy and parental autonomy, and the reciprocal liberty interest of parent and child in the familial bond between them, need no greater justification than that they comport with each state's fundamental constitutional commitment to individual freedom and human dignity. But the right of parents to raise their children as they think best, free of coercive intervention, comports as well with each child's biological and psychological need for unthreatened and unbroken continuity of care by his parents.[6] No other animal is for so long a time after birth in so helpless a state that its survival depends upon continuous nurture by an adult. Although breaking or weakening the ties to the responsible and responsive adults may have different consequences for children of different ages, there is little doubt that such breaches in the familial bond will be detrimental to a child's well-being.[7] But "so long as a family is intact, the young child feels parental authority is lodged in a unified body which is a safe and reliable guide for later identification."[8] Court or agency intervention without regard to or over the objection of parents can only serve to undermine the familial bond that is vital to a child's sense of becoming and being an adult in his or her own right.

Beyond these supplemental biological and psychological justifications for insulating parent–child relationships and safeguarding each child's entitlement to a permanent place in a family of his or her own, there is a further justification for a policy of minimum state intervention. It is, as Bentham recognized, that the law does not have the capacity to supervise the delicately complex interpersonal bonds between parent and child. As *parens patriae* the state is too crude an instrument to become an adequate substitute for parents. The legal system has neither the resources nor the sensitivity to respond to a growing child's ever-changing needs and demands. It does not have the capacity to deal on an individual basis with the consequences of its decisions or to act with the deliberate speed required by a child's sense of time and essential to his or her well-being. Even if the law were not so incapacitated, there is no basis for assuming that the judgments of its decision-makers about a particular child's needs would be any better than (or indeed as good as) the judgments of the parents. Only magical thinking will permit the denial of these self-evident, but often ignored, truths about the limits of law.[9]

To recognize how vulnerable the developmental processes are between infancy and adulthood and how essential parents are for continually safeguarding children from never-ending risks is also to recognize that parents may fail. They may place their children at unwarranted risk rather than promote their survival to adulthood. That danger justifies a policy of *minimum* state intervention rather than one of *no* state intervention.

Yet recognition that parents may disserve their children's interests still does not mean that the state necessarily can or will do better. Nor does it justify acceptance of the vague and subjective language of neglect and abuse statutes that give the state unguided discretion to supervene parental decisions with regard to health care for their children. If legislatures are to give full recognition to a child's entitlement to a permanent family and the entitlement of parents, no matter how poor, to raise their children as they think best, they must acknowledge the need for a realistic reappraisal of abuse and neglect statutes—statutes that generally provide, vaguely and overbroadly, that a child who is being denied proper care may be found "neglected." Legislatures must be made to see that the requisite of parental consent to medical care for children becomes meaningless if refusal to consent automatically triggers state inquiry or a finding of neglect. State statutes then must be revised to hold in check, not release, the rescue fantasies of those it empowers to intrude, and thus to safeguard families from state-sponsored interruptions of ongoing family relationships by well-intentioned people who "know" what is "best" and who wish to impose their personal health care preferences on others.

It is in this value-laden setting that an examination of cases is made to determine how and to what extent the state should seek to supervise or supervene parents in their decisions to secure or deny medical care for their children.

Life-or-Death Decisions

State supervention of parental judgment would be justified to provide any proven, nonexperimental, medical procedure when its denial would mean *death* for a child who would otherwise have an opportunity for either a *life worth living* or a *life of relatively normal healthy growth* toward adulthood[10]—to majority, when a person is freed of parental control and presumed competent to decide for himself or herself. The state would overcome the presumption of parental autonomy in health care matters only if it could establish: (1) that the medical profession is in agreement about what nonexperimental medical treatment is right for the child; (2) that the expected outcome of that treatment is what society agrees to be right for any child, a chance for normal healthy growth toward adulthood or a life worth living; *and* (3) that the expected outcome of denial of that treatment would mean death for the child.

These criteria for intervention were met by Judge Murphy, for the Superior Court of the District of Columbia, in *In re Pogue*.[11] He authorized blood transfusions for an otherwise healthy newborn infant who would have died had his parents' decision to reject the treatment been honored. At the same time Judge Murphy, recognizing the distinction between being an adult and being a child with regard to medical care choices, declined to order blood transfusions for the infant's mother, who, in the face of death, refused to consent to such intervention. Over the objection of the "adult" parents' wishes and without regard, of course, to the infant's "wishes," Judge Murphy, as a substitute parent, decided to protect the child's right as a person to reach the age of majority, when he will become entitled to make such life-or-death decisions for himself. The judge implicitly found the infant's parents temporarily incompetent to care for the child, while simultaneously acknowledging the adult status of the mother by declining to use her refusal of blood as a basis for declaring her a danger to herself and thus incompetent, as if a child, to decide for herself.

The scientific "fact" that death, for both the infant and the mother, was inevitable without transfusion—the nonexperimental medical procedure—was not in dispute. Nor was there any societal doubt about the desirability, the "rightness," of the predicted outcome of the transfusion—an opportunity for normal healthy growth, a life worth living. The issue was whether the judge and doctors, as adults with an unqualified value preference for life, could use the power of the state to impose their "adult" judgment on adults in law whose own "adult" judgment gave greater weight to another preference. On behalf of the adult, the answer was no; on behalf of the child, the answer was yes. Thus coercive intervention by the state was justified where the parents' decision would have deprived a child of proven medical treatment and consequently of an opportunity for healthy growth and development to adulthood.

There would be no justification, however, for coercive intrusion by the state in those life-or-death situations (1) in which there is no proven medical procedure, *or* (2) in which parents are confronted with conflicting medical advice about which, if any, treatment procedure to follow, *or* (3) in which, even if the medical experts agree about treatment, there is less than a high probability that the nonexperimental treatment will enable the child to pursue either a life worth living or a life of relatively normal healthy growth toward adulthood. These standards are anchored in such common law notions as that of plain duty, given expression in Justice Field's jury charge regarding criminal liability for acts of omission:

> [T]he duty omitted must be a plain duty, by which I mean that it must be one that does not admit of any discussion as to its obligatory force; one upon which different minds must agree, or will generally agree. Where doubt exists as to what conduct should be pursued in a particular case, and intelligent men differ as to the proper action to be had, the law does not impute guilt to anyone, if, from omission to adopt one course instead of another, fatal consequences follow to others.[12]

Outside of a narrow central core of agreement, "a life worth living" and "a life of relatively normal healthy growth" are highly personal terms about which there is no societal consensus. There can thus be no societal consensus about the "rightness" of always deciding for "life," or of always preferring the predicted result of the recommended treatment over the predicted result of refusing such treatment. It is precisely in those cases in which reasonable and responsible persons can and do disagree about whether the "life" after treatment would be "worth living" or "normal," and thus about what is "right," that parents must remain free of coercive state intervention in deciding whether to consent to or reject the medical program proffered for their child.

The "high probability of a life worth living or of relatively normal healthy growth" standard is, it must be remembered, designed not to facilitate but to inhibit state intervention. This broad standard is meant to reinforce a policy of minimum state intervention. In its breadth and in its evidentiary demands, it saddles the state with the burden of overcoming the presumption of parental autonomy. Intervention would thus be limited to those individual life-or-death cases in which the state could establish that the medical profession agreed upon the rejected medical treatment and that the treatment would provide the dying child with an opportunity for what societal consensus held to be either a life worth living or a life of relatively normal healthy growth. The state, of course, would remain without authority to challenge parental decisions to provide medical treatment in order to *save* their dying child even if the state could establish that there was a societal consensus that the expected outcome of such treatment was not a "life worth living."

Absent medical agreement about what treatment is indicated, or absent a societal consensus about the rightness of the predicted result of treatment, there would be no justification for disqualifying parents from (or for qualifying agents of the state for) making the difficult choice—for giving their personal meaning to "right" or to "worth living" or to "normal healthy growth." No one has a greater right or responsibility and no one can be presumed to be in a better position, and thus better equipped, than a child's parents to decide what course to pursue if the medical experts cannot agree or, assuming their agreement, if there is no general agreement in society that the outcome of treatment is clearly preferred to the outcome of no treatment. Put somewhat more starkly, how can parents in such situations give the wrong answer, since there is no way of knowing the right answer? In these circumstances the law's guarantee of freedom of belief becomes meaningful, and the right to act on that belief as an autonomous parent becomes operative within the privacy of one's family. Precisely because there is no objectively wrong or right answer, the burden must be on the state to establish "wrong," not on the parent to establish that what is "right" for them is necessarily "right" for others. Indeed, it is in just such cases that the Constitution, which separates church and, to a different degree, science from state, dictates abstention from imposing one group's orthodoxy about health care or truth about the meaning of life or, for that matter, death upon another.

Ultimately, then, it must be left to the parents to decide, for example, whether their congenitally malformed newborn with an ascertainable neurologic deficiency and highly predictable mental retardation should be provided with treatment that may avoid death, but that offers no chance of cure—no opportunity, in terms of societal consensus, for life worth living or a life of relatively normal healthy growth. Dr. Raymond Duff has argued persuasively:

> Families know their values, priorities and resources better than anyone else. Presumably they, with the doctor, can make the better choices as a private affair. Certainly, they, more than anyone else, must live with the consequences. Most of these families know they cannot place that child for adoption because no one else wants the child. If they cannot cope adequately with the child and their other responsibilities and survive as a family, they may feel that the death option is a forced choice. . . . But that is not necessarily bad, and who knows of a better way.[13]

For the law to adopt the Duff position would not mean abandonment of its commitment to defend human life. Special procedures could be established within hospitals to protect infants and their parents from possible misdiagnoses, though not from "erroneous" moral judgment. The function of such a procedure would be to verify the medical prognosis, not the ethical base, on which the parental decision relied. If the prognosis proved to be incorrect and if the parents refused to accept the revised finding, the state would be empowered, as it was in the blood transfusion case, to order the recommended treatment. If the tragic prognosis is warranted, then the law, as Duff argues, should treat the decision as a "private affair"—whether it be for medical means to sustain life or for humane shelter and care not necessarily designed to avoid death.

If parental autonomy is not accorded the recognition argued for in this chapter, and if society insists through law that such children, indeed any children, receive medical treatment rejected by their parents, the state should provide the special financial, physical, and psychological resources essential to making real for the child it "saves" the value it prefers. The state should become fully responsible for making "unwanted" children "wanted" ones.[14] Minimally and ideally the state should fully finance their special care requirements; in the event their parents do not wish to remain responsible for them, the state should find adopting parents who with unbroken continuity could meet not only the child's physical needs but also his or her psychological requirements for affectionate relationships and emotional and intellectual stimulation.

Except for meeting the child's physical needs, the task, however large the allocation of financial resources, may well be beyond the limits of law. The law is too crude an instrument to nurture, as only parents can, the delicate physical, psychological, and social tissues of a child's life. Even if it could force, and it may not, unwilling adults to adopt children, the law does not have the capacity to make an "unwanted" child a "wanted" one. If the past and present provide a basis for prediction, an institutional setting (not adoption or long-term foster care with the same family) is the more likely but hardly satisfactory prospect for the after-"care" of such children until their majority or death. Institutional arrangements have not provided the affectionate and other psychological ties such children—no matter how limited their potential for healthy growth and development—demand and deserve. As long as the state offers institutions that provide little more than storage space and "hay, oats, and water"[15] for medical science's achievements, the law must err on the side of its strong presumption in favor of parental autonomy and family integrity. Thus for the state to do other than either *assume* full responsibility for the treatment, care, and nurture of such children or *honor* the parent's decision to consent to or refuse authorization for treatment would be but to pay cruel and oppressive lip service to notions of human dignity and the right to life.

The case of Karen, a teenage patient suffering from an irreversible kidney malfunction, provides another life-or-death example in which the standard of an opportunity for a life worth living or a life of relatively normal healthy growth toward adulthood would preclude state supervention of parental judgments. Karen's case poses the question whether state intervention should be authorized to review the choice of an adolescent who, with her parents' permission and concurrence, decides to choose death over "life." Following an unsuccessful kidney transplant, Karen and her parents refused to consent to the continuation of "intolerable" life support devices. The decision to proceed as if family privacy and parental autonomy were, or at least should be, protected was described in an article by her doctors:

> [F]ollowing the transplant's failure, thrice-weekly hemodialysis was performed. Karen tolerated dialysis poorly, routinely having chills, nausea, vomiting, severe headaches and weakness. . . .
>
>   . . . .
>
> [A]fter it was clear that the kidney would never function, Karen and her parents expressed the wish to stop medical treatment and let "nature take its course." . . . [S]taff members conveyed to the family that such wishes

were unheard of and unacceptable, and that a decision to stop treatment could never be an alternative. The family did decide to continue dialysis, medication, and diet therapy. Karen's renal incapacity returned to pre-transplant levels and she returned to her socially isolated life, with diet restriction, chronic discomfort, and fatigue.

On May 10, Karen was hospitalized following ten days of high fever. Three days later the transplant was removed. Its pathology resembled that of the original kidneys, and the possibility of a similar reaction forming in subsequent transplants was established.

On May 21, the arteriovenous shunt placed in Karen's arm for hemo-dialysis was found to be infected, and part of the vein wall was excised and the shunt revised. During this portion of the hospitalization, Karen and the parents grudgingly went along with the medical recommendations, but they continued to ponder the possibility of stopping treatment. . . . On May 24, the shunt clotted closed. Karen, with her parents' agreement, re-fused shunt revision and any further dialysis.

. . . .

Karen died on June 2, with both parents at her bedside. . . . Shortly [before] her death she thanked the staff for what she knew had been a hard time for them and she told her parents she hoped they would be happy. We later learned that before her death she had written a will and picked a burial spot near her home and near her favorite horseback riding trail. In the final days she supported her parents as they faltered in their decision; she told her father, "Daddy, I will be happy there (in the ground) if there is no machine and they don't work on me any more."[16]

For Karen and her parents no medical treatment offered the possibility of re-suming a relatively normal life or a life worth living. The recommendation of the nursing and medical staff to continue the life support system was not a scientific, but a moral judgment. The rightness of forcing the consequences of their choice upon Karen rather than honoring her and her parents' decision could not be established. There was then no basis for exercising the power of the state to su-pervene the judgment of Karen's parents. Had Karen been an adult, on the law's chronological scale, there is no question, or there ought not to be, that out of respect for her dignity as a human being, the doctors would have had to abide by her request to end the treatment. As a New York court once declared, "[I]t is the individual who is the subject of a medical decision who has the final say and . . . this must necessarily be so in a system of government which gives the greatest possible protection to the individual in the furtherance of his own desires."[17]

For the doctors to have proceeded with dialysis against the wishes of teenage Karen and her parents would have constituted an assault in tort and in crime. Together as a family they must be entitled in law to be free, as they were, of the coercive force of the state or of the medical authorities. The law of torts and crime is designed, or ought to be, to protect family integrity by providing such safe-guards against the supervention of parental judgment by the medical staff or other "agents" of the state.

Had the situation been different, had Karen's parents insisted, over her objection, on continuing the life support system, would the state have been justified in supervening their judgment? Or had Karen insisted, over her parents' objection, on continuing the life support system, would the state have been justified in supervening their judgment? The answer to both questions should be "No," albeit an uneasy "No," particularly to the second question. It is, after all, the function and responsibility of parents to evaluate and make judgments about the wishes and requests of their children. It is, after all, the meaning of parental autonomy to make such decisions. Further, neither court nor hearing agency is likely to be as competent as, for example, were Karen's parents to determine her capacity for choice and whether to abide by it. The law should avoid giving the discretion for such subjective judgments to its agents.

But the uneasiness about the "no" answers remains. It stems from a fear that a few parents might not follow a child's express wish to undergo treatment that might seem intolerable to them, though not to the child. It also stems from a growing concern that for some matters, particularly with regard to health care, the general statutory age of adulthood, of emancipation, has been set too high. The question then, and one addressed in the next section, is not whether Karen specifically but whether all persons aged sixteen(?) in such circumstances as Karen found herself ought to have the controlling voice in law rather than their parents or guardians—whether it be for life or not to avoid death. But until legislatures or courts find a formula for determining under what circumstances and at what age below majority children may become their own risk-takers for certain health care decisions, ultimate responsibility must remain with parents or, if they be disqualified, with adult guardians, who may (as Karen's parents did) or may not decide to support their child's choice.

Emancipation of Children for Health Care Purposes

The law, both case and statutory, has begun to emancipate some minors to determine for themselves what health care course to pursue. For example, sixteen-year-olds have been granted the right to enter or leave mental institutions over the objection of parents, who, in the past, had the authority to arrange for their admission or release as voluntary patients. For another example, pregnant minors have been given adult status for purposes of determining whether to obtain an abortion.[18] In the case of "mentally ill" sixteen-year-olds, these modifications of parental autonomy silently rest on a not totally unwarranted suspicion that mental institutions provide little, if any, medical treatment, and more openly upon a fear of parental abuse, not unlike the exploitation of the system by members of a family wishing to put a difficult spouse, parent, or sibling out of sight. The reasons that seem to underlie renewed challenges to the commitment of adults for mental health care without their consent prompt and seem to justify a limited emancipation of children in this area. As for pregnancy, the justification for emancipation appears to stem from a recognition that those who insist on parental consent are concerned less with the child's well-being than with strengthening their general opposition to abortion, which they cloak in the magical notion that law can improve family communications by compelling a young woman in trouble to consult with her parents when such family trust does not exist.

There may, then, be situations that justify abiding by the health care choices of children without regard to the wishes of their parents—situations that justify emancipating children and thus relieving parents of the right, as well as the responsibility, to determine whether to consider or to accept the treatment preferences of their children. Unlike the life-or-death problems already addressed, the issue here is whether and when children, not the state, should be given the otherwise parental right to determine for themselves what medical course to pursue. The question, which could only arise in situations in which the state would not be authorized, under the standards proposed, to supervene parental autonomy, is: Under what specific circumstances should the law presume children to be as competent as are adults to be their own risk-takers for all or some health care purposes?

Any answers to this question which favor qualifying minors as adults for certain health care decisions should provide standards for establishing emancipation status that are as impersonal and as nonjudgmental as is the chronological-age standard for establishing adult status. Whatever the rationale for the emancipation, access to such status for all children in a designated category should be open and automatic. The right to partial emancipation should not rest on satisfying, on a case by case basis, some body of wise persons that the particular child is "mature enough" to choose or that the particular child's choice is "right." To introduce such a subjective process for decision would be not to emancipate the child but rather to transfer to the state the parental control and responsibility for determining when to consult and abide by the child's choice. To require relatively objective criteria for establishing emancipation status is not to take a simplistic view of children but rather to recognize how varied and complex all children are and how inadequate courts are for assessing a child's capacity for decision. The law then must limit the state to determining by some relatively objective standard *who* is entitled to decide, not *what* specific decision is to be preferred in a particular case nor whether a specific child has the "wisdom" to make a choice. To resolve the question of emancipation by authorizing a court or hearing agency to decide each case on the basis of which choice is "right" or which child in a given category is "mature enough" is to deny to both—parent as well as child—autonomy to decide and family privacy in which to decide. The question thus becomes: Under what specific circumstances should persons who are children in law and generally responsible to and the responsibility of their parents be presumed qualified and authorized to make medical treatment choices free of parental control?

The requisites of an acceptable answer would be satisfied by a law in furtherance of the strong societal commitment to safeguard "life" which provided, for example, that children of any age (or above twelve?) are emancipated who in a life-or-death situation wish, against their parents' decision, to pursue treatment. Although such a provision is not being proposed, it would meet the criteria set forth above only if emancipation carried with it the right of the child to change his or her mind—to agree with the parents—and to refuse or to withdraw consent for the proffered treatment. That right would have to be recognized, not for purposes of symmetry, but because to do otherwise would constitute a cruel hoax on child and parent. Far better to acknowledge from the outset in such situations that the child is not being emancipated for health care purposes, that the state knows what is right, and that its judgment is being imposed on both parent and child without regard to their wishes. Legislatures or courts could more easily satisfy the requisites of an acceptable answer by avoiding the express wishes of the minor as a standard of emancipation and by establishing, as some have done, such "impersonal," "objective" criteria as a chronological age fixed below that of majority (for example, sixteen), coupled with a specific medical diagnosis or prognosis (for example, pregnancy, irreversible kidney malfunction, or mental illness). Pregnancy alone, without regard to a child's age, would be a sufficiently objective standard for emancipation to determine whether or not to obtain an abortion.

This brief consideration is not meant to provide a definitive answer to this difficult question but rather to illustrate how age and diagnoses could and should be used as statutory criteria for the partial emancipation of children from parental authority in some health care decisions, whether or not they involve life-or-death choices. It is to non-life-or-death choices that this chapter now turns.

Non-Life-or-Death Decisions

When death is not a likely consequence of exercising a medical care choice, there is no justification for governmental intrusion on family privacy; nor is there justification for overcoming the presumption of either parental autonomy or the autonomy of emancipated children. Where the question involves not a life-or-death choice but a preference for one style of life over another, the law must restrain courts and medicine men from coercively imposing their "kindness"—their preferred lifestyles—in the form of medical care upon nonconsenting parents and their children. The law, in adopting such a position, cannot presume that parents do not make "mistakes." Nor can it challenge the scientific "facts," prognoses, or diagnoses upon which experts base their recommendations. Rather the law must recognize that it cannot find in medicine (or for that matter in any science) the ethical, political, or social values for evaluating health care choices. Courts must avoid confusing a doctor's personal preference for a certain style of living with the scientific bases upon which the recommendation rests. The presumption of parental capacity to decide is meant to hold in check judges or doctors who may be tempted to use the power of the state to impose their personal preferences, their "adult parental" judgments upon parents whose own adult judgment may give greater weight to another preference.

In implementing this basic commitment to parental autonomy and to family privacy, the law does not take a simplistic view of parents, of the parent–child relationship, or of the family. Rather, it acknowledges not only how complicated human beings are, but also how limited is its own capacity for making more than gross distinctions about human beings' needs, natures, and routes of development. The law recognizes and respects the diverse range of religious, cultural, scientific, and ethical beliefs and the overlapping and ever-changing modes of their expression within and between generations at all stages of the life cycle. Thus a prime function of law is to prevent one person's truth (here about health, normalcy, the good life) from becoming another person's tyranny. It is in terms of that function that parental decisions in non-life-or-death situations to reject medical care recommendations for their children will be analyzed.

The case of *In re Sampson*[19] illustrates how vaguely worded neglect statutes may be invoked in the name of health care to violate a family's privacy, to undermine parental autonomy, and to foster a community's, if not a judge's, prejudice against the physically deformed. Under the Family Court Act of New York,[20] Judge Hugh Elwyn declared Kevin Sampson, aged fifteen, "a neglected child."[21] He made this finding in order to establish his authority to veto a decision by Kevin's mother not to permit blood transfusions for Kevin during surgery. He ordered her to force Kevin to undergo a series of operations that had been recommended by the Commissioner of Health and by duly qualified surgeons to correct a facial condition called neurofibromatosis. Judge Elwyn observed that Kevin had "a massive deformity of the right side of his face and neck. The outward manifestation of the disease is a large fold or flap of an overgrowth of facial tissue which causes the whole cheek, the corner of his mouth and right ear to drop down giving him an appearance which can only be described as grotesque and repulsive."[22] He went on to psychologize and predict:

> [T]he massive deformity of the entire right side of his face and neck is patently so gross and so disfiguring that it must inevitably exert a most negative effect upon his personality development, his opportunity for education and later employment and upon every phase of his relationship with his peers and others.[23]

Judge Elwyn made this assertion with apodictic certainty even though he acknowledged that "the staff psychiatrist of the County Mental Health Center reports that 'there is no evidence of any thinking disorder' and that 'in spite of marked facial disfigurement he failed to show any outstanding personality aberration.'"[24] Nevertheless, the judge added, "this finding hardly justifies a conclusion that he has been or will continue to be wholly unaffected by his misfortune."[25] He also noted that Kevin had been exempted from school, not because he was intellectually incapable, but, it may be assumed, because he appeared to his classmates and teachers, as he did to Judge Elwyn himself, "grotesque and repulsive." But the judge's speculations on behalf of the state as *parens patriae* did not lead him to consider that under the protective cloak of family privacy, a loving, caring, accepting, autonomous parent had somehow been able to nurture in Kevin a "healthy personality." Kevin, after all, had developed in spite of state-reinforced prejudice and discrimination against the physically different in school, health agency, and court.

The testimony of the doctors who recommended surgery justified not a finding of neglect but rather a reaffirmation of parental autonomy. The doctors admitted that "the disease poses no immediate threat to [Kevin's] life nor has it as yet seriously affected his general health" and that surgery was very risky and offered no cure.[26] Further, the doctors found in the central nervous system no brain or spinal cord involvement and that delay until Kevin was twenty-one would decrease, not increase, the risk. The court replied with blind arrogance:

> [T]o postpone the surgery merely to allow the boy to become of age so that he may make the decision himself as suggested by the surgeon and urged by both counsel for the mother and the Law Guardian . . . totally ignores the developmental and psychological factors stemming from his deformity which the Court deems to be of the utmost importance in any consideration of the boy's future welfare and begs the whole question.[27]

And without regard to the relationship of Kevin's well-being to the integrity and support of his family, the court added: "'Neither by statute nor decision is the child's consent necessary or material, and we should not permit his refusal to agree, his failure to cooperate, to ruin his life and any chance for a normal, happy existence.'"[28]

The judge, who by an act of conjury had qualified himself as prophet, psychological expert, risk-taker, and all-knowing parent, described but ignored a powerful reason for concluding that state authority should not supervene parental judgments about the rightness for their child of a recommended medical treatment when death is not in issue. Judge Elwyn wrote:

> It is conceded that "there are important considerations both ways" and that the views expressed by the dissenting Judges in *Seiferth* have not been universally accepted. Moreover, it must also be humbly acknowledged that under the circumstances of this case "one cannot be certain of being right." Nevertheless, a decision must be made, and so, after much deliberation, I am persuaded that if this court is to meet its responsibilities to this boy it can neither shift the responsibility for the ultimate decision onto his shoulders nor can it permit his mother's religious beliefs to stand in the way of attaining through corrective surgery whatever chance he may have for a normal, happy existence, which, to paraphrase Judge Fuld [author of the dissent in *Seiferth*], is difficult of attainment under the most propitious circumstances, but will unquestionably be impossible if the disfigurement is not corrected.[29]

Were his humility real, the judge would not have allowed himself to believe that he, rather than Kevin's mother, was best qualified to determine the meanings of "a normal, happy existence" for her son. In Kevin's eyes either might be proven "wrong" retrospectively. But nothing, not even magic, can qualify a judge to make that prediction with equal or greater accuracy than the parent. Nor is any judge prepared, let alone obligated, as are parents, personally to assume day-to-day responsibility for giving the Kevins the care they may require as a consequence of such a personal value choice about lifestyle.

Laws of neglect must be revised to restore parental autonomy and safeguard family privacy, not only because judges cannot be substitute parents and courts cannot be substitute families, but also because the power of the state must not be employed to reinforce prejudice and discrimination against those who are cosmetically or otherwise different. When Judge Elwyn referred to Judge Fuld's dissent, it was to a case in which the court refused to find Martin Seiferth, aged fourteen, a neglected child even though his father would not compel Martin to undergo the surgery recommended for the repair of a cleft palate and harelip.[30] Martin's father, despite his own beliefs, would have consented to the surgery had Martin been willing. Their decisions were based not upon "religious" beliefs, but upon a belief that "forces in the universe" would allow Martin to cure himself. Despite evidence far less equivocal than that in Kevin's case, the majority of the court refused to be trapped by rescue fantasies of the health department and its doctors or by strong prejudices that the court was being asked to reinforce in an effort to "save" the child from himself and his parents. The court refused to order surgery, not because it thought it lacked authority, but because it thought Martin's reluctance to have the surgery foretold an unwillingness to participate in the therapy following the operations. Thus it was unwilling, unlike Judges Elwyn and Fuld, to substitute its or a state agency's value preferences about lifestyle and about who and what is beautiful or natural for those of the responsible parents.

If Martin Seiferth, as an adult, chose to undergo the recommended surgery, it would not invalidate the argument that the court should not even have had discretion to do other than to protect him and his parents from state intrusion. In fact, Martin Seiferth chose not to have the surgery. "After attending one of the vocational high schools in the city, where he learned the trade of upholsterer and was elected president of the Student Council, he set up in business on his own and is, despite his disfigurement, active and successful."[31] The county health department that originated the case reacted as if experience offered no lessons about the need for minimum state intervention on parental autonomy and family privacy:

> [He] had graduated . . . at the head of [his high school] class. It was his intention then to become an interior decorator. . . . [T]he Health Department [is] still of the opinion that the operation should have been performed in order to give this young man a fuller opportunity for the development of his talents.[32]

The law must be designed to protect its citizens from just such official blindness to the forceful imposition of personal wishes or beliefs on those who share neither the wish nor the belief about the value of medical care or "fuller opportunities" for their children.

Interrelated Decisions Not Involving Life or Death for One Child and Involving Life or Death for Another Child

Should the state have authority to invade the privacy of a family in order to review the deliberations of parents who have to decide whether to let one of their children die or whether to attempt to supply a life-saving organ for transplant by consenting to "unnecessary" surgery on one of their healthy children?

The answer ought to be "No." But that was not the answer of a Connecticut court in *Hart v. Brown*.[33] In that case doctors advised Mr. and Mrs. Hart that the only real prospect of saving their eight-year-old daughter Katheleen's life from a deadly kidney malfunction was to transplant a kidney from Margaret, her healthy twin sister. The doctors recommended and the Hart parents consented to the "unnecessary" surgery on Margaret to provide Katheleen with an opportunity to pursue a relatively normal life. But the hospital administration and the doctors refused to accept parental consent without a court review.[34] They acted out of a concern for their livelihood, not for the lives or well-being of Margaret or of Katheleen. Understandably, they feared becoming liable for money damages because the law might not accept parental consent as a defense to assault and malpractice, were such suits brought.

The Harts were thus forced to turn to the state to establish either their authority to decide or the rightness of their decision. They initiated a declaratory judgment action. There followed hearings and proceedings before Judge Robert Testo that intruded massively on the privacy of the family and set a dangerous precedent for state interference with parental autonomy. There was no *probable cause* to suspect that the parents might be exploiting either of their children, only that the doctors and administrators in refusing to accept the parental choice might be risking the well-being of both children and the family. The court upheld the parental choice, though not their autonomy to decide.

Although Judge Testo's decision avoided tragic consequences for the Harts, he did set a precedent for unwarranted and undesirable intervention by the state. He held:

> To prohibit the natural parents and the guardians ad litem of the minor children the right to give their consent under these circumstances, *where there is supervision by this court* and other persons in examining their judgement, would be most unjust, inequitable and injudicious. Therefore, natural parents of a minor should have the right to give their consent to an isograft kidney transplantation procedure *when their motivation and reasoning*

are favorably reviewed by a community representation which includes a court of equity.[35]

Had the Hart parents refused to consent to Margaret's surgery and the transplant of her kidney to Katheleen, equally unwarranted proceedings might have been brought to establish their neglect in order to obtain court authority to impose the doctors' recommendation. Doctors can, because of their special training, make diagnoses and prognoses; doctors can indicate the probable consequences for a Margaret or a Katheleen of pursuing one course or another. But absent a societal consensus, nothing in their training, or for that matter in the training of judges, qualifies them to impose upon others their preferred value choices about what the good or better is for such children or for their families. The critical fallacy is to assume as Judge Testo does in his declaratory judgment—as the legislature does in its laws of neglect and abuse—that the training and offices of doctors, legislators, and judges endow them not just with the authority but also with the capacity to determine what risks to take for someone else's child, in circumstances where there is no right or wrong answer or set of answers.

That some will object to and be uneasy about the substantial limits this chapter proposes be placed upon the power of the state to supervene parental decisions about health care for their children cannot be denied. But it is the absence of a substantial societal consensus about the legitimacy of state intrusion on parental autonomy, on the entitlement of children to autonomous parents, and on family privacy in situations beyond the proposed limits that is the best evidence for holding in check the use of state power to impose highly personal values on those who do not share them. Further, the limits set by the standard of normal healthy growth toward adulthood or a life worth living, by the life-or-death choice, and by the requirement of proven medical procedures has a built-in flexibility that can respond both to new findings in medicine and to new and changing consensuses in society.[36]

NOTES

1. Lewis, The Humanitarian Theory of Punishment, 6 Res Judicatae 224, 228 (1952).
2. 1 J. Bentham, Theory of Legislation 248 (Boston 1840). Similarly, Freud observed:

> The biological factor is the long period of time during which the young of the human species is in a condition of helplessness and dependence. Its intrauterine existence seems to be short in comparison with that of most animals, and it is sent into the world in a less finished state. . . . Moreover, the dangers of the external world have a greater importance for it, so that the value of the object which can alone protect it against them and take the place of its former intra-uterine life is enormously enhanced. This biological factor, then,

establishes the earliest situations of danger and creates *the need to be loved* which will accompany the child through the rest of its life.

S. Freud, Inhibitions, Symptoms, and Anxieties 139–40 (1926) (emphasis added).

3. *See generally* J. Goldstein, A. Freud, & A. Solnit, Beyond the Best Interests of the Child (1973) [hereinafter cited as Beyond the Best Interests].

4. *See* Jacobson v. Massachusetts, 197 U.S. 11 (1905) (upholding state compulsory vaccination law). Such laws may remain in force even though, with the passage of time, they may, as in the case of vaccination against smallpox, no longer be medically sound.

5. *See* Goldstein, On Being Adult and Being an Adult in Secular Law, 105 Daedalus, Fall 1976, at 72.

6. *See generally* Beyond the Best Interests, *supra* note 3, at 9–52.

7. The breaking of bonds by adolescents should not be confused with their forceful breaking by the state:

> With adolescents, the superficial observation of their behavior may convey the idea that what they desire is discontinuation of parental relationships rather than their preservation and stability. Nevertheless, this impression is misleading in this simple form. It is true that their revolt against any parental authority is normal developmentally since it is the adolescent's way toward establishing his own independent adult identity. But for a successful outcome it is important that the breaks and disruptions of attachment should come exclusively from his side and not be imposed on him by any form of abandonment or rejection on the psychological parents' part.

Beyond the Best Interests, *supra* note 3, at 34.

8. From a discussion with Anna Freud (notes on file with Yale Law Journal).

9. *See* Beyond the Best Interests, *supra* note 3, at 31–34, 49–52.

10. While a life of relatively normal healthy growth is assumed to be a life worth living, it is not assumed that all lives worth living from a societal-consensus point of view could be characterized as relatively normal or healthy. For example, a quadriplegic child in need of a blood transfusion for reasons unrelated to that condition might, for society, be a "life worth living" though not a life of normal healthy growth.

For an example of a decision about whether a life was worth living, *see* D. Kearns, Lyndon Johnson and the American Dream 89–90 (1976):

> During the summer Sam Johnson suffered another major heart attack. He was put in the hospital and kept in an oxygen tent for months. When Lyndon returned to Texas on his father's sixtieth birthday, Sam pleaded with his son to take him out of the lonely hospital and back to his home where he could be with friends and family. At first Lyndon resisted. The doctors said that Sam needed an oxygen tent, and none was available in Stonewall. But Sam Johnson would not listen to logical objections. "Lyndon," his son recalled him saying, "I'm going back to that little house in the hills where the people know when you're sick and care when you die. You have to help me."
>
> Finally, Johnson agreed. "I realized," Johnson said later, "how dangerous it was to let my father go home. But I also believed that a man had a right to live and to die in his own way, in his own time. God knows that hospital de-

pressed me something terrible and I was only visiting. No matter how sweet the nurses and the doctors are, they're not your family. They don't really know anything about you, they don't know anything about all the things that are going on in your head. . . . Yes, I understood why my daddy wanted to leave and I respected his wish. I brought him his clothes, I helped him dress, and I carried him home."

In his own room in the Johnson City house, Sam briefly seemed to improve. Then only two weeks later, on October 23, 1937, he died.

11. *In re* Pogue, Wash. Post, Nov. 14, 1974, § C, at 1 (No. M-18-74, Super. Ct., D.C., Nov. 11, 1974).

12. United States v. Knowles, 26 F. Cas. 800, 801 (N.D. Cal. 1864) (No. 15,540).

13. Kelsy, Shall These Children Live? A Conversation with Dr. Raymond S. Duff, Reflection, Jan. 1975, at 4, 7 (Yale Divinity School magazine).

14. For a discussion of the concept of a "wanted" child, *see* Beyond the Best Interests, *supra* note 3, at 5–7. The Model Child Placement Statute proposed by the authors states: "A wanted child is one who receives affection and nourishment on a continuing basis from at least one adult and who feels that he or she is and continues to be valued by those who take care of him or her." *Id.* at 98.

15. From a conversation with Judge James H. Lincoln, Judge of the Probate Court, Juvenile Division, Wayne County, Michigan.

16. Schowalter, Ferholt, & Mann, The Adolescent Patient's Decision to Die, 51 Pediatrics 97, 97–98 (1973).

17. Erickson v. Dilgard, 44 Misc. 2d 27, 28 (N.Y. Sup. Ct. 1962).

18. Planned Parenthood v. Danforth, 96 S. Ct. 2831, 2842–44 (1976).

19. 65 Misc. 2d 658 (N.Y. Fam. Ct. 1970), *aff'd*, 377 App. Div. 2d 668 (1971), *aff'd*, 278 N.E.2d 918 (N.Y. 1972).

20. N.Y. Fam. Ct. Act §§ 1011–1074 (McKinney 1975).

21. 65 Misc. 2d at 676.

22. *Id.* at 659.

23. *Id.* at 660.

24. *Id.*

25. *Id.* According to Judge Elwyn, a psychologist had found Kevin to be extremely dependent. The staff psychiatrist reported that Kevin demonstrated "'inferiority feeling and low self concept.'" *Id.*

26. *Id.* at 661.

27. *Id.* at 672.

28. *Id.* at 673 (quoting *In re* Seiferth, 127 N.E.2d 820, 824 (N.Y. 1955) (Fuld, J., dissenting)).

29. 65 Misc. 2d at 674.

30. *In re* Seiferth, 127 N.E.2d 820 (N.Y. 1955).

31. Letter from William G. Conable, attorney for Seiferth, to Joseph Goldstein (Apr. 20, 1964), *quoted in* J. Goldstein & J. Katz, The Family and the Law 993 (1965).

32. Letter from Elmer R. Weil, county attorney of Eric County, to Joseph Goldstein (Apr. 28, 1964), *quoted in id.* at 993–94.

33. 289 A.2d 386 (Conn. Super. Ct. 1972).

34. Interestingly, the doctors were willing to rely on parental consent, without

court review, to remove both of Katheleen's kidneys and thus leave her with "no potential kidney function" and with the "prospect of survival . . . because of her age, at best questionable." *Id.* at 388.

35. 289 A.2d at 391 (emphasis added).

36. For a draft of provisions of a child placement code that reflect the views expressed in this chapter, *see* J. Goldstein, A. Freud, & A. Solnit, Before the Best Interest of the Child, ch. 6 & app. II (1979).

CHAPTER TWENTY-SEVEN

Medical Care, Parental Autonomy, and Seriously Ill Newborns

Joel Frader, M.D.

BEGINNING IN APRIL 1982, a series of events led to unprecedented intervention by the federal government into medical practice in the United States. On the basis of concern about the treatment of a single child, "Baby Doe," with the genetic disorder Down's syndrome, the country saw a virtual cascade of proposed regulations; litigation opposing various federal actions; completed and signed Congressional legislation, the Child Abuse Amendments of 1984[1]; and the institution of a regulatory structure intended to limit parental and physician discretion involving medical decisions for seriously ill newborns.[2]

The most important innovation resulting from these developments is the creation of a new legal category of child abuse and neglect: "medical neglect."[3] The Child Abuse Prevention statute[4] now requires states that receive federal funds supporting child abuse prevention and treatment programs to have mechanisms for their child protective agencies "to pursue any legal remedies"[5] needed to "prevent the withholding of medically indicated treatment from disabled infants with life-threatening conditions."[6] Thus, physicians must "provid[e] treatment (including appropriate nutrition, hydration, and medication) which, in the treating physician's or physicians' reasonable medical judgment, will be most likely to be effective in ameliorating or correcting all such conditions."[7] Physicians need not provide these therapies if: (1) "the infant is chronically and irreversibly comatose";[8] (2) the "treatment would: (i) merely prolong dying, (ii) not be effective in ameliorating or correcting all of the infant's life-threatening conditions, or (iii) otherwise be futile in terms of the survival of the infant";[9] or (3) the treatment would be "virtually futile"[10] and "under the circumstances would be inhumane."[11]

Even when the three exceptions above apply, however, physicians must provide "appropriate nutrition, hydration, and medication."[12] The statute does not define any key terms, such as "appropriate," "futile," "virtually futile," or "inhumane." Neither does it discuss any role for parents—even to the extent of mentioning that physicians might want to follow standard legal practices concerning informed consent and shared decision making. It also places a heavy enforcement burden on states, including penalties for noncompliance. The latter involve denial of federal funds for state child abuse and neglect programs if the states do not create the required mechanisms for responding to complaints of suspected medical neglect.

This chapter critically examines the role of the state in medical decisions involving seriously ill newborns.[13] It concludes that proponents of government surveillance and regulation have not based their arguments on empirically or logically supported grounds, despite their political success.

A Definitional Note

Despite all the debate, legislation, and regulation, we still have no agreement on: (1) what constitutes a handicap for a newborn infant, and (2) which conditions establish a handicap that should trigger state action under the Baby Doe law and regulations. One problem seems to be that many antidiscrimination laws and regulations envisage a sharp separation between the physical condition (whether a simple feature, like skin color, or a major medical disorder) or personal characteristic of an individual, and the person's qualifications for a job, benefit, or service. For example, with Down's syndrome, historically the genetic disorder signaled mental retardation, which provided the "rationale" for allowing a life-threatening intestinal blockage to go untreated; the mental handicap could legitimately be said to have no relevance to the treatment of the condition. With respect to many seriously ill infants, however, we can provide no such simple "but for" description of the problem. In a great many cases, the set of medical problems includes several malformed or damaged body systems which affect one another, which may individually threaten life, and which individually and collectively interact in complex ways to influence the overall prognosis.

We should also note, in considering medical outcome or prognosis, the importance of rejecting attempts to measure medical success solely in terms of survival. Despite the unfortunate linkage of the phrase "quality of life" with notions of social worth, how patients experience their lives *does* count. Perhaps we need not worry about imposing life on individuals completely incapable of responding meaningfully to their environment, those called "irreversibly comatose" in the Baby Doe law[14]—they at least cannot in any sense themselves suffer. Most of us, however, will admit that for some sentient individuals life itself can become excessively burdensome. The difficulty in this discussion comes in judging which babies have so many troubles that they, along with their families, would be better served by forgoing life-sustaining therapy.

Empirical Issues

As noted by Joseph Goldstein[15] and Angela Holder,[16] individual states in the United States have for some time had the legal means to intervene on behalf of children when parents fail to seek or reject a child's "needed" medical care. The state of Indiana sought to use such authority in 1982 in the now famous Baby Doe case. Given government's longstanding interest in child welfare, and the concomitant legal means to support it, the question arises whether the prevalence or seriousness of alleged medical neglect of handicapped infants justifies expanding state authority, especially at the federal level. That is, can we reasonably say that there is empirical support for the proposition that infants whose lives could be saved or improved by medical intervention are not receiving treatment, and that this deficit warrants authorizing further state action?

We have no conclusive evidence. As John Lantos[17] and others[18] tell us, some reports suggested that at the start of the 1970s, pediatricians and surgeons fairly often agreed with parents to forgo life-saving surgery for infants with Down's syndrome and intestinal obstruction, or babies with spina bifida and hydrocephalus. But, as Arthur Caplan has noted, throughout that decade nontreatment practices "were rapidly changing from what they had been" based on advances in both medical and ethical understanding.[19] With respect to Down's syndrome, modern pediatrics and psychology had begun to show that given an appropriate loving and stimulating environment, most children with this disorder could have happy and fulfilling lives. The same phenomenon has occurred with spina bifida. While surgery to close openings in the coverings of the spinal cord still do not materially improve neurologic function, relatively recent surgical advances in the treatment of hydrocephalus have clearly reduced the incidence and severity of brain infections and resulted in substantial improvements in survival and quality of life. Therefore, there are sound reasons for believing that decisions to forgo treatment, like that which occurred in the Baby Doe case in 1982, are and were uncommon.[20]

Of course, not everyone views the situation the same way. The U.S. Commission on Civil Rights, in its report *Medical Discrimination against Children with Disabilities*, declared: "Available evidence suggests that decisions to withhold medically indicated treatment from infants born with disabilities continue to occur."[21] The report concluded that such decisions were not "isolated," though they acknowledged that "[a]ttempts to quantify denials of treatment, now or in the recent past, are subject to inherent limitations."[22] In a highly unusual move, the chairman of the Civil Rights Commission, William B. Allen, included a dissenting view with the report. He wrote that the final draft "did not contain any information whatever as to the rate of incidence of medical neglect of handicapped newborns. Nor did it include even raw numbers of the total births and deaths of severely afflicted infants in the United States."[23] He went on to say that no one could provide that important information. He "found this extraordinary, to say the least, and utterly unacceptable, to be candid."[24] In the end, the published report included a supplement with some statistical information about handicapped infants, but the data were insufficient to answer important questions about *prevent-*

able deaths, or deaths that, though technically preventable, would have resulted in children suffering from conditions excepted even by the 1984 Child Abuse and Neglect Amendments. Chairman Allen concluded that the report had both methodological and substantive problems indicating, overall, "that the interests of handicapped newborns have been sacrificed [in the report] to a political mission."[25]

It seems fair to conclude that there is no firm empirical basis for suspecting that handicapped infants frequently receive substandard or discriminatory medical treatment. Without some reason to believe that such children commonly suffer inadequate care, one must wonder about the justification for creating a federal program to "protect" them.

Before leaving this topic, we should note a growing concern about the opposite side of the nontreatment "coin" among social scientists,[26] ethicists,[27] and pediatricians, and most notably the neonatologists with the greatest investment in "advancing" the field of newborn care.[28] At least one account by parents calls attention to signs of abusive overtreatment, especially treatment extended to very small, very premature infants.[29] Epidemiologic studies and health care research continue to document the rising incidence of serious mental and physical impairment among survivors of neonatal intensive care,[30] with substantial burdens to the affected children and their families. All but the most zealous vitalists have noticed the awful irony, and possible cynicism, of the federal retreat from funding assistance programs for the handicapped just as new laws and regulations seek to dictate extremely expensive and marginally efficacious treatment.

In summary, an empirical analysis reveals that for part of our history some infants, especially those expected to have mental impairment, did not receive medical and surgical treatment that typically would have been extended to babies who were thought to be mentally normal. Almost no information exists, however, about the extent of such differential treatment and, as discussed, we have reason to believe that double standards of care were disappearing by the time of federal intervention in 1982. Finally, many of those most concerned about maltreatment of a few infants have virtually ignored the large-scale iatrogenic "production" of serious handicaps by modern neonatal intensive care. One has to wonder whether the attention to using the law to save "at-risk" babies from harm has been misdirected, both quantitatively and qualitatively.

Political Issues

One can hardly discuss the issue of state intervention in the treatment of handicapped infants without mentioning the role of politics. The reason for this is straightforward; a major issue in the treatment of babies with multiple health problems involves deciding how to allocate scarce medical resources. The United States faces a terrible political dilemma. The people, at least as reflected by the actions of their elected leadership over more than a decade, demand the impossible: complete medical treatment at little or no cost. Elected politicians have based their success on promises to reduce revenues generated through taxes. California's Proposition 13 and the Reagan tax cut in 1982 are obvious examples. These actions have clearly had their effect: dramatic reductions in governmental spending (especially at local and state levels) or, at a minimum, reductions in the rate of increase in spending with resultant real (noninflated) loss of spending power. Programs for inhome services for the handicapped have been cut, educational programs for those with special needs have suffered, and follow-up medical services no longer remain available to children and families once marginally getting by with what the "safety net" provided.

The peculiarities of our political heritage probably account for much of the popularity of actions designed to limit government's scope. The people of the United States have always had a healthy suspicion of the state, while holding individual initiative in high esteem. Many of us seem to favor the libertarian notion, clearly articulated with respect to medical care by H. Tristram Engelhardt and Michael Rie, that if we cannot provide something we want for ourselves, through our successful efforts, it may be unfortunate, but it is not necessarily unfair.[31] Our nation, however, seems to have trouble deciding when to judge the "little guy's" troubles as personal misfortunes not mandating our collective helping hand. We also have a tradition of rooting for the underdog, especially when we cannot easily hold the disadvantaged person responsible for his or her non-favored status.

Consequently, Americans find themselves caught in a very unpleasant situation. They want to minimize state interference in their lives, especially when the state action will require resources they believe should be reserved for their own discretionary use. But they also want to ensure that no one suffers simply because he or she differs from the majority, perhaps somehow remembering the persecution of outsiders (Pilgrims, Quakers, other religious minorities) that helped spur our national development. The result, in our recent political history, is contradictory and inconsistent government behavior. The movement to "get the government off the backs of the people" and limit state control over personal resources has reduced taxes and services. But at the same time, paradoxically, we have passed laws designed to protect the vulnerable, like the Baby Doe legislation, which have increased government intrusion into a realm widely regarded as personal and private, not to mention immensely complex. On the one hand we hear a movement to support "family values"; on the other hand we literally eliminate, in the Child Abuse Amendments of 1984, parents as decision-makers for critically ill infants. Our political vacillation is showing, and it seems to some quite an embarrassment.

Moral Issues

Given the lack of evidence of widespread neglect of handicapped infants, the growing concern about relatively common iatrogenic harm (some might say abuse) imposed by increased medical intervention, and the countervailing political currents regarding the appropriate role of the state in medical matters, is there a moral "common ground" regarding the government's place in the medical care of vulnerable children?

Goldstein provides an explication of the now dominant legal approach to state intrusion into medical decisions about children, namely that government can only require *"minimal* standards of child care," and must presume parents meet those standards in the absence of substantial evidence to the contrary.[32] In this view, as Goldstein says, "the state is too crude an instrument to become an adequate substitute for parents."[33] Even when those in the health care system (or others involved with specific children) suspect that parents have abandoned their obligations to a child, the state must act with great caution because of the importance and nature of family relationships and because "personal health care preferences" may reasonably vary widely.[34] Herein lies the crux of the matter: The Baby Doe law and regulations, or similar intrusions, assume we can readily recognize the "best interests" of particular children. In assuming, rather than analyzing critically, what "best interests" might mean, state intervention simply begs the important moral questions.

This chapter, of course, cannot establish the "proper" meaning of the best interests of incompetent children who are unable to express their own preferences. Once we set aside the metaethical question of whether the problem can be settled at all, the immediate issue becomes whether, given our politically and morally heterogeneous society, the state can justify extensive efforts to impose the particular view that all handicapped infants, with very narrow exceptions, have to receive *whatever* medical treatment might ameliorate or correct all their life-threatening conditions.

Three arguments suggest that comprehensive mandates such as the Baby Doe law constitute an improper approach to the problem of medical decisions that involve handicapped infants: (1) reasonable people disagree about what constitutes a life worth living; (2) enormous medical and technical uncertainty remains about the prognosis for many of the babies in question; and (3) families often have legitimate concerns besides the preservation of the life of a single child. We address each of these briefly, in turn.

Recent developments in law and bioethics concerning advance medical directives or so-called living wills, including federal laws that seek to protect the rights of patients,[35] make clear that neither doctors nor society at large have a singular solution regarding the bounds of treatment patients should accept or reject. We seem to have reached a consensus that various considerations, including the patient's religious beliefs, preferences about the use of his or her estate, attitudes toward mechanical devices used in modern medical technology, and so forth, may all legitimately contribute to the decision whether the patient will or will not receive life-sustaining treatment. Of course, with respect to the Baby Doe law, we must decide for infants who have not yet had the opportunity to reflect on and decide their preferences regarding medical care. Nevertheless, the general movement toward a patient- rather than physician-centered basis for medical decisions recognizes that we have few shared values that declare what constitutes, as Goldstein puts it, a *"life worth living."*[36]

Certainly, we believe we can make such judgments regarding children at some times. We often feel justified in seeking court-ordered treatment for relatively simple and low-risk therapy opposed by parents on religious or similar grounds. We sanction court-supervised blood transfusions of children of Jehovah's Witnesses, or medical interventions for ill children of Christian Scientists or others who refuse treatment for children for religious reasons.[37] But these examples highlight the second ethical problem with the Baby Doe treatment requirements. Blood products and appendectomies constitute relatively low-risk interventions with high degrees of certainty regarding outcome. We can hardly make this claim regarding, for example, a child with multiple congenital anomalies involving damage to many organ systems where treatment requires weeks, months, or years of hospitalization, repeated surgeries, and the often uncomfortable side effects of medical therapies. Not only do these interventions impose burdens some persons might reasonably choose to forgo, but much of the time the physicians cannot accurately predict the likelihood of success (even if defined solely in terms of survival) of the required course. When we look for guidance regarding the outcome of medical and surgical treatments, especially for rare conditions or therapies used on very small premature infants, the search often is futile. Courts considering this problem for young children other than newborns have recognized increased parental discretion under conditions of moderate medical risk and likely pain and suffering associated with the recommended treatment.[38]

Finally, radical child "advocacy," such as that seen in the Baby Doe law, assumes that the child's best interests should automatically trump the interests of other concerned parties. Along with other ethicists, I have begun to raise serious doubts about the cogency of this view.[39] Parents often have multiple responsibilities that involve other children, dependent elderly family members, and legitimate plans and projects for themselves and their loved ones. It is not obvious, for example, that a household with several children, a retired and frail grandparent, and two parents employed in at least one job each must sacrifice an income so one parent can remain at home full-time to care for a newly born child who is unlikely ever to interact with the environment beyond the level of a two-month-old, but who may well live for many, many years. Such a child, even if someone were to certify him or her "chronically and irreversibly comatose," would have to receive fluids and nutrition that could sustain life more or less indefinitely under the Baby Doe provisions. Do "family values" really mean imposing such a situation on one another?

Among bioethicists, then, something surprisingly like a consensus seems to have emerged: The greater the uncertainty of the medical outcome, especially insofar as treatment will allow the child to have "a reasonable potential for minimal personal capacities,"[40] and the higher the costs and risks of the treatment, the less physicians or the state have a legitimate claim to impose unwanted medical treatment.[41]

Conclusion

No clear need exists for a system of state intervention designed specifically for handicapped infants, and, as a nation, we have serious moral qualms about such a system. Our society does not agree on what constitutes a life worth living, we have a long tradition of permitting personal or family autonomy in such discretionary matters, and the kinds of medical treatments involved in these cases are full of uncertainty, risk, and burden. Finally, blind adherence to the purported needs of the handicapped child alone may well seriously harm other important values and interests within the child's own family, not to mention the economic and moral costs to the medical care system and society at large. Federal intervention on behalf of handicapped infants seems to have been an extremely misguided effort.

NOTES

1. *See* Child Abuse Amendments of 1984, Pub. L. No. 98-457, 98 Stat. 1749 (1984).
2. *See* Child Abuse and Neglect Prevention and Treatment Program, 45 C.F.R. § 1340.15 and Appendix (1992).
3. 42 U.S.C.A. § 5106a(b)(10) (Supp. 1992).
4. *See* 42 U.S.C.A. §§ 5101–5118 (Supp. 1992).
5. 42 U.S.C. § 5106a(b)(10)(C) (Supp. 1992).
6. *Id.*
7. 42 U.S.C.A. § 5106g(10) (Supp. 1992).
8. 42 U.S.C.A. § 5106g(10)(A) (Supp. 1992).
9. 42 U.S.C.A. § 5106g(10)(B) (Supp. 1992).
10. 42 U.S.C.A. § 5106g(10)(C) (Supp. 1992).
11. *Id.*
12. 42 U.S.C.A. § 5106g(10) (Supp. 1992).
13. For historical analysis of the 1982 "Baby Doe" case, and discussion of subsequent legal interventions, see generally Caplan, Hard Cases Make Bad Law: The Legacy of the Baby Doe Controversy, in Compelled Compassion: Government Intervention in the Treatment of Critically Ill Newborns 105, 107 (A. Caplan et al. eds., 1992); Frader, Forgoing Life-Sustaining Food and Water: Newborns, in By No Extraordinary Means: The Choice to Forgo Life-Sustaining Food and Water 180, 181 (J. Lynn ed., 1986); Frader, Selecting Neonatal Ethics, 20 Soc. Sci. Med. 1085, 1087 (1985); Lantos, Baby Doe Five Years Later: Implications for Child Health, 317 New Eng. J. Med. 444, 444–47 (1987); Shapiro & Frader, Critically Ill Infants, in Medico-Legal Aspects of Critical Care 61, 76–81 (K. Benesch et al. eds., 1986); Stevenson et al., The "Baby Doe" Rule, 255 JAMA 1909, 1909–1912 (1986); Frader, review of A. Kaplan et al., Compelled Compassion: Government Intervention in the Treatment of Critically Ill Newborns (1992), 327 New Eng. J. Med. 824, 824 (1992).
14. *See* 42 U.S.C.A. § 5106g(10)(A) (Supp. 1992).

15. *See* Goldstein, Medical Care for the Child at Risk: On State Supervention of Parental Autonomy, 86 Yale L.J. 645, 645–70 (1977), Chapter 26 in this volume.

16. *See* Holder, Parents, Courts, and Refusal of Treatment, 103 J. Pediatrics 515, 515–21 (1983).

17. *See* Lantos, Baby Doe Five Years Later, *supra* note 13, at 144.

18. *See* Todres et al., Life-Saving Therapy for Newborns: A Questionnaire Survey in the State of Massachusetts, 81 Pediatrics 643, 645–46 (1988); Todres et al., Pediatricians' Attitudes Affecting Decision-Making in Defective Newborns, 60 Pediatrics 197, 199–201 (1977).

19. *See* Caplan, Hard Cases Make Bad Law, *supra* note 13, at 111.

20. This was true even as the federal regulations and law were being put into place in 1982. During the initial phase of federal activism, the Department of Health and Human Services (HHS) established a telephone hotline for the reporting of suspected medical neglect of handicapped infants. One participant in the investigations that resulted from these reports reflected on his experience and concluded that in only one of nineteen cases he reviewed had treatment been "questionable." *See* Green, Caring and Communicating: Observations on 19 Baby Doe Patients, 139 Am. J. Diseases Children 1082, 1083 (1985). The case involved a very premature infant, born physiologically depressed, whose survival seemed, even to the reviewer, highly unlikely. That author's main criticism focused on the fact that the physician "did not take an active part in the care and clinical decision-making during [the] few terminal hours." *Id.* More to the point, perhaps, is the fact that although more than six hundred Baby Doe cases were investigated, in some fashion, by HHS, the government found no violations of rules barring discrimination against the handicapped. *See* Bucciarelli & Eitzman, Baby Doe: Where We Stand Now, 5 Contemp. Pediatrics 116, 121 (1988). Some of the onsite investigations, on the other hand, at least hindered efficient and efficacious treatment of the babies in question and others in the medical and nursing units providing their care. *See* Strain, The American Academy of Pediatrics Comments on the "Baby Doe II" Regulations, 309 New Eng. J. Med. 443, 443–44 (1983).

21. U.S. Commission on Civil Rights, Medical Discrimination against Children with Disabilities iii (1989).

22. *Id.* at 3.

23. *Id.* at 154.

24. *Id.* at 157.

25. *Id.* at 155.

26. *See* F. Frohock, Special Care: Medical Decisions at the Beginning of Life vii–viii (1986); J. Guillemin & L. Holmstrom, Mixed Blessings: Intensive Care for Newborns 7–8 (1986).

27. *See generally* Moskop & Saldanha, The Baby Doe Rule: Still a Threat, Hastings Center Rep., Apr., 1986, at 8, 9; T. Murray, "Suffer the Little Children . . .," in Which Babies Shall Live? 72–73 (T. Murray & A. Caplan eds., 1985); Rhoden & Arras, Withholding Treatment from Baby Doe: From Discrimination to Child Abuse, 63 Milbank Memorial Fund Q. 18, 36 (1985); Strong, The Neonatologist's Duty to Patient and Parents, Hastings Center Rep., Aug. 1984, at 10, 14.

28. *See generally* A. Campbell, Baby Doe and Forgoing Life-Sustaining Treatment: Compassion, Discrimination, or Medical Neglect? in Caplan et al., Compelled

Compassion, *supra* note 13, at 216; Kopelman et al., Neonatologists, Pediatricians, and the Supreme Court Criticize the "Baby Doe" Regulations, in *id.*, at 243–47; William Silverman, Overtreatment? special presentation, Clinical Bioethics Section, Annual Meeting of the American Pediatric Society and the Society for Pediatric Research, Baltimore, Md., May 4, 1992; Stahlman, Implications of Research and High Technology for Neonatal Intensive Care, 261 JAMA 1791, 1791 (1989).

29. *See, e.g.,* Stinson & Stinson, On the Death of a Baby, 244 Atlantic Monthly 64–72 (1979).

30. *See* Blank, Rationing Medicine in the Neonatal Intensive Care Unit (NICU), in Caplan et al., Compelled Compassion; *supra* note 13, at 168–69; Paneth & Stark, Cerebral Palsy and Mental Retardation in Relation to Indicators of Perinatal Asphyxia: An Epidemiologic Overview, 147 Am. J. Obstetrics & Gynecology 960, 965 (1983).

31. *See* Engelhardt & Rie, Intensive Care Units, Scarce Resources, and Conflicting Principles of Justice, 255 JAMA 1159, 1159 (1986).

32. *See* Chapter 26 in this volume (emphasis in original).

33. *Id.*

34. *Id.*

35. *See* Omnibus Budget Reconciliation Act of 1990, Pub. L. No. 101–508, § 4206, 104 Stat. 1388-115, 1388-115–17 (1990).

36. *See* Chapter 26 in this volume (emphasis in original).

37. *See, e.g.,* Jehovah's Witnesses v. King County Hosp. Unit No. 2, 278 F. Supp. 488 (W.D. Wash. 1967), *aff'd,* 390 U.S. 598 (1968); People *ex. rel.* Wallace v. Labrenz, 104 N.E.2d 769 (Ill. 1952), *cert. denied,* 344 U.S. 824 (1952); John F. Kennedy Memorial Hosp. v. Heston, 279 A.2d 670 (N.J. 1971).

38. *See, e.g.,* Newmark v. Williams, 588 A.2d 1108 (Del. 1991); In re Hofbauer, 393 N.E.2d 1009 (N.Y. 1979).

39. *See* Frader, Ethics in Pediatric Intensive Care, in Pediatric Critical Care 7–15 (B. Fuhrman & J. Zimmerman eds., 1992); Hardwig, What about the Family?, Hastings Center Rep., Mar./Apr. 1990, at 5–10; Strong, The Neonatologist's Duty, *supra* note 27, at 10–16.

40. *See* Walters, Approaches to Ethical Decision-Making in the Neonatal Intensive Care Unit, 142 Am. J. Diseases Children 825, 825 (1988).

41. *See id.* at 829; Strong, The Neonatologist's Duty, *supra* note 27, at 15; R. Weir, Selective Nontreatment of Handicapped Children 268–69 (1989).

CHAPTER TWENTY-EIGHT

"If I Can Say Yes, Why Can't I Say No?" Adolescents at Risk and the Right to Give or Withhold Consent to Health Care

Jan C. Costello

A MOTHER BRINGS her tearful daughter, sixteen, to the county rape crisis center. "She's been sexually molested. I want her examined. I know who's responsible, and I want the police called and charges filed against him." The daughter, alone with the doctor, says, "My mother walked in on me having sex with my boyfriend, who's seventeen. She's just trying to make trouble for us. I don't want you to examine me."

A fifteen-year-old boy goes to the family doctor's office for a routine examination he needs to qualify him for a part-time job. He complies with all the doctor's instructions, including requests for blood and urine samples, "to make sure you don't have diabetes." He does not know that his father, who called to make the appointment, has instructed the doctor, "When you have him there, take blood and urine samples—let me know if he's using drugs."

Anorexic and depressed, a twelve-year-old girl is admitted to the eating disorders program of a private hospital. Both she and her parents sign the application for her voluntary admission. A week later, after a family therapy session during which the girl expresses hostility toward her father, the father informs the hospital that he is taking his daughter home immediately. The girl protests, "But I want to stay here—I think it's helping me."

Twenty-five years ago, the outcome in all three cases would have been simple: The child, as a minor, is incompetent; the parent alone can give or withhold consent to health care. This sweeping principle, however, is no longer good law. State statutes granting adolescents limited or general powers to consent to health care and an increasing body of case law recognize the actual capacity of "mature

490

minors" to give such consent.[1] Moreover, courts—including the U.S. Supreme Court—have found both that the constitutional rights of liberty and privacy embrace a right to give or withhold consent to medical procedures, and that minors have such constitutional rights.[2] Developments in tort, contract, and constitutional law thus have changed dramatically the principle of consent from a time when even an older minor's incapacity was absolute.

Increasingly, the consent powers of parents and older minors overlap, leading to confusion for adolescents, parents, and health care providers. In each scenario described above, a state statute gave the child an independent right to give legally valid consent to certain health care procedures. Yet the statutes did not explicitly take away the parent's right to consent, on behalf of the same child, to the same procedures. In each situation, both parent and child are capable of giving legally valid consent to examination or treatment of the child.

If both parent and child can say yes, can the child say no—and have that refusal honored?

If both parent and child can say yes, can the child's yes outweigh the parent's no?

Is there a way to recognize the adolescent's actual capacity for decision making while preserving the parent's traditional role as the protector of the child's interests?[3]

This chapter explores these questions. It first considers the significance of three typical state laws: Do they give only a right to say "yes" (a right to "assent"), or a right also to refuse health care? Next, the chapter briefly summarizes "mature minor" case law, which has established that older adolescents have a right to refuse as well as consent to health care. Finally, the chapter draws on federal constitutional law for the idea that a competent minor has a constitutional right to make her or his own health care decisions, and that the state must at a minimum provide a mechanism for such a minor to demonstrate competency.

To resolve the current confusion of the law, this chapter recommends a presumption that an adolescent (age twelve and up) is competent to give or withhold consent to ordinary (nonexperimental, non-high-risk) health care procedures. Where an adolescent refuses such a procedure and the parent wishes to have it performed, the chapter recommends that there be a judicial determination of the adolescent's competency. If the adolescent is competent, her or his decision is final. If the adolescent is not competent, the parent may make a decision in the minor's best interest. In a situation involving an experimental, high-risk procedure, the parent's consent may still be necessary, but not sufficient; a competent minor's informed consent is also required.

The Role of Consent

At common law, a minor could not make a valid contract with a health care provider and could not give valid consent to treatment. These common law principles have become part of the civil code of virtually all states. Thus, a health care professional who treats a minor without parental consent faces two potential problems: inability to enforce the contract and receive payment for services, and liability in tort for battery.

There are two common exceptions to the principle of minor incompetency to make a contract: where the services contracted for are "necessaries"[4] and where the minor is authorized to consent by a state law. Exceptions to the requirement of parental consent in tort law include emergencies and emancipation.

This chapter is chiefly concerned with situations where state law authorizes the minor's consent. Such authorization typically is derived from statutes, although it may also rely upon the emerging body of case law finding valid consent by "mature" minors even in the absence of a statute.

State statutes intended to benefit children "at risk"[5] specifically authorize minors to consent to certain types of health care. These commonly include: examination of victims of sexual assault; pregnancy testing and prenatal care; treatment of sexually transmitted diseases; outpatient mental health care; and treatment for chemical dependency or alcohol abuse.[6] Legislatures hope that giving minors an independent ability to consent will enable them to be treated despite parental unavailability or outright refusal of care.

Obviously, a related issue is whether the parent even knows about the condition for which the minor is seeking treatment. Such statutes vary in whether they permit or require notice to the parents; some provide for an exception to parental notice where there is reason to believe the parent is abusive or where giving notice would be inappropriate.[7]

These statutes provide the basis for a defense by the health care provider of legally valid consent, should the parent or child bring a later tort claim. The contracts for services rendered under a statutory provision may not be disaffirmed; thus the health care provider may seek payments—but from whom? In some cases the statute provides that a parent is not liable for health care services to which the minor alone has given valid consent. But arguably, in the absence of such a disclaimer, parents may be liable for health care to which the minor has consented and which falls under "necessaries." In my experience, most health care providers treating minors under these statutes are publicly funded—and thus less worried about billing the parents than about being sued in tort.[8]

Three Typical Statutes Affecting Right to Consent

Statutes giving minors a right to consent to health care are usually of three types. The first permits a minor of *any* age to give valid consent to a specific type of health care—for example, to examination and treatment for venereal disease.[9] The second gives minors above a designated age general power to consent to a broad range of health care.[10] The third type is a combination, permitting minors above a designated age to consent only to a specific type of procedure.[11]

What difference would each type of statute make in the three cases above?

In Case 1 the minor, aged sixteen, refuses a gynecological examination for the purpose of determining whether she had been sexually molested. Before considering whether she can refuse such an examination, we must first determine whether she could consent to it—if she had come alone to the rape crisis center and alleged that she *had* been raped. Assume that she lives in a jurisdiction that uses the first type of statute: authorizing consent by any alleged victim of rape or sexual assault, regardless of age.[12]

Can the rape crisis center refuse to examine the minor? Or, rather, should the center honor the minor's refusal to be examined? I believe that the parent's presence on the scene and ability to consent to examination of the minor does not negate the minor's independent ability to give consent. The statute does not condition exercise of the minor's right on the unavailability of the parent. Moreover, if the parent were present but refused the examination, the rape crisis center physician could clearly have proceeded with the examination based solely on the minor's consent.

But does the independent right to give consent always imply an equivalent right to refuse?[13] Where the statute gives all minors the right to give consent, but does not specify an age limit, did the legislature really determine that these minors are competent, or is this just a legal fiction letting actually incompetent minors give "legally valid consent" to protect the health care provider from tort liability? At least two commentators has taken this position,[14] and in my experience this is often the opinion of health care professionals: that these statutes give a minor, even an adolescent, a right to say yes, but not to say no.

I would advise the rape crisis center director that the sixteen-year-old girl has a right to refuse the examination, but I could not base my opinion primarily on the non-age-specific statute. Rather, I would look for other laws of the same state that do specify an age of minimum consent for health treatment (chemical dependency, sexually transmitted diseases), to see if they state one well below sixteen. If the legislature in numerous other instances has recognized the actual capacity of older minors to give informed consent, this would support a right to refuse, not merely to "assent," for this sixteen-year-old. But this is a difficult argument to make given only a non-age-specific statute. After all, the physician may argue, since the legislature in other instances did give a specific age, perhaps here the omission indicates an intent only to allow "assent,"[15] but not refusal.

Case 2 presents a stronger case for a right to refuse as well as to consent, if we assume that the relevant statute gives minors above a specified age a general power to consent to ordinary medical and dental procedures.[16] The fifteen-year-old is above the specified age of consent, and the proposed procedures qualify as ordinary health care, so the statute applies.

Therefore, I advised the doctor that he must obtain the minor's informed consent to take the blood and urine samples, and to have them tested for drugs and alcohol abuse.

Although his father made the doctor's appointment for him and "instructed" the doctor, the fifteen-year-old could consent to have the tests done elsewhere—

for example, at a publicly funded drug rehabilitation center.[17] Thus he is competent to refuse to have them done by this doctor.

Can the doctor obtain blood and urine based on the minor's consent to test for diabetes, and then test for drugs? No—for informed consent to be valid, the patient must be told accurately what tests are proposed and for what purpose.[18] The information that the blood and urine will be used for drug testing is "material" to the informed consent; without this information, the minor's consent is not valid. Moreover, I believe that informed consent would require the doctor to tell the fifteen-year-old that she intends to communicate the test results to his parents. Assume that the doctor has a statutory discretion—or obligation—to inform the parent.[19] That is information "material" to the minor's decision; a reasonable patient in the minor's circumstances would wish to know it before giving consent.

Case 3, that of the anorexic and depressed twelve-year-old girl, is harder because she wishes to consent to treatment as a hospital inpatient. A statute granting minors a right to consent may exempt or not refer to inpatient treatment.[20] This may be for two practical reasons: First, it is very difficult for a minor who lives with a parent to receive inpatient hospital care without the parent's learning of it; second, inhospital procedures are likely to be more expensive, so that the hospital will insist on parental consent in order to establish financial liability.

The fact that the hospital asked both her and her parent to sign the consent form is probably irrelevant in the absence of a statutory exception on point. If her consent to continued inpatient treatment cannot be based on a statute, and she does not otherwise qualify as a "mature minor" (unlikely because she is only twelve), the hospital must discharge her if her father requests it. (This assumes that there is no other intervening health emergency. If her anorexia were so serious as to be life-threatening, the emergency exception could apply. Also in that case the father's refusal of continued treatment might trigger dependency court jurisdiction over her as a neglected child.)[21]

However, assuming that her anorexia is in the early stages and her life is not in danger, her only option is to find some kind of outpatient treatment to which she can give valid consent. Assume that her jurisdiction does permit consent to outpatient treatment for mental illness for minors age twelve and older,[22] although it does not specifically permit outpatient treatment for eating disorders. The minor's depression could qualify as a mental illness permitting treatment under the statute. What if the statute permitted treatment only of minors thirteen and older? The hospital might try to justify outpatient treatment of her even at age twelve, arguing that her statement that she believes counseling is helping her may be evidence of sufficient intelligence and maturity to give true valid consent. Thus, if the hospital is concerned about the minor's well-being, it may treat her without charge as an outpatient or refer her to a publicly funded outpatient program.

Can the outpatient treatment take place without the knowledge of her parents? Notice may not be an issue here, since the father is already aware of the daughter's desire for treatment. But what if the father is so threatened by his daughter's desire to continue in therapy that the hospital fears he will prevent her from following up on outpatient referral? In that case the treating professional can exercise discretion not to inform the father that a referral has been made, or that the daughter is participating in outpatient therapy.

Statutory Purpose: Access to Services or Minors' Autonomy?

Using the statutory framework, in each case I have tried to carve out a zone of competency within which the minor's decision can be respected as legally valid. But is this a misreading of the statutes?

In reading a right to consent as implying necessarily a concomittant right to refuse, I am simply applying basic tort law. Certainly for a legally competent adult there is no question of the correlation between the right to say yes and the right to say no.[23] But given minors' traditional incompetency, can we assume the same correlation, especially since in other areas[24] minors' rights have not always translated into identical treatment with adults?

I believe that these treatment statutes, at least those which specify an age of consent for minors, do not so much confer a right to consent as recognize that the right exists. As I shall argue later, a state that fails to permit consent by mature minors may violate their constitutional rights. The statutes simply codify a reality about the actual capacity of adolescents to make health care decisions.

Older Minors' Capacity for Informed Consent

Legally valid consent, whether given by parent or minor, must by definition be "informed" consent.[25] One way of assessing whether a minor is actually capable of giving or withholding consent is to review the tasks involved in informed consent. To give "knowing" consent, an individual must possess the cognitive ability to understand the information given about the proposed treatment: the nature of the procedure; the desired consequences; possible side-effects and their likelihood; and other alternatives. For consent also to be "voluntary," there must be an absence of coercion. Yet in addition to intellectually grasping the information provided, the individual must be able to process that information, to apply feelings, desires, needs, and values to reach a conclusion about whether to give or withhold consent.

Research in the area of minors' competency has consistently shown that children, especially adolescents, are remarkably similar to adults in both the choices they make and their decision-making process.[26] Minors fifteen years old and older make decisions regarding waiver of rights or consent to medical treatment in generally the same way that adults do. Children as young as nine or ten in some situations will choose outcomes congruent with adults', although their reasoning process differs more from that of adults.[27] Despite a stereotype of rebellious teenagers refusing to listen to their parents, research shows that adolescents, as opposed to young adults, are significantly more apt to be influenced by parental desires in making health care decisions.[28]

These research results lend support to the long-established "mature minor" rule. This rule is derived from decisions in which, even in the absence of parental consent, courts upheld as valid minors' consent to health care. Commentators have identified the common fact patterns of these "mature minor" cases: (1) The minor was near the age of majority (fifteen or older); (2) the treatment was less than "major" or "serious"; and (3) the treatment was for the minor's benefit rather than for that of a third party (as in cases of tissue or organ donation).[29] Courts have found "mature minors" capable of valid consent to a range of "nonmajor" medical procedures, including minor surgery on an injured finger and plastic surgery.[30] Administrative agency guidelines for research involving children refer to the "mature minor" criteria.[31]

As with the statutory exceptions, a "mature minor" principle under which a minor may give valid consent includes a right to withhold such consent. A state supreme court upheld a seventeen-year-old Jehovah's Witness's refusal of a blood transfusion.[32] The minor's doctor had found that she was a mature minor who understood the consequences of her decision; therefore, the court ruled, the state had no *parens patriae* authority to intervene. In another case, a state court of appeals found state intervention unwarranted, respecting a fourteen-year-old boy's objections to surgery to correct his cleft palate.[33] In both cases, the minor's decision was not at odds with the parent's; however, the courts made a point of ascertaining the minor's wishes and referred to them as an important factor in denying the state's petition to order the medical procedure.

The "mature minor" cases involve situations where parental consent is not required because of the de facto competency of the minor. A different line of cases involving tissue or organ donation by a minor indicates that parental consent, though necessary, may not be sufficient to authorize some kinds of medical procedures.[34] If the proposed procedure is not for the minor's benefit and is life-threatening or high-risk, the adequacy of the parent's consent is questionable.[35] Courts approving donations by minors have emphasized the child's consent as an important factor. One commentator believes that the same courts would have respected a minor's refusal to be a donor as conclusive.[36] Thus the "mature minor" cases support the conclusion that de facto competent minors can give or withhold consent to "nonmajor" treatment for their own benefit—and that parental consent for "major" treatment, even where necessary, is not sufficient to override a competent minor's refusal.

Does the minor have a right to prove her or his competency in fact?

Constitutional Right to Privacy

Perhaps the most significant source of minors' increasing power to give or withhold consent has been case law recognizing their constitutional rights of liberty and privacy. The U.S. Supreme Court has held that minors possess such rights and that they encompass the right to make decisions concerning the use of contraception and abortion. In *Hodgson v. Minnesota*,[37] the Court stated that "the right to make this decision 'do[es] not mature and come into being magically only when one attains the state-defined age of majority.' "[38] The Court in an earlier case[39] had held that the state may not require in all cases parental *consent* to abortion. While a state interest in protecting *immature* minors will sustain a requirement of either parental or judicial consent, the state must provide an alternative procedure whereby a pregnant minor may demonstrate that she is sufficiently mature to make the abortion decision herself or that, despite her immaturity, an abortion would be in her best interests.[40] Moreover, a state may not make a blanket decision that *all* minors under the age of fifteen are too immature to make this decision.[41]

While the Supreme Court has upheld parental *notice* requirements in the abortion context,[42] it has done so only where the state provides a "judicial bypass" procedure by which the mature minor may demonstrate to the satisfaction of the court that she is capable of exercising her constitutional right to choose an abortion.[43] Even while acknowledging the state's interest in encouraging pregnant minors to consult their parents,[44] the Court has consistently recognized that this interest cannot unduly burden the mature minor as she exercises her right to make this health care decision. The state has a legitimate interest in protecting immature (and presumptively incompetent) minors; once a minor's competency is determined, however, she presumably has the same right as an adult to decide for or against an abortion.

The right of a mature minor to consent to abortion, of course, implies a right to refuse an abortion. In one case a pregnant minor's decision, despite parental pressure, not to have an abortion was upheld by the court.[45] In some cases state constitutions have been found to offer independent protection of minors' right to choose or refuse abortion.[46]

The right of privacy is much broader than simply the right to consent to or refuse abortion, of course. Even if the right to abortion is restricted—by constitutional amendment or a later Supreme Court decision—the minors' constitutional right of privacy may still have great importance for other health care decisions.[47] Indeed, even if the treatment statutes did not create specific exceptions to incompetency, decisions related to the minors' liberty and privacy rights strongly suggest that a state could not require parental consent for all health care treatment of minors, regardless of the minors' maturity.

Proposed Resolution

How do these statutes—and these issues—fit in with the sign in a local shopping mall: "Ear piercing. You must be over 18 or have parental consent?" Most people seeing a mother carrying an infant with pierced ears would not question whether the parent has a right to make this decision for the baby. But what if the mother wants her seventeen-year-old's ears pierced and the minor says no? Should the ear-piercer be able to hold the seventeen-year-old down (calling for reinforcements if necessary) and pierce the holes, because the parent said, "Do it"? I think most lay people would instinctively say no, that there is a difference between an infant and an adolescent. Because the adolescent has greater actual capacity to understand and make decisions, a more developed sense of autonomy, the older child's "no" should outweigh the mother's "yes."

By the same reasoning, the rape crisis center should respect the "no" of the sixteen-year-old who says she was not raped, and refuses an examination. If the fifteen-year-old boy says he does not want to have his blood and urine tested for drug use, his refusal should be honored, too, because his autonomy outweighs his father's desire for information—at least on the facts given. But what if the boy has a diagnosed chemical abuse problem, and the parent has strong reasons for wanting the information? I believe that the mature minor is still competent to refuse; she or he cannot be "treated" involuntarily unless the parent can successfully obtain the authority of the state to impose the procedure.[48] If it is argued that even a mature minor's refusal should not be honored because there is a demonstrated need for treatment—that the welfare of the child is the paramount concern—does that mean that the anorexic, depressed girl should be able to continue inpatient treatment over parental objections, and at parental expense?

Before the expansion of mature minors' rights, the working rule was "the parent's decision always controls, unless it will kill or severely damage the minor." In light of the "mature minor" rule, the specific treatment statutes, and the minors' constitutional right of privacy, I believe there should be a different principle: From age twelve on, there should be a presumption of competency to make treatment decisions, at least in situations meeting the "mature minor" criteria of non-major health care intended to benefit the minor. In most such cases, therefore, the minor's "yes" or "no" should be dispositive. In situations involving high-risk, experimental, or life-threatening procedures, the state could require informed consent from a parent as well as from the minor. However, precisely because of the importance of the decision involved,[49] the parental consent in such cases may be required but not sufficient—the procedure cannot be performed if a competent minor refuses it. Where there is such a conflict of decision-makers, there should be a judicial determination of the competency of the minor. If the minor is competent, her or his refusal must be honored. If the minor is incompetent, the parent may make the decision in the minor's "best interests."

The treatment statutes, "mature minor" rule, and constitutional law cases acknowledge that there are "competent" mature minors. In the contexts discussed here, such minors' health care decisions must be respected, whether they decide to say yes or no.

NOTES

Acknowledgments: Thanks are due to Michael L. Perlin, Deborah L. Rhode, and Richard A. Rothschild for comments on an earlier version of this chapter.
1. *See infra* notes 5–11 and accompanying text.

2. *See infra* notes 37–47 and accompanying text.

3. *See infra* notes 25–28 and accompanying text.

4. "Necessaries" include food, clothing, shelter, and medical care. *See* M. Soler et al., Representing the Child Client 3.03[1][b](1991).

5. For the purposes of this chapter, "at risk" means the children have a condition that will endanger their health or life unless they are given appropriate health care treatment. An example of such a condition acknowledged by all states is sexually transmitted disease. *See* A. Holder, Legal Issues in Pediatric and Adolescent Medicine 130 (2d ed. 1985).

6. *See* Soler, Representing the Child Client, *supra* note 4, at 3.03[1][c][ii].

7. *See, e.g.,* Cal. Civ. Code § 25.9 (1990); Md. Gen. Code Ann. § 20-103(c)(1990).

8. Private health care providers, because they are used to billing parents or to treating children under family health insurance plans, are often unfamiliar with the statutes permitting consent by older minors. Minors living separately from their parents may be more likely to seek out publicly funded health care providers, such as birth control clinics that have a contract with the state.

9. *See, e.g.,* Ala. Code § 22-8-6 (1990) (venereal disease, pregnancy, drug addiction); Cal. Civ. Code § 34.9 (victim of sexual abuse).

10. *See* Ala. Code § 22-8-4 (1990) (fourteen and older general consent to medical, dental, and mental health care); Cal. Civ. Code § 34.6 (1990) (fifteen and older general consent to medical and dental care).

11. *See* Ala. Code § 22-8-9 (1990) (minors fourteen and older may consent to bone marrow donation); Cal. Civ. Code § 34.8 (1990) (minor twelve years or older, who is alleged to have been raped, may consent to medical care and treatment "related to the diagnosis or treatment of such condition, and the collection of medical evidence with regard thereto"); Md. Gen. Ann. Code § 20-104 (1990) (minors sixteen and older may consent to mental health treatment).

12. Cal. Civ. Code § 34.9 (1990) permits a minor of any age "who is alleged to have been sexually assaulted" to give consent to diagnosis, treatment, and collection of medical evidence. Possibly because there is no age limit, the sexual assault statute requires the health care provider to attempt to contact parents—unless the provider "reasonably believes that the parent, parents or guardian of the minor committed the sexual assault on the minor."

13. "In any case where a child can be treated at his own request and without the consent of his parent, under a minor treatment statute or otherwise, it is quite probable that the same child has the right to refuse treatment, at least if the condition is not life-threatening. The two concepts appear to be interlocked: a child who has the right to consent has an equal right to refuse to consent." Holder, Legal Issues, *supra* note 5, at 141.

See also Soler, Representing the Child Client, *supra* note 4, at 3.02[1][iv] ("Where minors have the right to consent to treatment, particularly reproductive health care, minors probably have the correspondent right to refuse treatment").

14. G. Koocher & P. Keith-Spiegel, Children, Ethics & the Law 108 (1990) ("[G]ranting authority to minors to consent to treatment is often intended to protect either the state or the minor who would not otherwise be able to obtain treatment, not to promote the autonomy of minors").

15. In the context of research involving minors, "[c]onsent, a legal concept implying full competence to make a binding decision that affects oneself and in most circumstances reserved for those who have reached the age of majority, cannot be appropriately delegated to others. Thus, currently it is *permission* that is sought from parents or guardians. The affirmative agreement, termed *assent*, is to be obtained (with exceptions), from the children themselves." Koocher & Keith-Spiegel, Children, Ethics & the Law, *supra* note 14, at 105.

Professor Winnick argues that a lower standard of competency should be required for assent than for refusal of treatment, at least in situations where no coercion is involved. Winnick, Competency to Consent to Treatment: The Distinction between Assent and Objection, 28 Hous. L. Rev. 15, 21 (1991).

16. *See, e.g.,* Alaska Stat. § 09.65.100(1) (1991); Cal. Civ. Code § 34.6 provides: A "minor 15 years of age or older who is living separate and apart from his parents or legal guardian, whether with or without the consent of a parent or guardian and regardless of the duration of such separate residence, and who is managing his own financial affairs, regardless of the source of his income, may give consent to" medical or dental care. The physician may, with or without the consent of the minor, advise the parent of the treatment given or needed. *See* Carter v. Cangello, 105 Cal. App. 3d 348, 351 (1980) (seventeen-year-old could consent to medical care under statute, even though still receiving some financial support from parents).

Not all state legislatures distinguish between minors who are living with their parents but who seek health care independently, and children who, although not formally emancipated, are on their own. *See* Miss. Code Ann. § 41-41-3(h)(1981).

17. Cal. Civ. Code § 34.10 (1990).

18. Battery arises when a patient has consented to one particular treatment and another is performed. *See, e.g.,* Bang v. Charles T. Miller Hosp., 88 N.W.2d 186 (Minn. 1958) (plaintiff consented to a prostate resection but was not informed that his sperm ducts would be tied off); Corn v. French, 289 P.2d 173 (Nev. 1955) (consent to exploratory surgery but not to mastectomy).

"If the patient, adult or minor, does not understand all material facts, any consent that is given will be held legally invalid." Holder, Legal Issues, *supra* note 5, at 138.

19. Cal. Civ. Code § 34.6 (1990) (physician has discretion to inform parents); Md. Gen. Code Ann. § 20-102(e) (1990) (physician may inform parents even over objection of minor).

20. Cal. Civ. Code § 25.9 permits the minor to consent to outpatient mental health treatment only. *Cf.* Cal. Civ. Code § 34.10 (1991) (permitting a minor thirteen and older to give consent to outpatient and inhospital treatment for chemical dependency). *But see In re* Roger S., 569 P.2d 1286 (Cal. 1977) (minor aged fourteen can assert due process right to challenge his confinement in state mental hospital).

21. Cal. Welf. & Inst. Code § 300 (Supp. 1992) (juvenile court has jurisdiction over minors deprived of necessary medical care).

22. Since she is over twelve, she can consent to outpatient mental health treatment or counseling if the treating professional determines that she "is mature enough to participate intelligently in mental health treatment or counseling on an outpatient basis, and . . . would present a danger of serious physical or mental harm to herself or to others without such mental health treatment or counseling."

Cal. Civ. Code § 25.9(a). *Cf.* Ala. Code § 22-8-3 (1990); Md. Gen. Code Ann. § 20-104 (1990).

23. *See infra* note 47. *See also* Holder, Legal Issues, *supra* note 5, at 141–42.

24. *See* Soler, Representing the Child Client, *supra* note 4, at 3.02[2][e] (curfew laws); 6.06 (freedom of expression in schools).

25. *See* Holder, Legal Issues, *supra* note 5, at 137–38.

26. Koocher & Keith-Spiegel, Children, Ethics & the Law, *supra* note 14, at 111, state: "[R]esearch on the capacity of children to weigh benefits and risks to requests to participate in research or treatment decisions has revealed much of what common sense would suggest—namely, that older teenagers still legally defined as minors are no less capable than are adults." *See also* Grant, Consent in Paediatrics: A Complex Teaching Assignment, 17 J. Med. Ethics 199, 202 (1991) (fourteen-year-old girl requested pregnancy and AIDS test; cognitive development sufficient to weigh advantages and disadvantages). For an outline of research in the general area of minors' competence, *see* S. Shah & B. Sales, Law and Mental Health: Major Developments and Research Needs 120–23 (1991).

27. *See* Shah & Sales, Law and Mental Health, *supra* note 26, at 121–22.

28. *See* Scherer, The Capacities of Minors to Exercise Voluntariness in Medical Treatment Decisions, 15 Law & Hum. Behav. 431 (1991) (stating that little difference exists between adolescents and young adults in voluntariness, except that adolescents are more likely to defer to parental pressure). For an analysis of the older child's increasing desire and capacity for autonomy, see Eccles et al., Control versus Autonomy during Early Adolescence, 47 J. Soc. Issues 53 (1991).

29. Wadlington, Minors and Health Care: The Age of Consent, 11 Osgoode Hall L.J. 115 (1973).

30. Younts v. St. Francis Hosp., 469 P.2d 330, 332, 337 (Kan. 1970) (seventeen-year-old girl gave valid consent to surgery on injured fingertip; citing exception to general rule requiring parental consent "when the child is close to maturity and knowingly gives an informed consent"); Lacey v. Laird, 139 N.E.2d 25, 34 (Ohio 1956)(concurring opinion that "performance of a surgical operation upon an 18 year old girl with her consent will ordinarily not amount to an assault and battery"); *but see* Baird v. Attorney General, 360 N.E.2d 288, 296 (Mass. 1977)(although "mature minor" rule applies in jurisdiction, legislature may constitutionally impose parental consent requirement for abortion).

31. In the context of research involving children, "assent" from the minor alone is sufficient if certain criteria are met: (1) the proposed research involves minimal intrusion; (2) the research will benefit either the child or the group of which the child is a member; (3) the child is mature enough to give actual informed consent. *See* Koocher & Keith-Spiegel, Children, Ethics & the Law, *supra* note 14 at 105–106. Koocher and Keith-Spiegel give an example similar to the cases with which this chapter deals: A fifteen-year-old girl, who by state statute can receive confidential birth control information without parental consent, wishes to participate in research. Since the girl here can consent to birth control treatment, the authors conclude that she *may* be able to give assent to a program where she would be "followed up" and periodically interviewed about her perceptions of the experience of being a patient at the birth control clinic.

32. *See In re* E.G., 549 N.E.2d 322 (Ill. 1989). For a discussion of the case, *see* Soler, Representing the Child Client, *supra* note 4, at 3.02[1].

33. *See In re* Seiferth, 127 N.E.2d 820 (N.Y. 1955). Although this case is often classified as one in which the court upheld the *parents'* religious objections to the surgery, the New York Court of Appeals stressed the importance of fourteen-year-old Martin's refusal. Martin would have had to cooperate in lengthy speech therapy following surgery. The court believed that it was important to "view the case from the psychological viewpoint of this misguided youth" and concluded that he should not be forced to undergo surgery against his "sincere and frightened antagonism." *Id.* at 823.

34. *See, e.g.,* Bonner v. Moran, 126 F.2d 121 (D.C. Cir. 1941).

35. "[I]t is highly questionable whether a parent can give consent to any medical procedure carrying a serious risk to a minor for the benefit of another in which the donor child receives no medical benefit." Holder, Legal Issues, *supra* note 5, at 169.

36. "The right to refuse to donate should be as carefully preserved for a minor as for an adult. In the decisions in which opinions are available, it is obvious that trial judges made sincere efforts to elicit the donor's views on the subject and included the stated willingness of the donor child among their reasons for allowing the transplant. The implication is that they all would have respected a refusal as conclusive." *Id.* at 177.

37. Hodgson v. Minnesota, 497 U.S. 417 (1990).

38. *Id.* at 2937, *citing* Planned Parenthood v. Danforth, 428 U.S. 52, 74 (1976).

39. *See Danforth,* 428 U.S. at 74.

40. *See* City of Akron v. Akron Center for Reproductive Health, 462 U.S. 416, 439–40 (1983).

41. *See id.* at 440.

42. *See* H.L. v. Matheson, 450 U.S. 398 (1981).

43. *See, e.g.,* Hodgson v. Minnesota, 497 U.S. at 473, 478.

44. *See* Planned Parenthood v. Danforth, 428 U.S. at 52, 94.

45. *See, e.g., In re* Smith, 295 A.2d 238 (Md. 1972); *see also* Arnold v. Board of Educ., 880 F.2d 305 (11th Cir. 1989). *See generally* Soler, Representing the Child Client, *supra* note 4, at 3.02[1][iv].

46. *See, e.g.,* American Academy of Pediatrics v. Van De Kamp, 214 Cal. App. 3d 831 (1989); *In re* T.W., 551 So. 2d 1186 (Fla. 1989).

47. Building on *In re* Quinlan, 355 A.2d 647, *cert. denied,* 429 U.S. 922 (1979), many courts have based the right to refuse treatment either on the common law right to informed consent or on both the common law right and a constitutional privacy right. The right to make health care decisions, including the refusal of treatment, may fall under the constitutional right to liberty; the state may not deny this right to a competent person without due process. *See* Cruzan v. Director, Missouri Dep't of Health, 497 U.S. 261, 278–81 (1990). In *Cruzan* the Court noted in dicta that it had not, in its earlier decision of Parham v. J.R., 442 U.S. 584 (1979), reached the question whether an *incompetent* minor's liberty interest included the right to refuse treatment. 497 U.S. at 279. However, it upheld the state's requirement of clear and convincing evidence of an incompetent adult's desire to refuse life-sustaining treatment, reasoning that although the incompetent adult's right to refuse could be exercised by a surrogate decision-maker, the state "may legitimately seek to safeguard the personal element of this choice." *Id.* at 281.

48. If the minor is found to be incompetent, the parent can make a "best interests" decision on his or her behalf. Minors found competent should be subject to involuntary treatment only if they satisfy the requirements of the state civil commitment law.

49. For an argument that the level of competency required, or the presumption of competency, should vary with the importance of the decision involved, see Saks, Competency to Refuse Treatment, 69 N.C. L. Rev. 945, 997–98 (1991).

AIDS and Children

■ CHAPTER TWENTY-NINE

Undoing a Lesson of Fear in the Classroom: The Legal Recourse of AIDS-Linked Children

Lisa J. Sotto

AIDS, implacable and thus far incurable, comes as a shock. It arrives like a cannibal at the picnic and calmly starts eating the children.[1]

THIS STATEMENT characterizes the "epidemic of fear" we are presently experiencing as a result of the recent dramatic rise in cases of acquired immunodeficiency syndrome, more commonly known as AIDS. The American public has attached to this disease a stigma far worse than that which the medical community believes is justified. Although medical experts have claimed "with assurance" that AIDS is "an extremely difficult disease to catch"[2] and is not transmitted by casual contact, one poll shows that more than one-half of the American public believes otherwise.[3] Indeed, this chapter maintains that it is the fear of AIDS, rather than AIDS itself, which gnaws at the flesh of children.

This overwhelming fear, based primarily on misinformation and ignorance of medical data, has created a class of people considered to be "the new untouchables."[4] Many individuals who are suffering from AIDS or an AIDS-related condition, who are related to an AIDS patient, or who are members of groups at high risk of contracting AIDS experience groundless discrimination, isolation, and ostracism. Such discrimination is manifested prominently in controversies concerning the decision of several local school boards to exclude from the regular class-

Reprinted in redacted form with permission from the University of Pennsylvania Law Review. Originally in 135 U. Pa. L. Rev. 193 (1986). Copyright 1986 The University of Pennsylvania Law Review.

room children who either have been diagnosed or are perceived as having AIDS. These exclusions are unwarranted because they are based on irrational fears. The weight of available medical evidence clearly demonstrates that AIDS is transmissible only through acts that would not occur in the normal school setting.

In this chapter, I argue that children facing AIDS-related discrimination are protected by several federal laws that prohibit discrimination against disabled individuals, as well as by the equal protection clause of the Fourteenth Amendment to the Constitution.[5] Each of these enactments prohibits school officials from segregating or excluding an AIDS-linked child from the regular classroom.[6] The discussion will proceed on the following assumptions: First, that the AIDS-linked children at issue are physically capable of withstanding a normal school day; second, that such children have no unusual behavioral problems, are in complete control of their bodily secretions, and do not have uncoverable, oozing skin lesions; and third, that medical experts will continue to regard AIDS as posing no danger to other students in the normal classroom setting.

AIDS: The Medical Background

AIDS is a physical disorder that, among other things, destroys the body's ability to fight certain infectious diseases. The virus responsible for causing AIDS is human immunodeficiency virus (HIV). A person may carry the virus for months or years without suffering any symptoms. Eventually, virtually all HIV carriers become symptomatic and develop full-blown AIDS.[7] There is no cure for AIDS and no preventive vaccine, and neither will be available soon. The only present possibility for treatment "is to treat intensively each infection as it arises and when that particular infection has been eradicated, return the patient to the milieu in which he lives."[8]

In 1981, AIDS was first identified under the name by which it is currently known. In the first five years of the epidemic, more than 30,000 cases resulting in more than 15,000 deaths were reported nationwide. During that period, more than 200 cases of juvenile AIDS were diagnosed, and the mortality rate was high.

The two groups at highest risk for contracting AIDS are homosexual or bisexual men, and male or female intravenous (IV) drug users. Together, these groups account for about 90 percent of AIDS cases in the United States. Other risk groups include sexual partners of individuals at risk for AIDS, infants born to parents at risk for AIDS, and people who received transfusions of blood or blood products prior to the development of the HIV antibody test now used to ensure that all blood donated for use is free from HIV. The majority of children with AIDS received the disease from their infected mothers, either during pregnancy or during the birth process. Blood transfusions administered before the use of the HIV antibody test have also caused AIDS in a number of juvenile victims. In addition, children, like adults, may acquire the disease through use of IV drugs or sexual contact with an infected partner.

Thus, AIDS has been transmitted in three ways: Through sexual contact, through injection of a substantial amount of infected blood directly into an individual's body, and through infection from mother to child in utero or during the birth process. Although HIV has been detected in saliva and tears, there are no documented cases of AIDS resulting from transmission by these bodily fluids. Health experts contend that "transmission through ordinary social contact is virtually impossible."[9] None of the identified AIDS cases in the United States is known to have been transmitted through casual contact between individuals. AIDS is not spread by any airborne method, such as coughing or sneezing, nor is it transmitted by sharing food, water, or eating utensils with infected persons.

In studies of children afflicted with AIDS who were monitored for periods of a few months to five years, no other member of any child's family acquired either AIDS or HIV as a result of contact with the infected child.[10] These children shared drinking cups, beds, and even toothbrushes with their siblings; nevertheless, the siblings remained healthy. In fact, some families took no special precautions against contracting the disease because it was not known for many years that a child in the family had AIDS. Even so, there is no evidence that the healthy siblings of these children were infected with HIV as a result of contact with infected family members. It seems clear, then, that while a theoretical risk of transmission from casual contact remains a remote possibility, such transmission is virtually impossible as a practical matter. Indeed, the director of the CDC has stated that the risk of contracting AIDS from a child in the classroom is comparable to that of "being struck by lightning when you walk out the front door in the morning," and the risk of getting the disease as a result of the casual contact that occurs in a school setting is "much less than the chance of the boiler that heats the building blowing up."[11]

Federal Enactments Prohibiting Discrimination against AIDS-Linked Children

Because the risk of contagion by the type of casual contact that occurs in a school setting is "nil or infinitesimally small,"[12] any attempt to exclude or segregate AIDS-linked children from the regular classroom is unwarranted and therefore constitutes unlawful discrimination. Although the AIDS "epidemic" raises a reasonable health concern in many circumstances, the fear some parents and school administrators have displayed with regard to the presence of AIDS-linked children in regular schools is unfounded.

In other contexts, such fear has failed to justify the exclusion of AIDS victims. In *LaRocca v. Dahlsheim*,[13] for example, healthy prisoners sought to expel infected prisoners from the same correctional facility. After reviewing the medical data, the court held that removing AIDS-linked prisoners from the facility was wholly unwarranted.[14] Because the conditions of interaction among students in the classroom are much less confined than those among incarcerated prisoners, the result in *LaRocca* clearly argues against segregating AIDS-linked children from the regular schoolroom.

Nevertheless, several school administrators and school boards have attempted to bar AIDS-related children from unrestricted learning in their normal classrooms. One such resolution passed by a community school board in Queens, New York, stated that because

> the health and safety of the pupil/staff population of the thirty-five schools under its jurisdiction would be endangered by a case, contact or carrier, or suspected case, contact or carrier of AIDS . . . said child[ren] shall not be admitted to any school register and/or shall be removed from any school register[15]

in that school district. This resolution would bar from the classroom (i) any child diagnosed as having AIDS; (ii) any child who has tested positively for HIV; (iii) any child with AIDS-Related Complex (ARC); and (iv) any child who has a relative with AIDS, is a member of a high-risk group, or has a friend or relative who is a member of a high-risk group.

The federal enactments that could protect AIDS-linked children from these and other discriminatory regulations are section 504 of the Rehabilitation Act of 1973,[16] which prohibits discrimination against the disabled; the Education of the Handicapped Act,[17] which evidences a strong federal policy favoring full education for the handicapped; and the equal protection clause of the Fourteenth Amendment.[18] Each will be discussed in turn.[19]

The Rehabilitation Act of 1973

The Rehabilitation Act of 1973 provides a legal basis on which AIDS-linked children may assert a right to a regular, nonsegregated education. Section 504 of the act mandates: "No otherwise qualified handicapped individual in the United States . . . shall, solely by reason of his handicap, be excluded from the participation in, be denied the benefits of, or be subjected to discrimination under any program or activity receiving Federal financial assistance."[20] Since public schools in all states but one utilize federal funds for their educational programs, federal law prohibits these schools from discriminating against handicapped schoolchildren.

The Rehabilitation Act defines a "handicapped individual" as "any person who (i) has a physical . . . impairment which substantially limits one or more of such person's major life activities, (ii) has a record of such impairment, or (iii) is regarded as having such an impairment."[21] The act's coverage of "otherwise qualified handicapped individual[s]" means that a person suffering from a disability may not be treated differently from a nondisabled individual. Furthermore, the act includes within its scope persons who presently have no incapacity at all, or who have a disability that does not substantially limit major life activities, but who are merely perceived as having an impairment that substantially limits such activities.[22] The act's language and the case law interpreting it indicate that individuals with contagious diseases are included within the act's coverage. Although

AIDS cannot be transmitted by casual contact, it is among the contagious diseases addressed by the act. In fact, the act prohibits public schools that receive federal aid from discriminating not only against children who have been diagnosed as having AIDS, but also against children who are perceived by the public or by school administrators as being AIDS victims.

Children diagnosed as having AIDS fall within the purview of the act. An AIDS patient suffers from a "physical . . . impairment which substantially limits one or more of such person's major life activities."[23] The regulations promulgated under the act define "physical or mental impairment" to mean, among other things, any physiological condition affecting the lymphatic system.[24] Because AIDS interferes with the body's ability to produce certain leucocytes, which comprise part of the lymphatic system, children diagnosed as having AIDS have a "physical impairment" within the scope of the Act.[25] AIDS-linked children who have not been diagnosed as having the disease are protected by the act as well, because they are "regarded as having . . . an impairment."[26]

The underlying policy of the act is to ensure that individuals with actual or perceived disabilities will not be prevented from performing activities they are capable of performing, simply because of discriminatory views that "unfairly ignore their individual qualifications and [are] based on prejudicial beliefs about [that] class [of persons]."[27] The spirit of the act would be violated if AIDS-linked children were summarily barred from the regular classroom rather than judged on the basis of their present ability to benefit from a normal education.

Furthermore, section 84.34 of the regulations promulgated under the act provides that a recipient of federal financial assistance should offer education to a handicapped person in the least restrictive setting possible.[28] In other words, the state should provide an education to handicapped persons in a setting with non-handicapped individuals whenever feasible. In accordance with this principle, AIDS-linked children must not be excluded from receiving an education in the same classroom with their peers. Indeed, to exclude these children from a state program that is normally available to all children is, in effect, a quarantine. An executive order concerning quarantines identifies certain easily communicable diseases, among which neither AIDS nor any of the opportunistic diseases associated with AIDS appears.[29] Clearly, AIDS does not pose the kind of threat that warrants quarantine from society.

Section 504 of the act imposes a rebuttable presumption of illegality upon any defendant who bars handicapped children from their regular classrooms.[30] Since the real or perceived handicaps of AIDS-linked children are totally unrelated to their potential for successful performance in school, a segregated AIDS child needs to establish only a prima facie case of discrimination.[31] At that point, the school board that separated the child would have to present evidence to rebut the claim of discrimination. If it could not, it would then have to integrate the child.[32]

Existing case law offers limited guidance regarding the rights of AIDS victims under the act. To analyze properly the issues involved in the case of a child diagnosed as having AIDS, it is helpful to analogize to cases involving other contagious diseases in which similar issues have arisen. The application of section 504 in two cases, one dealing with tuberculosis and the other with hepatitis B, strongly supports the argument that the act also protects AIDS patients.

In *Arline v. School Board*,[33] the Eleventh Circuit interpreted section 504 to include coverage of a contagious disease. It held that tuberculosis constitutes a handicap within the meaning of the Rehabilitation Act. In this case, a public school teacher had been dismissed after contracting tuberculosis, an illness transmitted much more easily than AIDS and, unlike AIDS, certainly transmissible through casual contact in a school setting. The court stated that the language of the act and its implementing regulations "in every respect supports a conclusion that persons with contagious diseases are within the coverage of section 504."[34] The court concluded that "coverage . . . clearly . . . promote[s] Congress's intent to reduce instances of unthinking and unnecessary discrimination against those who are the focus of the statute's concern."[35] The teacher was ordered reinstated. AIDS patients should receive the same or greater consideration because AIDS poses less of a threat of infection than tuberculosis. As in *Arline*, the rationale of any school board choosing to segregate an AIDS child would not "reflect a well-informed judgment grounded in a careful and open-minded weighing of the risks and alternatives"; rather, the board simply would be yielding to "reflexive reactions grounded in ignorance or capitulat[ing] to public prejudice."[36]

New York State Association for Retarded Children v. Carey[37] also suggests that children diagnosed with AIDS are protected by the act. In *Carey*, the Second Circuit overturned a decision by school administrators to segregate from their regular classrooms certain mentally retarded children infected with hepatitis B. The court based its decision solely on section 504's mandate that handicapped children should not be excluded from regular public school sessions simply because of their handicap.[38]

AIDS is often compared with hepatitis B. Like AIDS, hepatitis B has no known cure and can be transmitted through sexual contact, exposure to contaminated blood or blood products, or infection in utero from a mother to her offspring. Hepatitis B, however, is "both hardier and more infectious than HTLV-III/LAV,"[39] and some experts believe hepatitis B, unlike AIDS, may be transmitted through infected saliva.[40] The CDC has stated that the hepatitis B mode of transmission approximates the worst-case scenario for the spread of AIDS because the risk of acquiring hepatitis B is "far in excess" of the risk of contracting AIDS.[41] The CDC maintains that if the precautions followed to prevent the spread of hepatitis B are used to prevent transmission of AIDS, exposure to an AIDS patient will pose no danger of infection to a healthy individual.[42] *Carey* presents an excellent model for analysis of the issues involving AIDS children, the only difference being that hepatitis B is transmitted far more easily than AIDS.

Carey involved the actions of school administrators who yielded to pressure from parents of healthy children and the fear of adverse publicity. The school board had devised a plan under which some known carriers of hepatitis B would be segregated within the school from their healthy peers, thereby disrupting the normal course of the segregated children's education.[43] The district court stated that the potential health risk involved in exposing these children to uninfected classmates was not clearly demonstrated to be "significant":[44] the "medical evidence upon which the proposal is based is sparse and fails to demonstrate any causal relationship between the classroom setting and transmission of the virus."[45] Indeed, segregating the children was "an unwarranted and unnecessarily restrictive reaction to the purely theoretical risk of transmission that the [School] Board has shown."[46] The court also discussed the important role schooling plays in socializing handicapped children:

> A child's chance in this society is through the educational process. A major goal of the educational process is the socialization process that takes place in the regular classroom, with the resulting capability to interact in a social way with one's peers. It is therefore imperative that every child receive an education with his or her peers insofar as it is at all possible. . . .
>
> [P]lacement of children in abnormal environments outside of peer situations imposes additional psychological and emotional handicaps upon children which, added to their existing handicaps causes them greater difficulties in future life. A child has to learn to interact in a social way with its [sic] peers and the denial of this opportunity during his minor years imposes added lifetime burdens upon a handicapped individual.[47]

The district court held that the segregation plan violated section 504 of the act.[48] Under the act, the schools were obligated to provide education for the infected children in the least restrictive environment possible.[49] The court emphasized that the defendant could not demonstrate even a single instance of transmission of hepatitis B within the school environment;[50] the school board's "showing of a purely theoretical risk of spread of hepatitis B predicated upon a philosophical concept of causation is insufficient to offset the weighty countervailing educational needs of the affected children. No substantial justification for the proposed discrimination has been demonstrated, which absence compels [the] conclusion" that segregating carriers of the disease violates section 504 of the act.[51]

Agreeing that the school board had failed to make a "substantial showing" that segregation was warranted,[52] the Second Circuit affirmed the district court's decision. The court found that the school board was unable to demonstrate any more than a "remote possibility" that the disease could be transmitted in the normal classroom setting. The merely theoretical possibility of contagion did not pose the "significant risk" necessary to justify segregation.[53]

There are striking parallels between the situation in *Carey* and that involving AIDS-linked children. If a segregation plan were implemented for AIDS-linked children, school administrators would be yielding to public pressure rather than considering medical facts, just as the school board in *Carey* succumbed to the desires of the parents of healthy children. As the *Carey* courts did not echo the public's fears, no court should blindly accept the public's opinion regarding AIDS. *Carey* stands for the proposition that the unrestricted education of a child is far more important than a "purely theoretical risk of transmission" of disease in the classroom setting.

In 1986 a New York State trial court adopted the reasoning of *Carey* when it held that automatic exclusion of juvenile AIDS victims from the classroom violated their rights under the act. In *District 27 Community School Board v. Board of Education*,[54] two local school boards sought an injunction to prohibit the New York City Board of Education from admitting a child thought to have AIDS to any public school in the city. The court refused to issue injunctive relief, partly on the ground that providing the relief sought would violate the mandates of the act.[55] Because the effect of the AIDS virus on the lymphatic system qualified its victims as persons with a physical impairment, as defined in the regulations promulgated under the act,[56] both AIDS victims and, presumably, those perceived as having AIDS were entitled to the act's protection.[57] The court relied in part on the Second Circuit's decision in *Carey*; in fact, because "several medical experts described the hepatitis B virus as being 'far more contagious' than the AIDS virus, the failure of proof in [the instant case was] even greater than . . . in *Carey*."[58] The petitioners were unable to establish anything beyond a "remote theoretical possibility" of transmitting the AIDS virus in a school setting.[59] Thus, the Board of Education could not be enjoined from admitting AIDS-linked children to their normal classrooms.

Section 504 of the Rehabilitation Act of 1973 protects AIDS-linked children from discrimination. Another federal act, the Education of the Handicapped Act, complements the Rehabilitation Act and provides similar protection.[60]

The Education of the Handicapped Act

The Education of the Handicapped Act[61] (EHA) was enacted to "meet the educational needs of handicapped children in order to assure equal protection of the law."[62] The EHA requires state and local school boards receiving federal funding to establish and maintain "a policy that assures all handicapped children the right to a free appropriate public education,"[63] and provide a "full educational opportunity to all handicapped children."[64] Furthermore, Congress wrote into the law a strong preference for mainstreaming, requiring the states to establish

> procedures to assure that to the maximum extent appropriate, handicapped children . . . are educated with children who are not handicapped, and that special classes, separate schooling, or other removal of handicapped children from the regular educational environment occurs only when the nature or severity of the handicap is such that education in regular classes . . . cannot be achieved satisfactorily.[65]

The statute defines handicapped children as those who are "mentally retarded, hard of hearing, deaf, speech or language impaired, . . . *or other health impaired children*."[66] Under the regulations that implement the statute, "other health impaired children" include those who suffer from "limited strength [or] vitality . . . due to chronic or acute health problems."[67]

Like the Rehabilitation Act, the EHA appears to include AIDS-linked children within its coverage. AIDS patients suffer from a chronic health impairment that affects their strength and vitality. Their inability to fight off infections, however, does not automatically warrant their removal from the regular classroom setting. A decision by school administrators to separate a child who does not require removal constitutes a prima facie violation of the EHA's mainstreaming provisions.[68] In addition, the EHA mandates that the state assess each disabled child individually and place her according to her particular needs, rather than treat all such children in a uniform manner. The procedures required under the EHA ensure that all children reviewed will be mainstreamed "to the maximum extent appropriate" for each child.[69]

The relevant question under the EHA is whether the proposed placement of an AIDS-linked child is appropriate. If it is feasible to place a child in an integrated setting, then to place the child elsewhere violates the EHA. With respect to children diagnosed with AIDS, medical evidence indicates that they pose no practical danger to other children. The remaining question is whether other students pose such a risk to the infected child that it is necessary to remove her from the regular classroom.

A reduced immunological ability to combat illnesses that frequently affect schoolchildren might justify the segregation of children with AIDS. Not all AIDS victims, however, face equal risks of infection. The CDC has stated: "Assessment of the risk to the immunodepressed child is best made by the child's physician who is aware of the child's immune status."[70] Thus, a child who has been judged by her physician to be capable of attending school should not be prevented from doing so by a school board resolution that summarily bars all AIDS-linked children from the classroom. For infected schoolchildren who have been deemed by their physicians to be capable of attending school, the benefits of learning in a classroom with nonhandicapped peers outweigh the risks of contracting potentially harmful infections.

The stigma of being labeled as abnormal severely damages the sense of self-worth of segregated AIDS-linked children. Restricted access to socializing and learning with peers does not "represent a full educational opportunity for [a child] as it isolate[s] him and tend[s] to call undue attention to his handicap."[71] A Texas district court has noted that "[f]ull social interaction is an important part of today's educational curriculum and is even more vital to a child . . . who necessarily suffers a certain degree of isolation as a result of his handicap."[72] Psychologists and educators have agreed that "face-to-face contact between students"[73] plays an essential role in a proper education; indeed, appropriate schooling "consists of many elements, ranging from the desk [at which the child sits] to the child who sits next to him, and includ[es] the teacher who stands at the front of his class."[74] Without all these elements, an education is surely incomplete. AIDS-linked children must not be required to suffer the consequences of segregation. Educating these children in separate classrooms or allowing them to communicate with their teachers and classmates only by telephone clearly denies them the full benefits of a proper education.

Furthermore, if healthy children are made to believe that AIDS-linked children are somehow unfit for social interaction and therefore must be separated from the rest, these children will learn a lesson of fear, mistrust, and intolerance that they will carry into their adult lives. School administrators may unconsciously impart to healthy children a dangerous message about those who are different and who are not responsible for their disabling condition. After all, attitudes promoted in the classroom merely reflect the misconceptions and stereotypes of society as a whole. Allowing AIDS-linked children to be integrated into the regular classroom would promote for all children a greater understanding and acceptance of those with differing personal characteristics.

Under the mandates of the EHA, both children diagnosed as having AIDS and children perceived as having AIDS would be protected from arbitrary discrimination in the school setting. The EHA reveals a strong preference in favor of mainstreaming. Unless a child is deemed by her doctor to be unable to attend school, the EHA, in accordance with the underlying values served by mainstreaming disabled children, requires that the child be placed with her peers in the regular classroom.

The Equal Protection Clause

The Rehabilitation Act of 1973 and the Education of the Handicapped Act prohibit discrimination against AIDS-linked children in public schools. Federal statutes, however, do not offer the only protection for these children. This chapter argues that segregating AIDS-linked children also violates their rights under the equal protection clause of the Fourteenth Amendment.

The equal protection clause guarantees that no state shall "deny to any person within its jurisdiction the equal protection of the laws,"[75] thereby mandating that "all persons similarly circumstanced shall be treated alike."[76] This chapter maintains that AIDS-related children and healthy children with no link to AIDS are similarly situated with regard to AIDS because neither group can transfer the disease in the normal, unrestricted school setting. Thus, by classifying AIDS-linked children in a discriminatory manner, a resolution such as the one proposed in New York City denies these children their constitutional right to equal protection of the laws and burdens them with a stigmatizing classification. Whether the examining court chooses to apply strict scrutiny or an intermediate level of scrutiny to legislation barring AIDS-related children from regular classes, or whether a higher level of deference is deemed to be proper, the court should find that such legislation denies to these children equal protection of the law.[77]

Strict Scrutiny

For a court to apply strict scrutiny in reviewing a regulation that segregates AIDS-linked children from their peers, the regulation must either adversely affect a fundamental right explicitly or implicitly protected by the Constitution, or operate to the disadvantage of a discrete class of people that is a "suspect class."[78] To withstand strict scrutiny, the legislative body that passes such a regulation must demonstrate that the classification scheme is necessary to promote a compelling government interest, and that it is precisely and narrowly tailored to serve legitimate objectives.[79]

In *San Antonio Independent School District v. Rodriguez*,[80] the Supreme Court ruled that education is not a fundamental right; despite its "undisputed importance," it is "not among the rights afforded explicit protection under our Federal Constitution."[81] One of the two bases for applying the strict scrutiny standard to allegedly discriminatory AIDS legislation is therefore unavailable. AIDS-linked children appear, however, to fit the definition traditionally used to describe a suspect class. This chapter argues that AIDS-linked children constitute a suspect class and that government efforts to segregate them from their normal classrooms should be reviewed under a standard of strict scrutiny.

A government regulation that classifies all AIDS-linked children so as to bar them automatically from their regular schoolrooms fits the definition of suspectness presented by Justice Brennan in *Plyler v. Doe*.[82] Such a classification

> reflect[s] deep-seated prejudice rather than legislative rationality in pursuit of some legitimate objective. Legislation predicated on such prejudice is easily recognized as incompatible with the constitutional understanding that each person is to be judged individually and is entitled to equal justice under the law. . . . Legislation imposing special disabilities upon groups disfavored by virtue of circumstances beyond their control suggests the kind of "class or caste" treatment that the Fourteenth Amendment was designed to abolish.[83]

The government regulation described above would create stark differences between the treatment of AIDS-linked children and non-AIDS-linked children. Furthermore, AIDS-linked children would all be classified under one category, even though no medical justification exists for such uniform treatment. Indeed, the only justifiable classification scheme would be one that distinguished between those children who are deemed by their physicians to be well enough to attend school and those who are deemed to be physically unable to do so.

Such a government regulation would promote no government interest at all, much less a compelling one, as is required to withstand strict scrutiny. The medical evidence presently available indicates that there is no practical risk of transmission in the normal school setting. No government interest exists in removing, and in effect quarantining, AIDS-linked children from their normal environments. A permissible government objective of such segregation might be to protect a child diagnosed with AIDS from contracting a potentially harmful disease from peers in school. This objective should not be achieved, however, by simply barring all children with AIDS from the classroom. Because the risks of infection differ in every case, the risks should be weighed separately for each AIDS patient.

Furthermore, automatic removal of AIDS-linked children from their normal classrooms must fail under a standard of strict scrutiny because it is not narrowly tailored; such segregation is, in fact, fatally flawed in that it is both overinclusive and underinclusive. It is overinclusive in that it restricts AIDS-linked children entirely, because none can transmit the disease by the casual contact that occurs in a classroom. It is also overinclusive because it bars from the classroom diagnosed AIDS patients who have been deemed by their physicians to be healthy enough to attend school. Automatic removal is underinclusive because it fails to segregate many who in fact may be carriers of AIDS, such as untested children who are infected with HIV but are asymptomatic, or children who have been very recently contaminated with the virus and therefore would generate negative antibody test results. Because AIDS-linked children can be classified as a suspect group, a government regulation that automatically deprives these children of the benefits of a meaningful public education is "presumptively invidious"[84] and therefore unconstitutional under the Fourteenth Amendment.

Intermediate Scrutiny

Although strict scrutiny seems to be an appropriate standard to apply to a government regulation that automatically bars AIDS-linked children from their regular classrooms, it is necessary to consider alternative standards because the Court traditionally has been extremely reluctant to name any class as suspect.[85] Accordingly, one must examine the other levels of scrutiny used by the Court to determine whether such action would be unconstitutional at those levels as well.

The Court has applied a standard of heightened scrutiny in cases where government classifications affect neither a fundamental right nor a suspect class but nonetheless "give rise to recurring constitutional difficulties."[86] Although strict scrutiny does not apply, any regulation examined under a standard of heightened scrutiny must serve an important government objective and must be substantially related to achieving that objective.[87] Several courts of appeals and commentators have acknowledged that an intermediate level of deference has been applied to "legislative restrictions on access to education."[88] The particular case to which these authorities refer is *Plyler v. Doe*,[89] which involved a Texas statute that denied a public education to undocumented alien children.[90] Although the majority opinion referred to a framework of rational relation in its decision to strike down the statute, the Court's requirement that the statute further a "substantial state interest"[91] clearly indicates that the statute was reviewed under a standard of heightened scrutiny.[92]

Justice Brennan, writing for the majority, evaluated the importance of education:

> Public education is not a "right" granted to individuals by the Constitution. But neither is it merely some governmental "benefit." . . . [E]ducation has a fundamental role in maintaining the fabric of our society. We cannot ignore the significant social costs borne by our Nation when select groups are denied the means to absorb the values and skills upon which our social order rests.
>
> In addition . . . denial of education to some isolated group of children poses an affront to one of the goals of the Equal Protection Clause: the

abolition of governmental barriers presenting unreasonable obstacles to advancement on the basis of individual merit. . . . The inestimable toll of that deprivation on the social, economic, intellectual, and psychological well-being of the individual, and the obstacle it poses to individual achievement, make it most difficult to reconcile the cost or the principle of a status-based denial of basic education with the framework of equality embodied in the Equal Protection Clause.[93]

Equality of educational opportunity traditionally has been recognized as a highly important attribute of education. In *Plyler*, Justice Brennan addressed the complete denial of a public education to a group of children. In contrast, the AIDS-related regulations with which this chapter is concerned do not purport to wholly deny formal learning to AIDS-linked children, because home instruction would be available for them. Despite the probable contention of the school board, however, that these children would be receiving an education equivalent to that of their peers, any government regulation that automatically segregates or bars such children from their regular classrooms violates the spirit of the equal protection clause. These children are denied a meaningful opportunity to enjoy a benefit granted to others. The exclusion operates to prevent them from ever fully assimilating into society. Isolated from other children at a young age, AIDS-linked children will feel permanently alienated from a society that has separated them from their peers.

In the absence of medical evidence that AIDS can be spread by casual contact, one important government interest, the protection of healthy children from contracting the disease, is not implicated. Another government objective, to protect AIDS-diagnosed children from contracting potentially harmful diseases in school, need not be achieved by summarily barring all such children from the schoolroom. Indeed, no reasonable basis exists for segregating every AIDS-linked child from the normal classroom. Under an intermediate level of scrutiny, then, the type of government regulation at issue must fail.

Rationality Standard

If a court reviewing the regulation in question considers neither strict scrutiny nor intermediate scrutiny to be the applicable standard, the regulation would be tested under the rationality standard. This standard applies to regulations that are not based upon a "suspect classification," do not affect a "fundamental right," and do not involve a "quasi-suspect" category. Under the rational relation standard, the court would determine whether the classification at issue bears a rational relation to a legitimate public purpose.[94] The Supreme Court traditionally has granted considerable legislative deference to government regulations reviewed under this standard. Recently, however, the Court has demonstrated its willingness to strike down classification schemes that are not rationally related to a legitimate state purpose.

The question with respect to AIDS-linked children is whether it is rational to treat such children differently from their peers. It is true that children diagnosed with AIDS suffer a disability not shared by others; in the classroom setting, however, their particular disability does not warrant the distinction imposed by the government regulation at issue. Although the purpose of such a regulation, the prevention of the spread of AIDS, is a legitimate end, it is not rationally served by distinguishing between AIDS-linked children and non-AIDS-linked children within the educational setting. The Supreme Court recently asserted: "The state may not rely on a classification whose relationship to an asserted goal is so attenuated as to render the distinction arbitrary or irrational."[95] In the case of AIDS-linked children in the regular school setting, medical evidence clearly shows that allowing such children to remain with their peers would not pose any threat to the public's legitimate interests. A government regulation that would automatically bar them from the classroom fails to withstand equal protection review even under a rationality standard.

Conclusion

Medical evidence currently available indicates that AIDS is transmitted only by sexual contact, the sharing of hypodermic needles, blood transfusions, and in utero infection from a mother to her offspring. There appears to be no risk of spreading the disease by casual contact, such as that which occurs in the classroom. In addition, the risk that a child diagnosed with AIDS will contract a potentially harmful disease from her peers in school should be assessed on an individual basis. School administrators who arbitrarily segregate all AIDS-linked children from their classmates are yielding to the pressure of uninformed public fear. By preventing these children from obtaining the full measure of educational benefits to which they are entitled, a school board acts in violation of the Rehabilitation Act of 1973, the Education of the Handicapped Act, and the equal protection clause of the Fourteenth Amendment. Instead of classifying such children as a single group, the proper authorities should separately assess each AIDS-linked child to determine the most appropriate educational placement for him or her.

There is no evidence that AIDS has ever been contracted through casual contact. This society must not allow an innocent minority to be ruled by a misinformed majority. The consequences of segregating AIDS-linked children and unjustifiably granting them an inferior education "may affect their hearts and minds in a way unlikely ever to be undone."[96]

NOTES

1. Morrow, The Start of a Plague Mentality, Time, Sept. 23, 1985, at 92.
2. Phillip M. Boffey, U.S. Counters Public Fears of AIDS, N.Y. Times, Sept. 20, 1985, at A15 (quoting Dr. James O. Mason, director, Centers for Disease Control).
3. *See* Erik Eckholm, Poll Finds Many AIDS Fears That the Experts Say Are

Groundless, N.Y. Times, Sept. 12, 1985, at B11. A New York Times/CBS poll found that 51 percent of the participants believed that AIDS was one of the two or three "most serious medical problems facing the country," although almost all of those polled claimed to be aware of the very limited number of ways in which AIDS could be transmitted. *See id.*

4. Thomas, The New Untouchables, Time, Sept. 23, 1985, at 24.

5. U.S. Const. amend. XIV, § 1. The federal statutes to be discussed are the Rehabilitation Act of 1973, 29 U.S.C. §§ 701–796(i) (1982 & Supp. III 1985 & West 1986), and the Education of the Handicapped Act, 20 U.S.C. §§ 1400–1454 (1982 & Supp. III 1985). The latter statute is also known as the Education for All Handicapped Children Act because "that was the official name of the 1975 statute which extensively amended and expanded the EHA." Goodwin, Public School Integration of Children with Handicaps after Smith v. Robinson: "Separate but Equal" Revisited? 37 Me. L. Rev. 267, 271 n.25 (1985).

6. Future references to "AIDS-linked children" and "AIDS-related children" will include: (1) children who have been diagnosed as having AIDS; (2) children with AIDS-related conditions; (3) children who have tested positively for HIV, the virus which causes the disease, but who show no symptoms of AIDS and may never contract it; and (4) children who are in a high-risk group or who have family members in a high-risk group for contracting AIDS. Because all of these children face similar forms of discrimination, and because medical evidence indicates that none of these children can transmit AIDS in the normal school setting, this chapter generally will not distinguish among them for purposes of discussing their legal options. In certain sections of this chapter, however, it may be necessary to distinguish between children diagnosed with AIDS and children merely perceived as having AIDS.

7. *See* Wallis, You Haven't Heard Anything Yet, Time, Feb. 16, 1987, at 54; *see also* Smilgis, The Big Chill: Fear of AIDS, Time, Feb. 16, 1987, at 50, 51 (more than 90 percent of those thought to be infected with the AIDS virus do not know that they are carriers; additionally, the incubation period for the virus may be as long as ten years).

Most statistics used in this chapter represent current figures at the time the piece first went to press in 1986.

8. Johnson, Editorial, 52 Medico-Legal J. 3 (1984).

9. Doctors' Unit Urges Schools to Admit AIDS Victims, N.Y. Times, Oct. 24, 1985, at A19 (discussing recommendations of the American Academy of Pediatrics).

10. *See* Department of Health, State of New York, Public Health Series 85-92, Guidelines for the Education and Day-Care of Children Infected with Human T-Lymphotropic Virus Type III/Lymphoadenopathy-Associated Virus (HTLV III/ LAV) 2 (Sept. 4, 1985); Boffey, *supra* note 2, at A15.

11. Eckholm, *supra* note 3, at B11 (quoting Dr. James O. Mason, director, CDC). Dr. Pauline Thomas, a pediatric AIDS specialist with two young children, was asked under oath whether she would allow one of her children to be given the HIV antibody test if the child had been bitten by a known AIDS patient. The doctor quickly and unequivocally replied that she would not. *See* Joseph P. Fried, Reporter's Notebook: Few Answers in AIDS Suit, N.Y. Times, Sept. 23, 1985, at B5.

12. Boston Globe, May 12, 1985, at 29, 36.

13. 120 Misc. 2d 697 (N.Y. Sup. Ct. 1983).

14. *Id.* at 709–710.

15. Community School Board–District 27, City of New York, Addendum to the Community School Board 27 Open Meeting Agenda of August 22, 1985 (on file with the University of Pennsylvania Law Review) [hereinafter Addendum]. The school board asserted that "a conservative attitude toward the care and teaching of our children is the most sensible and responsible approach." *Id.*

16. 29 U.S.C. § 794 (1982 & Supp. III 1985).

17. 20 U.S.C. §§ 1400–1454 (1982 & Supp. III 1985) (subsequently renamed Individuals with Disabilities Education Act).

18. U.S. Const. amend. XIV, § 1.

19. This chapter does not treat as distinguishable children diagnosed with AIDS and children merely perceived as having AIDS. The two groups are indistinguishable with respect to the issues presented here because it is assumed that no child in either group can transmit AIDS in the typical school setting.

20. 29 U.S.C. § 794 (1982 & Supp. III 1985).

21. 29 U.S.C. § 706(7)(B) (1982). "Major life activities" include functions such as caring for oneself, performing manual tasks, walking, seeing, hearing, breathing, learning, and working. 45 C.F.R. § 84.4(j)(2)(ii) (1985).

22. *See* 45 C.F.R. § 84.4(g)(2)(iv) (1985).

23. 29 U.S.C. § 706(7)(B) (1982).

24. *See* 34 C.F.R. § 104.3(j)(2)(i)(A) (1986).

25. *See* 45 C.F.R. § 84.4(j)(2)(iii) (1985).

26. 29 U.S.C. § 706(7)(B) (1982).

27. Leonard, Employment Discrimination against Persons with AIDS, 10 U. Dayton L. Rev. 681, 696 (1985).

28. *See* 45 C.F.R. § 84.34 (1985).

29. *See* Exec. Order No. 12,452, 48 Fed. Reg. 56, 927 *reprinted in* 42 U.S.C. § 264 (Supp. III 1985).

30. *See* 29 U.S.C. § 794 (1982 & Supp. III 1985); *see also* New York Ass'n for Retarded Children v. Carey, 612 F.2d 644, 649 (2d Cir. 1979) (construing section 504 of the act as creating a rebuttable presumption).

31. To present a prima facie case of discrimination, the plaintiff must demonstrate that the defendant, by having received federal financial assistance, is subject to the mandates of section 504, that the plaintiff is handicapped, and that the defendant has segregated the plaintiff from the normal classroom. *See* Goodwin, Public School Integration, *supra* note 5, at 291.

32. *See Carey*, 612 F.2d at 649; *see also* Goodwin, Public School Integration, *supra* note 5, at 289. Goodwin suggests that section 504 allows the plaintiff an easier case than does the Education of the Handicapped Act, because the latter legislation requires that the AIDS child "prove both the existence of segregation and the feasibility of education in an integrated setting." *Id.*

33. 772 F.2d 759 (11th Cir. 1985), *cert. granted*, 475 U.S. 1118 (1986). [Editor's Note: This case was later affirmed by the U.S. Supreme Court; *see* 480 U.S. 273 (1987); *see also* Chapter 30 in this volume.]

34. *Id.* at 764.

35. *Id.*

36. *Id.* at 765.

37. 612 F.2d 644 (2d Cir. 1979).

38. *See id.* at 649.

39. Centers for Disease Control, Summary: Recommendations for Preventing Transmission of Infection with Human T-Lymphotropic Virus Type III/Lymphadenopathy-Associated Virus in the Workplace, 34 Morbidity & Mortality Weekly Rep. 681 (1985) [hereinafter Summary].

40. *See* New York State Ass'n for Retarded Children v. Carey, 466 F. Supp. 487, 489 n.1 (E.D.N.Y. 1978), *aff'd*, 612 F.2d 644 (2d Cir. 1979).

41. Summary, *supra* note 39, at 683.

42. *See id.* at 681.

43. *See Carey*, 466 F. Supp. at 492.

44. *See id.* at 500.

45. *Id.* at 499.

46. *Id.* at 500.

47. *Id.* at 496–97 (quoting Hairston v. Drosick, 423 F. Supp. 180, 183 (S.D. W. Va. 1976)).

48. *See id.* at 502.

49. *See id.* at 503.

50. *See id.*

51. *Id.* The court held that the segregation plan also violated the Education of the Handicapped Act, the equal protection clause of the Constitution, and several other laws not .directly related to the issues under discussion here. The court of appeals affirmed the district court's decision solely on the ground that segregating the carriers violated the Rehabilitation Act. *See* New York Ass'n for Retarded Children v. Carey, 612 F.2d 644, 649 (2d Cir. 1979).

52. *See Carey*, 612 F.2d at 650.

53. *Id.* at 651.

54. 130 Misc. 2d 398 (N.Y. Sup. Ct. 1986).

55. *See id.* at 413–15. The court also held that the relief sought would deny to the child in question the equal protection of the laws. *See id.* at 416–17.

56. *See id.* at 414.

57. *See id.*

58. *Id.* at 415.

59. *Id.*

60. The Supreme Court held in Smith v. Robinson, 468 U.S. 992 (1984), that a handicapped child who asserted the right to have the state provide a special education could not base his claim on the Rehabilitation Act of 1973 or the equal protection clause. The Court stated that the child's only remedy was founded on the Education of the Handicapped Act (EHA). *Smith* did not address the issue of a child who desired to be mainstreamed, but was limited to a situation in which a child's choice was between two or more nonmainstreamed educational placements. For a discussion concerning the dichotomy between those sections of the EHA dealing with mainstreaming versus those addressing specialized education, *see* Goodwin, Public School Integration, *supra* note 5, at 279–84; *see also* Roncker v. Walter, 700 F.2d 1058 (6th Cir. 1983), *cert. denied*, 464 U.S. 864 (1983) (holding that the free appropriate education and integrated placement requirements are two distinct mandates of the EHA).

61. 20 U.S.C. §§ 1400–1454 (1982 & Supp. III 1985).

62. *Id.* § 1400.

63. *Id.* § 1412(1).

64. *Id.* § 1412(2)(A)(i).

65. *Id.* § 1412(5)(B). This provision is commonly referred to as the "least restrictive environment" or "mainstreaming" section. The implementing regulations of the EHA are grouped under the category heading "least restrictive environment"; the statute itself does not include such language. *See* 34 C.F.R. §§ 300.132, 300.550–.556 (1986).

66. 20 U.S.C. § 1401(a)(1) (1982 & Supp. III 1985) (emphasis added).

67. 34 C.F.R. § 300.5(b)(7) (1986).

68. *See* Espino v. Besteiro, 520 F. Supp. 905, 911 (S.D. Tex. 1981).

69. 20 U.S.C. § 1412(5)(B) (1982 & Supp. III 1985).

70. Centers for Disease Control, Education and Foster Care of Children Infected with Human T-Lymphotropic Virus Type III/Lymphadenopathy-Associated Virus, 34 Morbidity & Mortality Weekly Rep. 517, 519 (Aug. 30, 1985) [hereinafter Education and Foster Care of Children]. Furthermore, the CDC has indicated that "[t]he risk of acquiring some infections . . . may be reduced by prompt use of specific immune globulin following a known exposure." *Id.*

71. Espino v. Besteiro, 520 F. Supp. 905, 909 (S.D. Tex. 1981) (evaluating the isolation within a regular classroom of a seven-year-old boy "medically diagnosed as a quadriplegic and . . . confined to a wheelchair," *id.* at 906).

72. *Id.* at 913.

73. Crockenberg & Bryant, Socialization: The "Implicit Curriculum" of Learning Environments, 12 J. Res. Dev. Educ. 69, 71 (1978).

74. Coleman, Equality of Educational Opportunity, in The School in the Social Order 114 (F. Cordasco et al. eds., 1970).

75. U.S. Const. amend. XIV, § 1.

76. F. S. Royster Guano Co. v. Virginia, 253 U.S. 412, 415 (1920).

77. A court may choose from three levels of scrutiny in reviewing legislation alleged to violate the equal protection clause. The choice depends on the nature of the challenged legislation. If a statute affects a "suspect class" or impinges on a "fundamental right," the statute will be strictly scrutinized. If a "classification, while not facially invidious, nonetheless give[s] rise to recurring constitutional difficulties," Plyler v. Doe, 457 U.S. 202, 217 (1982), the legislation will be reviewed under an intermediate level of scrutiny. If neither strict scrutiny nor intermediate scrutiny is appropriate, the legislation will be reviewed under a rational relation standard, which accords great deference to legislative judgment. *See generally* G. Gunther, Cases and Materials on Constitutional Law 670–76 (10th ed. 1980) (discussing the historical development of equal protection analysis).

78. *See* San Antonio Indep. Sch. Dist. v. Rodriguez, 411 U.S. 1, 16–17 (1973).

79. *See Plyler*, 457 U.S. at 217.

80. 411 U.S. 1 (1973).

81. *Id.* at 35.

82. 457 U.S. 202 (1982). Although *Plyler* was decided on the basis of intermediate scrutiny, Justice Brennan included in his discussion of the equal protection clause the definition of suspectness quoted in the text.

83. *Id.* at 216 n.14. AIDS-linked children arguably constitute a "discrete and insular" minority, United States v. Carolene Prods. Co., 304 U.S. 144, 152 n.4 (1938). They form a clearly defined and bounded group with an "immutable" characteris-

tic, Frontiero v. Richardson, 411 U.S. 677, 686 (1973). The disability thrust upon them as a result of their exclusion from the regular classroom is certainly harmful. Furthermore, from a political perspective, AIDS-linked children are a particularly vulnerable group: As children, they have no voting power; over half are black, and almost one-quarter are Hispanic; most are indigent and have at least one parent infected with AIDS. Many have a parent who is an IV drug user. *See* Center for Infectious Diseases, Centers for Disease Control, Acquired Immunodeficiency Syndrome (AIDS) Weekly Surveillance Report—United States AIDS Activity 2 (Sept. 16, 1985). Given these conditions, AIDS-related children seem to be in "such a position of political powerlessness as to command extraordinary protection from the majoritarian political process." *Rodriguez*, 411 U.S. at 28 (discussing the "traditional indicia of suspectness").

84. Plyler v. Doe, 457 U.S. 202, 216 (1982).

85. Only classifications based on "race, alienage or national origin" have been considered suspect. City of Cleburne v. Cleburne Living Center, 105 S. Ct. 3249, 3255 (1985).

86. *Plyler*, 457 U.S. at 217.

87. *See, e.g.*, Craig v. Boren, 429 U.S. 190, 197 (1976). The Court invalidated an Oklahoma statute that discriminated on the basis of gender as being insubstantially related to achieving the purported governmental objective. *See id.* at 199–204.

88. Sklar v. Byrne, 727 F.2d 633, 637 n.5 (7th Cir. 1984); Halderman v. Pennhurst State Sch. & Hosp., 707 F.2d 702, 709 n.7 (3d Cir. 1983) (citations omitted) (the right of parents "to direct and control the upbringing of their children without unnecessary governmental interference" is protected under "an 'intermediate' level of scrutiny"); *see also* Comment, Intermediate Equal Protection Scrutiny of Welfare Laws That Deny Subsistence, 132 U. Pa. L. Rev. 1547, 1555–60 (1984) (interpreting *Plyler* as implicitly holding that denial of a very important interest closely related to the exercise of constitutional rights probably triggers intermediate scrutiny).

89. 457 U.S. 202 (1982).

90. *See id.* at 205.

91. *Id.* at 230.

92. It is possible that the majority simply would have preferred to have stated explicitly that education is a fundamental right. To obtain Justice Powell's vote, however, it probably was necessary to avoid such a statement; Powell had voted with the majority in San Antonio Indep. Sch. Dist. v. Rodriguez, 411 U.S. 1 (1973), which held that education is not a fundamental right. *See id.* at 35. Indeed, the dissenters in *Plyler* asserted that the *Plyler* majority had applied a "quasi-suspect-class and quasi-fundamental-rights analysis." *Plyler*, 457 U.S. at 242, 244 (Burger, C.J., dissenting).

93. *Plyler*, 457 U.S. at 221–22 (citations omitted).

94. *See* City of Cleburne v. Cleburne Living Center, 105 S. Ct. 3249, 3254 (1985).

95. *Id.* at 3258.

96. Brown v. Board of Educ., 347 U.S. 483, 494 (1954), *quoted in* San Antonio Indep. Sch. Dist. v. Rodriguez, 411 U.S. 1, 70, 71–72 (1973) (Marshall, J., dissenting).

CHAPTER THIRTY

Among Schoolchildren: AIDS, the Law, and the Public Schools

Barry Sullivan

And the leper in whom the plague is, his clothes shall be rent, and his head bare, and he shall put a covering upon his upper lip, and shall cry, "Unclean, unclean." —Leviticus 13:45

IN 1988, the American Bar Association's Coordinating Committee on AIDS noted that "[c]hildren with HIV [human immunodeficiency virus] experience many of the legal problems common to their adult counterparts. . . . [as well as] compelling legal problems unique to their age and status."[1] The truth of these observations is clear. That children and adults with HIV should experience many of the same legal problems is not surprising because they share many other problems as well. Although the most widely publicized cases of discrimination against children with HIV have involved white, middle-class children who acquired the disease through blood transfusions, those cases are not representative.[2] Indeed, the demographic reality could not be more different. Approximately 80 percent of children with AIDS have acquired the disease from their mothers, either perinatally or at birth, and most of the mothers (disproportionately minority and low-income women) have acquired the disease through intravenous (IV) drug use, or from sexual partners who are IV drug users.[3] This pattern of transmission underscores the National Commission's recent observation that HIV disease cannot be understood without reference to racism, homophobia, poverty, and unemployment—that "web of associated social ills" which "foster the spread of the disease."[4] To the extent that children and adults are caught up together in this web of social ills, it is not surprising that they should experience many of the same legal problems.

It is also true that children with HIV encounter legal problems that are unique to their age and status. Indeed, children at various stages of development will experience legal problems that are different from those experienced by children who are younger or older. They also will have problems associated with specific contexts. Some children with HIV will experience legal problems in connection with the child welfare and juvenile justice systems, while others will face legal problems as children of divorce. Of central importance, however, is the school setting. Virtually all children aged five to eighteen spend thirty hours each week, nine months each year, in school with their peers. For most children with HIV, school is their most intensive and prolonged occasion for social interaction, and they will undoubtedly experience social and legal problems as a result of those interactions.[5]

When parents have learned that children with HIV are attending school with their children, their reaction often has been emotional and violent opposition.[6] In many instances, parents have found little solace in assertions that HIV is not transmitted through casual contact. Nor have they taken comfort from the absence, in the entire history of this disease, of a single documented case of school-based transmission. Instead, they often have chosen to focus on the admitted inability of medical science to vouch for the absolute impossibility of transmission in the school setting. Because medical scientists have typically described the probability of transmission in such circumstances as "theoretically possible," "slight," or "negligible," they implicitly have conceded the existence of some risk. According to the proponents of exclusion, that concession settles the issue because children should not be exposed to any risk. To counter such arguments, other interlocutors take the position that we simply misunderstand when we take the testimony of medical science at face value. According to that argument, scientists can never express themselves in unqualified terms. Thus, when they say that the risk of transmission is theoretically possible, slight, or negligible, we should take them to mean that there is, as a practical matter, no risk at all.[7]

In this chapter I take the position that the debate about exclusion should not be framed in these terms. On the one hand, I view the categorical exclusion of children with HIV as unnecessary and unwise. On the other hand, we must acknowledge the exceedingly remote but nonetheless real possibility of transmission in the school setting and avoid building arguments against exclusion based on unrealistic views regarding the impossibility of transmission. If impossibility of transmission becomes the bedrock of case law in this area, then one case of transmission in the school setting necessarily will shake the law to its foundations. That is precisely what has happened in the health care context, where the apparently substandard infection-control practices of one Florida dentist have been accorded mythic significance, at least in part because of extravagant claims that previously were made with respect to the absence of risk in the health care field, and have therefore undermined previously settled law.[8] Given the virtually endless variety of activities that may go on in school, there is no reason to believe that a similar case could not occur in that setting, and a case law built on an absolute denial of such a risk will offer little assistance in dealing with the inevitable.

My aim in this chapter, then, is to demonstrate that we need to talk more responsibly about risks of transmission, to acknowledge the competing values at stake, and to ensure that the logic of our case law does not fall victim to its own hyperbole. The analysis proceeds in four parts. First, consideration is given to the arguments for and against exclusion by examining the positions advanced by Lisa J. Sotto (see Chapter 29) and Carolyn Kasler,[9] whose works have defined the debate in this area. Second, the relevant case law is considered to see how the courts have dealt with the issue of exclusion under relevant statutory and constitutional principles. Third, the problem of identifying students with HIV and the claims of personal privacy are examined. Finally, the analysis concludes with suggestions for improving legal discourse concerning children and AIDS, drawing upon recent scholarship in the philosophy of science, which suggests that risk analysis is neither purely objective nor merely a social construct. In other words, determinations about risks cannot be defended entirely on scientific or objective grounds, but neither can they be dismissed as merely subjective. Thus, we can talk about risks in a reasoned way, and we can conclude that some risk judgments are more warranted than others.[10] In this way, it can be shown that the "mainstreaming" of children with HIV, and the recognition of their interest in privacy, is a justifiable strategy.

The Exclusion Debate

When Lisa Sotto's essay appeared in 1986, President Reagan still had not personally acknowledged the existence of the HIV epidemic;[11] the Supreme Court had not yet decided *School Board v. Arline;*[12] and the Department of Justice adhered to the view that section 504 of the Rehabilitation Act[13] afforded no protection against discrimination based on fears of contagiousness, no matter how unfounded those fears might be.[14] Moreover, because a small number of pediatric AIDS cases had received massive media attention, the problem of schoolchildren with AIDS had become a matter of widespread public concern. Sotto was therefore sailing largely uncharted waters when she engaged in the analyses that led to her central conclusions: that is, that the exclusion of children with HIV would violate section 504, the Education of the Handicapped Act,[15] and the equal protection clause of the Fourteenth Amendment.[16] The accuracy of these conclusions is less important, for present purposes, than the assumptions and reasoning upon which they are based.[17]

In Sotto's view, the medical evidence should be interpreted to mean that "the risk of contagion . . . is 'nil or infinitesimally small.'" Thus, the central challenge for public policy is educational. The great need is to make people believe that they effectively face no real risk, and to ensure that public policy choices are based on this objective, medical fact, rather than on irrational fears of transmission. As Sotto recognizes, however, the gulf between "fact" and "belief" was both broad and deep: "Although medical experts have claimed 'with assurance' that AIDS is 'an extremely difficult disease to catch' and is not transmitted by casual contact, one poll shows that more than one-half of the American public believes otherwise." In these circumstances, Sotto asserts, "it is the fear of AIDS, rather than AIDS itself, which gnaws at the flesh of children." This fear, "based primarily on misinformation and ignorance of medical data," had given birth to "groundless discrimination, isolation, and ostracism."[18] In Sotto's view, the problem is far from intractable. Indeed, it could easily be resolved if only the credibility gap could be bridged, and people could be convinced of the truth of medical science.

Carolyn Kasler's 1989 response to Sotto reflects a far different approach to the legal issues raised by HIV infection among schoolchildren. Kasler joins issue with Sotto on the threshold question whether the medical evidence, which Sotto treats as the unquestionable foundation for her analysis, is in fact sufficiently reliable to supply the factual predicate for analyzing the relevant legal issues. Basically, Kasler argues that fear of children with HIV is neither irrational nor unreasonable. It is one thing to say that HIV appears not to be transmitted by casual contact. It is another to treat that observation as a "truth," or even to equate the myriad of behaviors that are to be found in the school setting, from nursery school through high school, with "casual contact."[19] The thrust of Kasler's approach is exemplified by her opening paragraph:

> Imagine two scenarios: Two third graders, playing at recess, decide to form a club. Initiation to be a member is to become a blood brother for life . . . or death. Later one child is found to have AIDS and the second child is added to the list of carriers. Or, two high school students certain that they are in love, make a decision to consummate their relationship for better . . . or worse. Perhaps the young man was unaware of his illness, or perhaps he was told not to publicize the fact that he had AIDS. He was an innocent victim of a blood transfusion, and he has a right to privacy, to avoid being ostracized, until his symptoms actually get the best of him. His needs have now caused the disease to get the best of another innocent victim.[20]

These scenarios are wholly imaginary, as Kasler acknowledges. In the decade since AIDS was first described, no case of school-based transmission has been reported. For Kasler, however, these horrific scenarios demonstrate that "supporters of AIDS victims' rights should be able to *guarantee* that events like those . . . do not occur in our schools."[21] That is not possible, because "incidents like these, and innumerable other risky situations occur every day when children meet."[22] For this reason, Kasler argues, "[p]ublic fear about AIDS is not hysteria and is not unreasonable fear, but fear of the unknown and of what is yet to be learned about this 'young' disease."[23] Indeed, "[i]t is a fear based on many real possibilities not as unlikely to occur as the medical profession, government officials and politicians would have us believe."[24] Moreover, we must not be distracted by the slightness of the risk of transmission, which is "outweighed by . . . its effect [as] a death sentence."[25]

In Kasler's view, the problem clearly requires strong medicine. First, a student's HIV status must be disclosed. "In a school setting, revealing the identity of the victim is necessary to protect the health of both the victim and the non-victim, to promote the goal of finding a cure for this disease, and to permit the community to enforce precautions against the spread of AIDS."[26] Moreover, "[n]ot informing *everyone* who may be in daily contact with an AIDS victim is a paternalistic deprivation of the non-victim's right to protect himself."[27] Second, it must be recognized that "[c]ertain school-related activities present a higher risk of transmission, *i.e.*, physical education, biological sciences, fun play, and even bathroom visits," and these "must be curtailed, monitored, and/or prohibited."[28] In this way, Kasler concludes, courts "will be better able to address the problem with rules and tangible standards rather than with the tenuous medical findings on this changeable new disease."[29]

Not surprisingly, Kasler concludes that exclusion is not prohibited by section 504, which she characterizes as "an obstacle which school boards must face when seeking to restrict a child with AIDS,"[30] by the Education for the Handicapped Act,[31] or by the equal protection clause.[32] In addition, Kasler finds no substance to the "one last right to which [persons with HIV] cling—the right of individual privacy."[33] Based on an expansive reading of the Supreme Court's decision in *Whalen v. Roe*,[34] Kasler concludes that any interest in confidentiality must give way to the public health.[35] Kasler also asserts, based on a similarly expansive reading of *Tarasoff v. Board of Regents*,[36] that a physician or public health official has a duty "to tell all those in contact with the AIDS patient of the fact that this individual has AIDS."[37]

Exclusion in the Courts

The Sotto and Kasler essays reflect fundamentally different attitudes, not only with respect to the specific problem of HIV in the schools, but also with respect to the more general problem of making decisions and dealing with risks when the truth cannot be known with absolute certainty. They also reflect fundamentally different views as to the meaning of "the normal school setting." On the one hand, Sotto treats the behaviors associated with school attendance as if they all could be described as "casual contact." Kasler, in contrast, recognizes that school attendance encompasses a far greater diversity of behaviors, but she provides no basis for distinguishing among the many and various behaviors that may amount to something more than "casual contact." In neither case, therefore, does the commentator provide any rigorous discussion of "significant risk" and "otherwise qualified"—two concepts that are central for section 504 purposes. With these considerations in mind, we will review the present state of the law with respect to section 504, the Education of the Handicapped Act, and the equal protection clause.[38]

Section 504

Although the Supreme Court has not yet expressly considered the question, it seems relatively well settled that section 504 generally protects children with HIV. The leading case in this area, *Chalk v. United States District Court*,[39] involves an AIDS-diagnosed teacher of hearing-impaired students, rather than a student, but its reasoning and holding seem equally applicable to students. In *Chalk*, the teacher invoked section 504 to challenge the school district's decision to reassign him to administrative duties. On appeal from the denial of Chalk's motion for a preliminary injunction, the Ninth Circuit held that Chalk was a handicapped person within the meaning of the act, and that the district court had erred in holding that he was not "otherwise qualified." The district court had denied relief to Chalk, notwithstanding the "overwhelming consensus of medical opinion," solely on the basis of "speculation for which there was no credible support in the record."[40] The district court had rejected the sufficiency of the medical evidence, stating:

> It seems to me the problem is that we simply do not know enough about AIDS to be *completely certain*. The plaintiff has submitted massive documentation tending to show a minimal risk. . . . The likelihood is that the medical profession knows exactly what it's talking about. But I think it's too early to draw a definite conclusion, as far as this case is concerned, about the extent of the risk.[41]

The Ninth Circuit concluded that the district court had placed "an impossible burden of proof" on Chalk, and that its language simply misconceived the *Arline* decision, which allows an employee to be excluded "only if there 'is a *significant* risk of communicating an infectious disease to others.' "[42] The court also observed: "Little in science can be proved with complete certainty, and Section 504 does not require such a test."[43]

The *Chalk* court correctly articulated and applied the "significant risk" test. The court made clear, not only that evaluations of risk must be based on fact, rather than speculation or general misgivings about the nature of scientific knowledge, but also that the presence of *some* risk would not necessarily demonstrate the existence of a *significant* risk. In this respect, *Chalk* may usefully be compared with two later decisions, *Doe v. Dolton Elementary School District No. 148*[44] and *Doe v. Washington University*.[45] Those cases demonstrate considerable confusion on both points.

In *Dolton*, the Northern District of Illinois held that a student with AIDS, who had been excluded from regular classes and extracurricular activities, was "likely to be considered a handicapped individual," either by virtue of having a physical impairment which substantially limits his life activities, or by virtue of being regarded as having such an impairment. The court also concluded that the student was "otherwise qualified" because, "[i]n this case, . . . there is no significant risk of transmission in the classroom setting."[46] On this point, the court noted, "the consensus of medical authority is overwhelming."[47]

The *Dolton* court relied extensively on *Chalk,* and seemed not to think that the case raised any particularly close question. At the end of its opinion, however, the court struck an almost apologetic note: "Any public misperception associated with this student's reentry into the classroom should be reduced, if not removed altogether, by the court's conscientious attempt to protect the interests of all concerned."[48] In addition, the court did not simply order the student to be readmitted, but also ordered that he not engage in any contact sports, that he be examined each month by his personal physician, that he be examined each week by the school nurse, and that his identity be disclosed to all faculty and staff.[49] The court gave no explanation as to the purported need for these measures.

The *Dolton* court expressed its misgivings only in its decree, whereas the court in *Doe v. Washington University* simply held that the existence of *some* risk of transmission precluded a dental student with HIV from being considered "otherwise qualified" under section 504. In reaching that conclusion, the court noted that the dispute turned on assessing the probability that the virus would be transmitted to a patient during clinical training. The court observed:

> This area is at the heart of this country's debate surrounding HIV infected individuals, as there has been only limited study of the risk of HIV transmission from infected health-care workers to patients. Although since the filing of this lawsuit a number of cases have been publicized that indicate the realistic possibility of transmission of HIV from an infected health care worker to a patient, there is no nationwide consensus on the precise probability that an HIV-infected dental student will transmit HIV to a patient.[50]

The court further noted the parties' agreement that the risk of transmission was "a low but existent risk, not now capable of precise measure."[51] Although the student claimed that the use of proper barrier techniques could remove that risk, the court argued that "[t]his absolute is refuted in light of the Bergalis tragedy in which a Florida dentist infected five of his patients with the same virus/strain of AIDS that caused the dentist's death."[52] The court acknowledged that the risk of transmission may be minimal, but concluded that the student could not be deemed "otherwise qualified" because "there is still *some risk* of transmission."[53]

The Education of the Handicapped Act

The availability of relief under the Education of the Handicapped Act (EHA) will depend upon the existence of something more than mere seropositivity. In *Doe v. Belleville Public School District No. 118,*[54] the court held that children with HIV would not automatically be considered "handicapped" under the act.[55] To come within that definition, a student's physical condition must be such that it adversely affects her ability to learn and do the required classroom work.[56] Obviously, the mere fact that a student is seropositive would not meet that test, as a New York state court held in *District 27 Community School Board v. Board of Education*.[57]

In *Martinez v. School Board*,[58] the Eleventh Circuit exhaustively considered the proper relationship of the two statutes, holding that a student with HIV was entitled to seek relief under the EHA, in addition to section 504, not by virtue of her seropositivity, but because she was mentally handicapped. Based on evidence suggesting a "'remote theoretical possibility' of transmission of the AIDS virus through tears, saliva and urine," the trial court had found that the appropriate educational placement for the student was for her to be taught, until she was toilet-trained and no longer placed her fingers in her mouth, in a separate classroom with a glass window and sound system to allow her to see and hear her fellow students.[59]

The Eleventh Circuit, holding that the student was entitled to the benefits of both statutes, found that the evidence did not support the placement ordered by the trial court. According to the Eleventh Circuit, the trial court should have made the following inquiry:

> Applying the standards under these two statutes to the facts of this case, the trial court first had to determine the most appropriate educational placement . . . under the [EHA]. Next, it had to consider whether [she] was otherwise qualified to be educated in this setting. If the trial court found that [she] was not otherwise qualified, it then had to consider whether reasonable accommodations would make her so. If, after reasonable accommodations, a *significant risk* of transmission would still exist, [she] would not be otherwise qualified.[60]

The trial court never made this inquiry because it mistakenly relied on evidence of a "remote theoretical possibility" of transmission, with respect to tears, saliva, and urine, to substitute for the "significant risk" required to justify exclusion from the classroom. The case required remand because the trial court "made no findings with respect to the overall risk of transmission from all bodily substances, including blood in the saliva, to which other children might be exposed in [this particular] classroom."[61]

Equal Protection

With respect to the equal protection questions raised by the exclusion of children with HIV, there seems little to add to the Sotto and Kasler essays. In Sotto's view, "AIDS-related children and healthy children with no link to AIDS are similarly situated with regard to AIDS because neither group can transfer the disease in the normal, unrestricted school setting." For that reason, according to Sotto, any classification of children based solely on seropositivity would violate the equal protection clause under any available standard of review. In Kasler's view, however, "[c]hildren with diseases are not similarly situated with non-victims and may necessarily, for the protection of everyone, be addressed separately."[62] According to Kasler, therefore, differential treatment of children with HIV would not violate equal protection.[63]

Whether such exclusionary policies would pass constitutional muster seems now, as then, to be a matter for debate. There are no more recent cases on point, and that situation appears unlikely to change. In most circumstances, the values embodied in the equal protection clause will be enforced in this area through section 504 of the Rehabilitation Act, the EHA, and the Americans with Disabilities Act. There will be little reason to address the constitutional question. At all events, it is unlikely that the Supreme Court would apply strict scrutiny in these circumstances,[64] and it seems improbable that the Court would strike down many policies under a less searching standard of review.[65] On the other hand, it is unlikely that the courts would simply accept Kasler's facile distinction between "children with diseases" and "non-victims." Certainly, the courts would inquire into the nature of a particular disease, whether it is contagious, and the means by which it can be transmitted, before they approved any differential treatment afforded to children with that disease. In addition, the courts necessarily would inquire into the nature of the exclusionary or other treatment afforded to "children with diseases," and consider the relationship of that treatment to the ends sought to be achieved. Thus, one can readily imagine circumstances, such as the enforcement of a policy categorically prohibiting students with HIV from attending regular high school classes, where no reasonable argument in favor of constitutionality could be made.

Identifying Students with HIV and the Claims of Personal Privacy

In the preceding discussion, we have set to one side the feasibility of identifying students with HIV. We have simply assumed that all such students are identifiable. That assumption is unwarranted, however, and an additional series of problems arises from that fact. For example, Sotto has argued that the automatic removal of children known to be seropositive "is underinclusive because it fails to segregate many who in fact may be carriers of AIDS, such as untested children who are infected . . . but are asymptomatic, or children who have been very recently contaminated with the virus and therefore would generate negative antibody test results." The point is well taken. If one assumes that children with HIV do constitute a serious threat to the public health, one cannot consistently depend upon self-identification to identify and deal with all of them. On the other hand, a policy of universal, mandatory testing of schoolchildren would be objectionable on numerous grounds, not the least of which would be the huge monetary cost that would have to be incurred to secure information of admittedly limited value.[66] In fact, of course, no reasonable strategy for dealing with HIV, in the schools or elsewhere, can be predicated upon the assumption that we can always distinguish between those who are seropositive and those who are not. That is simply a vain hope, which necessarily distracts our attention from more efficacious responses such as education and the formulation of protocols that require people to act in certain circumstances as if they knew that they were in danger of exposure.

Some consideration must also be given to the related issue of confidentiality. An argument can be made for the proposition that some school officials should be given known information about a student's HIV status, notwithstanding the questionable utility of such information where schools will doubtless include many other children whose seropositivity is either unknown or unknowable.[67] Where there is some risk of transmission attendant upon a particular event, however, knowledge as to a student's seropositivity simply should not determine the response. In such circumstances, all students should be treated as if they were seropositive. Nonetheless, some states make elaborate provision for the notification of school officials. For example, Illinois requires that the Department of Public Health notify a student's school principal whenever the department has knowledge that the student has been exposed to HIV.[68] The principal, in turn, must notify the district superintendent. As a matter of discretion, the principal may also notify certain other persons who may have responsibility for or contact with the student. In each case, the principal may identify the particular student by name. Certain other persons also may be informed, but only that an unidentified child with HIV is enrolled.

In 1989 the American Bar Association noted that "[t]he privacy interests of children with respect to their HIV status are similar to those of adults. Without confidentiality, children with AIDS or HIV infection and their families may suffer discrimination, harassment and ostracism in school and in employment."[69] Given the student's obvious need for confidentiality, the broad discretion granted to principals by the Illinois statute seems unwise at best. In view of the numbers of persons to whom the principal is authorized to convey this theoretically protected information, it is not difficult to imagine the kind of investigation that would be required to ascertain the source of any subsequent disclosure. Certainly, any such subsequent disclosure should be subject to substantial civil or criminal penalties, but the deterrent effect of such penalties is at least open to question in these circumstances.

State disclosure statutes may well be subject to constitutional attack. Notwithstanding Kasler's assertions,[70] the question remains open as to whether a student's HIV status may be constitutionally protected. In *Whalen v. Roe*,[71] the Supreme Court recognized a constitutional right to privacy in certain personal information.[72] Subsequently, in *Nixon v. Administrator of General Services*,[73] the Supreme Court indicated that the precise limits of that right depend upon the application of a balancing test.[74] In line with these decisions, the District of New Jersey has held that a police officer's disclosure of an arrestee's HIV status violated his Fourteenth Amendment right to maintain the privacy of such information.[75] Several other courts have upheld a prisoner's right to maintain the confidentiality of his or her HIV status.[76] In the somewhat different context of civil discovery, the

Florida Supreme Court has concluded that the privacy rights of blood donors outweigh an infected plaintiff's right to know the donors' names.[77] It does not seem unlikely that the courts would reach similar results in the event that forced disclosure is challenged in the school setting.[78]

In sum, state disclosure statutes may well be subject to constitutional attack. They certainly do not represent good public policy, because they neither acknowledge nor accommodate the existence of competing values. They pay insufficient attention to the legitimate privacy interests of the individual student and her parents, while at the same time giving undue weight to a risk that may be only theoretical, and is very small at best. Even the Illinois scheme is preferable, however, to Kasler's assumption that mandatory disclosure is the entitlement of everyone whose path happens to cross that of a student with HIV.

Improving the Conversation

The conversation about HIV in the schools is characterized by an extraordinary lack of precision, even in terms of defining the problem. For example, Sotto talks about "the normal school setting" and "casual contact" as if the terms were not only synonymous but also adequate for describing the full range of behaviors in which schoolchildren engage from nursery school through adolescence and high school. Kasler, on the other hand, recognizes that problem but then proceeds to supply an arbitrarily chosen list of activities that purportedly "present a higher risk of transmission" and therefore should be "curtailed, monitored, and/or prohibited." Why a properly conducted high school biology class or bathroom visits should be characterized in this way is a matter that Kasler never explains. Nor does she explain how a "tough policy" of disclosing the identities of children known to have HIV will enhance the public health, despite our admitted inability to identify many other children with HIV, including those who might have identified themselves if reasonable assurances of confidentiality had been available. In neither case does one feel that the real problems are being addressed at all, let alone in a helpful or rigorous way.

To the extent that the conversation seems unsatisfactory, a large part of the problem is due to the imprecise language that the interlocutors have used to discuss risk. Moreover, that imprecision is not merely linguistic, but conceptual as well. For example, Kasler and Sotto do not simply differ as to what amount of risk may be acceptable; they differ as to the very possibility of quantifying and evaluating risks. Indeed, there is a sense in which they do not join issue at all. They are like ships passing in the night because their unarticulated assumptions make communication impossible. On the one hand, Sotto takes the position that risk analysis is simply a matter of scientific evidence. The facts are ascertainable, and once they are ascertained, the answer will follow as a matter of pure logic. In other words, questions in this realm can be resolved by resort to objective facts. As Kristin Shrader-Frechette has demonstrated, this view (which she calls naive positivism) is erroneous because "risk estimates are not purely objective and capable of being determined by experts." On the other hand, Kasler's absolute rejection of the authority of scientific evidence is both unhelpful and indefensible. Thus, "although hazard assessments can never be wholly value free (as many naive positivists claim), nevertheless it is false to assert (as many cultural relativists do) that any perspective on risk can be justified." As Shrader-Frechette suggests, "some risk judgments are more warranted than others are, although none is value free."[79]

To be sure, there is no perfect judgment about risk, and the term "significant risk" itself suggests a false possibility of avoiding normative judgments. To frame the question properly, we must recognize the need to determine not only whether the level of risk can be known, but also whether the level is "acceptable." In any event, it does not follow that "all risk attitudes are equally imperfect."[80] "Reasonable people accumulate observations and inferences about judgments until the probability of those judgments is so great that they do not doubt them. They make assumptions when their inferences and evidence support them, but they do not demand empirical confirmation for everything."[81] That certainly is the case here. Available scientific evidence may not be capable of demonstrating the categorical impossibility of HIV transmission in the school setting, but the evidence is sufficient to show, with respect to most activities that normally and legitimately take place in the school setting, that the risk of transmission is slight and not unlike other risks that we accept without question or alarm, and therefore tolerable in the main. We do indeed yearn for certainty, but there is little worth knowing, in science or elsewhere, that can be known with absolute certainty.[82] In practice, we tolerate a great deal of uncertainty, and we necessarily take risks because we do. We could not live, or act, if we did not.[83] In addition, the sheer volume of risks that we face is overwhelming. As a practical matter, therefore, there may be some comfort to be had in the scientific evidence. Likewise, there may be some persuasive power in the Centers for Disease Control's judgment that the risk of transmission in the school setting is "much less than the chance of the boiler that heats the building blowing up."[84] With this framework in mind, there are four points to be made.

First, we can say with assurance that we cannot predicate a strategy for dealing with the problem of HIV in the schools on the assumption that we can identify and segregate all children with HIV. Even if we thought that such identification and segregation were desirable as a matter of public policy, we would have to admit that the identification of all such children is simply not possible at the present time. This is so for at least three reasons: First, HIV tests cannot identify all persons who are seropositive and capable of transmitting the infection to others. No test is perfect, and the administration of any test is subject to human error. More important, currently available testing protocols are designed to detect antibodies, rather than the virus itself, and antibodies may not develop (and thus will not be detectable) for several months after transmission has occurred. Thus, a person may be seropositive, and capable of infecting others, while producing consistently negative test results.[85] Second, even if it were technologically possible to determine seropositivity with certainty, the cost of doing so with respect to all of the schoolchildren in America, at sufficiently short intervals to make the information more or less reliable (consistent with its inherent unreliability), would be prohibitive.[86] Third, we are more likely to identify students with HIV through voluntary self-identification, but self-identification is not likely to occur if such students are afforded unnecessary publicity or differential treatment. Thus, a policy that depends on our ability to identify all schoolchildren with HIV, and to treat them in a special way, is simply not feasible.

Second, there is sufficient scientific evidence for us to say with assurance that HIV is not transmitted through casual contact. Unlike some other viruses, HIV is not transmitted environmentally, and early studies showing the absence of transmission between family members in ordinary living situations remain substantially uncontroverted.[87] Thus, as one commentator has observed:

> Public health authorities, following CDC research and recommendations, emphasize that HIV cannot be transmitted through "casual" contact, such as living in the same household, attending the same school, or working with a person who has HIV infection. Studies of the household contacts of persons with HIV infection found no evidence of transmission through nonsexual contacts. Researchers examined a variety of activities, including sharing household items (such as eating utensils, drinking glasses, toothbrushes, towels), sharing household facilities (such as beds, bath/showers, toilets), washing items used by HIV-positive individuals (such as dishes and clothes), and interacting with HIV-positive individuals (such as hugging, kissing, helping someone to bathe or eat).[88]

To be sure, most of the interactions that occur in the school setting may reliably be described as "casual contact." It would be a mistake, however, to suggest that "casual contact" necessarily exhausts the universe. For example, one would have to be very disconnected to take the view that consensual (or even nonconsensual) sexual intercourse is unthinkable in today's schools, and sexual intercourse necessarily involves the same degree of risk, regardless of where the conduct occurs. The same might well be said of needle sharing. Similarly, blood to blood contact is an effective means of transmission. It may well be very unlikely that transmission will result from the kinds of blood-to-blood contact that typically occur in the school setting, but the literature reflects one case in which transmission of the virus is believed to have resulted from an exceptionally bloody fistfight that broke out during a wedding reception.[89] There is no reason to rule out the very possibility of such an occurrence in school.

Third, having recognized the possibility that some conduct capable of transmission may occur in the school setting, we need to consider how to deal with it. In this connection, we should consider sexual intercourse, miscellaneous opportunities for exposure to blood, and contact sports.

Although Kasler gives great prominence to the problem of sexual intercourse in the schools, opening her essay with the example of two high school students who wish to consummate their relationship,[90] one would be remiss if one failed to emphasize that sexual intercourse, whether consensual or not, has no claim to being an integral part of the school experience. At the same time, however, it is unlikely that we can do anything to make sexual intercourse appear so unappealing to adolescents that the problem will cease to exist. The central point must be that consensual sexual intercourse is a matter of choice. Certainly, the schools should do their best to ensure that students are not using school property for such activities, but one would hope that the schools would take that view in any event. Moreover, the schools certainly should undertake strong educational efforts to ensure that students understand the risks they face from HIV and other sexually transmitted diseases, and students should have access to information about minimizing those risks. It is a bit far-fetched, however, to assume that the schools have a legitimate role to play in attempting to identify those sexual partners who may not be appropriate because of their HIV status.

Similarly, our concern about the possible transmission of HIV through coerced sexual intercourse should be focused on preventing predatory conduct in the schools, rather than on identifying those students who, because of their HIV status, would present a special danger if they engaged in that activity. It is not too much to expect that our schools be safe, and, to the extent that decisions must be made about allocating scarce resources, those resources should be devoted to ensuring that students are not sexually abused or raped, rather than being squandered on mandatory HIV testing, which is likely to have little effect outside the realm of public relations. If students are to be excluded, it should be those who will not conform their conduct to appropriate behavioral standards, not those who happen to be seropositive.

Opportunities for exposure to blood present a slightly different problem. In most cases, exposure to seropositive blood will not pose a "significant risk" of transmission. For transmission to occur, there must be blood-to-blood contact. In addition, we know that not all blood-to-blood contact will result in transmission of the virus. Perhaps the best proof of that fact is the many look-back studies showing that seropositive surgeons, engaged in highly invasive procedures, have not transmitted the virus to their patients.[91] On the other hand, the wedding brawl reported in *The Lancet* suggests that transmission may be possible in the context of an exceptionally bloody fistfight. Again, the most reasonable solution to this problem would not seem to be exclusion, but the formulation and enforcement of policies aimed at avoiding such occurrences in the school setting, and for the speedy implementation of universal precautions in cleaning up after such an event. Bloody fistfights are largely avoidable from the individual student's perspective, and school officials certainly can take strong measures to see that they do not occur.

With respect to contact sports, the American Academy of Pediatrics (AAP) has noted: "Although it is theoretically possible that transmission of HIV could occur in sports such as wrestling and football in which bleeding and skin abrasions are common, no such transmission has been reported in these sports."[92] The AAP therefore takes the position that athletes with HIV should be permitted to participate in all competitive sports; that those engaged in a sport involving blood exposure should be counseled with respect to the theoretical risk of contagion to others and encouraged to consider another sport; that physicians should not disclose a patient's HIV status to the participants or staff of athletic programs; and that all athletes should be made aware that the athletic program is operating pursuant to these policies. In addition, the AAP would place great weight on the use of certain universal precautions, such as the prompt cleaning of all injuries.[93] Given the absence of any documented case of transmission in the athletic context, and the voluntary nature of participation in contact sports, the AAP's resolution of this issue seems appropriate and consistent with existing legal requirements.

Fourth, the courts have talked about this problem in the terms laid down by *Arline,* but that language has been debased by subsequent decisions, and it needs to be reclaimed if the rule itself is not to be altered. On the one hand, the *Chalk* court recognized that there must be a "significant risk" of transmission before a person should be considered not "otherwise qualified" under section 504—a standard that seems unlikely to be met in the school context. On the other hand, the *Dolton* court purported to follow *Chalk,* found that the student's presence in the classroom presented no "significant risk," and then proceeded, without any explanation (apart from a perceived need to avoid "public misperception"), to frame a decree that imposed on the student conditions having no obvious connection to that finding. Moreover, the courts have routinely invoked "significant risk" as the legal standard governing their analysis, while at the same time perceiving the need for emphasizing that the actual risk of transmission in a particular situation could be characterized, as a factual matter, as negligible, close to zero, or "trivial to the point of non-existence."[94] That is fair enough, and it may well serve an important rhetorical purpose in a particular case. But such a repeated emphasis on the total absence of risk may well have a tendency to transform a serendipitous factual circumstance into a controlling legal standard. In this way, the absence of *all* risk tends to replace the absence of *significant* risk as the benchmark. Indeed, that is precisely what happened in *Washington University,* where the court went even further than the *Dolton* court, concluding that the plaintiff dental student was not "otherwise qualified" under section 504 because there was "*some* risk of transmission."[95] In other cases, adverse decisions have been rendered on the basis of an "extremely low" risk or "any" risk at all.[96]

Such reasoning is erroneous and bears no resemblance to the inquiry mandated by section 504. If the concept of "significant risk" is to be a useful concept in this area, the standard simply cannot be satisfied by the mere presence (or an inability to prove the absence) of "some risk." At the same time, we cannot deny the reality represented by these cases, or that embodied by Kasler's *cri du coeur*— that fear of children with HIV is not irrational. They reflect a basic but unachievable human desire to know with certainty and avoid risk categorically. It would be folly for us to ignore them.

Conclusion

In sum, we need to focus more carefully, and talk more precisely, about questions of risk. At the threshold, we need to establish a common ground for analyzing risks. In that respect, we must understand the unspoken assumptions underlying various views of risk. We also need to focus on specific conduct, and, to the extent we can, on the precise risk presented by that conduct. There are a number of legitimate questions to be raised: how large the risk is, how the risk compares to other risks that we routinely accept, what precisely is the cause of the risk, whether the risk can be reduced, how the risk can be reduced, what values are to be weighed against measures aimed at reducing the risk, what costs would be reasonable to incur in securing various levels of risk reduction. What level of risk is "significant," and what criteria should we use to determine whether a particular level of risk is unacceptable?

These questions are not easy, and they may well lead to other questions, themselves raising important moral issues. Where risks are indeed thought to be significant, for example, one might wish to probe the grounds upon which society properly may cause individuals to be subjected to those risks. Likewise, if risks are to be avoided, we must not only ascertain the costs, but determine by whom they are to be borne. We must recognize that considerations of fairness and safety will not point invariably in the same direction, and that we cannot therefore be spared from the demands of judgment. By pursuing these questions, we may well be persuaded that the risks presented by mainstreaming children with HIV are not so daunting as the proponents of exclusion have proclaimed. More important, we may avoid having our public policy determined by irrational fear in the event that a case of school-based transmission actually occurs. And we may even make some progress in dealing with the problem of HIV in the schools. At the same time, we must remember that this problem is but a small part of that larger "web of associated social ills"[97] that cry out for inclusion in our public agenda. Those issues also urgently require that we find a common ground for conversation and action. This chapter has attempted to suggest some openings in aid of that greater project, which necessarily will be left for another day. In the interim, we would do well, as Emerson suggested, to place our faith in the power of "common-sense and plain dealing."[98] We cannot afford to do otherwise.

NOTES

Acknowledgments: The views expressed in this chapter are those of the author and should not be attributed to the American Bar Association or the Coordinating Committee on AIDS. The author would like to thank Patricia A. Davidson, S. Michelle Malinowski, Thaddeus J. Nodzenski, Leonard Rubinowitz, and Winnifred F. Sullivan for helpful comments on an earlier draft.

1. American Bar Association, AIDS: The Legal Issues: Discussion Draft of the

American Bar Association AIDS Coordinating Committee 188 (1988) [hereinafter ABA Discussion Draft]; *see also* American Bar Association, American Bar Association Policy and Report on AIDS, 21 U. Tol. L. Rev. 9, 16, 89–99 (1989) [hereinafter ABA Policy and Report].

2. *See generally* D. Kirp, Learning by Heart: AIDS and Schoolchildren in America's Communities (1989). The incidence of AIDS transmission through blood transfusions has decreased substantially since 1985, when testing of the blood supply became commonplace. *See* ABA Discussion Draft, *supra* note 1, at 87–89.

3. *See* ABA Discussion Draft, *supra* note 1, at 206; *see generally* Arras, AIDS and Reproductive Decisions: Having Children in Fear and Trembling, 68 Milbank Memorial Fund Q. 353, 356–57 (1990); Lovell Banks, Women and AIDS—Racism, Sexism and Classism, 17 N.Y.U. Rev. L. & Soc. Change 351, 352–53 (1989–90).

4. National Commission on Acquired Immune Deficiency Syndrome, America Living with AIDS: Transforming Anger, Fear and Indifference into Action: Report of the National Commission on Acquired Immune Deficiency Syndrome 14 (1991); *see also* Dalton, AIDS in Blackface, in Living with AIDS 237 (S. Graubard ed., 1990). Similarly, Susan Sontag has observed: "That it is a punishment for deviant behavior and that it threatens the innocent—these two notions about AIDS are hardly in contradiction. Such is the extraordinary potency and efficacy of the plague metaphor: it allows a disease to be regarded both as something incurred by vulnerable 'others' and as (potentially) everyone's disease." S. Sontag, AIDS and Its Metaphors 64 (1989).

5. *See* ABA Discussion Draft, *supra* note 1, at 188; ABA Policy and Report, *supra* note 1, at 89–91. Many younger children will, of course, spend comparable amounts of time in day care settings. Much of the analysis in this chapter will also apply to them.

6. *See, e.g.,* Kass, Schoolchildren with AIDS, in AIDS and the Law: A Guide for the Public 66 (H. Dalton & S. Burris eds., 1987); *see also* Sontag, AIDS and Its Metaphors, *supra* note 4, at 27.

7. These counterarguments, which are diametrically opposed in one sense, nonetheless share a common premise. The proponents of exclusion assert that children should not be subject to any risk of HIV, and that the absence of conclusive proof as to the absolute impossibility of transmission in the school setting therefore requires exclusion. Some opponents of exclusion do not take issue directly with the view that no risk is acceptable, however negligible, but attempt to show that a negligible risk may be redefined as no risk at all. By failing to challenge the assumption that the categorical avoidance of risk is an achievable goal, those opponents of exclusion concede a significant part of the argument.

8. In Doe v. Washington Univ., 780 F. Supp. 628 (E.D. Mo. 1991), for example, the trial judge was greatly influenced by reports that Dr. David Acer had most probably infected five of his patients. The judge found no reason to analyze the question further once he had found *"some risk* of transmission." *Id.* at 633 (emphasis in original); *see generally* Sullivan, AIDS and the Medical Boards: Some Legal Issues, 78 Fed. Bull. 266, 266 (1991). This tendency to end the inquiry once *some* risk is demonstrated has been replicated in decisions involving physicians, nurses, firefighters, and paramedics. *See, e.g.,* Behringer v. Medical Center, 55 Fair Empl. Prac. Case. 1145, 1164–67 (N.J. Super. 1991); Leckelt v. Board of Comm'rs

of Hosp. Dist. No.1, 909 F.2d 820, 829–30 (5th Cir. 1990); Severino v. North Fort Myers Fire Control Dist., 935 F.2d 1179, 1182 (11th Cir. 1991); Anonymous Fireman v. Willoughby, 779 F. Supp. 402, 416 (N.D. Ohio 1991). In such cases, the courts have effectively found that no risk of HIV transmission can be tolerated.

9. *See* Kasler, Comment, Reading, Writing, but No Biting: Isolating School Children with AIDS, 37 Clev. St. L. Rev. 337 (1989) [hereinafter Kasler Comment].

10. *See* Shrader-Frechette, Reductionist Approaches to Risk, in Acceptable Evidence: Science and Values in Risk Management 218, 219 (D. Mayo & R. Hollander eds., 1991).

11. R. Shilts, And the Band Played On: Politics, People, and the AIDS Epidemic 578–79, 594–96 (1987).

12. 480 U.S. 273 (1987). In *Arline,* the Supreme Court held that persons with a contagious disease were not necessarily precluded from relief under section 504 of the Rehabilitation Act of 1973, 29 U.S.C. § 794 (1985), but should be evaluated individually to determine whether they are "otherwise qualified." 480 U.S. at 285.

13. *See* 29 U.S.C. § 794 (1985).

14. The Department of Justice stated: "[A] person who is discriminated against because he is (or is regarded as) seropositive [is not handicapped and thus] has no claim under section 504. Nor can he challenge the reasonableness of the defendant's judgment about the risk that he will spread the disease; defendants are not prohibited by section 504 from making incorrect, and even irrational, decisions as long as their decisions are not based on handicap." Memo from Assistant Attorney General Cooper on Application of Section 504 of Rehabilitation Act to Persons with AIDS, BNA Daily Labor Report at D-10 (June 25, 1986) (footnotes omitted). In 1988, the department reversed course. *See* Justice Department Memorandum on Application of Rehabilitation Act's section 504 to HIV-Infected Persons, BNA Daily Labor Report at D-1 (Oct. 7, 1988).

15. *See* 20 U.S.C. §§ 1400–1454 (1982 & Supp.III 1985) (subsequently renamed Individuals with Disabilities Education Act).

16. *See* U.S. Const. amend. XIV, § 1.

17. For example, Sotto had little difficulty in finding a qualifying "physical impairment" for section 504 purposes (*see* Chapter 29), even though there was a serious question as to whether asymptomatic HIV infection actually could be deemed to limit a "major life activity," which was defined by regulation to include functions such as caring for oneself, performing manual tasks, walking, seeing, breathing, learning, and working. *Id., citing* 45 C.F.R. § 84.4(j)(2)(ii) (1985). Similarly, Sotto found that children with asymptomatic HIV infection were protected by the Education of the Handicapped Act (EHA) based on a regulation that defined "other health impaired children" to include children who suffer from "limited strength or vitality . . . due to chronic or acute health problems." *Id., citing* 34 C.F.R. § 300.5(b)(7) (1986). That conclusion seems questionable.

18. To say the least, Sotto's approach to these problems is based on a naive view as to the existence, certainty, and ascertainability of "medical facts." She does not recognize that "[t]he core methodological concern . . . is how to use the partial regularities disclosed by scientific investigation to fortify, without overpowering, the introspective element needed to make net judgments on particular cases." Lerner, Preface to the issue "On Evidence and Inference," 87 Daedalus 3, 7 (1958);

see also Shrader-Frechette, Reductionist Approaches to Risk, *supra* note 10, at 219. On the other hand, Kasler seems to suggest that controlling weight should be afforded to popular fears, presumably because of the impossibility of identifying any legitimate, objective criteria for evaluating risks. *See* Kasler Comment, *supra* note 9, at 339. Sanford Kuvin makes a similar point: "[I]f you are pricked with HIV-infected blood your chances of acquiring HIV are less than half of 1%. But what about the risk to the 40 health care workers known to be HIV-infected in this country from patients, and what about Kimberly Bergalis and the other four patients infected from one dentist in Florida? All of these HIV victims view their risk as 100%." Kuvin, A Proactive Public Health Policy for the Mandatory Testing of Health Care Workers and Patients Involved in Invasive Procedures, 2 Cts. Health Sci. & L. 115, 117 (1991) (footnotes omitted).

19. Kasler chides the medical profession for its inability to provide irrefutable proof that HIV will not be transmitted in the school setting, while at the same time refusing to agree that quarantine or isolation is a necessary strategy for dealing with children with HIV. *See* Kasler Comment, *supra* note 9, at 338-53. Thus, she asserts that "[i]f doctors and the medical profession present the courts with medical facts, perhaps they must meet the *Jacobson [v. Massachusetts,* 197 U.S. 11 (1905),] test of proven, statistical knowledge, rather than the tenuous assumptions surrounding AIDS." Kasler Comment, *supra* note 9, at 351. It might be argued that Kasler's point shows little sophistication about the nature of scientific evidence or theory. Indeed, Kasler seems to be faulting medical science for its inherent inability to prove a negative. But such criticisms have no force if one starts, as Kasler does, from the proposition that children with HIV must be excluded from school unless medical science can establish, categorically and beyond a reasonable doubt, that transmission cannot occur in the school context.

20. *See* Kasler Comment, *supra* note 9, at 337.

21. *Id.* at 338.

22. *Id.*

23. *Id.*

24. *Id.* at 339 (emphasis added); *see also* Sontag, AIDS and Its Metaphors, *supra* note 4, at 82.

25. Kasler Comment, *supra* note 9, at 366. Taken to its logical conclusion, Kasler's view necessarily would preclude any weighing of costs and benefits in connection with health or safety matters. On this basis, for example, how could one deny the need for perfectly clean air? The degree of personal autonomy assumed by Kasler is certainly inconsistent with membership in a modern industrial society, and is probably inconsistent with membership in any civil society. *See* Sontag, AIDS and Its Metaphors, *supra* note 4, at 73. Kasler's analysis therefore preempts consideration of the truly nettlesome and most important issues—that is, the normative questions of justly apportioning costs and benefits when costs and benefits do not necessarily involve the same populations or individuals, and determining what levels of risk should be deemed acceptable.

26. Kasler Comment, *supra* not 9, at 362.

27. *Id.* at 365 (emphasis added).

28. *Id.* at 366.

29. *Id.* (footnote omitted). Two points should be made. First, Kasler provides no

factual basis for selecting the particular activities that she deems to present a higher risk of transmission. Second, by asserting that the courts will be better able to address the problem with "rules and tangible standards," Kasler nicely sums up the predicament she has created. She does not want to credit well-established medical evidence, and she does not want that evidence to play any role in the formulation of legal standards in this area. But if legal standards are not to be based on the best available medical evidence, upon what will they be based? The source and basis of Kasler's "rules and tangible standards" simply remain unidentified.

30. *Id.* at 353. Unlike Sotto, Kasler published her essay after *Arline* had been decided and the Department of Justice had changed its position as to the applicability of section 504 to persons with HIV. According to Kasler, *Arline* is distinguishable on the ground that tuberculosis, unlike AIDS, is treatable and controllable. *Id.* at 355. The proper approach, therefore, is to weigh the possible harm to the child with HIV against the possible harm to other children. If a school system affords alternative educational opportunities to the child with HIV, the harm to her will be minimized, and the balance will therefore tip heavily in favor of protecting other children from the seropositive child. *Id.*

31. Although the EHA provides that children with disabilities generally should be afforded a free appropriate public education in a classroom with their peers to the maximum extent possible, *see* 20 U.S.C. § 1400(c) (1988), Kasler takes the words "appropriate" and "maximum extent possible" as affording ample room for excluding students with HIV. *See* Kasler Comment, *supra* note 9, at 357–58. In these circumstances, "[t]he maximum extent possible may be limited by the reasonable assumption of harm to others." *Id.*

32. Kasler likewise sees no constitutional difficulty in affording disparate treatment to children with HIV. First, strict scrutiny is unnecessary because education is not a fundamental right, and children with HIV do not constitute a suspect class. Second, the classification necessarily passes constitutional muster because "[c]hildren with diseases are not similarly situated with non-victims and may necessarily, for the protection of everyone, be addressed separately." *Id.* at 358.

33. *Id.* at 359.

34. 429 U.S. 589 (1977).

35. *See* Kasler Comment, *supra* note 9, at 362.

36. 551 P.2d 334 (Ca. 1976).

37. *See* Kasler Comment, *supra* note 9, at 363 (footnote omitted).

38. In the future, it will also be necessary to consider the effect of the Americans with Disabilities Act, 42 U.S.C. § 12101 *et seq.* (1990). A full discussion of that act is beyond the scope of this Chapter, but it should be noted that Titles II and III of the act will cover various types of public and private educational institutions. *See* 42 U.S.C. §§ 12131 *et seq.* (Title II, Public Services); 42 U.S.C. §§ 12181 *et seq.* (Title III, Public Accommodations and Services Operated by Private Entities). It also should be noted that the act affords protection, not only to those who have or are perceived to have HIV disease, but also to those who are "known to have a relationship or association" with someone with HIV. *See* 42 U.S.C.A. §§ 12112(b)(4), 12182(b)(E) (1992); 56 Fed. Reg. 35, 737 (July 26, 1991). Timothy Bishop has provided a preliminary analysis of the relationship between the Americans with Disabilities Act and previous antidiscrimination statutes. *See* Bishop, Discrimination against Persons with HIV Disease: The Americans with Disabilities Act §§ 9.4, 9.5, in AIDS Practice Manual (P. Albert et al. eds., 4th ed. 1992).

Since 1988, the Department of Justice has taken the position that section 504 protects persons with HIV, whether asymptomatic or not. Although Gary Lawson has strongly criticized that position, he also has predicted that it is likely to prevail, if and when the Supreme Court addresses the issue. *See* Lawson, AIDS, Astrology and *Arline:* Towards a Causal Interpretation of Section 504, 17 Hofstra L. Rev. 237, 298–99 (1989).

39. 840 F.2d 701 (9th Cir. 1988).

40. *Id.* at 708.

41. *Id.* at 707 (emphasis by court of appeals).

42. *Id.* at 707–708, *quoting* Sch. Board v. Arline, 480 U.S. 273, 288 n.16 (1987) (emphasis by court of appeals).

43. *Id.* at 707; *see also id.* at 712 (Sneed, J., concurring). While some question was initially raised as to whether an asymptomatic person with HIV could be considered handicapped for purposes of section 504, it now seems settled that an asymptomatic person will be deemed to be one who "has a physical or mental impairment which substantially limits one or more of such person's major life activities." *See* 29 U.S.C.A. § 706(8)(B)(i) (1991). In addition, an asymptomatic person may qualify for protection as one who "is regarded as having such an impairment." *See* 29 U.S.C.A. § 706(8)(B)(iii) (1991); Doe v. Dolton Elementary Sch. Dist. No. 148, 694 F. Supp. 440, 443–44 (N.D. Ill. 1988).

44. 694 F. Supp. 440 (N.D. Ill. 1988).

45. 780 F. Supp. 628 (E.D. Mo. 1991).

46. *Dolton*, 694 F. Supp. at 445.

47. *See id.* at 444–47. The court also rejected the school district's argument that the availability of home instruction precluded a finding of irreparable harm. *Id.* at 446–48.

48. *Id.* at 449.

49. *See id.*

50. Doe v. Washington Univ., 780 F. Supp. at 632.

51. *Id.* at 633.

52. *Id.*

53. *Id.* at 632–33 (emphasis in original). One would have to agree that a dental student is distinguishable from other students in the sense that there is some basis for believing the virus actually may have been transmitted through dental procedures. That fact, however, would seem to provide the starting point, rather than the conclusion, for analyzing the issue under the "significant risk" standard. Moreover, very little is actually known about the practices followed in Dr. Acer's office, and what is known has led most experts to believe that he followed substandard infection-control procedures. *See* National Commission on Acquired Immune Deficiency Syndrome, Preventing HIV Transmission in Health Care Settings 12 (1992). Certainly, there is no basis for asserting that Dr. Acer's practices demonstrate the insufficiency of "proper barrier techniques." Indeed, the *Washington University* court's conviction as to the power of its evidence is belied by the fact that it relies on the Acer case on several different occasions, giving the impression on each occasion that it is discussing yet another confirming case, rather than merely repeating the same example. *See* Doe v. Washington Univ., 780 F. Supp. at 633–34 & n.8.

54. *See* 672 F. Supp. 342 (S.D. Ill. 1987).

55. In *Belleville*, the school district was claiming that the student's rights were to be determined under the EHA, rather than under the Rehabilitation Act, a strategy aimed at securing a dismissal of the complaint for failure to exhaust administrative remedies. *Id.* at 343. Where section 504 and the EHA provide concurrent rights, the plaintiff must exhaust administrative remedies before filing suit under section 504. *See* 20 U.S.C. § 1415(f) (1988).

56. *See Belleville*, 672 F. Supp. at 344–45; *accord* Robertson v. Granite City Community Unit Sch. Dist. No. 9, 684 F. Supp. 1002, 1005 (S.D. Ill. 1988).

57. *See* 502 N.Y.S.2d 325 (N.Y. Sup. Ct. 1986).

58. 861 F.2d 1502 (11th Cir. 1988).

59. *Id.* at 1504.

60. *Id.* at 1506 (emphasis added); *see also* Thomas v. Atascadero Unified Sch. Dist., 662 F. Supp. 376, 381–82 (C.D. Cal. 1986).

61. *Martinez*, 861 F.2d at 1506.

62. Kasler Comment, *supra* note 9, at 358.

63. *Id.* at 358–59.

64. *See, e.g.*, City of Cleburne v. Cleburne Living Center, 473 U.S. 432, 442–446 (1985).

65. *See, e.g.*, Gregory v. Ashcroft, 111 S. Ct. 2395, 2406 (1991) (rational basis test); Clark v. Jeter, 486 U.S. 456, 461–64 (1988) (intermediate scrutiny test).

66. *See* Bloom & Glied, Benefits and Costs of HIV Testing, 252 Sci. 1798 (1991); Gerberding, Expected Costs of Implementing a Mandatory Immunodeficiency Virus and Hepatitis B Virus Testing and Restriction Program for Healthcare Workers Performing Invasive Procedures, 12 Infection Control & Hosp. Epidemiology 443 (1991). The value of the information is admittedly limited because testing is inherently imperfect and subject to human error. In addition, currently available tests detect antibodies rather than the virus itself, and therefore fail to identify persons who are infected and therefore capable of infecting others, but are not yet seropositive.

67. The National Association of State Boards of Education has taken the position that information about a student's HIV status should be shared with as few persons as possible. *See* National Association of State Boards of Education, Someone at School Has AIDS: A Guide to Developing Policies for Students and School Staff Members Who Are Infected With HIV 15–17 (1989); *see also* S. Rennert, AIDS/HIV and Confidentiality: Model Policy and Procedures 50 (1991).

68. *See* 410 Ill. Comp. Stat. 315/2a(1993). *See also* 410 Ill. Comp. Stat. 305/9(d)(1993).

69. ABA Policy and Report, *supra* note 1, at 98; *see also* Current Trends: Education and Foster Care of Children Infected with Human T-Lymphotropic Virus Type III/Lymphadenopathy-Associated Virus, 34 Morbidity & Mortality Weekly Rep. 517, 520 (recommendation 10) (1985); Report of the Presidential Commission on the Human Immunodeficiency Virus Epidemic 125 (1988); Task Force on Pediatric AIDS, Education of Children with Human Immunodeficiency Virus Infection, 88 Pediatrics 645, 646–47 (1991).

70. *See* Kasler Comment, *supra* note 9, at 359–63.

71. 429 U.S. 589 (1977).

72. *Id.* at 599–600; *see also* Thornburgh v. American College of Obstetricians and Gynecologists, 476 U.S. 747, 766 (1986); Moody, Note, AIDS and Rape: The Constitutional Dimensions of Mandatory Testing of Sex Offenders, 76 Corn. L. Rev. 238, 261 (1990).

73. 433 U.S. 425 (1977).

74. *Id.* at 458, 465.

75. *See* Doe v. Borough of Barrington, 729 F. Supp. 376, 382–85 (D.N.J. 1990). *See also* Doe v. City of New York, 1994 WL 24213 (2d Cir. Jan. 28, 1994) (New York Human Rights Commission violated right to privacy by revealing details of conciliation agreement, including complainant's HIV status); Doe v. Town of Plymouth, 825 F. Supp. 1102, 1107 (D. Mass. 1993) ("plaintiff has a constitutional right to privacy which encompasses nondisclosure of her HIV status"). On the other hand, the Illinois Supreme Court recently upheld mandatory HIV testing for persons convicted of prostitution, notwithstanding the absence of any standards to govern the trial judge's discretion in determining to whom, or in what circumstances, the test results may be disclosed. *See* People v. Adams, 597 N.E.2d 574 (Ill. 1992). Illinois courts also have held that the news media may disclose such mandatory testing of convicted prostitutes without violating the Illinois AIDS Confidentiality Act, 410 Ill. Comp. Stat. 305/1 *et seq.* (1993), the information already being a matter of public record. *See* Doe v. Alton Telegraph, 805 F. Supp. 30, 32 (C.D. Ill. 1992); *In re* Application of Multi Media KSDK, Inc., 581 N.E.2d 911, 914 (Ill. App. Ct. 1991).

76. *See, e.g.,* Nolley v. County of Erie, 776 F. Supp. 715, 731 (W.D.N.Y. 1991); Woods v. White, 689 F. Supp. 874, 876 (W.D. Wis. 1988), *aff'd,* 899 F.2d 17 (7th Cir. 1990); Doe v. Coughlin, 697 F. Supp. 1234, 1241 (N.D.N.Y. 1988). The Eleventh Circuit has held that prisoners have a constitutionally protected privacy interest in nondisclosure of their HIV status, but that interest is outweighed by the government's interest in segregating inmates with HIV to prevent violence and transmission of the virus. *See* Harris v. Thigpen, 941 F.2d 1495, 1521 (11th Cir. 1991).

77. *See* Rasmussen v. South Florida Blood Serv., Inc., 500 So. 2d 533, 535 (Fla. 1987). *See also* Coleman v. American Red Cross, 979 F.2d 1135, 1139 (6th Cir. 1992) (affirming district court's denial of motion to compel discovery of donor's identity); Doe v. American Nat'l Red Cross, 790 F. Supp. 590, 594 (D.S.C. 1992) (upholding South Carolina's statutory privilege barring disclosure of donor's identity); Estate of Hoyle v. American Red Cross, 149 F.R.D. 215, 217 (D. Utah 1993) (granting motion to prevent disclosure of donor's identity based on right to privacy). A contrary result was reached by the Texas Court of Appeals. *See* Tarrant County Hosp. Dist. v. Hughes, 734 S.W.2d 675, 679 (Tex. Ct. App. 1987). Many of the courts which have permitted disclosure of the names of blood donors have taken steps to prevent public disclosure, such as restricting disclosure to the party's attorney, or to an attorney appointed to represent the donor, and requiring that documents containing confidential information be filed under seal. *See* Watson v. Lowcountry Red Cross, 974 F.2d 482, 487–88 (4th Cir. 1992); Borzillieri v. American Nat'l Red Cross, 139 F.R.D. 284, 289 (W.D.N.Y 1991); Sampson v. American Nat'l Red Cross, 139 F.R.D. 95, 99–100 (N.D. Tex. 1991).

78. The Family Educational Rights and Privacy Act protects the confidentiality of certain student records. *See* 20 U.S.C. § 1232g(b)(1)–(2) (1988). The protection afforded by this statute is somewhat limited, however, in that it purports to address only "a policy or practice of releasing" certain personally identifiable information. In addition, the sole remedy for violations of the statute is the termination of federal funding. Several courts have held that this statute does not afford any private right of action. *See* Tarka v. Franklin, 891 F.2d 102, 104 (5th Cir. 1989), *cert. denied*, 494 U.S. 1080 (1990); Fay v. South Colonie Cent. Sch. Dist., 802 F.2d 21, 33 (2d Cir. 1986).

79. Shrader-Frechette, Reductionist Approaches to Risk, *supra* note 10, at 220. Thus, Shrader-Frechette observes: "Just as the cultural relativists attempt to reduce risk evaluations to sociological constructs, so the naive positivists attempt to reduce hazard estimates to allegedly objective calculations determined by scientists. The cultural relativists overemphasize values in risk assessment, and the naive positivists underemphasize them. Both groups err, however, in believing that categorical value judgments are purely relative and matters of taste. The naive positivists ignore such values precisely because they believe that they are subjective. The cultural relativists embrace alleged subjective values because they believe that relativism is unavoidable." *Id.* at 230. If some risk judgments were not better than others, however, "insurance companies and actuaries would go out of business; that they do not indicates that there are better and worse accounts of risk." *Id.* at 224–25.

80. *Id.* at 242.

81. *Id.* at 241. Thus, Shrader-Frechette recalls Aristotle's claim that "wise persons realize the reliability characteristic of different kinds of judgments and . . . demand only that assurance appropriate to the particular type of investigation." *Id.* at 233; *see, e.g.,* Aristotle, Nicomachean Ethics, Bk. 1, ch. 7, 1098a (M. Ostwald ed., 1962) ("One should not require precision in all pursuits alike, but in each field precision varies with the matter under discussion and should be required only to the extent to which it is appropriate to the investigation").

82. *See* Powell, Rules for Originalists, 73 Va. L. Rev. 659, 678–83 (1987).

83. *See* ABA Policy and Report, *supra* note 1, at 9, 26–27; Sullivan, AIDS: Law, Public Policy, and the Work of the American Bar Association, 21 U. Tol. L. Rev. 1 (1989).

84. *See* note 11 to Chapter 29. Of course, there also are limits to the logical force of such information. Whether we find certain risks tolerable depends not only on the perceived degree of the risk, but also on other factors such as the ease with which a less risky substitute may be acquired. Thus, questions of "acceptable" risk necessarily involve normative considerations.

85. Sanford Kuvin has argued that "[t]his 'window' is in reality virtually shut because if it weren't our blood supply would be totally unsafe since a donor might donate his or her blood during a period of infectivity and not be detected." Kuvin, A Proactive Public Health Policy, *supra* note 18, at 119. In fact, of course, great efforts have been undertaken to divert persons at risk from the pool of blood donors, which may well account for the apparent "closing" of the window in this context.

86. *See* Bloom & Glied, Benefits and Costs of HIV Testing, *supra* note 66, at 1798; Gerberding, Expected Costs, *supra* note 66, at 444–46. This situation may well change in the future, with the creation of cheaper tests. In that event, our society will be pressed to think more seriously about the weight that it wishes to give to the substantial but not readily quantifiable costs attendant upon mandatory testing.

87. *See, e.g.,* Transmission: Brother-to-Brother Infection Not Likely "Casual," CDC Says, AIDS Pol'y & L., Apr. 30, 1992, at 3; Friedland & Klein, Transmission of the Human Immunodeficiency Virus, 317 New Eng. J. Med. 1125, 1132 (1987); Friedland et al., Lack of Transmission of HTLV-III, 314 New Eng. J. Med. 344, 348 (1986). But see Fitzgibbon et al., Transmission from One Child to Another of Human Immunodeficiency Virus Type 1 with a Zidovudine Resistance Mutation, 329 New Eng. J. Med. 1835 (1993) (reporting on transmission from one young child to another, apparently in the home and probably through unrecognized exposure to blood); Brownstein et al., HIV Transmission Between Two Adolescent Brothers with Hemophilia, 42 Morbidity & Mortality Weekly Rep. 948 (1993) (reporting on transmission most likely through blood contact).

88. Rennert, AIDS/HIV and Confidentiality, *supra* note 67, at 93.

89. *See* O'Farrell et al., Transmission of HIV-1 Infection After a Fight, 339 The Lancet 246, 246 (1992).

90. *See* Kasler Comment, *supra* note 9, at 337.

91. *See* National Commission on Acquired Immune Deficiency Syndrome, America Living with AIDS, *supra* note 4, at 2, 14–18.

92. Human Immunodeficiency Virus [Acquired Immunodeficiency Syndrome (AIDS) Virus] in the Athletic Setting, 88 Pediatrics 640 (1991).

93. *See id.* at 640–41.

94. *See* Glover v. Eastern Nebraska Community Office of Retardation, 686 F. Supp. 243, 250 (D. Neb. 1988), *aff'd,* 867 F.2d 461 (8th Cir.), *cert. denied,* 493 U.S. 932 (1989). The United States supported the Eighth Circuit's decision, in an *amicus* brief filed on petition for a writ of *certiorari,* "as a routine application of settled Fourth Amendment principles to the special facts of HIV testing," but nonetheless observed that "the absence of an empirically verified health or safety problem ordinarily [does not] disable governments from taking preventive measures, fully consistent with the Fourth Amendment." Curran, Note, Mandatory Testing of Public Employees for the Human Immunodeficiency Virus: The Fourth Amendment and Medical Reasonableness, 90 Colum. L. Rev. 720, 753 (1990), (quoting No. 88-1805 Brief of the United States as Amicus Curiae, at 6–7, 13) (footnotes omitted).

95. Doe v. Washington Univ., 780 F. Supp. at 633–34 & n.8.

96. Leckelt v. Board of Commr's of Hosp. Dist. No.1, 909 F.2d at 829; Behringer v. Medical Center, 55 Fair Empl. Prac. Case. at 1164.

97. National Commission on Acquired Immune Deficiency Syndrome, America Living with AIDS, *supra* note 4, at 13–14.

98. R. Emerson, Art, in Essays: First Series (1841), *reprinted in* Emerson: Essays and Lectures 436 (Library of America ed., 1983).

CHAPTER THIRTY-ONE

Moving toward Effective
HIV Policies for Youth

Karla Kinderman

DURING THE SUMMER of 1992, the *Chicago Tribune* published an article entitled "HIV No Longer Sounds School Alarms."[1] It signaled a departure from what Lisa Sotto has characterized as the "epidemic of fear" that gripped the United States in the mid-1980s.[2] At that time, the presence of a child infected with human immunodeficiency virus (HIV) in the school setting terrified parents and educators. The fear associated with HIV resulted in many school board decisions to exclude infected children from normal classroom activities. Fortunately, this anxiety has, for the most part, subsided. School boards can no longer exclude children from school solely because they carry HIV.

Society's better understanding of the disease partially explains the shift in policy. People do, in fact, know more about HIV infection in the 1990s than they did in the mid-1980s. Studies have shown that a majority of people know how HIV is transmitted and how it is not; however, exceptions abound. Some people, for example, continue to believe that HIV is transmitted through insect bites.[3]

As a nation, we must continue to promote education about the actual risks of HIV transmission because discrimination against HIV-infected individuals, which still occurs in certain school systems, is the result of fear and ignorance. In the second decade of AIDS, any further attention devoted to the analysis of the remote risks of HIV transmission, including the risk posed by the continued school attendance of an HIV-infected child, must be brought into proper perspective. Researchers in this country have spent an exorbitant amount of time trying to prove that some transmissions through remote modes have occurred, at a time when transmissions through known modes, sex and intravenous (IV) drug use, continue to occur at an alarming rate. As David Rogers, the executive director of the National Commission on AIDS, whose term has now expired, observes, "[W]e are milling about, arguing with one another about the trivial facets of the epidemic, and fail to apply what we already know would significantly reduce rates of spread."[4]

AIDS policies should not reflect a preoccupation with remote risks. Rather, they should give realistic attention to the risk behaviors in which school-age children engage—sex and IV drug use. AIDS policies must include the following elements: (1) prevention; (2) early diagnosis followed by prompt treatment, continuing care and support, which can only occur if the confidentiality of the youth's medical condition is preserved; and finally (3) *funded* programs that allow us to achieve these important objectives.

Support for Continued School Attendance of HIV-Infected Children: Science, Policies, and Laws

HIV is a bloodborne pathogen that can be transmitted by exchanging body fluids (semen or vaginal secretions) during sex, sharing contaminated needles, and receiving infected blood or blood products. Infants may acquire HIV through the placenta or breast milk of their infected mothers. HIV transmission does not occur through contact with the saliva, sweat, or tears of an HIV-infected person, even though the virus can be isolated from these fluids. There have been no reported cases of transmission in school, day care, or foster care settings. Studies have found that no transmission occurs through close personal contact or the sharing of household utensils.[5]

The Centers for Disease Control and Prevention (CDC) issued guidelines in August 1985 concerning the school placement of HIV-infected children. The CDC stresses that students infected with HIV, including those with AIDS,[6] pose *no risk* of HIV transmission to other children through casual contact and, in general, recommends the following: (1) An HIV-infected child should be allowed to attend school after a case by case review to determine whether any circumstances exist that would tend to pose increased risks to others or require special precautions; (2) knowledge of the child's HIV status should be restricted to those individuals who "need to know"; and (3) education about HIV/AIDS should be encouraged for parents, students, and educational staff.[7] Following the CDC's leadership, the American Academy of Pediatrics (AAP) and the American Medical Association (AMA) issued policy statements that supported the continued school attendance of HIV-infected children.[8]

Future proposals to exclude HIV-infected youths from classrooms, absent a rational basis such as the presence of a secondary infectious disease like tuberculosis, will not only be against the recommendations of the CDC, AAP, and AMA, but will most assuredly run afoul of a developed legal scheme that guarantees the continued school attendance of HIV-infected children.[9] Section 504 of the Rehabilitation Act of 1973[10] and the newly enacted Americans with Disabilities Act (ADA)[11] prohibit discrimination against HIV-infected children, symptomatic and asymptomatic, in public schools and private schools that receive federal financial assistance.[12] In Title II of the ADA, all public entities (including public schools) are prohibited from discriminating against a "qualified individual with a disability" solely on the basis of that disability.[13] HIV infection, symptomatic and asymptomatic, is a "disability" under the ADA.[14] Cases that involve HIV-related discrimination in the schools were decided under section 504 before the ADA's enactment.

Section 504 prohibits discrimination against an otherwise qualified handicapped individual solely on the basis of the handicap. The case law dictates that an HIV-infected individual is handicapped and otherwise qualified if he or she does not pose a significant risk of harm to others. In *School Board v. Arline*,[15] the Supreme Court agreed with the AMA's brief *amicus curiae*, which argued that persons with infectious diseases are "handicapped" within the meaning of section 504.[16] The *Arline* Court stated in reference to that provision: "Congress acknowledged that society's accumulated myths and fears about disability and disease are as handicapping as are the physical limitations that flow from actual impairment."[17]

Arline left open the question whether an asymptomatic carrier of an infectious disease, such as HIV, is also handicapped under the act. This issue was addressed in *Ray v. School District*.[18] In that case, when the local school board discovered that the Ray children had tested positive for HIV, the board isolated them from contact with all other students. The family sued the board under section 504 to have the brothers returned to their regular classes. The district court found that the asymptomatic HIV-infected boys were "handicapped" within the meaning of section 504; and by employing a four-part analysis, originally proposed by the AMA and articulated in *Arline,* the Court further determined that the children did not pose a "significant risk" of transmission to others. This analysis requires a court to make an individualized inquiry into the facts "based on reasonable medical judgments, given the state of medical knowledge, about (1) the nature of the risk (how is the disease transmitted), (2) the duration of the risk (how long is the carrier infectious), (3) the severity of the risk (what is the potential harm to third parties), and (4) the probabilities the disease will be transmitted and will cause varying degrees of harm."[19] The Court then required the school board to allow the boys to return to their regular classes because they did not pose a significant risk of HIV infection to other children.

Thus, despite numerous emotion-filled pleas to exclude HIV-infected children from the classroom, groundless fears generally have not had much influence on the way courts have decided the issue of whether HIV-infected children should be allowed to attend school. The courts instead have relied expressly on the views of medical authorities and science-based decision making to support the continued school attendance of HIV-infected children.[20]

The Second Decade of AIDS:
Addressing Actual Risks and Adequate Care

Rather than continue to focus on the evaluation of theoretical risks, including the risk, if any, of HIV transmission in the classroom, our country should devote its energies to preventing HIV among youths and providing adequate health care for those infected with HIV. The school placement cases typically have involved children with hemophilia who acquired HIV through transfusions before 1985; most of these children were white males—the group most likely to have hemophilia. The majority of children living with HIV, however, are African-American or Hispanic. Although African-Americans represent approximately 12 percent of the United States population, they constitute approximately 30 percent of AIDS cases. Hispanics, who represent approximately 9 percent of the U.S. population, constitute approximately 17 percent of all AIDS cases. The representation of these two minority groups among HIV-infected women and children is even more dramatic. African-American and Hispanic women account for more than 70 percent of all AIDS cases among women, and their children for more than 80 percent of the cases among youths.[21] The majority of infected children are newborns who acquired HIV from their mother and adolescents who acquired HIV mostly through heterosexual sex, but also through IV drug use. The majority of HIV-infected youths already have multiple health and social problems, such as sexually transmitted diseases (STDs), child abuse, drug use, and poverty.

To continue to focus our country's time and resources on immeasurably small risks does a grave injustice to youths who face known risks or who are already infected with HIV.[22] The following discussion highlights just a few of the prevention, health care, and financing issues that warrant our attention in the second decade of AIDS.

Prevention

HIV and AIDS education in the schools alone is not enough to stop the spread of HIV among our nation's youth. Information about preventing HIV infection must reach school dropouts who engage in high-risk behaviors, and the reasons why youths engage in high-risk behaviors, such as IV drug use, must be addressed. Nevertheless, school-based education currently seems to be one of the best weapons we have to prevent most youths from taking risks involving HIV transmission.

Besides problems with the present scope of educational initiatives, deficiencies also exist in the content of the information presented. While there have been innovative educational programs in all of the states and the District of Columbia,[23] moral strictures have limited their effectiveness. For example, the CDC, which channels at least $200 million per year to groups interested in delivering HIV education, was forced to prohibit funding of materials and activities that promote or encourage drug abuse or heterosexual or homosexual activities.[24] Under CDC funding guidelines, AIDS education materials must be free of "offensive" (i.e., sexually explicit) information and should promote abstinence from extramarital sex and IV drug use.[25] The CDC's publication, *Guidelines for Effective School Health Education to Stop the Spread of AIDS*, does not advocate changing behavior through skills training, such as teaching a student to persuade a sexual partner to use a condom.[26]

Prevention efforts in school-based clinics also have been stymied. School-based clinics typically offer substance abuse programs, family planning, and screening for STDs. One of the more recent innovations in school health services is making condoms available to students through school-based clinics (or through comprehensive AIDS prevention programs). Despite estimates that 72 percent of teenagers have had intercourse at least once by the twelfth grade, condom availability programs are typically strongly opposed.[27] This opposition seems misplaced because, although there are not an overwhelming number of AIDS cases among adolescents, the number of AIDS cases among persons aged twenty to twenty-nine indicates considerable transmission among adolescents, given that the latency period between HIV infection and the onset of AIDS can be as long as ten years.[28]

Moral strictures also have had an impact on both school-based and public efforts to prevent transmission through IV drug use. Despite the tremendous need to provide drug treatment to help individuals stop using or injecting drugs or to adopt safer drug use practices, many programs aimed at reducing transmission through IV drug use are forbidden. Following several years of the "just say no" approach, it is estimated that more than 1.1 million Americans inject drugs and put themselves, their sexual partners, and their children at high risk of HIV infection. The primary federal act designed to assist in HIV prevention efforts, the Ryan White Comprehensive AIDS Resources Emergency Act of 1990,[29] forbids the use of funds made available under the act for needle-exchange programs.[30] This is unfortunate, given the role that IV drug use plays in the transmission of HIV. In 58 percent of the cases where the newborn carries HIV, the mother was infected with HIV through heterosexual contact with an IV drug user or through her own IV drug use.[31] Expert opinion indicates that a needle-exchange program will actually reduce the risk of transmission without encouraging increased drug use.[32] Some legislatures do recognize these opinions. Connecticut, for example, has decriminalized the possession of needles obtained without a prescription if the needles are provided or sold by a licensed pharmacy or pharmacist, a needle-exchange program, other health care facility, or licensed health care practitioner.[33]

Building Trust: Confidentiality and Care of the Already Infected

HIV-infected adolescents need a wide range of services, including HIV testing, education and counseling, medical care, and social services.[34] Many adolescents who are already infected with HIV, however, may suppress relevant information or avoid medical treatment out of fear of being exposed as carriers of HIV.[35] For these reasons, confidentiality is essential to the provision of adequate care. Inadequate protection of confidential care stems from disclosure laws, informed consent requirements, and the method of payment for services rendered.

Laws that govern physician disclosure of an adolescent's health records vary among states. Some states mandate that only the minor, who provided consent to care, can authorize disclosure of his or her health records, and prohibit notification of the minor's parents if the minor objects. Other states allow the physician to notify the parents over the minor's objection. Illinois, for example, is in the latter category and allows health care providers to notify the minor's parent or legal guardian that the minor tested positive for HIV.[36] Regardless of specific disclosure laws, under the Family Educational Rights and Privacy Act of 1974, parents may be able to access any information the physician sends to the school.[37]

Confidential care for adolescents is further complicated by informed consent requirements, which dictate whether the adolescent can provide informed consent to medical care independently or whether consent must be obtained from a parent or legal guardian.[38] Some states have enacted laws that allow the minor to give consent for HIV testing, but the majority of states are silent as to the rights of minors to do so. Where there is no specific statute, a strained construction of statutes related to venereal disease (VD), STDs, or mature/emancipated minors would allow minors to consent to HIV testing. The VD and STD statutes enable minors to consent to the diagnosis and treatment of STDs or VD; only twelve states, however, have classified HIV infection or AIDS as a STD or VD. The mature/emancipated minor statutes allow minors to consent to testing, but most statutes require that the minor be pregnant or married.[39]

In addition, the method of payment for medical services typically compromises the confidentiality of adolescent health care.[40] Bills are usually sent to the minor's parents. Adolescents who rely on their parents' private insurance typically will find that the insurance claim lists the services provided. This may not be the case when the adolescent is covered by a health maintenance organization or other prepaid plan. These plans can provide confidential care because services are provided without sending a bill that discloses the nature of the service. In the public sector, it seems that a similar mechanism should be used to make confidential care obtainable. Adolescents covered under Medicaid may find that their family receives a monthly itemized list of services provided, or they may not be able to use Medicaid without first obtaining the Medicaid "card" or "sticker" from the parent.

Many states are struggling to ensure necessary confidential care for adolescents. In Connecticut, newly enacted legislation allows a physician to examine and treat a minor for HIV without parental consent if the minor requests that a parent or guardian not be notified.[41] The physician must determine that the minor either would be denied treatment or would not seek, pursue, or continue treatment if a parent is notified.[42] The minor's medical information is protected by confidentiality requirements that extend to the provision of payment. The bill for services goes to the minor and not the parents, unless the minor consents. A minor who is tested without parental consent is required to receive counseling that encourages him or her to work toward involving parents or guardians.

Financing Prevention and Care

Currently, the states bear the brunt of the public's cost for uninsured people with HIV infection.[43] It is estimated that more than 40 percent of people with AIDS are served by the Medicaid program. In geographic areas with a large number of IV drug users, Medicaid covers as much as 75 percent of the cost of health care. This cost is significant because HIV-related disease is expensive to treat and to manage; it requires substantial expenditures in the closing months of life and demands considerable expenditures for drugs, physicians' services, and long-term care. Although Congress has recognized this insurmountable burden and enacted the Ryan White Act to assist the states in financing this epidemic, that measure is not fully funded and provides minimal relief. As the burden continues to increase, states are struggling with ways to finance the care of an increasing number of youths and their children, including a growing number of children who acquired HIV perinatally. Many of these infants are abandoned and left to spend their lives as "boarder babies" in hospitals or long-term care facilities at an extremely high cost.

After paying on average an annual cost of $38,300 for an HIV-infected patient's care,[44] states and localities are looking at HIV prevention as a way to save money. Many states and localities have mounted effective prevention programs, but many others have not. According to the National Commission on AIDS, prevention programs at the state and local levels are not likely to have strong fiscal structures. They rely primarily upon seed money or demonstration grants from governmental or private foundation sources. Because this does not provide a steady funding stream, it is impossible to plan, implement, and evaluate programs. Not only is the funding stream erratic, but it comes attached to rigid requirements that hinder the development of the most meaningful programs, including needle-exchange and condom availability programs. Delayed reimbursement also jeopardizes HIV prevention activities nationwide. Until prevention programs are adequately funded, the number of AIDS cases likely will increase, as will the financial burden on the states.

Conclusion

HIV prevention, confidentiality, care, and financing issues are complex, particularly as they relate to youth. These are the issues that warrant our continued attention in the second decade of AIDS. We must move away from being preoccupied with the extremely remote risks of HIV transmission in the classroom setting, and concentrate instead on the actual risk behavior in which school-age children may engage—sex and IV drug use. Only in this way can we develop effective policies for youth.

NOTES

1. *See* Donato, HIV No Longer Sounds School Alarms, Chic. Trib., Aug. 26, 1992, at 1.

2. Sotto, Comment, Undoing a Lesson of Fear in the Classroom: The Legal Recourse of AIDS-Linked Children, 135 U. Pa. L. Rev. 193 (1986), Chapter 29 in this volume.

3. *See* Adams and Hardy, AIDS Knowledge and Attitudes for July–September 1990, Advance Data, Apr. 1, 1991, at 3.

4. Rogers, Report Card on Our National Response to the AIDS Epidemic—Some A's, Too Many D's, 82 Am. J. Pub. Health 522, 523 (1992).

5. *See, e.g.,* Friedland et al., Lack of Transmission of HTLV-III/LAV Infection to Household Contacts of Patients with AIDS or AIDS-Related Complex with Oral Candidiasis, 314 New Eng. J. Med. 344, 344–49 (1986); Rogers et al., Lack of Transmission of Human Immunodeficiency Virus from Infected Children to Their Household Contacts, 85 Pediatrics 210, 210–14 (1990). *But see* Fitzgibbon et al., Transmission from One Child to Another of Human Immunodeficiency Virus Type 1 with a Zidovudine Resistance Mutation, 329 New Eng. J. Med. 1835 (1993); Brownstein et al., HIV Transmission Between Two Adolescent Brothers with Hemophilia, 42 Morbidity & Mortality Weekly Rep. 948 (1993).

6. Acquired immune deficiency syndrome (AIDS) is a condition of immunological deficiency associated with the infection of the cells of the immune system with a retrovirus known as human immunodeficiency virus (HIV). Because a person with AIDS is immunologically deficient, he or she can develop a variety of life-threatening illnesses. Approximately half of the HIV-infected people develop AIDS within ten years of the initial infection; however, the time between HIV infection and the onset of AIDS can vary greatly. A person who is infected with HIV but has not yet developed AIDS can be without symptoms but can still transmit the virus.

7. *See* Education and Foster Care of Children with Human T-Lymphotrophic Virus Type III/Lymphadenopathy-Associated Virus, 254 JAMA 1430, 1435–36 (1985). Many school districts adopted these guidelines. The CDC recommended a more restricted environment for preschool children, neurologically impaired children, and children with open lesions because of the early uncertainty about possible transmission of HIV, for example, through scratching and biting. The suggested restrictions were perceived as contradicting the assertion that the risk was negligible. The guidelines applied to all children who were infected with HIV, not only to children with AIDS. As a result, the focus of those wishing to restrict school attendance was broadened, and some communities called for mandatory testing of all children or those perceived to be at risk to determine which children were infected. Today, this restriction is no longer necessary and is outdated.

8. *See* American Academy of Pediatrics, Committee on School Health/Committee on Infectious Diseases, School Attendance of Children and Adolescents with Human T-Lymphotrophic Virus III/Lymphadenopathy-Associated Virus Infection, 77 Pediatrics 430, 430–32 (1986); AMA Council on Ethical and Judicial Affairs, AMA HIV Policy Update, Proceedings of the House of Delegates 85 (1989).

9. *See infra* notes 10–14.

10. *See* 29 U.S.C.A. § 794 (Supp. 1992).

11. *See* 42 U.S.C.A. § 12101–213 (Supp. 1992).

12. If a private school does not receive federal assistance, the situation may still be covered by a state or local antidiscrimination law, including HIV/AIDS-specific statutes.

13. *See* 42 U.S.C.A. §§ 12131, 12132 (Supp. 1992).

14. *See* S. Rep. No. 116, 101st Cong., 1st Sess. 22 (1989).

15. 480 U.S. 273 (1987).

16. Brief of the American Medical Association as Amicus Curiae, Sch. Board v. Arline, 480 U.S. 273 (1987) (85-1277).

17. 480 U.S. at 284.

18. 666 F. Supp. 1524 (M.D. Fla. 1987).

19. 480 U.S. at 288, *citing* Brief of the American Medical Association as Amicus Curiae, at 19.

20. In the unlikely event that a court does not take this view and finds that a child poses a significant risk of transmission, the child could still exert the right to educational programs or services especially appropriate or specifically designed for children with HIV and/or AIDS under the Education of the Handicapped Act (subsequently renamed Individuals with Disabilities in Education Act, IDEA). *See* 20 U.S.C.A. §§ 1400–1485 (1988 and Supp. 1993). States receiving federal financial assistance for special education programs must provide a public school education to handicapped children (now children with disabilities). *See id.* This includes children with AIDS, although it may not include children who are asymptomatic unless they also have an unrelated developmental disability.

21. *See* National Commission on AIDS, The Challenge of HIV/AIDS in Communities of Color 3–6 (1992).

22. *See* House Select Committee on Children, Youth, and Families, A Decade of Denial: Teens and AIDS in America, 102nd Cong., 2d Sess. iv (1992).

23. *See* Association for the Advancement of Health Education, HIV Prevention for Teachers of Elementary Education and Middle School Grades (1992); D. Kerr et al., School-Based HIV Prevention: A Multidisciplinary Approach (1990) (American School Health Association); National Commission on the Role of the School and the Community in Improving Adolescent Health, Code Blue: Uniting for Healthier Youth 27, 38–39 (1991).

24. Pub. L. No. 100–436, 102 Stat. 1692 (1988).

25. *See* 57 Fed. Reg. 10794 (1992); 56 Fed. Reg. 65109 (1991); 55 Fed. Reg. 23414 (1990); 54 Fed. Reg. 10049 (1989).

26. *See* Centers for Disease Control, Guidelines for Effective School Health Education to Prevent the Spread of AIDS, Morbidity & Mortality Weekly Rep., Jan. 29, 1988, at 1, 1–14 (Supp.).

27. *See* Roper, Linking Science, Policy, and Practice, address before the Prevention '92 Conference in Baltimore, Maryland (Mar. 24, 1992).

28. *See* Kipke & Hein, Acquired Immunodeficiency Syndrome (AIDS) in Adolescents, 1 Adolescent Med. 429, 429–30 (1990).

29. Pub. L. No. 101-381, 104 Stat. 628 (1990).

30. 42 U.S.C.A. § 300ff-1 (Supp. 1991).

31. *See* National Commission on AIDS, The Challenge of HIV/AIDS in Communities of Color, *supra* note 21, at 29.

32. *See id.*

33. *See* Needle-Sharing Reductions Cited as Result of New Connecticut Law, 8 AIDS Pol'y & L. 3 (1993).

34. National Commission on AIDS, America Living with AIDS 47–60 (1992).

35. *See* AMA Council on Scientific Affairs, Confidential Health Services for Adolescents, Proceedings of the House of Delegates 2 (1992); *see generally* Holder, Minors' Rights to Consent to Medical Care, 257 JAMA 3400, 3400–3402 (1987).

36. *See* 1992 Ill. Legis. Serv. P. A. 87-1104.

37. *See* 20 U.S.C § 1232g (Supp. 1990).

38. *See* Holder, Disclosure and Consent Problems in Pediatrics, 16 Law Med. Health Care 219, 219–28 (1988).

39. *See* English, Points to Consider, Adolescents and HIV: Legal and Ethical Issues, read before the panel on Women, Adolescents, and Children with HIV Infection and AIDS, Public Health Service, Jan. 1992, at 6.

40. *See generally* Fisher et al., Are Adolescents Able and Willing to Pay the Fee for Confidential Health Care? 107 J. Pediatrics 480, 480–83 (1985).

41. *See* 1992 Conn. Acts 119 (Reg. Sess.).

42. The law is remarkable because it resulted from student lobbying efforts. Governor Lowell Weicker signed the bill on May 22, 1992, at a rally with students who led the campaign for testing without parental permission.

43. *See* Fox, Financing Health Care for Persons with HIV Infection, 16 Am. J. Law & Med. 223, 226 (1990).

44. *See* Hellinger, Forecasts of the Costs of Medical Care for Persons with HIV: 1992–1995, 29 Inquiry 356, 360–61 (1992).

■ PART V

*Children and the
Criminal Justice System*

■ CHAPTER THIRTY-TWO

Re-Imagining Childhood and Reconstructing the Legal Order: The Case for Abolishing the Juvenile Court

Janet E. Ainsworth

JUVENILE COURTS exist in all fifty states of the United States and the District of Columbia, as well as in virtually all of the industrialized nations of the world. So ubiquitous is the institution of the juvenile court in the contemporary world that one easily might forget that it did not always exist. In fact, the juvenile court is a relatively recent invention.

The juvenile court system has come under increasing attack in recent years from both the right and the left ends of the political spectrum. The right complains that the system coddles young criminals and sets them loose to prey on society after lenient sanctioning;[1] the left decries the arbitrary railroading of predominantly lower-class juveniles by paternalistic juvenile court judges. Ironically, as this chapter will explain, both criticisms are predicated on identical views about the essential nature of childhood, views embodying a vastly different conception of childhood from the one that gave birth to the juvenile court.

In this chapter I examine the development of the juvenile court, noting that the system is premised on certain historically contingent beliefs and assumptions about the unique nature of childhood. After presenting a historical account of the socially constructed nature of childhood and adolescence, I explore how those constructs informed the ideology and practice of the juvenile court. Next follows a discussion of how perceptions of youth have changed in the late twentieth century, showing that these changes undermine the ideological legitimacy of a separate juvenile court system. As a result, juvenile court has undergone both ideological and institutional change from its original form. These shifts in theory and practice are outlined here, with specific attention given to several U.S. Supreme Court decisions that have significantly affected juvenile court. The Court's jurisprudence both reflects and shapes the current social reality for juveniles in America.

Finally, this chapter calls for the abolition of the juvenile court,[2] suggesting that such a course would better reflect current American beliefs about adolescence. I discuss the ideological costs of maintaining an institution that no longer comports with our cultural reality and the practical consequences of abolishing the juvenile court. In considering these consequences, this chapter contends that the supposed benefits of juvenile jurisdiction do not depend on the existence of a separate juvenile court, and that juveniles would receive positive advantages from being tried within a unified criminal justice system.

On one level, this chapter is an interpretive study of one institution, the juvenile court, which begins with a thick description of its historical and cultural context and proceeds to a call for specific legal reform. On a more abstract level, it argues that consciousness of the nature of our interpretive constructs in general can have real-world consequences if we, as legal actors, choose to reshape our legal world in light of that consciousness.

The Invention of Childhood

The choice of the word "invention" for this subheading is meant to be subtly jarring. After all, it is human creations that are ordinarily said to be "invented," whereas aspects of the natural world are said to be "discovered." By calling childhood an invention, I am suggesting that childhood is better seen as a social fact than as a biological one.

Before further exploring the nature of childhood, I will first lay out the theoretical underpinnings for the remainder of this discussion. I premise this chapter explicitly on social constructivism, a social theory of knowledge; therefore, a precis of social constructivist theory and its influence on contemporary thought will provide background for this study.

Constructivist Social Theory

Social constructivist theory originates in a radical epistemological skepticism, which holds that human knowledge cannot be grounded in either eternal or universal truths, be they truths of human nature, of the physical world, or of principles of logic or reason. Rejecting empiricism, with its reliance on experiential verification of reality, constructivism denies that commonly accepted categories of knowledge can be validated through objective observation. It instead posits that without preexisting categorization, we could derive no meaning from our observations of reality.

To the constructivist, categories within which we understand reality do not correspond to a mapping of that reality, but rather are humanly created artifacts, produced by culturally and historically situated participants in a collective social enterprise. These socially created categories are propagated through social discourse, which is itself a culturally and historically situated practice. Thus, constructivism insists that all human knowledge, whether composed of experientially gathered information or the shared categories that impose meaning on that information, takes its form through social discourse.

These categories of knowledge are open-textured; in other words, they can be extended to accommodate circumstances and information outside the original parameters of the category. Consequently, these humanly fashioned interpretive constructs allow for competing understandings and are susceptible to change over time. Changes in these constructs, however, do not necessarily result from changes in external reality. Whether our shared understanding prevails over time depends not on the objectively verifiable validity of the constructs but rather on the cultural and social processes that generate the constructs in the first place. Constructs may be abandoned or modified as the community comes to question their coherence and perspicuity. Conversely, interpretive constructs may be retained even in the face of what an outsider might see as contradiction or illegitimacy.

To say that all knowledge is situated—that our experience of reality is both culturally and historically contingent—is not to say that our constructs are invalid or false. The social constructivist critique of foundationalist epistemology is often misinterpreted as an attack on the value of certain categories of knowledge, a mistaken conflation of the real with the natural. Constructivism does not say that everyday visions of reality are false but rather that they are artificial and, being humanly made, conceivably can be unmade and remade in a different way. For this reason, social constructivism provides the intellectual premises for a social critique, as well as a mechanism to explain and promote social transformation.

Across the spectrum of academic disciplines, a large and influential group of scholars has based its scholarship on a constructivist view of social reality, asserting that the constituent elements of a society—its institutions, customs, practices, conceptual categories, values, and ideology—are socially constructed artifacts. The modern germinal exposition of this theory is Peter Berger's and Thomas Luckmann's *The Social Construction of Reality*.[3] Berger and Luckmann acknowledge the intellectual antecedents of modern social constructivism in such disparate sources as the relativistic historicism of Wilhelm Dilthey, the phenomenological sociology of Alfred Schutz, and the self-styled ontogenetic social psychology of George Herbert Mead. Locating their theoretical project within the field of the sociology of knowledge, Berger and Luckmann address the epistemological and sociological implications of constructivism. The key insight derived from looking at society as a composite of humanly constructed artifacts is that even basic aspects of social life are neither natural nor inevitable, as they may appear to members of that society, but rather are culturally and historically contingent and mutable. The contingency and mutability of social reality are largely invisible to those within the society. Therefore, dramatic changes may occur in the created meaning of a social artifact—be it a concrete artifact such as an institution or practice, or an abstract artifact such as a value system or conceptual category—without members of the society expressly desiring or even consciously registering those changes. Instead, members of a society tend to impose their current belief structures onto the past, attributing their version of social reality to those who came before them. Eternally proceeding from one state of certainty about the nature of reality to another different, incommensurate state of certainty, people are seldom if ever aware of how completely their world is their own creation.

As Berger and Luckmann emphasize, the fact that reality is socially produced does not mean that the individual within society can, by an exercise of will, escape the coercive force of reality.[4] Rather, change in the social order occurs through a dialectic process in which the constituent aspects of society affect and are affected by the actions of the human beings who create them and who are created as subjects by them.

Social constructivist theory has been enormously influential in the humanities and in the social sciences, particularly in history, psychology, sociology, and anthropology. Antifoundationalists such as the philosophers Richard Rorty[5] and Nelson Goodman,[6] the literary critic Stanley Fish,[7] and the political theorist Don Herzog[8] share the fundamental constructivist perceptions about the socially created nature of meaning and reality.

Given the impact of constructivist thought throughout the academy, it is unsurprising that contemporary social science scholarship on the law has incorporated its insights. Social scientists see the role of law in society as, in the words of Clifford Geertz, "constructive, constitutive and formational. . . . [L]aw is local knowledge not placeless principle and . . . is constructive of social life not reflective or anyway not just reflective of it."[9]

Constructivist theory has deeply influenced scholarship within legal academia as well. More than fifty years ago, legal realists rejected the received wisdom that law was determined by abstract legal principles or reasoning; rather, they believed that law was created by judges influenced by external social conditions. Contemporary constructivist legal scholarship carries this insight one step further, describing law as both constituent of social reality and as created by it in a dialectic process,[10] a kind of constitutive hermeneutics.[11] This constructivist view of the law has two corollary implications: First, that the apparent intrinsicality and immutability of basic legal doctrine is illusory;[12] and second, that understanding the process through which reality is constructed provides a mechanism for meaningful change in the law.[13]

The Social Construction of Childhood and Adolescence

It is one thing to recognize that aspects of society such as parliamentary democracy, the exclusionary rule, and rugged individualism are socially contingent artifacts, but perhaps harder to accept that the life stage we call "childhood" is likewise a culturally and historically situated social construction. Of course, infants and young children are physiologically and psychologically different from older youths and adults; these differences undoubtedly persist across time and place. As the anthropologist Ruth Benedict once observed, however, "The facts of nature are 'doctored' in different ways by different cultures."[14] Human biology may set the outside limits on our social definition of ourselves, but because biological constructs are themselves human artifacts, social reality constrains what we imagine to be biological necessity as well.

Social definitions of reality determine which biological attributes will be considered authentic, meaningful, and constituent of identity, and which will be trivialized, ignored, suppressed, or even explicitly denied. For example, the biological differences between human males and females might seem to be an obvious instance in which immutable biology invariably overrides any of society's attempts to deny or evade its constraints. No human society, one might think, could define males as the producers of young in light of the inescapable biological fact that males cannot give birth. Yet for many years Western natural science actually did credit males with creating the fetus without any contribution from the female; scientists even "observed" tiny homunculi when they examined sperm under primitive microscopes. More generally, much research in psychology, sociology, and anthropology, as well as feminist theory, confirms the socially constructed nature of gender identity and many of what are often assumed to be natural gender characteristics.

Similarly, the socially constructed aspects of human life stages such as childhood and adolescence far outweigh their invariant biological attributes. The number of stages into which an individual's life is divided and the essential qualities deemed characteristic of each stage in the life cycle have varied over time and across cultures.[15] Indeed, the very concept that human lives pass through life stages with distinct characteristics has not always held the social and legal significance that it does in the contemporary West.

The definition of childhood—who is classified as a child, and what emotional, intellectual, and moral properties children are assumed to possess—has changed over time in response to changes in other facets of society. The historian Philippe Ariès first pointed out the dramatic contrast between the modern Western conception of childhood and the conception held in the medieval European world.[16] As he observed, "In medieval society, the idea of childhood did not exist. . . . [The] awareness of the particular nature of childhood . . . which distinguishes the child from the adult . . . was lacking."[17] At that time, the primary age-based boundary was drawn between infancy, a time of physical dependence ending roughly at age seven, and full personhood. Those persons older than seven, especially those in the lower social classes, participated in the normal range of adult activities: They were apprenticed to begin their working lives, drank in taverns, shared the same games and amusements as adults, gambled, and were exposed to sexual behavior and jokes. Wearing the same kind of clothing, these young people even looked like adults. Not surprisingly, then, medieval art depicted them as miniature adults. In short, within the medieval world, the young were fully integrated members of the community. No one believed that young people were innocent beings who needed to be quarantined from a harsh adult world.

In later centuries, the period between the end of infancy and sexual maturity was redefined as a discrete state in human development. Two seemingly contradictory strands of Western thought gave rise to this refiguration of childhood. On the one hand, the Calvinist doctrine of infant depravity characterized the young as inherently sinful and doomed to spiritual death absent coercive discipline by adults. In contrast, Enlightenment philosophy and the later romanticism of Rousseau saw children as innately innocent beings whose potential should be nurtured by parents without corrupting their natural goodness. What both of these conceptions of childhood shared, however, in contrast to the earlier medieval construction, was the belief that children are essentially different from adults and that one aspect of that difference is their intrinsic malleability.

The late nineteenth and early twentieth centuries saw an extension of this dramatic reconstruction of childhood. In the academy, experts dedicating their scholarship to the study of the child placed great emphasis on how inherently and essentially different children are from adults. The so-called child study movement was predicated on the belief that childhood is composed of stages, each with characteristic emotions, capacities, and needs. Appropriating from the theory of evolution the slogan "ontogeny recapitulates phylogeny," proponents of child study now had a model justifying a scholarly focus on childhood. Because they believed that the chronological development of the individual human echoes the historical development of human civilization, studying childhood was thought to provide a window on the otherwise unknowable human past. By the same token, child study proponents reasoned, what society knew of the past would teach it how best to socialize the young.

As this "child study" movement gained momentum, prominent universities such as Harvard, Yale, and Princeton rushed to set up departments of child development. In medicine, the perception of the uniqueness of childhood led to the birth of pediatrics and the founding of specialized children's hospitals. On the political front, Congress in 1912 passed a federal bill to establish a special Children's Bureau within the Department of Commerce and Labor.[18]

At the same time that academic and governmental attention was focusing on childhood, the temporal contours of childhood were extended through the creation of a new stage of preadulthood—adolescence.[19] Although the word "adolescence" was not invented during this period, the term was rarely was used prior to the late nineteenth century, and little or no attention was paid to any special characteristics that teenagers might have. By the turn of the century, the attributes of childhood were being applied to teenagers, who only a generation earlier would not have been distinguished from older adults. Since as children they were assumed to be vulnerable, malleable, and in need of adult guidance, training, and control before they could graduate to full personhood, adolescents now became targets of paternal adult attention. Compulsory school attendance laws, which earlier had been ignored in those few jurisdictions that enacted them, were passed in state legislatures and were increasingly enforced. Between 1900 and 1930, the number of high school graduates increased 600 percent. At the same time, legislatures promulgated child labor laws establishing a minimum age for workers, limiting the hours that could be worked, and regulating the conditions of employment. As a result, the number of people between the ages of ten and fifteen who were gainfully employed declined 75 percent from 1910 to 1930.[20] The minimum age for marriage was raised to discourage early marrying.[21] The consequences of this spate of law reform prolonged the economic dependence of adolescents, increased the amount of age stratification in society,[22] and established a greater degree of formal social control over the young than had existed previously.

The Invention of Adolescence and the Ideology of the Juvenile Court

Among all of the law reforms adopted during the Progressive Era to accommodate the new perception of the adolescent's nature and needs, the creation of the juvenile court undoubtedly ranks as the most far-reaching achievement. The rapidity with which the concept spread is striking. In 1899, Illinois passed the Juvenile Court Act, founding a juvenile system widely acknowledged at the time as the model for other states to follow.[23] And follow they did; within twenty years all but three states had similar juvenile justice systems in place.[24]

The desirability, even necessity, for a separate court system to address the problems of young people appeared obvious, given the newly emerging view of the adolescent as an immature creature in need of adult control. When parental control failed, the benevolent, if coercive, hand of the state could provide the corrective molding needed by the errant youth. By categorizing the adolescent as a subclass of the child rather than as a type of adult, the Progressives fashioned a discrete juvenile justice system premised upon the belief that, like other children, adolescents are not morally accountable for their behavior. Thus, ordinary retributive punishment for the adolescent would be inappropriate. The Progressives treated lawbreaking by juveniles as a symptom justifying—in fact, humanely requiring—state intervention to save them from a life of crime that might otherwise be their fate.

The allusion to medical treatment suggested by the word "symptom" is not accidental; the Progressives frequently compared social deviance to physical disease.[25] Although Progressive ideology entertained an eclectic set of conflicting notions about the causes of deviant behavior, including physiological, genetic, and environmental theories, the belief that criminal behavior was caused by unwholesome environment, especially the baneful influence of squalid urban life, came to dominate correctional thinking.[26] Juvenile misbehavior was seen as merely the overt manifestation of underlying social pathology. Like physical pathology, social pathology could not be ignored or the "disease" might progressively worsen. With proper diagnosis and treatment, however, social pathology was considered as susceptible to cure as physical ailments. Particularly in light of the supposedly malleable nature of juveniles, the Progressives exuded confidence in their ability to cure juvenile delinquency.[27]

The juvenile court movement gained momentum from the proselytizing efforts of some of its early judges.[28] In stump speeches to civic groups, in editorials in the popular press, and in articles in professional journals, these advocates of the new juvenile court system tirelessly promoted the redemptive message embodied in juvenile court ideology. One such advocate, Judge Julian Mack, attributed the necessity for a separate juvenile court system to its exclusive concern for the social rehabilitation of needy youths. In contrast, criminal courts focused on the judgment of whether the accused had violated the law and, if so, what penalty was warranted. He wrote, "The problem for determination by the judge is not, Has this boy or girl committed a specific wrong, but What is he, how has he become what he is, and what had best be done in his interest and in the interest of the state to save him from a downward career."[29] To the advocates of the juvenile court, the essential difference between the moral and cognitive capacities of the juvenile and those of the adult did not serve merely to mitigate juvenile culpability for breaking the law, but to absolve the juvenile completely from criminal liability.

Juvenile court philosophy made no distinction between criminal and noncriminal behavior, as long as the behavior was considered deviant or inappropriate to the age of the juvenile. Behavior such as smoking, sexual activity, stubbornness, running away from home, swearing, and truancy could trigger juvenile court jurisdiction as validly as could breaking a criminal law. Because the child was not being punished, but rather protected by the state, juvenile court had a mandate to assume liberal jurisdiction over the wayward young, much as it might over other helpless and needy members of society. The idea that the peculiar vulnerability of children justified state control over them was analogized to the well-established chancery court principle, *parens patriae*, which gave the state authority over parentless children. Invoking a chancery court pedigree for juvenile court jurisdiction, the *parens patriae* doctrine lent legitimacy to the new court system while it obscured the extent to which juvenile court marked an unprecedented expansion of state social control over adolescents.

Every aspect of the *parens patriae* juvenile court was designed to mold wayward youths into good citizens. The hallmark of the system was its disposition, individually tailored to address the needs and abilities of the juvenile in question. To that end, judges were given almost limitless discretion in crafting the disposition to facilitate whatever the judge thought would "cure" the youth. Juveniles could be put on probation until their majority, giving the juvenile court total control over every aspect of the probationer's life. If the juvenile was incarcerated in a juvenile detention facility, the commitment would be for an indeterminate period, because the judge could not perfectly predict in advance the amenability of the youth to rehabilitative treatment. Once rehabilitated, the youth would be released from further court control, regardless of the seriousness of the offense that gave rise to juvenile court jurisdiction, because the basis for the court's disposition was treatment, not punitive sanction. Indeed, the juvenile court judge could, at least in theory, discharge the juvenile offender immediately after the dispositional hearing if the judge believed that the youth had no need for court-monitored treatment or services, even if the juvenile had committed a serious offense.

Some states deliberately eliminated the usual procedural formalities of criminal adjudication from juvenile court. These formalities were considered both unnecessary and undesirable: unnecessary because the role of the court was not to adjudicate guilt and punish, but to prescribe treatment; undesirable because informality itself was deemed a part of the rehabilitative process.[30] For this reason, trial by jury was eliminated in most juvenile courts as irrelevant to the proper determination before the court, because the court was less concerned with factually determining whether the child had broken the law than with sensitively diagnosing and treating the child's social pathology. As the Pennsylvania Supreme Court observed, "Whether the child deserves to be saved by the state is no more a question for a jury than whether the father, if able to save it, ought to save it."[31] The object of what Judge Mack termed "not so much the power, as the friendly interest of the state"[32] was invariably referred to as "the child," the "boy or girl," or "the lad."[33] Calling teenage lawbreakers "children" was not disingenuous rhetoric. Rather, it demonstrates that the social construction of adolescence as a species of childhood powerfully informed the ideology and practice of the *parens patriae* juvenile court.

The Refiguration of the Life Cycle in the Late Twentieth Century

From our vantage point in the late twentieth century, the Progressives' use of the word "child" to describe the adolescent youth accused of violating the law seems incongruous if not willfully perverse. Just as the turn-of-the-century Progressives reconstructed childhood and adolescence, so too Americans in the last half of the twentieth century have limned a new refiguration of the human life cycle in which childhood and adolescence have been re-imagined. As a result, the Progressives' view of childhood now seems so foreign to our current assumptions that it may be difficult for us to credit that they seriously believed in it.

When adolescence was conceived at the turn of the century, it was assimilated into the familiar category of childhood. Children and adolescents were seen as subcategories of one larger category, whose members were considered more like infants in their nature and needs than they were like adults.[34] The dichotomy between the essential natures of the child and adult remained intact. During the latter half of the twentieth century, however, the human life cycle increasingly was subdivided into more and more stages of life.[35] Beyond adolescence, but before full adulthood, "youth" was defined as a new life stage encompassing those from their late teens into their twenties and even early thirties, roughly corresponding to the years spent in college and graduate education.[36] Even adulthood was fragmented into life stages with attributed characteristics—old age was divided into the vigorous "young-old" and the truly "old-old,"[37] and the prime of life was subdivided into salient stages as well.[38] Nor was this reconstruction of the life cycle a preoccupation limited to academics; the mass media contributed "yuppies," "midlife crisis," and the "menopausal male" to our vocabulary and to our vision of ourselves. By the latter part of the twentieth century, everyone was "just going through a phase."

As the life cycle became fragmented into more stages, it became harder to see each stage as absolute and dichotomous. Age segregation, which followed from viewing life stages as discrete periods with characteristic attributes and needs, makes less sense when the life cycle is seen more as a continuum than as a sharply divided passage between childhood and adulthood. Boundaries delineating age-appropriate behavior have blurred, especially among the young, with both younger children and young adults adopting styles, attitudes, and activities that society formerly considered characteristic of adolescence. Although at the turn of the last century, G. Stanley Hall confidently could delineate the quintessential and definitive characteristics of adolescence, researchers in the closing decades of this century see a multiplicity of adolescences. From this later vantage point, adolescence does not seem to have any intrinsic and invariant characteristics.

Nor do the young appear to be as inherently and essentially different from adults as formerly had been assumed. Psychological research shows that even comparatively young children possess cognitive and reasoning abilities equivalent to those of adults.[39] The newer research shows that children are not as incompetent (nor adults as competent) as earlier psychologists had believed.[40] In the words of one sociologist, "In the post-industrial era . . . the institutional and psychological basis for conceiving childhood and adulthood as distinct stages of life may no longer exist."[41]

Today we are witnessing the breakdown of the binary opposition between child and adult that provided the conceptual foundation of juvenile court jurisprudence. Conservatives and liberals may disagree on the policies that ought to be implemented to deal with youthful criminal offenders, but both ends of the political spectrum agree that the child–adult distinction is a false dichotomy that can no longer support disparate justice systems.

Legal Implications of the Re-Imagination of Childhood

As the socially constituted perception of adolescence and childhood has evolved during the late twentieth century, the premises of the *parens patriae* juvenile court no longer correspond to our cultural image of the young. Just as the invention of adolescence at the turn of the century made the Progressives' child welfare law reforms both possible and necessary, so, too, the contemporary change in the images of adolescence and childhood has legal implications that both reflect the change and at the same time reinforce it.

The "Just Deserts" Juvenile Court

Rejection of Parens Patriae Ideology

The history of correctional philosophy in the second half of the twentieth century is a tale of steadily increasing loss of faith in positivistic penology.[42] The original architects of the juvenile court were confident that juvenile delinquents could be rehabilitated, as long as judges possessed the expertise, information, and resources necessary for proper diagnosis and treatment. Despite several decades of experience with rehabilitative penology in the adult and juvenile justice systems, however, criminal recidivism stubbornly refused to wither away. Dozens of studies were undertaken to find out what program, what methodology, what theory might work. The depressing conclusion, by and large, was that nothing worked.[43]

As a consequence of the general disillusionment with rehabilitative penology, the focus of the criminal justice system turned from assessing the social needs of the offender to assessing the social harm that the offender caused—in short, from rehabilitation to retribution. This trend occurred in juvenile justice systems as well, underscoring the magnitude of change in the social perception of the culpability of young offenders. From a world in which the child by definition was morally incapable of committing a crime, we have now passed to a world in which juveniles are to be held strictly accountable for their crimes. As a result of this shift in juvenile justice philosophy, state juvenile court hearings have come to resemble adult criminal trials.

Consonant with this new philosophy, sentences in the new punitive juvenile court are designed to hold the youth accountable for the offense committed; any rehabilitative services or programs provided during incarceration are incidental to the punishment meted out. The "just deserts" sentencing model bases the length of incarceration on how much punishment the offense merits, not on how long it might take to reform the offender. In rejecting rehabilitation as the justification for incarcerating the offender, determinate sentencing strikes at the very heart of the parens patriae dispositional framework. The proliferation of "just deserts" juvenile sentencing laws in the 1980s[44] is telling evidence of the demise of the older juvenile court model.

A Model of the New Juvenile Court

In 1977, Washington state enacted a complete overhaul of its juvenile court system.[45] Washington's Juvenile Justice Act has been called "the most substantial reform of a state juvenile code that has occurred anywhere in the United States."[46] Often cited as the paradigmatic embodiment of the new juvenile court philosophy, the Washington system is widely acknowledged as the model for reforms in juvenile court systems throughout the country.

Washington's Juvenile Justice Act exemplifies a rejection of both the philosophy and the practice of the traditional *parens patriae* juvenile court.[47] According to Representative Mary Kay Becker, the principal sponsor of the bill in the state legislature, the new "just deserts" system enacted by the Juvenile Justice Act represents a move "away from the *parens patriae* doctrine of benevolent coercion, and closer to a more classical emphasis on justice. . . . The presumptive sentencing scheme . . . makes [it] clear that youngsters who are being sentenced—i.e., deprived of liberty—are being punished rather than 'treated.'"[48]

The core provision of Washington's new system is its determinate sentencing scheme, which sets the length of sentence on the basis of two objective characteristics: the offense, legislatively ranked by level of seriousness, and the prior criminal record of the offender.[49] Judges may deviate from the standard sentences only if mitigating or aggravating factors pertain to the offense; moreover, judges may not base sentencing deviations on their perception of the offender. The law expressly forbids sentencing judges to take into account information showing that the offender has been abused or neglected.[50] Nor may prosecutors exercise discretion on the basis of such factors. Instead, they must prosecute serious cases regardless of any perceived treatment needs of the child.[51] Even the prosecutorial decision to divert minor offenses from the formal adjudication process cannot be made with reference to the social needs of the child in question.[52] In short, the new juvenile justice system has divorced consideration of the social needs of the offender from the issue of imposition or duration of confinement.

The punitive focus of the Juvenile Justice Act was sharpened by Washington's establishment in 1984 of the Juvenile Disposition Standards Commission to implement the "clear policy" on sentencing called for by the act.[53] Charged with the responsibility of developing a policy and standards on juvenile sentencing, the commission produced the *Washington State Juvenile Disposition Standards Philosophy and Guide* in order to "provide direction for the various professionals in the juvenile justice community and help the public understand the reasons and methods behind the juvenile disposition standards."[54] The *Guide* adopted a youth justice model with three major components: justice and accountability; community safety; and youth development.[55] The *Guide* emphasized that proportional punishment of offenders both furthers justice[56] and promotes community safety.[57] While acknowledging that providing treatment services during incarceration might be desirable, the *Guide* cautioned that social services must be only incidental to sanctions, and never the actual rationale for the sentence.[58]

Disposition is not the only aspect of juvenile court to undergo a transformation. Washington replaced the intimate, informal proceeding in which the judge might "put his arm around his shoulder and draw the lad to him"[59] with procedures that, with one exception,[60] precisely mirror those of the adult criminal trial. The juvenile, like an adult, is charged by prosecutorial information, and must enter a plea of guilty or not guilty.[61] The arraignment hearing is explicitly governed by the same court rules pertaining to adult defendants.[62] Like an adult accused, the juvenile has the right to be represented by counsel[63] and to receive the services of investigators and expert witnesses necessary to a defense.[64] The juvenile is entitled to the same notice of charges, discovery of prosecution evidence, opportunity to be heard, and confrontation of adverse witnesses that an adult enjoys.[65] Severance and joinder likewise are governed by the same rules that apply in adult criminal cases.[66] Admissibility of evidence is governed by the same constitutional standards,[67] and the normal rules of evidence apply with full rigor.[68] In essence, except for the lack of trial by jury, the juvenile court fact finding in Washington is, by statute and court rule, procedurally identical to that in an adult criminal trial.

As the Washington juvenile justice model shows, the juvenile court of the late twentieth century bears little procedural resemblance to the Progressive vision of juvenile court. No matter how procedurally congruent the juvenile and adult court hearings become, however, juvenile court dispositions unavoidably differ from adult dispositions in one key regard: The potential length of incarceration is limited by the juvenile court's inevitable loss of jurisdiction over offenders when they reach the age of majority. Because sentences proportionate to offenses therefore may not be available to the juvenile court judge, the trend toward a just deserts model of juvenile court has sharpened the perception that juvenile court sanctions are inappropriate for many youthful offenders.

Bypassing Juvenile Court Jurisdiction

When a judge perceives that the maximum length of confinement available in the juvenile system is too short to be an appropriate sanction in a particular case, a mechanism long has existed to transfer jurisdiction from juvenile court to the adult criminal justice system. Traditionally, the *parens patriae* juvenile court judge could waive juvenile jurisdiction over an offender if the judge determined that the youth was not amenable to the rehabilitative treatment of the juvenile correctional system.[69] In making the waiver decision, the juvenile court judge focused solely on the individual characteristics of the youth. The criminal act itself was relevant only insofar as the nature of the offense committed might indirectly shed light on the likelihood that the child who had done such an act could be reformed.[70]

The shift from a rehabilitative to a just deserts sentencing philosophy, however, has greatly transformed the waiver process. This shift in focus was presaged in the Supreme Court's 1966 decision *Kent v. United States*.[71] That decision required an adversary hearing before a juvenile could be transferred to adult court for federal prosecution, and ordered the judge to articulate the specific basis for the waiver decision.[72] The Court listed several appropriate factors that the judge must consider in making the waiver decision, including "[t]he seriousness of the alleged offense to the community and whether the protection of the community requires waiver[,] . . . [w]hether the alleged offense was committed in an aggressive, violent, premeditated or willful manner[,] . . . [and] whether the alleged offense was against persons or against property."[73] In addition, the judge could also take into account the more traditional considerations, such as:

> The sophistication and maturity of the juvenile as determined by consideration of his home, environmental situation, emotional attitude and pattern of living[,] . . . [t]he record and previous history of the juvenile[,] . . . and the likelihood of reasonable rehabilitation of the juvenile . . . by the use of procedures, services and facilities currently available to the Juvenile Court.[74]

Despite the *Kent* Court's recognition that a judge must look at the offense itself in making the waiver decision, the *Kent* opinion still used the nature and seriousness of the offense as predictors of future dangerousness to be factored into the determination of whether the offender could successfully be rehabilitated. In the Court's discussion of the issue, one finds no intimation that a juvenile who commits certain offenses consequently deserves a specific punishment, only that juvenile correctional treatment might well be fruitless under those circumstances.

In contrast, under the just deserts model, the discretionary waiver procedures,[75] which once centered on an assessment of whether an offender could be salvaged, now direct the judge to focus on how the community can be made safe. Although the individualized waiver determinations made by juvenile court judges invariably are inconsistent because of the varying philosophical bents of the individual judges and the subjective nature of weighing the factors in any particular case, judges nonetheless appear to be responding to the new philosophy by emphasizing the nature of the offense over the characteristics of the offender even in their discretionary waiver decisions.

On the political front, state legislatures have acted to limit judicial discretion in the waiver decision in two ways. Since 1970, half of the states have amended their judicial waiver statutes to restrict waiver to certain types of offenses or presumptively to require trial as an adult for specific enumerated offenses. A considerable and growing number of states have gone even further, passing laws that automatically try juvenile offenders accused of certain crimes, or with specified prior records, as adults.

Automatic waiver statutes represent a total repudiation of the philosophy of the *parens patriae* juvenile court, which stemmed from the belief that juveniles were so different in nature from adults as to justify a separate justice system for them. Whereas the traditional juvenile court saw "child" and "adult" as mutually exclusive and essentially dichotomous age-based categories, waiver of juveniles into the adult criminal justice system appears rational only when this categorization has blurred. Discretionary waiver rests on the assumption that, although most juveniles differ enough from adults that they ought not be held accountable for their law violations, some persons who are chronologically juveniles share enough adult attributes to be treated as adults and punished for their crimes. In contrast, automatic waiver statutes break down the child–adult dichotomy completely, assuming that nothing inherent in the nature of children generally or in the individual juvenile in particular prevents holding the juvenile offender criminally responsible for breaking the law. Because the nature of the offense rather than the nature of the offender triggers adult jurisdiction under automatic waiver statutes, the proliferation of these laws is another indication of the impact on the law of the refiguration of childhood and adolescence.

The Supreme Court and the Juvenile Offender

Examining U.S. Supreme Court decisions that deal with the juvenile justice system serves two valuable functions. First, because Supreme Court justices are themselves culturally and historically situated actors, tracing the Court's developing juvenile jurisprudence provides tangible evidence of the general social refiguration of childhood. But the Court's opinions are not merely products of larger social processes; these decisions also actively produce social reality. Supreme Court pronouncements have direct, real-world consequences, reshaping institutions or permitting institutions to resist change, according to the Court's decree. Second, and more broadly, the Supreme Court's impact on society transcends the direct consequences of its decisions. The language used in Supreme Court opinions constitutes a powerful rhetorical resource, reconstructing the framework within which public debate is conducted. That being the case, Supreme Court opinions can be seen as both cultural context and content, as artifact and architect of legal reality.

The Procedural Challenge to the Parens Patriae *Juvenile Court*

Beginning in the mid-1960s, the Supreme Court undertook a systematic reexamination of the procedural manifestations of the *parens patriae* juvenile court. The opening salvo of the juvenile court's "constitutional domestication"[76] was fired in the 1967 decision *In re Gault*.[77] That case arose when a neighbor called the police to complain that fifteen-year-old Gerald Gault had made a lewd telephone call to her.[78] The police arrested Gault and held him in custody overnight. The following day, he appeared in court without a lawyer to answer an allegation specifying only that he was "a delinquent minor . . . in need of the protection of this Honorable Court."[79] No witnesses were sworn, and no transcript was made of the proceedings. In fact, the neighbor whose complaint triggered Gault's arrest did not appear in court at all. Instead, the Arizona juvenile court judge questioned Gault about the telephone call. As a result of incriminating admissions that Gault made during this questioning, the judge ordered Gault committed to a state juvenile facility until his twenty-first birthday, unless earlier paroled. Had Gault been an adult, however, the maximum possible sentence would have been a two-month jail sentence and a fifty-dollar fine.

In his habeas corpus petition, Gault claimed that the Arizona juvenile court hearing violated his constitutional rights to notice of the charges, to counsel, to confront and cross-examine witnesses against him, to a transcript, and to appellate review, and also that the hearing deprived him of his privilege against self-incrimination. The U.S. Supreme Court agreed, finding that much of the procedural informality of juvenile court failed to provide due process of law.

In reaching this conclusion, the Court looked beyond the articulated *parens patriae* philosophy of the juvenile court and critically examined its implementation in practice.[80] Despite "the highest motives and most enlightened impulses" of the founders of the juvenile justice system, the Court concluded that the reality of juvenile court had failed to live up to its promise.[81] Informal procedures and unfettered discretion resulted in arbitrariness, not in the "careful, compassionate [and] individualized treatment" imagined by the proponents of juvenile court.[82]

Although the *Gault* majority expressed skepticism about much of the asserted rationale for a separate juvenile court, the Court still apparently accepted the belief that children and adults are sufficiently different in nature to justify a separate court system. Although the majority acknowledged the brute reality of juvenile incarceration despite the euphemistic labels its institutions might bear, the Court nevertheless declined to hold that juvenile delinquency adjudications are the equivalent of criminal prosecutions. As a result, the *Gault* holding was grounded in the due process clause of the Fourteenth Amendment rather than the more specific Sixth Amendment guarantees.[83] If the Court was prepared to say that "the condition of being a boy does not justify a kangaroo court,"[84] it was not ready to say that being tried as a boy made no difference to the scope of his constitutional rights.

The consequences of regulating juvenile court procedure through the due process clause rather than through the Sixth Amendment became obvious four years after *Gault* in *McKeiver v. Pennsylvania*.[85] In *McKeiver*, the Court held that juveniles are not constitutionally entitled to trial by jury in delinquency hearings.[86] The plurality opinion reaffirmed that the juvenile delinquency adjudication had "not yet been held to be a 'criminal prosecution,' within the meaning and reach of the Sixth Amendment."[87] Thus the Court framed the issue as whether "fundamental fairness" required jury trials under the due process clause.[88] In answering this question, the Court interpreted "fundamental fairness" as mandating only those procedural safeguards that enhanced accurate fact finding.[89]

As the *McKeiver* plurality recognized, jury trial is the procedural right most inimical to the traditional juvenile court model.[90] With a trial by jury, the juvenile delinquency adjudication would so closely resemble a criminal trial as to make a separate juvenile justice system superfluous. If a state chose to maintain a separate (if concededly unequal) justice system for the young, the Court was unwilling to make that choice constitutionally invalid.

The Breakdown of the Child–Adult Dichotomy

As an institution, juvenile court depends for its legitimacy upon the belief that the young inherently differ from adults in their capacity to make responsible choices, thus making it wrong to hold them legally accountable for breaking the law. One might expect courts subscribing to this ideology to reason analogously that juveniles lack the inherent capacity to be held legally accountable for the purported waiver of their constitutional rights. Yet the U.S. Supreme Court rejected this argument in *Fare v. Michael C.*,[91] holding that no special bright-line age-based rules are constitutionally required to assess the validity of a juvenile's waiver of the privilege against self-incrimination.[92]

In *Fare v. Michael C.*, a sixteen-year-old juvenile who had been implicated in a homicide was in police custody. As is constitutionally required prior to custodial police interrogation, he was read his *Miranda* rights.[93] Instead of requesting an attorney, Michael C. asked that his probation officer be present during questioning. After that request was denied, Michael C. agreed to speak with the police, and during that interrogation made statements that incriminated him in the homicide.[94] On appeal, Michael C. argued, and the California Supreme Court agreed, that interrogation of a juvenile must cease whenever the juvenile asks for "an adult who is obligated to protect his interests."[95] The California high court accepted Michael C.'s contention that being a juvenile in and of itself automatically justifies a different bright-line rule to define when the privilege against self-incrimination is invoked.

The U.S. Supreme Court reversed the California high court, holding that juveniles are not entitled to a special rule that automatically would constitute an invocation of the privilege against self-incrimination.[96] The Court further rejected any suggestion that a juvenile's purported waiver of his rights should be judged by a different standard than an adult's waiver would be. Although the trial judge could consider the age and experience of the suspect in judging whether a waiver was knowing, voluntary, and intelligent, the Court concluded that the same "totality of the circumstances" balancing test is appropriate in evaluating waiver of *Miranda* rights, whether by adults or juveniles. The Court opted for a case by case evaluation of juvenile waiver of rights, with the trial judge free to consider how much weight, if any, to accord to an individual juvenile's immaturity. The holding in *Michael C.* represents a repudiation of the view that adult and child are members of binary, dichotomous categories whose inherently differing cognitive capacities justify separate waiver rules.

The issue of whether the law ought to recognize the adult–child dichotomy also arises with the question of the constitutionality of the death penalty for juveniles. Whether a bright line should be drawn prohibiting executions of juveniles below a certain age is a question that divided the Supreme Court in *Thompson v. Oklahoma*[97] and again a year later in *Stanford v. Kentucky*.[98] Both cases were plurality decisions, with Justice O'Connor providing the swing vote in each case.[99] The *Thompson* plurality adopted a bright-line rule that the Constitution forbids executing persons under the age of sixteen at the time of the commission of their crimes.[100] In *Stanford*, the *Thompson* dissenters assembled a plurality of the Court to reject extending the *Thompson* holding to those under eighteen.[101]

Writing for the plurality in *Thompson*, Justice Stevens asserted that a bright-line rule prohibiting executions of those under sixteen is necessary given the nature of adolescents.[102] Citing psychological evidence, he insisted that youths are inher-

ently less culpable than adults because of their special impulsiveness and suscep-
tibility to peer pressure.[103] He noted the prevalence in our legal system of age-
based laws reserving certain rights and duties for those over a certain age.[104]
These laws "reflect . . . this basic assumption that our society makes about children as a class; we assume that they do not yet act as adults do."[105]

Justice O'Connor, however, expressed reluctance to draw a line on the basis of
the invariant nature of adolescents. In her view, even though some juveniles
under sixteen are sufficiently impulsive and immature to make imposition of the
death penalty unacceptable, not all people under sixteen share those characteristics.[106] She based her concurrence instead on a finding that a national consensus
exists against executing those under sixteen.[107]

The dissenters in *Thompson*, Justices Scalia, Rehnquist, and White, rejected the
proposition that persons under sixteen necessarily exhibit attributes that make
capital punishment disproportionate to their culpability.[108] In the opinion of the
dissenters, many juvenile offenders are "indistinguishable, except for their age,
from their adult criminal counterparts."[109] Instead of drawing a line below which
no juvenile could be executed, the dissent would have allowed juries to make
case by case decisions.[110] The opinions in *Stanford v. Kentucky*[111] are mirror images
of those in *Thompson*, with the *Thompson* plurality, now in dissent, arguing for a
bright-line rule prohibiting execution of those under eighteen,[112] and the former
Thompson dissenters, now writing for the Court, declining to mandate such a rule.[113]
Given Justice O'Connor's continued refusal to draw a line based on the intrinsic
nature of youths[114] and the addition to the Court of Justice Kennedy, who voted
with the *Stanford* plurality, four of the current Supreme Court justices have explicitly rejected the notion that chronological age ought to divide those eligible for the
death penalty from those who are not.[115] In the context of capital punishment, just
as in the context of juvenile waiver of rights, it is very likely that, given its current
membership, the Supreme Court will continue to repudiate a bright-line dichotomy between child and adult.

Abolishing the Separate and Unequal Juvenile Court

Having an autonomous juvenile justice system with its own distinctive procedures made sense in a world that viewed the categories of "child" and "adult"
as inherently antithetical in their essential attributes. Once the imagined nature of
childhood changed and the child–adult dichotomy blurred, however, the ideological justification for a separate juvenile jurisprudence evaporated. With its philosophical underpinnings no longer consonant with the current social construction
of childhood, the juvenile court now lacks a rationale for its continued existence
other than sheer institutional inertia. All things being equal, inertia might not be
an insupportable basis for maintaining the juvenile court. After all, dismantling
the system would entail at least some political and economic costs. Indeed, overcoming the vested interests of such an entrenched institution could take a heroic

political effort of will. Yet all things are not equal. Perpetuating an anachronistic juvenile court exacts its own costs, both ideological and practical. These costs compel me to conclude that the juvenile court ought to be abolished.

Ideological Costs of an Autonomous Juvenile Court

To the extent that today's juvenile court preserves its legacy of greater procedural informality than the adult criminal court, the procedural contrast between the two systems is the most salient feature of the juvenile justice system. This contrast may be more of a liability to the juvenile court than traditionally has been assumed, however. When juvenile court practice diverges from that observed in other courts, juvenile court seems less like a court at all. As Martha Minow observed, "Due process notions are familiar to every child in this culture."[116] Raised on a steady television diet of fictional courtroom drama and local news coverage of notorious criminal trials, American young people have an image of what a court proceeding should look like. The perfunctory bench trial typical of the juvenile court is not what they imagine a trial to be.

The gulf between the archetypical trial and its actualized caricature has significance for juveniles beyond the obvious conceptual dissonance it engenders. Like any other litigants, juvenile defendants invest the legal system with legitimacy only insofar as they see it to be a just system. That perception of justice is affected not merely by the litigants' degree of satisfaction with the outcome of the case, or its distributive justice, but also by their belief in its prescriptive fairness, or its procedural justice.

Extensive sociological research has explored the somewhat counterintuitive notion that how one is treated in court may be at least as important as the ultimate verdict in shaping one's opinion about whether a system is just. According to these studies, the key factors contributing to a sense of procedural justice are consistency in the process, control of the process by the litigant, respectful treatment of the litigant, and ethicality of the fact-finder.[117] Consistency in the process means both that the system always follows prescribed rules and that everyone is treated equally within the system. Process control is the litigant's ability to determine which issues will be contested and upon what basis the contest will proceed. Respectful treatment of the litigant connotes more than just courteous interchange; it also includes investing the litigant with the full complement of rights possessed by other actors in the system. Ethicality of the fact-finder entails a sense that the judge is honest, nonbiased, forthright, and nonarbitrary in adjudication.

Even in its current "constitutionally domesticated" version, juvenile court procedural practice cuts against these core notions of procedural justice. Treating juveniles differently from adults—by denying them jury trials, for example—violates the consistency norm of equal treatment for all and reminds the young that they do not have all of the rights assigned to full-fledged members of the society.

Similarly, the paternalistic tendencies that juvenile court engenders in its functionaries undermine the norm of litigant process control. From judges to probation officers to defense counsel, juvenile court professionals all too frequently assume that juvenile accuseds are incapable of exercising sound judgment in making the decisions that affect their cases. Confidence in the ethicality of the fact-finder is undercut by the dual roles of the juvenile court judge as finder of fact and sentencing authority. Particularly for the repeat offender, the judge's knowledge of the accused's background and previous criminal record creates the unseemly appearance that guilt has been prejudged. In the sentencing role, expression by the judge of paternalistic concern for the juvenile accused coupled with stern judicial sanctioning likewise is inconsistent with the normative model of adjudicatorial behavior. All of these divergences from procedural justice norms strongly suggest that, in the eyes of juvenile respondents, the legitimacy of juvenile court is suspect.

As a consequence of this loss of legitimacy of the juvenile court, the process of legal socialization for a large segment of our youth has broken down. Legal socialization, or the inculcation of a society's approved norms and values regarding the law, has been described as a primary mechanism of social control.[118] The legal system, along with the schools, has been considered the most important institution involved in legal socialization.[119] In a legal culture as deeply permeated by due process concepts as ours, strict observance of procedural rights in and of itself contributes to an inculcation of the values of the social and political order. If juveniles perceive their exposure to the legal system as unjust, however, the legal socialization process fails. Ironically, conserving the current legal order may be possible only at the expense of abolishing the present dual system of adult and juvenile criminal jurisdiction.

Practical Consequences of Abolishing the Juvenile Court

The Availability of Jury Trials

The most striking difference between juvenile court adjudications and those in criminal court is the lack of jury trial for juveniles. In the majority of states and in the federal system, juveniles are denied jury trial unless they are bound over upon a prosecution request to be tried as adults. Three states give the juvenile judge discretion to allow trial by jury,[120] and thirteen states guarantee juvenile jury trials by case law or statute.[121] Even in those states where juveniles may opt for a trial by jury, such trials are apparently extremely uncommon.[122] The juvenile court ethos exerts powerful institutional and ideological constraints on the accused's exercise of the right to jury trial. The result, whether by legal code or local custom, is that juveniles seldom see jury resolution of the charges against them.

Being deprived of a jury trial hurts juveniles in a number of ways. Juries traditionally have been treasured as a protection against biased judges and overzealous prosecutors, because the jury has no access to background information about the accused that might cause them to prejudge the case. Moreover, because the jury embodies community values, it functions as the symbolic conscience of the community.

Further, it is one of the less well-kept secrets of our criminal justice system that juries acquit more frequently than do judges. In their germinal comparison of judge and jury fact finding, Kalven and Zeisel empirically demonstrated[123] what every trial lawyer knows: A defendant ordinarily stands a far better chance with a jury trial than with a bench trial.[124] A recent California study comparing juvenile to adult court convictions confirms Kalven and Zeisel's findings; on comparable offenses it is easier to get a conviction in juvenile court than in the adult criminal justice system.[125]

Why do judges convict more often than juries? One explanation is that the nature of judicial decision making is intrinsically different from the process of fact finding for juries. Judges try hundreds, even thousands, of cases every year, while jurors hear only a few during their service. Over and over again, the juvenile court judge hears testimony from the same police and probation officers, inevitably forming a settled opinion on their credibility. Worse yet, the judge may well have heard earlier charges against the accused, and thus may come to hold a fixed view on the juvenile's credibility and character. In any event, the judge hears pretrial motions to suppress evidence; even if the motions are granted, the judge will have heard the damning information.

Another explanation for the discrepancy in conviction rates between judges and juries is that sitting in high-caseload courts such as the typical juvenile court, judges invariably begin to slip into a routine that may make them less meticulous in considering the evidence. Judges grow "weary of fact-finding whereas jurors find it novel and nothing escapes their attention."[126] Not only may judges consider the facts more casually than would jurors, but they also may apply less stringent concepts of reasonable doubt and presumption of innocence.

Moreover, as a general proposition, fact finding by a single person necessarily differs from that by a group because the sole fact-finder does not have to discuss the law and the evidence with others before reaching a verdict. The back-and-forth, give-and-take of a discussion can cause the fact-finders to reconsider their opinions in light of the arguments and observations of others. Being forced to articulate the basis for an opinion forces the fact-finder to spell out the logical connections between the evidence and conclusions, "giv[ing] contours to items previously apprehended in a fleeting and unclear manner."[127]

Not only is the judicial decision-making process different from that of juries, but the personal characteristics of judges differ from those of most jurors. In terms of economic status, social class, race, and gender, it is an understatement to say that judges as a group do not reflect the composition of the community at large. That jury pools include men and women, blacks and whites, adds valued dimension to jury fact finding that judges cannot share.

Additionally, the litigants in a jury trial may probe the jurors for hidden biases through searching voir dire examination, inquiring about attitudes, beliefs, and experiences that may affect the way in which jurors would hear the case. In a bench trial, no analogous opportunity exists to explore the judge's background. Without voir dire scrutiny to detect the possibility of judicial bias, one must assume that judges are persons of superhuman powers of self-reflection, able to attend to their conscious and unconscious mental processes and set aside any biases they might reveal.

The value of the availability of jury trials for juveniles goes beyond curing the problems of biased judges or disadvantageous fact finding, however. A jury trial requires the trial judge to articulate in detail the law to be applied in the case through the mechanism of jury instructions. Any error of law in the instructions is reviewable by an appellate court. If no jury instructions exist to make explicit the trial judge's understanding of the law, the reviewing court has no way of knowing whether the juvenile court judge misunderstood or misapplied the law to the juvenile's detriment. As a result, juveniles denied a jury trial lose out twice. They are more likely to be convicted in the first place, and are unlikely to be able to prove an error of law that would allow them to prevail on appeal.

Denying jury trials has symbolic costs as well, undermining the perceived legitimacy of the judicial process in the eyes of the juvenile. Given its centrality in the popular cultural vision of the legal system, it is not surprising that young people share the general public's regard for the jury trial, ranking it highly among their constitutional rights.[128] Thus, the right to jury trial is important both symbolically and substantively. If abolishing the juvenile court is the only practical means of securing jury trials for juveniles charged with criminal offenses, then abolition would be well worth it for that benefit alone.

Achieving Effective Assistance of Counsel

In the literature on the contemporary juvenile court, a harsh indictment of the legal counsel available to juveniles is a repeated refrain.[129] Notwithstanding that more than twenty years ago the Supreme Court constitutionally guaranteed legal counsel to juveniles charged with crimes,[130] the most recent empirical studies reveal that a shockingly high proportion of juveniles still are tried without lawyers.[131] As it turns out, those juveniles may be the lucky ones; over and over again, studies have shown that juveniles with lawyers fare worse in juvenile court than those proceeding without counsel and are more likely to be incarcerated and jailed for longer periods than if represented pro se.[132]

These statistics reveal only the correlation between legal representation and more severe dispositions, and not why this disadvantage exists. One possibility is that lawyers hurt their clients through sheer incompetence and inadequacy in their advocacy. Another is that lawyers in juvenile court may deliberately solicit harsher penalties, believing that such dispositions are in their clients' best interests in the long run. Still another explanation is that juvenile court judges may display conscious or unconscious antagonism toward the idea of attorneys in juvenile court, and take out their hostility on the represented clients. Or it may be that the juvenile court judge has prejudged the case and predetermined the likely sentence before the proceedings began and, to save the system time and money, encourages waiver of counsel in those cases where the probable sanction is comparatively light. What is clear, however, is that all of these factors find factual support in current studies of the juvenile court.

As is demonstrated in two in-depth examinations of juvenile court procedures,[133] trials in juvenile court are frequently "only marginally contested,"[134] and marked by "lackadaisical defense efforts."[135] Defense counsel generally make few objections,[136] and seldom move to exclude evidence on constitutional grounds.[137] Defense witnesses rarely are called,[138] and the cross-examination of prosecution witnesses is "frequently perfunctory and reveals no design or rationale on the part of the defense attorney."[139] Closing arguments are sketchy when they are made at all.[140] Watching these trials, one gets the overall impression that defense counsel prepare minimally or not at all.[141] The New York State Bar Association study estimated that in 45 percent of all juvenile trials, counsel was "seriously inadequate"; in only 5 percent could the performance of defense counsel be considered "effective representation."[142]

One explanation for the abysmal performance of defense counsel is that lawyers in juvenile court are all too frequently both inexperienced and overworked. Particularly in jurisdictions where juveniles have no right to jury trial, public defender offices often assign their greenest attorneys to juvenile court to season them.[143] Supervision from senior attorneys is not always what might be desired, and caseloads in these high-volume courts are crushing. Moreover, in a forum without jury trials, there is a tendency for lawyers to cut corners in these cases of comparatively low public visibility, a tendency often tacitly encouraged by judges anxious to process cases as expeditiously as possible. Under these circumstances, it is no wonder that juvenile bench trials are seldom models of zealous defense advocacy.

In addition, defense lawyers who routinely practice in juvenile court face tremendous institutional pressures to cooperate in maintaining a smoothly functioning court system.[144] The defense lawyer who is seen as obstreperous in her advocacy will be reminded subtly, or overtly if necessary,[145] that excessive zeal in representing juvenile clients is inappropriate and counterproductive. If she ignores these signals to temper her advocacy, the appointed defense lawyer is vulnerable to direct attacks, such as having her fees slashed or being excluded from the panel of lawyers from which the court makes indigent appointments.[146] Seldom are such crude measures necessary, however. For most defense lawyers, withstanding the psychological debilitation attendant upon being the sustained focus of judicial and prosecutorial disapproval is hopeless.[147]

Perhaps the most pervasive and insidious reason for less-than-zealous defense advocacy is the ambiguity felt by many juvenile court lawyers concerning their proper role.[148] The legacy of decades of paternalistic *parens patriae* ideology is still evident in the attitudes of many defense lawyers, who cannot help thinking of themselves as charged, at least in part, with a responsibility to act in their clients' long-term best interests rather than scrupulously to safeguard their legal rights.[149]

Despite the clear ethical mandate to represent juveniles on the same terms and with the same zeal as they would adults,[150] many defenders nevertheless find themselves deeply torn between their professional obligation to press their clients' legitimate legal claims and their paternalistic inclination to help the court address their clients' often desperate social needs. Even lawyers who have not internalized this role conflict may face external pressure from judges and probation officers to conform to a guardian-like role.

In all of these ways, the institution of the autonomous and distinct juvenile court inherently discourages effective assistance of counsel for juvenile defendants. As long as a separate juvenile court system exists, separate advocacy models appear to be the inevitable result. Although rooting out paternalistic attitudes toward children cannot be accomplished by fiat, abolishing the juvenile court would go a long way toward ensuring that juveniles charged with crimes get the same caliber of legal counsel, operating under the same standards of zealous advocacy, as adult defendants receive.

Dispositional Needs of Juveniles

One objection to the abolition of the separate juvenile justice system is that juvenile court sentencing practices shield young people from the draconian sentences meted out to adult offenders. This objection, however, both overstates the protections of the juvenile system and underestimates the degree to which the ordinary criminal justice system could and undoubtedly would adapt to the extension of its jurisdiction over minors.

First, the recent trend extending the scope of judicial and statutory waiver procedures already has deprived many young offenders of supposedly palliative juvenile court sentences. Even for those juveniles remaining within the juvenile court system, however, it may be anachronistic to think of their sentences as radically less severe than those they might receive as adults. For example, one study of juvenile sentences indicates that, compared with earlier times, in recent years the juvenile court is incarcerating more offenders[151] and their sentences are longer, even though the juvenile arrest rate has been declining since 1975. The gap between juvenile and adult sentencing practices thus appears to be narrowing.

Nor must adult sentences necessarily ignore the fact of youth as a mitigating factor. In those jurisdictions that still maintain indeterminate adult sentences, parole boards and judges alike could consider the age of the offender in setting the appropriate sentence. For states with determinate sentencing grids, an express mitigation factor for youth could be accommodated within the ordinary sentencing matrices. There are neither theoretical nor practical bars to the use of age to mitigate the harshness of average adult sentences. Furthermore, available historical evidence suggests that judges considered youth as a mitigating factor in the past before the advent of the juvenile court.[152] Recent sociological data suggest that judges currently give lighter sentences to younger adults in the criminal justice system.[153] There is no reason to suppose that what has been termed the "punishment gap"[154] between younger and older offenders will not continue to exist when the juvenile court has been dismantled.

Nor is there any need for a special adjudicatory system to justify incarcerating young offenders separately from older criminals, any more than we must have a separate women's court or be forced to imprison females in male penal facilities. Preserving a separate juvenile court system tends to obscure from the public the extent to which juvenile sentencing already fails to protect juveniles from exploitation in adult facilities. The grim truth is that, even under a separate juvenile justice regime, all too many juveniles currently are incarcerated in adult penal institutions.[155] Worse yet, the current dichotomous juvenile and adult system often forces the use of adult prisons to incarcerate juveniles waived into the adult system. While there may be sound reasons for holding certain young teenagers criminally responsible and trying them as adults, their subsequent incarceration is a prison administrator's nightmare. In the prison world, these youngest inmates face a horror of unimaginable violence and victimization. If we abolish the separate juvenile court, we detach the question of what place of incarceration would be appropriate from the question of criminal accountability. Serious young offenders could be given sentences proportionate to the gravity of their crimes without necessarily requiring that they serve the first part of the sentence alongside older convicts. In reconstructing childhood as a developmental continuum in which the development of different capacities may proceed at different rates, we are comfortable today concluding that a particular fifteen-year-old may have sufficient cognitive and moral maturity to justify holding him fully responsible for his criminal conduct, while at the same time realizing that he may not be physically and psychologically competent to hold his own in the world of an adult prison. Abolishing the juvenile court is thus compatible with our contemporary sentencing and correctional ideology, and consistent with the current social construction of childhood.

Conclusion

This chapter is a case study applying social constructivist theory in a critical examination of a legal institution—in this case, juvenile court. This theory asserts that the collective social process of constructing systems of shared significance makes it possible for the individual to ascribe meaning to the actions of both self and others. Therefore, this chapter outlines the historical and cultural construction of childhood and adolescence in our society, and explores the consequences of that interpretive construct for the legal order in its treatment of law violations by the young. The turn-of-the-century invention of adolescence and its assimilation to childhood made an autonomous juvenile justice system imaginable and, indeed, indispensable within its social context. Because our interpretive construct of childhood and adolescence has changed, and we no longer view young people as essentially and uniformly different from adults, we can no longer justify maintaining a procedurally and practically inferior justice system for juveniles; hence the call for its abolition.

The reader may question why a normative claim need be made to abolish the juvenile court, assuming that the current refiguration of the life cycle must inevitably lead to change in our legal institutions to make the legal order consistent with our social context. Here I wish to emphasize that the legal order is not merely a passive reflection of the social context in which it is embedded, but rather is in addition a dynamic part of that context. As has been noted, juvenile court would not have been created absent the Progressive Era's attitudes and beliefs about the nature of young people. But it is equally true that in its ideological articulation of purpose and in its practice, the Progressive juvenile court itself helped to change our shared social understanding of what it means to be a child.

Social constructivism does not imply a deterministic clockwork universe in which "superstructural" aspects such as legal institutions respond to overarching social processes. On the contrary, constructivism insists that it is through the intentional actions of human actors that society collectively creates and recreates our world. In short, the fact that our social order is culturally and historically contingent does not make it immune from criticism or proof against consciously effectuated change. Not only can we examine and understand our shared interpretive constructs, but also we have the power and indeed the moral obligation to judge our constructs and to change them if we find them unsatisfactory. In this study, I have suggested that a separate juvenile court system is no longer consonant with our current cultural and historical context. I have further argued that this institution exacts insupportable social costs. As intentional actors in the legal order, we ought to choose to dismantle it.

NOTES

1. A succinct and forceful exposition of this position was given by Alfred Regnery, administrator of the federal Office of Juvenile Justice and Delinquency Prevention under the Reagan Administration. *See* Regnery, Getting Away with Murder: Why the Juvenile Justice System Needs an Overhaul, 34 Pol'y Rev. 65 (Fall 1985).

2. In pressing for the abolition of the juvenile court in this chapter, I am referring to juvenile court adjudication of criminal charges, a function of every state juvenile court system now in place.

3. P. Berger & T. Luckmann, The Social Construction of Reality (1966).

4. *Id.* at 60–62.

5. *See generally* R. Rorty, Philosophy and the Mirror of Nature 155–64, 315–94 (1979) (rejecting Cartesian foundationalism in favor of a pragmatic relativistic epistemology).

6. *See* N. Goodman, Ways of Worldmaking 1–22, 109–29 (1978) (reality can be experienced or described under one or more systems of interpretive const which Goodman calls "frames of reference").

7. *See* S. Fish, Is There a Text in This Class? The Authority of Interpretive munities 1–17, 338–55 (1980) (interpretive communities produce meaning, reality, through shared values, assumptions, and ideology).

8. D. Herzog, Without Foundations: Justification in Political Theory 224–43 (1985) (urging contextual justification over foundationalist justifications in grounding the moral and political order).

9. C. Geertz, Local Knowledge: Fact and Law in Comparative Perspective, in Local Knowledge 218 (1983).

10. *See, e.g.,* Boyle, The Politics of Reason: Critical Legal Theory and Local Social Thought, 133 U. Pa. L. Rev. 685, 780 n.270 (1985) ("[T]his suggests the operation by which we make sense of the world—using the available reservoirs of cultural meaning for purposes that both shape and are shaped by the process in which we are engaged").

11. I borrow the term from Steven Mailloux, who used it to describe constructivist epistemology in literary theory. Mailloux, Truth or Consequences: On Being against Theory, in Against Theory 65, 68 (W. J. T. Mitchell ed., 1985).

12. Gordon, New Developments in Legal Theory, in The Politics of Law 288–89 (D. Kairys ed., 1982).

13. *See* Kelman, Interpretive Construction in the Substantive Criminal Law, 33 Stan. L. Rev. 591, 600–669 (1981); Winter, Bull Durham and the Uses of Theory, 42 Stan. L. Rev. 639, 677–93 (1990).

14. Benedict, Continuities and Discontinuities in Cultural Conditioning, 1 Psychiatry 161 (1983), *quoted in* Skolnick, The Limits of Childhood: Conceptions of Child Development and Social Context, 39 Law & Contemp. Probs. 38, 43 (Summer 1975).

15. Anthropological evidence suggests that adolescence, for example, is by no means universally recognized. Some cultures recognize a gradual transition from childhood into adult activities and responsibilities; others observe puberty as the event marking the passage from childhood to adulthood without any intermediate transitional phase corresponding to adolescence in the modern West. Skolnick, The Limits of Childhood, *supra* note 14, at 61–63.

16. P. Ariès, Centuries of Childhood: A Social History of Family Life (1962).

17. *Id.* at 128.

18. S. Tiffin, In Whose Best Interest? Child Welfare Reform in the Progressive Era 236 (1982); *see* Children's Bureau Act, Pub. L. No. 116, ch. 73, 37 Stat. 79 (1912).

19. The emergence of adolescence as an accepted social "fact" in the late nineteenth and early twentieth centuries has been well-documented. *See* J. Kett, Rites of Passage: Adolescence in America—1790 to the Present 111–264 (1977).

20. Lapsley et al., Toward a Theoretical Perspective on the Legislation of Adolescence, 5 J. Early Adolescence 441, 450 (1985).

21. H. Chudacoff, How Old Are You? Age Consciousness in American Culture 86 (1989).

22. One obvious instance of this age stratification occurred in education. Age-grading in the classroom was based on the assumption that a child's abilities, needs, and interests were most compatible with those of children of a similar age, and that age segregation in a child's daily life was both natural and beneficial. Before the turn of the century, the practice was almost unknown. *Id.* at 30–40.

23. A. Platt, The Child Savers: The Invention of Delinquency 9–10 (2d ed. 1977).

24. *Id.;* D. Rothman, Conscience and Convenience: The Asylum and Its Alternatives in Progressive America 215 (1980); E. Ryerson, The Best Laid Plans: America's Juvenile Court Experiment 81 (1978).

25. Boston Juvenile Court Judge Baker, in a 1910 article promoting the juvenile court system, compared the judge to a "physician" engaged in diagnosing an "outbreak" of criminal behavior. Once treatment had begun, the judge must check up on the progress of the probationer, "just as a physician might do in the case of a burn or a bruise." Even tighter supervision would be needed to cure more intransigent cases of deviance, which Judge Baker likened to "tuberculosis or typhoid." Baker, Procedure for the Boston Juvenile Court, quoted in L. Empey, American Delinquency: Its Meaning and Construction 499–50 (1978).

26. Platt, The Child Savers, *supra* note 23, at 18–55; Rothman, Conscience and Convenience, *supra* note 24, at 210–12.

27. Ryerson, The Best Laid Plans, *supra* note 24, at 120.

28. Among the most influential advocates of the juvenile court were the architects of the model system in Illinois, including Timothy Hurley, the chief administrator of the system; Richard Tuthill, an Illinois juvenile court judge; and Julian Mack, the Cook County juvenile court judge whose 1909 Harvard Law Review article, Mack, The Juvenile Court, 23 Harv. L. Rev. 104 (1909), was extremely influential.

29. *Id.* at 119–20.

30. Procedural informality extended even to the recommended physical layout of the courtroom. The judge was not to be seated above the courtroom on a bench, but was to be "[s]eated at a desk, with the child at his side, where he can on occasion put his arm around his shoulder and draw the lad to him." *Id.* at 120.

31. Commonwealth v. Fisher, 62 A. 198, 200 (Pa. 1905).

32. Mack, The Juvenile Court, *supra* note 28, at 117.

33. I have culled those appellations from Judge Mack's law review article, The Juvenile Court, *supra* note 28, at 117, 119, 120, where he repeatedly uses them.

34. Skolnick, The Limits of Childhood, *supra* note 14, at 74.

35. *See* Chudacoff, How Old Are You? *supra* note 21, at 157–90; J. Demos, Past, Present, and Personal: The Family and the Life Course in American History 114–31 (1986); L. Friedman, The Republic of Choice: Law, Authority, and Culture 169–75 (1990).

36. Keniston, Youth: A "New" Stage of Life, 39 Am. Scholar 631, 635 (1970); K. Keniston, Youth and Dissent 7 (1971).

37. Neugarten, Age Groups in American Society and the Rise of the Young-Old, 415 Annals Am. Acad. Pol. & Soc. Sci. 187 (1974).

38. Dannefer, Adult Development and Social Theory, 49 Am. Soc. Rev. 100, 101–04 (1984); Levinson, A Conception of Adult Development, 41 Am. Psychologist 3, 5–6 (1980); D. Levinson, The Seasons of a Man's Life 18–33 (1978) (subdividing middle age).

39. For a survey of the psychological literature suggesting that children as young as ten years old are as competent at decision making as adults, see L. Houlgate, The Child and the State: A Normative Theory of Juvenile Rights 61–73 (1980); Melton, Developmental Psychology and the Law: The State of the Art, 22 J. Fam. L. 445, 463–64 (1984); Melton, Taking *Gault* Seriously: Toward a New Juvenile Court, 68 Neb. L. Rev. 146, 153–58 (1989). Lawrence Kohlberg conducted the foundational study of moral reasoning in children. *See* Kohlberg, The Development of Children's Orientations toward a Moral Order, 6 Vita Humana 11, 16 (1963) (observing that by age fourteen, the average child has reached the level of moral reasoning possessed by most adults); *see also* Skolnick, Children's Rights, Children's Develoment, in The Future of Childhood and Juvenile Justice 138, 144–48 (L. Empey ed., 1979) (providing later research on moral reasoning); Skolnick, The Limits of Childhood, *supra* note 14, at 52–55 (same).

40. Skolnick, The Limits of Childhood, *supra* note 14, at 56.

41. *Id.* at 74.

42. By positivism in penology, I mean the assumption that external, deterministic factors such as heredity, environment, or social conditions cause criminal behavior, not an evil exercise of free will on the part of the criminal, and that unraveling the causes of crime will tell us what sentencing policies to adopt. S. Cohen, Against Criminology 4–7 (1988).

43. Among the many studies finding that rehabilitative treatment was ineffective in preventing recidivism are D. Lipton et al., The Effectiveness of Correctional Treatment (1975); National Research Council Committee on Law Enforcement and Criminal Justice, The Rehabilitation of Criminal Offenders: Problems and Prospects (1979); Bailey, Correctional Outcome: An Evaluation of 100 Reports, 57 J. Crim. L., Criminology & Police Sci. 153 (1966); Martinson, What Works?—Questions and Answers about Prison Reform, 35 Pub. Interest 22 (1974); Robinson & Smith, The Effectiveness of Correctional Programs, 17 Crime & Delinq. 67 (1971). *See generally* N. Shover, A Sociology of American Corrections 274–312 (1979) (reviewing the research on correctional effectiveness).

44. Some "just deserts" statutes provide determinate sentencing matrices, some require mandatory minimum sentences for many offenses, and some rely on administratively promulgated sentencing guidelines. Even in jurisdictions without statutory "just deserts" sentencing, judges appear to be exercising their sentencing discretion by basing juvenile dispositions on "just deserts" principles. Feld, The Juvenile Court Meets the Principle of Offense: Punishment, Treatment, and the Difference It Makes, 68 B.U. L. Rev. 821, 882–91 (1988).

45. Basic Juvenile Court Act, ch. 291, §§ 1–83, 1977 Wash. Laws 1002.

46. Schneider & Schram, Responses of Professionals to the Washington (State) Law, in Current Issues in Juvenile Justice 101, 101 (R. Corrado et al. eds., 1983).

47. *See* Becker, Washington State's New Juvenile Code: An Introduction, 14 Gonz. L. Rev. 289, 305–307 (1979).

48. *Id.* at 307–308.

49. Wash. Rev. Code § 13.40.150(3)(h)–(i) (1977).

50. *Id.* § 13.40.150(4)(e).

51. *Id.* § 13.40.070(3).

52. *Id.* § 13.40.070(7).

53. *Id.* §§ 13.40.010(2)(j); 13.40.027(1).

54. Washington State Juvenile Disposition Standards Commission, Washington State Juvenile Disposition Standards Philosophy and Guide 3 (1984).

55. *Id.* at 9.

56. "[T]he community should obtain justice by the fair and prompt imposition of sanctions upon youthful offenders. . . . The more serious the youth's offense, the greater the sanction the youth should receive." *Id.*

57. "The safety of the community is addressed when sentences and sanctions are based upon the youth's offense history." *Id.* at 12.

58. The commission's *Guide* stated that:

> Punishment, under the guise of rehabilitation, is unjust and will be perceived as such by the youth. A sentence that is geared to the treatment needs of the youth undercuts the significance of the crime committed. The need for treatment services should not influence the severity of the youth's sentence or sanctions.

Id. at 15.

59. Mack, The Juvenile Court, *supra* note 28, at 120.

60. The exception is that jury trials are not available to Washington's juveniles. Wash. Rev. Code Ann. § 13.04.021 (Supp. 1991); State v. Schaaf, 743 P.2d 240, 247 (Wash. 1987).

61. Wash. Rev. Code Ann. § 13.40.130(1) (Supp. 1991).

62. Wash. Juv. Ct. R. 7.6; Wash. Crim. Ct. R. 4.1, 4.2.

63. Wash. Rev. Code Ann. § 13.40.140(2) (Supp. 1991).

64. *Id.* § 13.40.140(3); Wash. Juv. Ct. R. 9.3; Wash. Crim. Ct. R. 3.1(f).

65. Wash. Rev. Code Ann. § 13.40.140(7) (Supp. 1991).

66. Wash. Juv. Ct. R. 7.9, 7.10; Wash. Crim. Ct. R. 4.3, 4.4.

67. Wash. Rev. Code Ann. § 13.40.140(8) (Supp. 1991).

68. Wash. Juv. Ct. R. 7.11(b).

69. *See* S. Davis, Rights of Juveniles: The Juvenile Justice System §§ 4.1–.4 (2d ed. 1980).

70. *Id.*

71. 383 U.S. 541 (1966).

72. *Id.* at 557, 561.

73. *Id.* at 566–67.

74. *Id.* at 567.

75. There are two classes of discretionary waiver procedures: judicial waiver and prosecutorial waiver. Except for New York and Nebraska, all states and the District of Columbia provide for a judicial determination of whether a court should waive juvenile jurisdiction.

Several states provide concurrent jurisdiction for some or all offenses in both juvenile and criminal court, allowing prosecutors to exercise their discretion in filing charging documents in either court system. *See* Ark. Stat. Ann § 41-617 (1977 & Supp. 1983) (concurrent jurisdiction over all criminal violations); Neb. Rev. Stat. § 43-247 (1989) (same); Wyo. Stat. § 14-6-203(c) (1986) (same); *cf.* Colo. Rev. Stat. § 19-1-104 (Supp. 1990) (concurrent jurisdiction only over specific listed offenses); Fla. Stat. Ann. §§ 39.02 (West 1989) (same); Ga. Code Ann. § 15-11-5 (1990) (same); Utah Code Ann. § 78-3a-25(6) (1990) (same).

76. Paulsen, The Constitutional Domestication of the Juvenile Court, 1967 Sup. Ct. Rev. 233, 236.

77. 387 U.S. 1 (1967).

78. *Id.* at 4.

79. *Id.* at 5.

80. *Id.* at 14–22, 28–30.

81. *Id.* at 17–18.

82. *Id.* at 18–19.

83. The Sixth Amendment explicitly mandates many of the rights that the Court denied Gault. It applies "[i]n all criminal prosecutions," giving the defendant "the right to a speedy and public trial, by an impartial jury . . . to be informed of the nature and cause of the accusation; to be confronted with the witnesses against him; . . . and to have the Assistance of Counsel for his defence." U.S. Const. amend. VI.

84. *Gault*, 387 U.S. at 28.

85. 403 U.S. 528 (1971) (plurality opinion).

86. *Id.* at 545.

87. *Id.* at 541.

88. *Id.*

89. *Id.* at 543.

90. *Id.* at 545–50.

91. 442 U.S. 707 (1979).

92. *Id.* at 725.

93. Miranda v. Arizona, 384 U.S. 436, 444–45, 473–74 (1966).

94. *Fare*, 442 U.S. at 710–11.

95. *Id.* at 729–30 (Marshall, J., dissenting).

96. *Id.* at 724.

97. 487 U.S. 815 (1988).

98. 109 S. Ct. 2969 (1989).

99. *Stanford*, 109 S. Ct. at 2980 (O'Connor, J., concurring in part and concurring in the judgment); *Thompson*, 487 U.S. at 848 (O'Connor, J., concurring).

100. *Thompson*, 487 U.S. at 838.

101. *Stanford*, 109 S. Ct. at 2980 (Justice O'Connor concurred with Justices Scalia, Rehnquist, White, and Kennedy to form the plurality).

102. *Thompson*, 487 U.S. at 833–38.

103. *Id.*

104. *Id.* at 823–24, 839–48.

105. *Id.* at 825 n.23.

106. *Id.* at 853 (O'Connor, J., concurring).

107. *Id.* at 849–59 (O'Connor, J., concurring).

108. *Id.* at 864 (Scalia, J., dissenting).

109. *Id.* at 865 (Scalia, J., dissenting).

110. *Id.* The dissent noted that the jury exercised "particularized judgment" in sentencing Thompson to death. *Id.* at 863 (Scalia, J., dissenting).

111. 109 S. Ct. 2969 (1989).

112. *Id.* at 2987–94 (Brennan, J., dissenting).

113. *Id.* at 2979–80.

114. In *Stanford*, Justice O'Connor rested her concurrence on her finding that no national consensus forbids executing those between sixteen and eighteen. *Id.* at 2980–82 (O'Connor, J., concurring).

115. The *Thompson* holding, which prohibited capital punishment for those under sixteen, must be considered tenuous authority in light of the limited basis of Justice O'Connor's concurrence in that case. *See supra* notes 106–107 and accompanying text. Presumably if the national mood shifted to favor execution of those under sixteen, Justice O'Connor would find their execution constitutional. The three justices most recently appointed to the Court, Justices Souter, Thomas, and Ginsburg, have yet to rule on any case posing this issue. However, it seems nearly certain that at least one of these justices will adopt the position taken by the *Stanford* plurality.

116. Minow, Are Rights Right for Children? 1987 Am. B. Found. Res. J. 203, 212 (1987).

117. E. Lind & T. Tyler, The Social Psychology of Procedural Justice 93–127, 131–32 (1988).

118. Tapp & Kohlberg, Developing Senses of Law and Legal Justice, in Law, Justice and the Individual in Society 89 (J. Tapp & F. Levine eds., 1977).

119. *Id.* at 104.

120. The three states giving the judge authority to allow juvenile jury trials are: Alabama, Kansas, and South Dakota.

121. States providing juvenile jury trials include: Alaska, Colorado, Massachusetts, Michigan, Montana, New Mexico, Oklahoma, Tennessee, Texas, West Virginia, Wisconsin, and Wyoming.

122. Statistics compiled in a 1978 study showed that the percentage of juvenile adjudications taking advantage of the right to jury trial ranged from a low of 0.36 percent in Alaska to a high of 3.2 percent in Denver. Note, The Right to a Jury under the Juvenile Justice Act of 1977, 14 Gonz. L. Rev. 401, 418 n.125 (1979).

123. Kalven and Zeisel used a database of 3,576 cases to study how often the jury's verdict differed from that which the judge would have pronounced. They found that the jury convicted in 64.2 percent of the cases, acquitted in 30.3 percent, and failed to reach a verdict in 5.5 percent of them. Judges, on the other hand, convicted 83.3 percent of the defendants, and acquitted the remaining 16.7 percent. H. Kalven & H. Zeisel, The American Jury 55–81 (1966). Adding together the statistics for acquittals and hung juries, juries failed to convict more than twice as often as did judges.

124. *Id.*

125. P. Greenwood et al., Youth Crime and Juvenile Justice in California 30–31 (1983) (after controlling for seriousness of offense, juveniles are convicted of a higher proportion of charged crimes than adults).

126. Norton, What a Jury Is, 16 Va. L. Rev. 261, 266 (1930).

127. Berger & Luckmann, Social Construction, *supra* note 3, at 153; *see also id.* at 152–55.

128. In a recent sociological study, eighth graders were told to imagine that Americans could retain only some of their constitutional rights, and then asked to rank which basic rights they most valued. The right to jury trial was judged more valuable than any other right associated with the criminal trial process. The right to privacy was rated most highly, chosen by 84.3 percent of the respondents, followed by freedom of speech (82.4 percent), the prohibition against cruel and unusual punishment (72 percent), freedom of religion (55 percent), the right to trial by jury (49 percent), the privilege against self-incrimination (38 percent), the right to counsel (23.5 percent), freedom of assembly (23.5 percent), freedom of the press (22 percent), and the right to bear arms (16 percent). Sibley, Child's Play: The Origins of Hegemony, Acquiescence and Obligation in Adolescents' Studies of Law 7 (1989) (unpublished paper presented at annual meeting of Law and Society Association at Madison, Wis., 1989).

129. *See* M. Bortner, Inside a Juvenile Court: The Tarnished Ideal of Individu-alized Justice 136–39 (1982); M. Finkelstein et al., Prosecution in the Juvenile Court: Guidelines for the Future 40–42, 51–62 (1973) [hereinafter Prosecution in the Juvenile Court] (describing Boston Juvenile Court); B. Flicker, Providing Counsel for Accused Juveniles 2 (1983); J. Knitzer & M. Sobie, Law Guardians in New York State: A Study of the Legal Representation of Children 8–9 (1984) [here-inafter Law Guardians in New York State]; E. Lemert, Social Action and Legal Change: Revolution within the Juvenile Court 178 (1970); Platt, The Child Savers, *supra* note 23, at 163–75; Clarke & Koch, Juvenile Court: Therapy or Crime Control and Do Lawyers Make a Difference? 14 Law & Soc'y Rev. 263, 297–300 (1980); Davidson & Saul, Youth Advocacy in the Juvenile Court: A Clash of Paradigms, in Legal Reforms Affecting Child and Youth Services 29, 40–41 (G. Melton ed., 1982); Duffee & Siegel, The Organization Man: Legal Counsel in the Juvenile Court, 7 Crim. L. Bull. 544, 548–49 (1971); Feld, The Right to Counsel in Juvenile Court: An Empirical Study of When Lawyers Appear and the Difference They Make, 79 J. Crim. L. & Criminology 1185, 1207–1208 (1989); Ferster et al., The Juvenile Justice System: In Search of the Role of Counsel, 39 Fordham L. Rev. 375, 398–99 (1971); Fox, Juvenile Justice Reform: An Historical Perspective, 22 Stan. L. Rev. 1187, 1236–37 (1970); Platt & Friedman, The Limits of Advocacy: Occupa-tional Hazards in Juvenile Court, 116 U. Pa. L. Rev. 1156, 1168–81 (1968).

130. *In re* Gault, 387 U.S. 1, 41 (1967).

131. For a survey of statistical studies on the percentage of juvenile offenders represented by counsel, see Feld, The Right to Counsel in Juvenile Court, *supra* note 129, at 1199–1200.

132. Even when comparing offenders accused of similar crimes, and controlling for prior record, the sociological research has demonstrated that, all things being equal, lawyers appear to hurt, not help, their clients appearing in juvenile court. *See* Bortner, Inside a Juvenile Court, *supra* note 129, at 139–40; L. Stapleton & V. Teitelbaum, In Defense of Youth: A Study of the Role of Counsel in American Juvenile Courts 64–65 (1972); Clarke & Koch, Juvenile Court, *supra* note 129, at 304–306; Duffee & Siegel, The Organization Man, *supra* note 129, at 548–53; Feld, *In re Gault* Revisited: A Cross-State Comparison of the Right to Counsel in Juve-nile Court, 34 Crime & Delinq. 393, 393 (1988); Hayeslip, The Impact of Defense Attorney Presence on Juvenile Court Dispositions, 30 Juv. & Fam. Ct. J. 9, 12 (1979). For a detailed regression analysis controlling for disparities in seriousness of offense, prior criminal history, and detention status, see Feld, The Right to Counsel in Juvenile Court, *supra* note 129, at 1239, 1250, 1260, 1306–12.

133. Prosecution in the Juvenile Court, *supra* note 129, at 51–62 (a federally funded examination of the Boston Juvenile Court); Law Guardians in New York State, *supra* note 129 (a study of New York's juvenile courts commissioned by the state's bar association).

134. Prosecution in the Juvenile Court, *supra* note 129, at 51.

135. *Id.* at 41.

136. *Id.* at 52; Law Guardians in New York State, *supra* note 129, at 8.

137. Prosecution in the Juvenile Court, *supra* note 129, at 52.

138. *Id.* at 51.

139. *Id.*

140. In the Boston Juvenile Court, summations by the defense were "the exception rather than the rule." *Id.* at 52.

141. Law Guardians in New York State, *supra* note 129, at 8–9.

142. *Id.*

143. Feld, The Right to Counsel in Juvenile Court, *supra* note 129, at 1331. Barbara Flicker notes, "[I]n some defender offices, assignment to 'kiddie court' is the bottom rung of the ladder, to be passed as quickly as possible on the way up to more visible and prestigious criminal court assignments." Flicker, Providing Counsel, *supra* note 129, at 2; *see also* Lemert, Legislating Change in the Juvenile Court, 1967 Wis. L. Rev. 421, 431 (noting low priority given to juvenile court work by many defenders).

144. The process of cooptation, or being rendered unthreatening to a system through assimilation of its values and practices, has long been a problem for defense attorneys in juvenile court. *See* Bortner, Inside a Juvenile Court, *supra* note 129, at 136–39; Flicker, Providing Counsel, *supra* note 129, at 2A; Platt, The Child Savers, *supra* note 23, at 163–75; Feld, The Right to Counsel in Juvenile Court, *supra* note 129, at 1207–1208; *see also* Clarke & Koch, Juvenile Court, *supra* note 129, at 297–300 (1980) (providing statistical support for ineffectiveness of juvenile counsel).

145. Bortner, Inside a Juvenile Court, *supra* note 129, at 137.

146. Flicker, Providing Counsel, *supra* note 129, at 4.

147. *See* Feld, The Right to Counsel in Juvenile Court, *supra* note 129, at 1207–1208.

148. *See generally* Ferster et al., The Juvenile Justice System, *supra* note 129, at 398–401 (discussing various roles counsel assumes when representing juvenile clients and systemic influences on these roles).

149. A survey of defenders in New York State showed that 85 percent of those lawyers considered their role to be that of a guardian ad litem. Law Guardians in New York State, *supra* note 129, at 8–9.

150. The American Bar Association stipulates that the lawyer with a juvenile client must represent that client's legal interests, and that it is up to the client to decide what those interests are, after consultation with the lawyer. Institute of Judicial Administration/American Bar Association, Juvenile Justice Standards: Standards Relating to Counsel for Private Parties § 3.1(a), (b) (1980). The lawyer has the same obligation as to an adult client to keep his juvenile client informed of the progress of his case, and the same requirement to keep his client's confidences and secrets inviolate. *Id.* §§ 3.3, 3.5.

151. Krisberg et al., The Watershed of Juvenile Justice Reform, 32 Crime & Delinq. 5 (1986).

152. The historian Anthony Platt suggests that, prior to the juvenile court, young people were not often charged with crimes. Even when charged, they frequently were acquitted by juries instructed on the matter of the criminal responsibility of the young, and almost never executed. In tracking down some of the widely cited examples of child executions in the nineteenth century, he discovered a number to be apocryphal, and most of the rest to be cases involving child slaves. He concludes that the child-saving literature exaggerated the extent to which young people were previously subjected to severe penalties. Platt, The Child Savers, *supra* note 23, at 193–212.

153. Several studies have shown that both juveniles waived into adult court and young adults normally subject to adult criminal jurisdiction receive lighter sentences than somewhat older adults with similar offenses and records. Feld, The Juvenile Court Meets the Principle of the Offense: Legislative Changes in Juvenile Waiver Statutes, 78 J. Crim. L. & Criminology, 471, 500–501 (1987); P. Greenwood et al., Factors Affecting Sentence Severity for Young Adult Offenders 13–14 (1984).

154. Feld, The Principle of the Offense, *supra* note 153, at 501.

155. Most states statutorily require certain juveniles to serve their juvenile sentences in adult prisons. To illustrate, the state of Washington permits the administrative transfer of juveniles if they "present a continuing and serious threat to the safety of others." Wash. Rev. Code § 13.40.280 (Supp. 1991). Those juveniles who receive adult sentences to be served consecutively to their juvenile sentences also may be mandatorily transferred to adult prisons to serve their juvenile terms. *Id.* § 13.40.285. In addition to this kind of statutory transfer, many juveniles are held in adult prisons and jails without legal authorization. For a discussion of this situation and the litigation it has spawned, *see* Soler, Litigation on Behalf of Children in Adult Jails, 34 Crime & Delinq. 190, 190–205 (1988).

CHAPTER THIRTY-THREE

Re-Imagining the Juvenile Court

Mark I. Soler

In "Re-Imagining Childhood and Reconstructing the Legal Order: The Case for Abolishing the Juvenile Court," Chapter 32 in this volume, Janet Ainsworth joins a distinguished group of commentators who have called for major reform or outright abolition of the juvenile court.[1] Professor Ainsworth brings an important new perspective to this issue in her constructivist analysis of changing attitudes toward children in this country and the effects of those changes on the role and operations of the juvenile court. She also demonstrates a keen sensitivity to the significance of juveniles' own perceptions of the juvenile court and its processes.

On the other hand, her argument that abolition of a separate juvenile court should follow from society's recent perceptions of juveniles as little different from adults is somewhat problematic. In her consideration of changing attitudes toward children during the 1980s, she fails to give sufficient weight to the role of the federal Office of Juvenile Justice and Delinquency Prevention, which influenced those attitudes in the service of the Reagan administration's political agenda. Moreover, in the portion of her argument based on the allegedly changing tenor of U.S. Supreme Court decisions, she overlooks a leading case that substantially undermines her premise. Finally, it is questionable whether the procedural reforms she suggests really address the underlying problems of juvenile courts throughout this country. Ultimately, however, her basic approach is quite useful, and can pave the way to a very productive vision of a truly new juvenile court.

Rather than abolishing the juvenile court, it may be possible to "re-imagine" juvenile court reform. One of the most serious problems affecting children and families at risk is the fragmentation and lack of coordination of available services. Although children and families often have multiple problems, it is frequently impossible to develop comprehensive, interagency, multidiscipline services to meet those problems. Several federal and state statutes, however, explicitly or implicitly authorize juvenile courts to monitor the provision of services to children and families. As will be discussed below, focusing on the role of the juvenile court in coordinating services may lead to a more useful vision for juvenile court reform.

The Constructivist Contribution

In discussing the "invention" of childhood, adolescence, and the juvenile court, Ainsworth concludes through constructivist analysis that "basic aspects of social life are neither natural nor inevitable, . . . but rather are culturally and historically contingent and mutable." Therefore, the "life stage[s]" we call "childhood" and "adolescence" are "likewise . . . culturally and historically situated social construction[s]." In describing how the institution of the juvenile court developed out of attitudes toward childhood and adolescence held by Progressives at the turn of the century, Ainsworth asserts:

> The desirability, even necessity, for a separate court system to address the problems of young people appeared obvious, given the newly emerging view of the adolescent as an immature creature in need of adult control. When parental control failed, the benevolent, if coercive, hand of the state could provide the corrective molding needed by the errant youth.[2]

By comparison, Ainsworth maintains that the late twentieth century has witnessed a "refiguration of the human life cycle" where new social attitudes have broken down the clear dichotomy between child and adult.[3] Recent studies rejecting the rehabilitative potential of the juvenile justice system[4] have accompanied these changing societal perceptions of childhood.

As a result, juvenile courts have changed their focus from rehabilitation of youngsters to retribution for the offenses they have committed, while legislatures have adopted "just deserts" statutes emphasizing accountability and punishment. In addition, state statutes mandating the automatic transfer or "waiver" from juvenile court to adult criminal court for children accused of certain crimes have proliferated. Lastly, the Supreme Court, in cases involving invocation of the privilege against self-incrimination and the validity of the death penalty, has considered juveniles to be little different from adults.[5]

Ainsworth's discussion, as outlined above, is valuable in several respects. First, it is, for the most part, a careful, detailed, and accurate description of evolving social, judicial, and legislative approaches to the problem of juvenile delinquency in this country. Second, it focuses on the pivotal role of attitudes in determining the character of the law and legal institutions, directly considering changed attitudes of society generally and acknowledging the changed attitudes of judges and legislators. This analysis is creative and insightful.[6] Third, it provides a broad-scale view of the entire juvenile justice system. It is a *macro*-constructivist analysis, looking at the relationship between perceptions of children by society at large and the institutions created by society to care for those children.

Ainsworth next considers the ideological costs of an independent juvenile court, providing a *micro*-constructivist analysis that complements the previous discussion. At this juncture, Ainsworth looks at the juvenile court from the *child's* point of view. She asserts that the procedural contrasts between adult court and juvenile court may well convince children that they are not receiving procedural justice, and that this in turn will undermine the legitimacy of the juvenile court in children's eyes. This discussion builds on landmark studies that have considered other aspects of government intervention (e.g., out-of-home placement) from the child's point of view.[7] Taken together with her broad social and historical analysis, Ainsworth's chapter provides both an overview and an inner view of the evolution and workings of the juvenile court. It fails, however, to thoroughly address several important aspects of the juvenile justice system.

The Political Agenda in the Reconstruction of Childhood

Ainsworth mentions the political context of the juvenile justice system only briefly, with a passing reference to Alfred Regnery, the administrator of the Office of Juvenile Justice and Delinquency Prevention (OJJDP) under the Reagan administration.[8] This cursory treatment is unfortunate, for Regnery and the Reagan-era OJJDP had a significant impact on both the juvenile justice system and attitudes toward juvenile justice in this country, in ways that are quite relevant to Ainsworth's analysis.

The OJJDP is the federal government's principal agency dealing with juvenile justice issues. The agency conducts research, funds and evaluates programs, and provides money directly to state and local governments for juvenile justice resources.[9] Although small in comparison to other federal agencies,[10] the OJJDP, through its funding authority, wields enormous influence over the development of juvenile justice policies throughout the country.

Regnery came to the OJJDP with no background in juvenile justice.[11] At his Senate confirmation hearing, he was questioned about a bumper sticker on his car that asked, "Have You Slugged Your Kid Today?"[12]

Regnery dramatically changed the OJJDP's direction. Whereas the agency had previously focused on stopping the widespread incarceration of children in adult jails and the locking up of "status offenders" such as truants and runaways,[13] under Regnery it focused on "making the predators accountable" and "restoring traditional values."[14]

The awarding of noncompetitive grants for questionable studies by the OJJDP during Regnery's directorship has been widely criticized. For example, Regnery approved a grant of more than $700,000 to Judith Reisman, a former songwriter for the "Captain Kangaroo" show, to study cartoons and other visual images in *Penthouse, Playboy,* and *Hustler*.[15] Because of "multiple serious flaws in the methodology,"[16] Reisman's study went unpublished.

The OJJDP under Regnery provided special financial support to one project that is particularly relevant to Ainsworth's research on the proliferation of "just deserts" sentencing laws. The OJJDP grant, administered by Claremont McKenna College, was to draft a model "just deserts" juvenile code.[17] The model code was completed, and, with training and instructional materials, was distributed and presented to state legislators throughout the country.[18]

The importance of the OJJDP's funding priorities during the 1980s should not be underestimated.[19] By funding and publicizing research[20] and programs[21] that supported their view that violent juvenile crime was overwhelming society—and that the "deterrent" approach was the only way to handle the problem effectively—the OJJDP and the Reagan administration played a major role in the "re-imagining of childhood" that occurred during the 1980s. Thus, Ainsworth's conclusion is certainly correct: There was a dramatic change of attitude toward children and juvenile crime during the 1980s. The reasons for that change of attitude, however, lie as much with the political agenda of the Reagan administration as with the perceived failures of juvenile rehabilitation programs.

The Supreme Court's *Schall v. Martin* Decision

During the 1980s, the Supreme Court's most important decision on the juvenile court was *Schall v Martin*.[22] Inexplicably, Ainsworth does not discuss the case, although it is directly relevant to her thesis. The issue in *Schall* was the constitutionality of a provision of the New York Family Court Act[23] that authorized pretrial detention of an alleged juvenile delinquent based on a finding of a "serious risk" that the youth "may before the return date commit an act which if committed by an adult would constitute a crime."[24] Noting that preventive detention of juveniles accused of crime is permitted by every state and the District of Columbia, as well as by several model juvenile justice codes, the Court found that preventive detention under the New York statute served legitimate state interests.[25] The Court held that, "[g]iven the regulatory purpose for the detention and the procedural protections that precede its imposition," the act was constitutional.[26]

The Court's opinion casts serious doubt on Ainsworth's premise that there has been a "breakdown of the child–adult dichotomy" in Supreme Court jurisprudence. In fact, the very beginning of the Court's discussion demonstrates that the "child–adult dichotomy" was the *foundation* for the *Schall* decision. The Court noted:

> [T]he Constitution does not mandate elimination of all differences in the treatment of juveniles. The State has 'a *parens patriae* interest in preserving and promoting the welfare of the child,' . . . which makes a juvenile proceeding fundamentally different from an adult criminal trial.[27]

Further, in weighing society's interest in protecting the community against the juvenile's interest in personal liberty, the Court declared:

> The juvenile's countervailing interest in freedom from institutional restraints . . . must be qualified by the recognition that juveniles, unlike adults, are always in some form of custody. Children, by definition, are not assumed to have the capacity to take care of themselves. They are assumed to be subject to the control of their parents, and if parental control falters, the State must play its part as *parens patriae*.[28]

This reasoning hardly heralded a "breakdown of the child–adult dichotomy" in Supreme Court jurisprudence. Indeed, because of the apparent differences between juveniles and adults, the Court seemed more concerned about juvenile than adult crime. The Court declared that "[s]ociety has a legitimate interest in protecting a juvenile . . . from the downward spiral of criminal activity into which peer pressure may lead the child."[29] Furthermore, the Court warned that "the harm to society generally may even be greater in [the juvenile offender] context given the high rate of recidivism among juveniles."[30]

In conclusion, given the reasoning in *Schall*, it is not at all certain that the "Supreme Court . . . has repudiated a bright-line dichotomy between child and adult."[31] Therefore, while the argument for reform or abolition of the juvenile court has merit, Supreme Court jurisprudence may not provide a sound basis for that argument.

Re-Imagining Juvenile Court Reform

The Current System: Fragmented Services for Children and Families

In looking at the future of the juvenile court, it should first be noted that the basic tenet of conservative criticism—that "nothing works"—is of doubtful validity. Researchers have conducted many significant studies that demonstrate the value of rehabilitative programs.[32] Effective rehabilitation programs have been established in states such as Florida, Maryland, Massachusetts, Pennsylvania, and Utah.[33]

Ainsworth's chapter raises a more fundamental question: What are the goals of juvenile court reform? Ainsworth posits that abolishing the "separate and unequal juvenile court" would engender procedural reforms, notably more effective legal counsel and jury trials for juveniles charged with crimes. Other commentators have also focused on procedural issues in considering juvenile court reform.[34] Even when they have considered substantive issues, such as culpability defenses,[35] these commentators have focused on the adjudicatory or fact-finding phase of juvenile court jurisdiction.

Significantly, Ainsworth does consider "dispositional needs of juveniles" as well, discussing the treatment of juveniles after their delinquency is established.

However, her discussion is limited to the issues of shrinking sentencing disparities between juveniles and adults and the inadvisability of incarcerating juveniles in adult institutions. It is unfortunate that, during her discussion of the dispositional needs of juveniles, Ainsworth does not consider the broader needs of children in the juvenile justice system, and therefore omits a fruitful area for consideration.

Processing juveniles in the adult courts would not trigger meaningful reform. The physical environment of many adult criminal courts, particularly in major metropolitan areas, is as oppressive and depressing as that of juvenile courts.[36] Budget crises at all levels of government and "get tough" attitudes on the part of law enforcement personnel, judges, and other public officials have generated enormous caseloads for overworked public defenders. In both the adult and the juvenile systems, institutions are overcrowded, and there are few resources for the development of noninstitutional community-based programs.[37] It would hardly be sufficient to provide delinquent children with enhanced due process in a bankrupt system.

The underlying problems of juvenile justice may have less to do with the procedural inadequacies during adjudication than with the pervasive inadequacy of services and programs for children and families. Ainsworth writes that the "original architects of the juvenile court were confident that juvenile delinquents could be rehabilitated, as long as judges possessed the expertise, information, and resources necessary for proper diagnosis and treatment." But neither juvenile courts nor any other youth programs or services have sufficient information and resources at their disposal. On the contrary, these services have failed to avert a crisis among America's children.[38]

Two related problems are pervasive in service systems for children and families. First, children at risk are channeled into services and programs that are categorical and narrowly defined. Children labeled "neglected" or "abused" are placed in foster care, but rarely given family support or individualized mental health services. Children with mental health problems are sent to psychiatric hospitals, and kept out of most community-based, family-centered programs. Children labeled "delinquent" are locked up in correctional institutions but excluded from comprehensive mental health services or "programs aimed at resolving underlying family problems."[39] Second, in part as a consequence of the narrow tracking and labeling of children at risk, services are fragmented.

These critical deficiencies in service systems are well-recognized by government officials,[40] policy-making bodies,[41] researchers,[42] and the private sector.[43] The National Commission on Children reported, under the heading "Categorical Programs in a Fragmented System":

> In fiscal year (FY) 1989, the federal government spent approximately $59.5 billion, or 5.2 percent of total federal program outlays, on programs and services for children. . . . These funds support at least 340 programs administered by offices and agencies scattered across 11 cabinet-level departments. . . . In FY 1989, state and local governments spent at least $180.3

billion—or approximately 31 percent of their budgets—on programs and services for children, similarly dispersed across a range of state and municipal agencies and offices.[44]

The National Commission on Children concluded that, in such a fragmented and categorical system, programs have:

> different, and sometimes conflicting, eligibility criteria and administrative procedures. Service providers generally operate in separate locations, with different professional orientations, and subject to distinct governance arrangements. Typically, there is little communication or coordination among them. Families seeking assistance thus encounter a service delivery system that is often confusing, difficult to navigate, and indifferent to their concerns.[45]

In response to these problems, federal,[46] state,[47] and local governments,[48] and major foundations,[49] have begun to support "services integration" projects aimed at encouraging separate agencies to provide more comprehensive and more effective service. Most of these activities have involved educational, child welfare, health, and mental health systems. There has been relatively little effort to develop interagency collaboration among the juvenile justice systems. The best-known efforts include the *Willie M.* program for violent and seriously disturbed juveniles in North Carolina, which provides extensive case management and comprehensive services to severely disruptive youth;[50] the Ventura County Children's Mental Health Project, which provides community-based comprehensive services to seriously emotionally disturbed, multi-problem children in the juvenile justice, child welfare, mental health, and educational systems;[51] and the programs of the New York City Department of Juvenile Justice, which provide case management for adolescents during and after pretrial detention, as well as family support services.[52]

The Juvenile Court: Forum for Social Services Coordination

There has been even less effort to develop a role for the juvenile court in combatting fragmentation and coordinating services for children under the court's jurisdiction. The only significant attempt has been with children in the dependency system, under the guidelines of the federal Adoption Assistance and Child Welfare Act,[53] and that effort has had mixed results. The statute requires that before a child is removed from the home on account of neglect or abuse, the social services agency must make "reasonable efforts"[54] to enable the child to remain in the home with her or his parents. Similarly, after a child is removed from the home, the agency must make "reasonable efforts" to allow the child to return home to her or his family.[55] Most states have enacted parallel legislation.[56]

The federal statute does not define "reasonable efforts." A number of juvenile and family courts have provided working definitions,[57] and it is clear that such efforts must, in appropriate circumstances, include alcohol and other substance abuse treatment for biological parents, other medical care, and counseling services[58]—that is, services from health and mental health agencies. As a practical matter, attempts to have juvenile court judges require reasonable efforts from other agencies have had only limited success,[59] and the juvenile court has not been perceived as having the role of services coordinator.

There are good reasons, however, why the juvenile court should serve that function. First, the juvenile court has the appropriate responsibility: Under all juvenile codes the court must act in the best interests of the child,[60] and under statutes like the Adoption Assistance and Child Welfare Act, it has the specific responsibility to ensure that services are provided to preserve the family. Second, the juvenile court has the necessary authority: The child, the parents, and the social services agency are before the court, and pursuant to its mandate the court can bring other agencies within its jurisdiction, and adopt such orders as are necessary to carry out its functions.[61] Third, the juvenile court periodically reviews the child's situation to monitor progress and the implementation of its orders.[62] Finally, juvenile court judges can serve a coordinating function by enforcing federal and state statutes, an attorney responsibility for which they have some degree of training and experience.

There are other statutes that could serve as vehicles for a juvenile court coordination function. For example, the Individuals with Disabilities in Education Act (IDEA)[63] guarantees disabled children a free education appropriate to their individual needs. The statute also guarantees the provision of "related services" that are necessary for each child to effectively utilize the educational resources that are provided, including counseling and other mental health services.[64] Those children in juvenile justice systems who are placed in pretrial detention facilities or state correctional institutions are entitled to special education services under the federal statute.[65] Thus, the juvenile court could serve a coordinating function to ensure that such services are provided.

Similarly, the federal Early and Periodic Screening, Diagnosis and Treatment program (EPSDT)[66] is the nation's primary health screening and treatment program for poor children. Since many children coming before the juvenile court are eligible for EPSDT, the court could ensure the provision of health and dental services to such children.

In addition, the Supplemental Security Income program (SSI)[67] is the major federal program that provides payments for health care to low-income disabled children. In *Sullivan v. Zebley*,[68] the Supreme Court invalidated the SSI criteria that had been used to evaluate children's disabilities. The Social Security Administration has now promulgated substantially revised eligibility guidelines,[69] resulting in new entitlements to health care for large numbers of disabled children. Again, the juvenile court could serve as a focal point to ensure that children receive proper SSI evaluation and health care.

How would the juvenile court implement coordination mechanisms? The court already receives reports from probation officers, social workers, and other social service personnel; several statutes already require agencies to prepare detailed plans for each child. For example, under the federal Adoption Assistance and Child Welfare Act, the social services agency must prepare a written case plan for each dependent child that describes the services to be offered and the plan for reuniting the child with her or his family or for other permanent placement.[70] Under the IDEA, the educational agency must prepare an individualized education program (IEP) that sets forth educational goals and the projected timetable for achieving them.[71]

An even more effective planning model for the court would be the Family Service Plan for *family*-centered support for handicapped infants and toddlers[72] required by the Early Intervention Program for Infants and Toddlers,[73] which is comparable to the IEP required for individual disabled students.

For the juvenile court to serve this coordinating function requires a significant re-imagining effort.[74] Many would welcome a restructured juvenile court. The significance of procedural fairness in the adjudicatory phase would be undiminished, but, in the dispositional phase, there would be a new determination to provide comprehensive services critical for children and families, rather than simply relegating young miscreants to the available local or state lockups. It would *not* be necessary for the juvenile court to become more like a social welfare agency; it *would* be necessary for juvenile court judges to affirmatively enforce statutory rights of children under federal and state statutes. This would undoubtedly require substantial new training of juvenile court judges, but their basic role—enforcing the law—would not be unfamiliar.

It may be that a truly effective juvenile court, coordinating and ensuring the provision of a wide range of services, is as different from today's juvenile court as the juvenile court envisioned in 1899 was different from the adult criminal courts of the time. But if we are serious about providing effective intervention in the lives of children and families at risk, we must advocate changes of that magnitude. And therein lies the value of Ainsworth's analysis. The widespread alarm at the failure of fragmented service systems, and the recognition of the need for comprehensive interagency services, informs and influences a new vision of the juvenile court. This is becoming a shared vision across the nation. Just as the attitudes toward the needs of children in the Progressive era shaped the origins of the juvenile court at that time, so can new attitudes toward the needs of children and families shape a new vision of the juvenile court in the 1990s.[75]

NOTES

Acknowledgment: I am indebted to Frank Montes of Boalt Hall School of Law, University of California, Berkeley, for his research for this chapter.

1. *See, e.g.,* Feld, Juvenile Court Legislative Reform and the Serious Young Offender: Dismantling the "Rehabilitative Ideal," 65 Minn. L. Rev. 167 (1980); Feld, The Juvenile Court Meets the Principle of Offense: Punishment, Treatment, and

the Difference It Makes, 68 B.U. L. Rev. 821 (1988); Gardner, Punitive Juvenile Justice: Some Observations on a Recent Trend, 10 Int'l J.L. & Psychiatry 129 (1987); Guggenheim, A Call to Abolish the Juvenile Court System, Children's Rights Report (ACLU Juvenile Rights Project, New York, N.Y.), June 1978, at 3–4; Melton, Taking *Gault* Seriously: Toward a New Juvenile Court, 68 Neb. L. Rev. 146 (1989); Wizner & Keller, The Penal Model of Juvenile Justice: Is Juvenile Delinquency Jurisdiction Obsolete? 52 N.Y.U. L. Rev. 1120 (1977). *Cf.* Dawson, The Future of Juvenile Justice: Is It Time to Abolish the System? 81 J. Crim. L. & Criminology 136 (1990) (arguing against abolishing the juvenile justice system).

2. For a skeptical view of the "reforms" of the juvenile court, see Fox, Juvenile Justice Reform: An Historical Perspective, 22 Stan. L. Rev. 1187 (1970).

3. "Today we are witnessing the breakdown of the binary opposition between child and adult that provided the conceptual foundation of juvenile court jurisprudence." *See* Chapter 32 in this volume (footnote omitted).

4. *Id.*

5. *Id.*

6. *See also* Feld, The Transformation of the Juvenile Court, 75 Minn. L. Rev. 691, 693–94, 724 (1991) (changing conceptions of childhood during the Progressive Era influenced the development of the juvenile court).

7. J. Goldstein et al., Beyond the Best Interests of the Child 31–33 (1973). *See generally* J. Goldstein et al., Before the Best Interests of the Child (1979); J. Goldstein et al., In the Best Interests of the Child (1986); Melton, Taking *Gault* Seriously, *supra* note 1, at 168–69.

8. Ainsworth states: "The [political] right complains that the system coddles young criminals and sets them loose to prey on society after lenient sanctioning." She notes that Alfred Regnery presented a "succinct and forceful exposition" of this position, citing his article entitled Getting Away with Murder: Why the Juvenile Justice System Needs an Overhaul, 34 Pol'y Rev. 65 (Fall 1985).

9. 42 U.S.C. §§ 5611–14 (1988).

10. The budget for OJJDP was $81 million for FY 1982, $70.3 million for 1988, and $68.6 million for FY 1989. Children's Defense Fund, A Children's Defense Budget: An Analysis of the President's Budget and Children 4 (1982); Children's Defense Fund, A Children's Defense Budget FY 1988: An Analysis of Our Nation's Investment in Children xxiv (1987); Children's Defense Fund, A Children's Defense Budget FY 1989: An Analysis of Our Nation's Investment in Children xx (1988).

11. Prior to his appointment, Regnery had worked in the Lands and Natural Resources Division of the U.S. Department of Justice. Regnery Approved for OJJDP by Judiciary Committee, Crim. Just. Newsl., May 23, 1983, at 3.

12. Waas, Al Regnery's Secret Life, New Republic, June 23, 1986, at 17.

13. 42 U.S.C. §§ 5601, 5633 (a)(12)(A), (a)(13) (1988); J. Brown & M. McMillen, U.S. Department of Justice, Residential Environments for the Juvenile Justice System 4 (1979).

14. Regnery, A Federal Perspective on Juvenile Justice Reform, 32 Crime & Delinq. 39, 43, 50–51 (1986).

15. Kurtz, 'Serious Flaws' Shelve $734,371 Study, Wash. Post, Nov. 19, 1986, at A17; Waas, Secret Life, *supra* note 12, at 17–18.

16. *Id.*

17. Regnery, A Federal Perspective, *supra* note 14, at 48. *See also* W. Treanor & A. Volenik, American Youth Work Center, The New Right's Juvenile Crime and Justice Agenda for the States 1, 2 (1987).

18. *Id.* at 1.

19. *See* I. Schwartz, (In) Justice for Juveniles 115 (1989); Sylvester, Attorneys Who Teach 'Street Law,' Nat'l L.J., June 20, 1983, at 1.

20. Krisberg, Are You Now or Have You Ever Been a Sociologist? 82 J. Crim. L. & Criminology 141, 142–45 (1991).

21. For example, the OJJDP "spent $3.5 million in 1984 to set up special teams of prosecutors in 13 major cities" to prosecute "habitual, serious, and violent juvenile offenders." Regnery, A Federal Perspective, *supra* note 14, at 44.

22. 467 U.S. 253 (1984).

23. New York Jud. Law § 320.5(3)(b) (McKinney 1983), *quoted in Schall,* 467 U.S. at 255.

24. 467 U.S. at 255 (quoting New York Jud. Law § 320.5(3)(b) (McKinney 1983)). The lawsuit was brought as a habeas corpus class action "on behalf of a class of all juveniles detained [preventively] pursuant to [§ 320.5(3)(b)]." *Schall,* 467 U.S. at 255–56, 261.

25. *Id.* at 266–68.

26. *Id.* at 281.

27. *Schall,* 467 U.S. at 263 (citations omitted).

28. *Id.* at 265 (citations omitted).

29. *Id.* at 266.

30. *Id.* at 265.

31. Chapter 32 in this volume.

32. *See, e.g.,* D. Altschuler & T. Armstrong, Intervening with Serious Juvenile Offenders: A Summary of a Study on Community-Based Programs, in Violent Juvenile Offenders 187 (Robert A. Mathias et al. eds., 1989); Gendreau & Ross, Revivification of Rehabilitation: Evidence from the 1980's, 4 Just. Q. 349 (1987); *see also* B. Krisberg, National Council on Crime and Delinquency, Juvenile Justice: A Critical Examination 45–48 (1989).

33. *See, e.g.,* S. Lerner, The Good News about Juvenile Justice (1990).

34. *See, e.g.,* Feld, Principle of Offense, *supra* note 1, at 903–909; Feld, The Transformation of the Juvenile Court, *supra* note 6, at 718–22; Gardner, Punitive Juvenile Justice, *supra* note 1, at 147; Melton, Taking *Gault* Seriously, *supra* note 1, at 172–74.

35. *See, e.g.,* Feld, Principle of Offense, *supra* note 1, at 898–99; Gardner, Punitive Juvenile Justice, *supra* note 1, at 143–46.

36. A recent description of the Baltimore City Juvenile Court is all too typical of juvenile and adult courts:

> The building's massive columns, vaulted ceilings and dimly lighted corridors conjure fleeting images of a dungeon. Children wander the hallways, a few in tears. The water fountains are too high for most to reach. Lawyers, their arms spilling over with folders, bustle about. Sheriff's deputies cast jaundiced eyes on it all.

Riley, Corridors of Agony, Time, Jan. 27, 1992, at 48, 49.

37. California Department of Youth Authority, Overcrowding in Juvenile Detention Facilities and Methods to Relieve Its Adverse Effects 7 (1983); I. Schwartz, The Death of the *Parens Patriae* Model, in The Young Offenders Act 146, 150–56 (A. Leschied et al. eds., 1991).

38. *See* J. Simons et al., Children's Defense Fund, The Adolescent and Young Adult Fact Book (1991) [hereinafter CDF Fact Book]; National Commission on Children, Beyond Rhetoric: A New American Agenda for Children and Families 4 (1991). The Children's Defense Fund has reported disturbing statistics that testify to this children's crisis:

> One million teenagers—about the equivalent of the entire population of San Antonio, Texas—got pregnant in 1988.
>
> . . . .
>
> Homicide is the second leading cause of death among adolescents and young people ages 15 to 24. . . .
>
> Black teenage males are three times more likely to be killed by guns than to die of natural causes.
>
> . . . .
>
> More than half of seventh- to twelfth-graders nationwide drink alcohol. Eight million—about 40 percent—drink weekly. . . .
>
> . . . .
>
> One in 15 teenagers and one in six young adults say they currently use both alcohol and illegal drugs.

CDF Fact Book, *supra*, at viii–ix.

> Every day in America, seven teenagers and 10 young adults are the victims of homicide.
>
> . . . .
>
> 10 teenagers and 13 young adults are killed by firearms.
>
> . . . .
>
> 39 youths ages 15 to 24 are killed in motor vehicle accidents.
>
> . . . .
>
> 604 teenagers contract syphilis or gonorrhea.
>
> . . . .
>
> [A]n estimated 1,140 teenagers have abortions.
>
> . . . .
>
> 2,478 teenagers drop out of school.
>
> . . . .
>
> 4,901 teenagers and 2,976 young adults are victims of violent crimes.
>
> . . . .
>
> 7,742 teenagers become sexually active.
>
> . . . .
>
> 8,826 teenagers and 6,235 young adults are the victims of theft.

Id. at 2.

39. Soler & Shauffer, Fighting Fragmentation: Coordination of Services for Children and Families, 69 Neb. L. Rev. 278, 280 (1990).

40. House Select Committee on Children, Youth, and Families, No Place to Call Home: Discarded Children of America, H.R. Rep. No. 395, 101st Cong., 2d Sess. 62–65 (1990).

41. National Commission on Child Welfare and Family Preservation, A Commitment to Change 17 (1990).

42. S. Kamerman & A. Kahn, The Annie E. Casey Foundation, Social Services for Children, Youth and Families in the U.S. xiii–xiv (1989); A. Melaville & M. Blank, Education and Human Services Consortium, What It Takes: Structuring Interagency Partnerships to Connect Children and Families with Comprehensive Services 6–9 (1991). *See also* Gardner, Failure by Fragmentation, California Tomorrow, Fall 1989, at 18, 19–20.

43. Research and Policy Committee of the Committee for Economic Development, The Unfinished Agenda: A New Vision for Child Development and Education 6, 12–13 (1991).

44. National Commission on Children, Beyond Rhetoric, *supra* note 38, at 314–16 (footnotes omitted).

45. *Id.* at 317.

46. The federal government is supporting model collaboration projects in several areas, evaluations of ongoing interagency programs, and a national clearinghouse for information on services integration. Community-Based Service Integration Projects: Announcements of the Availability of Funds and Request for Proposals, 56 Fed. Reg. 29,656 (1991).

47. Several state governments have implemented novel programs. For example, the state of New Jersey initiated its School-Based Youth Services Program in 1988 to provide mental health, family counseling, health, and employment services in schools to at-risk adolescents. *See, e.g.,* Sylvester, New Strategies to Save Children in Trouble, Governing, May 1990, at 32, 34; Office of the Inspector General, U.S. Department of Health and Human Services, Services Integration for Families and Children in Crisis A-23 (1991). California has begun a similar program. Cal. Educ. Code §§ 8800–8807 (West 1993). Iowa has undertaken a "de-categorization" project in several counties that combines state and local funding streams from a variety of areas, including foster care, day care, juvenile detention, state juvenile institutions, and mental health services. C. Bruner, Improving Children's Welfare: Learning from Iowa (National Conference of State Legislatures 1990).

48. Nationwide, there are numerous local programs underway, such as the "New Beginnings" school-based services program in San Diego. *See* City of San Diego et al., New Beginnings: A Feasibility Study of Integrated Services for Children and Families ix–x (1990). Another such program is the Ventura County (California) Children's Mental Health Project for seriously emotionally disturbed youth. *See* Soler & Shauffer, Fighting Fragmentation, *supra* note 39, at 288–89.

49. For example, the Annie E. Casey Foundation has sponsored comprehensive service initiatives in the education and child welfare area. *See* Center for the Study of Social Policy, New Futures: Plans for Assisting At-Risk Youth in Five Cities 2 (1989). Similarly, the Robert Wood Johnson Foundation has launched a multi-city effort to develop interagency services for children with mental health problems. Developing Community-Based Systems of Care, Family Matters 2 (Robert Wood Johnson Foundation, Fall 1991).

50. Behar, A State Model for Child Mental Health Services: The North Carolina Experience, Children Today, May–June 1986, at 16, 17; L. Garner, Leadership in Human Services: How to Articulate and Implement a Vision to Achieve Results 18–19 (1989); J. Knitzer & L. Olson, Children's Defense Fund, Unclaimed Children: The Failure of Public Responsibility to Children and Adolescents in Need of

Mental Health Services 97–99 (1982); M. Soler & L. Warboys, Services for Violent and Severely Disturbed Children: The *Willie M.* Litigation, in Stepping Stones: Successful Advocacy for Children 61–112 (1990).

51. Soler & Shauffer, Fighting Fragmentation, *supra* note 39, at 288–89.

52. Department of Juvenile Justice, City of New York, Listen to the Dreams: Annual Report 1990, at 16–17 (1990); Department of Juvenile Justice, City of New York, Case Management System for Children in Detention (1990). *See also* Schiraldi, Hawaii's Juvenile Justice System: A Model for Reform, Fed. Probation, Sept. 1990, at 58.

53. Pub. L. No. 96-272, 94 Stat. 500 (codified as amended at 42 U.S.C. §§ 620–28, 670–79a (1988)).

54. 42 U.S.C. §§ 671(a)(15), 672(a)(1) (1988). *See generally* National Council of Juvenile and Family Court Judges et al., Making Reasonable Efforts: Steps for Keeping Families Together 104–105 (1987) [hereinafter Steps for Keeping Families Together].

55. 42 U.S.C. §§ 671(a)(15), 672(a)(1) (1988).

56. *See, e.g.,* Cal. Welf. & Inst. Code §§ 319(d), 361(c), 11,404(b)(B)(2), (4) (West 1992). *See generally* Shotton, Making Reasonable Efforts in Child Abuse and Neglect Cases: Ten Years Later, 26 Cal. W. L. Rev. 223, 234–35 (1990).

57. *See* Shotton, Making Reasonable Efforts, *supra* note 56, at 237–53.

58. *Id.* at 245–48; Steps for Keeping Families Together, *supra* note 54, at 89.

59. *See* Shotton, Making Reasonable Efforts, *supra* note 56, at 227.

60. *See, e.g.,* Cal. Welf. & Inst. Code § 202(b) (West 1992).

61. Cal. Welf. & Inst. Code § 727 (West 1992).

62. 42 U.S.C. § 675(5)(B), (C) (1988).

63. 20 U.S.C. §§ 1400–1485 (1988). The statute is commonly known as Public Law 94-142 (Education for All Handicapped Children Act of 1975, 89 Stat. 773).

64. 20 U.S.C. § 1401(a)(17) (1988).

65. Green v. Johnson, 513 F. Supp. 965 (D. Mass. 1981). *See* Warboys & Shauffer, Legal Issues in Providing Special Education Services to Handicapped Inmates, Remedial Special Educ., May/June 1986, at 34; Keenan & Hammond, The Institutionalized Child's Claim to Special Education: A Federal Codification of the Right to Treatment, 56 Det. J. Urb. L. 337 (1979).

66. 42 U.S.C. § 1396d(a)(4)(B) (1988).

67. 42 U.S.C. §§ 1381–83c (1988).

68. 493 U.S. 521, 541 (1990).

69. 20 C.F.R. Part 416 (1991) (amending 20 C.F.R. §§ 416.901–.946).

70. 45 C.F.R. § 1356.21(d)(4) (1988). *See* Steps for Keeping Families Together, *supra* note 54, at 104–105.

71. 20 U.S.C. §§ 1401(a)(19), 1412(4), 1414(a)(5) (1988); 34 C.F.R. §§ 300.340–.349 (1991).

72. Under the statute, "infants and toddlers" are defined as "individuals from birth to age 2." 8 U.S.C. § 1472(1) (1988).

73. 20 U.S.C. §§ 1471–85 (1988). The statute is commonly known as Part H of the IDEA or Public Law 99-457 (Education of the Handicapped Act Amendments of 1986, 100 Stat. 1145).

74. The characteristics of effective coordinated service systems include: (1) having a clear value statement for the service system, (2) maintaining a family-centered orientation, (3) ensuring broad community involvement, (4) involving the educational system in a central way, (5) having a readily accessible intake location, (6) evaluating all child and family needs at intake, (7) providing active and effective case management, (8) developing a comprehensive service plan, (9) providing methods of dispute resolution within the system, (10) being able to provide high-quality services, (11) ensuring stable and flexible funding, (12) maintaining an effective management information system, (13) developing measures of effectiveness of service, (14) providing an ongoing planning mechanism, (15) being able to develop others in the field, and (16) avoiding the problem of "reverse discrimination" against those not in the target population for coordinated services. *See* Soler & Shauffer, Fighting Fragmentation, *supra* note 39, at 289–97. That there is no service system in the country that meets all of these criteria is a measure of the difficulty of developing such systems.

75. At least one juvenile court judge has articulated a similar vision. *See* Gelber, The Juvenile Justice System: Vision for the Future, 41 Juv. & Fam. Ct. J. 15 (1990). In describing the juvenile court of the twenty-first century, Judge Seymour Gelber writes: "In the cards is a complete fusion of the three major systems: juvenile court, public school, social services. It will be one single operation, housed in one location, with one communications network and one counselor to see the child from arrest through all three systems." *Id.* at 15.

CHAPTER THIRTY-FOUR

Imagining Legal Scholarship: The Case for the Juvenile Court and for Teaching Juvenile Law and Procedure

Hunter Hurst

IT WAS LATE in the nineteenth century, and we the people perceived some among us to be physically small, psychologically immature, socially incapable, and morally incomplete. Having thus subjectively framed the issue, we then constructed empirical measures, such as intelligence tests, social maturation scales, moral development scales, and physical skill and endurance tests to validate objectively our subjective perceptions and create that peculiarly American class of people known as Children. (Other cultures seem to have engaged in similar endeavors at various points in their history, but that is another paper.)

To complete our objective validation of this class among us called Children, we created a uniquely American institution called the Juvenile Court and sent proselyting judges far and wide to urge the establishment of these unique courts. These proselyting judges (not to be confused with proselyting law professors such as Roscoe Pound), though restricted to travel by horse and buggy, soon spread the word throughout the land, and legislatures belched forth in unison Juvenile Courts in all fifty states and the District of Columbia. This is the real truth about the history of the Juvenile Court according to Janet Ainsworth.[1]

Ninety years later, we the people no longer perceive any difference between this class we call Children and the class we call Adults. Accordingly, Professor Ainsworth issues a clarion call for a new subjectively perceived, but objectively validated, reality to begin. The new reality calls for us to get on with the task of developing measures to validate the nonexistence of Children, and legislate them out of being—if not for all time and for all aspects of existence, at least for their criminal law violations. She stops short of calling for proselyting judges to hit the

road and whip legislatures into a feeding frenzy as a condition precedent to dis-
gorging statutes to accomplish this goal and, instead, implies that a few proselyting law professors and the legal profession's trade union are equal to the task.

Ainsworth labels the process of subjectively framing the issue and then developing objective measures to validate subjective perceptions as Constructivist
Social Theory. I am no student of Constructivist Social Theory, but must con-
fess that I am a strong believer in the tendency of human beings to create their
own subjective realities and then offer objective evidence for their existence.
In my subjective life experience, that tendency is especially pronounced among
those who perceive themselves as scientists, lawyers, scholars, accountants, social workers, and doctors and who have accumulated the requisite objective validation to perpetuate the perception of their expertise. The tendency is most viru-
lent among those carrying multiple labels from the above group.

Though Ainsworth tends to speak critically of those who subjectively frame
issues and then set about developing objective validation, empirical and otherwise, she seems to have resorted to the same machinations and sought to make
her case (that our subjective impression of childhood has changed) by recounting
all of the objective evidence for what she calls the new phenomenon of a childless
society. This chapter will essentially take the same approach. In it I argue that (1)
children still abound, and the juvenile court is the preferred medium for hearing
delinquency cases; (2) the juvenile court is superior to the criminal court as measured by constitutional performance, rehabilitation of offenders, protection of
children, and flexibility to provide individualized justice for children in their for-
mative years; and (3) that the existing imperfections of the juvenile court can be
better resolved by improving the teaching of juvenile law and procedure in
schools of law than through emulation of criminal courts.

The Dubious Case for the Disappearance of Childhood

While Ainsworth relies on arguments from social, anthropological, and psychological disciplines about the blurring of boundaries delineating age-appropriate
behavior, the only real evidence she offers for the new reality are a few carefully
selected state statutes defining the conditions for waiver or transfer of juvenile
cases to criminal court, several even more carefully chosen case decisions, two
juvenile code revisions, one occurring in the state of Washington in 1977 and the
other occurring in New York in 1978, and the assertion that, since children have
been raised on a steady diet of television portrayals of justice, the juvenile court
must comport with these portrayals to be perceived as just. In other words, since
Judge Wapner and "L.A. Law" have predetermined the public perception of justice, we must behave accordingly.

In consonance with the habits of competent counsel, Ainsworth did not permit the introduction of any evidence that might diminish the power of her argu-

ment. Since I am in basic agreement with her contention that cultures create their own reality and then set about creating evidence to verify that reality, I will not attempt to present a contrary argument. Rather, I shall attempt a complete presentation of the evidence and let the reader decide whether Children exist and whether the criminal justice system is the preferred tribunal for hearing their cases.

Exhibit A: The Original Juvenile Court Act

The original vision of the juvenile court was neither as solicitous of children nor as blind to fundamental fairness as its critics claim.[2] The original Illinois Juvenile Court Act, the one Julian Mack is charged with proselyting, defined a Child as a person under the age of sixteen, and permitted the commitment of children over age eleven to jails and prisons and provided for their confinement in separate quarters. The act also made provision for any interested party, including the judge, to demand a jury trial—that seldom used and often abused crown jewel of our civil and criminal justice system in the United States. Jury trials occur rarely in criminal trials in the United States and are used more as a plea bargaining tool by defense counsel than as a medium for assuring fair treatment for defendants. In my own experience, juries enjoy a greater reputation in the legal community for discriminating against minorities, being corruptible, and awarding exorbitant damage claims against perceived "deep pockets" than they do for any manifestation of ideal justice.

Exhibit B: What State Statutes Really Say about Juvenile Court Jurisdiction

Too many contemporary social reformers masquerading as zealous defenders of individual rights choose to define the juvenile court only in terms of its jurisdiction over law violators.[3] Of course the juvenile court has jurisdiction over law violators, but it also has jurisdiction over neglected, abused, and dependent children and their families and, if a rapidly moving trend continues, it will soon have jurisdiction over all family matters. The reason that the juvenile court's critics tend to define it only in terms of its jurisdiction over law violators is that to do otherwise might be tantamount to admitting that there is ample evidence after all for the existence of childhood. Otherwise, why would it need to have a protective jurisdiction?

Consider the following provisions of state statutes specifying age distinctions between adults and children:

- The majority of states continue the juvenile court's jurisdiction to age twenty-one, if jurisdiction attaches prior to the age of eighteen. Indeed, in the state of California—which now contains 10 percent of the U.S. population—the court's jurisdiction extends to age twenty-five for delinquent youth.[4]

- No state permits a person under the age of eighteen to vote.[5]
- In no state may anyone below the age of eighteen serve on a jury.[6]
- No state permits a person under the age of eighteen to participate in a valid contract without first being emancipated for this purpose by the court of juvenile jurisdiction on a case by case basis.[7]

Of course, the litany of such protective statutes is much longer, so it is entirely possible, if not probable, that they represent some of the contemporarily perceived reality of the existence of childhood, but they do not by any means exhaust all of the statutory evidence for it. Consider the following provisions of statutes regarding delinquency.

Thirty-nine states explicitly specify in their juvenile codes a purpose for the juvenile court in dealing with delinquent behavior. Thirty-eight of these frame that purpose in terms of acting in the interest of children; and those states that have in any way revised their purpose clauses and/or their waiver statutes in recent years have taken deliberate care to ensure that the courts' handling of delinquent children be free of the taint of criminality.[8] Thus, not only is the state of Washington alone—and alone now for fourteen years—in treating juveniles as criminals in its juvenile court system,[9] but it is alone in believing that criminal procedure is without "taint." Criminal processing and the label of criminality in the United States do indeed have taint—huge taint, taint that can deprive you of the right to vote, taint that can deprive you of the right to hold public office, taint that can prevent you from enjoying the liberty and freedom rights guaranteed under our Constitution, taint that can subject you to the death penalty in thirty-eight of the states; and the taint list goes on.

Second, most state statutes call for juvenile court proceedings and records to be presumptively closed.[10] However, this is one area of law and practice where the trend is in the opposite direction. But the trend toward open proceedings and open records is not driven by a reconceptualization of childhood, legal or otherwise. It is grounded in the assumption that open government is the bedrock of freedom.[11]

Finally, statutes in all states and the District of Columbia make provision for persons under the age of eighteen to be tried as criminals, either through excluding designated acts from the jurisdiction of the juvenile court, mandating waiver, or authorizing waiver. Of those states that articulate a minimum age for waiver, fourteen is the most frequently occurring age; however, eighteen states and the District of Columbia specify no minimum age for the waiver of children to criminal court.[12]

Exhibit C: U.S. Supreme Court Cases and Findings

In my thirty years in the juvenile justice profession, I have yet to find a critic of the juvenile court who likes the Supreme Court decision in *McKeiver v. Pennsylvania*[13] very well. The Court held in *McKeiver* that juveniles have no constitutional right to trial by jury. Seventeen states nonetheless make provision for jury trial in juvenile court, although in most of these states it is not an unfettered right, just as is the case with adult criminals.

But the Supreme Court decision that is absolutely abhorred by critics of the juvenile court is *Schall v. Martin.*[14] Martin appealed a New York Family Court Act that authorizes pretrial detention of an accused juvenile delinquent, based on a finding that there is a serious risk that the juvenile may, before the return date, commit an act that if committed by an adult would constitute a crime. The U.S. Supreme Court held that the New York statute was not invalid under the due process clause of the Fourteenth Amendment because preventive detention serves a legitimate state objective, held in common with every state, of protecting both the juvenile and society from the hazards of pretrial crime. That finding, while disturbing to juvenile court critics, is more acceptable than the second holding, which was that the procedural safeguards afforded by New York's Family Court Act to juveniles detained under the statute provide sufficient protection against erroneous and unnecessary deprivation of liberty. The Court found no merit to the argument that the risk of erroneous and unnecessary detention is too high, since there is nothing inherently unattainable about a prediction of future criminal conduct. Of course, much of the juvenile court's raison d'être with regard to delinquent as well as neglected children is predicated on the assumption that behavior is predictable and therefore preventable. In fact, the Supreme Court found that the Family Court Act of New York provided more predetention procedural safeguards for juveniles than are constitutionally required for adults.[15]

Other examples reluctantly cited by juvenile court reformers and critics are the death penalty cases of Kevin Stanford of Kentucky and Heath Wilkins of Missouri.[16] In language that would have done credit to social constructivist theorists, the Court concluded that "'Eighth Amendment judgments should not be, or appear to be, merely the subjective views of individual Justices; judgment should be informed by objective factors to the maximum possible extent.'"[17] The Court went on to say that "statutes passed by society's elected representatives" constitute such a factor.[18] More significantly for our purposes, the *Stanford* majority opinion found that the determinations required by the transfer statutes in Kentucky and Missouri to certify a juvenile for trial as an adult ensured individualized consideration of the maturity and moral responsibility of sixteen- and seventeen-year-olds before they are held to stand trial as adults. The majority thought it was those particularized laws that demonstrated society's views on the age at which no youthful offender should be held responsible.[19]

Exhibit D: The Efficacy of Criminal Justice Procedure in Protecting the Rights of Individuals and Society

A particularly hollow argument of those legal reformers who would try juvenile offenders as criminals is found in their descriptions of the beauties of fundamental fairness within the criminal justice system.[20] They elaborate eloquently on the marvelous legal protections and assurances of individual rights, but they say nothing about the fact that minorities are overrepresented fivefold in America's adult prisons; they do not present any evidence on the prevalence and effectiveness of counsel for adult defendants; and they never mention how many criminal justice facilities are under court order in the United States. As of June 30, 1990, in thirty-five states the entire department or one or more adult corrections institutions was under court order for various violations of constitutional protections. This situation contrasts with that of the juvenile justice system, where a total of six states and the District of Columbia were under court order.[21]

It is not surprising that juvenile court critics have failed to expose any documentation for the superiority of justice within the criminal justice system. For example, in touting the superiority of the state of Washington's simulated criminal justice system for juveniles, Ainsworth missed the opportunity to point out that, in that state, persons under the age of eighteen are placed in secure detention both for pretrial purposes and for punishment at a rate two times that of the nation.[22] In fact, when Washington's use of detention for punishment is compared with figures for the rest of the country, it becomes apparent that Washington commits youth to detention at a rate eight times the U.S. average. Washington's rate of commitment is 12.3 per 1,000, and the U.S. average is 1.42 per 1,000. Part of this discrepancy can be explained by the fact that some states prohibit the use of detention facilities as a place of commitment. However, when Washington's experience is compared with that of jurisdictions that permit the use of detention facilities as a place of commitment—California, the District of Columbia, and Utah—Washington's rate of commitment is still enormously disparate.[23] It is inconceivable that Washington's bloated detention rates mean that children are getting more justice. It is, however, entirely possible that these rates are indicative of a mechanistically successful emulation of the criminal justice system. The adult jails of this country have been a revolving door for at least four decades because of a procedurally correct but substantively defunct criminal justice system. Washington may be approaching the same Nirvana with its juvenile justice system.[24] Of course, these phenomena could be aberrations, because Washington state has at this writing only fourteen years of experience with its new code, but there is some real evidence in the state of New York, whose juvenile code is one of the state codes that Ainsworth frequently cites as validation for the new reality.

With the passage of the Juvenile Offender Act in 1978, the state of New York subjected every child in that state who was thirteen years of age and older and charged with a Class A or B felony (e.g., arson, assault, manslaughter, rape, and burglary) to criminal prosecution. The practices created with the passage of that act have received the benefit of at least three qualitative and quantitative evaluations. All three studies, though using different approaches, reached similar conclusions. They found that exposing very young children to criminal prosecution for their acts did not improve the protection of their individual rights, did not improve the protection of the public, did not improve the efficiency of government, and did not systematically punish serious offenders for their behavior.

Only 4 percent of all those arrested and charged as juvenile offenders under the statute were sentenced to terms longer than they might have received from the family court.[25]

More recent data from the New York State Division for Youth, Bureau of Program Evaluation and Research, reveal that very little has changed since the above-mentioned evaluations were conducted. In 1991, approximately two-thirds of all juvenile offender cases received by the criminal court were either dismissed or removed to the family court. Of the one-third who were convicted, three out of four were placed on probation. Half of the remainder were placed in secure facilities but served a sentence quite similar to that of juvenile delinquents placed by the family court. Moreover, only 4 percent of persons receiving institutional sentences under the Juvenile Offender Act are white, 65 percent are African-Americans, and 26 percent are Latinos of various races. Of juveniles admitted to secure facilities, 94 percent were fifteen years of age or older.[26] According to the Division for Youth,

> The large number of older [juvenile offender] admissions to the Division can, for the most part, be explained by the fact that the Criminal Court process takes considerably longer than that of Family court. Inasmuch as youth prosecuted in Criminal Court are more likely to have spent longer periods of time in detention than those processed in Family court, it is not unusual to see such admissions of older youth.[27]

Exhibit E: Concept versus Practice in Criminal Court

The reality of our criminal justice system is quite different from that painted by scholars who propose to abolish the juvenile court and move juvenile offenders into the criminal justice system. Former Chief Judge Sol Wachtler of New York's highest court explains this reality. He speaks of "a court system in which criminal proceedings often last only two to four minutes, and judges dispose of 90 percent of cases through plea bargaining instead of trials statewide"; in New York City, he contends, "fewer than 5 percent of all felony cases go to trial, and in the New York City Criminal Court fewer than 1 percent of cases filed are tried."[28] He says that plea bargaining has become the accepted method of resolution of criminal charges. What he did not say is even more damning, and that is that plea bargaining has been the accepted rule now for many years in the criminal justice system, and few in the legal community really seem to care. Due process and the Bill of Rights mean little when the advice of counsel is to waive all of these protections by pleading guilty.

Former Chief Judge Wachtler is not alone in his criticism of practice in criminal courts. Attorneys who have practiced in both criminal and juvenile courts prefer the latter. "[A]s bad as the juvenile courts are, the adult criminal courts . . . are worse."[29] If criminal courts were to be preferred, attorneys would have discovered it a long time ago. Most states permit any youth who is charged with a waivable offense to select criminal court as the forum to hear the case. In spite of such provisions, however, juvenile offenders are not clamoring to get into criminal court. This reluctance stems from the fact that "[f]or the most part, the typical criminal court in urban areas is a harsh, tough, mean institution cranking out pleas with no pause for individualized attention. It is no place for an adult defendant to be, much less a child."[30]

Exhibit F: Recidivism as a Measure of Performance

Anyone who thinks that our justice system, either juvenile or criminal, is capable of controlling crime adequately has never thought very seriously about the matter. To begin with, we have no idea who commits most of the crime in the United States, because most crime goes undetected; as a result, the formal system never sees most of the people whose behavior it might punish or attempt to correct. The reported clearance rate for 1991 for all crime was 21 percent; in other words, only one in five crimes reported to the police was cleared by the arrest of an individual.[31] So even if the system were totally effective in preventing future crime for those who are criminally charged, 80 percent of the crime problem might be unaffected. In the juvenile justice system, one out of every two offenders appearing in juvenile court in any given year had never been there before, so the juvenile court could be 100 percent effective in correcting the behavior of young people and it would still receive approximately 600,000 cases of delinquency each year.[32]

Even though no court has ever solved or will ever solve the crime problem, juvenile or otherwise, juvenile court critics—especially legal scholars—repeatedly use recidivism rates as a cudgel with which to bludgeon the court. Invariably, the statistics cited are those of juveniles who have been committed to state correctional institutions. Critics point to recidivism rates as high as 70 percent and cite these as the proof of the juvenile court's failure. But they persistently ignore the fact that youngsters committed to state correctional institutions are among the most intractable offenders received by this system and account for 5 percent or less of the juvenile court's workload.[33] This trend continues in spite of the fact that there is considerable evidence that juvenile courts and the juvenile justice system do not have a deleterious effect on the future behavior of delinquents and may even be doing a far better job than we realize.

In his study of a birth cohort of males born in Philadelphia in 1945, the noted criminologist Marvin Wolfgang found that 35 percent of them were arrested for committing a crime prior to reaching their eighteenth birthday. Of those who were arrested, 54 percent were recidivists, but only 18 percent of those who were arrested persisted in their delinquent behavior.[34] In a similar study in Racine, Wisconsin, Lyle Shannon studied cohorts of males and females born in 1942, 1949, and 1955. Shannon found that 44 percent of members of these birth cohorts had a contact with the police. Half (51 percent) of those having such a contact had more than one contact, but only 18 percent of those who engaged in delinquent behavior in the first instance persisted in their delinquency.[35]

Across the Atlantic, Donald West and David Farrington followed a birth cohort of urban white working-class males in a London neighborhood and found that 20 percent of them had "been convicted" of an offense prior to their eighteenth birthday. Sixty-two percent of the members of the British cohort were found to be recidivists in that they were convicted on more than one occasion, but only 17 percent of the original 20 percent persisted in their delinquent behavior to the point of being classified as chronic delinquents.[36]

All three of the above studies were conducted in communities with juvenile courts. In each instance, less than one of five youths who were the subject of juvenile justice system intervention persisted in their delinquent behavior. These studies may not be testimony to the efficacy of the system, but they present a rather compelling case for the proposition that juvenile courts are doing no harm.

In a more recent study of youths with juvenile court careers, Howard Snyder found that 34 percent of the young people born between the years 1962 and 1965 in the state of Utah and in the county of Maricopa (Phoenix), Arizona, had a least one court referral prior to their eighteenth birthday. He also found that 59 percent of those who had a court referral had only one court referral, and that 84 percent of those who had at least one referral had no more than three referrals.[37]

Rivers and Trotti followed a cohort of juvenile offenders in the state of South Carolina on into their adult careers to determine whether they were ever convicted of a criminal offense. The oldest members of the cohort were followed for seven years from age seventeen to age twenty-four. This age span is demonstrably the prime crime time for all offenders. Yet in the South Carolina study, only 27 percent, or one in four of the total cohort, had acquired any kind of criminal record seven years later.[38] This finding provides further assurance that the juvenile court is not a training ground for criminal offenders. Without question, some do become criminal offenders, and certainly the number could probably be reduced, but to argue that juvenile courts should be abolished because some of the youths referred to these institutions grow up to be criminals is, based on the evidence, somewhat akin to arguing that hospitals ought to be abolished because some of the people who enter there die.[39]

The Deepest Flaw in Our System of Justice

Most critics of the juvenile court who would repair its deficits by replacing it with criminal procedure are apparently blind to the most fatal flaw in our system of justice—our reliance on adversarial process without benefit of effective counsel.[40] In our system of justice, as in any adversarial system, the quality of the outcome is directly dependent on the quality of the adversaries, and in this country the quality of the adversaries is directly related to the defendant's or the plaintiff's ability to pay the bill. As a consequence, the more materially deprived persons in our system of justice are, the less justice they get. It matters not whether one is deprived because one is a child who has no right to property, or an adult without skills and unable to acquire property; the degree of fairness our system accords hinges on the quality of counsel. This observation is not intended to demean public defenders or prosecutors. Public defenders are among the most knowledgeable and effective practitioners of juvenile and criminal defense among the practicing bar. However, public defenders work for the state, not for the defendant; and if they try to take the time required to produce an effective defense for every client, they soon go mad or lose their job. Adversarial systems of justice are simply not designed to have both adversaries employed by the state, especially in the matter of criminal law violations.

The absence of counsel is felt most deeply in courts of juvenile jurisdiction. There is no living to be made in juvenile court as a practitioner of law, not because there is nothing for counsel to do, but because children have no right to property and no ability to engage and direct counsel. To ensure further that, if counsel does appear in juvenile court, he or she will appear unprepared, accredited schools of law in the United States do not require that their students master a course in juvenile law and procedure in order to obtain a degree, and no state bar association requires attorneys to demonstrate any competence in juvenile law in order to be licensed to practice law. This dilemma is quite understandable, if not entirely defensible, and seems unlikely to change in the near term. As a consequence, the efficacy of adversarial decision making is beginning to be challenged as never before, especially in matters involving juvenile and family jurisdiction.

The frustration with adversarial procedure in matters involving children and families is almost complete. The state of Nevada recently passed a statute creating a family court. Prominent among the mandates of that statute is the provision that the Family Court of the State of Nevada shall utilize nonadversarial procedures wherever possible to resolve cases presented to that court.[41] Nevada is the first state to mandate that the court utilize nonadversarial decision-making procedures for the entire range of the court's jurisdiction, including juvenile delinquency, but it is unlikely to be the last. Since the Nevada statute does not specify what nonadversarial technique is to be used, the Nevada Family Court judges are free to innovate lawfully as they see fit. Conceivably, Nevada may decide to emulate New Mexico and consider a tiered approach to handling delinquency cases.[42] A tiered approach would limit the amount of due process and the severity of possible dispositions for younger, less serious offenders and escalate procedural protections and the severity of dispositions as the age, culpability, and seriousness of the offender's crimes increased.

Juvenile Law in Legal Education

The juvenile court is certainly not without imperfection, but to propose that it be replaced by the criminal court is unacceptable.[43] It is discouraging but not surprising that legal scholars continue to call for such actions. Schools of law generally do an excellent job of teaching the theory of criminal law and procedure but a poor job of teaching the reality of criminal justice in the United States. As a consequence, law graduates, especially those who pursue careers without a deep immersion in the practice of criminal law, tend to romanticize our criminal justice system.

Conversely, when schools of law do offer a course in juvenile law, it is offered as an elective and invariably compares juvenile law and procedure with criminal law and procedure. In such a comparison, juvenile law and procedure is forever destined to be the loser because the theory of criminal justice is used as the standard for measurement. If the reality of criminal law and procedure were used as the standard, the outcome would be reversed. The teaching of juvenile law as a unique body of law has seldom been seriously considered by schools of law. It is quite simply a losing proposition. There is no career ladder for attorneys who want to specialize in juvenile law, so there is no demand for such a curriculum. Accordingly, courses in juvenile law attract few serious students of law. It is thus no wonder that many scholars do not view neglect, abuse, and dependency as a critical piece of juvenile court jurisdiction.

Unless and until we the people—but especially the legal community—face the fact that pro bono and publicly funded legal services for children and disenfranchised adults do not now and never will equate to basic fairness, much less equal justice under the law, we will continue to engage in the sterile exercise of scholarly critique and rebuttal without ever reaching the desired level of thesis, antithesis, and synthesis. In the meantime, community after community builds larger and larger institutions to accommodate more and more delays generated by a crippled and archaic adversarial system that makes little procedural distinction between those charged with capital crimes and those charged with minor theft; a system that is oblivious to the gradations of the moral imperative for retribution inherent in crimes involving children and those involving adults; a system that knows only win/lose, even when the defendants are children in need of protection, and reason begs for a win/win decision-making method.

Conclusion

The juvenile court can be improved, but that improvement cannot come from emulation or substitution of the criminal justice system. Our system of criminal justice is too deeply and irrevocably flawed to serve as a model. One should realize that what defense lawyers call "justice" and the rest of us call "fairness" is in short supply in our criminal justice system. The juvenile court sits somewhere between equity law, criminal law, and civil law. For the more compulsive social and legal reformer, that is an ambiguous and untidy posture requiring clarification and sanitization. But we should move with caution because the juvenile court possesses both the flexibility to resolve minor offenses promptly through diversion, conciliation, consent, and other effective means of nonadversarial decision making and the capacity to ensure fairness and protection for the child. And when a child has committed an offense egregious enough to invoke the primacy of community protection, the court has the capacity to transfer the case to the criminal court for prosecution.

But perhaps most importantly, the juvenile court has the dual mandate of protecting society and acting in the interest of children. The criminal court has no such mandate. But it is self-evident that the state has a compelling interest in both protecting society and acting in the interest of children. Consequently, unless and until we have a vision of a forum that can better attain these ideals, we should continue our quest to improve the juvenile court but steadfastly resist all efforts to replace it. And we should be especially firm in our resolve to maintain it when the proposed alternative is anything resembling our current criminal court.

NOTES

1. *See* Chapter 32 in this volume.

2. 2 Children and Youth in America: A Documentary History 506–511 (R. Bremner et al. eds., 1970).

3. *See* Federle, The Abolition of the Juvenile Court: A Proposal for the Preservation of Children's Legal Rights, 16 J. Contemp. L. 23 (1990); Feld, The Transformation of the Juvenile Court, 75 Minn. L. Rev. 691 (1991); Holstein, Slamming the Door on Prodigals: Changing Conceptions of Childhood and the Demise of Juvenile Justice, 9 N. Ky. L. Rev. 517 (1982). For a more balanced analysis of the rights of children charged with a criminal act, see Clark, Procedural Rights in the Juvenile Court: Incorporation or Due Process? 7 Pepp. L. Rev. 865 (1980); Rosenberg, The Constitutional Rights of Children Charged with Crime: Proposal for a Return to the Not So Distant Past, 27 UCLA L. Rev. 656 (1980).

4. *See* L. Szymanski, Extended Age of Juvenile Court Jurisdiction Statutes Analysis (June 1990) (available from the National Center for Juvenile Justice).

5. Thompson v. Oklahoma, 487 U.S. 815, 839 (1988).

6. *Id.* at 840.

7. *See* M. Soler et al., Representing the Child Client 3.05 (1987).

8. *See* L. Szymanski, Juvenile Code Purpose Clauses (Apr. 1991) (available from the National Center for Juvenile Justice). For example, Pennsylvania law provides:

> (b) Purposes.—This chapter shall be interpreted and construed as to effectuate the following purposes:
> (1) To preserve the unity of the family whenever possible. . . .
> (2) Consistent with the protection of the public interest, to remove from children committing delinquent acts the consequences of criminal behavior, and to substitute therefor a program of supervision, care and rehabilitation.
> (3) To achieve the foregoing purposes in a family environment whenever possible.

42 Pa. Cons. Stat. § 6301 (1990).

9. Washington law provides that: "It is the further intent of the legislature that

youth, in turn, be held accountable for their offenses and that both communities and the juvenile courts carry out their functions consistent with this intent." Wash. Rev. Code. § 13.40.010 (1992).

10. *See* L. Szymanski, Confidentiality of Juvenile Proceedings (Mar. 1991) (available from the National Center for Juvenile Justice); L. Szymanski, Confidentiality of Juvenile Records (Mar. 1991) (available from the National Center for Juvenile Justice).

11. *See* H. Hurst, Confidentiality of Juvenile Justice Records and Proceedings: A Legacy under Siege 16 (1985) (unpublished manuscript, on file with author).

12. *See* L. Szymanski, Waiver/Transfer/Certification of Juveniles to Criminal Court: Age Restrictions—Crime Restrictions at tables 1 & 2 (Mar. 1991) (available from the National Center for Juvenile Justice); L. Szymanski, Statutory Exclusion of Crimes from Juvenile Court Jurisdiction at table 1 (Mar. 1991) (available from the National Center for Juvenile Justice).

13. 403 U.S. 528 (1971).

14. 467 U.S. 253 (1984).

15. *See* Gerstein v. Pugh, 420 U.S. 103 (1975).

16. *See* Stanford v. Kentucky, 492 U.S. 361 (1989) (decided with Wilkins v. Missouri) (holding that it is not cruel and unusual punishment to impose the death penalty on sixteen- and seventeen-year-old murderers).

17. *Id.* at 369 (quoting Coker v. Georgia, 433 U.S. 584, 592 (1977)).

18. *Id.* at 370.

19. *Id.* at 375.

20. *See, e.g.*, Feld, The Transformation of the Juvenile Court, *supra* note 3.

21. *See* Juvenile and Adult Correctional Departments, Institutions, Agencies and Paroling Authorities, United States and Canada, 1991 Directory xx (1991) (published by the American Correctional Association).

22. *See* M. Sickmund et al., Rate Analysis of Children in Custody Data: 1986/87 and 1988/89 at table 2 (Feb. 1991) (available from the National Center for Juvenile Justice).

23. The District of Columbia, with a rate of 4.86/1,000, is Washington's closest competitor for the use of detention as punishment, followed by California at 4.11/1,000 and Utah at 3.76/1,000.

24. *See* M. Sickmund & R. Poole, Juvenile Detention in the United States: Admissions Awaiting Hearing and Court Commitments—1990 (1992) (available from the National Center for Juvenile Justice).

25. *See* M. Fabricant, Juvenile Injustice: Dilemmas of the Family Court System (Sept. 1981) (Community Service Society of New York). *See also* Citizens' Committee for Children of New York, Inc., The Experiment That Failed: The New York State Juvenile Offender Law (Dec. 1984); M. Sobie, The Juvenile Offender Act: A Study of the Act's Effectiveness and Impact on the New York Juvenile Justice System (Feb. 1981) (published by the Foundation for Child Development, New York).

26. Juvenile Offenders, Research Focus on Youth (New York State Division for Youth, Bureau of Program Evaluation and Research), Winter 1992, at 3, table 2.

27. *See id.*

28. State Judiciary News, 16 State Ct. J. 28, 32 (1992) (quoting from Judge Wachtler's 1991 State of the Judiciary Message).

29. I. Rosenberg, Leaving Bad Enough Alone: A Response to Barry Feld 8 (1992) (unpublished manuscript, on file with the author).

30. *Id.* at 8–9.

31. U.S. Department of Justice, Federal Bureau of Investigation, News Release at 4 (Aug. 30, 1992).

32. *See* H. Snyder, Court Careers of Juvenile Offenders 37 (1988) (published by Department of Justice). *See also* H. Snyder et al., Juvenile Court Statistics 1988 (1990).

33. *See* Snyder et al., Juvenile Court Statistics 1988, *supra* note 32, at 15, 22, 26, 30.

34. M. Wolfgang et al., Delinquency in a Birth Cohort (1972).

35. L. Shannon, Assessing the Relationship of Adult Criminal Careers to Juvenile Careers (1982).

36. D. West, Delinquency: Its Roots, Careers and Prospects (1982); D. Farrington, Delinquency from 10 to 25 (Nov. 1981) (paper presented at the Society for Life History Research Meeting, Monterey, California; on file with author).

37. *See* Snyder, Court Careers of Juvenile Offenders, *supra* note 32, at 22.

38. J. Rivers & T. Trotti, South Carolina Delinquent Males: A Follow-up into Adult Corrections (Aug. 1989) (unpublished manuscript, on file with the author).

39. Gable & McFall, What to Do about Serious Delinquency: Do Good? Do Bad? Do Nothing? 2 Today's Delinquent 7 (1983).

40. *See generally* J. Knitzer and M. Sobie, Law Guardians in New York State: A Study of the Legal Representation of Children 8 (1984) ("Overall, 45% of the courtroom observations reflected either seriously inadequate or marginally adequate representation").

41. "The family court shall, whenever practicable and appropriate, encourage the resolution of disputes before the court through nonadversarial methods or other alternatives to traditional methods of resolution of disputes." Nev. Rev. Stat. Ann. § 3.225 (Michie 1991).

42. Springer, Rehabilitating the Juvenile Court, 5 Notre Dame J.L. Ethics & Pub. Pol'y 397 (1991). *See also* New Mexico Children's Code, N.M. Stat. Ann. § 32A-1-1 et seq. (ch. 32A) (Michie 1978 & Supp. 1993).

43. See Edwards, The Juvenile Court and the Role of the Juvenile Court Judge, 43 Juv. & Fam. Ct. J. 1 (1992), for a balanced assessment of what the juvenile court is and is not, plus a vision of what it needs to become. *See also* Hirschi & Gottfredson, Rethinking the Juvenile Justice System, 39 Crime & Delinq. 262–71 (1993).

■ CHAPTER THIRTY-FIVE

Schall v. Martin and Juvenile Detention

Robert G. Schwartz

In 1967, *In re Gault*[1] signaled that children had reached constitutional maturity. *Gault* recognized children as "persons" within the meaning of the Fourteenth Amendment, entitled to numerous procedural protections at trial. In 1984, before *Gault* reached the age of majority, *Schall v. Martin*[2] warned of a new constitutional discipline. *Martin* departed radically from *Gault* and eliminated most federal court challenges to unnecessary incarceration of youths in juvenile detention centers. Since *Martin*, lawyers for children have had to create new litigation and nonlitigation strategies to diminish unnecessary juvenile detention.

Schall v. Martin Revisited

Plaintiffs in *Schall v. Martin* brought both substantive and procedural due process claims. Plaintiffs asserted substantively that they could not be deprived of liberty prior to an adjudication of delinquency. Procedurally, plaintiffs challenged the absence of safeguards in the New York statute and the undisciplined discretion that family court judges exercised in making pretrial detention decisions.

The U.S. Supreme Court disposed of both due process claims, though in doing so it blended its substantive and procedural analyses. The majority framed the substantive claim by asking whether "preventive detention . . . serve[s] a legitimate state interest."[3] To answer the substantive question, the Court further inquired "whether, *in the context of the juvenile system*, the combined interest in protecting both the community and the juvenile himself from the consequences of future criminal conduct is sufficient to justify such detention."[4] Unfortunately for plaintiffs, the Court's view of the "context of the juvenile system" was an avuncular regression to pre-*Gault* times.

In re Gault

Martin analyzed pretrial detainees' rights within the "context" of a juvenile justice system that was similar to the "context" that *Gault* had rejected. The *Gault* Court had echoed the claim of *Kent v. United States* that a juvenile has "the worst of both worlds: that he gets neither the protections accorded to adults nor the solicitous care and regenerative treatment postulated for children."[5] *Gault* sought to remedy this concern by reshaping long-held juvenile justice doctrines, particularly that of *parens patriae*, in order to recognize juveniles as "persons" who command Fourteenth Amendment protection.[6]

The *parens patriae* doctrine fully emerged in 1839 in *Ex parte Crouse*,[7] which permitted the state to act as a substitute for unfit parents. Over sixty-five years later, the Pennsylvania Supreme Court in *Commonwealth v. Fisher*[8] built upon *Crouse* and upheld the state's first juvenile court act, reasoning that: "Every statute which is designed to give protection, care and training to children, as a needed substitute for parental authority and performance of parental duty, is but a recognition of the duty of the state, as the legitimate guardian and protector of children where other guardianship fails."[9] The *Fisher* court further declared that the juvenile court act, designed for the "salvation of children,"[10] had no impact on a child's liberty. The court reasoned that since a parent could confine a child in the home to prevent a career of crime, the state, in its role as *parens patriae*, could also confine a child without having "to adopt any process."[11]

Even though *Fisher*'s reasoning came to prevail in state practice throughout the United States, the *Gault* Court rejected this view that the juvenile court's benign intentions eliminated the need for fundamental fairness. In particular, the *Gault* Court dismissed the argument that "a child . . . has a right 'not to liberty but to custody.'"[12]

Martin Rewrites Gault

In order to find a legitimate state interest in preventive detention, thereby minimizing a minor's liberty interest, the *Martin* Court had to find a way around *Gault*. *Martin* circumvented *Gault* by disingenuously cementing unrelated cases into a foundation of juvenile justice case law to build a hybrid constitutional theory that could hold the weight of its revisionist juvenile justice "context" argument. The *Martin* Court acknowledged *Gault*'s application of due process to juveniles.[13] However, in determining how the due process clause applies to juvenile proceedings, the Court utilized the *parens patriae* rationale of *Santosky v. Kramer*[14] to differentiate between juvenile and adult proceedings.[15]

However, *Santosky*, which followed *Gault*, did not address delinquency proceedings. Rather, it established the standard of proof for judicial proceedings to terminate parental rights. Nonetheless, the Court used *Santosky* as a convenient, if mislaid, building block.

Similarly, in assessing the strength of plaintiffs' claim to a protectable liberty interest, the *Martin* Court cited *Lehman v. Lycoming County Children's Services Agency*[16] for the proposition "that juveniles, unlike adults, are always in some form of custody."[17] *Lehman*, like *Santosky*, did not involve delinquency proceedings; it instead explored whether federal habeas corpus jurisdiction should extend to state domestic relations matters.

By inappropriately applying cases such as *Santosky* and *Lehman* to the juvenile detention setting, the *Martin* Court reinvented a pre-*Gault* juvenile "context" through which it diminished children's rights by exalting the state's interest in acting as *parens patriae* to protect the community and to protect juveniles from themselves.

Martin's Due Process Analysis

Other commentators effectively rebut the Court's argument that the state may use the *parens patriae* rationale to act as unrestrainedly as parents can, and also refute the Court's crucial argument that children have a diminished liberty interest by virtue of their inherent custodial status.[18] This point deserves elaboration.

The Martin Court did not examine the extent to which detained minors are deprived of liberty. Rather, it relied upon and accepted the state's interest to determine that there is no loss of liberty at all. The Court's endorsement of *Lehman* enabled it to overlook conditions at the Spofford Detention Center, a maximum security facility known at the time for its Dickensian conditions,[19] and thus made a very real loss of liberty harmlessly disappear.

Trivializing the minor's liberty interest allowed the Court to curtail the procedural safeguards available to juvenile detainees. As in cases such as *Goss v. Lopez*,[20] the *Martin* Court correlated the amount of process due with the severity of the liberty deprivation.[21] Since the Court had already established that such deprivation was minimal because of a compelling *parens patriae* state interest, the Court easily concluded that little procedural protection was required. Had the Court used a different procedural due process analysis, however, the outcome of the case might have been different.

In *Mathews v. Eldridge*,[22] for example, the Court offered an alternative analytic framework for determining the scope of the due process clause. The Mathews Court explained that:

[O]ur prior decisions indicate that identification of the specific dictates of due process generally requires consideration of three distinct factors: First, the private interest that will be affected by the official action; second, the risk of an erroneous deprivation of such interest through the procedures used, and the probable value, if any, of additional or substitute procedural safeguards; and finally, the Government's interest, including the function involved and the fiscal and administrative burdens that the additional or substitute procedural requirement would entail.[23]

Under the *Matthews* test, outcomes in procedural due process cases relating to juveniles often hinge on the Court's assessment of the private interest at stake. In particular, these decisions depend upon whether the Court deems parents' and children's interests as shared or competing. For example, in *Parham v. J.R.*,[24] which involved parents voluntarily placing children in state mental hospitals, the Court considered the parents' interests to be allied with government interests, thereby rendering weightless the opposing private interest of children who opposed hospitalization.[25]

Given the *paired* parent–child private interest in *Schall v. Martin*, it is likely that an application of the *Matthews* test in that case would have resulted in heightened due process for juveniles. Significantly, it is possible to view *Gault* as a parents' rights as much as a children's rights case.[26] The *Martin* Court, however, again discarded *Gault's* analysis in favor of a *Fisher*-like characterization of parental failure that minimizes the private interests at stake.[27] The *Martin* Court presumed parental irresponsibility; otherwise, it suggested, the child would not have been arrested.[28] It is not surprising, then, that the private interest here is given the back of the Court's hand: Neither the child nor the parent has a liberty interest large enough to warrant consideration.

Thus, the *Martin* Court selectively and arbitrarily relied on precedent to make children's liberty interests disappear, thereby licensing a process that has harmed countless juveniles and has been used to hide problems in the nondetention components of the juvenile justice system.[29] Inevitably, *Martin* has challenged lawyers for children to develop new litigation and nonlitigation strategies to undo the damage.

Martin's Legacy

In 1989, over a quarter of a million children were held in detention.[30] Between 1982 and 1989 national admissions to detention centers increased by 30 percent.[31] A 1989 one-day census of youths in detention revealed that half of those detained were confined in overcrowded facilities.[32] Fewer than half of those detained were charged with Part I offenses.[33]

In Pennsylvania, for example, where litigation continues to illuminate issues of preventive detention and overcrowding, admissions to juvenile detention centers continue to grow.[34] However, the Pennsylvania experience, like that of other states, also suggests two issues worthy of exploration. First, detention following arrest, the triggering event in *Martin*, is only one cause of rising detention populations. An advocacy focus that merely addresses detention following arrest for new offenses therefore would be misplaced. Second, litigation, coupled with policy and program changes, may reduce the harmful effects of detention in spite of *Martin's* devaluation of children's liberty interests.

Limiting *Martin*'s Reach: A Case Study of Pennsylvania

The Coleman *Consent Decree*

In 1981, plaintiffs in *Coleman v. Stanziani*[35] filed a federal court class action challenging the constitutionality of a Pennsylvania law permitting the secure detention of a child "to protect the person or property of others or of the child or because the child may abscond or be removed from the jurisdiction."[36] Even though the constitutional complaints in *Coleman* were similar to those in *Martin*, for several reasons the *Coleman* lawsuit resulted in a negotiated settlement.

The usual uncertainty about the outcome of litigation if pursued to trial or summary judgment was one reason for the settlement. On the same day that the Supreme Court decided *Martin*, the Third Circuit Court of Appeals offered encouragement to the *Coleman* plaintiffs by affirming the district court's dismissal of Pennsylvania's motion for judgment on the pleadings.[37] However, the plaintiffs remained uneasy because even though the *Martin* Court's decision appeared to rest in part on New York's requirement that judges who order detention state their reasons for doing so, the *Martin* holding had unequivocally upheld preventive detention.[38] Although Pennsylvania had no analogous "statement of reasons" requirement, it was unclear how a court might reconcile the two cases.

Another reason for the *Coleman* settlement stemmed from a study[39] commissioned by *Coleman* plaintiffs that examined detention practices in six Pennsylvania counties in 1981. The study, like the case sampling offered into evidence in *Martin*, showed wide and troubling variation in detention practices in the six counties.[40] The study was instrumental in convincing defendants that, as a policy matter, Pennsylvania needed a more uniform system of detention.

Coleman was settled by consent decree in 1986. The settlement required judges and juvenile probation officers to give "statements of reasons" for pretrial detention decisions and to consider the use of nonsecure detention alternatives. The decree prohibited secure detention based solely on the absence of a parent or guardian. Most importantly, the settlement established binding detention standards, promulgated by Pennsylvania's progressive Juvenile Court Judges' Commission (JCJC).[41]

These standards for judges and probation officers define who may be held in secure detention during the pretrial, posttrial awaiting disposition, and postdisposition periods. They list fifteen offenses for which secure detention may be authorized. They also list circumstances under which a court or probation officer may order detention because the juvenile is already under the supervision of the court and is being charged with a new offense.

The standards further permit detention when a child is a fugitive, or when the child has a record of failing to appear at previous juvenile proceedings. The standards permit postadjudication and postdisposition detention under specified circumstances, and, through an "exceptional circumstances" clause, provide some flexibility in decision making to judges and probation officers. Judges or probation officers who detain a juvenile for "exceptional circumstances" must, however, file written reasons with JCJC.[42]

The Impact of the Coleman *Settlement*

At first, the mere filing of *Coleman* and the subsequent settlement so diminished the use of secure detention in Pennsylvania that between 1982 and 1989 about one-quarter of the state's detention centers closed because of underutilization. In the late 1980s, however, Pennsylvania juvenile detention center populations began to rise significantly. Populations grew even though the *Coleman* standards placed limitations on detention after arrest for many new offenses, implementing one of the key outcomes that had been sought by plaintiffs in *Martin*. But because it was limited to detention following arrest, *Coleman* had limited effect on (1) new admissions for other reasons, such as probation violations, and (2) length of stay in detention, which correlates directly with overcrowding.

JCJC's January 1992 data[43] show that Pennsylvania detention center[44] admissions for the first half of 1991 were over 70 percent higher than for the same period in 1987,[45] the first full year of implementation of the Coleman settlement. Only 22 percent of admissions during the first six months of 1991 were for new, *Martin*-like offenses,[46] that would trigger permissible detention. Probation violations accounted for 15 percent of all new admissions,[47] and 35 percent of new admissions followed findings that the juvenile was likely to abscond;[48] of the latter group, 41.7 percent (14.5 percent of all new admissions) were detained because they had escaped from court-ordered placements.[49]

JCJC's August 1991 report[50] revealed that admissions to detention centers rose from 5,875 in 1987 to 8,426 *and* that the average length of stay rose by almost one full day.[51] Even though plaintiffs were able to overcome *Martin* and to settle *Coleman,* Pennsylvania juvenile detention centers were almost full.[52] This phenomenon, not unique to Pennsylvania, suggests that new options to prevent unnecessary detention of juveniles must be explored.

Post-*Martin* Opportunities

One commentator has observed that:

Detention does not deserve to be a major part in the juvenile justice process. It should be brief, terribly selective and modest in its aims. If the rest of the system behaves, it should almost disappear [. . .] [D]etention should not be, as it is now, the hidden closet for the skeletons of the rest of the system.[53]

Ironically, by detaining youths for technical probation violations, detention centers hold more than the system's skeletons. This policy also impedes successful systemic reform and unintentionally triggers increased detention.

The only two ways of decreasing detention center populations are: (1) reducing admissions, and (2) reducing lengths of stay. Because *Martin* gave carte blanche to states to detain youths for new offenses, it is increasingly appropriate for advocates, like the plaintiffs' lawyers in *Coleman,* to develop nonlitigation policy approaches that narrow a state's definition of detainable offenses. The *Coleman* experience suggests, however, that entry into detention for non-offense-related reasons is not limited as easily.

One unfortunate obstacle to limiting detention for non-offense-related reasons is the movement to use intensive probation as an alternative to placing youths in training schools after adjudication and to use aftercare probation as an alternative to extended postadjudication confinement. Intensive and aftercare probation, otherwise known as parole, provides close community-based supervision, but also results in more technical probation violations and, consequently, in detention.[54] Thus, it will be difficult to reduce juvenile detention unless policy-makers or courts eliminate technical probation violations as offenses for which detention is permissible.[55]

Another problem with non-offense-based detention is overcrowding that results from prolonged pretrial detention, triggered by lengthy waiting periods between arrest and trial. For example, a jurisdiction that takes twenty days to bring detained youths to trial will need twice as many detention beds as a jurisdiction that brings the same number of juveniles to trial in ten days. Speedy trials for detained youths thus have a major impact on detention center populations.[56]

It is generally overlooked that overcrowded facilities may also be a product of delay in bringing *non*-detained youth to trial. This is because detention is a risk-management tool for many judges, whose experience suggests that released youths are unlikely to commit new offenses between the time of arrest and time of trial if that period is brief. The risk increases, however, the longer youths are on the street. Under these circumstances, detention center populations are likely to rise, not only because some youths will be rearrested before the distant trial date, but because judges will tend to order detention to prevent that scenario. The absence of speedy trials for *all* youths is inevitably a cause of overcrowding.[57]

Another cause of detention center overcrowding is the increase in the length of stay in overcrowded training schools, where youths are sent after disposition (sentencing). Many young people are held in detention centers after disposition while they wait for treatment beds to open up in training centers. Few states have regulations analogous to Florida's requirement that youths be freed unless they are moved to the place of disposition within five days of sentencing.[58]

Conclusion

Unfortunately, few jurisdictions manage to control the flow of youths through their juvenile justice systems in ways that minimize the use of secure detention. The unhappy result is a combination of systemic failure and *Martin*-sanctioned state discretion. When the result is serious overcrowding, litigation is inevitable.[59] Even then, alternative dispute resolution may be the wiser way to resolve the controversy.[60] Litigation to reduce overcrowding *has* resulted in limits to admissions following arrest,[61] but in the post-*Martin* era, such challenges are sporadic.

There is thus a glimmer of opportunity for successful litigation after *Martin*, but such litigation must be creatively conceived and must emphasize the creation of detention alternatives.[62] It is most likely, unfortunately, that in an age when the due process clause is a chisel that reduces liberty, advocates' greatest opportunities for success may well lie in policy arenas over which the Supreme Court will not have review.

NOTES

Acknowledgment: The author thanks Kendra Stetser for her editorial assistance.

1. 387 U.S. 1 (1967).

2. 467 U.S. 253 (1984).

3. *Id*. at 263–64.

4. *Id*. at 264 (emphasis added).

5. *In re* Gault, 387 U.S. at 18 n.23 (citing Kent v. United States, 383 U.S. 541, 556 (1966) (quoting Handler, The Juvenile Court and the Adversary System: Problems of Function and Form, 1965 Wis. L. Rev. 7)).

6. *See Gault*, 387 U.S. at 27–28.

7. 4 Whart. 9, 11 (Pa. 1839).

8. 62 A. 198 (Pa. 1905).

9. *Id*. at 56–57.

10. *Id*. at 50.

11. *Id*. at 53.

12. *Gault*, 387 U.S. at 17, 21.

13. *See* Schall v. Martin, 467 U.S. 253, 263 (1984).

14. 455 U.S. 745, 766 (1982).

15. *See Schall*, 467 U.S. at 263.

16. 458 U.S. 502, 510–11 (1982).

17. *Martin*, 467 U.S. at 265.

18. *See, e.g.,* Worrell, Pretrial Detention of Juveniles: Denial of Equal Protection Masked by the Parens Patriae Doctrine, 95 Yale L.J. 174 (1985).

19. *See Martin*, 467 U.S. at 290 n.13 (Marshall, J., dissenting).

20. 419 U.S. 565, 584 (1975).

21. *See Martin*, 467 U.S. at 275.

22. 424 U.S. 319 (1976).

23. *Id*. at 334–35.

24. 442 U.S. 584 (1979).

25. *See id*. at 603–606.

26. "No notice was given to Gerald's parents when he was taken into custody. . . . There is no requirement [under Arizona law] that the petition be served and it was not served upon, given to, or shown to Gerald or his parents." *In re* Gault, 387 U.S. 1, 31–32 (1967).

27. The Pennsylvania Supreme Court had upheld the state's new juvenile court law: "To save a child from becoming a criminal, or from continuing in a career of crime . . . the legislature surely may provide for the salvation of such a child, if its parents or guardian be unable or unwilling to do so." Commonwealth v. Fisher, 62 A. 198, 200 (Pa. 1905).

28. In *Fisher*, there was at least an adjudication of delinquency before the Court presumed parental neglect; in *Martin*, on the other hand, the mere fact of a child's arrest raised the specter of parental nonfeasance. *See* Schall v. Martin, 467 U.S. 253, 265 (1984).

29. *See infra* under "Post-*Martin* Opportunities."

30. *See* National Center for Juvenile Justice, National Estimates of Juvenile Delinquency Cases: 1989 (Easy Access, Version: 1.10) (computer printout by the National Center for Juvenile Justice, Pittsburgh, Pa., on file with author).

31. *See* I. Schwartz et al., University of Michigan School of Social Work, Juvenile Arrest, Detention, and Incarceration Trends: 1979–1989, at 3 (1991).

32. *See id.*

33. *See id.* Part I offenses are defined by the U.S. Department of Justice as criminal homicide, forcible rape, robbery, aggravated assault, burglary (breaking or entering), larceny-theft, motor vehicle theft, and arson. *See, e.g.,* Federal Bureau of Investigation, U.S. Department of Justice, Uniform Crime Reports for the United States app. II at 320 (1988).

34. *See infra* text accompanying note 50.

35. 570 F. Supp. 679 (E.D. Pa. 1983), *aff'd*, 735 F.2d 118 (3d Cir. 1984), *cert. denied*, 469 U.S. 1037 (1984).

36. Pa. Cons. Stat. Ann. § 6325 (1982 & Supp. 1991).

37. Coleman v. Stanziani, 735 F.2d 118, 120 (3d Cir. 1984), *cert. denied* 469 U.S. 1037 (1984).

38. *See* Schall v. Martin, 467 U.S. at 255 n.3.

39. *See* Goldkamp, Characteristics of Detention Populations in Selected Pennsylvania Counties (1984) (unpublished manuscript, on file with author).

40. In five of the six counties, more than half of the detained juveniles were held on felony charges, while only 36 percent were held for felonies in the sixth county. *Id.* at 3. In one suburban county, 65 percent of detainees were held for crimes against persons, while in another suburban county only 18 percent were held for such offenses. *Id.* at 3–4. Weapons, robbery, and drug-related charges and offenses involving injury to persons were rare in five of the six counties. *Id.* at 4. Furthermore, in one rural county, over half of detained juveniles had never been previously arrested. *Id.*

41. *See* 237 Pa. Code. § 101 (1986). *See also* Secure Detention Juveniles in Pennsylvania: The *Coleman* Decree, Children's Rts. Chron. (Juv. L. Center, Philadelphia, Pa.), 1986–87, at 1, 2–9.

42. For a more complete discussion of *Coleman*, see Anderson & Schwartz, Secure Detention in Pennsylvania, 1981–1990: The Experience After *Coleman v. Stanziani* (1990) (unpublished manuscript, on file with author).

43. M. Szumanski, Juvenile Court Judges' Commission, 1991 Monitoring Report: Use of Secure Detention in Pennsylvania (1992). Under the *Coleman* decree, JCJC provides the court and parties with semiannual reports. These reports summarize compliance with JCJC's detention standards. JCJC's obligation ends with the expiration of the consent decree in September 1996.

44. *Coleman* governs all Pennsylvania detention centers except the Youth Study Center in Philadelphia, which since 1974 has been the subject of separate litigation. *See infra* note 55.

45. *See* Szumanski, 1991 Monitoring Report, *supra* note 43, at 2.
46. *See id.* at 17.
47. *See id.* at 2.
48. *See id.* at 17.
49. *See id.* at 5.
50. *See* M. Szumanski, Juvenile Court Judges Commission, 1990 Monitoring Report: Use of Secure Detention in Pennsylvania (1991).
51. *See id.* at 7, 8.
52. *See id.* at 5.
53. Council of Judges, National Council on Crime and Delinquency, Recommendations on Juvenile Detention: Background Statement 5–6 (1989) (quoting Patricia M. Wald).
54. *See* R. Wiebush, Evaluation of the Lucas County Intensive Supervision Unit: Diversionary Impact and Youth Outcomes 35 (1991) ("[T]hose who are intensively supervised are more likely to have [technical probation] violations *discovered* than those who are not").
55. This is one reason that a Philadelphia federal court consent decree in a conditions case involving the city's Youth Study Center prohibits detaining youth at the center solely because they have committed technical probation violations. Santiago v. City of Philadelphia, No. 74–2589, at 25 (E.D. Pa. 1988) (order approving third amended stipulation in partial settlement of this action).
56. Most jurisdictions have provisions in their juvenile codes that require speedier trials for detained than for nondetained youths. *See, e.g.,* 42 Pa. Cons. Stat. Ann. § 6335 (a) (1982 & Supp. 1991).
57. For example, in the mid-1980s, when Philadelphia juvenile court was suffering a shortage of judges, the mean time between arrest and disposition for released youths rose to over three months. Juvenile Court Judges' Commission, Pennsylvania Juvenile Court Dispositions 1986, at 16 (1987). Under such circumstances, it is not surprising that Philadelphia judges, seeking to intervene more quickly or worried about juveniles committing new offenses if released prior to trial, would be inclined to order detention to compel a speedy trial.
58. *See* Fla. Stat. Ann. ch. 39.044(11) (West Supp. 1992) (recently amended to permit the Florida Department of Health and Rehabilitation Services to apply for an additional ten days of detention). In 1988, the Philadelphia district attorney, concerned that the *Santiago* court would close admissions to the Youth Study Center, brought a suit in state court to require the Pennsylvania Department of Public Welfare (DPW) to move youths committed to DPW training schools out of the center within ten days of disposition. Castille v. Pennsylvania Dep't of Pub. Welfare, No. 2533 C.D. 1988 (Pa. Cmmw. Ct. Dec. 27, 1989). The district attorney correctly recognized that opening the back door of a detention facility would have just as much impact on overcrowding as closing the front door. Unfortunately, the successful litigation affected only youths committed to training schools, not those committed to private residential treatment centers. An unintended result of the suit was that judges then committed more youths to training schools in order to speed their flow out of the Youth Study Center.
59. *See* Dale, Lawsuits and Public Policy: The Role of Litigation in Correcting Conditions in Juvenile Detention Centers (Jan. 21, 1992) (unpublished manuscript, on file with author).

60. *See generally*, Sturm, A Normative Theory of Public Law Remedies, 79 Geo. L.J. 1355 (1991); Schwartz, Litigation and Mediation Reduce Detention Center Overcrowding, 71 Prison J. 68 (1991).

61. *See* Schwartz, Litigation and Mediation, *supra* note 60, at 75 (discussing litigation in Pennsylvania); Dale & Sanniti, Litigation as an Instrument for Change in Juvenile Detention: A Case Study (paper presented at the annual meeting of the American Society of Criminology, Nov. 21, 1991; transcript on file with author) (discussing litigation in Florida).

62. *See* F. Orlando et al., Center for the Study of Youth Policy, Broward County Juvenile Detention Project: Summary of Results, June 1990, at 2 (1990) (describing a project that put forth alternatives to detention in one Florida jurisdiction).

■ CHAPTER THIRTY-SIX

Pretrial Detention: Law and Policy from the Juvenile Court Perspective

Gerald E. Radcliffe

EVERYTHING SAID about juveniles seems to be glamorous, spectacular, and attention-getting. This, of course, creates an emotional climate which draws strong statements. Amid the turmoil, decent persons are challenged and motivated to improve the system which administers a noble but vague commodity known as justice to juveniles. The problems of juveniles change as our social conditions vary.

We as a democratic society hope that those charged with fashioning a code of behavior for the citizenry will enact laws that do more than simply protect the child and community. Ideally, the juvenile justice system we adopt should allow sufficient flexibility to permit each case to be based upon the needs of the child; such a system would disallow treatment that fails to take into account the child's mental, physical, and moral development.

Nearly all states, as well as the federal government, provide for the pretrial detention of juveniles.[1] The language of these statutes is typically couched in terms of public safety and assurance that the juvenile will appear for trial. In 1984, the U.S. Supreme Court held that pretrial detention of juveniles is constitutionally permissible.[2] Although a number of Supreme Court decisions have extended constitutional safeguards to juveniles, the scope of this protection is not absolute.[3] Several legal scholars and commentators continue to criticize the underlying goals and assumptions of the juvenile justice system that allows preadjudicatory and predispositional detention of juveniles (pretrial detention).[4] After considering the specific legal status of pretrial detention, this chapter examines the issue in the broader context of the nature and goals of the juvenile justice system. This system's priorities are the individualized rehabilitation of juvenile delinquents and the preservation of the family unit; pretrial detention is often a useful tool in achieving these goals. Also, pretrial detention is an important way to protect society from juvenile offenders when these goals cannot be completely achieved.

The Law of Pretrial Detention

Bail-Bondsmen or Parents?

There is no requirement, under the U.S. Constitution, that juveniles be granted monetary bail or bond.[5] As a practical matter, the granting of monetary bail or bond would be a vain act, given that few juveniles would have the financial resources to post bail. The theory of bail in the adult criminal system is "that the threat of forfeiture of one's goods will be an effective deterrent to the temptation to break the conditions of one's release."[6] Bail is properly employed only "to release accused with assurance that he will return at trial."[7] In practice, the bail system is seriously flawed.

Release or Detention

Ohio statutes and the Ohio Rules of Juvenile Procedure provide prototypical and illustrative examples of pretrial detention practices. For example, section 2151.31 of the Ohio Revised Code Annotated provides in pertinent part:

> A child taken into custody shall not be confined in a place of juvenile detention or placed in shelter care prior to the implementation of the court's final order of disposition, unless his detention or shelter care is required *to protect the child from immediate or threatened physical or emotional harm, because the child may abscond or be removed from the jurisdiction of the court, because the child has no parents, guardian, or custodian or other person able to provide supervision and care for him and return him to the court when required, or because an order for placement of the child in detention or shelter care has been made by the court pursuant to this chapter.*[8]

Thus, Ohio statutes provide for pretrial detention under certain circumstances. Moreover, Rule 7 of the Ohio Rules of Juvenile Procedure prescribes standards for the detention of juveniles, requires detention hearings and rehearings, and mandates separation from adults in confinement:

> (A) Detention: standards. A child taken into custody shall not be placed in detention or shelter care prior to final disposition unless his detention or care is required to protect the person and property of others or those of the child, or the child may abscond or be removed from the jurisdiction of the court, or he has no parent, guardian, or custodian or other person able to provide supervision and care for him and return him to the court when required.

. . . .

(F) Detention hearing. When a child has been admitted to detention or shelter care, a detention hearing shall be held promptly, not later than seventy-two hours after the child is placed in detention or shelter care or the next court day, whichever is earlier, to determine whether detention or shelter care is required. . . .

. . . .

(G) Rehearing. Any decision relating to detention or shelter care may be reviewed at any time upon motion of any party. . . .

(H) Separation from adults. No child shall be placed in or committed to any prison, jail, lockup or any other place where he can come in contact or communication with any adult convicted of crime, under arrest or charged with crime.[9]

Typically, a judicial decision to detain juveniles accused of either acts of delinquency or status offenses is motivated by various factors, including: (1) a substantial risk to the community, in cases of offenders charged with dangerous offenses, (2) a perceived likelihood that the accused may flee from the court's jurisdiction, (3) the inability of a parent to control the behavior of the child, and (4) the absence of a parent or other appropriate person to accept custody during the pendency of the proceeding.

Pretrial detention of delinquents may occur in either a secure facility, such as a juvenile detention center, or a nonsecure setting, such as a group home or foster home; status offenders may be held only in a nonsecure setting. Whatever the place of detention, the holding of a child pending trial is a deprivation of liberty.

Childhood Was Not Abolished

The Constitution does not mandate elimination of all differences between the treatment of adults and juveniles.[10] Children are assumed to be subject to the control of their parents, and if parental control falters, the state must play its part as *parens patriae*. It is well established that the constitutional liberty interest of juveniles may, in appropriate circumstances, be subordinated to the state's *parens patriae* interest in preserving and promoting the welfare of juveniles.[11]

The U.S. Supreme Court has held that due process is applicable in juvenile proceedings. The Court stated wisely that the issue remaining "is to ascertain the precise impact of the due process requirement upon such proceedings."[12] Thus, certain basic constitutional protections enjoyed by adults accused of crimes also apply to juveniles.[13] However, the state has "a *parens patriae* interest in preserving and promoting the welfare of the child,"[14] which makes a juvenile proceeding fundamentally different from an adult criminal trial. Therefore, the U.S. Supreme Court has attempted to strike a balance: to respect the "informality" and "flexibility" that characterize juvenile proceedings[15] while ensuring that such proceedings comport with the "fundamental fairness" demanded by the due process clause.[16] Stated briefly, the law of the land constitutionally permits pretrial detention of an arrested juvenile upon certain findings.

The "legitimate and compelling state interest" in protecting the community from crime cannot be doubted.[17] Crime prevention is "a weighty social objective,"[18] and this interest persists undiluted in the juvenile context.[19] The harm suffered by the victim of a crime is not dependent upon the age of the perpetrator. And the harm to society generally may even be greater in this context, given the high rate of recidivism among juveniles.[20]

The interest of the juvenile in being free from institutional restraints, even for the brief time involved, is undoubtedly substantial.[21] But that interest must be tempered by the recognition that juveniles, unlike adults, are always under some form of custodial care.[22] Children, by definition, are assumed to lack the capacity to take care of themselves. The widespread use and judicial acceptance of preventive detention for juveniles confirm the substantial state interests involved. Every state, as well as the District of Columbia, permits preventive detention of juveniles accused of crime.[23]

Pretrial Detention in Broader Context

Parens patriae—the theoretical underpinning for state intervention in the lives of children, including pretrial detention—manifests itself in the continuing debate over the legitimate role of the juvenile court. In recent years, rapidly increasing levels of juvenile crime, neglect, and abuse have exacerbated this debate. Clearly, it is a debate that presents the fundamental issue of how we, as a society, should react to the needs of our children.

Some commentators have been critical of pretrial detention. Nevertheless, important as reforming the proceeding may be, there is deep concern that focusing our efforts exclusively on the juvenile court procedure will allow the crucial issue of how we care for our children to recede into the background once the court makes its recommendations.[24] Pretrial detention is but one aspect of the complicated workings of the juvenile court. The procedure should not be considered in isolation but in the context of the juvenile court's functions and ideals. Furthermore, pretrial detention should not be seen as a measure to which juvenile judges uncritically resort, but as a protective and necessary measure that juvenile judges employ because the juvenile court's primary goals—rehabilitation of the juvenile and preservation of the family—cannot always be adequately met.

Treatment or Punishment

From its inception the judicial process for juveniles was conceived of as a hybrid between the criminal justice system and the rehabilitative mental health process.[25] In theory, juveniles brought before a court of law were to be given benevolent adult supervision to reform their behavior.[26] While societal protection is a goal of both criminal and juvenile justice systems, the punishment inflicted upon adult criminals was deemed cruel and inappropriate for juvenile offenders.

The concept of rehabilitation is integral to this country's policy toward juveniles. Judge David Lionel Bazelon said: "[T]he law increasingly recognizes that every man has certain entitlements as a citizen. It is difficult to think what more basic entitlements there could be than a child's right to a fair start in life."[27] Another commentator noted, however, "If indeed this is a right, . . . then thousands of our children never experience full citizenship. The price we as a society pay for denying this right can be measured in one dimension by the constant increase in juvenile court caseloads and the mounting difficulty of finding adequate rehabilitative services."[28]

Original concepts of the juvenile court movement may now appear too unworkable, and perhaps even too naive, to provide substantive justice and adequate care.[29] Unfortunately, the growing body of decisions indicates that the principle of flexibility through benevolent discretion and sympathy has sometimes led to punitiveness, arbitrary decisions, and serious violations of fundamental rights.

While there have been efforts to improve the process, legislators have lost that early impetus to guarantee that juveniles be given the humanitarian care originally envisioned as the objective of the juvenile justice system.[30] Without coordinated efforts by legislatures and all aspects of juvenile reform, the courts will be unable unilaterally to transform statements of principle into reality. Quality care and an adequate judicial system for our children cannot be established independently of one another.[31] In response to legislative inaction, the courts have expanded the developing right to treatment of institutionalized juveniles.[32]

Recent case law has, in many important respects, converted the promise of treatment into a right to treatment.[33] There is a judicial consensus that, unless an adjudication of delinquency is followed by an actual rehabilitation-oriented disposition, the juvenile proceeding becomes nothing more than a criminal court for minors. Thus, court decisions have come to recognize that the concept of treatment is often employed as mere rhetoric, in a smokescreen attempt to place "dangerous" children well away from a threatened community. It is even possible that the real purpose of the juvenile and family courts in establishing a right to treatment for juveniles is to coerce legislatures, communities, and service agencies into providing adequate care for children whose needs are being so woefully neglected by our society.[34] Right to treatment can exist only when a comprehensive analysis is undertaken of the types of services suitable to the needs of the children and families who are coming before the court. Moreover, in order for the analysis to be more than an empty vessel, it must be followed by implementation and funding on the part of governmental agencies. Legislative action must provide the crucial initiative.[35]

In the meantime, the juvenile court judge, the agencies that serve the needs of children, and the community must understand the mission of the juvenile court. Its purposes encompass the legitimate goals of society on behalf of its children. These goals include ensuring that children are reared to become productive citizens, protected from abuse and neglect, educated,[36] and corrected and rehabilitated if they violate the law, and also that society be protected from their delinquent behavior.

The juvenile court system—judges, social workers, and others—strives to achieve these goals. In doing so, it is sometimes necessary to place the juvenile in a special setting. For example, foster care placement is often necessary to protect the child from abuse or neglect. Likewise, pretrial detention is often necessary to make possible and facilitate any rehabilitative treatment that may be available, and to protect society from further offenses.

Juveniles as Members of a Family

An equally important purpose of the juvenile justice system is to preserve and strengthen families so that they can rear their children without state interference. The family offers our best opportunity for providing care, control, supervision, and accountability for children on a day-to-day basis. As a society our first response on behalf of at-risk children should be to strengthen the family. Out-of-home care may be necessary in some cases, but it is overutilized as a solution to problems facing children and families.

Strengthening and empowering families is the most effective strategy for the juvenile justice system. Before a child is removed from the family, or as soon after removal as possible, the goals of an enlightened society are best promoted by preservation of the family. The family has the greatest incentive to maintain its integrity, but often lacks the skills or resources to accomplish the task. The state can and should provide support to strengthen the family and empower it to provide adequate care and control for its children. In those cases in which the danger to the child or to the community is great and the family is unable to provide the necessary care and control of the child, substitute care in constructive and sound rehabilitation facilities is necessary.

There must be resources to support and strengthen families; schools, community-based organizations, and rehabilitative services must be available to provide the necessary care, control, and nurturance on behalf of at-risk children. Resources must be sufficient to provide an effective response to the problems facing the children and families in the juvenile justice system, regardless of the label—"delinquent," "dependent," "status offender"—placed on the child. Without these resources the juvenile court is likely to become an "abysmal failure."[37]

Clearly, preservation of the family is not always possible. For an abused or neglected child, the goals of protection and family preservation may conflict. Maintaining or returning a child to the home in which abuse occurred involves obvious risks of further abuse. Likewise, for the delinquent, family preservation and societal protection may be in conflict.[38] Separation from the family in the form of pretrial detention is sometimes indispensable to societal protection, but it may also be the first step toward a rehabilitative process that may eventually lead to long-lasting family unity.

The existence of these tensions does not make the juvenile court's mission useless or hopeless. Instead, they are a constant reminder of the challenges facing the juvenile court system in dealing with the complex problems surrounding the rearing of children in our society.

Do We Need a "Gavel"?

No other societal institution has such awesome powers over the lives of youths as does the juvenile court. Juvenile and family court jurisdictions number over 3,000, with over 7,000 judges and referees and more than 100,000 support and administrative personnel. In 1991, these courts heard and disposed of nearly 1.5 million juvenile delinquency and "unruliness" proceedings, as well as more than 400,000 child abuse and neglect cases, reviewed an estimated 700,000 protective services orders, and determined the custody of over 3.0 million children.[39]

As a result of its prominent position in our society, the juvenile court has been the focus over the years of numerous and constantly varying legal, political, and sociological forces. The court's history has been marked by responses to these strong currents, as the juvenile court attempts to adjust its philosophy and operations to meet the changing needs of our society.[40]

In the midst of such frequent changes, the court has endeavored to fulfill its paramount responsibility of maintaining the delicate balance between serving the needs of troubled youth and serving the self-protective needs of an orderly society. By both design and default, the juvenile court has been placed in the position of discharging its legal responsibilities while serving as a primary vehicle in the delivery of social rehabilitative services to a large segment of our population.

The delivery of social rehabilitative services sometimes becomes almost academic and devoid of meaning to the juvenile judge on the bench confronted with the momentous decisions, affecting the lives of many people, that must be rendered each day. Often, as these families and youngsters pass before the judge, there is no time to debate the fine points of judicial or social philosophy. The judge only knows that the responsibilities to society and to that individual child must be discharged in the best way possible with whatever resources are made available by the community.[41]

Conclusion

The juvenile court is the best institution available for holding society responsible for raising its children to adulthood. The success of the juvenile court will depend, however, on society's desire to address the needs of its children and families.[42] We who work in the juvenile court system do our best to protect the weak and rehabilitate the delinquent. Harsh realities and our duty to protect society often make pretrial detention mandatory. When resorted to, however, pretrial detention must have as its backdrop the twin goals of rehabilitation and family preservation. In its undisputed *parens patriae* capacity, the juvenile court system has pretrial detention as one of its tools.

The questions of policy surrounding pretrial detention exist among many others that involve juveniles in this country. To address the problems encompassed by the jurisdiction of the juvenile court, we as a society will have to improve our commitment to our children and families.[43]

NOTES

1. *See* F. Bailey & H. Rothblatt, Handling Juvenile Delinquency Cases § 1:11 (1982).

2. *See* Schall v. Martin, 467 U.S. 253 (1984).

3. *See In re* Gault, 387 U.S. 1 (1967).

4. *See, e.g.,* Worrell, Pretrial Detention of Juveniles: Denial of Equal Protection Masked by the Parens Patriae Doctrine, 95 Yale L.J. 174 (1985).

5. *See* State *ex rel.* Peaks v. Allaman, 115 N.E.2d 849 (Ohio Ct. App. 1952). The Supreme Court has never addressed the question of whether juveniles are entitled to monetary bail; in McKeiver v. Pennsylvania, 403 U.S. 528 (1971), the Court rejected the notion that juveniles are entitled to all procedural rights guaranteed to adults charged with committing a crime.

6. Bandy v. United States, 81 S. Ct. 197, 197 (Douglas, Circuit Justice 1960).

7. D. Freed & P. Wald, Bail in the United States: 1964, at 105 (1964).

8. Ohio Rev. Code Ann. § 2151.31 (C) (Baldwin 1991)(emphasis added).

9. Ohio R. Juv. P. 7.

10. *See, e.g.,* McKeiver v. Pennsylvania, 403 U.S. 528 (1971) (no right to jury trial in juvenile proceeding).

11. *See* Schall v. Martin, 467 U.S. 253 (1984); Santosky v. Kramer, 455 U.S. 745, 766 (1982); State v. Gleason, 404 A.2d 573, 580 (Me. 1979); People *ex rel.* Wayburn v. Schupf, 350 N.E.2d 906, 910 (N.Y. 1976); Baker v. Smith, 477 S.W.2d 149, 150–51 (Ky. 1971).

12. *In re* Gault, 387 U.S. 1, 13–14 (1967).

13. *See id.* at 31–57 (notice of charges, right to counsel, privilege against self-incrimination, right to confrontation and cross-examination); *see also In re* Winship, 397 U.S. 358 (1970)(proof beyond a reasonable doubt); Breed v. Jones, 421 U.S. 519 (1975)(double jeopardy).

14. Santosky v. Kramer, 455 U.S. 745, 766 (1982).

15. *See In re* Winship, 397 U.S. at 366.

16. *See* Breed v. Jones, 421 U.S. 519, 531 (1975); *see also McKeiver,* 403 U.S. at 543 (plurality opinion).

17. *See, e.g.,* De Veau v. Braisted, 363 U.S. 144, 155 (1960); *see also* Terry v. Ohio, 392 U.S. 1, 22 (1968).

18. Brown v. Texas, 443 U.S. 47, 52 (1979).

19. *See In re* Gault, 387 U.S. at 20 n.26.

20. *Id.* at 22.

21. *See id.* at 27.

22. *See, e.g.,* Lehman v. Lycoming County Children's Servs. Agency, 458 U.S. 502, 510–11 (1982); *In re* Gault, 387 U.S. at 17.

23. *See* National Council of Juvenile and Family Court Judges, Directory and Manual (1964).

24. *See* Harris, Children's Lack of Political Voice Leaves Needs Unmet, L.A. Times, May 16, 1991, at A1 (summarizing the views of children's advocate Marian Wright Edelman and others).

25. *See* M. Moore, From Children to Citizens: The Mandate for Juvenile Justice (1987).

26. *See* J. Goldstein et al., Beyond the Best Interests of the Child (1973); Krisberg, The Politics of Juvenile Justice: Then and Now, 15 Law & Soc. Inquiry 893 (1990).

27. Bazelon, Racism, Classism, and the Juvenile Process, 53 Judicature 373, 378 (1970).

28. Rangel, Juvenile Justice: A Need to Reexamine Goals and Methods, 5 Cap. U. L. Rev. 149, 152 (1976).

29. *See, e.g.,* Lucas, Is Inadequate Funding Threatening Our System of Justice? 74 Judicature 292 (1991) (the author is the chief justice of the Supreme Court of California).

30. *See, e.g.,* Kent v. United States, 383 U.S. 541, 555 (1966) (decrying that "the child receives the worst of both worlds: that he gets neither the protection accorded to adults *nor the solicitous care and regenerative treatment postulated for children*")(emphasis added); Jackson v. Indiana, 406 U.S. 715, 738 (1972)("At the least, due process requires that the nature and duration of commitment bear some reasonable relation to the purpose for which the individual is committed").

In Nelson v. Heyne, 491 F.2d 352, 360 (7th Cir. 1974), the court held that juveniles incarcerated in a correctional institution "have a right under the Fourteenth Amendment due process clause to rehabilitative treatment." The court also noted:

> When a state assumes the place of a juvenile's parents, it assumes as well the parental duties, and its treatment of its juveniles should, so far as can be reasonably required, be what proper parental care would provide. Without a program of individual treatment the result may be that the juveniles will not be rehabilitated, but warehoused, and that at the termination of detention they will likely be incapable of taking their proper places in free society; their interests and those of the state and the school thereby being defeated.

Id.

31. *See* S. McCully, Why Not the Best of Both Worlds? The Permissible and the Desirable (presentation at the Utah Juvenile Court Workshop, Mar. 28, 1991) (speaker is a Utah juvenile court judge).

32. *See* Rangel, Juvenile Justice, *supra* note 28.

33. See Gladstone, Juvenile Justice: How to Make It Work, Miami Herald, June 3, 1990, at C1.

34. *See* Edna McConnell Clark Foundation, Making Reasonable Efforts: Steps for Keeping Families Together (1987).

35. *See* Academy for Contemporary Problems, Major Issues in Juvenile Justice Information and Training Project: Services to Children in Juvenile Courts, The Judicial Executive Controversy (1981).

36. *See* National Council of Juvenile and Family Court Judges, Deprived Children: A Judicial Response, 73 Recommendations, 37 Juv. & Fam. Ct. J. 3, 3 (1986).

37. Gelber, The Juvenile Justice System: Vision for the Future, 41 Juv. & Fam. Ct. J. 15, 15 (1990).

38. *See* Edwards, The Juvenile Court and the Role of the Juvenile Court Judge, 43 Juv. & Fam. Ct. J. 1 (1992).

39. *See* H. Snyder et al., Juvenile Court Statistics 1989 (published by U.S. Department of Justice) (1992).

40. Hearings before the Subcommittee on Juvenile Justice of the Senate Committee on the Judiciary, 102d Cong., 2d Sess. (1992) (statement of Gerald E. Radcliffe, trustee and chairman of the Governmental Relations Committee of the National Council of Juvenile and Family Court Judges).

41. *See generally* Bailey & Pyfer, Deprivation of Liberty and the Right to Treatment, 7 Clearinghouse Rev. 519 (1974); Blasko, Saving the Child: Rejuvenating a Dying Right to Rehabilitation, 11 New Eng. J. on Crim. & Civ. Confinement 123 (1985); Edwards, Specific Objectives for the Treatment of Juveniles, 35 Fed. Probation, Sept. 1971, at 26; Fox, Reform of Juvenile Justice: The Child's Right to Punishment, 25 Juv. Just., Aug. 1974, at 47; Gustaitis, Juvenile Offenders: Is Locking Them Up the Only Answer? 3 Cal. Law., Mar. 1982, at 24; Kapner, The Juvenile's Right to Treatment—The Next Step, 47 Fla. B.J. 228 (1973); Keenan & Hammond, The Institutionalized Child's Claim to Special Education: A Federal Codification of the Right to Treatment, 56 U. Det. J. Urb. L. 337 (1979); Levine, Disaffirmance of the Right to Treatment Doctrine: A New Juncture in Juvenile Justice, 41 U. Pitt. L. Rev. 159 (1980); Malmquist, Juvenile Detention: Right and Adequacy of Treatment Issues, 7 Law & Soc'y Rev. 159 (1972); McNulty & White, The Juvenile's Right to Treatment: Panacea or Pandora's Box? 16 Santa Clara L. Rev. 745 (1976); Pyfer, The Juvenile's Right to Receive Treatment, 6 Fam. L.Q. 279 (1972); Rangel, Juvenile Justice, *supra* note 28; Reaves, The Right to Treatment for Juvenile Offenders, 7 Cumb. L. Rev. 13 (1976); Renn, The Right to Treatment and the Juvenile, 19 Crime & Delinq. 477 (1973); Volenik, Right to Treatment: Case Developments in Juvenile Law, 3 Just. Sys. J. 292 (1978); Frisch, Note, Constitutional Right to Treatment for Juveniles Adjudicated to Be Delinquent—*Nelson v. Heyne*, 12 Am. Crim. L. Rev. 209 (1974); Klaber, Note, Persons in Need of Supervision: Is There a Constitutional Right to Treatment? 39 Brook. L. Rev. 624 (1973); Levidow, Note, Overdue Process for Juveniles: For the Retroactive Restoration of Constitutional Rights, 17 How. L.J. 402 (1972); Marshall, Comment, The Right to Treatment for Juveniles in Texas: A Legislative Proposal, 13 St. Mary's L.J. 142 (1981); Simpson, Comment, Rehabilitation as the Justification of a Separate Juvenile Justice System, 64 Cal. L. Rev. 984 (1976); Skemp, Note, Establishment of a Constitutional Right to Treatment for Delinquent Children, 26 Baylor L. Rev. 366 (1974); Sorg, Comment, Due Process for Juveniles Facing Strict-Security Confinement, 26 Syracuse L. Rev. 1017 (1975); Note, A Right to Treatment for Juveniles? 1973 Wash. U.L.Q. 157; Developments—Limits on Punishment and Entitlement to Rehabilitative Treatment of Institutionalized Juveniles: *Nelson v. Heyne*, 60 Va. L. Rev. 864 (1974); Note, The Supreme Court Sidesteps the Right to Treatment Question—*O'Connor v. Donaldson*, 47 U. Colo. L. Rev. 299 (1976).

42. Dugger, Care Ordered for Children in Abuse Case, N.Y. Times, May 29, 1991, at B5 ("I don't want children to survive, I want them to thrive")(quoting New York Family Court Judge Edward Kaufmann).

43. *See* National Commission on Children, Beyond Rhetoric: A New American Agenda for Children and Families (1991).

Capital Punishment

■ CHAPTER THIRTY-SEVEN

Perspectives on the Juvenile Death Penalty in the 1990s

Victor L. Streib

THE U.S. SUPREME COURT has recently decided a number of cases on the juvenile death penalty, leaving a changed constitutional landscape. This previously uncertain area of law now seems fairly settled, but the issues relating to criminology, politics, and "the right thing to do" remain vigorously contested. In this vein, the juvenile death penalty still raises most starkly the clash between criminal children and the punitive state.

To explore the dimensions of this issue in the 1990s requires information concerning both the relevant law and the actual practice. This chapter begins with the basic legal foundation, namely the requirements of the U.S. Constitution as expounded by the Supreme Court. Explored next is the practice of sentencing to death and actually executing juvenile offenders in the current era. Finally, given the context of law and practice, appropriate criteria are suggested for resolving this issue today.

U.S. Supreme Court Decisions, 1982–1992

Pre-1988

The Supreme Court toyed with the issue of the juvenile death penalty for several years before facing it squarely. In 1981 the Court considered a certiorari petition putting forward the specific issue of the constitutionality of capital punishment for an offense committed when the defendant was only sixteen years old.[1] When the Court decided *Eddings v. Oklahoma*[2] the following year, however, it sidestepped the direct constitutional issue, observing only that "the chronological age of a minor is itself a relevant mitigating factor of great weight."[3] A four-Justice dissent[4] would have reached the ultimate constitutional issue and would have rejected any constitutional bar to the execution of sixteen-year-olds.[5]

After *Eddings* in 1982, the Court continued to appear to be tempted by the issue but for several years did not grant certiorari on the question. *Burger v. Kemp*[6] was decided in 1987, a case in which the offender was only seventeen years old at the time of his crime but which did not directly raise the age issue. In his dissent, Justice Powell questioned the constitutionality of the death penalty for seventeen-year-olds and lamented the majority's unwillingness to wait for a decision squarely on this issue.[7] As *Kemp* was being decided, the Court had already granted certiorari in the case of a fifteen-year-old offender in *Thompson v. Oklahoma*.[8] It was to decide that case one year later.[9]

Thompson v. Oklahoma

In *Thompson*[10] the issue was couched as "whether the execution of [a death] sentence would violate the constitutional prohibition against the infliction of 'cruel and unusual punishments' because petitioner was only 15 years old at the time of his offense."[11] *Thompson* held that such an execution would be unconstitutional. The *Thompson* ruling resulted from a four-Justice plurality[12] to which Justice O'Connor added the crucial fifth vote on narrower grounds.[13] *Thompson* had three dissenters.[14]

Justice Stevens' *Thompson* plurality opinion began with the obligatory benchmark of consideration of the "'evolving standards of decency that mark the progress of a maturing society.'"[15] According to Justice Stevens, determining such standards required consideration of (1) current legislation on the acceptance or rejection of the death penalty for offenders younger than certain age limits, (2) jury willingness to impose death sentences on juveniles where authorized, and (3) views of informed organizations and other nations on the acceptability of the juvenile death penalty.[16]

The *Thompson* plurality noted that every state that had enacted a minimum age in its death penalty statute had chosen an age of at least sixteen.[17] The *Thompson* plurality included consideration of the many distinctions in other, non-death-penalty statutes pertaining to children, either denying them basic adult rights and privileges or granting them special children's rights and privileges.[18]

This opinion also considered the frequency of death sentences for and actual executions of juvenile offenders.[19] The *Thompson* plurality interpreted the extreme rarity of such sentences as evidence that they must be considered generally abhorrent by juries.[20] Finally, Justice Stevens based the plurality's conclusions in part on the rejection of the juvenile death penalty by almost all foreign nations and by many significant organizations, such as the American Law Institute and the American Bar Association.[21]

The *Thompson* plurality concluded that the Court is the ultimate arbiter of the limits of cruel and unusual punishment under the Eighth Amendment to the Constitution.[22] The Court measured the unique culpability of juveniles and the contribution of the juvenile death penalty to the acceptable social purposes of that penalty.[23] The *Thompson* plurality concluded that juveniles generally have less culpability for their misdeeds and have a significant capacity for growth.[24] These unique characteristics, when blended with society's fiduciary obligations to its children, led the plurality to conclude that retribution "is simply inapplicable to the execution of a 15-year-old offender."[25] The other major criminological purpose of the death penalty—general deterrence of other similarly minded, homicidal juveniles—was also discounted by the plurality as inconsistent with what is known about the manner in which adolescents contemplate and evaluate the consequences of their behavior.[26]

Since Wayne Thompson was only fifteen years old at the time of his crime, the Court had no compelling need to address the argument in his brief that age eighteen was the most logical point at which to draw the line.[27] Whatever might be the zenith of this constitutional age limitation, the *Thompson* plurality held that line was certainly no lower than age sixteen.[28]

The crucial fifth vote to reverse Wayne Thompson's death sentence was added to the *Thompson* plurality's four votes by Justice O'Connor's solitary concurring opinion.[29] In her *Thompson* concurrence, Justice O'Connor began with a survey of death penalty statutes and found that all express minimum ages were age sixteen or above.[30] While she went on to consider sentencing and execution statistics as well as treaties and other information,[31] in the end Justice O'Connor returned to the legislative issue and found that states such as Oklahoma apparently had not given the minimum-age issue the careful consideration it must receive.[32] Until they do, she would neither allow such states to execute offenders under age sixteen at the time of their crimes nor reach the broader question of the constitutionality of the juvenile death penalty.[33]

Justice Scalia's dissent in *Thompson* began with the unarguable premise that when first enacted the Eighth Amendment did not prohibit the death penalty for crimes committed by persons under age sixteen.[34] Scalia then turned to the conventional indicators of the evolving standards of decency and found no clear position from state legislative minimum-age standards.[35] The fact that actual sentences and executions of such offenders had been rare indicated to the dissent simply a community reluctance to impose such drastic measures, not a new constitutional standard.[36] Finally, the dissenters rejected the majority's principle that it is ultimately the Court's responsibility to determine whether a punishment is cruel and unusual instead of simply measuring the apparent societal standard.[37]

Stanford v. Kentucky

Stanford[38] was decided one year after *Thompson*. This decision dealt also with the death penalty for juvenile offenders but here the petitioners were aged sixteen and seventeen at the time of their crimes.[39] The *Stanford* plurality began with the premise that the death penalty for crimes committed by persons aged sixteen and seventeen was not prohibited by the Eighth Amendment when it was first adopted.[40] Only then did the analysis move to the "evolving standards of decency" to see if that original Eighth Amendment standard has "evolved."[41]

Justice Scalia's *Stanford* plurality agreed with Justice Stevens' *Thompson* plurality that any "evolution" must be manifested primarily in action by the various legislatures[42] and juries[43] facing the issue. It is in his *Stanford* plurality opinion that Justice Scalia expanded upon most of the points he had made in his *Thompson* dissent. This is particularly true in characterizing the legislation and jury sentences for offenders aged sixteen and seventeen in comparison to the issue of fifteen-year-olds in *Thompson*. Several states had express minimum ages of sixteen and seventeen for the death penalty in their statutes,[44] and Justice Scalia added those jurisdictions without any express minimum ages whatsoever on the premise that they meant to include juveniles of sixteen and seventeen.[45]

The practice of sentencing and executing offenders aged sixteen and seventeen clearly had not been as rare as the sentencing and execution of fifteen-year-olds.[46] As with his dissent in *Thompson*, Justice Scalia's plurality in *Stanford* interpreted such rarity as understandable prudence rather than a clear signal of an evolved standard of decency rejecting the practice.[47]

The primary thrust of the *Stanford* plurality opinion essentially ended there. Justice Scalia already had rejected the practices of other nations as irrelevant to the American societal standard[48] and next rejected the minimum ages of American statutes on non-capital-punishment issues as irrelevant to the individualized analysis uniquely required in capital punishment cases.[49] Justice Scalia ignored the positions of various professional and learned societies, suggesting that such views may be appropriate for legislative policy decisions but certainly not for Supreme Court constitutional determinations.[50]

The *Stanford* plurality rejected the principle that the Court should refer to its own sense of Eighth Amendment requirements, dismissing proportionality analyses based upon relative moral culpability and measurable contributions to acceptable goals of punishment.[51] Finding no societal consensus against the death penalty for offenders aged sixteen and seventeen, the opinion concluded that such punishment is not cruel and unusual under the Eighth Amendment.[52]

Justice O'Connor's *Stanford* concurrence began with a reminder that her *Thompson* concurrence required a specific, express minimum age in the pertinent death penalty statute before an eligible offender can be executed unless such execution is clearly not forbidden by a national consensus.[53] Justice O'Connor concluded, however, that the executions challenged in *Stanford* could proceed, since "it is sufficiently clear that no national consensus forbids the imposition of capital punishment on 16- or 17-year-old capital murderers."[54]

Justice Brennan's dissent in *Stanford*[55] tracked closely the analytical scheme of Justice Stevens' plurality opinion in *Thompson*. After finding the juvenile death penalty generally rejected by legislatures, juries, informed organizations, and other nations,[56] the *Stanford* dissent noted the lesser moral culpability of juveniles

TABLE 37.1
EXECUTIONS OF JUVENILE OFFENDERS, JANUARY 1, 1973–MARCH 1, 1992

Name	Date of Execution	Place of Execution	Race	Age at Crime	Age at Execution
Charles Rumbaugh	Sept. 11, 1985	Tex.	White	17	28
J. Terry Roach	Jan. 10, 1986	S.C.	White	17	25
Jay Pinkerton	May 15, 1986	Tex.	White	17	24
Dalton Prejean	May 18, 1990	La.	Black	17	30
Johnny Garrett	Feb. 11, 1992	Tex.	White	17	28

and the failure of the juvenile death penalty to make any measurable contribution to acceptable goals of punishment under the Eighth Amendment.[57] The four *Stanford* dissenters would have drawn the minimum-constitutional-age line at eighteen.[58]

Current Status

Since 1989 the Court has not taken any juvenile death penalty cases and shows no apparent interest in doing so. The effect of *Thompson* in combination with *Stanford* is to draw the constitutionally mandated minimum-age line for capital punishment at age sixteen. No state may go below that line unless its capital punishment statute includes an express provision to do so and reflects a clear legislative intent to permit such executions. No current state capital punishment statute has an express minimum age lower than sixteen, and no state legislature has attempted to lower the capital punishment age below sixteen. Absent the Court's revisiting this issue, sixteen will remain the minimum age for capital punishment permitted by the Constitution.

Juvenile Death Sentences and Executions

Executions

Executions for juvenile crimes have always been part of American capital punishment practice. Beginning in 1642, when sixteen-year-old Thomas Graunger was executed in Plymouth Colony, Massachusetts,[59] a total of 332 such juvenile executions have been documented.[60] In the current era, 1973–1992, only 5 of the 162 executions have been for juvenile crimes.[61] Table 37.1 lists these cases.

All five of these recent juvenile executions were of the oldest juvenile offenders, aged seventeen at the time of their crimes. No persons have been executed for crimes committed at age sixteen or younger since 1959.[62] Included as executed juvenile offenders are the three seventeen-year-olds in Texas, even though under Texas law an offender must be sixteen or younger to be in juvenile court.[63] Since seventeen is by far the most common maximum age for juvenile court nationally,[64] for consistency all seventeen-year-olds are included within this juvenile death penalty analysis regardless of any specific state's age provisions.

TABLE 37.2
EXECUTIONS AND DEATH SENTENCES OF JUVENILE OFFENDERS
BY CENSUS DIVISION AND REGION, JANUARY 1, 1973–MARCH 1, 1992

Census Divisions and Regions	Juvenile Death Sentences	Juvenile Death Sentence Reversal Rate (Rev/Sent)	Juvenile Death Sentence Execution Rate (Ex/Sent)	Juvenile Offenders Currently under Death Sentences
New England Div.	0	$0/0$	$0/0$	0
Mid-Atlantic Div.	6	$3/6$	$0/6$	3
NORTHEAST REGION	6	$3/6$	$0/6$	3
E. North Central Div.	9	$9/9$	$0/9$	0
W. North Central Div.	3	$1/3$	$0/3$	2
NORTH CENTRAL REGION	12	$10/12$	$0/12$	2
South Atlantic Div.	41	$30/41$	$1/41$	10
E. South Central Div.	18	$11/18$	$0/18$	7
W. South Central Div.	28	$14/28$	$4/48$	10
SOUTH REGION	87	$55/87$	$5/87$	27
Mountain Div.	3	$3/3$	$0/3$	0
Pacific Div.	1	$0/1$	$0/1$	1
WEST REGION	4	$3/4$	$0/4$	1
Totals	109	$71/109$	$5/109$	33

Although it is too early to be certain, a pattern may be emerging in these juvenile executions. In the mid-1980s, when the national execution rate for all offenders reached the now typical level of about twenty each year,[65] juvenile executions also began, with three occurring within nine months in 1985 and 1986. Then, when major constitutional challenges to juvenile executions were mounted, such executions ceased until the U.S. Supreme Court had decided *Thompson* in 1988 and *Stanford* in 1989. Less than a year after *Stanford* was decided, juvenile executions recommenced at a low but steady rate.

Three (60 percent) of the five juvenile executions during this period occurred in Texas, despite the fact that Texas law precludes offenders aged sixteen or younger from being given the death penalty. Of the 157 adult offenders executed during this same period, forty-two (27 percent) have been executed in Texas, by far the highest level in the nation, but a far lower level than that for juvenile executions.[66]

Recent Juvenile Death Sentences

In the current era, approximately 4,500 offenders have been sentenced to death, 109 (2.4 percent) of whom have been juvenile offenders.[67] As Table 37.2 indicates, these juvenile death sentences have been spread across the United

States, excepting only the New England census division. However, 87 (80 percent) of these juvenile death sentences have been concentrated in the South census region, with nearly half of those in the South Atlantic division of that region.

Of the 109 juvenile death sentences imposed by trial courts during this nearly twenty-year period, only five sentences have resulted in actual execution of the offender (see Table 37.1). Two-thirds of the sentences (71/109) have already been reversed, a portion that will rise even higher as the more recent juvenile death sentences make their way through the appellate and postconviction processes.

As a result of these 109 sentences, 71 reversals, and 5 executions, 33 persons remain under sentences of death for juvenile crimes. While located in every census region, 82 percent (27/33) are in the South region. Given past experience, it can be assumed that a high proportion of these 33 juveniles will have their sentences reversed, although probably not as high as the two-thirds reversal rate of the past twenty years.

Table 37.3 lists the ten states in which recent juvenile death sentences have been most common and compares the states' total juvenile executions with these recent sentences. The top ten states listed account for 82 percent (89/109) of all recent juvenile sentences, but only 48 percent (160/332) of all juvenile executions. This suggests that the practice of sentencing juvenile offenders to death is now much more concentrated among a relatively few states, at least as compared with the much more widespread practice of executing juvenile offenders over the last several centuries.

Six of the top ten states in recent sentencing are also in the top ten in total juvenile executions, suggesting fairly consistent policies over three and a half centuries. Other states, particularly Pennsylvania and Oklahoma, are among the leaders in recent juvenile death sentences but have comparatively few actual juvenile executions. Questions arise as to what might have prompted these apparent changes in state practices.

Appropriate Criteria for Legislative Decisions

The juvenile death penalty issue is now in the legislative arena. *Thompson* and *Stanford* have constitutionally mandated a minimum age of sixteen for the death penalty, but selection of any age higher than sixteen has been left to legislatures. It is theoretically possible, given Justice O'Connor's concurrence in *Thompson*,[68] for a legislature to enact a constitutionally acceptable minimum age lower than sixteen, but none has shown any inclination to try to do so. In essence the Court's foray into this area has channeled the jurisprudential controversy over the juvenile death penalty into a narrow, line-drawing debate concerning the ages sixteen, seventeen, and eighteen.

What criteria should a legislative body consider when engaged in this debate? In addition to the constitutional and other legal issues described above, any legis-

TABLE 37.3
TEN STATES WITH THE MOST JUVENILE DEATH SENTENCES,
JANUARY 1, 1973–MARCH 1, 1992, COMPARED WITH
TOTAL JUVENILE EXECUTIONS SINCE 1642

State	Juvenile Death Sentences, 1973–1992		Juvenile Executions since 1642	
	Rank	Number	Rank	Number
Florida	1	20	10	14
Texas	2	15	5	18
Georgia	3	10	1	46
Alabama	4	9	8	15
Louisiana	5	7	13	11
Mississippi	5	7	14	10
Ohio	7	6	4	19
North Carolina	8	5	3	20
Pennsylvania	8	5	20	5
Oklahoma	8	5	25	2
Totals		89		160

lative body should consider a wide range of criminological, jurisprudential, and political factors in deliberations concerning the minimum-age issue. Following is a brief sketch of factors that might militate toward an age higher than the absolute minimum age required by the Constitution.

1. The punishment of capital crimes must consider in part the harm inflicted but must also evaluate the criminal intent involved.[69] While adolescents can intend an action, it is unlikely that they have thought about it deeply with insight and understanding and thus seldom would have this criminal intent to the fullest extent.

2. Even the extreme retributive feelings generated by heinous homicides may be blunted somewhat by the knowledge that children cannot be expected to behave as adults all of the time. Nonetheless, the strong need for retribution may be satisfied by long-term imprisonment.

3. Deterrence of homicide by juveniles may not be enhanced by choosing the death penalty.[70] The alternative of long-term imprisonment may be a punishment more feared by adolescents.

4. The goals of reform and rehabilitation for juvenile offenders should not be ignored. Behavior patterns change significantly as persons mature from adolescence to adulthood and into middle age, and long-term imprisonment holds out the possibility of a destructive teenager's becoming an acceptable adult at some time in the future.

5. Given the reluctance of juries and judges to impose juvenile death sentences and the high reversal rate once a juvenile death sentence is imposed at trial, juvenile death penalty systems produce very few executions for the amount of public money, time, and energy invested. The resulting cost of several million

dollars per juvenile execution might be better used for other criminal and juvenile justice needs.[71]

6. If we are attempting to "send a message" to teenagers through the juvenile death penalty, we should remember that young people often are more influenced by what role models do than by what they say. Stern lectures from government officials on the evil of killing people (murder) may ring hollow when those same government officials undertake to kill people through execution. Perhaps like smoking, abusing alcohol, shunning seatbelts, and other unrecommended adult habits, killing people may be seen as just another exclusively adult prerogative unfairly denied teenagers striving for adult accoutrements.

7. Although a variety of ages from sixteen to twenty-one commonly are used in law to separate children from adults, by far the most common age line is eighteen. If persons under age eighteen are considered legally unable to think in an adult manner to vote, drink, marry, or buy a car, is it likely that they are able to think in an adult manner in life-or-death situations?

8. Abolition of the death penalty for juveniles may be a common ground on which death penalty proponents and opponents can meet and agree. If there is consensus on this specific issue, avenues of dialogue and understanding may be explored for constructive discussion of the death penalty for adults and the appropriate application of criminal punishment in general.

If we put behind us the death penalty for juveniles, what can be done about violent juvenile crime? Two answers to this problem suggest themselves. The temporary solution is to impose long-term prison sentences on such violent juveniles, probably with minimum terms of twenty to twenty-five years. This would ensure that they are reasonably mature adults and have been subjected to whatever rehabilitative programs are available before they would ever be eligible for parole. As stated above, long sentences would satisfy society's need for retribution and would possibly have some deterrent value.

The long-term solution to violent juvenile crime, or all crime for that matter, is unlikely to come from extreme criminal punishment, whether imprisonment or death. Instead of seeking to eradicate violent crime by imposing violent punishment, we must be willing to devote enormous resources to the search for the causes of violent juvenile crime. Despite the pronounced need for investment of governmental resources in such research, such resources have almost totally disappeared in the past twenty years. From a sophisticated understanding of those causes can come a rational search for cures. Allegiance to such a scientific method may well reject the juvenile death penalty as belonging to the dark ages of criminal justice.

NOTES

1. *See* Eddings v. Oklahoma, 450 U.S. 1040 (1981) (granting certiorari in Eddings v. State, 616 P.2d 1159 (Okla. Crim. App. 1980), *rev'd*, 455 U.S. 104 (1982)).
2. 455 U.S. 104 (1982).
3. *Id.* at 116.

4. *Id.* at 120. The dissent was written by Chief Justice Burger and joined by Justice White, Justice Blackmun, and Justice Rehnquist.

5. *See id.* at 128.

6. 483 U.S. 776 (1987).

7. *See id.* at 822 n.4, 823 n.5 (Powell, J., dissenting).

8. Thompson v. Oklahoma, 479 U.S. 1084 (1987) (granting certiorari in Thompson v. State, 724 P.2d 780 (Okla. Crim. App. 1986), *vacated and remanded,* Thompson v. Oklahoma, 487 U.S. 815 (1988)).

9. Thompson v. Oklahoma, 487 U.S. 815 (1988).

10. *Id.*

11. *Id.* at 818–19 (Stevens, J., plurality opinion) (footnote omitted).

12. *See id.* at 818 (Stevens, J., plurality opinion).

13. *See id.* at 848 (O'Connor, J., concurring).

14. *See id.* at 859. The dissent was written by Justice Scalia and joined by Chief Justice Rehnquist and Justice White.

15. *Id.* at 821 (quoting Trop v. Dulles, 356 U.S. 86, 101 (1958) (Warren, C.J., plurality opinion)).

16. *See id.* at 821–22 (Stevens, J., plurality opinion). These factors are discussed in detail in Vanore, Note, The Decency of Capital Punishment for Minors: Contemporary Standards and the Dignity of Juveniles, 61 Ind. L.J. 757 (1986).

17. *See id.* at 829.

18. *See id.* at 823–25.

19. *See id.* at 831–33.

20. *See id.* at 832.

21. *See id.* at 830.

22. *See id.* at 833.

23. *See id.*

24. *See id.* at 833–37.

25. *Id.* at 837.

26. *See id.* at 837–38.

27. *See id.* at 838; Petitioner's Brief at 22–24, 46–49, Thompson v. Oklahoma, 487 U.S. 815 (1988) (No. 86-6169).

28. *Thompson,* 487 U.S. at 838 (Stevens, J., plurality opinion).

29. *See id.* at 848 (O'Connor, J., concurring).

30. *See id.* at 849.

31. *See id.* at 851–55.

32. *See id.* at 857.

33. *See id.* at 857–58.

34. *See id.* at 864 (Scalia, J., dissenting).

35. *See id.* at 868.

36. *See id.* at 869–70.

37. *See id.* at 873.

38. 492 U.S. 361 (1989). The *Stanford* ruling also applied to its companion case, Wilkins v. Missouri. *See id.*

39. *See* Stanford v. Kentucky, 492 U.S. 361, 365–68 (Scalia, J., plurality opinion).

40. *See id.* at 368.

41. *See id.* at 369.

42. *See id.* at 370–73.

43. *See id.* at 373–74.

44. *See id.* at 370.

45. *See id.* at 370–72.

46. *See id.* at 373–74.

47. *See id.*

48. *See id.* at 369 n.1.

49. *See id.* at 374–77.

50. *See id.* at 378.

51. *See id.* at 379.

52. *Id.* at 380.

53. *Id.* at 380–81 (O'Connor, J., concurring).

54. *Id.* at 381.

55. *See id.* at 382 (Brennan, J., dissenting).

56. *See id.* at 384–90.

57. *See id.* at 390–405.

58. *See id.* at 405.

59. *See* V. Streib, Death Penalty for Juveniles 73 (1987).

60. *See* W. Espy, List of Confirmations, State-by-State, of Legal Executions as of March 2, 1992, at 2 (unpublished report available from the Capital Punishment Research Project, 100 East Main Street, Headland, Ala. 36345) (on file with author).

61. *See* NAACP Legal Defense and Educational Fund, Death Row, U.S.A. 1, 5–8 (Winter 1991) (available from NAACP National Office, Suite 1600, 99 Hudson Street, New York, N.Y. 10013) [hereinafter Death Row].

62. *See* Streib, Death Penalty, *supra* note 59, at 118–19.

63. Tex. Penal Code Ann. § 8.07(d) (West Supp. 1992).

64. *See* S. Davis, Rights of Juveniles: The Juvenile Justice System § 2.1, at 2–2 (2d ed. 1980 & Supp. 1991).

65. *See* Death Row, *supra* note 61, at 4.

66. *See* Texas Executes Convicted Slayer, N.Y. Times, Mar. 4, 1992, at A8; Texas Inmate Executed for Killing 2 in 1987, N.Y. Times, Feb. 29, 1992, at 7.

67. V. Streib, The Juvenile Death Penalty: Present Death Row Inmates under Juvenile Death Sentences and Executions for Juvenile Crimes, January 1, 1973, to December 31, 1991, at 3, 5–8 (Jan. 17, 1992) (unpublished report available from author).

68. Thompson v. Oklahoma, 487 U.S. 815, 848–59 (O'Connor, J., concurring).

69. *See* Tison v. Arizona, 481 U.S. 137 (1987); Enmund v. Florida, 458 U.S. 782 (1982).

70. *See, e.g.,* Stanford v. Kentucky, 492 U.S. 361, 404–405 (Brennan, J., dissenting).

71. Several recent studies have found the cost per execution of a death penalty system to be many times the cost of incarcerating a prisoner for life. *See, e.g.,* Nakell, The Cost of the Death Penalty, 14 Crim. L. Bull. 69, 76–77 (1978); Spangenberg & Walsh, Capital Punishment or Life Imprisonment? Some Cost Considerations, 23 Loy. L.A. L. Rev. 45, 47–57 (1989); Tabak & Lane, The Execution of Injustice: A Cost and Lack-of-Benefit Analysis of the Death Penalty, 23 Loy. L.A. L. Rev. 59, 135–36 (1989); Garey, Comment, The Cost of Taking a Life: Dollars and Sense of the Death Penalty, 18 U.C. Davis L. Rev. 1221, 1245–70 (1985).

CHAPTER THIRTY-EIGHT

On the Death Penalty for Juveniles

Joseph L. Hoffmann

IN THE PAST few years, the U.S. Supreme Court decided three important cases regarding the constitutionality of the death penalty for juveniles under the Eighth Amendment. These decisions make up the current constitutional framework within which the issue of capital punishment for juvenile killers must be addressed. This chapter will start by reviewing the state of the law on the juvenile death penalty. It will then argue that one's view of the juvenile death penalty depends on one's concept of what a juvenile can do or should be expected to do. It will conclude that the juvenile death penalty should be a matter of policy, not of constitutionality.[1]

The View from the Supreme Court

In 1988, in *Thompson v. Oklahoma*,[2] a fragmented Court struck down the death sentence that had been imposed against the defendant, who was only fifteen when he and three accomplices brutally murdered his former brother-in-law. In *Thompson*, a plurality of four Justices found the death penalty to be a disproportionately severe punishment for a fifteen-year-old killer. Justice Stevens, writing for the plurality, presented evidence of a growing societal consensus against executing fifteen-year-olds, and added his own personal view that such punishment was too severe: "Given the lesser culpability of the juvenile offender, the teenager's capacity for growth, and society's fiduciary obligations to its children, [the retributive justification for punishment] is simply inapplicable to the execution of a 15-year-old offender."[3]

Justice O'Connor provided the fifth vote for reversal of Thompson's death sentence, but she did not join Justice Stevens' opinion. Instead, she based her decision on the fact that Oklahoma had not enacted a statute specifically making fifteen-year-olds eligible for the death penalty; the age of fifteen simply fell within the range of ages that qualified for potential treatment as an adult in criminal cases. This, according to Justice O'Connor, created "considerable risk that the Oklahoma Legislature either did not realize that its actions would have the effect of rendering 15-year-old defendants death eligible or did not give the question the serious consideration that would have been reflected in the explicit choice of some minimum age for death eligibility."[4]

Justice Scalia, joined by Chief Justice Rehnquist and Justice White, dissented, arguing that societal trends pointed in the direction of *lowering*, not raising, the age of criminal responsibility, and that the Court should not overrule society solely on the basis of its own views about proportionality of punishment.[5] Justice Kennedy, the ninth member of the Court, took no part in the *Thompson* decision.

In 1989, in *Stanford v. Kentucky* and *Wilkins v. Missouri*,[6] the Supreme Court upheld death sentences imposed against sixteen-year-old and seventeen-year-old murderers. As in *Thompson*, the Court was badly divided. In *Stanford* and *Wilkins*, Justice Scalia wrote an opinion that was joined in part by four other Justices and in part by only three others.[7] In the majority portion of his opinion, Justice Scalia concluded that society had not rejected the death penalty for those who kill at the ages of sixteen and seventeen. In the plurality portion of his opinion, he restated his *Thompson* position that the Court has no business evaluating a particular punishment solely on the basis of its own views about proportionality.

Justice O'Connor refused to join the proportionality part of Justice Scalia's opinion in *Stanford*, and wrote separately to reiterate her view that the Court must exercise independent moral judgment under the proportionality prong of Eighth Amendment doctrine. Because she felt that proportionality analysis was not helpful in assessing the validity of the death penalty for defendants as diverse as sixteen-year-old and seventeen-year-old juvenile killers, however, she agreed with Justice Scalia that the death sentences in *Stanford* and *Wilkins* should be upheld.[8]

Justices Brennan, Marshall, Blackmun, and Stevens dissented, citing "strong indications"[9] that society *had* rejected the death penalty for all killers under age eighteen, and finding such punishment to be disproportionately severe as well.

Although no single rationale emerged from the *Thompson*, *Stanford*, and *Wilkins* cases, the Supreme Court in the three cases effectively ruled that the death penalty for juveniles violated the Eighth Amendment only when applied to a killer who had not yet reached the age of sixteen at the time of the crime. The decisions may have ended (at least for now) the constitutional debate, but they certainly did not end the controversy that surrounds the death penalty for juveniles. As the number of violent crimes attributed to juveniles has continued its alarming rise,[10] the public demand for tougher adult-type punishments—including, but not limited to, the death penalty—has also increased.[11] Yet, since 1989, a number of legislatures have revisited the juvenile death penalty issue, and most of those legislatures have *raised* the minimum age for the death penalty.[12]

The continuing existence of controversy over the death penalty for juveniles helps to explain why the Supreme Court, despite the arguments made by others to the contrary, properly declined to fix a constitutional age limit for capital punishment at eighteen. In construing the Eighth Amendment, the Court is necessarily constrained by what a societal consensus believes to be "just" or "moral." The Eighth Amendment, after all, bars only "cruel and unusual" punishments.[13] If one defines "cruel and unusual" punishment in terms of society's "evolving standards of decency,"[14] then one is clearly asking whether *society* believes the punishment to be "cruel and unusual." But even if one asks, instead, whether the punishment is "disproportionate" or "excessive" under a "dignity of man" principle,[15] the essential inquiry remains the same: It is virtually impossible to define such words as "disproportionate" or "excessive" except by reference to what *society* believes about the seriousness of particular crimes, or about the relative severity of particular punishments.[16]

Of course, the mere fact that many states have authorized the death penalty for juveniles by means of legislative enactments, and that the citizens of those states have chosen to impose the death penalty in individual cases involving juvenile killers (through sentencing verdicts rendered by a jury or judge ostensibly representing the larger community), cannot completely resolve the Eighth Amendment question. It is possible, after all, for a legislature, judge, or jury to be out of step with society's moral values. But the existence of such evidence places a "heavy burden"[17] upon those who contend that such death sentences violate society's norms.

The Eighth Amendment has rarely been invoked by the Supreme Court to invalidate legislatively authorized punishments, even when society's moral rejection of the challenged punishment has seemed clear. And history reveals that the Court quickly finds itself on extremely shaky ground when it reaches out to strike down a punishment in the face of mixed societal signals concerning the punishment at issue. Perhaps the best example of this is the Court's 1972 decision in *Furman v. Georgia*,[18] striking down the then existing death penalty statutes on Eighth Amendment grounds. In *Furman*, two Justices (Justice Brennan and Justice Marshall) found the death penalty to be "cruel and unusual" under all circumstances, but neither could point to a clear societal consensus in support of their respective positions. Justice Brennan argued that society was *moving* toward rejection of the death penalty, even if it had not yet reached that conclusion.[19] Justice Marshall argued that society *would* reject the death penalty, if it only knew enough about the administration of capital punishment.[20] The remaining Justices who joined with Justice Brennan and Justice Marshall to strike down the statutes relied on procedural objections, implicitly suggesting that the death penalty could be constitutionally valid if it were administered differently.[21] Constructed on a shaky foundation, *Furman* proved to be an unusually short-lived decision. Between 1972 and 1976, almost two-thirds of the states reenacted their death penalty statutes, hoping to satisfy the procedural objections identified in *Furman*. And in 1976, the Court overruled *Furman* by a 7–2 vote, with only Justices Brennan and Marshall dissenting.[22]

With respect to the death penalty for juveniles, the Court has tried to "hedge its bet" as much as possible. Thus, in *Thompson v. Oklahoma*,[23] Justice O'Connor, speaking only for herself but providing the crucial fifth vote to invalidate the sentence, did not rule out a legislative rebuttal. Instead, she seemed to leave open the possibility that a legislature might give "serious consideration"[24] to the question and adopt a constitutionally valid death penalty statute applicable to fifteen-year-old killers; however, such tentative legislative authority remains untested.

Justice O'Connor's attempt to "remand" the juvenile death penalty issue to state legislatures for reconsideration provoked a sharp dissent from Justice Scalia, who noted that Justice O'Connor had turned the usual judicial deference toward elected legislatures on its head. Nonetheless, Justice O'Connor's view, albeit highly unusual, serves the salutary purpose of allowing the Court to "test" the views of society before imposing a blanket Eighth Amendment ban that might not comport with evolving, and conflicting, societal values.

Justice Brennan, who would have invalidated the death penalty for juveniles in *Stanford*, did not want to leave the matter to state legislatures at all. He therefore turned to sources outside American society for support. For example, Justice Brennan cited the fact that more than fifty nations from around the world have formally abolished the death penalty, or have severely limited its use; moreover, 65 nations that retain the death penalty prohibit its imposition against juveniles. According to Justice Brennan, only Pakistan, Bangladesh, Rwanda, and Barbados, in addition to the United States, have executed a juvenile offender since 1979.[25] By these citations, Justice Brennan hoped to broaden the scope of the relevant "society" for purposes of the Eighth Amendment; he seemed to be saying that, even if *American* society has not yet reached the point of clearly rejecting the death penalty for juveniles, maybe *world* society (or at least the "civilized" world) has.

The Juvenile Death Penalty as a Matter of Policy

The main problem of discussing, or of thinking about, the issue of capital punishment for juveniles is that we do not have a single, shared concept in mind when we use the term "juvenile." In the case of juveniles who commit serious, violent crimes, it seems that there are two competing prototypes, each reflected in the popular culture.

One image is that of James Dean in the movie *Rebel without a Cause*—a sensitive, mixed-up kid who gets in trouble because of his inability to control his emotions, and who often acts before thinking about the consequences of his actions, but who is basically good at heart. Thus, in *Stanford*, Justice Brennan describes juveniles as "'more vulnerable, more impulsive, and less self-disciplined than adults,' "[26] "particularly impressionable and subject to peer pressure."[27] He refers to killers like the defendants as "delinquent juveniles."[28]

The other image is that of the gang members who threaten Kevin Kline and Danny Glover in the movie *Grand Canyon*—tough, street-wise, inner-city man-children (in the minds of white people usually, although not always, seen as black), who are, for whatever reason, without conscience or remorse and therefore highly capable of committing senseless acts of violence. This is the image conjured up by Justice Scalia's vivid descriptions of the crimes committed by the defendants in *Stanford* and *Wilkins*. For example, Stanford shot his victim, a kidnapped female gas-station attendant, "point-blank in the face and then in the back of her head"; he "started laughing"[29] after telling the story of the murder to a corrections officer. Wilkins, in turn, stabbed a female convenience-store clerk eight times as she begged for her life, leaving her to die on the floor of the store; he had previously committed burglary, theft, and arson, and had tried to kill his mother by putting insecticide into Tylenol capsules.[30]

Of course, in the real world, juvenile murderers may not be very much like either movie prototype, but that is precisely the point: Juveniles are, in all ways except chronological age, impossible to categorize with any kind of certainty. Juveniles are as unique as any other group of people, and only by reducing the category of juveniles to the "average juvenile," or to a "prototypical juvenile," can they be seen as homogeneous.

Even if juveniles shared many of the same characteristics, that would not necessarily lead to the conclusion that they all must be spared the death penalty. Moral culpability or responsibility is not a trait that can be determined in a scientific or pseudo-scientific manner. Rather, it is a normative judgment, based in part on what actually "caused" the defendant's actions, and in part on what society believes *should* have been allowed to "cause" the defendant's actions.

The ultimate question, for purposes of moral culpability, is not whether the particular defendant *is*, or *is not*, responsible for his or her actions in some factual or scientific sense; rather, the ultimate question is whether society believes that the defendant *should be* held responsible for his or her actions, regardless of whatever influences or pressures may have weighed upon the defendant at the time.

Take, for instance, the infamous case of Jeffrey Dahmer. The sole issue in Dahmer's case was whether the defendant should be held morally responsible for the torture, murder, and mutilation of numerous young men and boys in Milwaukee over a period of several years, which Dahmer admitted that he did.[31] Dahmer certainly suffered from severe mental disturbances, which no doubt influenced (or "caused") his bizarre behavior. But the questions posed to the Dahmer jury—namely, whether despite his mental illness, Dahmer knew right from wrong and could control his actions—could not be answered in any scientific or pseudo-scientific manner. These questions required the jury to determine the moral significance of *whatever* degree of awareness and self-control Dahmer actually had.

In a similar way, the juvenile death penalty cases are more about what we think a juvenile defendant *ought* to be able to do to conform his or her conduct to the norms of society, in light of the characteristics of the particular defendant involved, than they are about what the defendant can actually do. Who can say, as a factual matter, whether a particular defendant (juvenile or adult) commits murder because he is evil, or because he is the product of a broken home, a failed support system, or a corrupt and uncaring society? Perhaps all are true.

Nevertheless, we still must make moral judgments in these cases, and we inevitably manage to do so. If there can be any certainty about the legitimacy of such moral judgments, it is provided by the fact that most members of society share similar moral values, and can thus often agree about how to resolve such cases. When society cannot agree to treat a particular category of cases in a particular way (as is the case with juvenile killers and the death penalty), it means that society believes there are morally significant differences among the cases in that category and, therefore, the differences take on moral significance.

Why, then, does society make so many other legal decisions on the basis of youth, treating all juveniles alike for purposes of voting, drinking, driving, and serving in the military? Some critics argue that these age limits reflect society's view that juveniles are less morally responsible, as a class, than adults. This ostensibly supports the conclusion that the death penalty for juveniles is unconstitutional.

What these critics overlook is that, in these instances, chronological age is used as a "proxy" for other, more directly relevant characteristics such as maturity, responsibility, and experience. For example, the reason seventeen-year-olds are barred from voting is *not* that *all* seventeen-year-olds would be incapable of voting wisely and responsibly; surely there are some seventeen-year-olds who would make much better voters than many so-called adults. Rather, the problem is that *some* (or many or most) seventeen-year-olds are not ready to vote, and we simply cannot, or will not, spend the enormous amounts of time and money that would be needed to separate the ones who should vote from the ones who should not. We use chronological age (in this instance, age eighteen) as a "proxy" for what *really* counts, and we are willing to tolerate the resulting errors.

In other words, our use of (essentially arbitrary) age limits for voting, drinking, driving, and military service does *not* reflect the existence of societal consensus about the degree of responsibility attributable to all juveniles. Sixteen-year-olds and seventeen-year-olds cannot be categorized and labeled that easily. Rather, such age limits are the result of a simple cost–benefit analysis: Given the particular context, including the importance of the particular legal right at stake, is it worth the time and trouble that would be required to resolve each juvenile's eligibility on an individual case by case basis? Or should we settle for a rough approximation of the correct outcome, by using chronological age as a "proxy"?

The use of age limits in other contexts thus cannot provide a foundation for the constitutional attack on the juvenile death penalty. Each context is different.

In the context of the criminal law generally, and the death penalty in particular, an individualized determination of guilt and moral responsibility—that is, the criminal trial—is already required. Moreover, the matters to be determined at such a trial are far more important, to both the defendant and society, than the question whether an individual seventeen-year-old should be allowed to vote, drink, or drive. Thus, for constitutional purposes, there can be no persuasive argument by analogy based on the use of chronological age as a "proxy" in other contexts—even if we are unwilling to make individualized determinations of a juvenile's eligibility for voting, drinking, or driving, we might be willing to bear the high costs of making such an individualized determination of a juvenile's moral responsibility for a capital crime.

And, then again, we might not. Because critics of the juvenile death penalty do not claim that *all* juveniles are morally irresponsible and thus ineligible for the death penalty, it is irrelevant to the Eighth Amendment issue that the Court faced in *Thompson, Stanford,* and *Wilkins.* But it is highly relevant to the ongoing policy debate over the juvenile death penalty. The argument, rephrased in policy terms, is as follows: Although we prefer individualized determinations of moral responsibility in death penalty cases, our juries and judges are not very good at making such determinations. Moreover, given the severity and irrevocability of the death penalty, we should be unwilling (on both policy and constitutional grounds) to tolerate any significant risk of error in making such determinations. But even if the risk of error can be reduced to an insignificant level (as it probably can) by the use of more elaborate procedures (e.g., expanded hearings on whether to try the juvenile defendant as an adult), such procedures would likely be so costly, and would turn up such a small number of death-eligible juvenile killers, that as a matter of policy we should choose not to incur them. In short, even if we can implement a constitutionally valid juvenile death penalty (which we probably can), it would cost too much to do so.

This argument, which is not often made, might well persuade a state legislature to abolish the juvenile death penalty. Death penalty cases are always time-consuming and costly, even without the added complication of a juvenile defendant. Society might be better served by concentrating its limited prosecutorial resources on cases that are more likely to lead to a proper death sentence. If so, the state legislatures seem to be the appropriate place to resolve this issue.

As death penalty critics seem to suggest, maybe we will ultimately feel better about ourselves, as parents and as morally responsible adult members of society, if we make the symbolic gesture of sparing juveniles the death penalty. If we are to do so, however, we should do so through our elected legislatures, not by compulsion at the hands of the Court. In addition, if we choose to do so, we should recognize that we do so not because the death penalty is necessarily immoral as applied to all juveniles (and, hence, not because the juvenile death penalty violates the Eighth Amendment), but because there might be other good reasons to abolish it. On the other hand, the problem of juvenile violent crime is doubtless severe, and the death penalty, in particular cases involving juvenile defendants, may be morally appropriate. In the end, the juvenile death penalty becomes largely a matter of policy, not of constitutionality.

NOTES

Acknowledgments: I would like to thank Craig Bradley, Dick Fraher, Victor Streib, Bill Stuntz, and Scott Sundby for helping me develop and refine the views expressed in this chapter. I remain solely responsible, however, for those views, as well as for any errors contained in the chapter.

1. For a criticism of the juvenile death penalty based on a constitutional analysis, see Vanore, Note, The Decency of Capital Punishment for Minors: Contemporary Standards and the Dignity of Juveniles, 61 Ind. L.J. 757 (1986).

2. 487 U.S. 815 (1988).

3. *Id.* at 836–37 (Stevens, J., plurality opinion).

4. *Id.* at 857 (O'Connor, J., concurring).

5. *See id.* at 865–74 (Scalia, J., dissenting).

6. 492 U.S. 361 (1989). The cases were consolidated for decision.

7. *See id.* at 368–80.

8. *See id.* at 380–82 (O'Connor, J., concurring).

9. *Id.* at 405 (Brennan, J., dissenting).

10. In *Thompson v. Oklahoma*, 487 U.S. 815 (1988), Justice Stevens cites statistics from the Uniform Crime Reports showing that from 1982 through 1986, 1,861 juveniles under the age of sixteen were arrested for some kind of willful criminal homicide. *See id.* at 832–33 & nn. 38, 39 (Stevens, J., plurality opinion).

11. *See Thompson*, 487 U.S. at 865–74 (Scalia, J., dissenting) (citing examples from federal and state law in support of his contention that society has recently tended to impose greater criminal responsibility upon defendants who committed their crimes at an earlier age).

12. For example, both Indiana's and Missouri's revised death penalty statutes set the minimum age for the death penalty at sixteen. *See* Ind. Code Ann. § 35-50-2-3(b) (West 1986 & Supp. 1991); Mo. Rev. Stat. 565.020 (Vernon 1992).

13. U.S. Const. amend. VIII.

14. Trop v. Dulles, 356 U.S. 86, 101 (1958) (plurality opinion); *see also* Vanore, Decency of Capital Punishment, *supra* note 1, at 768–83.

15. *See* Vanore, Decency of Capital Punishment, *supra* note 1, at 783–90.

16. "A punishment is inordinately cruel, in the sense we must deal with it in these cases, chiefly as perceived by the society so characterizing it. The standard of extreme cruelty is not merely descriptive, but necessarily embodies a moral judgment. The standard itself remains the same, but its applicability must change as the basic mores of society change." Furman v. Georgia, 408 U.S. 238, 382 (1972) (Burger, C.J., dissenting).

17. *See* Gregg v. Georgia, 428 U.S. 153, 175 (1976).

18. 408 U.S. 238 (1972).

19. *See id.* at 299–300 (Brennan, J., concurring).

20. *See id.* at 362–68 (Marshall, J., concurring).

21. *See id.* at 240 (Justice Douglas); *id.* at 306 (Justice Stewart); *id.* at 310 (Justice White).

22. Gregg v. Georgia, 428 U.S. 153 (1976).

23. 487 U.S. 815 (1988).

24. *Id.* at 857.

25. *See* Stanford v. Kentucky, 492 U.S. 361, 389 (1989) (Brennan, J., dissenting).

26. *Id.* at 395 (quoting Twentieth Century Fund Task Force on Sentencing Policy toward Young Offenders, Confronting Youth Crime 7 (1978)).

27. *Id.*

28. *Id.* at 396 n.11.

29. *Id.* at 365.

30. *See id.* at 366–67.

31. *See* Jury Deliberates Sanity of Dahmer, N.Y. Times, Feb. 15, 1992, at 10.

ABOUT THE CONTRIBUTORS

JANET E. AINSWORTH is an Assistant Professor at Law at the University of Puget Sound School of Law.

MARTIN MAZEN ANBARI received his medical and law degrees from the University of Pennsylvania. He was an editor of the University of Pennsylvania Law Review from 1991 to 1992, and editor-in-chief from 1992 to 1993. He is a resident at the Mallinckrodt Institute of Radiology, Barnes Hospital, in St. Louis.

DONNA MASCARI BAKER is an associate with the law firm of Morrison and Foerster, Los Angeles.

STEVEN BANKS is Coordinating Attorney for the Homeless Family Rights Project of the Legal Aid Society of New York City.

ELIZABETH BARTHOLET is a Professor of Law at Harvard Law School. She is also the adoptive parent of two children born in Lima, Peru.

DONALD L. BESCHLE is an Associate Professor at The John Marshall Law School, Chicago, Illinois.

WILLIAM SCOTT BIEL received his law degree from the University of Pennsylvania. He was an editor of the University of Pennsylvania Law Review from 1990 to 1991, and editor-in-chief from 1991 to 1992. He is now an attorney with the law firm of Luce, Forward, Hamilton and Scripps in San Diego.

PAUL BLATT has over fifteen years of management and administrative experience in child welfare at the county and state levels.

JENIFER D. C. CARTLAND is a research analyst in the Division of Research on Health Policy at the American Academy of Pediatrics and a doctoral student in political science at Loyola University of Chicago.

HARVEY CATCHEN is an Associate Professor of Community Health at the State University of New York College at Old Westbury.

ANDREA CHARLOW is an Associate Professor at Drake Law School, Des Moines, Iowa.

JAN COSTELLO is a Professor of Law at Loyola Law School, Los Angeles.

JUDITH COHEN DOLINS is Director of the Division of State Government Affairs at the American Academy of Pediatrics, Elk Grove Village, Illinois.

JOEL FRADER, M.D., is an Associate Professor in the Departments of Pediatrics and Anesthesiology/Critical Care Medicine, and Associate Director of the Center for Medical Ethics, University of Pittsburgh.

JOSEPH GOLDSTEIN is Sterling Professor of Law at Yale University, and Professor, Yale University Child Study Center.

MARK GOODMAN is Executive Director of the Student Press Law Center, Washington, D.C.

MARTIN GUGGENHEIM teaches law at New York University Law School.

BRUCE HAFEN is University Provost and Professor of Law at Brigham Young University, Provo, Utah.

CHRIS HANSEN is Associate Director of the American Civil Liberties Union's Children's Rights Project, New York.

JOSEPH L. HOFFMANN is a Professor of Law, Indiana University School of Law, Bloomington.

S. RANDALL HUMM holds degrees from Yale University, the Wharton Business School, and the University of Pennsylvania Law School. He was an editor of the University of Pennsylvania Law Review from 1990 to 1992, and a law clerk to Federal Judge Sarah Evans Barker from 1992 to 1994.

HUNTER HURST is Director of the National Center for Juvenile Justice, a private nonprofit research organization in Pittsburgh.

BRENDA KELLEY is Assistant Secretary in the Office of Community Services of the Louisiana Department of Social Services, Baton Rouge.

KARLA KINDERMAN is an analyst in the Department of HIV of the American Medical Association, Chicago.

WENDY S. LADER received her law degree from the University of Pennsylvania. She was an editor of the University of Pennsylvania Law Review from 1990 to 1992. She is now an attorney in Washington, D.C.

PAUL A. LOGLI is the elected State's Attorney for Winnebago County, Illinois.

DORETTA MASSARDO MCGINNIS is an associate with the law firm of Pepper, Hamilton & Sheetz, Philadelphia.

PAUL MINORINI is an associate with the Washington, D.C., law firm of Hogan & Hartson.

MICHAEL B. MUSHLIN is a Professor of Law at Pace University, New York.

BEATE ANNA ORT holds degrees from the University of Virginia and the University of Pennsylvania Law School. She was an editor of the University of Pennsylvania Law Review from 1990 to 1992. She is now an assistant general counsel with the Immigration and Naturalization Service, Washington, D.C.

JAMES G. PAWELSKI is a legislative analyst in the Division of State Government at the American Academy of Pediatrics, Elk Grove Village, Illinois.

GERALD E. RADCLIFFE is Judge of the Probate and Juvenile Divisions of Common Pleas Court of Ross County, Ohio, and Trustee and Chairman of the Governmental Relations Committee of the National Council of Family and Juvenile Court Judges (NCFJCJ).

GERSHON M. RATNER is General Counsel and Director of Litigation, National Veterans Legal Services Project, Washington, D.C.

ALICE SARDELL is an Associate Professor of Urban Studies at Queens College, City University of New York.

ROBERT G. SCHWARTZ is Executive Director of the Juvenile Law Center, Philadelphia.

ANNE I. SEIDEL is Trial Attorney at the Equal Employment Opportunity Commission Office, Seattle.

AMY SINDEN is a staff attorney at Community Legal Services of Philadelphia, on a Skadden Fellowship.

MARK I. SOLER is Executive Director of the Youth Law Center, a public interest law office based in San Francisco that works throughout the United States on juvenile justice issues.

LISA J. SOTTO is an associate with the law firm of Hunton & Williams, New York.

VICTOR L. STREIB is a Professor of Law at Cleveland State University.

BARRY SULLIVAN is a partner in the firm of Jenner & Block and an Adjunct Professor of Law at Northwestern University School of Law.

CATHLEEN TUCKER is the project manager for the Association of Administrators of the Interstate Compact on the Placement of Children. She is also the policy associate for the Association of American Public Welfare Attorneys and the National Council of Local Public Welfare Administrators.

WALTER J. WADLINGTON is James Madison Professor of Law and Professor of Legal Medicine, University of Virginia.

PAUL WECKSTEIN is Co-Director of the Center for Law and Education, a national support center for legal services attorneys and others working on the educational rights of low-income students and parents.

STEPHEN WIZNER is William O. Douglas Clinical Professor of Law, Yale Law School.

BARBARA BENNETT WOODHOUSE is an Assistant Professor at the University of Pennsylvania Law School.

JAY WORONA is General Counsel for the New York State School Boards Association, Albany.

BETH K. YUDKOWSKY is the Director of the Division of Research on Health Policy at the American Academy of Pediatrics, Elk Grove Village, Illinois.

INDEX

Public schools, duty of, to provide basic skills education (*cont.*)
against recognizing, 318–20; conclusions on, 338–40; failure of, as background to, 313–18; focus on educational failure in urban areas, 313, 340 n.7; judicial enforcement of, 337–38; legal sources for, 320–37
Public schools, financing, 364–73; costs of effective education and, 317–18, 319; educational adequacy theory and, 364, 367–71; funding equity theory for, limitations of, 365–67; litigation on schemes for, 364
Public utility model of health care delivery, 453–54

Quality Education Acts (QEA I and II), New Jersey, 366

Race: selective enforcement of laws linked to, 96, 133; as suspect class, 55, 57, 64 n.48, 71–72, 80 n.10. *See also* Adoption, race matching in
Race discrimination, laws on, 71–75; "but for" causation, 81 n.23; Civil Rights Act, 75, 83 n.33; employment qualifications, 82 n.30; housing, 82 n.29; necessity doctrine, 72
Railway Express Agency v. New York, 285 n.179
Rational basis test, equal protection claims based on, for legal duty to educate effectively, 326, 329–31
Rationality standard, public education of AIDS-linked children and, 516–17
Ray v. School District, 550
R.C. case, 228–29
Reagan administration, 259, 525, 598–99
Regents of the University of Michigan v. Ewing, 378
Regnery, Alfred, 598–99
Rehabilitation Act of 1973, section 504; application of, to AIDS-linked students, 507–11, 519 n.5, 525, 527, 528–29, 540 n.14, 550; application of, to education of students with disabilities, 355–56, 507, 510
Rehabilitation vs. retribution in juvenile court, xxi, 567–69, 571–73, 589 nn.43, 44, 597–98, 600, 639–41, 644 n.30
Religion, 36–50; in American society, 36–37, 46 nn.1, 2, 48 n.32; best interests test and, in child custody, 40–44; definitions of, 41–42, 44, 49 nn.51, 56; as factor in child custody, 38–40, 44–46, 47 n.14; First Amendment standards on, 37–38; mental health and, 40–41, 44, 48 n.36; in public schools, 379, 384 n.38; social attitudes and, 42–43, 45, 48 n.32, 49 n.59, 50 nn.67, 69
Religiosity, measuring, 41, 48 n.37
Remedies: for educational adequacy, 367, 368;

educational standards and, 358–59, 367–68; for foster children as victims of abuse, 198–99
Rights: to association, child custody for parents in same-sex relationships and, 54; to education, 332–33, 352–53; of women vs. fetal, 90–92, 129. *See also* Children's rights; Parental rights; Privacy rights; Student speech rights
Riis, Jacob, 289
Risks: of AIDS and HIV transmission in public schools, 523–25, 527–31, 534–37; to children's health, 436–37
"Robin Hood" plans for public school financing, 365
Robinson v. California, 91
Roe v. Wade, 88, 90, 101 n.15
Roisman, Florence, 293–94
Rose v. Council for Better Education, 370–71
Ryan White Act, 554

Same-race parents, attempts to match adoptable children to, 68–70
Same-sex relationships, denial of child custody to parents in, 51–57; cases involving, 52; equal protection clause of Fourteenth Amendment and, 51–52; heightened equal protection scrutiny in, 52–56; purported state interests inadequate to equal protection scrutiny, 56–59
San Antonio Independent School District v. Rodriguez, 286 n.185, 331, 333, 346 n.69, 347 n.75, 358, 514
Santosky v. Kramer, 626–27
Savage v. Aaronson, 301
Schall v. Martin, 599–600, 615, 625–35; effect of, on *In re Gault* decision, 626–27; due process analysis of, 627–28; legacy of, 628–31
School Board v. Arline, 509, 525, 528, 537, 540 n.12, 542 n.30, 550
Schutz, Alfred, 563
Scrutiny, 521 n.77: heightened, burdening same-sex relationships, 53–54, 62 n.23; intermediate, in legal duty to educate, 328–29, 347 n.75; intermediate, in public education of AIDS-linked children, 515–16; strict, and legal duty to education, 326–28; strict, in public education of AIDS-linked children, 513–15, 542 n.32
Seattle School District No. 1 v. Washington, 323–24
Section 504. *See* Rehabilitation Act of 1973, section 504
Select Committee on Children, Youth and Families, in House of Representatives, 438
Self-incrimination, 577
Serrano v. Priest (Serrano I), 332–33
Sex discrimination: child custody cases and preference for one gender, 6, 7–8, 22 n.17; in de-